Social Struggles in Archaic Rome

Social Struggles in Archaic Rome

New Perspectives on the Conflict of the Orders

EDITED BY

Kurt A. Raaflaub

with contributions by
T. J. Cornell, R. Develin, W. Eder,
J. Linderski, R. E. Mitchell, A. Momigliano,
K. A. Raaflaub, J.-C. Richard, M. Toher,
and J. von Ungern-Sternberg

UNIVERSITY OF CALIFORNIA PRESS
Berkeley Los Angeles London

University of California Press
Berkeley and Los Angeles, California

University of California Press, Ltd.
London, England

© 1986 by
The Regents of the University of California
Library of Congress Cataloging in Publication Data

Main entry under title:
Social Struggles in Archaic Rome: New Perspectives
on the Conflict of the Orders

Bibliography: p.
Includes index.
1. Plebs (Rome)—Addresses, essays, lectures.
2. Rome—Social life and customs—Addresses, essays,
lectures.   3. Social classes—Rome—Addresses, essays,
lectures.   4. Estates (Social orders)—Rome—Addresses,
essays, lectures.   5. Rome—History—Republic, 510–265
B.C.—Addresses, essays, lectures.   I. Raaflaub, Kurt.
II. Cornell, Tim.
DG83.3.C65   1986   937'.01   85-13935
ISBN 0-520-05528-4 (alk. paper)

Printed in the United States of America

1 2 3 4 5 6 7 8 9

Contents

Chronological Table   vii
List of Abbreviations   xi
Editor's Preface   xv

I. The Conflict of the Orders in Archaic Rome:
A Comprehensive and Comparative Approach:
K. A. Raaflaub *(Brown University)*   1

II. The Value of the Literary Tradition Concerning
Archaic Rome: *T. J. Cornell (University of London)*   52

III. The Formation of the "Annalistic Tradition":
The Example of the Decemvirate:
J. von Ungern-Sternberg (University of Basel)   77

IV. Patricians and Plebeians: The Origin of a Social
Dichotomy: *J.-C. Richard (University of Nantes)*   105

V. The Definition of *patres* and *plebs*: An End to the Struggle
of the Orders: *R. E. Mitchell (University of Illinois)*   130

VI. The Rise of the *plebs* in the Archaic Age of Rome:
A. Momigliano (Universities of London and Chicago)   175

VII. From Protection and Defense to Offense and Participation:
Stages in the Conflict of the Orders:
K. A. Raaflaub *(Brown University)*   198

VIII. Religious Aspects of the Conflict of the Orders: The Case
of *confarreatio*: *J. Linderski (University of North Carolina)*   244

IX. The Political Significance of the Codification of Law in
Archaic Societies: An Unconventional Hypothesis:
W. Eder (Free University, Berlin) 262

X. The Tenth Table and the Conflict of the Orders:
M. Toher (Union College) 301

XI. The Integration of the Plebeians into the Political Order
after 366 B.C.: *R. Develin (University of Tasmania)* 327

XII. The End of the Conflict of the Orders:
J. von Ungern-Sternberg (University of Basel) 353

Bibliography 379
Contributors 435
Index of Subjects 439
Index of Persons and Places 447
Index of Scholars 453
Index of Sources 456

Chronological Table

Based on the lists of traditional dates and events in *CAH* VII: 321; H. H. Scullard, *History*[4] (1980): 420–25; and M. Cary and H. H. Scullard, *A History of Rome down to the Reign of Constantine*[3] (London, 1975): 559–61.

753–16	Romulus.
715–673	Numa Pompilius.
673–42	Tullus Hostilius. Destruction of Alba Longa.
642–17	Ancus Marcius.
616–579	L. Tarquinius Priscus. Roman Forum drained.
578–35	Servius Tullius. "Servian Reforms" introduced. Temple of Diana on the Aventine.
535 (?)	Naval battle off Alalia: Phocaeans defeated by Etruscans and Carthaginians.
534–10	L. Tarquinius Superbus. Capitoline temple erected.
524	Etruscans defeated at Cumae.
509	Fall of monarchy; soon thereafter war with Porsenna; annual magistracy established; dedication of Capitoline temple; first treaty between Rome and Carthage.
506	Battle of Aricia: Porsenna's son Arruns defeated by Latins and Aristodemus of Cumae.
501	First dictator appointed.
496	Battle of Lake Regillus between Rome and Latin League; Cult of Liber, Libera, and Ceres introduced.
494	First secession of the *plebs*; tribunes of the *plebs* introduced.
493	*Foedus Cassianum* between Rome and the Latins.
486	Agrarian law of Spurius Cassius; wars with Aequi and Volsci intermittently for next fifty years.
483–74	War with Veii.

479	Battle of the Cremera.
474	Naval battle off Cumae: Etruscans defeated by Hiero of Syracuse.
471	*Lex Publilia Voleronis: concilium plebis* and tribunes recognized.
456	*Lex Icilia de Aventino publicando.*
451–50	The first and second Decemvirates; publication of the Twelve Tables.
449	Secession of the *plebs*; Valerio-Horation laws.
445	*Lex Canuleia*; military tribunes with consular power introduced.
443	Censorship established.
431	Aequi defeated on Mt. Algidus.
425	Rome wins Fidenae from Veii.
406–396	War with Veii.
396	Military pay introduced; fall of Veii; peace with Volsci.
390	Battle of the Allia; Gauls sack Rome; wars with Latins and other neighbors intermittently over next fifty years.
367	Licinio-Sextian laws; consulship restored; curule aedileship created.
366	First plebeian consul; praetorship created.
358	Renewal of treaty with Latins.
357	Maximum rate of interest fixed.
356	First plebeian dictator.
354	Alliance with Samnites.
351	First plebeian censor.
348	Rome's treaty with Carthage renewed.
343–41	First Samnite War.
342	*Leges Genuciae.*
340–38	Great Latin War.
339	*Leges Publiliae.*
338	Latin League dissolved.
337	First plebeian praetor.
326	*Lex Poetelia* concerning debts (or 313); Roman alliance with Neapolis.
326–304	Second Samnite War.
312	Censorship of Appius Claudius.

306	Third Treaty with Carthage.
304	Appius Claudius's reforms repealed; Flavius publishes the *legis actiones*.
300	*Lex Valeria de provocatione; lex Ogulnia*, opening priesthoods to plebeians.
298–90	Third Samnite War.
293 (?)	*Lex Maenia*, concerning patrician sanction for elections.
289	Mint and *tresviri monetales* established.
287	*Lex Hortensia*, giving *plebiscita* the force of law.
280–75	War with Pyrrhus.
264–41	First Punic War.
232	Distribution of *ager Gallicus* carried by Flaminius.
218	*Lex Claudia*.
218–201	Second Punic War.

List of Abbreviations

A&A	*Antike und Abendland*
AAH	*Acta Antiqua Academiae Scientiarum Hungaricae*
AArch	*Acta Archaeologica*
ABSA	*Annual of the British School at Athens*
AC	*L'Antiquité classique*
AJA	*American Journal of Archaeology*
AJP	*American Journal of Philology*
ANRW	*Aufstieg und Niedergang der römischen Welt*; ed. H. Temporini and W. Haase (Berlin, 1972–)
ASNP	*Annali della Scuola normale superiore di Pisa*
BAGB	*Bulletin de l'Association G. Budé*
BCAR	*Bullettino della commissione archeologica communale in Roma*
BCH	*Bulletin de correspondance hellénique*
BEFAR	*Bibl. des Ecoles françaises d'Athènes et de Rome*
BIDR	*Bollettino dell'Istituto di diritto romano*
BJ	*Bonner Jahrbücher*
BSA	*(Annual of the) British School at Athens*
CAH	*Cambridge Ancient History*
CB	*Classical Bulletin*
CIL	*Corpus inscriptionum Latinarum*
CISA	*Contributi dell'Istituto di storia antica dell'Univ. del sacro cuore, Milano*
CJ	*Classical Journal*
CQ	*Classical Quarterly*

CRAI	Comptes rendus de l'Académie des inscriptions et belles-lettres
CSCA	California Studies in Classical Antiquity
CW	Classical Weekly/World
DArch	Dialoghi di archeologia
FGrHist	Die Fragmente der griechischen Historiker, ed. F. Jacoby
FIRA	Fontes iuris Romani anteiustiniani, ed. S. Riccobono et al.
GIF	Giornale italiano di filologia
G&R	Greece and Rome
GRBS	Greek, Roman and Byzantine Studies
HdAW	Handbuch der Altertumswissenschaft
HRR	Historicorum Romanorum reliquiae, ed. H. Peter
HZ	Historische Zeitschrift
IG	Inscriptiones Graecae
ILS	Inscriptiones Latinae selectae, ed. H. Dessau
JHS	Journal of Hellenic Studies
JRS	Journal of Roman Studies
LEC	Les Etudes classiques
LCM	Liverpool Classical Monthly
MEFR	Mélanges d'archéologie et d'histoire de l'Ecole française de Rome
MH	Museum Helveticum
NJAB	Neue Jahrbücher für Antike und deutsche Bildung
OCD	The Oxford Classical Dictionary^2 (Oxford, 1970)
OLD	Oxford Latin Dictionary (Oxford, 1982)
ORF	Oratorum Romanorum fragmenta, ed. H. Malcovati
PBSR	Papers of the British School at Rome
PCPhS	Proceedings of the Cambridge Philological Society
PP	La parola del passato
RAL	Rendiconti della cl. di sc. mor., stor. e filol. dell'Accademia dei Lincei
RD	Revue historique de droit français et étranger
RE	Pauly-Wissowa's Real-Encyclopädie der klassischen Altertumswissenschaft (Stuttgart, 1893–)
REA	Revue des études anciennes
REL	Revue des études latines
RFIC	Rivista di filologia e di istruzione classica
RhM	Rheinisches Museum für Philologie
RH	Revue historique

RIDA	*Revue internationale des droits de l'antiquité*
RIL	*Rendiconti dell'Istituto lombardo*
RISG	*Rivista italiana per le scienze giuridiche*
RM	*Mitteilungen des Deutschen Archäologischen Instituts: Römische Abteilung*
RPh	*Revue de philologie*
RSA	*Rivista storica dell'antichità*
RSI	*Rivista storica italiana*
SDHI	*Studia et documenta historiae et iuris*
SE	*Studi etruschi*
SMSR	*Studi e materiali di storia delle religioni*
SR	*Studi romani*
Syll.	*Sylloge inscriptionum Graecarum*, ed. W. Dittenberger
TAPA	*Transactions and Proceedings of the American Philological Association*
TLL	*Thesaurus linguae Latinae* (Leipzig, 1900–)
WdF	*Wege der Forschung*
ZPE	*Zeitschrift für Papyrologie und Epigraphik*
ZRG	*Zeitschrift der Savigny-Stiftung für Rechtsgeschichte (Romanistische Abteilung)*

Editor's Preface

1

The archaic period of the ancient Mediterranean world was characterized by the emergence of the *polis* ("city-state") type of political community in Phoenicia, in Greece, and in Etruria and other parts of Italy, and by its rapid spread along the coastal areas of the Mediterranean and Black Seas. These communities all shared certain characteristics, and in their early history many of them seem to have gone through a crisis roughly similar in origin, development, and results. In a long and difficult process, often marked by a sequence of violent conflicts and compromises, the rule of exclusive aristocracies was replaced by a political system that allowed the responsible participation of large segments of the nonaristocratic citizen body and gave the lower classes important economic, social, military, religious, and judicial rights.

This process of social and political struggle and transformation, which the historians of Rome often call the Conflict (or Struggle) of the Orders, proved an indispensable precondition for the remarkable achievements of the ancient world. Its results enabled Athens to withstand the attack of the Orient in the Persian Wars, to develop democracy, and to rise to the political and cultural brilliance of the Periclean period. The social and political system that was developed during the Conflict of the Orders gave the Roman state the internal strength, homogeneity, and cohesiveness that were needed to conquer and then rule Italy and the whole Mediterranean world.

Despite the profound historical significance of the Conflict of the Orders, it is only partially understood. The reason is easy to find:

the ancient sources are few, and for many aspects nonexistent. This is especially true for Rome, where contemporary evidence is almost completely lacking, and the picture drawn by the literary sources, which were written many centuries later, is in many ways gravely deformed. Modern scholarship has therefore focused on the discussion of constitutional developments, and is still largely influenced by the legalistic approach used in the late nineteenth century. Few attempts have been made to break the impasse by applying different methods.

With this situation in mind, Timothy Cornell, Walter Eder, Jerzy Linderski, Richard Mitchell, and I presented papers and discussed various aspects of the Conflict of the Orders at two colloquia held at Brown University in the fall of 1981. The discussion was continued in a seminar at the annual meeting of the American Philological Association at San Francisco in December 1981. The resulting papers form the core of this volume (chapters I, II, V, VII, VIII, and IX). A few other scholars working in the field of early republican history—Robert Develin, Arnaldo Momigliano, Jean-Claude Richard, and Jürgen von Ungern-Sternberg—were invited afterwards to contribute papers on specific topics. Mark Toher's contribution grew out of a paper delivered in a seminar that served as preparation for the colloquia of 1981.

The resulting volume offers a representative cross section through current international scholarship on the Conflict of the Orders and through the range of problems posed by it. In both respects the selection is, of course, far from complete: the number of scholars working in this area is considerably larger, and several important aspects are either omitted completely or treated only insufficiently.[1] Ten of the twelve contributions are published here for the first time. The exceptions are easily justified: Momigliano's paper (chapter VI, published in 1967 in Italian) offers the best summary of the contributions to the present topic by an eminent scholar whose work has been seminal in this as in many other areas; Ungern-Sternberg's second paper (chapter XII, published in 1980 in German) deals with a

---

1. Such as the economic background of the Conflict of the Orders or the conflict's relation to Rome's contemporary "foreign policy" and wars. In both cases attempts to solicit contributions failed, but these topics will be pursued at another conference planned for the near future.

crucial question never seriously discussed before, namely whether the Conflict of the Orders did indeed end at the traditional date of 287 B.C.

We hope that this volume will provoke discussion and collaboration among a larger group of specialists and nonspecialists, and that it will stimulate more intensive and systematic research on a subject that is both truly important and highly challenging. To quote Momigliano: "As early Rome is the ideal place to combine archaeological exploration and source criticism, the study of archaic Rome remains an ideal school of historical method."[2] The important question is, however, whether the exploration of archaic Rome, besides offering an ideal training ground, can also yield new insights and improved understanding. A pessimistic prognosis has recently been formulated by L. Capogrossi Colognesi: "Les problèmes d'histoire archaïque romaine me semblent en effet de plus en plus insolubles."[3] Few might agree with such a radical statement, but the objective difficulties posed by the miserable source situation are indeed formidable. Moreover, as always when contemporary sources are scarce and uncertain,[4] scholarly discipline and soundness tend to be threatened in various ways: some stick at any cost to the deceptive safety offered by the literary sources; others, on the contrary, feel free to discard and select according to their own (mostly unstated) principles; not infrequently methodological anarchy seems to rule, imagination is given free rein, one-sided theories abound, and open discussion among scholars is replaced by fierce insistence on one's own opinion and harsh polemics against opposing views. In his review of a volume that was published in 1967 after a colloquium on the origins of the Roman Republic, E. J. Bickerman made the following comments:

> At a symposium held near Geneva, nine distinguished specialists in Roman archaeology, history and law, from six countries, ably discussed the present state of our knowledge (or should I say, ignorance) of the early history of Rome. They presented imaginative and generally credible reconstructions of various aspects of

2. Momigliano, *JRS* 53 (1963): 108 (= *Contr. III* [1966]: 371).
3. Capogrossi Colognesi, *Dial. d'hist. anc.* 5 (1979): 137.
4. The history of early Sparta offers another example.

this history. They are learned and judicious, yet they have no faith in the hypotheses of their co-authors; they disagree on all essential points of the early Roman history, from the dating of the foundation of the city to the meaning of the struggle between the Patricians and the Plebeians, and their theories cancel each other out. When the authors are in accord, they often share the conventional errors of our handbooks. A very average reader, such as the writer of these lines, begins to wonder why the early history of Rome is both so obscure and so controversial and whether there is hope that it may become less opaque.[5]

There is no lack of such "qualities" in the present volume either. In fact, diametrically opposed views stand side by side on such issues as the value of the literary sources, the function of religion in determining social status and influencing social conflict, the power or weakness of aristocracies, the political significance of the codification of law, the meaning of the ban on intermarriage, the end of the Conflict of the Orders, and a few others. Disagreement in itself, however, is not necessarily a disadvantage. It is negative only if it is the unshakable result of a clash of preexisting and absolutely fixed opinions, and if there is no readiness to listen, to accept challenges, to adapt and progress. It is positive and fruitful if it opens the way to productive debate and eventually to compromise and agreement because it is based on openness, readiness to listen, and an explicit discussion of approach and methodology.

The last point seems to me extremely important. Not only do we have to shed some of our scholarly vanity, but there surely must be something wrong if it is possible to defend mutually exclusive theories with seemingly good arguments on the basis of the same evidence. Even scarce and uncertain sources usually do not allow totally divergent interpretations if they are treated with sound methodology. There may be a range of possibilities, even a "grey zone" of considerable breadth, within which it is hard or impossible to locate precisely the correct interpretation. That "grey zone" may be close to black or to white, but it cannot be both at the same time. In other words, if we are faced with mutually exclusive and radically diver-

---

5. Bickerman, *RFIC* 97 (1969): 393; cf. the similar reaction of G. Poma, *Studi* (1974): 19.

gent theories on the same topic, we should suspect that the fault lies not only with the sources but also with the scholars and the methodology used by them to establish one or both of these theories.

It is on the basic level of methodology and approach, therefore, that our discussions have to begin and remain focused if we want to establish a solid foundation for the discussion of individual problems and, from there, make real progress toward agreement and a better understanding of the Conflict of the Orders. Unfortunately, there is widespread reluctance among ancient historians to talk in detail about methods and theories. I consider such reluctance to be unjustified and harmful. The darker the age we are dealing with, the more it is an indispensable precondition for sound and acceptable results that we render account to ourselves and to our fellow researchers of the methodology and theories underlying these results. I am convinced that in such openness lies one of our chances to overcome the deadlock that haunted the participants in the colloquium of 1967.

Another chance lies in the exploration of new approaches. In my abstract announcing the colloquia and the seminar on the Conflict of the Orders in 1981, I suggested a few approaches that might help us to find new answers to old questions.[6] These suggestions are elaborated in my opening chapter in the present volume. The other authors were encouraged to test these approaches in their own contributions, to take issue with my views, to discuss explicitly the methods, theories, and approaches used in their own work, and to explore possibilities rather than insisting on fixed solutions. As might be expected, some of them followed this invitation more eagerly than others. As it is, however, this volume seems to me to contain an unusual amount of such basic exploration and discussion and of novel approaches; various well-established views and time-honored concepts are challenged vigorously, and new interpretations are proposed on several crucial issues; the debates between individual contributions reflect the interaction going on among the authors while this volume was being prepared. To repeat, it is our hope that our ideas will provoke not only approval, criticism, or rejection, but an open, intensive, and fruitful dialogue.

---

6. See R. S. Bagnall, ed., *American Philological Association, Annual Meeting 1981, Abstracts* (Chico, Calif., 1981): 80–81.

2

No effort has been made to cover all aspects of the Conflict of the Orders. The first three papers deal with problems and the value of our sources. In my opening chapter these problems are discussed and ways of overcoming the limitations of the evidence are explored. A program of systematic and imaginative research is outlined that would make it possible to reach beyond the problematic testimony of the annalistic historians and to supplement the Roman material with comparative evidence from other societies. In particular, a systematic comparison with phenomena occurring in archaic Greece promises valuable insights.

T. J. Cornell (chapter II) defends the basic credibility and usefulness of the annalistic tradition. He sees it supported in its earliest parts by recent archaeological evidence that generally enhances the tradition's trustworthiness, although such evidence is almost completely lacking for the Conflict of the Orders itself. Cornell emphasizes the number of sources the annalists could rely on and the familiarity of the educated Roman public with the history of its city. He distinguishes between the "structural facts" that underlie the tradition, and are basically sound, and the "narrative superstructure," which contains distortions of all kinds, and he argues strongly against those who believe that the annalists deliberately falsified the record and freely invented additions to it.

J. von Ungern-Sternberg (chapter III) judges the reliability of our literary sources more skeptically. He applies an approach developed and used successfully early in this century mostly by German scholars, but widely ignored or forgotten in recent decades. By comparing various extant versions, he demonstrates how a specific story (in this case that of the Decemvirate) was gradually developed, refined, and transformed by several generations of historians, who through the experiences and problems of their own times became aware of new aspects and meanings of the story. In this view, the share of "structural facts" is rather limited, that of the "narrative superstructure" (elaboration, not necessarily falsification) extremely large.

The next three contributions for the most part discuss the origins of the dichotomy between patricians and plebeians, the origins of the Conflict of the Orders, and related questions. J.-C. Richard (chapter IV) summarizes, updates, and occasionally modifies some of the views presented in his important book on the origins of the Roman *plebs* (published in 1976 in French). He focuses on a range of problems connected with the emergence of the social differentiation that resulted in the opposition between patricians and plebeians. The patriciate developed gradually in a long process that began under the first kings, and it became a closed order only in the first decades of the Republic. Roughly at the same time, and partly in reaction to that development, the *plebs* emerged as a political entity with an organization that enabled it to contest the patricians' claims. Richard offers a challenging reconstruction and presents all the key issues for further discussion.

In probably the most radical and provocative paper of this volume, R. E. Mitchell (chapter V) challenges the whole concept of a "Conflict of the Orders." Unlike most scholars, who adopt the framework of a contest between patricians and plebeians as presented in the sources and then discard individual episodes and details, Mitchell accepts many of the particulars (especially those of a legal or religious nature) but interprets them in a different and largely nonpolitical framework. In his view the main difference between *patres* and *plebs* was not one between two social orders but between groups defined by religious and legal criteria. He suggests that the original regal Senate was composed primarily of priests, the *patres*; accordingly, in the early Republic too, the *patres* were priests who were automatically senators by virtue of their priesthoods; initially, their heirs automatically succeeded to their priesthoods and thereby to their Senate seats. Only gradually did the number of *conscripti* increase; these were nonpriests who became senators by virtue of office or personal political or military merits. Mitchell supports his thesis with an analysis of a wide range of terms and issues. He concludes that, whatever social, economic, or political conflicts may have troubled the early Republic, the opponents in such conflicts were not the *patres/patricii* and *plebei*. The Conflict of the Orders, as it is traditionally understood, is therefore a construction by ancient and modern historians, based on fundamental misunderstandings about archaic Roman society.

A. Momigliano's paper (chapter VI) was written in 1969, in the heat of the debates provoked by the innovative work of A. Alföldi, G. Dumézil, and others. Although it is a "historic" paper, and as such partially outdated, it is timeless as a testimony to the intellectual vigor, the seminal ideas, and the innovative approaches of one of the truly great historians of our time. Many of his suggestions still serve as stimulating starting points for further analysis. Momigliano places the question of the Conflict of the Orders in the context of recent research on early Rome, emphasizes the lack of focused and systematic research in this particular area (which is still to a large extent the case), and offers an avenue of fruitful investigation by examining a number of key terminological oppositions. He concludes with a few suggestions as to how the underprivileged and powerless plebeians eventually gained the strength to challenge patrician supremacy effectively.

Chapters VII–X deal with various aspects of the earlier part of the Conflict of the Orders. The starting point of my contribution (chapter VII) is the observation that we cannot expect there to have been an unchanging struggle over the same issues for roughly two centuries. Using as much of the Roman evidence as can safely be retained, and supplementing it with comparative evidence mostly from archaic Greece, I try to establish criteria enabling us more clearly to distinguish several stages within that long period. Furthermore, I argue that the "closure of the patriciate" left the plebeians without an aristocratic leadership of families equal to the patricians in status, wealth, and ambition. Accordingly, in the first phase the plebeians almost exclusively fought for economic improvements and protection against the overwhelming power of the patricians. In later stages the plebeian families that emerged as leaders in the struggle against the patricians and acquired wealth, influence, and a large *clientela* of their own began to aim at social, military, and finally also political equality with the patricians.

J. Linderski (chapter VIII) sheds new light on an important aspect of the Conflict of the Orders by demonstrating patrician manipulation of certain religious institutions. He concentrates on the marriage *per confarreationem* and reconstructs the social and political framework as an aid to understanding the concept of *confarreatio* as an archaic private institution, subsequently overlaid by an official component that transformed it into the instrument of a hereditary aristocracy. Linderski also offers an interesting new explanation of the ban on intermarriage.

W. Eder (chapter IX) examines the political function of codification of law both in archaic Greece (especially in Athens) and in Rome. After carefully establishing his methodological and theoretical basis, he argues that the articulation of custom into law in these archaic *poleis* primarily served the needs and advantages of the ruling class, not those of the lower classes. He demonstrates on the one hand the urgent need of the aristocracies to support institutionally not only their control of power but, even more, the unity of and equality within their ranks. On the other hand, he emphasizes the absence of evidence for pressure by the lower classes in promoting the legislation in question, the continued aristocratic predominance after its promulgation, and the failure of the *plebs* to gain substantial political or economic benefits or even real equality before the law. In the final part of his paper, Eder analyzes a number of individual regulations and shows how they fit into the picture previously drawn.

M. Toher (chapter X) provides another example of how comparison can be used to reach a better understanding of early Roman problems. He focuses on the funerary restrictions in the tenth of the Twelve Tables and sets against them a comprehensive examination of the content and purpose of similar legal restrictions in the Greek world. He shows that the tenth Table belongs to a uniquely Greek tradition and has no counterpart in Italic practice. He suggests that funerary restrictions were not part of general sumptuary legislation and therefore did not serve the same purposes. Plato's and Cicero's discussions of the meaning of such regulations confirm that they must have been prompted by religious aims and ancestral practice. Consequently, Toher concludes, they have nothing to do with the Conflict of the Orders.

The last two papers are concerned with the final phase and the end of the Conflict of the Orders. In the opening section of his contribution, R. Develin (chapter XI) forcefully defends his opinion that for the fourth and early third centuries the literary sources deserve more credit than is often admitted, especially when they talk about legislation and other official business. We should therefore believe them when they describe a prolonged contest between patricians and plebeians throughout the fourth century and even into the third. Setting forth various possible explanations and arguing strongly against mechanical application of popular factional theories, he describes the incidence of repeated legislation on plebeian privileges, and of apparent patrician violation of those privileges, as an accurate reflection of the long-drawn-out and difficult process by which the plebeians became fully integrated into the system. Passage of laws did not always entail implementation; patrician authority, Roman conservatism, and plebeian acceptance of the traditional system prevented speedy solutions and a linear development.

J. von Ungern-Sternberg (chapter XII) proposes that the Conflict of the Orders did not end with the *lex Hortensia* of 287, as is commonly assumed. He combines scattered pieces of information (all that we have, inasmuch as Livy's second decade is lost) to show that distinction between the orders and conflicts over privileges continued into the late third century, as is particularly visible in C. Flaminius's measures and policies and the disputes provoked by them. In this view, the Conflict of the Orders between patricians and plebeians was gradually transformed into a conflict between the *plebs* (in the narrow sense) and the patrician-plebeian Senate. The end of the Conflict of the Orders can then be located in the emergency of the second Punic War, although there even is a certain amount of continuity into the period of the Gracchi and the efforts of the late republican *populares*.

The Bibliography is intended as a tool for further work in this area. It lists not only all the books and articles on the early Republic and the Conflict of the Orders and on comparable developments in archaic Greece mentioned in this volume, but also other literature on the Conflict of the Orders gathered from various bibliographies and *L'Année philologique*. Accordingly, throughout this volume footnote references to articles and monographs will be given only in abbreviated form.

Contributions to this volume are identified by their Roman numerals ("chapter X"). Cross-references refer not to pages but to notes ("see below n. 00" or "see below chapter X, n. 00") or to passages in which those notes occur ("see below at n. 00" or "see below chapter X, following n. 00" or "see Smith, below chapter X, before n. 00").

The papers in this volume were essentially completed in 1983. With few exceptions, publications that appeared after that date could not be taken into consideration.

3

It remains for me to acknowledge all those who helped to prepare and improve this volume. Besides the authors themselves, I wish in particular to thank Erich S. Gruen, whose substantial comments at a preliminary stage helped us all to rethink and reformulate parts of our work. Aaron Baker, Michael Flower, John Marincola, Mary Elizabeth Murphy, Elli Mylonas, Panetha Nychis, Walt Stevenson, and Mark Toher improved some of the translations, helped to compile and check the bibliography, and assisted me in many other important ways. Ruthann Whitten, the secretary of the Department of Classics at Brown University, patiently and cheerfully typed the texts and innumerable changes. The university and the department, which also paid for an additional typist, were extremely generous in providing me with all this support; without it, it would have been impossible for me to produce this volume. The readers, copyeditor, and staff of the University of California Press deserve high praise for their courteous and painstaking assistance. Finally, my wife, Deborah Boedeker, not only supported me with her interest and encouragement, but also spent many hours improving the style of my own contributions and some others originally written in French or German.

KURT A. RAAFLAUB

I

The Conflict of the Orders in Archaic Rome: A Comprehensive and Comparative Approach

1. The Problems and the Task

In the introduction to his *Roman Antiquities*, Dionysius of Halicarnassus criticizes the works of the earliest Roman historians, Q. Fabius Pictor and L. Cincius Alimentus, both contemporary with the second Punic War. He says: "Each of these men related the events at which he himself had been present with great exactness, as being well acquainted with them, but touched only in a summary way upon the early events that followed the founding of the city" (1.6.2). As a

An earlier version of this paper was read as a programmatic introduction to the first of two colloquia on the Conflict of the Orders at Brown University in the fall of 1981. I am convinced that no real progress can be made toward a better understanding of the Conflict of the Orders unless we first establish a sound methodological basis, and it is the purpose of this essay to contribute to that indispensable preliminary task. It is to be hoped that it will provoke scholarly discussion on a fundamental level rather than on the usual level of individual historical problems.

general statement, this may be fairly correct. But the reality seems to have been somewhat more complex. Many scholars have observed that the preserved fragments of most Roman annalists show a characteristic pattern.[1] For example, the *Annales* of L. Calpurnius Piso Frugi contained seven books, the first two of which covered the origins and the period of the kings, while the third went down to at least the end of the fourth century. In the *Annales* of Ennius, the first three books described the time of the kings; by the fifth the Samnite Wars had been reached. In these and many other works, the early history of Rome to the end of the monarchy was, it seems, described in considerably more detail than the first two centuries of the Republic. Only with the Samnite Wars did narratives expand again, becoming ever more detailed as they approached the writer's own time. Fabius Pictor wrote about a hundred years after the Great Samnite War. A century might have been roughly the period that could be spanned by memory and documentary evidence available without difficult research.[2] On the other hand, there existed in the third century not only a wealth of legends and a firmly established Greek tradition about the origins of Rome and the period of the kings in general, but also oral traditions (that were at least partially connected with surviving buildings, monuments, and documents) about Rome's grandeur under the Tarquins, the fall of the monarchy, and the events of the very first years of the Republic. In between, however, there was a big gap: from at least the first decade of the Republic to the Samnite Wars the sources were extremely scarce and made a detailed report difficult.[3]

In Livy, however, we find a different distribution of the material. Book I covers the origins and the whole regal period, the next four

---

1. Cf., e.g., E. Gabba, "Tradizione letteraria" (1967): 133ff.; Cornell, "Tradizione storiografica" (1980): 19ff. For recent surveys on the republican annalists, cf. E. Badian, "Early Historians" (1966): 1ff.; and B. W. Frier, *Annales* (1979): 201ff. Cf., further, A. Momigliano, *Contr. III* (1966): 55ff.

2. Even so Livy complains about the confusion and contradictions in the existing accounts of the Great Samnite War, about the distortion in existing documentary evidence, and the lack of "any writer contemporary with that period, on whose authority we may safely take our stand" (8.40). Polyb. 4.2.1–3 even restricts reliable oral memory to the previous generation. See also below n. 111.

3. Cf. E. Meyer, "Untersuchungen über Diodor's römische Geschichte," *RhM* 37 (1882): 610ff.; Gabba, "Tradizione letteraria" (1967): 137f. For a more cautious assessment of the Greek and a more positive and comprehensive one of the Roman tradition, see now Cornell, "Tradizione storiografica" (1980): esp. 26ff.

books the time from the beginning of the Republic to the sack of Rome; the Great Samnite War is reached in book eight. Dionysius needs four books for the monarchy, but six for just the next fifty years. All this represents a remarkable reversal. Dionysius certainly did not condense the material about regal Rome, and even if we assume that Livy did, the increase of information about the early Republic is quite amazing. Given the character of the pontifical *Annales Maximi*, it is quite unlikely that much valuable material came from there, even if the myth of their publication in the late second century had not been shattered recently by B. Frier.[4] Two authors, it seems, were mainly responsible for the vastly expanded reports on the early Republic: Cn. Gellius, who around 130 B.C. wrote *Annales* not in five to ten books, as was usual before and after him, but in ninety-seven, the fifteenth of which only reached the year 389. His verbosity and "lush antiquarianism" are as exceptional as his lack of influence on later authors. But he was intensively used by Dionysius (who loved him for the antiquarian details) and by Licinius Macer, the well-known tribune of 73, for whom Gellius was an ideal source, rich in plausible detail on precisely the period in which Macer was chiefly interested. According to Frier,

> Macer deliberately confined his *Annales* to the great plebeian revolution, from the foundation of Rome down to the *lex Hortensia* of 287 and its immediate aftermath in the conquest of Italy. His motives were in part his desire to glorify his plebeian ancestors . . . , in part his general love of plebeian institutions and history.[5]

Knowing these authors, their methods, experiences, and intentions, we are allowed to wonder whether there was really much of an increase in authentic and valuable information in their works. But Macer was, directly or indirectly, one of Livy's prime sources for the early Republic.[6]

Modern scholarship seems, however, to have adopted the pattern of the earlier annalists. There is intensive research going on into

---

4. Frier, *Annales* (1979): 179ff. For Livy's dealing with the regal period and the early Republic, see now Cornell, "Tradizione storiografica" (1980): esp. 22ff.
5. Frier, *Annales* (1979): 154. On Macer: ibid., 154ff. On Gellius: ibid., 186ff.; Badian, "Early Historians" (1966): 11f.; E. Rawson, *Latomus* 35 (1976): 713ff.
6. Ogilvie, *Comm.* (1965): 7ff.

Roman expansion in Italy and the conquest of the Mediterranean world, and there is a never-ending flow of publications on the origins of Rome (the city, its society and institutions), the "grande Roma dei Tarquini" and the origins of the Republic. But the early Republic is one of very few underresearched periods in ancient history. Not that there is a dearth of publications—quite the contrary. But they focus mostly on aspects of legal and institutional history, and they are often written by historians of law.[7] Typically, one of the most comprehensive (although rather one-sided) discussions of the period is to be found in F. De Martino's *Storia della costituzione romana* I–II², (1972–73). Generally speaking, the aspect of "origins" still dominates the approach and focus of interest. The Conflict of the Orders has rarely been recognized as an object of research worthy and important in itself.[8] Accordingly, it has hardly been touched upon in surveys of recent scholarship.[9] A. Momigliano, who for decades appeared best qualified in every respect to deal comprehensively with the whole range of problems and the entire period, has offered a series of stimulating suggestions and reopened the debate on several important points. He, too, however, was mainly interested

---

7. This is especially true for Italy and Germany where the history of early Rome has long been the domain of specialists in Roman law and the main organs of publication are periodicals in the history of law. Cf. J. Bleicken, *Republik* (1980): 110: Distrust of the annalistic tradition has brought it about, "dass alle Gelehrten, die sich mit Themen der römischen Frühgeschichte beschäftigen, das Schwergewicht ihrer Forschungen auf die Verfassungsgeschichte (unter Einbeziehung selbstverständlich der Sozial- und Religionsgeschichte) gelegt haben, weil wir zu ihr Daten besitzen, die von der Annalistik unabhängig sind."

8. Cf. Momigliano, *Contr. IV* (1969): 441f.; J.-C. Richard, *Origines* (1978): xii.

9. J. Heurgon, *Rise* (1973), has a rich and well-organized bibliography and useful discussions of many aspects of recent scholarship, but does not contain a chapter on social development and conflicts in the fifth and fourth centuries. The surveys of E. S. Staveley, *Historia* 5 (1956): 74ff., and W. Kunkel, *ZRG* 85 (1955): 288ff.; 86 (1956): 307ff.; and 90 (1960): 345ff. (now combined in id., *Kleine Schriften* [Weimar, 1974]: 441ff.), as well as E. Meyer's extremely useful *Staat*³ (1964), focus exclusively on constitutional and institutional history. In vols. I.1 and 2 (1972), *ANRW* features several articles on law, institutions, and foreign relations, but none on the social history of the early Republic. Poma, *Studi* (1974), covering the years 1963–73, at least contains one chapter on the political and social structure of Rome in the fifth century (69ff.), and L. Zusi, *Critica storica* 12 (1975): 177ff. (dealing with the publications of 1966–71), discusses recent theories on several issues tackled in the present volume. Still, a comprehensive survey of the results of, and tendencies in, modern scholarship on the Conflict of the Orders remains an urgent desideratum: cf. E. Bickerman, *RFIC* 97 (1969): 408.

in the "origins" and, regrettably, never really carried his analysis beyond the initial stage.[10]

In the past decade, at last, two monographs have been published on the Conflict of the Orders, both written by experts in Roman law who have explored the field for many years. Both offer a number of new and stimulating insights. They are rather different in approach and interest, and complementary in focus and content, and neither can properly be called a social and political history of the Conflict of the Orders. In his *La rivoluzione della plebe* (1975), A. Guarino is mostly interested in the prehistory and emergence of the contrasting orders and in the preconditions for what he understands as a full-scale plebeian revolution against a system controlled and exploited by the patricians. He therefore concentrates on the period before the first *secessio* and gives only a brief survey of the highlights of the conflict itself and of its results. In addition, the value of many of his suggestions is in various ways impaired by his legalistic approach and a lack of methodological clarity and of consistency in the use of the ancient literary sources.[11] E. Ferenczy's *From the Patrician State to the Patricio-plebeian State* (1976), on the other hand, has a clear focus on the last phase of the Conflict of the Orders, on the political integration of the plebeian elite, and especially on Appius Claudius Caecus, the great censor of 312. For this period, Ferenczy's contributions are at least in part substantial and valuable; in several areas they are challenging, innovative, and truly improve our understanding. The first part, however, which deals rather cursorily with the history of the patrician state and its institutions from its beginnings to the Gallic disaster, is much less satisfactory and often marred by a surprisingly uncritical belief in the reliability of our literary sources.[12]

---

10. See the articles collected in Momigliano's various *Contributi* and listed in the Bibliography. Cf. now Cornell, "Failure of the Plebs" (1983): 102ff., for a summary of Momigliano's "model" and a stimulating sketch of how, based on that model, the history of the Conflict of the Orders might be reconstructed (108ff.).

11. Cf. esp. the reviews by J.-C. Richard, *Gnomon* 49 (1977): 592ff.; O. Behrends, *ZRG* 94 (1977): 392ff.; A. Drummond, *JRS* 72 (1982): 177ff. Most of Guarino's earlier articles pertinent in this context have been collected in id., *Origini* (1973). His views are also presented in his *Storia del diritto romano*^{5} (1975) and *Diritto privato romano*^{5} (1976). They would merit detailed discussion.

12. Cf. the reviews by J.-C. Richard, *REL* 55 (1977): 39ff.; *Gnomon* 51 (1979): 401ff.; J. Béranger, *REL* 56 (1978): 541ff.; F. Wieacker, *ZRG* 96 (1979): 359ff.; E. Gabba, *Athenaeum* 56 (1978): 424ff.; R. M. Ogilvie, *CR* 29 (1979): 109f. For se-

What is still urgently needed, therefore, is a comprehensive examination of the entire Conflict of the Orders from the point of view of social and political, not legal and institutional, history.[13] Despite all that has been said about it, it is still one of the least known and understood periods of Roman history. That is both regrettable and challenging, not so much because a white or grey spot on the map of history is a nuisance, but because it is an extremely important period, in which the foundations were laid for historical developments that shook and changed the world. After all, it was toward the end of this period that the Romans definitively ceased to be just one of many comparable communities in the Mediterranean world that fought for survival against invaders, battled with their neighbors about cattle and fields, suffered from famine and internal struggles, and tried to secure for themselves a bigger share of security and prosperity than fortune seemed to have allotted them.[14] The extent and speed of the Roman expansion that began in the late fourth century are amazing. After two hundred years, a community with a territory only slightly larger than modern Rhode Island, or slightly smaller than ancient Corinth, had established its control over most of the then known civilized world and eliminated every serious challenge to its power. And this was not done in one great effort by one great personality like Cyrus or Alexander, but was achieved over many generations by the aristocracy and citizen body of a city-state. Nor was it just a flash of lightning against the sky of history. Whatever terminal date we choose for the Roman empire, it lasted close

---

rious reservations about Ferenczy's methodology, see A. Drummond, *JRS* 72 (1982): 176f. Ferenczy's previous contributions are listed by Richard, *REL* 55 (1977): 39, many of them also in the Bibliography of this volume.

13. At present, the best accounts are to be found in Brunt, *Conflicts* (1971): 42ff., and in some general surveys of Roman history, esp. in H. H. Scullard and M. Cary, *A History of Rome down to the Reign of Constantine*³ (New York, 1975): 62ff., 75ff.; Scullard, *History*⁴ (1980): 78ff., 115ff.; F. Altheim, *Röm. Geschichte* II (1953): 170ff., 329ff.; Bleicken, *Republik* (1980): 22ff., 215ff. (with critical bibliography), and "Rom und Italien" (1963): 60ff.

14. Whatever we think about Rome's economic and political power under the Etruscan kings, there seems to be substantial agreement that the situation was much worse and more difficult internally and externally at least between c. 485 and 425 (see chapter VII below at n. 29ff.), and again after the Gallic invasion. For a new assessment of the situation around 300 B.C., see Starr, *Beginnings* (1980); the catalogue of the exhibition *Roma medio repubblicana* (Rome, 1973); and T. Hölscher, *RM* 85 (1978): 315ff.

to, or more than, a thousand years, and in history that is an eternity. Its effects, moreover, reach well into our own immediate past, and its achievements were the foundations of our civilization.

The preconditions for all this, as far as they are to be found in Rome itself and in the Roman people, were created in the two dark centuries of the early Republic. Externally, they were marked by frequent and intensive fighting either against Rome's Latin neighbors or together with them against the Etruscans in the north and the mountain tribes in the east and south that were pushing down into the plains of Latium. Internally, they were dominated by a long series of bitter struggles between the patrician aristocracy and the plebeians: the Conflict of the Orders. The successes in fighting back external threats and in overcoming internal tensions were interconnected.[15] The extended exposure to this double pressure and challenge shaped the Romans and prepared them for their great future.

There is no doubt, therefore, that we can only understand the later achievements of the Romans if we really understand the Conflict of the Orders, its causes, content, stages, results, and historical function. What is called the Conflict of the Orders, and somewhat artificially dated by the first secession of the *plebs* (traditionally 494) and the Hortensian law (287), was really a long process of fundamental transformations in several respects. The exclusive aristocratic society of early Rome was replaced by a unified and cohesive citizen body, and although this was still led by an almost equally exclusive aristocracy, all classes were integrated and had their defined rights, obligations, and functions. Solutions were found for most of the problems that had caused a deep economic, social, and political crisis and brought Rome to the brink of civil war soon after the foundation of the Republic and repeatedly thereafter. During this period, Rome passed from the prepolitical stage, where there was little political organization, and power was primarily defined and exercised as social power, to the political stage, with defined and differentiated institutions and a well-balanced constitution. As opposed to the process of *Stadtwerdung*[16] (the formation of the city in the seventh and sixth centuries), this was the process of *Staatswerdung*, the formation of the Roman state that Polybius described and the later Roman authors took for granted.

15. Ferenczy emphasizes this repeatedly; it is one of the merits of his book.
16. The formulation of H. Müller-Karpe, *Stadtwerdung* (1962).

However, the difficulties and obstacles we face in trying to understand these developments are enormous, if not insurmountable. There are very few contemporary sources. The archaeological evidence is limited and often subject to vastly differing interpretations.[17] The analysis of the development of constitution and institutions is marred by errors and falsifications in our sources.[18] There is hardly a single piece of documentary evidence (such as laws, treaties, and lists of magistrates) whose authenticity and historical value is not fiercely debated.[19] And the literary sources, with their elaborate and detailed reports, were produced many centuries later by authors who were separated from their early Roman ancestors by a deep cultural and developmental gap that made it almost impossible for them to imagine early Roman life and actions, whose perception and methods of historiography were very different from ours, and who did not see any reason why they should not use the experiences of their own troubled times in reconstructing the history of the past. For the modern historian of the early Republic, Livy and Dionysius present an intractable jungle of traps and pitfalls. In many ways we might be better off if we took their description of the monarchy and early Republic as prose epics or historical novels and treated them as we do Homer and Vergil.

The modern historian of the early Republic is thus faced with a seemingly impossible task. However, there are at least two approaches that have not been exhausted so far and might help to advance our understanding sufficiently to make the effort worthwhile. Both are by no means new or sensational, and gains can only be expected

---

17. Cf. the debate on the chronology of the beginning of the Republic, adequately summarized by Poma, *Studi* (1974): 11ff., and discussed by M. Pallottino, *ANRW* I.1 (1972): 22ff. See further below at n. 29ff. On the lack of contemporary sources, see now M. I. Finley, "Ancient Historian" (1983): 207ff.

18. Cf. the summary of the ongoing scholarly debate in Meyer, *Staat*³ (1964), and Heurgon, *Rise* (1973): 106ff., 156ff., 186ff.

19. It suffices to mention the early treaties with Carthage and the *foedus Cassianum*, the *fasti*, and the laws of the early Republic. For the treaties, see H. Bengtson and R. Werner, *Die Staatsverträge des Altertums* II (Munich, 1962): nos. 121 (p. 16) and 126 (p. 22); Heurgon, *Rise* (1973): 250ff.; K.-E. Petzold, *ANRW* I.1 (1972): 364ff. On the *fasti* of the early Republic, cf. P. Fraccaro's review of Beloch's *Röm. Geschichte* (1926) in *RFIC* 56 (1927): 551ff.; and, more recently, Bengtson, *Grundriss*² (1970): 42ff.; E. Meyer, *MH* 9 (1952): 176ff.; Werner, *Beginn* (1963): 219ff.; R. T. Ridley, *Athenaeum* 58 (1980): 264ff. On the laws of the early Republic, cf. Bleicken, *Lex* (1975): 72ff., and Elster, *Studien* (1976).

through an intensified and comprehensive exploitation of a partly well known, partly still hidden potential. It is the purpose of this paper to explore and discuss those two approaches.

2. *The Comprehensive Approach*

The first is what might be called the "comprehensive approach," meaning that all available sources must be used adequately and to their full extent. "All" means not only the historiographical, epigraphical, and archaeological sources but also information scattered in the works of antiquarians and lexicographers, which is often hard to discover, and the evidence provided by linguistic analysis and social, political, military, religious, and legal institutions. Even though generations of historians have been working on this neverending task, recent studies (e.g., by A. Momigliano and A. Alföldi) have taught us how much ancient religious practices, costumes, names, and the forgotten remarks of antiquarians can still reveal to us.[20] There is quite probably not only more to be found, but a comprehensive analysis of such scattered material, which is frequently scrutinized only by specialists in a very limited context, could yield important results.

If, on the other hand, it is true that every generation has to write its own history books, this is not only the case because new evidence forces historians continually to reassess their conclusions, but because every generation has its own questions to ask. In recent decades the generally renewed interest in archaic societies and the fruitful exchange of ideas, methods, and insights between the disciplines of history, anthropology, sociology, and political science have created better conditions than have ever existed for a new attempt at solving some of the problems connected with the Conflict of the Orders in archaic Rome. What is needed, therefore, is not only a more systematic exploitation of the whole range of sources, but a more comprehensive approach to the material offered by them and a sound methodological basis for their interpretation. In particular, there must be a clear understanding of what the different categories of

---

20. See below at n. 56ff.

sources can and cannot tell us, what we can expect from them, and how we can use them most fruitfully.

This is especially true for the thorny problem of the historical value of our ancient historiographical sources. There is in our discipline an increasing and detrimental tendency (encouraged by the flood of new publications) to consult only recent scholarship and to lose sight of some of the fundamental and lasting results of the work of our predecessors. With good reason, some of them had grave doubts about the general reliability of the annalistic reports on the history of the early Republic. Occasionally, they went too far. The dangers connected with the position of extreme skepticism (which had its most radical representative in E. Pais around the turn of the century) have long been recognized. But at least that was a well-defined and clearly argued position. More recently, historians have tended to waver rather weakly between overcredulity and skepticism, practicing a happy but fruitless methodological eclecticism. Unfortunately, they often do not seem to understand sufficiently how deeply these questions affect any attempt at historical reconstruction. J. Heurgon describes the present situation as follows:

> What we see today is a full-scale rehabilitation . . . of the literary tradition; in some writers this goes so far as to believe its literal truth and to treat it as so authoritative that the slightest doubt . . . becomes rank blasphemy. . . . [This] reversal of the former situation . . . has been engendered in large part . . . by the weariness and discouragement with which one saw so many systematic and conflicting reconstructions rise up on the ruins of the tradition, only to collapse one after another. Confronted by the failure of these sometimes forced theories . . . hypercriticism has been driven to self-criticism. . . . A return to the sources has gradually forced itself upon us, as a return to a basic collection of data which deserves more credit than all the structures that we might build on its ruins.[21]

Undoubtedly it is true that hypercriticism is no longer feasible (it never is, anyway), and that the annalistic tradition has been at least partially rehabilitated, mainly through archaeological discoveries in

21. Heurgon, *Rise* (1973): 245; cf. Alföldi, *Early Rome* (1965): 318f.

I. A Comprehensive and Comparative Approach 11

several areas and of various kinds.[22] Undoubtedly, archaeology will provide us with more exciting discoveries—after all, our main prospect of really new information lies in excavation—and it may be hoped that it will also continue to be instrumental in confirming or modifying the literary tradition. So far, however, the remarkable discoveries of recent years have mostly improved our knowledge of prehistoric Latium and regal Rome; relatively few are of importance for the fifth and fourth centuries,[23] and in some cases, they have even further damaged the credibility of the ancient historians' reports.[24] At any rate, this, too, is a tool to be used carefully and with a good methodological foundation. The post-holes of the cabins on the Palatine, the sixth-century sanctuaries on the *Forum Boarium*, the gold tablets from Pyrgi, and the name of Poplios Valesios on an early inscription from Satricum, like many other items, prove and confirm some things but not everything.[25] The fact that Livy and Dionysius contain more reliable information about prehistoric and archaic Rome than was believed is most welcome. But it may not be taken as blanket authority for treating them as eyewitnesses. What we need more than ever before, precisely because of the increasingly significant contribution of archaeology, is a clear and differentiated concept of the possibilities and limitations of the historical exploitation and interpretation of archaeological evidence.

We especially need to separate and define different categories of information. Some kinds of information were available to the ancient authors. For example, the names of officials and generals and details of wars, triumphs, treaties, embassies, dedications of temples

---

22. Cf. Cornell, *Archaeological Reports* (1979–80): 71ff., esp. 83ff., and the literature quoted there; see also chapter II below at n. 38ff. For a comprehensive interpretation and a summary of our present state of knowledge, cf. G. Colonna, "Preistoria e protostoria" (1974): 273ff.; C. Ampolo and G. Bartolini, *DArch*, n.s., 2 (1980): 165ff.

23. Cf. Cornell, chapter II below at n. 43.

24. Especially remarkable is the archaeologists' failure to find evidence for the allegedly complete destruction of Rome by the Gauls: F. Castagnoli, *SR* 22 (1974): 426f.; M. Torelli and F. Coarelli at 226ff. and 229f. respectively in the exhibition catalogue *I Galli e l'Italia* (Rome, 1978); Cornell, *Archaeological Reports* (1979–80): 84; and, especially, Coarelli, "Sviluppo urbanistico" (1982): 22f.

25. See below at n. 35f. For the gold tablets of Pyrgi, cf. the bibliography in *Lamine di Pyrgi* (1970): 63ff., and the literature mentioned by Poma, *Studi* (1974): 39, with n. 13 on p. 120. Cf. also the general remarks by Finley, "Ancient Historian" (1983): 210ff.

and shrines, disasters and famines, miracles and omens, and the consultation of oracles and the Sibylline books may have been contained in the records of the *pontifices*[26] and, in one way or another, have provided the later authors with a framework of facts. Together with the information available from the Twelve Tables and some other early documents,[27] this helped to establish the course of (mostly external) events and to form at least a rough picture of the economic, religious, and political situation. Given the importance of military success and public service for the concept of *dignitas*, the (frequently expanded and exaggerated) memories and records kept in many noble families may have added more material in the same areas.[28]

Apart from making available some of the rare epigraphical monuments that have survived, archaeology, on the other hand, is able to confirm, refute, or modify some of this evidence and to add more to it: building activity or lack thereof, size and adornment of public and private buildings, size and patterns of settlements, customs and wealth or poverty of burials, patterns of trade or gift exchange, influx of foreign materials and influences, quality of art, architecture, and much more. By observing the appearance and disappearance, or the increase and decrease in quantity, of certain items, it can establish changes and indicate development; by noticing abrupt changes or major disturbances, it can occasionally even pinpoint

---

26. In a similar listing, Cornell (chapter II below after n. 31) calls this the "basic outline" or the "structural elements" of historical tradition. Cato's famous fragm. 77 P. may well be too narrow. Cf. Frier, *Annales* (1979): 83ff., 107ff., who reconstructs the late republican view of the content of the *tabulae* and the pontifical chronicle and rightly points out that the reality, especially in the fifth and fourth centuries, may have been different (104); but see also n. 41 below. We should be aware, however, that, with the probable exception of the religious elements, even those structural "facts" could be invented; the famous embassy to Athens before the decemviral legislation (see Poma, *Studi* [1974]: 41ff., with literature cited in n. 33 on p. 124f., and Toher, chapter X below, n. 2ff.) and the equally famous trial of the Scipios (literature in Ungern-Sternberg, *Capua* [1975]: 8 n. 33f.) should be enough of a warning.

27. Listed by Frier, *Annales* (1979): 127f. Ampolo, "Storiografia e documenti" (1983): 14ff., discusses the (often extremely unscholarly and uncritical) way such documents were used by most Roman historians and antiquarians (if they were used at all). Cornell, "Tradizione storiografica" (1980): 25, rightly emphasizes that all these documents date to the late sixth and early fifth centuries, whereas for a full century after the Twelve Tables none are mentioned at all.

28. Plut. *Numa* 1.2; Cic. *Brut.* 62; Livy 8.40.4f., with the comments of Frier, *Annales* (1979): 121ff.

historical events. Such findings undoubtedly help to improve our understanding of the material culture and to some extent, therefore, of the economic and social situation in a given community.

When trying to use archaeological finds for historical reconstruction, however, we are faced with several serious problems. In pointing these out, I do not want to belittle the importance of archaeological contributions—quite the contrary—but to scale unreasonably optimistic expectations down to a realistic level. First, most of the early Roman evidence is not only controversial in itself, and therefore subject to contradictory interpretations, but in addition it is often not interpreted in a sufficiently broad historical and methodological context. Let me give two examples. On the one hand, if the excavated foundations of the Capitoline temple indeed go back to the late sixth century (which is probable), and if the dimensions of the temple corresponded to those of the platform (which is not at all certain), Rome had one of the largest archaic temples in central Italy.[29] Does that allow us to conclude that it was one of the most powerful cities as well, ambitiously competing with its Etruscan neighbors? Such a conclusion would only be justified if there were strong evidence that the erection of large temples by archaic kings or tyrants was an expression of their power and ambition in foreign, rather than internal, politics. Whether or not scholarship on Greek tyrannies is correct in doubting this, the political significance of the Roman temple can only be determined in such a larger context.[30] On

---

29. Cf. Cornell, chapter II below at n. 54. The foundations, with the large temple known from later sources, are dated to the fourth century by Alföldi, *Early Rome* (1965): 323ff., and (with more arguments and new literature), *Frühgeschichte* (1976): 114ff.; cf. also H. Riemann, *RM* 76 (1969): 110ff., and *Gymnasium* 72 (1965): 338ff. The weighty counterarguments are summarized by F. Castagnoli, *SR* 22 (1974): 433ff. It seems hard, indeed, to contest the sixth-century origin of the platform. But the temple may be an entirely different matter. Based on comparative evidence from the Latino-Etruscan region, Castagnoli, *RM* 73/74 (1966–67): 12ff., and esp. *SR* 22 (1974): 433ff., proposes an attractive alternative—a much smaller temple on the large sixth-century platform. F. Coarelli tells me, however, that recent finds in Cerveteri indicate an archaic temple of similarly large proportions. The question therefore remains open.

30. Similar reservations should be expressed regarding conclusions drawn from the size of the city at the end of the sixth century, since such calculations are often based on the assumption that an (almost completely hypothesized) sixth-century *agger* at least partially followed the course of the later "Servian Walls." Against this assumption and the existence of a complete city fortification in the sixth century:

the other hand, the sherds found in various excavation sites indicate that the importation of figured Attic pottery declined sharply in the first and second quarters of the fifth century. This seems a safe statement despite the continuing debate about precise chronology.[31] Roughly at the same time (484 B.C.) a phase of intensive temple construction, recorded by the annalistic tradition, came to an end.[32] Both these factors are generally interpreted as strong indications of a severe economic crisis, which the Romans were able to overcome only toward the end of the century. Now there may indeed be good reasons to believe that there was such a crisis,[33] but it seems questionable to me whether these two factors alone are sufficient for such a belief. What I miss so far is a thorough discussion of the problem of why and how the increase and decrease in pottery imports and in temple building indicate economic prosperity or recession. In addition, "crisis" is a very loose term. What kind of a crisis? Whom did it affect: only the rich, only the poor, or the whole community? These certainly are questions that go beyond the task of an archaeologist, but since the conclusion (economic crisis) is based on archaeological

---

A. v. Gerkan, *RM* 55 (1940): 24ff.; H. Riemann, *RM* 76 (1969): 103ff.; Alföldi, *Early Rome* (1965): 320ff., with literature; Castagnoli, *Roma* (1978): 28f. F. Coarelli, "Sviluppo urbanistico" (1982): 24, summarizes what can reasonably be said for a sixth-century fortification on the basis of recent archaeological evidence. For the fourth-century "Servian Walls," see the catalogue of the exhibition *Roma medio repubblicana* (1973): 7ff., with literature. Beloch suggested c. 285 hectares for the "City of the Four Regions," i.e., two-thirds of the area surrounded by the "Servian Walls." Even so the size of Rome would have been enormous, much larger than any city in Latium and comparable to the very greatest Etruscan cities (see Cornell, chapter II below, n. 49). Accordingly, Beloch, Ed. Meyer, and others talked of "one of the largest cities in Italy and the Mediterranean World." Cornell concludes that "an urban community of these dimensions would have been more than a match for most Etruscan cities" (chapter II below at n. 49). Unfortunately, the territory surrounded by city walls is not in itself a reliable indication of the population or power of a city (cf. Castagnoli, *Roma* [1978]: 30; Coarelli, "Sviluppo urbanistico" [1982]: 24). Unless we count on constant importation of food (impossible for the fifth century), it was the size and productivity of the *ager* belonging to the city that determined the size of the population, whatever the proportion living in the city and the extension of the city territory (see below at n. 112ff.).

31. Cf. the recent discussion by J. C. Meyer, *Analecta Rom. inst. Danici* 9 (1980): 47ff.

32. Latte, *Religionsgeschichte* (1960): 415; R. Bloch, *Origins* (1960): 98f.; Frank, *Economic Survey* I (1933): 24. Opinions on the causes and (political) purpose of these foundations vary widely, cf. chapter VII below, n. 57.

33. Cf. chapter VII below, part 3, with literature cited in n. 29.

evidence (potsherds), I have to insist that the historical significance of archaeological finds can only be determined within a sufficiently broad framework.

Second, most of the archaeological evidence claimed as support for the basic reliability of the annalistic tradition belongs to an earlier period than we are concerned with in this volume. Indeed, as Cornell states, "the fifth century . . . is something of a blank."[34] Much of it, moreover, pertains to areas concerning which the ancient historians had some (and, relatively speaking, the most reliable) information anyway. And, if scrutinized for its support of specific facts claimed by our literary sources, the value of archaeological data is often quite limited, because it is too general. For example, what has been found on the Alban Hills indicates decline (though not total discontinuity) in roughly the right period, but does not confirm Roman responsibility.[35] The sanctuaries under the church of Sant' Omobono on the archaic *Forum Boarium* prove that the Romans indeed built sanctuaries in the sixth century, but, much as we are inclined to think so, they do not automatically confirm all the traditions about Servius Tullius.[36] Nor do the legendary exploits of Valerius Publicola or the Vibenna brothers become any more historical simply because their names have been discovered on contemporary documents from Veii and Satricum, and the persons themselves were probably historical.[37] There is no question that these are extremely important discoveries, but what is often made of them is

34. Cornell, chapter II below at n. 43; id., "Tradizione storiografica" (1980): 30.
35. Livy 1.28ff.; cf. Ogilvie, *Comm.* (1965): 120f.; Alföldi, *Early Rome* (1965): 238ff.
36. Cornell, *Archaeological Reports* (1979–80): 85 (with literature), cautiously speaks of "the most striking of a number of correspondences between archaeological data and the literary tradition about Servius Tullius." Cf. also Thomsen, *Serv. Tullius* (1980): 260ff., esp. 267ff. Eder, chapter IX below at n. 18f., is more cautious.
37. Cf. E. Bickerman, *RFIC* 97 (1969): 397. Aulus Vibenna in Veii: M. Pallottino, *SE* 13 (1939): 455ff.; Alföldi, *Early Rome* (1965): 215ff.; Thomsen, *Serv. Tullius* (1980): 23, 86f.; C. Ampolo, *Opus* 2 (1983): 397. Poplios Valesios on the *lapis Satricanus*: M. Pallottino, *Quad. del centro di studi per l'arch. etr.-ital.* 1 (1978): 99; id., in the introd. to C. M. Stibbe et al., *Lapis Satricanus* (1980); id., *SR* 27 (1979): 12f.; H. Versnel, "Historical Implications" (1980): 128ff., and *Gymnasium* 89 (1982): 202ff. The identity seems to be more certain in the case of Aulus Vibenna than in that of Publicola. Another strong case for historical identity may be found in the Sostratos from Aegina mentioned in Herod. 4.152 and on a stele recently found in Gravisca: M. Torelli, *PP* 26 (1971): 55ff. Cf. in general the important remarks by Ampolo, *Opus* 2 (1983): 397.

reminiscent of the "Troy syndrome": neither the heroic names on the Linear B tablets nor, despite all the efforts of Schliemann and his followers, the ruins of Hissarlik prove that the Greek epic tradition is historically valid even in its most basic content.[38] The problem of the correspondence between literary sources and archaeological data needs further and more comprehensive discussion.[39]

More importantly, unless it uncovers epigraphical evidence, archaeology does not precisely identify the human agent and rarely offers insight into historical causation. This statement can be expanded: what archaeology can neither give us[40] nor confirm in the narrative of the Roman historians, and what they could, with very few exceptions, not find in their written sources either,[41] is the whole area of internal and social politics, of social change and relations, of human behavior and thought, deliberation and decision, of cause and effect, purpose, intention, motivation. These aspects, however, are indispensable for a coherent social history and especially for a coherent explanation of social conflict. Livy and Dionysius give us both; we should, therefore, be extremely suspicious.

Especially for the early Republic and for social history, such suspicion is amply confirmed by our understanding of the development, intentions, and working methods of Roman annalistic historiography. As a genre, it has had its important historical function in more than one respect; there is no need to ridicule, despise, or condemn

---

38. Cf., e.g., M. I. Finley, "Lost: The Trojan War," in id., *Aspects of Antiquity*² (Harmondsworth, England, 1977): 31ff.; F. Hampl, "Die Ilias ist kein Geschichtsbuch," in id., *Geschichte als kritische Wissenschaft* II (Darmstadt, 1975): 51ff.; J. Cobet, "Gab es den Trojanischen Krieg?" *Antike Welt* 14, no. 4 (1983): 39ff.

39. M. Torelli, *DArch* 4 (1970): 83; id., "Roma arcaica" (1980): 16f.; Eder, chapter IX below at n. 18.

40. Cf. Momigliano, *Contr. IV* (1969): 442.

41. Exceptions are mentioned in chapter VII below at n. 31ff. It seems especially questionable to me whether the pontifical chronicle contained many notes, let alone detailed notes, on matters pertaining to the Conflict of the Orders. The few vague ancient references (discussed by Frier, *Annales* [1979]: 83ff.) do not allow such an assumption (even Livy 8.18.12f. is contradicted by 7.3.3). According to Frier (96), "conceived from the viewpoint of the aristocratic government of early Rome, the brief notes of the *tabula* provided evidence of the continuous and orderly operation of government; the notices leaked important information downward to the populace, in discrete and summary fashion." If this view of one of the main purposes of the *tabula* were correct (which I seriously doubt), we certainly should not expect many references to social unrest and the like.

it. But there are a number of characteristics that undeniably reduce its value for historical reconstruction—as much for the modern historian as for those like Livy and Dionysius who wrote at the end of the tradition itself, two hundred years after its founders. It seems necessary to recall these characteristics because they tend to be forgotten by those who work with, but not specifically on, those sources.[42]

The genre of *annales* was created in the time of the second Punic War with a strong explanatory and patriotic purpose, among others. It went through several stages clearly distinguishable in time and intent. Eventually, it "literally became the historical record of Rome, at least of the regal and early Republican periods," and it therefore seemed generally superfluous to seek out whatever primary or independent evidence still existed. But the source basis had been extremely poor from the beginning, and the need to compete with the Greek historical tradition, which was so rich in factual detail and plausibility, made it compulsory to "flesh out" the framework of data transmitted from the distant past. Several quarries were readily available: antiquarian interest in, and collections of, archaic customs and institutions; chronologically uncertain legends and stories that had been elaborated into juristic case studies;[43] familiarity with Roman society, institutions, and values (which in their essence, if not in detail, were thought to have remained unchanged for centuries); knowledge of the city itself, its surroundings and its empire; analogies and models especially in Greek history and offered by Greek historiography; the political experiences of the author's own time, contemporary or recent, that provoked deep partisan emotions; and, finally, the realm of imagination and fiction.[44] All these areas

---

42. The following remarks are based on Frier, *Annales* (1979) 201ff. (quotes: 223, 215, 276). For additional support, see E. Badian, "Early Historians" (1966): 1ff.; E. Gabba, "Tradizione letteraria" (1967): 133ff., and in *ANRW* II.30.1: 799ff.; D. Timpe, *ANRW* I.2: 928ff., and *A&A* 25 (1979): 97ff.; M. I. Finley, "Ancient Historian" (1983): 201ff.; cf. also Ungern-Sternberg, chapter III below at nn. 17ff., and *Capua* (1975): 1ff.

43. The story of the maiden in Ardea (Livy 4.9) offers a good example; cf. Ogilvie, *Comm.* (1965): 547f.; for another, see Peppe, *Esecuzione* (1981): 186.

44. For examples of late republican experiences, see Ogilvie, *Comm.* (1965), passim, for Livy, and Gabba's articles on Dionysius of Halicarnassus, listed in the Bibliography, especially *Athenaeum*, n. s., 42 (1964): 29ff., on the *rogatio agraria* of Sp. Cassius. H. Hill, *JRS* 51 (1961): 88ff., and Peppe, *Esecuzione* (1981): 24, emphasize

were exploited systematically by many generations of historians. Especially under the impression of late republican factional strife and civil war, the tradition, firmly embedded in its annalistic framework, underwent several reinterpretations.[45] Whereas the outlook of the early annalists had been dominated by foreign politics and Rome's ability to overcome external challenges, for the later ones the hitherto comparatively insignificant area of internal politics and social conflict acquired prime importance.

In addition, the documentary background of the *annales* was increasingly criticized and deemed insufficient for a continuing narrative of early Roman history. By the beginning of the first century, such doubts seemed so serious for at least one annalist that he decided to exclude the entire period before 390. Another historian, elaborating on thoughts already expressed by Polybius, condemned the whole annalistic genre as ill suited for serious historiography because it concentrated too heavily on military history and was generally ill informed as to the motives of the principal actors and consequently not capable of decent historical explanation.[46] In reaction to such attacks, later annalists tried "to present a more convincing narrative of Roman history (often through outrageous invention of documents and statistics)." At the same time, literary and moral concerns, the striving for entertainment and effect as well as for education, definitely gained the upper hand.

In the end, trust in the historical reliability of the tradition concerning early and archaic Rome was sufficiently weakened, and the desire for literary achievement so predominant, that Livy could feel free to reinterpret "all of Roman history before 390 more as a moral lesson than a strictly historical narrative." This reinterpretation made major rearrangements of facts and causation inevitable, but this had been done regularly, although for various reasons, by all his prede-

---

that the problem of debt and debt-bondage was understood and presented by Dionysius by analogy to Solonian Athens. As Finley remarks ("Ancient Historian" [1983]: 203), "The ability of the ancients to invent and their capacity to believe are persistently underestimated."

45. Ungern-Sternberg provides a good example in chapter III below.
46. Q. Claudius Quadrigarius (Plut. *Numa* 1.2), cf. Frier, *Annales* (1979): 121ff.; Sempronius Asellio, fr. 1–2 P., cf. Frier 219f. (with literature and references to Polybius); cf. also Frier 152ff.

cessors,⁴⁷ and by his own time the material was considered legendary enough⁴⁸ to allow such artistic freedom—just as, I would suggest, the Greek myths were changed and adapted by the tragic poets to their specific needs.

The difference, of course, is that we do not try to reconstruct early Greek history from tragedy—at least not on the level of facts and events—but do try to reconstruct the history of archaic Rome from Livy. He and Dionysius are our richest and—with few exceptions—earliest sources. Nevertheless, it may be wondered how we can seriously base our historical reconstruction on these authors, knowing the many motives and opportunities for, and the generally uncritical attitude to, the transformation, elaboration, and deformation of the record in the tradition of annalistic historiography; knowing, furthermore, the techniques and preferences of Licinius Macer, Livy's—or more probably his predecessors'—main source on the "history of the plebeians and the plebeian revolution."⁴⁹

There is an additional difficulty. Looking back from the late third century, the first Roman historians had within their reach of roughly a hundred years only the very last stages of the Conflict of the Orders. This final phase was dominated by a few issues: the distribution of *ager publicus* and the abolition of debt-bondage, the formalization of the *ius provocationis*, the constitutional integration of the *concilium plebis* and the tribunate, and, most of all, the access of the plebeian elite to offices and priesthoods. In our sources these very issues play a decisive role from the beginning to the end of the conflict. We are given the impression that for over two hundred years the plebeians were struggling for those very goals they finally attained at the end of the fourth century and the beginning of the third.⁵⁰ It is well known that there is in Livy and Dionysius an enormous amount of retrojection, schematic construction, and juggling around of a few given elements. Unfortunately, the ancient authors do not seem to have had a profound understanding of the character

---

47. For Livy, cf. the recent demonstration by T. J. Luce, *TAPA* 102 (1971): 265ff. and especially 299ff. See, on a larger scale, Ferenczy, *Patr. State* (1976): 84ff., on the "invention" of the first Samnite War by some early annalist.
48. Cf. Florus, *Epitome* 1.10.3.
49. See n. 6 above.
50. Cf. the discussion in chapter VII below.

of the conflict they were describing, especially not of its early stages.[51] I would suggest that the final successes of the plebeians and the social and political situation of the late fourth and early third centuries worked for them like scenery in a theater or on a screen. They knew that there was something behind it, that the picture they could see represented the result of a long evolution, but they did not know exactly where this evolution had begun and how it had developed. They knew a few factors involved and could locate a few important stations of this process, and they tried to make sense of it as best they could by incorporating all the known facts and constructing a linear evolution leading up to the final, visible result. But they could not imagine that the early stages might have been radically different from the later ones, and different not only in quantity but in quality. In other words, the origins of the system familiar to them were not only beyond their knowledge but also beyond their imagination.

On the one hand, of course, what seems to be an inability to reckon consciously with the unfamiliar, and a tendency to retroject contemporary phenomena and attitudes into the distant past without question, is common to practically all of Greco-Roman historiography.[52] On the other hand, this inclination corresponded to, and was encouraged by, another characteristic view that became increasingly predominant in the annalistic tradition and was used and formulated in an exemplary way by Livy. Annalistic history saw itself—and was certainly seen by others—as the history of the free Republic, and that meant "in essence, the history of the free and aristocratic government of Rome; it spoke for the endurance of an aristocratic ideal that was the essence of the Republic." As Livy finally and most clearly understood it, setting up a strong contrast to the

---

51. Cf. Momigliano, *Contr. IV* (1969): 437ff., esp. 438, and "Patrizi e plebei" (1967): 199ff. More generally: T. J. Cornell, "Tradizione storiografica" (1980): 33, referring to the observations of A. M. Snodgrass, *The Greek Dark Age* (Edinburgh, 1971): 6ff.

52. M. I. Finley, "Ancient Historian" (1983): 210 (referring to M. Crawford, "Roman Economy" [1976]: 198) observes: "The Romans, like the Greeks, were 'relentlessly modernizing' in their attempts to deal with their own archaic institutions and behaviour." For Greece, Aristotle's *Athenaion politeia* is an obvious example; cf. C. Hignett, *A History of the Athenian Constitution to the End of the Fifth Century* B.C. (Oxford, 1952): 1ff.; Day and Chambers, *Ath. Pol.* (1962): 5ff.; E. Ruschenbusch, *Athenische Innenpolitik im 5. Jh. v. Chr.: Ideologie oder Pragmatismus?* (Bamberg, 1979): 3ff.; Rhodes, *Comm. Ath. Pol.* (1981): 15ff.

monarchy preceding and the principate following it, the "Republic was to be deemed a unity, stretching onward from 509: the acts of a free people, the annual government, the preeminence of statute and constitution." Certainly Rome—its society, constitution, and power—developed remarkably in the course of centuries and the knowledge of these developments became ever clearer and more detailed, "but the Republic itself, however much its moral fiber might alter, would not be essentially other than it was in 509." The modern historian who works with Livy has to be aware of the serious consequences that such a "unitarian view" of republican history must have had on the reconstruction and presentation of that history. It especially limited the amount and character of historical change allowed within the basic stability and unity. Linear development and changes in quantity were more easily compatible with it than changes in quality and uneven or interrupted developments. Growth (of institutions, numbers, size, and power) was easily conceivable and unproblematic; the concept of radical transformation was highly problematic, if not unthinkable.[53]

To put it concretely: that the structure of Roman society might originally have been much more complex than a simple dichotomy between patricians and plebeians presumed to go back to the very beginnings of Rome; that the number of senators might not always have been fixed and not necessarily in hundreds; that there might not always have been a great reserve of *equites* striving for admission to the offices and the Senate; that the two consuls with equal power might not have been introduced at the very beginning of the Republic, but as much as a century later, preceded by one or several other forms of leading magistracies; that the centuriate army of the third century might not have been created in one stroke, but might have been developed through several stages over a long period of time; that the organization of the plebeians might equally have emerged gradually and not sprung full-blown out of nothing in 494;

---

53. Quotes: Frier, *Annales* (1979): 202f., 205, with references. For the ancient historians' view that the Roman constitution was fully developed by 449, see the literature cited in chapter VII below, n. 11. Cornell points out in "Tradizione storiografica" (1980): 32f., that neither Livy nor probably any other Roman historian was aware of a "crisis" or "decline" of Rome in the fifth century, or of the existence of what we call the "Roman Dark Age." For "linear simplification," see also A. Fraschetti, "Inquadramento storico" (1982).

that concepts such as "citizenship" and "freedom" might have meant little or nothing for a long time and then emerged slowly and with difficulty—these and many other possibilities did not, and obviously could not, occur to our historians, partly because they did not have all the necessary information, partly because they could not adequately interpret some of the information they had, partly because they operated with preconceived ideas and specific intentions, and partly because they did not have that breadth of historical and anthropological knowledge that only recent generations have been able to acquire and apply.

I cannot, therefore, see how, for the problems we are concerned with here, we could start from any other position than serious and determined skepticism. This conclusion probably will not be popular; it does not allow easy compromises. That every historical analysis has to begin with, and to be based on, the written sources is a sound principle in the vast majority of cases.[54] But the Conflict of the Orders is one of the few exceptions. Our ancient historians are not safe guides to the distant past. At best, they were just what we are, historians wrestling with the desperately difficult task of putting together a coherent picture out of a few scattered fragments of evidence. At worst, they were historical novelists. Even if the former were true, we should take their reconstructions as suggestions worthy of our consideration rather than as statements of fact. That they lived in late republican Rome does not automatically make their guesses and conclusions better than ours. Especially for the early Republic and for social history, therefore, the only sound method is to

---

54. This is rightly emphasized by A. Momigliano, e.g., *JRS* 53 (1963): 98; cf. id., *Contr. III* (1966): 607: "Ad ogni modo è inutile illudersi di poter capire la storia di Roma arcaica su pure basi archeologiche. La preistoria è preistoria appunto perché manca la tradizione storiografica. Quando la tradizione c'è, le va dato il dovuto peso." *Il dovuto peso*, yes, but not a privileged position of a priori trust or even *in dubio pro reo*. In particular, I agree with Momigliano, *Contr. III* (1966): 662: "Una tradizione non è priva di valore, perché non confermata indipendentemente. Allo storico importa meno trovare conferma archeologica ai dati della tradizione storica che di spiegare l'origine di queste dati e come siano venuti ad acquistare autorità." This is precisely the objective of Ungern-Sternberg's contribution in chapter III below; cf. also Peppe, *Esecuzione* (1981): 27f. Unfortunately, however, though this approach is useful for understanding the character and formation of the annalistic tradition, it does not help us to analyze, understand, and reconstruct the history of the archaic period.

distrust the ancient historians unless their statements can be confirmed or made plausible by independent evidence.[55]

We must attempt to find and disentangle those very elements upon which the annalists based their reconstructions. Inter alia we have to take seriously what is often proclaimed—that Livy's first ten books are a better source for the history of the late Republic than for that of the early Republic. One of the first steps, therefore, would consist of systematically stripping away everything that might possibly derive from late republican experience. This very difficult task will leave us with little source material, but at least what remains will be sound. To that we must then add the other categories of evidence gained through the comprehensive approach described above.

Apart from possible archaeological data and information gained through the comparative approach described below, this evidence must be collected mainly from a variety of nonhistoriographical literary sources: antiquarians and grammarians, writers of "natural histories" and "various histories," collectors of curiosities, orators and jurists, lexicographers, commentators, and the authors of other learned works compiled in late antiquity. Most representatives of these genres wrote during the Empire; the earliest extant ones were contemporaries of the latest annalists. Like the latter, they incorporated earlier material in their work, but they were interested in a much broader range of evidence, and they exploited categories of sources that were rarely used directly by the historians. Many of these sources contained a wealth of historical information: orations, poems, and songs; customs, laws, and moral codes; religious formulas and details of cults and ceremonies; unusual and antiquated words and sentences; records of monuments and inscriptions; and anecdotes, legends, and historical traditions preserved not only among Roman families but also among other Italic tribes and in Greek or Etruscan cities. Occasionally, some of this material was

---

55. With these last few sentences I put myself into stark opposition to the conclusions formulated by T. Cornell and R. Develin elsewhere in this volume; see my critical remarks in the appendix to this contribution. Cf. M. I. Finley's recent remarks in "Ancient Historian" (1983): 204, 209f.; Bleicken, *Lex* (1975): 5ff. (with literature); *Republik* (1980): 105ff. Bleicken's position, however, is even more absolute than mine: "dass die gesamte annalistische Überlieferung, die vor dem letzten Drittel des vierten Jahrhunderts liegt, auf Grund der allgemein bekannten. . . . Genesis dieser Annalistik keine Glaubwürdigkeit verdient" (*Lex*, 5).

picked up by a late annalist like Dionysius or by Plutarch, but most of it was overlooked by the historians, who usually refrained from consulting the works of antiquarians.[56] It therefore represents an invaluable treasure of information that is independent of the annalistic tradition.

Of course there are problems here as well. Because a systematic collection and interpretation has never been undertaken, it is difficult to assess how much of this hidden treasure still awaits discovery and how much more can be derived from elements that have long been known if they are scrutinized more thoroughly and in a broader context. Moreover, the danger of overconfident and overimaginative reconstruction, if not wild speculation, is particularly great when working with this kind of scattered and uncertain evidence;[57] accordingly, the results of such research will only be acceptable if they are based on both imaginative and methodologically solid work. Finally, the fact that some of the most important advances realized through this approach pertain to the regal era could well indicate that in this respect too, the period of the origins and formation of Roman society claims a disproportionally large share of the evidence. How much there still is to be gained for the early Republic and the Conflict of the Orders remains an open question until we have completed a systematic search. Nevertheless, such a search should be considered urgent and worthwhile. A few examples, selected at random, may serve as illustration.

The recollection of very ancient cults, religious rituals, and sacrifices recorded by antiquarians and lexicographers has made it possible to reconstruct the urban development of Rome from the Palatine settlement to the unified city. On the basis of similar evidence, the extension of the *ager Romanus antiquus* can be determined with great certainty (whether or not this was still the Roman territory at

---

56. Cf. E. Rawson, *JRS* 62 (1972): 33ff.
57. Examples are provided in many of J. Gagé's contributions on early Rome, now collected in *Débuts* (1976) and *Enquêtes* (1977); see the reviews by F. Kolb, *Gnomon* 53 (1981): 26ff.; J. Poucet, *AC* 47 (1978): 329; J.-C. Richard, *Gnomon* 51 (1979): 459ff.; A. Bernardi, *Athenaeum* 58 (1980): 485ff. Even so, Bernardi is right in emphasizing that in this case, too, many unsuccessful hypotheses are the price we have to pay for those few brilliant and successful ones that are generally accepted and truly advance our understanding. Cf. J. Hellegouarc'h, *REL* 55 (1977): 547.

the beginning of the Republic).⁵⁸ The opinion still held by many scholars that at the beginning of the Republic there was a single supreme magistracy, which was replaced by the two consuls only much later, is founded upon the remembrance of the early existence of a *praetor maximus* and a *dictator clavi figendi causa*. The analysis of certain terminological contrasts in archaic formulas, preserved mostly by lexicographers and collectors of curiosities, has recently stimulated discussion of sixth- and fifth-century Roman society.⁵⁹ One of these contrasts, between *classis* and *infra classem*, preserved by Gellius from an oration given by Cato in 169 B.C., has helped distinguish an early, simpler centuriate organization, which may have been introduced in the sixth century, from the much later and more complex form known to Livy and Dionysius and attributed by them to Servius Tullius.⁶⁰ Through Cicero we know that the Twelve Tables contained a reference to the *comitiatus maximus*, which is commonly identified with, and taken as *terminus ante quem* for, the *comitia centuriata*.⁶¹ The fragments of the Twelve Tables themselves, our most precious source for Rome's situation in mid-fifth century, practically without exception have been gathered from nonhistoriographical sources. Without them, for example, we would not know something that many scholars still do not want to know—namely, that around 450 B.C. the Tiber still (or again) was Rome's border with Etruria.⁶² To Dionysius's Greek background and unusual antiquarian interest we owe the

58. Cf. Heurgon, *Rise* (1973): 24ff., 154f.; A. Momigliano, *JRS* 53 (1963): 96ff., especially 98ff.; and A. Alföldi, *Hermes* 90 (1962): 187ff., and *Early Rome* (1965): 304ff.

59. On magistracy, see the summary of this discussion in Momigliano, *Contr. IV* (1969): 273ff.; Meyer, *Staat*³ (1964): 37–41, with n. 8 on p. 481ff.; F. De Martino, *Cost.* I² (1972): 236 ff.; Heurgon, *Rise* (1973): 161ff.; Richard, *Origines* (1978): 433ff. On terminology, cf. Momigliano, *Contr. IV* (1969): 443ff. (see chapter VI, part 2 below); id., "Patrizi e plebei" (1967): 204ff.; id., "Origins of the Republic" (1969): 24ff. For a careful discussion of such archaic terms, see also Richard, *Origines*, passim.

60. Cf. the discussion in H. Last, *JRS* 35 (1945): especially 42ff.; De Martino, *Cost.* I² (1972): 161ff.; Meyer, *Staat*³ (1964): 48ff., especially 53f.; Ogilvie, *Comm.* (1965): 166ff.; Heurgon, *Rise* (1973): 146ff.; J.-C. Richard, *RPh* 51 (1977): 229ff.; Thomsen, *Serv. Tullius* (1980): 144ff.

61. Twelve Tables IX.2; Cic. *De leg.* 3.4.11; cf. *De re pub.*2.36.61.

62. Twelve Tables III.5–6 from Gell. *Noctes Atticae* 20.1.47. Cf. F. Wieacker, "XII Tafeln" (1967): 310f., with literature; ibid. 293ff., for the sources of the Twelve Tables; 300ff., on their historical value; cf. id., *RIDA*, 3rd ser., 3 (1956): 473ff.

information from the so-called "Cumaean Chronicle" on Aristodemus of Cumae and his involvement in the war of the Latins against Arruns, son of Porsenna, the master of Rome, at the very end of the sixth century.[63] Finally, J. Linderski's analysis of the social and political significance of marriage *per confarreationem* (chapter VIII below) is largely based on a thorough reexamination of evidence scattered in nonhistoriographical sources.

So much for examples. Precisely because of the problematic nature of the extant historical sources, it is crucially important to make all the other evidence as completely accessible as possible and to interpret it adequately in a broad context. Even so, we may not be able to write a full and coherent history of the Conflict of the Orders. At many points we may indeed have to practice the *ars nesciendi*. But we may still be able to understand better what the problems and conditions were, what solutions were found by what kind of society, and in what respects the Romans were similar to and different from other archaic societies. For this purpose (in the overall analysis and in many details) a second and very different approach should be helpful: comparison with other societies that went through comparable stages and had comparable experiences.

3. *The Comparative Approach*

The *polis* type of community was common in most of the Mediterranean area in the first millennium B.C. About the vast majority of these communities we know very little, but it seems that in the seventh and sixth centuries B.C. many Greek *poleis* went through a deep crisis. Their difficulties are so similar to aspects of the Roman crisis and to phenomena in Etruria that A. Heuss even considers it a typical developmental stage of the archaic *polis* in general.[64] A few years ago, A. Momigliano pointed out "the enormous advance in our knowledge of other Italian societies contemporary with archaic Rome," which he considered a decisive precondition for our understanding early Roman society and institutions better than was possible for our

---

63. Dion. Hal. 7.2–12; *FGrHist* no. 576. Cf. Alföldi, *Early Rome* (1965): 56f.; Heurgon, *Rise* (1973): 156ff.; Scullard, *History*¹ (1980): 75f.
64. A. Heuss, *HZ* 216 (1973): 8ff.

predecessors half a century ago. Such progress was made in regard to some Osco-Umbrian townships, which preserved their archaic structures and customs much longer than Rome;[65] tribes such as the Samnites;[66] the Celts; and, especially, the Greeks of southern Italy[67] and the Etruscans.

Because of their long cultural and political predominance in Italy, their immediate proximity to Rome, and the presence and leading role of Etruscan families in Rome itself, the Etruscans claim a position of prime importance in comparative research. M. Torelli, C. Ampolo, G. Colonna, and others have used comparison with Etruscan phenomena fruitfully for the early period to analyze problems such as the formation of the city, the emergence of aristocracies, the migration of families and clans from one city to another and their integration in a new society, and so on.[68] Since, however, despite the Etruscans' knowledge of writing, those categories of written evidence that are most important for the historian—political documents and historiography—are almost completely lacking,[69] comparative efforts for the early period (eighth to sixth or early fifth centuries) are restricted to those aspects that can be illuminated by the existing categories of evidence, mostly archaeological, artistic, and linguistic-onomastic. As far as our present interest in social and political conflicts is concerned, we are therefore faced with the same limitations we had to point out for archaic Rome. Typically, discussions of the violent social struggles afflicting the Etruscan cities in the fourth and third centuries have to be based on indirect reports

---

65. Momigliano, *Contr. IV* (1969): 440 (see chapter VI below), and *JRS* 53 (1963): 112ff., especially 115ff., where the *tabulae Iguvinae* are used to shed new light on the Roman *curiae*.

66. Cf. Salmon, *Samnium* (1967). See, e.g., Altheim, *Lex sacr.* (1940), and *Röm. Geschichte* II (1953): 179ff., where rituals customary among the Samnites and other Italic tribes are used to explain the *lex sacrata* of the Roman plebeians.

67. For the intensive and systematic research on the Greek *poleis* in Italy, see especially the acts of the *Convegni di studi sulla Magna Grecia* in Taranto, published annually since 1961. For the problem of Greek influence on Rome, see below at nn. 94ff.

68. Cf. inter alia M. Torelli, *DArch* 8 (1974–75): 3ff.; C. Ampolo, *DArch* 4/5 (1970–71): 37ff.; 9/10 (1976–77): 333ff.; and *MEFR* 92 (1980): 567ff.; G. Colonna, *SE* 45 (1977): 175ff.

69. Cf. Pallottino, *Etruscans* (1975): 124, 153f., 197f., and J. Heurgon, *La Vie quotidienne chez les Etrusques* (Paris, 1961): 293ff. For a recent discussion of Etruscan historiography, see T. J. Cornell, *ASNP* 6 (1976): 411ff.

in later Roman sources and are hampered by many misunderstandings, gaps, and prejudices in these sources.[70] In saying this, I do not want to discourage comparison—quite the contrary—but to keep expectations on a realistic level.

There are other areas that may offer themselves to fruitful comparative analysis: the Phoenician city-states and Israel, the city-states of medieval Italy, and modern anthropological studies of both historical and contemporary archaic or "primitive" societies.[71] That the last category must be used with the utmost care is obvious,[72] but thorough comparative analysis has already considerably advanced our understanding of archaic Greek society and deepened our awareness of its specific problems.[73] As for the medieval Italian city-states, various scholars have mentioned their importance precisely for our present context; recently E. J. Bickerman has demonstrated with a few splendid examples how our understanding of some puzzling aspects of the struggle between patricians and plebeians can be advanced by a close examination of constitutional development in medieval communes, which generally paralleled that of early Rome.[74]

70. For the sources, see K. O. Müller and W. Deecke, *Die Etrusker* I² (Stuttgart, 1877; repr. with introd. and bibliography by A. J. Pfiffig, Graz, 1965); for a recent discussion, see Harris, *Etruria* (1971): 114ff., especially 126ff.; for an attempt at comparison: M. Torelli, *DArch* 8 (1974–75): 67ff.

71. Of course, there are other areas as well, e.g., the medieval cantons of central Switzerland (cf., e.g., P. Ducrey, "Remarques sur les causes du mercenariat dans la Grèce ancienne et la Suisse moderne," in *Buch der Freunde für J.R. von Salis* [Zurich, 1971]: 115ff.), or the Scandinavian communities in the Middle Ages (the Vikings) and early modern times (for example, I found G. Gunnarson's novel *Die Leute auf Borg* very illuminating). A splendid example of comparative research across ancient societies is M. I. Finley's analysis of debt-bondage: *RD* 43 (1965): 159ff., repr. in id., *Soc.* (1981): 150ff.

72. Cf. the warning expressed by A. Momigliano, *JRS* 53 (1963): 112f., and "Patrizi e plebei" (1967): 202f.

73. For a random selection of successful examples, see K. Meuli, "Scythica," *Hermes* 70 (1935): 136ff.; H. Jeanmaire, *Couroi et Couretes: Essai sur l'éducation spartiate et sur les rites d'adolescence dans l'antiquité hellénique* (Lille, 1939); M. I. Finley, "Marriage, Sale and Gift in the Homeric World," *RIDA* 2 (1955): 167ff. (repr. in id., *Soc.* [1981]: 233ff., but see A. M. Snodgrass, "An Historical Homeric Society?" *JHS* 94 [1974]: 114ff.); W. Donlan, "Reciprocities in Homer," *CW* 75 (1981–82): 137ff.; P. Vidal-Naquet, "The Black Hunter and the Origin of the Athenian *ephebeia*," *PCPhS* 194 (1968): 49ff. (French in *Annales* 23 [1968]: 947ff., repr. in Gordon, ed., *Myth* [1981]: 147ff.). See further the other articles collected in Gordon's volume; Gernet, *Anthropology* (1981); Humphreys, *Anthropology* (1978); Humphreys and King, eds., *Mortality* (1981).

74. Cf. E. J. Bickerman, *RFIC* 97 (1979): 402ff.

But to my knowledge nobody thus far has tried anything like a systematic comparison. That indeed is the crux of the matter: it is one thing to talk about comparative research and to use one or two obvious examples; it is an entirely different thing carefully to establish the areas and limits of comparability between two or more societies and to carry through a comprehensive and systematic comparative analysis. Clearly, only the latter process can produce results that will help us to understand archaic Roman society better.

For a number of reasons, the greatest potential for comparison seems to lie in archaic Greece, including the Greek *poleis* in Asia Minor, southern Italy, and Sicily.[75] These were societies contemporary with archaic Rome, and we have a considerable number of contemporary Greek sources that cover the entire archaic period from the late eighth century onward. Thanks to Homer, Hesiod, and some early Lyric poets, we can say more with greater confidence about Greek society and its problems in the eighth and seventh centuries than about any period of Roman history before the Punic Wars.[76] These sources allow us to follow the emergence of political thought and the gradual differentiation of political terminology, and they also mention and occasionally even discuss the economic, social, and political problems of their time. All this is an invaluable advantage—if these *poleis* are indeed comparable to archaic Rome.

---

75. This comparison to my knowledge has never been systematically applied or explored. It has recently been suggested by A. Heuss, *HZ* 216 (1973): 8ff.; Spahn, *Mittelschicht* (1977): 72ff.; M. Pallottino, *SR* 5 (1957): 621; *ANRW* I.1 (1972): 24; and especially in an important contribution by J. Martin, *Soc. Hist.* 4 (1979): 285ff. Parallels and analogies have, of course, been noted frequently (e.g., by Ed. Meyer, *GdA* III² [1937]: 471ff.; *Kl. Schr.* I² [1924]: 335), but except for a few specific problems such as the hoplite phalanx and debt bondage, they have hardly been discussed profoundly. Moreover, the method of comparison has been neglected completely in the recent monographs of Guarino and Ferenczy. The question of Greek influence on Roman military, political, religious, and legal institutions and on Rome's cultural and economic life is related, but not at all identical; it has been discussed recently by D. van Berchem, "Rome et le monde grec" (1966): 739ff., and E. Bayer, *ANRW* I.1 (1972): 305ff. For Greek influence on the Twelve Tables, which has attracted the highest amount of scholarly attention, cf. chapter X, parts 1 and 5 below; for Momigliano's position, see below at n. 100.

76. It suffices to emphasize that it has been possible to reconstruct comprehensively the social, economic, and political structure as well as the value system of "Homeric society": cf. Finley, *Odysseus*² (1977), and the corresponding chapters in Hasebroek, *Wirtsch.* (1931); Adkins, *Merit* (1960); Starr, *Origins* (1961); Spahn, *Mittelschicht* (1977); and Donlan, *Ideal* (1980).

At least superficially, the range of structural and developmental similarities is quite impressive.[77] Rome certainly was a *polis* of the type we find in Greece: a community with an urban political and religious center and a limited territory cultivated by its citizen-owners. Around 500 B.C., Rome's territory was comparable to that of Corinth. As in most Greek *poleis*, in Rome the earlier monarchy was replaced by an aristocracy consisting of a limited number of families that dominated the life of their community in every possible respect: economically, socially, militarily, in religion and jurisdiction, and, through the council, public offices, and priesthoods, also politically. This group aimed at exclusiveness and tried to set up social and institutional barriers against potential competitors. Between these aristocrats (including the members of their extended households) and the rest of the population was a deep and decisive gap. Slavery was not yet significant and the concept of citizenship was not yet defined.[78] The process of urbanization was completed in this phase of exclusive aristocratic domination. In some places, however, a proper civic space or political center, with a defined area for the assembly, a meeting-place for the council, buildings for religious and other officials, and temples for the protector-deities, was created not by the initiative of the aristocracy as such, but rather by that of a narrow group or an individual family within the aristocracy that had monopolized power.[79]

For reasons that at least in part again seem to be common to Rome and Greece, these aristocratic communities were affected by a deep crisis. Impoverishment of many independent farmers, food short-

---

77. For Greece, cf. Starr, *Origins* (1961), especially part 3; *Growth* (1977), especially chs. 6–8; Ehrenberg, *Solon* (1968): 20ff., 50ff.; Spahn, *Mittelschicht* (1977): 52ff., 59ff., 112ff., and the literature mentioned in chapter VII, n. 42, below. For Rome as *polis*: Ed. Meyer, *GdA* III² (1937): 471ff. For the crisis in Rome: Brunt, *Conflicts* (1971): 42ff.; H. S. Jones and H. Last in *CAH* VII (1928): especially 468ff.; Piganiol, *Conquête*⁶ (1974), chapters 5–6, and the literature mentioned in chapter VII, n. 29, below. See also chapter VII, n. 31 (food shortage), n. 42 (debt and personal dependence), and n. 82 (hoplite phalanx).

78. On aristocracy, see chapter VII, n. 90, below. On slavery: Austin and Vidal-Naquet, *Econ.* (1977): 18ff., 44ff.; P. Debord, "Esclavage mycénien, esclavage homérique," *REA* 75 (1973): 225ff. On citizenship: J. K. Davies, *CJ* 73 (1977–78): 105ff.; H.-J. Reinau, *Die Entstehung des Bürgerbegriffs bei den Griechen* (Basel, 1981).

79. In Athens by the Peisistratids or even Cleisthenes: see H. A. Thompson and R. E. Wycherly, *The Agora of Athens: The History, Shape and Uses of an Ancient City Center*, The Athenian Agora 14 (Athens and Princeton, 1972): 25ff.; R. E. Wycherly, *The*

ages, and increases in debt are some of the economic symptoms we observe. The aristocrats' arbitrariness in jurisdiction and abuse of their social and economic power provoked dissatisfaction and finally violent resistance in large parts of the population.[80] Changes in status and self-consciousness, gradually brought about by the introduction of the hoplite phalanx, played a considerable role.[81] Eventually, laws were codified, debt-bondage was abolished, the economic situation of the lower classes was improved, nonaristocrats who bore responsibility for the safety of the community were given more and better-defined political rights, and political power was institutionally organized. At the end of the crisis, leadership was still an exclusively aristocratic privilege, but aristocracy itself had changed considerably and lost much of its total control of the community. Large segments of the nonaristocratic population had been integrated politically, and the gaps between citizens and noncitizens and between free men and slaves were now much more accentuated.[82]

If this were the whole picture, we would indeed have an ideal situation for comprehensive comparison. Unfortunately, it is not; there are some major differences. The Greek *poleis* were allowed a long period of undisturbed development. They were not confronted

---

Stones of Athens (Princeton, 1978): 27ff.; T. L. Shear, "Tyrants and Buildings in Archaic Athens," in *Athens Comes of Age*, edited by W. A. P. Childs (Princeton, 1978): 1ff. For the time of Cleisthenes: P. Lévêque and P. Vidal-Naquet, *Clisthène l'Athénien* (Paris, 1964): 18ff.; P. Siewert, *Gnomon* 49 (1977): 390ff.; id., *Kleisthenes* (1982): 61f. In Rome by the Etruscan kings in the sixth century: see, recently, C. Ampolo, *DArch*, n.s., 2 (1980): 166ff.; L. Quilici, *Roma primitiva e le origini della civiltà laziale* (Rome, 1979): 309ff. with literature on p. 330. For some important parallels, cf. Ampolo, *PP* 26 (1971): 443ff.

80. For all these aspects, see the literature cited in n. 77 above; for Rome, see the discussion in chapter VII below.

81. See the literature cited in chapter VII below, n. 82.

82. In Athens, these results were achieved by the reforms of Solon and Cleisthenes, and by the period of peace and prosperity under the tyrants; see Ehrenberg, *Solon* (1968), chs. 3 and 4; Spahn, *Mittelschicht* (1977): 112–73. For Cleisthenes, see also Meier, *Pol.* (1980): 91ff.; J. Martin, *Chiron* 4 (1974): 5ff.; and Siewert, *Kleisthenes* (1982): 154ff. For the position of the aristocracy in post-Cleisthenic Athens, see (besides Meier and Martin) F. Frost, "Themistocles' Place in Athenian Politics," *CSCA* 1 (1968): 105ff.; and K. Kinzl, "Between Tyranny and Democracy," in id., ed., *Greece and the Eastern Mediterranean in Ancient History and Prehistory: Studies . . . F. Schachermeyr* (Berlin and New York, 1977): 199ff. For the concept of citizenship, see Reinau, *Entstehung des Bürgerbegriffs* (as in n. 78): 43ff. For Rome, see the literature cited in n. 13 above, and the discussion in chapter XI below.

with strong outside pressures by foreign powers or superior civilizations. With the exception of Spartan expansionism (which came to an end in the early sixth century), their frequent wars had a limited objective: cattle, booty, fields. They were not forced to fight for survival or political independence; down to the Persian Wars, the notion of political subjection or foreign rule was unknown to them. In addition, for a long time the tensions created by overpopulation and social conflicts could be "exported" due to the almost unlimited possibility of colonization.[83]

Rome, on the other hand, was deeply influenced early in its development by two superior civilizations, the Greek and the Etruscan. For over a century it was at least partially an Etruscan city, and kings of Etruscan origin secured for it a prominent position in the region. In addition, due to their favorable geopolitical position, the Romans constantly had to defend themselves against intruders. When the power of the Etruscan cities declined in the early fifth century, the Romans were forced to fight for more than a century to preserve their position and survive against their Latin and Etruscan neighbors and several mountain tribes, which claimed their share of the fertile coastal plains.[84]

These are indeed radically different situations. Only Sparta after the conquest of Messenia was exposed to a comparable amount of permanent pressure, which in this case was caused by the enslavement of the helots.[85] The effects of these differences are visible in many areas. In Rome such pressure must have strengthened not only the quality and importance of aristocratic leadership, but also solidarity, cohesiveness, discipline, and willingness to subordinate oneself within both the aristocracy and the entire community. These factors at least partially explain such typically Roman phenomena as

---

83. In the case of Athens, the *polis* territory seems to have been large enough to make even that superfluous. The unification of Attica itself had not left any traumata, and the wars of the sixth century were fought about disputed border districts and never threatened Athens's independence or existence. For this assessment of the situation in archaic Greece cf. Raaflaub, *Entdeckung* (1985), ch. 3.1, part d; for the following comparison, cf. ibid., ch. 7.2; Raaflaub, *HZ* 238 (1984): 529ff., and J. Martin, *Soc. Hist.* 4 (1979): 285ff.

84. Cf. Altheim, *Röm. Geschichte* II (1953): 257ff.; Heurgon, *Rise* (1973): 178ff.

85. For the effects on Spartan society, cf. Finley, *Soc.* (1981): 24ff.; P. Oliva, *Sparta and Her Social Problems* (Amsterdam and Prague, 1971): 132ff.; Spahn, *Mittelschicht* (1977): 84ff.

the cohesion and lasting social and political significance of *gens* and *familia*, the comprehensive and unbroken power of the *paterfamilias* even in postarchaic periods, the perseverance and functional extension of the *clientela* system, the lack of challenge to aristocratic leadership despite severe social disagreements, the survival of a strong and independent magistracy despite the collective claim to leadership by the senatorial aristocracy, and much more.[86] Most importantly, from early on the aristocracy devoted itself almost totally to political excellence and leadership; accordingly, its value system was completely built upon, and geared toward, service to the community.[87] Moreover, the community as a whole developed a remarkable ability to solve even weighty internal conflicts by compromising within the existing structures and under the existing leadership.

In Greece, on the other hand, there was no need for strong and united leadership, for solidarity and cohesiveness. One could afford from early on to question the superiority of the aristocracy and the effectiveness of their leadership.[88] Accordingly, the aristocrats were not able to maintain their superiority, power, exclusiveness, and unity in the conflicts of the seventh and sixth centuries. They increasingly had to prove their excellence in extrapolitical activities such as sports, and they frequently exhausted their potential in power struggles and subordinated both class solidarity and the integrity of the community to the interest and power of faction and

---

86. For *gens, familia,* and the position of the *paterfamilias,* cf. Heurgon, *Rise* (1973): 106ff., 231ff.; De Martino, *Cost.* I² (1972): 11ff.; E. Meyer, *Staat*³ (1964): 30ff.; E. Burck, "Die altrömische Familie," in *Das Neue Bild der Antike* II (Leipzig, 1942): 5ff., repr. in id., *Menschenbild* II (1981): 5ff., and in H. Oppermann, ed., *Römertum,* WdF 18 (Darmstadt, 1970): 87ff.; Kaser, *Privatr.* I² (1971): 58f., 60ff., 68ff.; and Guarino, *Riv.* (1975): 45ff. For *clientela*: Kaser, *Privatr.* I² (1971): 117ff.; Bleicken, *Verfassung* (1975): 20ff.; *Ordnung* (1972): 64ff.; and especially Meier, *Res publica amissa* (1966): 24ff. On the functional extension: E. Badian, *Foreign Clientelae* (Oxford, 1958). Magistracy: E. Meyer, *Staat*³ (1964): 106ff.; A. Heuss, *ZRG* 64 (1944): 57ff.

87. Cf. Meier, *Res publica amissa* (1966): 45ff.; Bleicken, *Verfassung* (1975): 40ff., 120ff.

88. Cf. W. Donlan, *Historia* 22 (1973): 145ff.; P. W. Rose, "Class Ambivalence in the Odyssey," *Historia* 24 (1975): 129ff.; F. Gschnitzer, "Politische Leidenschaft im homerischen Epos," in *Studien zum antiken Epos,* Beitr. zur klass. Philol. 72, edited by H. Görgemanns and E. A. Schmidt (Meisenheim, 1976): 1ff.; E. S. Farron, "The Odyssey as an Anti-Aristocratic Statement," *Studies in Antiquity* 1 (1979–80): 59ff.; Spahn, *Mittelschicht* (1977): 47ff., 114ff.; Raaflaub, "Politisches Denken" (1981): 36ff., especially 44ff.

family by involving foreign supporters and even the lower classes in factional strife.[89] In many cities such internal struggles were intensified by social tensions and led to tyranny, which in turn further weakened aristocratic authority and structures. Eventually, these were superseded by new structures based on the equality of larger segments of the citizen body. Typically, the power of the head of the family and the cohesiveness of family and clan, probably never as strong as in Rome, declined before the end of the archaic period. So did the significance of patronage and *clientela*, which could finally be replaced by a new set of primarily political relations. Political reforms such as those of Solon and Cleisthenes in Athens inevitably reduced the strength and exclusiveness of aristocratic leadership; the offices never developed independence, and the aristocratic council lost the decisive function of preliminary debate and planning the agenda of the assembly (*probouleusis*) when the assembly itself acquired a more important role in political life.[90]

What results from this brief survey is a complex and contradictory picture: there is a broad spectrum of profound structural similarities and there are many fundamental differences.[91] Consequently, the question of comparability needs careful and comprehensive reexamination; superficial analogies may be dangerously misleading. In

---

89. Cf., e.g., Herod. 5.66ff. It is hard to imagine a Roman senator in the role of a competitor in the Olympic Games. For the crisis of Greek aristocracies: Ehrenberg, *Solon* (1968), chs. 3 and 4; Starr, *Growth* (1977), chs. 6 and 7; Forrest, *Emergence* (1966), chs. 2 and 6–8; Spahn, *Mittelschicht* (1977): 59ff., 112ff.

90. For clans and families: F. Bourriot, *Recherches sur la nature du genos* (Paris, 1976); D. Roussel, *Tribu et cité* (Paris, 1976); Humphreys, *Anthropology* (1978): 194ff., especially 200f.; Lacey, *Family* (1968). The Homeric epics show that the position of the head of the *oikos* and the role of relationships similar to *clientela* were much more important in earlier centuries: cf. Finley, *Odysseus*² (1977): 74ff.; Gschnitzer, *Sozialgesch.* (1981): 27ff. For the changes in sixth century Attica, cf. Meier, *Pol.* (1980): 96ff., 113ff. For the effects of tyranny and of the reforms of Solon and Cleisthenes, see Forrest, *Emergence* (1966), chs. 6–8; Spahn, *Mittelschicht* (1977): 139ff., 161ff.; Meier, *Pol.* (1980): 91ff. For the democratic council and *probouleusis*, see P. J. Rhodes, *The Athenian Boule* (Oxford, 1972): 208ff.; and E. Will, *Le Monde grec et l'orient* I (Paris, 1972): 71ff. For the weakness of the magistracy, see E. Badian, "Archons and Strategoi," *Antichthon* 5 (1971): 1ff.

91. The social and political effects of these differing constellations are clearly visible in the solutions found by Athens and Rome for the problems of debt-bondage and the integration of the hoplite farmers into the political system; cf. below chapter VII, part 3, especially at nn. 52f., 58ff.; Raaflaub, *HZ* 238 (1984): 552ff., especially 557ff.

addition, there is one major problem, which at this point can only be stated: did these differences already affect the causes and origins of the social conflict—which would possibly give the conflict itself a different character and make a comparison very hard? Or did they only influence the actions and reactions of the parties involved, their methods of dealing with problems, and the solutions they found during the conflict—which would not radically change the basis for comparison?[92]

There is another major obstacle: Rome was one city, "Greece" is a collective term for a plurality of communities. Some of them were *poleis*, others were not, and among the *poleis* we find considerable differences in development and structure. Our most important sources (Hesiod, Tyrtaeus, Solon, Theognis) lived in different places and at different times. Strictly speaking, we do not know whether the problems they describe and the views they express were valid only for their own communities and times or also for other communities at the same or a different time. But we do have enough information to know that many of the problems they were confronted with occurred at many places or were even common in archaic Greece. It seems justifiable, therefore, to work from the assumption that simi-

---

92. At present I favor the second alternative. In his short but splendid comparative analysis of archaic Greek and Roman history, J. Martin, *Soc. Hist.* 4 (1979): 285ff., seems to decide for the first (although his objective is more general than mine—namely, to explain why, despite their similar origins, Greeks and Romans developed the clearly divergent types of action, social values, and identity that we observe in their respective periods of highest power and achievement). Martin emphasizes the radically different external situation, which in turn explains the existence in Rome, and the absence in Greece, of a strong political organization both on the side of the aristocrats and on that of the nonaristocrats. Both these factors together account for the contrast between the confrontational model for solving socioeconomic conflicts (which we find in Greece) and the compromise type of historical development in Rome (Martin, 290–96). So far I agree. But I strongly object to Martin's attempt to characterize the conflict between patricians and plebeians in Rome as a purely political one between a ruling aristocracy and a group of their peers who were excluded from political power, each with their clients and followers. Social and economic tensions between the upper and the lower classes would thus have affected both sides equally, making compromises much easier. Accordingly, in Martin's view, the causes of the Roman Conflict of the Orders differ radically from those of the conflicts in archaic Greek *poleis*. Indeed, such a view restricts the function of comparison to the observation and explanation of differences. In my opinion, the causes were much more closely related; comparison can therefore be employed in more positive ways as well. For arguments and examples, see chapter VII below, passim.

lar symptoms of the great crisis appeared and created similar problems in many communities, although they may not all have appeared everywhere and at the same time and although actions and reactions may have differed considerably from place to place.[93] We cannot therefore compare the whole Roman crisis with its analogue in any one Greek *polis*, but we can compare single aspects and elements of the Roman crisis with analogous aspects in one or another Greek *polis*.

Furthermore, there was obviously a large amount of Greek influence on archaic Rome. Such influence, though by no means absent in the preceding period,[94] markedly increased in the first half of the fifth century: apart from other trade relations, embassies were sent to Greek cities in southern Italy and Sicily, and grain was imported from there to curb famine; Greek cults were established, some of which required Greek cult personnel; Greek craftsmen and artisans helped to build and decorate temples; the idea of codifying the law was Greek, not Italic, and at least in part the content of the laws corresponded to Greek models.[95] These are the areas of Greek influence known to us, but there may have been more. We do not really know how comprehensively Rome was affected by the process of "Hellenization" that was going on in the entire Mediterranean area. Although we may suspect that this process accelerated in Rome in the fourth and third centuries, recent scholarship has revealed an impressive network of contacts with Greek *poleis* as early as the sixth and fifth centuries.[96]

---

93. For example, Athens was conspicuously absent among the *poleis* participating in the process of colonization, and Solon's *seisachtheia* may have been quite unique even in the Greek world. De Martino, *Cost.* I² (1972): 223, emphasizes such differences to discourage overconfidence in comparison. On the other hand, G. Nagy, *Class. Ant.* 2 (1983): 82ff., stresses the pan-Hellenic character of Theognidean and other archaic poetry.

94. Cf., e.g., C. Ampolo, *PP* 25 (1970): 200ff., and *DArch* 9/10 (1976–77): 333ff.; G. Colonna, *Archeol. Class.* 16 (1964): 1ff.; D. van Berchem, "Rome et le monde grec" (1966): 739ff.; Altheim, *Röm. Geschichte* II (1953): 130ff., 136ff.; G. Pugliese Carratelli, *PP* 23 (1968): 327ff.; E. Bayer, *ANRW* I.1 (1972): 306ff., 317ff.; Poma, *Studi* (1974): 37ff.

95. Cf., in general, Pugliese Carratelli, *PP* 23 (1968): 330ff.; Bayer, *ANRW* I:1 (1972): 312ff.; Poma, *Studi* (1974): 40ff. For the import of grain, see Momigliano, *Contr. IV* (1969): 331ff. (contra: Bayer, *ANRW* I.1 [1972]: 321ff.). For Greek influence on the Twelve Tables, see chapter X below, nn. 2 and 4. Cf. also M. Pallottino, "Magna Grecia" (1969): 35ff.; M. Torelli, "Griechen und Etrusker" (1974): 823ff.; B. d'Agostino, *Annales* 32 (1977): 3ff., on relations between Greeks and Etruscans.

96. Massilia and Cumae were especially important; for an analysis of this network, see especially G. Pugliese Carratelli, *PP* 23 (1968): 329ff. passim; for the

The important question, then, is whether and to what extent Greek models and ideas also influenced the social and political life of the Roman community, its institutions, its internal conflicts, and its ways of resolving such conflicts.[97] More generally, in our present context we have to ask whether and to what extent comparability suffers if one of the two objects was heavily influenced by the other. This is a problem that needs systematic investigation. How, under what conditions, and in what areas were foreign influences accepted (with or without substantial adaptation) or refused by ancient (especially archaic) societies? One would probably find marked differences in the reactions to such influences in the fields of social and political institutions (including religion, jurisdiction, and the military), social attitudes and interaction, and terminology.[98] I would assume that the effect of such impulses would be determined largely, but not only, by the degree of similarity in structure and need in both the giving and the receiving society; the higher the correspondence, the more complete the acceptance of such influences. The hoplite phalanx, the division of the citizen body into timocratic and local units, and the codification of law suggest examples, but things might be much more complex.[99]

A. Momigliano has theorized that the plebeians were more affected and propelled by Greek influences than the patricians, and that such influences account for the remarkable efficiency and strength of the plebeian institutions.[100] I find this unconvincing for two reasons. First, the particular effect of such influences on only one part of the community is simply postulated and not analyzed on the basis and with the support of more general (anthropological, theoretical) con-

---

fourth century, see Hoffmann, *Rom* (1934); E. Bayer, *ANRW* I.1: 330ff.; F. Castagnoli, *SR* 22 (1974): 430ff. For the problem in general, see M. Pallottino, "Magna Grecia" (1969): 38.

97. A. Momigliano, "Origins of the Republic" (1969): 32–34, and G. Pugliese Carratelli, *PP* 23 (1968): 332ff., confidently assume much influence by Greek political ideas, too. I do not think that this should simply be taken for granted.

98. Cf. also Poma, *Studi* (1974): 50; J. Cels Saint-Hilaire and C. Feuvrier-Prévotat, *Dial. d'hist. anc.* 5 (1979): 111f. For the problem of political terminology, cf. Raaflaub, *HZ* 238 (1984): 538–40 and passim.

99. For an example, see the variety of answers proposed for the question of whether and how the introduction of Greek cults in Rome was politically motivated; cf. the survey in Poma, *Studi* (1974): 45ff.

100. Momigliano, *Contr. IV* (1969): 450ff., and "Origins of the Republic" (1969): 31ff. Doubts are also expressed in Bayer, *ANRW* I.1: 328.

siderations. Second, we do not know of a single example in the Greek world of a well-organized and efficient opposition to aristocratic power and prerogatives such as that which the Roman plebeians created, particularly not one set up by lowerclass people such as those who composed the Roman *plebs* according to Momigliano.[101]

The strength and cohesion of the aristocracy, the power gap between aristocracy and nonaristocracy, the high amount of organization among the nonaristocrats, the permanence of strong outside pressure, and the resulting ties of solidarity within the whole citizen body: these factors determined both the character and resolution of social conflicts in Rome. For the reasons discussed before, both differed widely from analogous conflicts in the Greek world, despite a considerable amount of similarity in structure and need and despite the existence of a variety of Greek models and the wide range of Greek influences on Rome at the time of the Conflict of the Orders. At least for the study of this conflict, therefore, I suggest that such influence does not exclude or decisively hamper the application of the comparative approach.

Having examined some of the preconditions for such an approach, we should ask ourselves what we can and cannot expect from comparison. Again success largely depends on our ability to develop a sound methodological basis and a clear and differentiated understanding of the possibilities and limitations of the comparative approach. It would certainly be naive simply to transfer Greek models to Rome in order to supplement missing information or to refute specific features of the Roman tradition. For example, it seems that in Athens the office of the *archon basileus* was the result of a long, gradual evolution, during which the king was stripped of his powers and became an annual magistrate and finally just one of nine archons, a man with religious prestige but no military powers. Accordingly, some scholars, including G. De Sanctis, have taken the Roman *rex sacrorum* to represent the original monarchy in a state of extreme decline, not (as tradition has it) a priest appointed for the specific purpose of replacing the king. Accordingly, in their view, there could not have been a violent overthrow of the monarchy in Rome.[102] Few historians today

---

101. See chapter VII below at nn. 85 and 89.
102. De Sanctis, *Storia* I² (1956): 385ff., especially 389; cf. E. Meyer, *Staat*³ (1964): 37f.

would support this opinion. The method of comparison must be applied much more subtly. What can it really teach us?

First, it can help us to understand the meaning of certain historical phenomena. Momigliano has demonstrated this with the same example of the *archon basileus* and *rex sacrorum*:

> What we observe in Greece, amounts to a separation of religious functions from political and military power. We observe a tendency to get rid of kings as political and military leaders and to avoid endowing their successors with religious powers. Certain specific religious ceremonies were considered inseparable from kingship and therefore had to be left in the hands either of the natural descendants of the kings . . . or of elected officials who were called kings for the sake of continuity.[103]

Second, the comparison may stimulate our thinking, give us ideas and suggestions, and provide possible solutions. This is true both for individual aspects and for the conflict as a whole. To give just a few examples, it is important to realize that in Greece the economic, social, and juridical aspects of the crisis by far preceded the political ones, and that changes in military organization played a decisive role in forcing political issues.[104] We further learn from Solon's poems that the concept of extended participation in political life and of sharing the responsibility for social and political peace and welfare was not at all eagerly embraced by those who were not directly involved in the existing conflicts. Moreover, there could be, and in fact was, a whole large group in the community that was not involved at all in these conflicts and was therefore obviously not affected directly or sufficiently by the crisis.[105] As Hesiod's complaints and incidents in both Homeric poems indicate, serious dissatisfaction with aristocratic leadership could be vividly expressed but still linger for many decades before it erupted in a violent confrontation.[106] Finally, the

---

103. Momigliano, "Origins of the Republic" (1969): 15f.; cf. De Martino, *Cost.* I² (1972): 223.

104. For recent discussions of the political effect of the military factor, see chapter VII below, n. 82.

105. These aspects are emphasized by Spahn, *Mittelschicht* (1977): 121ff., especially 135ff., 150ff., 156ff.

106. See the literature cited in n. 88 above.

traditional aristocracies had such an enormous advantage in education, training, experience, organization, and social and political connections that, despite economic changes and political reforms, even in democratic Athens the members of wealthy but not old aristocratic families only reached positions of highest influence many generations after Solon had formally replaced birth by wealth as the criterion for holding high office.[107] Given the basic comparability of the societies involved, such factors should not be neglected.

For another set of problems, this can be stated even more strongly. Etruria, Latium, and Campania in the seventh to fourth centuries formed a geographically coherent though (especially in the earlier period) unevenly developed system of *poleis* and emerging *poleis*—societies dominated by aristocracies and proto-aristocracies. As such, it was comparable to the systems emerging especially in central and southern Greece and on the western coast of Asia Minor between roughly the late eighth century and the Persian Wars. The patterns of peaceful or hostile relationships that existed among such communities and/or among their aristocrats, and that were compatible with each developmental stage of the archaic *polis*, can be reconstructed fairly reliably from contemporary evidence for the Greek *polis* system.[108] Nothing similar is possible for archaic Italy. However, once we know these patterns and realize how they were determined by the structural and organizational possibilities and limitations of the "aristocratic" *polis*, we shall be much better able to understand not only the nature of Etruscan domination and monarchy in Rome, but also Etruscan methods of expansion to the south and north, the forms of Rome's early dealings with its neighbors, and the structures upon which Roman influence and expansion were based in the fourth and early third centuries. On all these questions, scholarly opinions are still mostly vague, widely divergent, and disturbingly contradictory.[109]

107. Cf. W. R. Connor, *The New Politicians in Fifth-Century Athens* (Princeton, 1971); M. I. Finley, "Athenian Demagogues," *Past and Present* 21 (1962): 3ff., repr. in id., ed., *Studies in Ancient Society* (London and Boston, 1974): 1ff.

108. For the aspects of war, conquest, foreign rule, and the concept of freedom, cf. Raaflaub, *Entdeckung* (1985), ch. 3.1.

109. Alföldi, *Early Rome* (1965), much of which is summarized in Heurgon, *Rise* (1973): 137ff., 176ff., is a most stimulating, but also frequently mistaken, analysis; cf. also Scullard, *History*[1] (1980): 33ff., 59ff., 92ff. Much is to be expected from the new edition of *CAH*.

Third, closely related to its second use and sometimes almost inseparable from it, comparison can save us from mistakes and misjudgments in just about every area we are dealing with. The meaning of the funeral restrictions in the Twelve Tables provides a good example. Unlike other categories of sumptuary laws, such restrictions make their only appearance in Rome before the time of Sulla in this context. But they are well attested and much more frequent in the Greek world. By examining this larger body of evidence, M. Toher is able to show that the political explanations proposed for the inclusion of funeral restrictions in the Twelve Tables do not find support elsewhere. We should therefore be very cautious in connecting these restrictions with demands or pressures generated by the Conflict of the Orders.[110]

In a completely different field, Greek historiography illustrates impressively the short range of historical memory as far as the unrecorded past is concerned, and the tendency to project experiences and views from the writer's own time back even into periods for which ample documentation was available.[111]

Another example has to do with the calculation of population figures, which is by no means an academic hobbyhorse but an indispensable basis for many historical assessments, not least in the context of the Conflict of the Orders. Again, the data from contemporary sources that we possess for classical (though not archaic) Greece are somewhat more specific and reliable than those the late republican sources give for the early and middle Republic. In this case, however, the material from Greece mostly helps check the plau-

---

110. For Toher, see chapter X below. The political explanation has been proposed, e.g., by F. Wieacker, "XII Tafeln" (1967): 312ff. G. Colonna, *PP* 32 (1977): 131ff., and others have connected the funeral restrictions in table X with the puzzling progressive diminution and final elimination of funeral gifts in the tombs of the late orientalizing period (c. 600–580) in Latium (cf. T. J. Cornell, *Arch. Reports* [1979–80]: 76). They conclude that such regulations merely codified a limit that had been in existence for over a century. Toher, chapter X, at nn. 68f., 78, shows that such a connection is most likely untenable.
111. For the former cf., e.g., the lack of understanding of, and of precise information about, the content and purpose of Cleisthenes' reforms already found in Herodotus (5.66ff.; cf. Siewert, *Kleisthenes* [1982]: 7ff.). For the latter, see the fourth-century interpretation of Pericles' building program: Plut. *Per.* 12; cf. F. Frost, "Thucydides, Son of Melesias, and Athenian Politics before the War," *Historia* 13 (1964): 385ff. I cannot therefore share Develin's optimism (chapter XI below at nn. 10ff.) about the sources on archaic Greece.

sibility of Roman figures that are based on evidence completely independent from the historiographical sources. Since these calculations will be referred to in other contributions as well, it is advisable to present them in some detail.

As is well known, the census figures mentioned by the late republican historians are vastly exaggerated: 80,000 male citizens for the time of Servius Tullius, 130,000 for 508 B.C. T. Frank accepted them as figures of the entire citizen population, including women and children; J. Beloch rejected them flatly; P. A. Brunt for once proposes that "we should practise the *ars nesciendi*."[112] It seems, however, that there are ways to overcome this impasse. If we believe in the "grande Roma dei Tarquini," the incorporation of the mouth of the Tiber and other surrounding areas into the Roman territory already in the sixth century, then by 500 B.C. it covered about 820 square kilometers; if we do not believe in such territorial acquisitions, according to A. Alföldi's much more conservative calculation, there were only about 435 km^2.[113] Working with the larger figure and using as a basis the population densities more reliably reported for Campania in the time of the Hannibalic War (roughly 50 per km^2, which certainly is far too high for Latium),[114] Beloch estimated a total citizen-body of about 40,000; to these he added 10,000 for the city (which is problematic). He thought that of these 50,000, somewhat more than a third would be adult male citizens (about 20,000), and two-thirds of these would qualify as hoplites (about 13,500 *adsidui*), while 7–8 percent of the citizens, with 1,300–1,500 adult males, would be patricians.[115]

According to more recent research, these figures and ratios must be lowered. F. De Martino uses subsistence potential as a criterion for calculating the population of archaic Rome. On the basis of scattered information in ancient sources and his own estimates, he as-

---

112. T. Frank, *AJP* 51 (1930): 313ff.; Beloch, *Röm. Geschichte* (1926): 216ff.; id., *Bevölkerung* (1886): 339ff.; Brunt, *Manpower* (1971): 27 n. 1. For a list of the ancient census figures see Brunt, *Manpower*, 13, with discussion 15ff. See also n. 122 below.

113. Beloch, *Röm. Geschichte* (1926): 169ff. Alföldi's figure according to C. Ampolo, *DArch*, n.s., 2 (1980): 28, calculated on the basis of the discussion of the Roman territory by Alföldi, *Hermes* 90 (1962): 187ff.; *Early Rome* (1965): 288ff.; *Frühgeschichte* (1976): 202ff. F. De Martino, *BIDR* 80 (1977): 2, assumes as little as 250 km^2 for Alföldi's territory.

114. Cf. De Martino, *BIDR* 80 (1977): 12.

115. Beloch, *Röm. Geschichte* (1926): 216ff.

sumes that not more than a third of the territory could be cultivated or used for grazing; moreover, half of the fields had to be left fallow every year. He concludes that at the very most 50,000 people could have been supported by the resulting crops.[116] Following the same direction of research, C. Ampolo bases his calculations on a broader and more solid base.[117] He uses the results of palaeobotanical studies of materials from recent excavations in Rome and Latium, corroborates this evidence with information preserved in ancient agricultural writers and antiquarians, and checks it against comparative evidence from the Middle Ages and early modern times in order to establish a pattern and calculate agricultural production in prehistoric and archaic Latium. This in turn enables him to determine much more reliably the number of inhabitants that could have been sustained on Roman territory. According to his conclusions, 10,000 people would have needed an area of 233 km^2; Beloch's larger territory therefore could not have sustained more than 35,000 inhabitants, Alföldi's smaller area only 18,000. Ampolo assumes 20–30,000 for the larger territory.

As for the ratios, comparative evidence from Greece helps us to determine the proportion of male adult citizens, hoplites, and aristocrats we might reasonably expect in structurally similar societies. Long ago Beloch, and later A. W. Gomme, systematically collected all the information preserved in the ancient authors concerning population figures in classical Greece.[118] This material provided a fairly sound basis for calculations that have been accepted as plausible and used ever since. E. Ruschenbusch has more recently based his calculations mostly on the census figures of 1889 and 1928, when life was still almost exclusively founded on traditional agriculture in the rural districts and islands of modern Greece.[119] The supportable population density, which can hardly have differed much from antiquity, averaged 36.3 per km^2 (with a few exceptional cases of 50 or

---

116. De Martino, *BIDR* 80 (1977): 9ff. This figure corresponds with Beloch's. Since it presupposes an average population density of over sixty per km^2, and since De Martino himself rejects Beloch's use of the density figure of much more fertile Campania (ibid., 12), he contradicts himself, and his figure must be considered far too high.

117. C. Ampolo, *DArch*, n.s. 2 (1980): 27ff.

118. Beloch, *Bevölkerung* (1886): 57ff.; Gomme, *Population* (1933).

119. E. Ruschenbusch, *Untersuchungen zu Staat und Politik in Griechenland vom 7.–4.Jh. v.Chr.* (Bamberg, 1978): 8ff.

more). Taking into account all the ancient data collected by Beloch and Gomme, Ruschenbusch proposes that 20–25 percent of the total population were adult male citizens, about a third being of the hoplite class.[120] He emphasizes that the wealthy upper class (those who in Athens belonged to the census class of the *hippeis* and paid for the liturgies) did not average more than 3–4 percent of the citizens.

Deliberately using slightly higher ratios (33 percent male citizens, 40 percent of whom were hoplites and 6 percent of whom belonged to the upper class) for the population of 20–30,000 proposed by Ampolo on Beloch's territory of about 820 km^2, we would get 6,600–9,900 male citizens, 2,700–4,000 hoplites, and 400–600 adult male patricians. These figures are, of course, rough estimates, but they are hardly too low.[121] Their implications are to be taken seriously. On the one hand, according to all these calculations, the contingent of hoplites would stay far below Fraccaro's famous sixty centuries of *iuniores*.[122] On the other, for a patriciate of such limited size, a Senate

---

120. At Marathon the presumably complete Athenian hoplite army of 9,000 represented about one-third of the adult male citizens (Herod. 5.97.2; cf. Beloch, *Bevölkerung* [1886]: 60, 99). Gomme, *Population* (1933): 3ff., estimates c. 27–30,000 male citizens in 500. On the basis of much later statistical material, Brunt, *Manpower* (1971): 59, and R. Duncan-Jones, *The Economy of the Roman Empire: Quantitative Studies* (Cambridge, 1974): 259ff., especially 264 n. 4, both estimate the adult male citizens at c. 28 percent of the total free population.

121. Using a population density of forty per km^2 (lower than that transferred by Beloch from Campania, but higher than that considered reasonable for Greece by Ruschenbusch), and applying the same ratios, we would still get a total population of only 33,000, comprising 11,000 adult male citizens, 4,400 hoplites, and 600 adult male patricians.

122. Fraccaro, *Opuscula* II (1957): 287ff.; cf. Heurgon, *Rise* (1973): 149f. For more recent discussion, see F. De Martino, *BIDR* 80 (1977): 13ff.; J.-C. Richard, *RPh* 51 (1977): 229ff.; Thomsen, *Serv. Tullius* (1980), ch. 5. I have to emphasize here that many of the earlier and very sophisticated discussions of the "Servian" centuriate organization (see the surveys in De Martino and Thomsen) are unrealistic, not only because they reckon with overly high population figures, but also because they fail to take into account the character and scope (in time, space, and purpose) of Roman warfare in the fifth century. For that time it surely is absurd to think of a limited military obligation of a fixed number of campaigns per soldier, or of centuries recruited from much larger cadres of available hoplites. Certainly every able-bodied and sufficiently equipped citizen was required to help to defend Roman fields, cattle, and the city itself against marauding invaders from neighboring tribes or cities whenever that was necessary. This natural and unlimited obligation may have been modified temporarily during the extended siege of Veii, and permanently during the wars of expansion in the second half of the fourth century. See also chapter VII below at n. 78ff.

of 300 members is as implausible¹²³ as the 3,000 Fabians heroically dying at the Cremera and the 5,000 *gentiles* and *clientes* of Attus Clausus still migrating to Rome in the early fifth century in most of our books.¹²⁴ Moreover, since the centuries of *equites* must have consisted mostly of patricians, it seems highly improbable that the patricians, even together with their wealthier clients, were able to provide the manpower needed for a decent hoplite army.¹²⁵

Similarly, the use of Greek data may help finally eliminate another fable. It has been argued that at the time when Athens virtually held a monopoly of fine pottery for the whole Greek world, not more than five hundred people were simultaneously occupied in the production of such pottery, and that not more than two hundred were at any one time working on the construction of the Parthenon, many of whom were so specialized that they had to move on after the completion of a particular building.¹²⁶ Even the "grande Roma dei Tarquini" did not have an export industry, and the scale of public and private building was in no way comparable to Periclean Athens. We should therefore once and forever dismiss the theory that the Roman plebeian class consisted mainly of immigrants, craftsmen, traders, and other categories of nonfarming urban dwellers who would have been not only numerous, but also powerful enough to challenge the predominantly rural aristocracy.¹²⁷

---

123 De Martino, *Cost.* I² (1972): 111, 113, 146, 264f., expresses doubts but is uncertain. See further chapter VII, n. 126, below.

124. On the Fabians, see Livy 2.49.4; 50.11; Dion. Hal. 9.15.3; Festus, p. 451 L. On the followers of Attus Clausus, see Livy 2.16.4; Dion. Hal. 5.40.3. Cf. the Sabine Appius Herdonius, who formed a troop of 4,000 men out of his clients and slaves: Livy 3.16.5; Dion. Hal. 10.14.1. Amazingly enough, these figures are almost universally accepted; cf., e.g., Heurgon, *Rise* (1973): 107; E. Meyer, *Staat*³ (1964): 31; C. Ampolo, *DArch* 4/5 (1970–71): 37ff.; and H. Versnel, *Gymnasium* 89 (1982): 206, who assumes similar figures (i.e., several hundred adult male members) for the *gens Valeria*. Clearly, these figures follow the extremes of late republican reality.

125. See chapter VII below at nn. 78ff. For recent discussions of patricians and *equites*, see L. Zusi, *Critica storica* 12 (1975): 192ff.; Richard, *Origines* (1978): 248ff.

126. See A. Burford, "The Builders of the Parthenon," *G&R* Suppl. 10 (1963): 23ff., 34; eadem, *The Greek Temple Builders at Epidauros* (Liverpool, 1969): 247ff. (app. 3); and R. H. Randall, "The Erechtheum Workmen," *AJA* 57 (1953): 199ff., especially 201, table 1. On potters, see R. M. Cook, "Die Bedeutung der bemalten Keramik für den griechischen Handel," *Jahrb. Deutsch. Arch. Inst.* 74 (1959): 114ff. On migrating artists, see also M. Torelli, "Griechen und Etrusker" (1974): 826.

127. Cf. chapter VII below at nn. 84ff. Against this view of Rome as a great manufacturing and mercantile center, see also Brunt, *Conflicts* (1971): 27ff.; M. Crawford, "Roman Economy" (1976): 202 n. 25.

Fourth, there is also the possibility of a "negative comparison." We can learn not only from historical phenomena that are equal or similar to those we are studying, but also from those that are radically different. Religious aspects have been mentioned. How does the presence or absence of religious issues influence the development and solution of social conflicts? What does it mean that the Roman magistrates retained extensive religious duties despite the separation of religious and politico-military powers discussed above? That the plebeians were able to create for themselves a firm and powerful organization with special cults, officials, and a separate assembly was certainly a decisive factor in the Conflict of the Orders. In so doing, they both reacted against and provoked the patricians' efforts to close themselves off as an exclusive and cohesive aristocratic "order." There were comparable (though not equally radical and successful) efforts among aristocracies, but none among the lower classes in Greece, where, accordingly, we find social conflicts but not a "Conflict of the Orders." What does this tell us? On the other hand, both Athens and Rome had to face the problem of politically integrating and organizing those members of the nonaristocratic population who as hoplites fought in the same phalanx and bore the same military responsibility as the noblemen. In Athens the new census classes determined the degree of political participation and access to leading offices. In Rome they only determined membership in voting units; neither the possibility of holding office nor that of social promotion was connected with such membership. Important insight can be gained from the historical interpretation of such different solutions.

These are just four possible ways to exploit the comparative approach. Undoubtedly there are more. Many scholars have compared aspects of Greek and Roman history and tried to apply some of the obvious analogies and differences. Nobody, to my knowledge, has ever done so systematically. At this point, I can only speculate how much might be gained from such an attempt—which may also be considerably less than I am hoping for. But because of the extremely difficult source situation and our lack of familiarity with such early societies, it is certain that our understanding can only be advanced if our work is based on a variety of approaches and, for each of them, on a clear methodological concept. Perhaps more than in any other field of historical research, here we have to think before we even start to collect our evidence.

Appendix

My own conclusions concerning the use we can make of the annalistic tradition about the early Republic differ rather strongly from those formulated by Timothy Cornell and Robert Develin elsewhere in this volume. A brief discussion might help to clarify things. In particular, Cornell attributes considerable weight to the fact "that the Romans of the later Republic thought they knew a great deal about their own history, a claim that would be very hard to understand if there were not some sound basis for it." And he criticizes "the attitude of some skeptical historians, who are inclined to argue that all information about early Rome is to be rejected unless it can be independently corroborated or shown to be derived from a reliable source." Rather, Cornell finds it "reasonable to assume that if a certain piece of evidence is not inherently improbable and was believed by the Romans themselves to be the truth, the burden of proof must lie with those who wish to disbelieve it."[128] Since I support the view criticized by Cornell (above at n. 55) and this seems to be one of those cases of "diametrically opposed opinions" and "total disagreement" that I mentioned in the Preface, I feel obliged not so much to defend my own "attitude" as to point out where I see some weakness in Cornell's argument, where agreement seems possible, and why I consider our views to be much closer to each other than one might think at first sight.[129]

First, Cornell mostly argues against the view that charges the annalists with deliberate falsification, free invention, and politically motivated distortion of facts. It is true that earlier scholars assembled an impressive body of evidence for substantial changes, not

---

128. See chapter II below, before and after n. 32 and before n. 35. It has become fashionable to denounce as "hypercritical" any attempt at serious source criticism and determined distrust of the annalistic tradition. Unfortunately, such verbal attacks against "hypercriticism" are usually not followed by a proper discussion of the criteria to be applied in dealing with that tradition, even by those who are fully aware of its problems. This I find a fundamental weakness even of such eminent works as De Martino, *Cost.*² (1972–75); Richard, *Origines* (1978), whose remarks on p. xiv are certainly not sufficient; Guarino, *Riv.* (1975); and Thomsen, *Serv. Tullius* (1980). I very much agree with A. Drummond, *JRS* 72 (1982): 179.

129. See Editor's Preface above, after n. 5. Ungern-Sternberg's remarks (chapter III below at nn. 17ff.) should be considered here as well. I want to emphasize that despite my disagreement on this point, I consider Cornell's papers of 1980 ("Tradizione storiografica") and 1983 ("Failure of the Plebs") among the most important recent discussions of the subject.

only in the "narrative superstructure" but also in the factual basis of the tradition, made for various reasons (including political ones) by one or the other author.¹³⁰ This evidence has too often been ignored or lightly dismissed in recent scholarship. Nevertheless, I agree that the approach attacked by Cornell is by and large neither adequate nor productive, and that it is unjustifiable to condemn the annalists summarily on this account. It is necessary, however, to distinguish between various possible purposes or effects of such vindication of the annalists' reputation. Cornell, it seems to me, is mostly concerned with establishing that the annalists represent a reputable, serious, and important genre of historiographic literature that deserves to be taken seriously, and whose formation, character, and development are worth thorough investigation. With that I fully agree. For me, on the other hand, it is precisely the formation of this *literary* genre with its peculiar character and scientific shortcomings that drastically reduces its source value and disqualifies most of its content for the task of reconstructing the history of archaic Rome.¹³¹ As we shall see, implicitly (and, at times, even explicitly) Cornell agrees with that. Some of the contradictions in his paper (and, I propose, the contradiction between our opinions that was mentioned above, leading to the present discourse) are caused by the fact that he does not pay sufficient attention to two fundamental distinctions: that between the literary and the historical value of annalistic historiography and that between its value as a source for the history of archaic Rome and its value as a source for traditions and beliefs valid in the late Republic.

Second, Cornell's defense of the value of our sources seems to be much more appropriate for the period of the kings and for the third

---

130. See the literature mentioned in chapter III, nn. 17ff., below. See further, Sallmann, *Plinius* (1971): 1ff., 22ff., 165ff., for basic considerations on source criticism; Wiehemeyer, *Kritik* (1938), for variants in the tradition; C. Habicht, *Hermes* 89 (1961): 1ff., for the invention of documents in fourth-century Greek historiography and oratory; T. J. Luce, *TAPA* 102 (1971): 265ff., and id., *Livy* (1977), chs. 5 and 6, for the use of sources and factual rearrangement serving interpretative goals; Wiseman, *Clio's Cosmetics* (1979), *pace* Cornell's review, *JRS* 72 (1982): 203ff. Cicero's assertion that the historian's first task is to tell the truth (see Cornell, chapter II below, n. 7) should be balanced against his statements that the orator has the right to invent documents to make his case more compelling (*Brut.* 11.42), and that historiography is the genre closest to oratory (*De leg.* 1.2.5).

131. Cf. n. 54 above on Momigliano's position.

century[132] and beyond than for the early Republic, and particularly the fifth century. The Greek sources and Roman oral traditions available to the first annalists had focused on the "origins" and the kings, but knew little about the two centuries following the fall of monarchy (which is mirrored in the works of the early annalists);[133] archaeology, as Cornell admits, so far has had little to contribute, and is therefore unable to confirm the factual accuracy of the annalistic descriptions beyond the general impression of economic distress.[134] At least as far as the Conflict of the Orders is concerned, Cornell should therefore agree with the assessment of the source situation given earlier in this paper.

Third, once these two points are clarified, agreement on all important points is possible. For example, throughout his paper Cornell stresses the substantial body of reliable information represented by the "structural facts" passed on from generation to generation of annalists, as opposed to the "narrative superstructure," or *exornatio* and dramatization of these facts by the individual authors.[135] This is a useful distinction, but it prompts three questions: what is the ratio between the two elements? What is the character of these facts? How do we distinguish the two elements and how can we extricate the facts from the dense network of *exornatio*? On all three points I find myself in perfect agreement with Cornell's answers. His definition of the nature of the "structural facts" is very close to my own given above, but it is worth stressing the limited amount of information provided by them. Cornell uses as an example the story of Sp. Maelius. The factual basis of the detailed and dramatic story we read in the extant sources is simple: "Maelius was killed by Servilius Ahala while trying to make himself king." According to Ungern-Sternberg, the facts concerning the Decemvirate were equally terse: a college of ten men codified the law. In the latter case, the surviving body of laws adds substance and the *decemviri* are at least firmly located in the *fasti*. Not even that is true for the Maelius episode: all the monuments connected with the story are of much later origin, the date is uncertain, and the confrontation between Maelius and Ahala may

132. But see Ungern-Sternberg, *Capua* (1975): 1ff., 8ff.
133. See above at nn. 1ff.
134. See Cornell, chapter II below at nn. 42ff.; cf. above at nn. 31ff.; chapter VII below at nn. 40f.
135. Cornell, chapter II below at n. 6, after n. 31, and especially at n. 58.

already be a secondary combination of two originally separate legends lacking a precise chronological location.[136] At any rate, the proportion of narrative superstructure is immensely larger than that of structural facts, and the task of extricating them practically has to start at zero. In Cornell's own words,

> we must attempt to free ourselves from the conscious assumptions that inform the literary sources, and to replace them with more authentic historical models. That is the only way we can hope to use the evidence of the sources . . . to uncover something of the real nature of Roman society in the archaic age.[137]

Fourth, it is no surprise, therefore, that Cornell's characterization of annalistic historiography so closely parallels my own and Ungern-Sternberg's[138] that the logic of his arguments must lead him to the same conclusions. And indeed it does:

> We have to reckon with the fact that the Romans of the last centuries of the Republic had no understanding of the true character of the political and social realities of the archaic age. In their efforts to make use of the data at their disposal they inevitably applied inappropriate and anachronistic models. The result is that we cannot rely on the sources for answers to even the most basic questions.[139]

I fully agree with these and the other concluding remarks in Cornell's paper. I would therefore expect him to agree with the conse-

---

136. Definition of "facts": see above at n. 26, and Cornell, chapter II below, after n. 31. Maelius: Cornell, at nn. 21ff. (especially after n. 22) with literature cited in n. 21. Momigliano, *Contr. IV* (1969): 331ff., especially 336–39, is even more skeptical. Decemvirate: Ungern-Sternberg, chapter III below after n. 13.

137. Cornell at the end of chapter II below.

138. Since his paper is printed in this volume, it is unnecessary to quote him. But in view of his many pointed statements, it seems to be mostly wishful thinking that Cornell ends his justified attack against certain recent and unreasonably radical theories with the remark that they are "far less convincing than the traditional account, which at least has the authority of the sources to back it up."

139. Cornell, chapter II below before n. 63; id., "Tradizione storiografica" (1980): 33f., and "Failure of the Plebs" (1983): 102, 120.

quences I draw from this situation in regard to the actual use of these sources and the direction of further research.

Many of the preceding remarks also apply to Develin's comments on the value of the tradition (see the first part of chapter XI below). I merely want to add, first, that in the case of Greece, too, the main problem is not deliberate and politically motivated falsification by fourth-century authors, but rather naive misrepresentation and anachronistic reconstruction resulting from lack of sources and of awareness about the fundamentally different character and problems of archaic society. The extant histories provide ample indication of how little even the Periclean age knew about the sixth century.[140] Second, concerning Rome, I think Develin's argument would gain much if he did not apply it without differentiation to the whole archaic period. There may have been more and better sources and memories about the second half of the fourth than about the first half of the fifth century. For example, his explanation (in the second part of his paper) of the repetition of similar laws is worth serious consideration for subsequent laws separated by twenty or thirty years in the period after 366, but hardly for those attributed to 509 or 449. It would seem important in this context to consider the consequences of the fact[141] that in the view of several late republican authors, the Roman constitution had reached its fully developed form by the time of the Decemvirate, and that all important elements of the Conflict of the Orders had emerged by then as well.

140. See n. 111 above.
141. Emphasized by Cornell, chapter II below at n. 59; Ungern-Sternberg, chapter XII below at nn. 73f.; and myself, chapter VII below at n. 11.

TIMOTHY J. CORNELL

II

The Value of the Literary Tradition Concerning Archaic Rome

The main problem in studying the "Conflict of the Orders" in archaic Rome is the unreliable nature of the literary tradition. That tradition, preserved in the historical works of writers such as Livy and Dionysius of Halicarnassus, and supplemented by the notices of poets, orators, and antiquarians, is both extensive and rich in details of every kind. The problem for the modern historian is not that there is insufficient evidence; on the contrary, the available documentation on early Roman history is relatively abundant when compared, say, with the surviving information on the archaic history of the Greek states. Rather, the problem is that we do not know how much of it we can trust.

One particularly disconcerting fact is that the tradition was not fixed in writing until the last centuries of the Republic. The first Roman historian, Q. Fabius Pictor, lived at the time of the second Punic War. The earliest Latin epic poet, Cn. Naevius, was his contemporary, and antiquarian studies developed in the following generation with the work of writers such as Sex. Aelius Paetus and C. Cassius Hemina.[1]

Where these men obtained their information about the archaic period is a question that cannot at present be satisfactorily answered. It is certainly possible to imagine what kinds of sources might have been available to them. For example it goes without saying that certain documents, such as lists of magistrates and triumphs, the laws of the Twelve Tables, and the texts of ancient treaties must have been among the sources used by the earliest researchers. We may also surmise that they drew upon oral traditions, the recollections of the noble families, and the *Annales Maximi*, an archaic chronicle kept by the Pontifex Maximus, which apparently contained some sort of record of historical events. But we have only the vaguest notion of the particular contributions of these different kinds of sources. For example, a great deal has been written about the *Annales Maximi*, but in all honesty it must be admitted that we know virtually nothing about what they contained, or how extensively they were used by the Roman historians.[2]

Identifying the primary sources of the earliest historians and antiquarians is difficult enough. But it is even more difficult to establish the precise relation of the primary sources to the developed literary narratives that have come down to us. There can be no doubt that the surviving accounts present a highly contrived and unrealistic picture of the early age of Rome. By that I do not mean to imply that what our sources have to tell us about archaic Rome is necessarily false or legendary. On the contrary, I am convinced that much of the famous story is based on fact, and that our sources have preserved a great deal of what really happened. The point however is that the facts have been transmitted through the medium of a pseudo-

---

1. The fragments of the early Roman historians are collected in *HRR* I. For a good general discussion, see E. Badian, "Early Historians" (1966): 1–38. On Fabius Pictor, see D. Timpe, *ANRW* I. 2 (1972): 928–69, with full bibliography. On the early Latin annalists and the beginnings of antiquarian research at Rome, see E. Rawson, *Latomus* 35 (1976): 689–717; on Paetus, Cic. *De orat.* 1.240.

2. A full discussion of the *Annales Maximi* and related problems can be found in B. W. Frier, *Annales* (1979). On the sources of the early Roman historians, see, e.g., G. De Sanctis, *Storia* I² (1956): 1–48; P. Fraccaro, *Opuscula* I (1956): 7–11; Momigliano, *Contr. III* (1966): 547–49.

historical narrative constructed out of secondary interpretation and conjecture, and filled up with rhetorical embellishment and plausible fabrication.

The process of elaboration is usually conceived of as a purely literary phenomenon.[3] There is undoubtedly some truth in this view. It is obvious that the Roman historians felt entitled to add rhetorical color and incidental detail to the traditional story in order to enliven the narrative. Thus for example the bare record of a battle or campaign could be embellished with all sorts of fictitious, but plausible, details supplied by the historian's own imagination or drawn from some preexisting literary model.[4] In the same way historians were expected to compose imaginary speeches to put into the mouths of leading historical figures. These relatively harmless literary devices were an accepted feature of the Hellenistic style of historical writing that was fashionable in Rome in the late Republic.[5] We should note, however, that the convention was acceptable only so long as the rhetorical elaboration did not do violence to the traditional facts. This was clearly Cicero's view, as P. A. Brunt has recently shown.[6] For Cicero good historians should not be mere *narratores*, but *exornatores rerum*. On the other hand he believed that the historian's first and overriding duty was to tell the truth.[7] It would be quite wrong to assert that literary convention gave the Roman annalists license to manufacture evidence or to tell lies. In a revealing passage, Livy implicitly criticizes Coelius Antipater (a historian of the second century B.C. who wrote a work on the second Punic War) for inventing an imaginary storm during Scipio's crossing to Africa in 204 B.C.[8] The implication seems to be that a historian was entitled to write an excit-

---

3. Thus, e.g., P. G. Walsh, *Livy* (1961): 110–37; R. M. Ogilvie, *Comm.* (1965): 1–16 and passim; id., *Early Rome* (1976): 15–29; T. P. Wiseman, *Clio's Cosmetics* (1979).

4. For some examples (taken at random), see Ogilvie, *Comm.* (1965): 112, on Livy 1.24.9 and 25.2; 285–86; 359–61; 579, on 4.28.7; and passim. On Livy's battle pieces, see Walsh, *Livy* (1961): 197–204.

5. On "tragic" history, see B. L. Ullmann, "History and Tragedy," *TAPA* 73 (1942): 25–53; F. W. Walbank, "History and Tragedy," *Historia* 9 (1960): 216–34; id., *Polybius* (Berkeley and Los Angeles, 1972): 34–40; Wiseman, *Clio's Cosmetics* (1979), passim, especially 3–8, 27–40.

6. P. A. Brunt, "Cicero and Historiography" (1980). On Cicero and history, see also Rambaud, *Cicéron* (1953); E. Rawson, *JRS* 62 (1972): 33–45.

7. *De orat.* 2.36, 51–3, 62, etc. In general, see P. A. Brunt (as in n. 6).

8. Livy 29.27.13 = Coelius fr. 40 P.

ing and dramatic account of an event, provided that the event itself was historical. Livy obviously thought that by inventing an imaginary storm out of nothing Coelius had overstepped the bounds of what was permissible in the way of rhetorical embellishment.

It is often supposed, however, that Roman historians habitually abused the accepted conventions by consciously distorting the historical facts at their disposal and giving free rein to their imaginations when the facts were lacking. The historians of the first century B.C., men such as Valerius Antias and Licinius Macer, are thought to have been especially guilty in this respect, although the earlier historians, including Fabius Pictor, have also come in for their share of criticism in recent years.[9] These writers are alleged to have perpetrated lies and distortions on a large scale, not only for frivolous reasons (for example, to entertain their readers), but also, more mischievously, to promote political causes and to glorify the achievements of their own real or supposed ancestors. On this view the surviving accounts of early Roman history represent a bogus tradition, consisting largely of mendacious annalistic fabrications.

This hypothetical reconstruction is open to a number of serious objections. First, the Roman historians whose works we are able to read appear to be innocent of the charges that are commonly levelled at their less fortunate predecessors, whose works are lost. Many harsh things have been said, rightly or wrongly, about Livy and Dionysius of Halicarnassus. They have been variously described as tedious, naive, prejudiced, ignorant, and foolish; but no one has seriously suggested that they were downright dishonest. The theory that the Roman historical tradition consists largely of annalistic invention is therefore seriously weakened by the fact that there are no surviving examples of the kind of historical writing the theory necessarily presupposes. In fact we are no more able to judge the honesty of the republican annalists than we are to assess their competence in research. When A. Alföldi argued that Fabius Pictor invented much of the traditional story of early Rome, it was easy for critics to point

---

9. On Antias and Macer, see, e.g., E. Badian, "Early Historians" (1966): 18–23; Ogilvie, *Comm.* (1965): 7–16; Wiseman, *Clio's Cosmetics* (1979): 23–24, 115–21, etc. Reservations in Luce, *Livy* (1977): 165–69, and in my review of Wiseman in *JRS* 72 (1982): 203–6. On Fabius Pictor, see Alföldi, *Early Rome* (1965), especially 101–75, and the criticisms of Momigliano, *Contr.* IV (1969): 487–99, and *Contr.* VI (1980): 69–75.

out that not nearly enough is known about Fabius Pictor to support such allegations.[10] The same argument applies a fortiori to writers such as Licinius Macer and Valerius Antias, who are even more obscure to us than Fabius Pictor.

Secondly we should note that the Roman annalists were not in a position to impose a fraudulent version of Rome's history on their contemporaries and on succeeding generations of historians. The main outline of political and military events was a matter of public knowledge in the later Republic; it was clearly set out in the works of historians such as Fabius Pictor, Cato the Censor, and L. Calpurnius Piso Frugi, men who had themselves made history and knew what they were talking about. The constituent elements of the narrative were based securely on the *fasti* and other documents. It is simply inconceivable that relatively late writers such as Valerius Antias could have departed radically from the received tradition and hoped to get away with it.[11]

The same argument applies even to early historians like Fabius Pictor. One should not assume that because Fabius was the first Roman to write history he had carte blanche on which to scribble anything he pleased.[12] In fact it is probable that educated Romans of the third century B.C. were already familiar with the main elements of their historical tradition, and that Fabius broke new ground only in that he was the first of them to set it down in literary form. This is surely the most reasonable explanation of the fact that extensive information about Rome's history had already found its way into the works of earlier Greek writers, such as Theophrastus, Timaeus, Hieronymus, Callimachus, and Diocles of Peparethos (among others).[13] Again it is hard to believe that an intelligent and independent-minded historian like Cato the Censor would have meekly accepted Fabius's version of early Roman history if the primary evidence,

---

10. A. Momigliano (as in n. 9).
11. Cf. my comments in *JRS* 72 (1982): 206.
12. *Pace* Alföldi, *Early Rome* (1965): 173. On this see Momigliano, *Contr. IV* (1969): 490.
13. The evidence is assembled by Jacoby, *FGrHist*, no. 840. For discussion of Greek accounts of early Rome, see P. M. Fraser, *Ptolemaic Alexandria* (Oxford, 1972): 763–69; T. J. Cornell, *PCPhS* 21 (1975): 1–32; J. Hornblower, *Hieronymus of Cardia* (Oxford, 1981): 140ff.

which he knew well, had said something radically different.[14] Moreover, if the Roman historians had been in the habit of perpetrating wholesale fabrications and inventions of historical facts, we should expect to find more trace of disagreements and inconsistencies in the surviving literature. In fact the general structure of the narrative is remarkably uniform in all the sources, and only minor discrepancies are registered.[15]

My contention is that the annalists had only limited scope for tampering with the received facts, and that they did not, in fact, greatly alter the basic outline of events that had been handed down to them. They were not free to invent anything they pleased; if anything, they may have been responsible for the insertion of a certain amount of trivial and anecdotal matter. By way of analogy we may observe that though it was possible for Mason L. Weems to invent the story of the cherry tree, he was hardly in a position to alter the known facts about George Washington's public career.[16] We may reasonably assume that the Roman tradition has its fair share of cherry trees. But even so we must not suppose that all such anecdotes are invariably of literary origin; if anything, the literary ones are probably exceptions. For example, Livy's story of Maharbal's advice to Hannibal after Cannae[17] might seem at first sight to be an obvious rhetorical elaboration by some annalist. But in fact it can be shown to be a well-established tradition going back at least to Cato, who had himself fought in the war against Hannibal.[18] It is most unlikely that Cato invented the story, which was probably already current at the time of the events themselves.[19]

---

14. On Cato's *Origines*, see D. Timpe, *Atti Accad. patavina, cl. di sc. mor., lett. ed arti* 83 (1970–71): 5–33; Schroeder, *Cato* (1971); A. E. Astin, *Cato the Censor* (Oxford, 1978): 211–39.

15. Fraccaro, *Opuscula* I (1956): 1–23.

16. An interesting comment on the cherry tree story (and other matters) is to be found in A. B. Hart, "Imagination in History," *Am. Hist. Rev.* 15 (1909–10): 227–51, especially 242–43.

17. Livy 22.51.2.

18. Gellius *Noctes Atticae* 10.24 = Cato, *Origines*, fr. 86 P; Coelius Antipater, fr. 25 P. See E. Badian, "Early Historians" (1966): 17.

19. The creation of "instant myths" is a well-attested phenomenon, especially in time of war. See, for example, the fascinating pages of P. Fussell, *The Great War in Modern Memory* (Oxford, 1975): 114–54.

This example underlines the important point that in the Republic the story of the city's past was not confined to history books, but was rather a living tradition that formed part of the consciousness of the entire community of Roman citizens. In this sense the Roman historical tradition can be defined as the sum of what successive generations of Romans believed about their own past; and in a society in which tradition—the *mos maiorum*—provided the standard by which all political and moral actions were judged, the living past had an importance that is hard for us to appreciate. Moreover the record of past events was a matter of direct concern to the ruling class, whose position was sustained by it and whose members based their claim to high office on the historic achievements of their ancestors. The historical tradition of the Roman Republic was neither an authenticated official record nor an objective critical reconstruction, but rather an ideological construct, designed to control, to justify, and to inspire.

The functional role of historical tradition in the political and social life of the Republic meant that the generally accepted picture of Rome's history was subject to a process of continuous transformation as each generation reconstructed the past in its own image. The successive reappraisals were registered in the works of the annalists, whose accounts naturally reflected contemporary preoccupations. They were not the creators of the historical tradition, but rather its purveyors.

The process of constant reassessment is exemplified by the way in which the political history of the archaic period was rewritten in the age of the Gracchi and later. It is commonly, and rightly, assumed that great political and social crises tend to inspire historical writing and to generate historical controversy. Thus for example it has been said that "the political strife of the seventeenth century in England plunged almost the entire governing class into historical studies."[20] So, too, the upheavals of the Gracchan age caused men to look back to earlier periods of political strife and to examine them with new eyes.

As an illustration let us take the story of the demagogue Spurius

20. J. H. Plumb, *The Death of the Past* (London, 1969): 40–41. The whole of Plumb's study is important on this issue.

Maelius.²¹ Maelius was a rich equestrian who ingratiated himself with the *plebs* at a time of famine by providing them with grain at his own expense. The popularity he gained as a consequence led him to contemplate making a bid for kingship, but his plans were discovered and he was killed by the impetuous youth C. Servilius Ahala. Our sources record two different versions of this event. In one, Servilius Ahala was acting in an official capacity as *magister equitum* to Cincinnatus, who had been appointed dictator to deal with the emergency created by Maelius's plot. The alternative version maintains that Servilius was not a magistrate, but merely a private citizen doing his duty on behalf of the state. The former account was preferred by Cicero, Livy, and Dionysius of Halicarnassus, but Dionysius tells us that the second version had been given by two of the earliest historians, Cincius Alimentus and Calpurnius Piso.²² It is most probable that the disagreement arose in the years following the murder of Ti. Gracchus, when conservative politicians were attempting to propagate the theory that the assassination of would-be tyrants was justified. In the pre-Gracchan period the tradition probably said no more than that Maelius had been killed by Servilius Ahala while trying to make himself king. A straightforward story of this kind no doubt appeared in the work of Cincius Alimentus. But the calamitous events of 133 B.C. would have given the episode a new and startling relevance, and must surely have provoked renewed curiosity about the circumstances of Maelius's fall. The question of the legality of Servilius's deed is likely to have been a particularly sensitive issue, since it might have appeared to be a precedent for the action of P. Scipio Nasica, who had instigated the lynching of Gracchus and his followers even though he held no magistracy at the time.

In any event it would have been important to determine what Servilius's status was at the time when he killed Maelius, a question that no one had bothered to ask before. The different versions in our sources are the product of uncertainty over what the historical evi-

---

21. Livy 4.13–16; Dion. Hal. 12.1–4; Cic. *Cato Maior* 56; Zon. 7.20. The basic discussion is by Mommsen, *Röm. Forschungen* II (1879): 199–222. See also Momigliano, *Contr.* IV (1969): 331–39; Ogilvie, *Comm.* (1965): 550–57; id., *Early Rome* (1976): 144–45; A. W. Lintott, *Historia* 19 (1970): 13–18; most recently P. M. Martin, *Royauté* (1982): 349–51.

22. Dion. Hal. 12.4.2–5 = Cincius, fr. 6 P = Piso, fr. 24 P.

dence actually had to say on the matter, which raised complex questions concerning the dating of the episode and the interpretation of the *fasti*.[23] The results are far from being disinterested scholarly interpretations, however, since the two rival versions both in their own way seek to justify the killing of Maelius. On the other hand they provide no evidence of an attempt to make crude political propaganda out of the episode. The late Republican overtones are unmistakable in the surviving accounts, but they nevertheless contain a sufficient number of unique details to make it unlikely that the whole story was a politically motivated fiction, a possibility that seems in any event to be ruled out by Dionysius's statement that an account of the event appeared in Cincius.[24] The story was moreover associated with various monuments and relics in the city. A place called Aequimaelium was thought to mark the site of Maelius's house, which was razed to the ground on the orders of the Senate;[25] nearby at the Porta Trigemina stood the columna Minucia, a column with a statue, which had supposedly been erected in honor of the L. Minucius who had first warned the Senate of Maelius's intentions.[26] The column was represented on coins minted in the 130s by C. Minucius Augurinus.[27] The family of the Servilii derived their cognomen Ahala (= "armpit") from the fact that the killer of Maelius had concealed his dagger under his arm. It would however be hypercritical to dismiss the entire story as an aetiological fabrication;[28]

---

23. The sources place the Maelius episode in 439 B.C. (Vulg.). This may be due to the fact that Cincinnatus, Servilius Ahala, and L. Minucius were all recorded as holding office in this year (Cicero, *Cato* 56, places the story of Cincinnatus and the plough in this context), or that archival sources mention a famine at this time (Momigliano, *Contr. IV* [1969]: 336). But there are curious residual traces in Livy of a "doublet" in 436, when a second Sp. Maelius appears as tribune of the *plebs* and clashes with Servilius Ahala and L. Minucius (4.21.3–4). On this, see Momigliano, *Contr. IV*: 337–38.

24. The MSS have Κιρκέος, but the emendation to Κίγκιος seems reasonable. Mommsen's radical alteration of the text (*Röm. Forschungen* II [1879]: 199 n. 98) is rejected by G. De Sanctis, *Storia* II² (1960): 15 n. 44. De Sanctis nevertheless managed to persuade himself that the entire Maelius story is a worthless fiction.

25. Livy 4.16.1; Dion. Hal. 12.4.6; Cic. *Dom.* 101; Varr. *Ling.* 5.157; Val. Max. 6.3.1.

26. Pliny. *Nat. Hist.* 18.15; 34.21; Dion. Hal. 12.4.6.

27. Crawford, *Coinage* (1975), nos. 242 & 243 (135–34 B.C.).

28. As do E. Pais, *Storia* I.1 (1898): 545ff.; De Sanctis, *Storia* II² (1960): 14–16; most recently T. P. Wiseman, *LCM* 8 (1983): 21.

in fact it is much more likely that the fanciful etymologies (cf. also the derivation of Μηνύκιος from μηνύειν in Dion. Hal. 12.1.14, etc.) were suggested by the story, rather than the other way round, and consequently that the tradition about Maelius's putsch was based on an authentic memory of something that really happened.[29]

The example of the story of Sp. Maelius can help us to understand the process by which the record of historical events was handed down and gradually elaborated in the course of its transmission. In particular it should be emphasized that the possibility of wholesale fabrication of historical data is not the best explanation of the elaborate and detailed stories that make up the tradition as we have it. We should beware of exaggerating the effect of frivolous and dishonest invention by the annalists of the late Republic.

We are in fact entitled to conclude that the surviving literary accounts are firmly based on a common body of tradition that outlined the main developments in the history of the city. This tradition was constantly being reinterpreted in the light of new historical circumstances and filled out with rhetorical elaboration as the art of historical writing became increasingly sophisticated. On the other hand there is no reason to think that the tradition was consciously deformed or systematically contaminated in the course of its transmission. I have argued that the annalists of the late Republic were not in a position to alter the basic outline of events by inserting arbitrary manipulations and wholesale inventions, and there is no serious evidence to suggest that any of them tried. The contrary is often asserted by modern scholars, who are apt to attribute all kinds of mischief to writers such as Claudius Quadrigarius, Licinius Macer, and Valerius Antias; but the resulting portraits of these little-known writers are grotesque and fanciful caricatures that are not substantiated by any evidence.[30] Rather, the fact that the surviving accounts of Cicero, Diodorus, Dionysius, and Livy agree closely with one another on all fundamental points (and often in matters of fine detail) can only mean that there was a basic common tradition that is reflected in all of them. This received tradition must have been more or less faithfully reproduced in the works of earlier annalists, whose individual contributions were therefore effectively negligible. This

29. Thus, correctly, e.g., A. W. Lintott, *Historia* 19 (1970): 15, citing Mommsen.
30. See n. 9 above.

conclusion is further borne out by the fact that Livy and Dionysius record only minor discrepancies in their sources. Naturally I am assuming that Livy and Dionysius had actually read the sources to which they refer; the once standard view that Livy knew of the works of Fabius Pictor and Calpurnius Piso only from citations in secondary authorities has rightly been challenged in recent studies and is almost certainly wrong.[31] As for Dionysius, his erudition is generally acknowledged.

The foregoing discussion prompts the conclusion that in a critical analysis of the historical tradition it is not necessary to discuss the individual annalists who helped to pass it on. It goes without saying that they introduced a great deal of rhetorical elaboration and were responsible for numerous mistakes, duplications, and anachronisms in matters of detail. But this fact is hardly of decisive importance, since modern historians are not much concerned with the details per se, and are mostly content to skip the set speeches, battle pieces, character sketches, and circumstantial descriptions of particular events. The point at issue is whether the basic outline of events can be considered reliable.

The "basic outline" includes the bare record of military campaigns, triumphs, defeats, peace treaties, annexations of territory, and colonial foundations; and in domestic affairs the development of the constitution, political upheavals, legislative enactments, the construction of major public buildings, and so on. These structural elements were ordered in a regular chronological sequence under the headings of the eponymous magistrates listed in the *fasti*. The basic tradition included popular oral stories, folktales, legends, and exemplary sagas of heroism and virtue; it explained the origins of the major public cults, institutions, and monuments that were still extant in the historical age of the Republic; it incorporated the semi-public traditions of the great noble families, which were solemnly rehearsed at public funerals and legitimated the power and influence wielded by their living representatives; and finally it was able to account for the innumerable antique monuments, buildings, relics, place names,

---

31. For the standard view, see, e.g., Ogilvie, *Comm.* (1965): 5–7. The contrary opinion of M. L. W. Laistner, *The Greater Roman Historians* (Berkeley and Los Angeles, 1947): 83–88, has recently been taken up again by H. Tränkle, *Hermes* 93 (1965): 311–37; Luce, *Livy* (1977): 161–81; Briscoe, *Comm.* (1973): 9.

and the entire rigmarole of time-honoured cult practices, archaic formulae, and obsolete institutional survivals that made republican Rome a kind of living museum.

We may now turn to the question of the reliability of the structural facts contained in the tradition. It is important to observe that even if we exclude the possibility of large-scale forgery, deliberate manipulation, and frivolous invention, the authenticity of the traditional story is not thereby necessarily guaranteed. But it *does* follow that the traditional story represents the truth as the Romans themselves conceived it. This consideration cannot be lightly dismissed. We should never lose sight of the fact that the Romans of the later Republic thought they knew a great deal about their own history, a claim that would be very hard to understand if there were not some sound basis for it. It is difficult to imagine that the Romans were entirely mistaken about something to which they obviously attached great importance.

It is worth asking whether there are any serious objections to the view that the tradition is fundamentally sound in essentials. The principal difficulty seems to be that the case cannot be definitely proved. In particular there is no certainty about the means by which reliable information about the archaic period of the sixth and fifth centuries B.C. could have been transmitted to informed Romans of the second and first centuries. That does not of course mean that the phenomenon is inexplicable,[32] or that our ignorance in this matter necessarily justifies skepticism. The phrase "no evidence" in this context means literally what it says: *no evidence*. It is necessary to stress this point in view of the attitude of some skeptical historians, who are inclined to argue that all information about early Rome is to be rejected unless it can be independently corroborated or shown to be derived from a reliable source. This kind of approach was exempli-

---

32. One might perfectly well suppose, for example, that much information was preserved in archival sources, especially the pontifical chronicle (e.g., Ogilvie, *Comm.* [1965], index, s.v. *annales*), or alternatively that oral epic poetry and songs preserved a vivid memory of great men and their deeds (see, e.g., Cic. *Brut.* 75; *Tusc.* 4.2.3). This is the famous "ballad theory" propounded by Niebuhr (though it did not originate with him), and made popular in England by Lord Macaulay (see especially the introduction to his *Lays of Ancient Rome*). For a critical discussion of the ballad theory see Momigliano, *Contr. II* (1960): 69–87. These hypothetical explanations remain perfectly possible in theory; but the facts are still uncertain.

fied in Sir George Cornewall Lewis, M.P., whose two-volume work, *An Inquiry into the Credibility of the Early Roman History* (London, 1853),[33] illustrates the extreme consequences of this hypercritical stance. The attitude represented by Lewis continues to flourish. For instance, in a recent issue of the *Journal of Roman Studies* a book on the origins of the Roman *plebs* is criticised because its interpretation is based on the evidence of the sources, and because it adopts the principle that the evidence of the sources should not be rejected unless there is good reason to do so.[34] This admirable principle is denounced by the reviewer, who argues instead that we should only believe the report of an event if we can show how the memory of it survived into the historical period. Since this condition rules out almost everything in our sources, the argument is tantamount to saying that early Roman history cannot be studied at all.

In strict logic it is obvious that an unverifiable report should neither be accepted nor rejected. But no one except an extreme Pyrrhonist would attempt to apply this logical principle to the ancient sources. Historians always work on the basis of probability, and a great deal of what normally passes for historical evidence would not stand up in a court of law, let alone in the court of logic. In the present context it seems reasonable to assume that if a certain piece of evidence is not inherently improbable and was believed by the Romans themselves to be the truth, the burden of proof must lie with those who wish to disbelieve it.

A further argument against excessive skepticism is provided by the patently arbitrary character of most hypercritical accounts of early Roman history. The notorious efforts of E. Pais to dismiss the entire tradition of early Roman history as a mixture of legend and falsification are no longer taken seriously by anyone and have themselves become a historical curiosity.[35] The same fate surely awaits the theories of E. Gjerstad, who attempted to lower the date of the be-

33. On G. C. Lewis, see Momigliano, *Contr. I* (1955): 249–62.
34. A. Drummond, *JRS* 72 (1982): 177–79, reviewing Richard, *Origines* (1978), and Guarino, *Riv* (1975).
35. Pais, *Storia di Roma* (1898). Pais retreated somewhat from his original stance in the second edition, significantly entitled *Storia critica di Roma* (1913), and became positively conventional in the third (1927), and in the first volume of *Histoire Romaine*, in the *Histoire Générale* edited by G. Glotz (Paris, 1926). In 1937 Pais's pupil E. Ciaceri produced what was virtually a rehash of the sources in *Le origini di Roma*

ginning of the Republic to the time of the Twelve Tables and thus to impose kings on the Romans of the early fifth century B.C.,[36] and those of A. Alföldi, who dismissed the whole tradition of Roman power under the Tarquins as a fabrication, and tried to prove that Rome was a place of no significance before the end of the fifth century B.C.[37] These radical theories are demonstrably erroneous and have always been unlikely to win acceptance, since they offer historical reconstructions that are far less convincing than the traditional account, which at least has the authority of the sources to back it up.

The main positive argument in favour of the tradition is that it provides an account of Rome's historical development that is not only plausible and internally consistent, but also compatible with the continually increasing body of evidence that has come from more than a century of scientific archaeological research. The importance of this fact can scarcely be overestimated. Archaeology provides a reliable and independent means of checking the validity of traditional information, and it is clear that it has done more than anything else in recent years to bring about a radical change in scholarly attitudes to the subject in general.

The archaeological evidence that is now available has revealed the character of the settlement that grew up on the site of Rome in the early part of the first millennium B.C. Similar settlements existed at other sites in Latium Vetus, and recent excavations, at sites such as Ficana and Castel di Decima, have begun to give us an idea of their material culture.[38] In the earliest period of the so-called Latial Cul-

---

(on which see Momigliano, *Contr. II* [1960]: 401–7). For an impassioned critique of Pais and everything he stood for, see Barbagallo, *Problema* (1926): 93–104, which remains an invaluable statement of the case against hypercriticism.

36. Gjerstad's views of early Roman history, stated repetitively in numerous publications, are conveniently summarized in his *Early Rome* VI (1973). For a very strong criticism, see R. E. A. Palmer, *AJA* 79 (1975): 386–90.

37. A. Alföldi, *Early Rome* (1965), passim, especially 318–35.

38. For a summary of the results of recent work, see T. J. Cornell, *Archaeological Reports* (1979–80): 71–89. Other recent surveys include J. Poucet, *AC* 47 (1978): 566–601; 48 (1979): 177–220. The basic works of reference are Gjerstad, *Early Rome* I–VI (1953–73); Gierow, *Latium* I and II.1 (1964–66); G. Colonna, "Preistoria e protostoria" (1974): 273–346; the exhibition catalogues *Civiltà del Lazio primitivo* (Rome, 1976) and *Ricerca su una comunità del Lazio protostorico: Il sepolcreto dell'Osteria dell'Osa sulla Via Prenestina* (Rome, 1979); the papers in *La Formazione della città nel Lazio* (DArch, n.s., 2 [1980]); and the annual reports in *Archeologia laziale*.

ture these communities were characterized by a simple form of daily life based on subsistence agriculture and domestic craft production. At this stage there is no sign in the evidence of social stratification based on wealth. But during the eighth century B.C. the settlements grew in size and sophistication, with the development of external contacts through trade and other forms of exchange, and the emergence of a wealthy aristocracy. The appearance of chamber tombs and the spread of the gentile-name system in the early seventh century indicate the formation of dominant clans that had succeeded in concentrating the economic surplus of the community into their own hands and perpetuating their domination through inheritance.[39] The origin of the patriciate must be traced back to this period.[40]

During the last phase of the Latial Culture (i.e., toward the end of the seventh century B.C.) there is evidence of a profound change in the character of the settlements. This transformation is especially evident at Rome, which seems in fact to have outstripped the majority of its Latin neighbours by this date. In various parts of the city the huts that had formerly been the main form of dwelling were replaced by more substantial houses with stone foundations, timber frames, and tiled roofs. In the area of the Forum the huts were demolished, and in their place a formal public square was laid out. The process continued in the sixth century. Traces of the foundations of temples, public buildings, and sanctuaries have been unearthed, together with fragments of roof tiles, terracotta antefixes, and decorated architectural friezes. The evidence, though fragmentary, indicates beyond any serious doubt the development of a flourishing urbanised community on the site of Rome during the sixth century. Artefacts from votive deposits and other contexts attest a highly developed material culture and widespread external contacts.[41]

The appearance of these dramatic changes in the physical development of the centre of Rome coincides in date with the rule of the dynasty of the Tarquins, who according to our sources transformed

---

39. See the works cited in the previous note; also C. Ampolo, *DArch* 4/5 (1970–71): 37–68; M. Torelli, *DArch* 8 (1974–75): 3–78; G. Colonna, *SE* 45 (1977): 175–92; L. Ménager, *SDHI* 46 (1980): 147–235.

40. Richard, *Origines* (1978), ch. 4, and chapter IV, part 2 below.

41. The evidence is assembled in Gjerstad, *Early Rome* I–IV (1953–1966). On the formation of the city, see especially C. Ampolo, *MEFR* 92 (1980): 567–76; *DArch*, n.s., 2 (1980): 165–87, and "Stadtwerdung Roms" (1982): 319–24.

the monumental centre of the city and indulged in grandiose building projects. The archaeological evidence thus provides a general confirmation of the literary tradition, which in fact becomes much more informative and historical in appearance during the last century of the monarchy.

There are certain points at which the literary and archaeological sources coincide in precise detail. The most striking of these instances concerns the temples that Servius Tullius is said to have built in the Forum Boarium. The discovery beneath the church of Sant' Omobono of the foundations of an archaic temple dating from around the middle of the sixth century is obviously a dramatic confirmation of this tradition.[42] Other examples of precise correspondences between the archaeological data and the literary sources could be quoted, although it is important to note that they are necessarily rather exceptional. But it is surely unreasonable to expect traditional stories to be confirmed by archaeological discoveries in more than a very few instances; and to argue that no story can be believed unless it is confirmed archaeologically is hypercritical.

It remains true, however, that archaeological evidence can have only an indirect bearing on the study of the Conflict of the Orders. There are two reasons for this. First, and most obviously, although the remains of tombs, buildings, and artefacts can illuminate many aspects of a past society's material culture, in the nature of things they cannot tell us much about its social structures, institutions, ideologies, or political struggles. The archaeologists have not yet developed a technique for investigating the origins of the tribunate or the legal status of plebiscites. Secondly, the archaeological record fails us at the crucial point. As we have seen, the material evidence shows that Rome was a prosperous and rapidly expanding urban community in the sixth century. The fifth century, by contrast, is something of a blank. Our knowledge of the material culture of Rome in the fifth century is so poor that there is almost no known artefact or monument that can be safely ascribed to it.[43] The exception is imported Attic pottery; but here we should note that the quantity of Attic pottery found in Rome declines very sharply after c. 500 B.C.

---

42. M. Pallottino, *CRAI* (1977): 216–35; Thomsen, *Serv. Tullius* (1980): 267ff.
43. Cf. I. S. Ryberg, *Arch. Record* (1940), ch. 2.

(much more sharply than in the Etruscan cities, where a similar pattern can be observed), and dies out almost completely after 450.[44]

The poverty of the archaeological record for this period might conceivably be fortuitous (for example, it is possible that large amounts of fifth-century material are in existence somewhere and just awaiting discovery by archaeologists, or that we already possess such material but do not yet know how to recognise it as belonging to the fifth century); but this possibility seems remote. It is much more likely that the absence of archaeological material from this period is itself a product of historical circumstances and a sign of general recession in Rome in the fifth century. This conclusion is consistent with certain indications in the literary sources. For example, the record of temple building in the late regal period and the first decades of the Republic comes to an end in 484 B.C. The dedication of the temple of Castor in that year is the last known event of its kind before the temple of Apollo in 431—itself an isolated instance.[45] The annalistic record of military difficulties, famines, and pestilences during the fifth century accords with this general impression of economic decline and provides the background for the social and political conflicts of the period. The archaeological evidence (or lack of it) is therefore consistent with other evidence for the conditions of the fifth century, but at the same time it obviously cannot provide answers to more specific questions.

The positive value of archaeological evidence in the present context is that it creates a strong prima facie case for saying that the main outlines of the traditional account, from the early regal period onwards, are in touch with historical reality; and it confirms the view advanced earlier in this paper, that there can be no justification whatever for an a priori rejection of the traditional data. The two types of evidence, archaeological and literary, represent different facets of the same historic society, and they both complement and corroborate one another. Any serious critical investigation of early Roman history must make full use of both types of material in order to produce an integrated reconstruction that must answer to the demands of internal consistency and coherence.

As an example of how important historical evidence can be pro-

44. See J. C. Meyer, *Analecta Rom. inst. Danici* 9 (1980): 47ff.
45. See the list in Latte, *Religionsgeschichte* (1960): 415.

duced from a combination of literary and archaeological data, let us briefly consider the question of the power of the Roman state at the beginning of the Republic. Our sources maintain that, under the last kings, Rome was the most powerful city in Latium, with an extensive territory, a developed urban centre, a sophisticated institutional structure, and a strong army. This traditional picture is undoubtedly well founded. In the first place our sources tell us that Rome had conquered more than a third of the territory of Latium by the beginning of the fifth century B.C. This area was distributed among the local tribes, twenty-one of which had been established by 495 B.C.[46] The territory of the twenty-one tribes measured some 862 km^2 according to Beloch's estimate.[47] A recent study has calculated that if 15 percent of the total land surface was under cultivation each year, Rome's territory would have been able to sustain a maximum population of around 35,000.[48]

This hypothetical conclusion is compatible with other quantifiable data that can be obtained from the traditional account. For instance we are told that under Servius Tullius the urban centre of Rome had expanded to embrace an area of some 285 hectares.[49] An urban community of these dimensions would have been more than a match for most Etruscan cities, and would have dwarfed the other centres of Latium, the largest of which, among those that can be measured, covered no more than about 40 hectares each.

Another indication of the power of Rome in the late sixth century is the size of its army. The most probable reconstruction of the origi-

---

46. Livy 2.21.7.
47. Beloch, *Röm. Geschichte* (1926): 169ff. His view was that the territory of Rome measured 822 km^2 before the conquest of Crustumerium and the creation of the tribus Clustumina and Claudia. Livy's notice about the twenty-one tribes follows the capture of Crustumerium (2.19.1), and the twenty-one tribes include both the Clustumina and the Claudia. Beloch's figure of 822 km^2 is often cited as an indication of the size of the *ager Romanus* at the end of the monarchy. But we should note that Beloch himself did not credit the traditional account of the conquests under the kings, and dated the capture of Crustumerium to the end of the fifth century B.C.
48. C. Ampolo, *DArch*, n.s., 2 (1980): 15–31.
49. Beloch, *Röm. Geschichte* (1926): 208ff. This is the so-called "City of the Four Regions" enclosed within the Servian *pomerium* (Livy 1.44, etc.). The area within the fourth-century "Servian" walls is 426 ha. It is not, however, known whether these walls follow the course of an earlier circuit. Beloch's figures for some of the Etruscan cities can be cited for comparison: Caere 120, Tarquinii 150, Vulci 180, Veii 242 ha. (Beloch, *Bevölkerung* [1886]: 472ff.).

nal form of the centuriate organisation presupposes an army (*classis*) of 6,000 infantry.[50] Since these troops were heavily armed soldiers ("hoplites") who were obliged to provide their own armour, we must assume that the total population, including women, children, and old men, as well as those (plebeians?) who were unable to afford the necessary equipment and were designated "*infra classem*," must have been very numerous, perhaps over 30,000 in all.

These calculations are entirely consistent with the archaeological evidence, which as we have seen confirms the traditional picture of rapid urban development in the sixth century. The most important building was the great temple of Jupiter Capitolinus, which was built by the Tarquins and dedicated at the beginning of the Republic. Archaeological evidence, in the form of fragmentary architectural terracottas, confirms the date of the temple, and traces of the foundations and substructure serve to corroborate what the tradition tells us about the immense scale of the building. The platform on which it stood measured some 61 meters long by 55 meters wide, making it one of the largest temples in the Mediterranean world at the time. This fact in itself must lend support to the tradition that Rome under the Tarquins was the leading state in central Italy.[51]

The final witness is the treaty between Rome and Carthage, quoted by Polybius and dated by him to the first year of the Republic. The text of the treaty makes Rome the overlord of a miniature "empire" in Latium extending down the coast as far as Terracina.[52] Polybius is a reliable historian and his statements have authority in their own right. His account is moreover perfectly plausible, given what is otherwise known of Carthaginian interests at this date. It is sufficient merely to refer to the Pyrgi inscriptions.[53]

50. This is the figure arrived at by P. Fraccaro, *Opuscula* II (1957): 287ff., 293ff.; see now his posthumous work *Della guerra presso i Romani*, published as *Opuscula* IV (1975), especially 29–40. Fraccaro's interpretation of the problem is still the most convincing. For an alternative view, arguing for an original *classis* of 4,000, see Richard, *Origines* (1978): 363–65. This would imply a total population of around 20,000.

51. Dion. Hal. 4.61 gives a fairly accurate measurement for the temple. On the archaeological remains, see Gjerstad, *Early Rome* IV (1966): 388–98.

52. Polyb. 3.22. Note especially 3.22.11: "The Carthaginians shall do no wrong to the peoples of Ardea, Antium, Lavinium, Circeii, Terracina or any others of the Latins who are subject to Rome" (Loeb Classical Library).

53. See, e.g., Pallottino, *Etruscans* (1975): 90; J. Ferron, *ANRW* I.1 (1972): 189–216.

But the principal argument in favour of Polybius's evidence is the fact that the contents of the treaty accord with the historical circumstances of Rome in the late sixth century as we have reconstructed them from other evidence. A fairly precise picture of the military and political power of Rome at this period is thus given by a number of separate pieces of evidence: the archaeological record, the traditional narrative of military expansion under the kings, the calculations, based on the evidence of the sources, of the size of the population, the strength of the army and the extent of the urban area of the city, and, finally, the text of the Carthage treaty. These data are not necessarily very persuasive by themselves, and each of them could be individually called into question. But the fact that they agree precisely with one another is a firm guarantee of the authenticity of all of them; and in combination they form an irresistibly strong case in favour of the traditional account.

It is nevertheless worth noting that when A. Alföldi tried to argue that Rome was only a primitive village at the end of the sixth century B.C., he was obliged not only to dismiss the traditional narrative, but also to denounce the Romano-Carthaginian treaty as a forgery, to lower the date of the introduction of the hoplite army and the creation of the twenty-one tribal districts to the end of the fifth century, and to argue that the surviving foundations of the Capitoline temple belong to a secondary reconstruction of fourth-century date.[54] But the greatest difficulty he faced was the fact that all these supposedly false data combined to make a plausible and coherent historical picture. Alföldi was therefore obliged to contend that the traditional account was the product of deliberate and systematic falsification. On his view the internal consistency and general plausibility of the tradition came ultimately from the mind of Fabius Pictor, the man who created and organised the material of the story. But this theory, unacceptable in any case, is fatally flawed because many of the arguments that sustain the traditional account depend, not directly on ancient testimony, but on independent modern interpretations of ancient testimony.

54. Alföldi, *Early Rome* (1965): 323–28; cf. H. Riemann, *RM* 76 (1969): 110ff.; J. Poucet, *LEC* 47 (1979): 354–57; F. Kolb, *Gnomon* 53 (1981): 27. But the evidence for the traditional view, that the temple that burned down in 83 B.C. was the one constructed under the Tarquins, seems overwhelming. For example, Tacitus, *Hist.* 3.72, is alone sufficient to prove the point.

For example, it obviously never occurred to Fabius Pictor or to any other Roman historian that their accounts of the territorial annexations of the Roman state under the kings might have a bearing on the size of the population. As a matter of fact the Roman historians believed that the population of archaic Rome was far larger than was actually the case, and record impossibly high figures for the sixth and fifth centuries.[55] Moreover Fabius and his successors clearly misunderstood the character of the military organisation of Rome in the archaic age. They attributed to Servius Tullius an elaborate system that comprised five classes of infantry graded according to ascending levels of wealth and bearing different types of arms. In this form the system certainly reflects later conditions, and cannot date back to the sixth century. But our sources on the centuriate organisation clearly reveal traces of an earlier system in which there was only one class (the *classis*), consisting of sixty centuries of infantry.[56] This was obviously the system Servius introduced, which survived until the end of the fifth century, when the five classes were established. Thus our knowledge of the Servian army of 6,000 hoplites, a crucial piece of evidence for our interpretation of the position of Rome in the sixth century, derives from an inference of modern scholarship (specifically of P. Fraccaro), and not from Fabius Pictor, who, as we happen to know, believed that under Servius Tullius there were as many as 80,000 Romans capable of bearing arms.[57]

At this point it is necessary to explain that there is nothing contradictory in the twofold assertion that, on the one hand, the tradition is basically reliable, and on the other hand that we cannot rely on

55. Beloch, *Röm. Geschichte* (1926): 216ff.; id., *Bevölkerung* (1886): 340; id., *Ital. Bund* (1880): 89ff.; Toynbee, *Hannibal's Legacy* I (1965): 438ff.; Alföldi, *Early Rome* (1965): 129; Brunt, *Manpower* (1971): 126ff.; Ampolo, *DArch*, n.s., 2 (1980): 27. The early census figures are defended by T. Frank, *AJP* 51 (1930): 313ff. Ogilvie rejects the Servian figure, but considers those of the fifth century "just credible" (*Comm.* [1965]: 178, on Livy 1.44.2). The principal argument against the authenticity of the early figures is that they do not make sufficient allowance for the huge increases that must have taken place during the conquests of the late fourth and early third centuries B.C., when Rome's territory increased by over 1,300 percent (from c. 2000 km² in 340 to c. 26,000 km² in 264). See Afzelius, *Eroberung* (1942): 192; cf. Beloch, *Röm. Geschichte*, 621; Toynbee, *Hannibal's Legacy* I: 142.

56. Cato, *ap*. Gell. *Noctes Atticae* 6.13.3; Festus p. 100 L, s.v. "*infra classem*"; and see the discussion of P. Fraccaro in the works cited in n. 50 above.

57. Livy 1.44.2: *adicit scriptorum antiquissimus Fabius Pictor, eorum qui arma ferre possent, eum numerum (sc. milia octoginta) fuisse* (= Fabius Pictor, fr. 9 Jac. = fr. 10 P).

Fabius Pictor's account of it. A fundamental distinction must be drawn between the traditional data and the interpretations of those data in our sources. In other words we should be careful to separate the structural facts on which the tradition is based from the narrative superstructure within which the facts are recounted, interpreted, and explained.[58] This is not simply a matter of saying that the literary accounts of the Roman historians were secondary; as far as the archaic period is concerned that is a truism. The point is rather that the combination of structural facts and narrative superstructure is an inherent feature of all forms of historical tradition. The process of interpretation began long before the development of historical literature, and it is clear that information about the past was handed down in narrative form from the very earliest times. Thus for example the story of the rape of Lucretia, which purported to explain the genuine historical fact of the overthrow of the monarchy and the inception of the Republic, is almost certainly of preliterary origin.

The Roman historical tradition was the product of a long process of constant interpretation and reappraisal as succeeding generations attempted to make sense of their past and to harness it to their own present needs. To my mind there is not the slightest doubt that the Romans of the last two centuries of the Republic were able to dispose of a great deal of authentic historical information, preserved and transmitted from the remote past in ways that we are not now able to reconstruct with any precision. The problem is that the Romans themselves did not necessarily comprehend the difficulties of interpretation that faced them, and were not always able to account adequately for the data at their disposal.

This happened not so much because they were not trained in the techniques of historical criticism as because they were not in fact engaged in the process of historical research at all. The Romans' approach to their own early history was uncritical because it was not founded on the basic principle of historical criticism, which is that the past is different from the present. The preservation and transmission of traditional stories of the city's past should in no sense be seen as an attempt to understand the archaic period as it really was.

---

58. For the distinction between "structural facts" and narrative, see the comments of Momigliano, *Contr.* VI (1980): 484.

Rather, the Romans of the late Republic saw the remote past as an idealised and exemplary model of their own society. They seem to have been almost totally unaware of the gulf that separated them from the archaic world of the fifth century B.C. For example, in his remarkable account of the development of the Roman state in the *De re publica*, Cicero felt that it was unnecessary to go beyond the time of the Twelve Tables. In this he was following an old tradition, which is reflected also in Cato the Elder and Polybius, that the constitution had reached its fully developed form in the middle of the fifth century.[59] The Romans were (notoriously) very conscious of what they took to be a decline in the moral character of the Roman people, but they had no conception of structural change. Modern historians on the other hand tend to regard contemporary perceptions of moral decline as mere symptoms of structural transformation.

The chief consequence of this unhistorical approach to the past was that the tradition was constantly subjected to a largely unconscious process of systematic anachronism. It is not in the least surprising that the traditional data should have been modernised in the light of contemporary experience, or that the political, economic, and social conditions of the later Republic should have been imposed on the events of the distant past. Thus, for example, Servius Tullius, who seems to have instituted some kind of primitive monetary system, is credited in the tradition with the introduction of coinage (actually a development of the late fourth or early third century);[60] in the same way the fully developed organisation of the *comitia centuriata* was also mistakenly traced back to Servius. Fabius Pictor evidently had some information that seemed to him to indicate that 80,000 able-bodied men were counted at the first census, a mistake he is unlikely to have made if he had had any conception of the actual historical circumstances of the sixth century.

The modernising process was for the most part the result of an honest attempt at historical explanation and the source of unconscious error. It was not, as some scholars suppose, a dishonest literary device for filling gaps in the record and making the narrative

---

59. Cic. *Rep.* 2.2, citing Cato's *Origines*; Polyb. 6.11.1; cf. my comments in "Foundation of Rome" (1978): 135–36.

60. Crawford, *Coinage* (1975): 35–46; id., "Roman Economy" (1976): 197–207, with references and bibliography.

more entertaining. It was a natural result of the Romans' attempt to make sense of their own past and to derive inspiration from it. The fact that episodes of the Conflict of the Orders are described in terms of late republican politics does not mean that they were arbitrarily manufactured out of whole cloth, but rather that the traditional record of these events invited comparison with contemporary politics. We should not be surprised that the tribunes of the fifth and fourth centuries B.C. are represented as behaving like any *popularis* tribune of the post-Gracchan age; moreover the *populares* themselves no doubt claimed to be reviving the original character and function of the tribunate and to be continuing the old plebeian struggle. An obvious example is the attempted "secession" to the Aventine by C. Gracchus and his followers in 121 B.C.[61] Again it is not surprising that the record of continual plebeian agitation for access to the *ager publicus* in the fifth and fourth centuries should have been elaborated in the narrative accounts of historians in purely "Gracchan" terms.[62]

Inevitably the Romans of the late Republic tended to emphasise the similarities, and to overlook the differences, between the events of the archaic period and those of their own age. The result was that they unwittingly distorted the truth; having no conception of the structural changes that had taken place they mistakenly assumed that ancient political institutions such as the Senate, the magistrates, and popular assemblies had functioned in the same way in the early Republic as they did in their own day. The consequence of this understandable error was that they completely failed to appreciate the peculiar character of the archaic period.

In conclusion it may be observed that the surviving literary accounts of the early age of Rome contain many genuine details and provide a framework of historical fact that there is every reason to think is reliable, at least in outline. Nevertheless we have to reckon with the fact that the Romans of the last centuries of the Republic

---

61. Appian *Bell. Civ.* I.26.114–18; Plut. *C. Gracch.* 15–16; Livy *Epit.* 61; Vell. Pat. 2.6.4–7.
62. References in Ogilvie, *Comm.* (1965): 340, on 2.41.3. Ogilvie himself is unjustifiably skeptical about the authenticity of these notices. On the Gracchan elaboration, see especially E. Gabba, *Athenaeum*, n. s., 42 (1964): 29–41. The record is (rightly) defended by De Martino, *Econ.* I (1979): 14f.

had no understanding of the true character of the political and social realities of the archaic age. In their efforts to make use of the data at their disposal, they inevitably applied inappropriate and anachronistic models. The result is that we cannot rely on the sources for answers to even the most basic questions. For instance they give no acceptable definition of patricians and plebeians, and clearly fail to explain what the distinction meant in the archaic period. Among other things they were almost certainly wrong to assume that only patricians could hold the consulship in the early Republic, and to imply that the original Senate was an exclusively patrician body.[63] Fundamental matters such as the system of land tenure in early Rome, the nature of the role of the *gentes*, the legal definition of *nexum*, the structure of military institutions, and the character of warfare in early Italy are all equally uncertain. Our understanding of the history of early Rome depends absolutely on the view we take of these and other questions, to which our sources manifestly fail to provide adequate answers. We must therefore attempt to free ourselves from the conscious assumptions that inform the literary sources, and to replace them with more authentic historical models. That is the only way we can hope to use the evidence of the sources (which is all we have to go on, given the relatively minimal contribution of archaeology to this area of the subject) to uncover something of the real nature of Roman society in the archaic age.

63. Full discussion of these points (with bibliography) in Richard, *Origines* (1978): 232–38, 478–84, 519–23.

JÜRGEN VON UNGERN-STERNBERG

III

The Formation of the "Annalistic Tradition": The Example of the Decemvirate

For Robert Werner at the occasion of his sixtieth birthday

> Emilia: "Ehedem wohl gab es einen Vater, der seine Tochter vor der Schande zu retten, ihr den ersten den besten Stahl in das Herz senkte, ihr zum zweiten das Leben gab. Aber alle solche Taten sind von ehedem! Solcher Väter gibt es keinen mehr!"
> Odoardo: "Doch, meine Tochter, doch!"
>
> —Lessing, *Emilia Galotti*

Modern methods of systematic source criticism, developed by generations of historians, have largely been inspired by criticisms of the traditions about early Rome contained in the first ten books of Livy and in the work of his contemporary Dionysius of Halicarnassus. In the winter of 1810/11, Barthold Georg Niebuhr delivered his famous lecture on "Roman History" at the newly founded University of Berlin. Since then scholars have increasingly become aware that the Augustan authors, our main informants, were separated by several centuries from the period of the kings and the beginnings of the Republic, that the historiographical works available to them were not

Paper read at the Universities of Erlangen, Saabrücken, Frankfurt, Essen, Graz, and Tel-Aviv. I thank Iris Werthmüller, Mark Toher, and Kurt Raaflaub for the English translation. The translations of ancient authors are taken from the Loeb Classical Library.

written before the end of the third century B.C., and that for the whole previous period there existed only a few sources, the value of which, moreover, is much debated.

Like many generations before them, the eighteenth century and the French revolutionaries were deeply impressed by Livy's vivid and colorful pictures. But in the nineteenth century, interest in them quickly faded. They came to be considered fictions—perhaps of some literary merit, but certainly not deserving the attention of serious historians, let alone politicians.

Indeed, almost none of Livy's and Dionysius's stories can confidently be claimed as "historical tradition." In this paper, however, I want to raise the question of whether we can allow this to be the final judgment on their historical value, or whether they actually deserve our renewed attention from an entirely different point of view. For that purpose I have selected the account of the two Decemvirates of c. 450 B.C. that gave Rome the Twelve Tables, the city's first, and for many centuries only, codification of law. In order to assure a better understanding of my analysis, I shall first summarize in some detail the tradition according to the third book of Livy; second, I shall briefly discuss some general problems of Roman annalistic historiography as far as they are immediately relevant to the interpretation proposed in this paper; then we shall consider the question of how, and for what motives, the Roman historians developed and shaped the story.

Patricians and plebeians had been opposed to each other for more than a generation when they finally agreed in 454/52 to elect a committee of ten men who "might propose measures that should be advantageous to both sides and secure equal liberty" (Livy 3.31.7: *qui utrisque utilia ferrent quaeque aequandae libertatis essent*). The Decemvirate thus appears as a stage in the Conflict of the Orders. After a long confrontation, the plebeians obtained equality before the civil law. However, they had to make concessions: only patricians were eligible for the college of the decemvirs; there were to be no other magistrates besides them (a measure affecting not only the consuls but also the speakers and leaders of the plebeians, the tribunes); the right of appeal to the people against a capital sentence (*provocatio*) was to be suspended for the decemvirs' term of office. Since their tenure was limited to one year, all this must have seemed tolerable.

Accordingly, ten men were elected for the year 451. Among them,

Appius Claudius acquired a leading position from the beginning. Although earlier an enemy of the *plebs*, he now presented himself as the people's friend and quickly gained great popularity among the plebeians. The other decemvirs pursued an equally popular policy by making only moderate use of their unrestricted powers. For example, only the presiding decemvir was accompanied by the full number of twelve lictors, and the draft of the first ten tables was presented to the assembly for a detailed debate and revisions before it was ratified by the same assembly.

Since the opinion prevailed that two more tables were needed for a complete codification of Roman law, however, the decision was made to appoint decemvirs again for the following year (450). This decision was facilitated by the fact that, because the decemvirs had performed their duties with justice and moderation, the plebeians neither wanted the consulship to be restored nor missed the protection offered by the tribunes (3.34.8).

The election campaign suddenly and radically changed the former picture of ideal harmony. A general contest for the eagerly desired office broke out among the leading men. Ap. Claudius especially left an unpleasant impression with his agitation among the plebeians— all the more so since he violated the generally accepted custom of not holding the same office twice in succession. Even the trick of appointing him presiding magistrate in the election did not succeed; on the contrary, he seized the opportunity to have himself elected first and then arranged the election of nine of his supporters, while ignoring the most prominent *nobiles*.

From then on, Ap. Claudius no longer needed to strive for the people's favor. Even before they entered their office on the Ides of May, he and his colleagues were devising secret plots. Upon entering office, they demonstrated the style of the new regime by presenting all 120 lictors with their bundles of rods and axes. The tyrannical intentions that now unified the college precluded any appeal to one decemvir against another. It became evident that the plebeians had been unwise to rely on their positive experience with the just administration of the first Decemvirate, and to let their hatred and fear of the consulate dominate their considerations, thereby continuing to forego their institutional protections (tribunate and *provocatio*). For while the patricians were mostly left alone, the tyranny of the decemvirs was increasingly directed against the plebeians (3.36.7).

Although the patricians, too, were far from happy about the decemvirs, they took comfort in the people's oppression at first, expecting that the *plebs* would soon come to yearn for the restoration of the consulate and the previous conditions (3.37.2–3).

Nevertheless, the last two tables were eventually completed. They only needed to be ratified by the assembly to become law, thus accomplishing the mandate of the second Decemvirate (3.37.4). But nothing of the sort happened. The decemvirs did not intend to relinquish their office voluntarily; nor did they summon an election meeting in order to have their mandate prolonged for the following year (449). Instead, relying on a group of young patricians, they increased their oppression of the plebeians, rewarding their supporters with the confiscated property of those executed.

By the turn of the year 450/49, the effects of the tyranny in Rome had become obvious enough to encourage some neighboring tribes, the Sabines and Aequi, to undertake plundering raids. Finally, the decemvirs were compelled by the danger of war to summon the Senate for the first time in a long period (3.38.6). The first call met with no success, since the senators had withdrawn to their estates outside Rome. The plebeians believed that the patricians, by failing to appear, were denying the decemvirs the right to convoke the Senate and, accordingly, any magisterial authority (3.38.10). This interpretation, however, soon proved wrong: on the following day, the Senate meeting was well attended. In vain the plebeians hoped that, by refusing the levy, they might be able to form a joint front with the patricians against the decemvirs. The outcome of the debate in the Senate demonstrated once more that the political views of the patricians were still dominated by their opposition to the tribunate of the *plebs*. It was their intention to persuade the decemvirs to abdicate in order to restore the consulate but not the tribunate (3.41.5–6).

As a result of their continuing disagreement, the Senate and people were unable to prevent the decemvirs from levying two armies against Rome's external enemies. But the soldiers did not fight successfully. They preferred defeat to victory under such generals (3.42.2). Their morale deteriorated further when the decemvirs had one of their most prominent leaders secretly assassinated (3.43).

The reversal began at Rome. The presiding decemvir, Ap. Claudius, became infatuated with a beautiful plebeian girl, Verginia (3.44.1). When she refused him, he tried to gain possession of her by causing one of his clients to claim her as his slave. Although having a vested interest in the outcome, Ap. Claudius himself was the judge in the ensuing trial. Despite the efforts of Verginia's father, L. Verginius, and her fiancé, L. Icilius, a former tribune of the *plebs*, Ap. Claudius adjudicated for his client (3.47.5). The desperate father realized that death was the only way for his daughter to avoid dishonor. As a result of this tragedy, riots occurred in the city. More importantly, the armies now took the initiative and withdrew to the Aventine (3.50.13). When the decemvirs refused to resign, on the grounds that the last two tables had still not been ratified (3.51.13), the armies occupied the *Mons sacer* (3.52.1; this was the so-called second *secessio plebis*).

It was only then that the senators increased their pressure on the decemvirs. Finally, concerned only with their personal safety, the decemvirs agreed to resign their office after the people had temporarily renounced their vindictiveness. Consuls and tribunes of the *plebs* were now elected, and the former constitutional order was restored (3.54–55). It was one of the first tasks of the new consuls to publish the Twelve Tables put together by the decemvirs (3.57.10).

These are the main lines of Livy's narrative. It centers around the two colleges of decemvirs and their most prominent representative, Ap. Claudius. The antagonism between patricians and plebeians forms its background. Surprisingly enough, we do not learn anything about the contents of the Twelve Tables.[1] On the occasion of the completion of the first ten, Livy presents only terse praise for these codes, "which even now, in this great welter of statutes piled one upon another, are the fountain-head of all public and private law" (3.34.6: *qui nunc quoque in hoc immenso aliarum super alias acervatarum legum cumulo fons omnis publici privatique est iuris*).

We can therefore only reconstruct the content of the Twelve Tables from fragments preserved mainly in quotations by Roman jurists, antiquarians, and orators. The provisions of the tables

> concern procedure in court actions and enforcement, the law of family, of wills, succession, property, contracts, and torts, as modern lawyers would classify them. Others deal with questions of

---

1. This is caused by the different working methods of Roman historians and antiquarians; cf. E. Rawson, *JRS* 62 (1972): 33ff. For critical comments on Livy's praise of the Twelve Tables, cf. Guarino, *Diritto*[5] (1975): 129ff.; *Riv.* (1975): 319ff.

sacral law, public law, and criminal law, to adopt again a modern code of classification. Some regulate the behaviour of citizens, such as several provisions prohibiting . . . the display of excessive luxury in funerals.[2]

Obviously, the Twelve Tables represented a rather comprehensive codification of law, the mere accomplishment of which was a success for the *plebs*, as Greek analogies confirm.[3] The very fact that the regulations in force were no longer known only to the aristocratic judges, and therefore could no longer easily be manipulated, provided the plebeians with a considerably improved guarantee of due process and fairness of jurisdiction. The severity of the law was left unmitigated in Rome, however, as was the case with Draco's codification of homicide law at Athens. To be sure, there now existed equality before the law for patricians and plebeians; only in certain cases was a distinction made between landowning and nonlandowning citizens (*adsidui* and *proletarii*); and the prohibition of luxurious funeral rites might possibly be interpreted as an early attack on the distinctly aristocratic lifestyle of the leading families. But the rigidly formal definition of procedures offered rather little help to the common people, who still had to surrender their own persons to their creditors and risked being sold abroad (*trans Tiberim*) as the ultimate consequence of their debts and obligations. This basically unchanged continuity of material conditions must be taken into account if one agrees with F. Wieacker's characterization of the Twelve Tables as the severe and limited, but not hostile, response of the *res publica* to the complaints and accusations of the *adsiduus* and *proletarius* oppressed by debt and by arbitrariness in jurisdiction and procedure, who resented the luxurious and wasteful lifestyle of the upper classes, which was bound to worsen their plight.[4]

Since intermarriage between patricians and plebeians was now formally prohibited, the plebeians were forced to accept the continued separation of the orders. Since, moreover, only the assembly

2. H. J. Wolff, *Law* (1951): 59.
3. See Raaflaub, chapter VII, part 3 below. This view is modified by Eder (chapter IX below). For a different interpretation of the funeral restrictions, see Toher, chapter X below.
4. F. Wieacker, "XII Tafeln" (1967): 316 (translator's paraphrase); cf. Beloch, *Röm. Geschichte* (1926): 237.

of the entire citizen body, the *populus* (which was controlled by its wealthy members), was to pass sentence in capital trials, the *plebs* in fact had to renounce the revolutionary practice of prosecuting political crimes before the *concilium plebis*.[5]

Our survey of the content of the Twelve Tables therefore seems to confirm Livy's report that they were the result of a compromise between patricians and plebeians that aimed at establishing equality for both sides in matters of civil law (*quaeque aequandae libertatis essent*).[6] The dating of the law code to the middle of the fifth century B.C. is confirmed as well, since—to mention only the most conclusive argument—the Tiber formed Rome's border with Etruria only in that period; previously Rome itself had been ruled by an Etruscan dynasty, and later in the century it was expanding aggressively in the direction of Veii. Further confirming evidence is offered by E. Täubler's brilliant observation that the sponsoring magistrates are mentioned at the head of each Roman law.[7] The tradition that the Twelve Tables were written by a college of ten men therefore seems to be based on documentary evidence and can consequently be accepted.

But what should we make of Livy's colorful story about the circumstances in which the law code originated? Can we accept as authentic his account of the virtuous first and villainous second Decemvirates, and about the manner in which the ten tyrants were finally forced to resign? Clearly the answer must be no, since, according to unanimous ancient tradition, the first Decemvirate was formed of patricians only, whereas the majority of the second college allegedly were plebeian. It has been correctly asserted that this is quite improbable. The plebeians would hardly have been able to secure participation in the elections for the second college—long after the tribunate had been suspended—if they had failed or not desired to achieve this in the elections for the first Decemvirate.[8] Further, as R. Werner has shown,[9] it is even less likely that this second, predominantly plebeian, college would have been responsible for the prohibition of intermarriage, which is firmly attested for the eleventh table—especially

---

5. A. Heuss, *ZRG* 64 (1944): 115ff.; for a different view, see A. Giovannini, *Chiron* 13 (1983): 545ff.
6. Ch. Wirszubski, *Libertas* (1950): 10ff.; J. Bleicken, *Ordnung* (1972): 29ff.
7. E. Täubler, *Decemvirat* (1921): 78.
8. H. Siber, "Plebs," *RE* 21.1 (1951): 112.
9. R. Werner, *Beginn* (1963): 282.

if indeed only five years later the *plebs* succeeded in having the ban on intermarriage abolished. It should not be doubted, therefore, that the Romans elected only one committee to draft the whole set of laws, and that they expected this committee to remain in office until its task was fulfilled.[10]

Strangely enough, it seems to have been overlooked so far that there actually is some support for such a view in the ancient sources. In his brief summary of the development of Roman law and constitution (*Dig.* 1.2.2.4 and 24), Sextus Pomponius mentions only one college of decemvirs, which has no difficulty in extending its term of office in order to continue its legislation. But then, after the accomplishment of their mandate, the decemvirs refuse to have new magistrates elected because they want to perpetuate control over the state for themselves and their supporters (*ut ipsi et factio sua perpetuo rem publicam occupatam retineret*). Unfortunately, we do not know much about Pomponius's sources,[11] but undoubtedly as a jurist, standing outside the annalistic tradition, he relied largely on antiquarian ones,[12] which seem to have known nothing at all about the second Decemvirate.

We ought to take this strand of the tradition seriously and not counter it by simply referring to the allegedly authentic *fasti*. Moreover, by reducing the time between the beginning of the Republic and the Decemvirate to only twenty years, Pomponius again proves to be independent of the authority of the *fasti* (*Dig.* 1.2.2.3–4).[13] Whether he indeed had independent and better information about the Decemvirate than our other sources remains an open question. But his testimony makes it difficult naively to follow the report of the annalistic sources. Thus for several reasons the conclusion seems inevitable that at least the second Decemvirate, along with its deeds and misdeeds, must be pure fiction. Moreover, it is quite likely that the virtuous first Decemvirate as such only forms an equally fic-

10. Beloch, *Röm. Geschichte* (1926): 242; Siber, *RE* 21.1: 112.
11. Cf. D. Nörr, *ANRW* II.15 (1976): 518ff. Täubler, *Decemvirat* (1921): 34ff., is hardly satisfactory on these matters.
12. For this distinction, see the important remarks of E. Rawson, *JRS* 62 (1972): 33ff.
13. This point was made by E. Bickerman, *RFIC* 97 (1969): 408 n. 3. If for the reasons mentioned before (at nn. 6f.), the date of the Decemvirate is fixed around 450 B.C., Pomponius's observation splendidly confirms the date of the beginning of the Republic around 472/70 as it is postulated by R. Werner.

titious positive counterpart to the second—except of course for the undoubtedly historical fact that the law was codified by such a committee.

And yet the second Decemvirate owes its fictitious existence precisely to the ban on intermarriage,[14] the only law that explicitly mentions patricians and plebeians and at the same time segregates them. This flagrantly contrasts with the principle of equality before the law, which the Twelve Tables established for all citizens in every other respect. Later observers, it seems, simply could not believe that the great lawgivers of Rome were capable of such a contradiction. They preferred to invent a second college, which was credited with the addition of the last two tables.

Here already we discover a typical feature of Roman historical thought and method, which we shall encounter several times later on. Inventions and additions clearly have an inherent logic; they arise out of historical questions that are answered in a specific way that is typical for the Romans but does not conform to our standards and expectations.[15] One invention then inevitably leads to another. Thus decemvirs who write unjust laws must behave unjustly in other ways too. Consequently, their office must by necessity end in a violent confrontation. This is provoked most effectively, when one of them, following the pattern of tyrants, is guilty of attempting to rape a beautiful girl, in this case Verginia.[16]

What we have just formulated on the basis of one specific case can be explained with the following basic considerations. When the first Roman historians wrote down the history of the early Republic at the end of the third century B.C., they could not rely on contemporary reports; what they had at their disposal were hardly more than

---

14. R. M. Ogilvie, *Comm.* (1965): 452f. (generally assuming plebeian disappointment over the severity of the codified law); 461f. (on the names).

15. The obvious influence of Greek law on the Twelve Tables was thus "explained" by Roman embassies sent to Greek cities; cf. F. Wieacker, "XII Tafeln" (1967): 337ff., and the discussion in *Les Origines de la république romaine* (1967): 357ff.; E. Gabba, "Tradizione letteraria" (1967): 167 n. 1; J. Delz, *MH* 23 (1966): 69ff. For the leitmotiv of the Conflict of the Orders, *externus timor, maximum concordiae vinculum*, cf. Ungern-Sternberg, *MH* 39 (1982): 265 with n. 50.

16. Beloch, *Röm. Geschichte* (1926): 244ff., on the contrary believes the legend of Verginia to be the starting point of the invention. See generally on this topic H. Geldner, *Lucretia* (1972). Fabius Pictor's hatred of the *gens Claudia*, postulated by Alföldi, *Early Rome* (1965): 159ff.; *Frühgeschichte* (1976): 76ff., is completely hypothetical.

uncertain memories and, at best, a few documents. Nevertheless, according to what we know about the numbers of books in various historical works, the quantity of material incorporated in such works increased considerably over time.[17] Certainly such increase did not come from additional research in the archives[18] or, as E. Rawson has shown convincingly,[19] from the exploitation of the *Annales Maximi*. Rather, it was prompted by the authors' desire to integrate the events handed down by tradition into an increasingly dense and precise narrative. Probably in some cases the annalists started with the facts they found in earlier versions or in unwritten traditions, but— and this is decisive—they liberally supplemented these with fictitious elements, such as debates and decrees of the Senate, laws, descriptions of military campaigns and battles, and so on, and they did not hesitate to change and distort facts that did not fit in their picture. Thus they achieved a high degree of pseudo-precision or, in M. Gelzer's apt formulation, a *protokollartige Genauigkeit*.[20] It served both historiographical[21] and practical purposes—namely, to provide the magistrates and senators with *exempla* to be used in their conduct of office.[22] In addition, there could be ulterior motives. For example, one might wish to prove that Roman interference in the East in 200 B.C. had been compatible with the criteria established by Roman sacral law for the *bellum iustum*.[23] In another case, the method of chronological displacement (clearly attested in Livy 21.15.3–6) was used in order to eliminate the embarrassing fact that Rome had remained inactive during Hannibal's siege of Saguntum.

Undoubtedly, especially after the era of the Gracchi, we should also expect the influence of political interests, though not necessarily in the form of a consistent tendency on the part of any one historian in favor of either the *optimates* or the *populares*. The material avail-

17. Cf. chapter I above at nn. 1f.
18. U. Bredehorn, *Senatsakten* (1968), went farther than most in trying to prove that the accounts of the annalists were based on documentary evidence; see my review, *Gnomon* 43 (1971): 369ff., and L. F. Janssen, *Mnemosyne*, 4th ser., 26 (1973): 91ff.
19. E. Rawson, *CQ* 21 (1971): 158ff.; cf. B. W. Frier, *Annales* (1979).
20. M. Gelzer, *Kl. Schr.* III (1964): 95.
21. Ibid., 221ff., with the testimonia of ancient theory.
22. Ibid., 258.
23. K.-E. Petzold, *Die Eröffnung des Zweiten Römisch-Makedonischen Krieges: Untersuchungen zur spätannalistischen Topik bei Livius* (Berlin, 1940, repr. Darmstadt, 1968).

able to us hardly allows us to ascertain such a clear-cut partisan "tendency";[24] and, for many reasons, it seems incompatible with the structure of Roman politics.[25] Rather, the problems of the present were included in the presentation of the past either in order to make the narrative more lively, or to comment indirectly on matters of contemporary concern.

All this was argued in principle a long time ago.[26] In addition, for the tradition concerning the early Roman Republic as it is covered in the first decade of Livy, there exist many excellent analyses of individual cases. Each of these contributes to the program outlined by Mommsen in a letter to Wilamowitz. He proposed that for this legendary or at least half-legendary period one should try to isolate and analyze by itself each individual story or group of related stories and then to combine all those methodologically correlated analyses into a comprehensive picture less of the historical facts than of the tradition.[27]

It must suffice here to mention two groups of such investigations. On the one hand, E. Schwartz (for the conspiracy of the year 500 in its relation to the Catilinarian Conspiracy)[28] and, following others, E. Gabba (for the agrarian law of Sp. Cassius in its relation to the agrarian reforms of the Gracchi)[29] have demonstrated how whole episodes were retrojected from the late into the early Republic. On the other hand, following Mommsen's example, E. Täubler, K. von

24. T. J. Luce, *Livy* (1977): 168; D. Timpe, *A&A* 25 (1979): 108f.
25. More on that below at nn. 39f.
26. Cf. especially Gelzer's articles in *Kl. Schr.* III (1964); D. Timpe, *ANRW* I.2 (1972): 928ff., especially 962ff.; id., *A&A* 25 (1979): 107ff.; E. Gabba, *ANRW* II.30.1 (1982): 807ff. See also Ungern-Sternberg, *Capua* (1975): 1–10 (citing earlier literature).
27. *Mommsen und Wilamowitz: Briefwechsel 1872–1903* (1935): 62 (letter of February 21, 1879), quoted by K. Christ, *Römische Geschichte und Wissenschaftsgeschichte* III (Darmstadt, 1983): 50 n. 68: "Wäre ich jung wie Du, so ginge ich an eine kritische Geschichte Roms, indem ich für die ganz und halb fabelhafte Zeit den Versuch machte, jede einzelne Erzählung oder Gruppe von Erzählungen zu isolieren und isoliert zu behandeln und alle diese zusammen durch korrelate Behandlung zu einem Gesamtbild weniger der Tatsachen als der Überlieferung zu gestalten. Daran darf ich nicht denken; aber ein Gedanke der Art kann doch vielleicht irgendwo zünden."
28. E. Schwartz, *Gesammelte Schriften* II (Berlin, 1956): 337ff.
29. For previous work, cf. R. Werner, *Beginn* (1963): 458 nn. 2 and 3; E. Gabba, *Athenaeum*, n. s., 42 (1964): 29ff.; Ogilvie, *Comm.* (1965): 337ff.; M. Basile, in *Miscellanea greca e romana* 6 (Rome, 1978): 277ff. Unfortunately, the tendency to believe

Fritz, T. P. Wiseman, and others have analyzed the formation of the traditions about especially important personalities and events of the fifth and fourth centuries.[30] Those who need even more convincing, I suggest, might find it helpful to examine briefly the monograph of W. Wiehemeyer, which carefully studies all those (and only those) variants in the tradition that are explicitly mentioned as such by Livy.[31]

In view of all this, I find it somewhat astonishing that Timothy Cornell and Robert Develin[32] try to distinguish between "structural facts" and "narrative superstructure." Such a distinction may be feasible if we accept as "structural" only the most elementary facts, such as the following: the city of Rome at some time came into being (whether or not it was "founded") and gradually increased in size; during a certain period (whenever that was) it was ruled by Etruscan kings, who eventually were "expelled";[33] later (?) patricians and plebeians[34] confronted one another; externally, wars were fought against Etruscans and mountain tribes; and so forth. But there is no certainty about the details (when? by whom? why?) on which the

---

just about everything the annalists tell us about agrarian laws in the fifth century has become very strong again in recent years: see J. Gagé, *Latomus* 38 (1979): 838ff.; and D. Capanelli in *Legge e società nella repubblica romana* I, edited by F. Serrao (1981): 3ff.

30. Mommsen, *Röm. Forschungen* I (1864): 285ff. (about the patrician Claudii), II (1879): 153ff. (about Sp. Cassius, M. Manlius, and Sp. Maelius, the three demagogues of the early Republic); E. Täubler, *Decemvirat* (1921); K. von Fritz, *Historia* 1 (1950): 3ff.; T. P. Wiseman, *Clio's Cosmetics* (1979), on which see the review of T. J. Cornell, *JRS* 72 (1982): 203ff. Cornell certainly is right in emphasizing that there were proud Claudii before as well as during Cicero's time, and that they early on appear as such in the literary tradition. This, however, does not disprove most of Wiseman's arguments, it only corrects certain exaggerations (cf. Wiseman himself, *LCM* 8 [1983]: 20ff.). See further (on Camillus) F. Klingner's review of E. Burck, *Erzählungskunst* (1934), in *Gnomon* 11 (1935): 582ff., repr. in id., *Studien zur griechischen und römischen Literatur* (Zurich, 1964): 599ff.; Burck in *Wege zu Livius*, edited by E. Burck (Darmstadt, 1967): 310ff.

31. W. Wiehemeyer, *Kritik* (1938).

32. See chapter II above at nn. 30ff., 58, 63; and chapter XI below at n. 13.

33. See Raaflaub, chapter I above at nn. 23ff., especially the perceptive remarks at n. 36 on the problem of what the temples of Sant' Omobono do and do not prove (the contrary is argued by Cornell, chapter II above at n. 42). Views similar to those of Raaflaub were expressed by K. Hanell, *Amt* (1946): 49ff.

34. Whose nature, however, was not even clearly understood by the Romans themselves: Cornell, chapter II above at n. 63.

basic questions of historians remain focused.³⁵ At least Cornell knows and even says that himself, and he gives a good and insightful description of the process through which the tradition was transformed.

There remain the *fasti*, whose reliability at least for the first decades of the Republic is so controversial. Those who insist on the credibility of the early *fasti* ought first to prove that the five consuls of the first year of the Republic are authentic.³⁶ If that is not possible, we are free *a limine* to assume that this "document" was falsified or changed in other parts as well. For it is hardly justifiable in such matters to follow the maxim adopted by Nero in dealing with the conspiracy of Piso and simply to accept as not untrue even what is not proved true (Tac. *Ann.* 15.51: *suspectante Nerone haud falsa esse etiam quae vera non probabantur*).

Consequently, the first books of Livy and the parallel account of Dionysius cannot retain much value for our attempts at reconstructing early Roman history. But that does not mean that they are of no interest to us at all; quite the contrary. It is a priori clear that it is inappropriate simply to talk of annalistic "lies," "falsifications," and so on. No doubt, these are not lacking; Livy himself says so (8.40.3–5), and it is hard to understand why he is not believed here by precisely those who otherwise are ready to believe so much of what he says.³⁷ Yet the motives of the Roman historians were many and complex, and some of them were quite serious. They deserve, therefore, to be examined seriously on their own merits.

Certainly, the better we understand the underlying principles according to which Roman tradition was quite consciously developed and transformed by each generation of Roman historians, the less satisfied we are with the methods commonly used by modern histo-

---

35. Ogilvie, *Early Rome* (1976), provides an instructive example: fully aware of the problematic source situation, Ogilvie tries to write a consistent historical account, which is certainly based on the "structural facts," but also betrays a rather arbitrary way of accepting and discarding elements of the annalistic tradition.

36. Especially in view of Polyb. 3.22.1; see R. T. Ridley, *Athenaeum* 58 (1980): 264ff.

37. Such as Cornell, chapter II above before n. 20; Develin, chapter XI below after n. 18. Livy here follows Cic. *Brut.* 62: Hanell, *Amt* (1946): 43ff., 132f. Cf. now H. Chantraine, *Gymnasium* 90 (1983): especially 543ff.; R. T. Ridley, *Latomus* 42 (1983): 372ff., and, with due emphasis, M. I. Finley, "Ancient Historian" (1983): 203: "The ability of the ancients to invent and their capacity to believe are persistently underestimated."

rians in dealing with this tradition. It will no longer suffice to analyze the individual stages of the tradition, to determine that they are in most cases of little or no historical value, and then, in complimenting Livy on his good style, to hand over the task of interpretation to the neighboring discipline, classical philology. Although E. Burck used precisely the account of the Decemvirate as a particularly convincing example of *die Erzählungskunst des T. Livius*,[38] we should not ignore the fact that Livy himself had taken over this account from his predecessors in an already highly developed and impressively consistent form. By his time, several generations of Roman historians had been working at it assiduously. It should be a question of considerable interest to us what our ancient colleagues actually had in mind when they shaped the tradition in this way.

To assure understanding of the following analysis, a few short preliminary remarks are necessary. From the time of the Gracchi (i.e., the last third of the second century B.C.) political life in Rome was dominated by two political methods fundamentally opposed to each other. On the one side were those politicians who consistently tried to realize their goals in association with the majority of the Senate; they were called *optimates*. On the other side were those who at least occasionally aimed at succeeding primarily through the popular assembly; these were the *populares*.[39] By now it should be commonly known[40] that we are not dealing here with political "parties" in the modern sense of the word, but with political methods and ways of acting that were seen as diametrically opposed to each other. Cicero's orations in defense of Rabirius and Sestius document this clearly enough, and to quote just one example, in the Fourth Catilinarian, Caesar is characterized as a man who in public life has chosen to fol-

---

38. Burck, *Erzählungskunst*² (1964); id., "Livius als augusteischer Historiker," *Die Welt als Geschichte* 1 (1935), especially 449ff. (= *Wege zu Livius* [as in n. 30]: 97ff.); cf. now Lipovsky, *Livy* (1981).

39. C. Meier, "Populares," *RE*, suppl. 10 (1965): 549ff., is fundamental on the subject; see also J. Martin, *Die Popularen in der Geschichte der Späten Republik* (Freiburg i. Br., 1965); R. Seager, "Cicero and the Word *popularis*," *CQ* 22 (1972): 328ff.; id., *CQ* 27 (1977): 380f., who is right in calling our attention to the fact that the terminology preferred by the *populares* was at least partially in use before them; and L. Perelli, *Il movimento popolare nell'ultimo secolo della repubblica* (1982). For references to the Conflict of the Orders in the policies of the *populares*, cf. chapter XII below at n. 84.

40. It suffices to refer to C. Meier, *Res publica amissa*, 7ff.

low the road that is considered *popularis* (9: *quoniam hanc is in re publica viam quae popularis habetur secutus est*). It is easy to recognize a resemblance between this antithesis (*optimates/populares*) and the opposition between patricians and plebeians. For contemporaries such a resemblance was even more obvious, since the *populares* not only usually operated through the tribunate, which had been the traditional political instrument of the plebeians, but constantly referred to the tradition of the Conflict of the Orders.

Returning to the second Decemvirate, whose purely fictitious character we have previously established, we shall now try to explain the origin and intention of some of the motifs involved.

The sources preserving the earliest surviving stage of the tradition (Diodorus 12.24.2, and possibly Cicero, *De re publica* 2.63) indicate Verginia to have been of patrician birth.[41] It is only in the later versions that she becomes a plebeian (Cic. *De fin.* 2.66; Zonaras 7.18) and that her fiancé, Icilius, a former tribune of the *plebs*, makes his appearance. This variation has far-reaching consequences. In the first case, Verginia is simply the victim of the lascivious decemvir Ap. Claudius. In the second, the episode is embedded in the context of the Conflict of the Orders, which offered Roman historians the opportunity of associating it with the highly relevant contemporary conflict between *optimates* and *populares*.

Ap. Claudius, who is described throughout as a late republican *popularis*, thereby acquired a particularly high profile. Originally a proud aristocrat, he had already in the first Decemvirate used his popularity among the people to procure for himself a leading position, "and so novel a character had he assumed, that from being a harsh and cruel persecutor of the *plebs*, he came out all at once as the people's friend [*plebicola*] and caught at every breath of popularity" (Livy 3.33.7). While canvassing for a seat in the second Decemvirate, he used popular methods even more unscrupulously: "He vilified the nobles [*optimates*], praised all the most insignificant and low-born candidates, and, surrounding himself with former tribunes, like Duilius and Icilius [!], bustled about the Forum, and through them recommended himself to the *plebs*" (Livy 3.35.4–5: *criminari opti-*

---

41. Cf. Ogilvie, *Comm.* (1965): 476ff. Cicero, presumably following Polybius, considers the Decemvirate a patrician victory; see F. Taeger, *Die Archäologie des Polybios* (Stuttgart, 1922): 84f., 134; J.-L. Ferrary, *JRS* 74 (1984): 91.

mates, extollere candidatorum levissimum quemque humillimumque, ipse medius inter tribunicios, Duillios Iciliosque, in foro volitare, per illos se plebi venditare).

To be sure, this description reminds us of the Greek typology of tyrants. For example, Plato's account of the initial behavior of a tyrant could easily be understood as typological generalization of Livy's text: "Then at the start and in the first days does he not smile upon all men and greet everybody he meets and deny that he is a tyrant, and promise many things in private and public?" (*Rep.* 566d–e). In addition, Aristotle observes that "almost the greatest number of tyrants have risen, it may be said, from being demagogues, having won the people's confidence by slandering the notables" (*Pol.* 1310b15), subsequently mentioning that one way to establish a tyranny is to obtain high office, since power is already on hand in that case—again an approach consistent with the political methods of Ap. Claudius.[42]

Nevertheless, it seems rather doubtful whether in such cases we may assume even an indirect Greek influence on the formation of the later Roman tradition.[43] More likely, the Roman historians used as a model the propaganda of the *optimates* against the great *populares* of the late Republic, especially the events of the year 133 and the tribunate of Ti. Sempronius Gracchus. Although he belonged to a noble and highly distinguished family, the latter's plans and policies increasingly conflicted with the views of the majority of the Senate. Finally he fell victim to an improvised assault of the *optimates* when he attempted to be reelected tribune for 132. In their propaganda, his opponents vigorously accused Tiberius of attempting to secure a position of superior personal power through his ostensibly popular policy. To put it in Greek terms, they accused him of aiming at a tyranny, or in Roman terms, a *regnum*. Some years later, the suspicions of the *optimates* similarly precipitated the ruin of his brother Gaius and other leading *populares*.[44] In its account of the decemvir

---

42. Another obvious parallel can be drawn between Livy 3.42.2 and Herod. 5.78: subjects of tyrants deliberately act cowardly in war.

43. But see Wiseman, *Clio's Cosmetics* (1979): 80f.

44. For Ti. Gracchus, see inter alia Cic. *Lael.* 41; Sall. *Jug.* 31.7; Vell. 2.4.4; Plut. *Ti. Gracchus* 14. For C. Gracchus see Fannius (?) fr. 6 and 7 (*ORF*[4]); Diod. 34/35.28a; 37.9; Vell. 2.6.2. For L. Appuleius Saturninus, see Flor. 2.4.4; Oros. 5.17.6. In the present context, it is important to notice the *damnatio memoriae* after the death of the leading *populares* in all these cases, as in the year 88.

Ap. Claudius, the Roman tradition presents as fully realized precisely what the later *populares* were alleged to be aiming at.[45] After being reelected decemvir, Appius finally throws off his mask (Livy 3.36.1: *ille finis Appio alienae personae ferendae fuit*) and conducts himself as the unscrupulous tyrant he has always intended to be.[46]

In depicting Appius's reign of terror, however, the tradition available to Livy was by no means narrowly one-sided, but seems to have incorporated other experiences as well. It unmistakably alludes to the proscriptions by which Sulla, the self-nominated leader of the *optimates*, attempted to facilitate the restoration of an unchallenged senatorial government after 82 B.C. And it might also recall the crimes both of the young Catiline and of other junior aristocrats who knew how to seize an opportunity for their own enrichment:

> They bullied the *plebs* and plundered their possessions; for success attended the strong, no matter what they coveted. And now they ceased even to respect a man's person; some they scourged with rods, others they made to feel the axe; and, that cruelty might not go unrequited, they bestowed the victim's property upon his slayer. Corrupted by these wages, the young nobles not only made no stand against the wrongdoing, but frankly showed that they preferred licence for themselves to liberty for all. (Livy 3.37.6–8)[47]

On the other hand, the Decemvirate described by Livy's predecessors also anticipates the so-called first Triumvirate of 60 B.C., a coalition formed by Pompey, Crassus, and Caesar in order to eliminate the Senate's opposition to Pompey's eastern settlement and to Caesar's consular election. According to Suetonius, their agreement

---

45. We should remember Ap. Claudius Pulcher, *cos.* 143, *cens.* 136, *princeps senatus*, who was father-in-law of Ti. Gracchus and a member of the agrarian commission. On his disregard of a tribunician veto, cf. Cic. *Cael.* 34; Suet. *Tib.* 2.4. On the harshness of his censorship, cf. Dio fr. 81.

46. Characteristically, Dionysius did not understand the *popularis* tint of the narrative (10.54.7; 55.1; 57.4). In 58.3, the change comes suddenly and without motivation.

47. Cf. Dion. Hal. 10.60; 11.2 (without the thought of Livy: *aliquamdiu aequatus inter omnes terror fuit; paulatim totus vertere in plebem coepit*: 3.36.7; 37.6). "Young men" are also mentioned shortly before the fall of the decemvirs by Diod. 12.25. On the motif of the *adulescentes nobiles*, see in general A. W. Lintott, *Historia* 19 (1970): 24ff., and J. P. Néraudau, "Jeunesse et politique" (1980), whose conclusions I cannot, however, accept.

simply stated "that no step should be taken in public affairs which did not suit any of the three" (*Div. Jul.* 19.2: *ne quid ageretur in re publica quod displicuisset ulli e tribus*). This formulation has a close parallel in the account of the Decemvirate given by Livy's contemporary Dionysius of Halicarnassus, who relied on essentially the same sources as Livy:

> They first of all took a solemn oath, without the knowledge of the populace, and made a compact among themselves not to oppose one another in anything, but that whatever was approved by any one of them should be ratified by all the others; and they agreed that they would hold their magistracy for life and admit no other person into the government, that they would all enjoy the same honours and possess the same power. (10.59.2)[48]

To an amazing extent, therefore, past and present seem to be indissolubly interlaced in the accounts of the second Decemvirate.[49] This remarkable phenomenon has been explained, on the one hand, by asserting that the Roman historians were only capable of comprehending events of the remote past in terms of their own experiences; accordingly, their accounts rather naively reflect recent events. On the other hand, it has been emphasized that the history of the past was turned into a battlefield where contemporary conflicts were restaged and continued. Both explanations are correct, but both are unsatisfactory because they each touch only on certain aspects of the problem. I shall try to document this by discussing yet another element of the account.

In the oldest version available (Diod. 12.24–25), the second Decemvirate is overthrown before the end of its first year of office because of Ap. Claudius's assault on Verginia. Thus only external factors prevented the publication of the last two tables; this task then naturally fell to the consuls of the following year (12.26). But accord-

---

48. Cf. Livy 3.36.9; A. Klotz, *RhM* 87 (1938): 46. *Pace* Ogilvie, *Comm.* (1965): 464, there is not the slightest similarity to the oath Sulla demanded from Cinna in 88 B.C. (Plut. *Sulla* 10).

49. Cf. R. Seager, *CQ* 27 (1977): 382ff., on other examples in the first decade of Livy. Seager places too much emphasis on the part of Livy himself, however, because he without sufficient reason neglects the parallel tradition in Dionysius (380 n. 8).

ing to later versions of the tradition (Cic. *De re pub.* 2.62; Zonaras 7.18), the decemvirs were determined to keep indefinitely the comprehensive power they had received for one year only. Therefore they without authorization extended their term of office beyond the end of the first year, although the remaining part of the codification was finished by then.[50] They did not offer any justification; it was an act resulting from mere lust for power. This account is further changed in the final stage of the tradition as it is presented by Livy and Dionysius of Halicarnassus. According to that version, the decemvirs completed the last two tables but deliberately delayed their publication (Livy 3.37.4).[51] Even after the expiration of the appointed year, therefore, they could point to the fact that their task was not yet accomplished.[52]

Why did the common source of Livy and Dionysius choose to connect the task of the decemvirs with the prolongation of their term of office in precisely this way? A famous incident in the transition between Republic and Empire may have served as the model. In October of 43 B.C., Octavian, Antonius, and Lepidus agreed at a meeting near Bononia (Bologna) that by decree of the popular assembly a new office was to be created for them, which they would hold for five years as *triumviri rei publicae constituendae*.[53] Shortly thereafter, on November 27 of the same year, the three generals used military pressure to enforce at Rome the legalization of this measure (the *lex Titia*).

However, during the following five years, the war against Caesar's assassins, disputes among the triumvirs, and the conflict with Sex. Pompeius precluded the planned reorganization of the Republic—if it had been planned at all. The triumvirs therefore remained in power even after the terminal date of their office (December 31, 38 B.C.), and finally, in the fall of 37, with the treaty of Tarentum, extended it retroactively for another five years (until December 31,

---

50. Cassius Hemina, fr. 18 P, and Sempronius Tuditanus, fr. 7 P, probably belong to this stage of the tradition: *Tuditanus refert libro tertio magistratuum decem viros, qui decem tabulis duas addiderunt, de intercalando populum rogasse. Cassius eosdem scribit auctores.*
51. Dion. Hal. 10.60.5–6 should also be interpreted in this way; cf. 11.6.4–5.
52. Cf. Täubler, *Decemvirat* (1921): 52f.
53. Fadinger, *Prinzipat* (1969): 32.

33 B.C.).⁵⁴ Appian (5.95.398) states explicitly that the triumvirs thought the extension did not need to be ratified by the people. Antonius maintained this interpretation of the legal situation to the end. Octavian soon changed his mind and requested an official confirmation by popular decree,⁵⁵ but he, too, though officially resigning from the Triumvirate at the end of the second five-year term, retained the triumviral *potestas* until 27, when his task was completed and the Republic was formally restored.⁵⁶

There are obvious parallels between these events and the description of the second Decemvirate in Livy and Dionysius. In each case an extraordinary office created for the purpose of reorganizing the Republic is extended beyond its scheduled terminal date, allegedly because the mandated task is not yet accomplished; thus, the aim and purpose of the office (*Zweckfrist*) is given priority over its time limit (*Zeitfrist*).⁵⁷ The ancient tradition was therefore "modernized" by applying the historians' own contemporary experience or, to put it more precisely, the legal problem raised by the actions of the triumvirs shed new light on the similar behavior of the decemvirs several centuries earlier.

How are we to assess this? Is it simply another example of the well-known tendency of Roman annalists to project different chronological levels onto one another and to blend various periods together? Are we to assume that such a tendency in this case was enhanced by considerations of contemporary polemics—since any emphasis on the decemvirs' deliberate attempt to delay the completion of the law code, clearly an arbitrary act on their part, could be expected to raise unpleasant doubts about the motives of the triumvirs? Both explana-

---

54. De Martino, *Cost.* IV.1² (1974): 93ff.; for the other possibility (Dec. 31, 32), cf. recently E. Gabba, *Appiani bellorum civilium liber quintus* (Florence, 1970): lxviiiff.

55. Both views are represented in modern scholarship, too; cf. on the one hand, Mommsen, *Röm. Staatsrecht* II³ (1887): 718ff. ("Zeitgrenze ohne rechtsverbindliche Kraft"), on the other hand, De Martino, *Cost.* IV.1² (1974): 94 ("nell'età repubblicana . . . prevalevano le esigenze di temporaneità dell'ufficio").

56. Fadinger, *Prinzipat* (1969): 315ff. Politically, it would not have made any difference if Octavian had immediately secured for himself a plebiscite conferring on him full powers for the conflict with Antonius, "poteri non dissimili da quelli conferiti con il triumvirato e quindi consistenti in un imperium maius" (De Martino, *Cost.* IV.1² [1974]: 119).

57. Livy 3.40.12; 51.13; Dion. Hal. 11.6.4–5. Accordingly, after the end of their year of office, the decemvirs were regarded as *privati* by the opposition (cf., e.g., Horatius in Livy 3.39.3ff.; Dion. 11.5.2ff.).

tions are probably right, but there is more. Basically, what happened here, just as in each of the earlier stages of the tradition, is that a timelessly valid insight was reformulated in the light of the author's own contemporary experience. The subject, the problems caused by the temptation of unlimited and uncontrolled power, remains the same for each generation, but the means of presenting it are different. The oldest version uses the figure of Verginia to emphasize quite naively the moral corruption of the tyrant, just as it had frequently been described in Greek literature since Herodotus; in a similar way the Roman tradition connected the rape and suicide of Lucretia with the overthrow of the monarchy.[58] Later, the desire to retain power is recognized as the ultimate goal; accordingly, the Decemvirate is prolonged into a second year. There is no need for rational explanations; a legal pretext can be added, however, once one is "discovered" in a comparable case (the second Triumvirate). As Mommsen rightly pointed out,[59] in this version the narrative is turned into an urgent warning against endowing individuals with unlimited power, be it only for a fixed time; once established, such extraordinary power can easily override any legal time limit.

The experiences of our own century amply confirm the truth of this warning. The mandate established by the "Law for the alleviation of the distress of people and *Reich*" (*Ermächtigungsgesetz*) of March 24, 1933, was limited to April 1, 1937, and then prolonged twice by the *Reichstag* until May 10, 1943. When the second extension was coming to an end, Hitler stated in a decree of May 1, 1943:

> In view of the fact that the law of March 24, 1933, formally expires on May 10, 1943, I decree: the government of the *Reich* is to continue to carry out the responsibilities conferred upon it by the law of March 24. I reserve the ratification of these powers of the government of the *Reich* through the Greater German *Reichstag*.[60]

Hitler, of course, did not need the Roman model, which he had probably never heard of; but some of his contemporaries might have

---

58. Mommsen, *Röm. Forschungen* I (1879): 299.
59. Mommsen, *Röm. Staatsrecht* II^3 (1887): 717.
60. Editor's translation. For the text, see H. Schneider, *Vierteljahreshefte für Zeitgeschichte* 1 (1953): 212f. The parallel with the second Triumvirate is established by Fadinger, *Prinzipat* (1969): 144 n. 2.

profited by a careful reading of Livy, especially since Hitler's intentions were clearly recognizable.

What is true of one detail can be said of the whole story. In the course of Roman historiography, the second Decemvirate became more and more a timeless simile for the emergence and fall of tyranny. Let us check this by looking once more at the version of Livy and Dionysius. At the outset, there is the antagonism between plebeians and patricians. Each side is fiercely determined to weaken the other; in order to attain this goal, it is even willing to put up with heavy restrictions on its own power. Thus the plebeians renounce the institutions guaranteeing their protection and security (*provocatio* and tribunate) solely to prevent the election of consuls.[61] On the other hand, the patricians agree to suspend the consulate because they are primarily bent on getting rid of the hated tribunes of the *plebs*.[62] Both parties thereby unknowingly prepare the way for the tyranny of the second Decemvirate, which is able to establish itself to the detriment of both of them. The power usurped by the decemvirs is only available because the political forces previously existing in the state completely paralyze each other.

Equally, the continued existence of the Decemvirate depends upon the continuation of that antagonism.[63] Because of their aversion to the tribunes of the *plebs*, the patrician senators are even willing to endure, as the smaller evil, the violence and arrogance of the decemvirs—which mainly affect the *plebs* anyway. The plebeians' hope for a joint action against the tyrants, therefore, remains unfulfilled for a considerable time.[64] The senators, at best, trifle with the idea of overthrowing the decemvirs in order to control the power all by themselves; rather than restoring the former constitutional setting, they plan to introduce an order more attuned to their own interests.[65] It

61. Livy 3.34.8.
62. Livy 3.37.2–3; Dion. Hal. 10.58.1. Cf. the oration of Q. Cicero in Cic. *De leg.* 3.19.
63. Dion. Hal. 11.22.6–7.
64. Livy 3.37.1; 38.9–10, 13; 49.7. Not by chance, this thought is lacking in Dionysius (at most, it may be hinted at in 11.4.2); it corresponds to the ideal of Livy expressed in 4.6.12, which is characterized correctly as an "Unterordnung von Gruppeninteressen unter die *salus rei publicae*" by K.-E. Petzold, *Gnomon* 50 (1978): 186. Pabst, *Studien* (1969), and R. Seager, *CQ* 27 (1977): 377ff., of course correctly emphasize that, in case of doubt, Livy favors law and order.
65. Livy 3.41.5–6.

is only when the decemvirs blatantly fail as generals and politicians and the masses rise in revolt that the Senate, led by a few "liberals" among its members, finally turns against them. Now, at last, unified opposition results in determined action and quickly brings about a peaceful resignation of the decemvirs;[66] thereafter, the old offices, the consulate and the tribunate, are both restored.

Machiavelli's *Discorsi* contain a number of specific observations on the Decemvirate. I want to cite only one here:

> The senate and the people also made a very great mistake in appointing the Decemviri, for, in spite of what has been said earlier in the discourse which dealt with dictators, to the effect that self-appointed magistrates, not those appointed by the people, are prejudicial to liberty, the people should, none the less, in appointing magistrates, have chosen such as were too respectable to turn to evil ways. And, whereas they should have appointed guardians to see that they behaved properly, the Romans took the guardians away, for they made the Decemvirate the sole magistracy in Rome, and annulled all others, owing, as we have said above, to the excessive desire of the senate to get rid of tribunes and of the plebs to get rid of consuls, a desire so strong that it blinded them, and caused them to cooperate in the disorderly procedure. For men, as king Ferdinand used to say, resemble certain little birds of prey in whom so strong is the desire to catch the prey which nature incites them to pursue, that they do not notice another and a greater bird of prey which hovers over them ready to pounce and kill.[67]

This analysis is closely comparable to ours: the concrete details of Livy's story are abstracted into statements of general validity. We are now able to understand why this can be done so easily. The Roman tradition had been formed over two centuries in accordance with general views and maxims; it reflects the historical thinking and the historical experiences of several generations;[68] it is interested in

---

66. On this aspect, see H. Arendt, *Macht und Gewalt*¹ (Munich, 1981): 49ff. (= *On Violence* [New York, 1970]).
67. *The Discourses of Niccolò Machiavelli*, transl. by L. J. Walker (New Haven, 1950): 309 (I.40.12).
68. Täubler, *Decemvirat* (1921): 12f.

providing practical examples for the statesman and citizen. All this separates the Roman historical tradition (for all its delight in invention) from the historical novel.[69]

It is for these very reasons that Machiavelli is fascinated by Livy's "tales from early Rome." He, too, is not interested in the Roman past as an end in itself—he accepts it uncritically and naively, just as it is described by the ancient authors—but, to cite an apt formulation of O. Seel, he takes it as "encoded present" (*verschlüsselte Gegenwart*).[70] Had he lived in Cicero's or Augustus's time, he would have applied his own experience to the text of the tradition handed down to him; he would have shaped it accordingly and thus carried the transformation one step further. One and a half millennia later, however, the tradition had been frozen into canonical truth. All Machiavelli could do was to comment on it. But innumerable times contemporary Italian events quite naturally come to his mind as suitable illustrations and inseparably melt together with his reflexions on Livy. In exactly the same way for the writers in the days of the Gracchi, Sulla, or the triumvirs, contemporary concerns and experiences must have blended in most naturally with the old tales about the decemvirs. Of course, the close resemblance of conditions in fifteenth-century Italy to those of the Roman Republic made such combinations rather easy. Machiavelli could thus perceive aspects of his own time reflected in the Roman past; he could use Roman history as "ready-made experience."[71] His success justifies his procedure;

---

69. Cf. the excellent remarks of D. Timpe, *A&A* 25 (1979): 97ff. See also F. Wieacker, *Labeo* 23 (1977): 60: "Allgemeiner konfrontieren die antiken Berichte mit dem Paradox, dass der verstehenden und erklärenden Interpretation des modernen Historikers in diesen seinen Hauptquellen nicht blosse Daten entgegentreten, sondern die eigene 'Sinndeutung', Lehrfabel oder ethische Parabel des antiken Historikers." However, not all modernized scenes reach the standard of the description of the first and second Decemvirates. To slip into schematism was a constant danger (see my comments mentioned in n. 15 above).

70. O. Seel, *Verschlüsselte Gegenwart: Drei Interpretationen antiker Texte* (Stuttgart, 1972).

71. G. Sasso, *Niccolò Machiavelli: Geschichte seines politischen Denkens* (Stuttgart, 1965): 217ff. (in Italian, Naples, 1958); cf. E. J. Bickerman, *RFIC* 97 (1969): 399f.; R. T. Ridley, "Machiavelli and Roman History in the Discourses," *Quad. di Storia* 9 (1983): 197ff. For another recent parallel, see B. Ceva, *La storia che ritorna: La terza deca di Livio e l'ultimo conflitto mondiale* (Milan, 1979), with the review by E. Gabba, *Athenaeum* 58 (1980): 529f. Catalano, *Tribunato* (1971), offers a wealth of material.

at the same time, it justifies the sagacious and plausible inventions of the Roman annalists.[72]

Appendix: Some Thoughts on the Source Problem

The foregoing discussion analyzes the aims of the surviving accounts of the Decemvirate. It does not primarily intend to offer a contribution to unsolved questions of source criticism, although it is, of course, based on certain assumptions about the nature of the tradition, outlined earlier (see above at nn. 17–25). I would like to add here a few remarks on the tradition concerning the Decemvirate.

The accounts of the first and second Decemvirates given by Livy and Dionysius of Halicarnassus are so similar that we must assume a common source.[73] Although it is easy to point out sporadic contradictions or omissions by either author, there is no evidence that convincingly points to a second source. To be sure, Livy tells the story better and more concisely;[74] either he was more capable of appreciating the intentions of his source or his own political views were more precise and refined.[75] But the sequence of scenes in both accounts of the second Decemvirate is identical. Moreover, it is hard to imagine that two authors would independently have invented the very same succession of fictitious speakers in a fictitious senatorial debate.[76]

---

72. In this context it is worth considering Goethe's comments on the revolution brought about by Niebuhr in the historical discipline; they are collected by E. Grumach, *Goethe und die Antike* I (Berlin, 1949): 46ff.; cf. L. Wickert, "Goethe und der Historismus in der Altertumswissenschaft," in *Convivium: Beiträge zur Altertumswissenschaft, Festschrift K. Ziegler* (Stuttgart, 1954): 165ff.
73. Probably no one today would postulate that Livy and Dionysius depended on each other.
74. See Burck, *Erzählungskunst*² (1964).
75. Cf. nn. 46, 47, 64 above. There is no indication at all of an intermediate source with *popularis* tendency; contra: E. Schwartz, *RE* 5.1 (1905): 947f.
76. Livy 3.39–41; Dion. Hal. 11.4–21. Cf. A. Klotz, *Livius* (1940–41): 266f. Luce, *Livy* (1977): 226f., for general reasons doubts that Livy follows only one source through long passages in his first books. He is, however, clearly disproved at least as far as the account of the Decemvirate is concerned. G. Poma, *RSA* 6/7 (1976–77): 129ff., offers important observations on Cicero, but the differences with the other strands of the tradition are played down too much.

The actual problems begin when we attempt to date their common source. The only available criteria are allusions to certain events and circumstances of the late Republic. Such allusions, however, are usually so vague that they allow a variety of interpretations. For example, Sulla and Caesar share many similarities, as do the civil wars of the eighties and forties. But what I consider the central problem of the account—the contradiction between the legal time limit of the Decemvirate and the reference to its unfinished task of codification—was an actual political issue in Rome only once, during the second Triumvirate. Sulla's dictatorship was justified in a very similar way, but was not restricted by a time limit, and Caesar was not *dictator rei publicae constituendae*.[77] Livy himself,[78] and perhaps even Dionysius, might well have noticed the analogy between the second Decemvirate and the political conditions of the thirties, but it is unlikely that each of them would independently have addressed the subject in exactly the same way, particularly by introducing as an indispensable precondition to the story the assertion that the decemvirs did not publish the last two tables during their first year of office. The conclusion is therefore inevitable: the two authors used a common source, which cannot be dated earlier than the thirties.

So late a date will probably upset many scholars, since the *communis opinio* still basically attributes Livy's sources to the "era of Sulla," and, more precisely, to the seventies of the first century B.C.[79] However, there have always been differing views. The allusions in Livy's and Dionysius's account of the early Republic to events around the year 60 (the Catilinarian Conspiracy,[80] the first Triumvirate),[81] to the dictatorship of Caesar, and even to the years thereafter[82] are too numerous and too conspicuous to be ignored. It is impossible to present or examine them here. Although admittedly not all the assumptions proposed by various scholars will be able to withstand criticism, it is

77. H. Gesche, *Caesar* (Darmstadt, 1976): 154 n. 8.
78. Cf. basically Ogilvie, *Comm.* (1965): 19; Luce, *Livy* (1977): 169.
79. Cf. Ogilvie, *Comm.* (1965): 7ff. and passim (striking, e.g., the observations on p. 468); D. Timpe, *A&A* 25 (1979): 97 n. 2, 117; but see Walsh, *Livy* (1961): 115ff.
80. E. Schwartz, *RE* 5.1 (1905): 953; *Ges. Schriften* II (1956): 337ff.; A. Klotz, *RhM* 87 (1938): 33, 43ff.
81. Cf. n. 48 above.
82. Zohren, *Antias* (1910); Klotz, *RhM* 87 (1938): 45; R. A. Bauman, *Acta classica* 9 (1966): 129ff., especially 136ff.; A. Valvo, *CISA* 3 (1975): 157ff.; 5 (1978): 111ff.

an urgent desideratum to collect and carefully analyze all such proposals within a larger and more clearly defined framework. In the meantime, the evidence must be considered sufficiently strong to allow us to assume a late date for at least some of Livy's sources.

Nor is such a late date excluded by our knowledge of possible authors. Licinius Macer certainly wrote his work before 66 B.C. There is no positive evidence to reliably date Valerius Antias.[83] Cicero's silence in *De legibus* (1.6f.), however, may well suggest a *terminus post quem* of 50 B.C.[84] For the same reason, the work of Tubero cannot be dated any earlier, whether it be that of the father, Lucius,[85] or, as is more likely, of the son, Quintus.[86] It is highly probable, therefore, that new accounts of early Roman history were written in the forties and thirties of the first century B.C., which would suffice for our present purposes.

To go further and try to identify the common source of Livy and Dionysius of Halicarnassus would seem difficult,[87] for after Sempronius Tuditanus,[88] there is not a single fragment of a known author dealing with the two Decemvirates. Recently, however, in part following Mommsen, T. P. Wiseman has once more analyzed the image of the Claudians in Livy, and he suggests very plausibly that Valerius Antias published his work only at the beginning of the forties.[89] Consequently, the history of Tubero, who used both Licinius Macer

---

83. On Vell. 2.9.6 and Fronto p. 114 N (= 131–32 van den Hout), see the good remarks by Zohren, *Antias* (1910): 26ff., and J. D. Cloud, *LCM* 2 (1977): 225ff. (contra: Volkmann, *RE* 7A.2 [1948]: 2313ff.; Ogilvie, *Comm.* [1965]: 12f.). See also Ungern-Sternberg, "Die Einführung spezieller Sitze für die Senatoren bei den Spielen (194 v.Chr.)," *Chiron* 5 (1975): 157ff.
84. Beloch, *Röm. Geschichte* (1926): 106. E. Badian, "Early Historians" (1966): 20ff. with n. 102, is undecided but closer to assuming an early date.
85. Thus Klotz, *RhM* 87 (1938): 48f.; Badian, "Early Historians" (1966): 22; R. Werner, *Gymnasium* 75 (1968): 509ff.
86. Ogilvie, *Comm.* (1965): 16f.; G. W. Bowersock, *Augustus and the Greek World* (1965): 130; id., "Historical Problems in Late Republican and Augustan Classicism," in *Le Classicisme à Rome*, Entretiens sur l'ant. class. 25 (Vandoeuvres-Geneva, 1979): 64ff.; Wiseman, *Clio's Cosmetics* (1979): 135 n. 145.
87. Cf. the remarks by A. Guarino, *Labeo* 26 (1980): 139f.
88. Cf. n. 50 above.
89. Wiseman, *Clio's Cosmetics* (1979): 104ff., 113ff.; see Mommsen, *Röm. Forschungen* I (1864): 285ff. Note further the important observation of Wiehemeyer, *Kritik* (1938), passim, that in Livy Antias frequently appears as standing in opposition to the rest of the tradition.

and Valerius Antias,[90] is to be dated even later. This date in turn is confirmed by the fact that Tubero was the patron of Dionysius of Halicarnassus,[91] who quotes Tubero's work.

In conclusion, on the one hand, we find in the story of the Decemvirate elements that remind us of the time of the second Triumvirate. On the other hand, we know of a history that was most probably written at precisely that time and used by both Livy and Dionysius. It seems hardly objectionable, therefore, to assume that this is indeed the common source behind both surviving accounts of the history of the Decemvirate.

90. This is obvious, e.g., from Livy 4.23.1, or from Livy 4.7.1–12 in comparison with Dion. Hal. 11.62. See Klotz, *RhM* 86 (1937): 217ff.; 87 (1938): 47; *Livius* (1940–41): 209f.

91. Bowersock, *Augustus* (as in n. 86): 130; Wiseman, *Clio's Cosmetics* (1979): 135ff.; A. M. Biraschi, "Q. Elio Tuberone in Strabone V,3,3?" *Athenaeum* 59 (1981): 195ff.

JEAN-CLAUDE RICHARD

IV

Patricians and Plebeians: The Origin of a Social Dichotomy

Important work has been devoted to the problem of the patricio-plebeian dualism[1] since my doctoral thesis was defended in 1976 and published in 1978.[2] It is therefore the proper time to restate the question, and I propose not only to lay out the facts that appeared decisive to me for the orientation of my research, but also to revise my position on certain points on which the aid of distance invites me to make a *retractatio*.

Transl. by E. Mylonas and K. Raaflaub.
1. Guarino, *Riv.* (1975)—this work appeared before my thesis, but too late for me to have made proper use of it; Gagé, *Débuts* (1976); I. Hahn, *Oikumene* 1 (1976): 47ff.; Ferenczy, *Patr. State* (1976); Alföldi, *Frühgeschichte* (1976); A. Momigliano, *Labeo* 23 (1977): 7ff.; Angelini, *Patriziato* (1979); Capogrossi-Colognesi, *Istituzioni* (1978); *Legge e società nella repubblica romana*, edited by F. Serrao (1981); P. M. Martin, *Royauté* (1982); E. S. Staveley, *Historia* 32 (1983): 24ff.
2. Richard, *Origines* (1978). In order to keep the following notes short, I shall for the most part mention only bibliography subsequent to my book, to which the reader may turn for references to earlier scholarship.

1

The doctrine of a patricio-plebeian dualism that in its developed and final form went back to the very origins of Rome is common to all the texts that transmit the annalistic tradition to us. It gives credit to Romulus for dividing the population of the growing city into *patres* and plebeians,[3] the latter being most often confused with the clients of the former.[4] Furthermore, the tradition invites us to see in the patriciate the hereditary nobility of the senatorial families, and in the *plebs* the agglomeration of all elements outside this elite.

It is, of course, true that the canonic character of this tradition is not enough to guarantee its truth. As far as the patricians are concerned, throughout the previous century many scholars preferred to see in them not a nobility but the most ancient civic body of the *Urbs*[5] and the descendants of the "Founding Fathers." Most of the recent work devoted to the study of the structure of the archaic Roman population has, however, rejected this postulate and returned to the patriciate the dignity of a nobility (although there are different opinions about the time of its formation). Thus, basing their calculations only on the *fasti consulares*, R. E. A. Palmer and P. C. Ranouil[6] have fixed the number of patrician families at 16 and 43 respectively.

Let us note, however, for the sake of comparison, that Th. Mommsen stopped his count at 54, P. Willems at 114, and E. Pais decided on the number 74.[7] But quite a few fictitious *gentes* had found their place on these lists, whose authors believed that the most ancient rural tribes, except for the *Crustumina*, owed their names to extinct patrician families. Even more radically, Willems did not hesitate to make use of the most fantastic "prosopographic" facts in order to

---

3. Cic. *De re pub.* 2.14–16; Dion. Hal. *Ant. Rom.* 2.8.1–4; Livy 1.8.4–7 (a little less clear); Plut. *Rom.* 13.1–9 (a little less clear).
4. Cic. *De re pub.* 2.16; Dion. Hal. *Ant. Rom.* 2.9.2; Plut. *Rom.* 13.7; Fest. p. 262 L, s.v. *patrocinia*.
5. Cf. among others, Niebuhr, *Hist.* I (1828): 260; Mommsen, *Röm. Staatsrecht* III.1 (1887): 14–15; cf. most recently Guarino, *Riv* (1975): 131–34, 304, 323; Hahn, *Oikumene* 1 (1976): 61–71.
6. Palmer, *Arch. Comm.* (1970): 299 (16 families plus 4 doubtful ones); Ranouil, *Patriciat* (1975): 184–85.
7. Mommsen, *Röm. Forschungen* I (1864): 107–20; Willems, *Sénat* I (1878): 69–88; E. Pais, *Ricerche* II (1916), especially 394ff. (74 families, of which 50 are certain). Cf. also G. Bloch, *MEFR* 2 (1882): 241ff.; and id., *Sénat* (1883): 114, who counted 73 patrician families.

enlarge the ranks of the patriciate. At least in its absurdity, this example is instructive, since a theory that on the one hand reserves the right of citizenship *optimo iure* to patricians only down to the third century[8] and on the other hand identifies only such a limited number of *gentes patriciae* cannot possibly be reconciled. Judging by the "Hundred Families" that are remembered in the history of the Locrians of Greece and Magna Graecia,[9] the total of 114 is clearly more indicative of an aristocracy than of an entire civic population. Whatever their worth, the traditions about the size of the most ancient Senate of the *Urbs* allow the same conclusion. It is not irrelevant to this argument that the word *pater*, because of its potential connotations of power,[10] could designate the senators as well, and that the adjective *patricius* belongs to the formations in *-icius* derived from the terms of official functions.

That the annalistic tradition is correct in defining the patriciate as an aristocracy of actual or potential senators does not, however, necessarily imply that one must adhere to the dogma of an original patricio-plebeian dualism that is the cornerstone of the annalistic doctrine. It is obvious indeed that this doctrine is deeply influenced by Greek views on the origin and development of the polis and its society.[11] On the other hand, a series of consistent facts has preserved in many details the image of an early Roman society to which the division into patricians and plebeians does not apply. Thus already in the last century, H. Jordan[12] noted that three hills of the Septimontium (Caelius, Oppius, Cispius), and four of the seven canonic kings (Numa Pompilius, Tullus Hostilius, Ancus Marcius, and Servius Tullius) had names that at a later date belonged to exclusively plebeian *gentes*. Already significant in themselves, these two observations were reinforced recently by another: A. Magdelain[13] points out that the *gentilicia* to which three of the *curiae* that are

---

8. Willems, *Sénat* I (1878): 7, 17.
9. Pol. 12.5.6–8. L. Lerat, *Les Locriens de l'Ouest* (Paris, 1952): 137–39; D. Musti, "Problemi della storia di Locri Epizefirii," in *Atti del XVI conv. di studi sulla Magna Graecia* (Naples, 1977): 44, 76.
10. Ulp. *Dig.* 1.6.4: *patres familiarum sunt qui sunt suae potestatis, sive puberes, sive impuberes*; Ernout and Meillet, *Dictionnaire*[4] (1967): 487, s.v. *pater*.
11. Cf. most recently the contributions of K. Raaflaub to this volume (chapters I and VII).
12. H. Jordan and C. Hülsen, *Topographie der Stadt Rom im Alterthum* I.1 (Berlin, 1878): 187–89; id., *Die Könige im alten Italien* (Berlin, 1887): 15–37.
13. A. Magdelain, *CRAI* (1979): 698ff., especially 709.

known to us (*curia Aculeia, curia Faucia,* and *curia Titia*) owe their names are not attested in the classical period in any but plebeian families.

It is certainly true that the existence in the last century B.C. of plebeian *Cispii* or *Titii* does not imply that their ancient predecessors whose names were frozen in a toponym or *curia* necessarily were their ancestors. The history of the *gentes* must no longer be interpreted on the basis of outdated rigid principles. Nevertheless, coincidences that do not carry much weight taken individually become significant and convincing when they multiply. In short, the three facts noted above are interpreted most naturally by assuming that the patricio-plebeian dualism was not an original element of Roman society.

In fact, everything looks as if this division was ignored by the curiate organization that, despite all uncertainties, was undoubtedly the most ancient structure unifying the Roman population.[14] A number of observations lead the analysis in this direction. Thus, despite recurring criticism, I see no reason to doubt the etymology of the word *curia* proposed by P. Kretschmer,[15] who connects it with *kowiriya*. In other words, the term simply designated a group of *viri*; nothing allows us to recognize them as patricians. In the classical period the name *Quirites* is applied to the totality of the citizens, whom it addresses as a homogeneous body, omitting any reference to the patricio-plebeian dualism.

The preceding deductions are confirmed by the information on the *Fornacalia*,[16] the festival most characteristic of the curiate organization, since it was celebrated *curiatim* and on a moveable date fixed by the *curio maximus*. In fact, this celebration was closely connected with the *Quirinalia*: those Romans who *Furnacalibus suis non fuerant feriati*,[17] either because they did not know which *curia* they belonged to or because they had not been able to free themselves of their obli-

---

14. Richard, *Origines* (1978): 212–25; G. Piéri, *RD* 59 (1981): 583–92, especially 584.
15. P. Kretschmer, "Lat. *quirites* und *quiritare*," *Glotta* 10 (1920): 147–57.
16. Dumézil, *Arch. Rel.* I (1970): 159f.; Richard, *Origines* (1978): 216f. A. Magdelain, "Quirinus et le droit," *MEFR* 96 (1984): 194, 237, has a different opinion.
17. Varro *Ling.* 6.13. E. Mayer, "*Quirinalia—Stultorum feriae*," *Ann. Univ. Budapest.* 2 (1974): 51–57.

gations, could always collectively redeem themselves by performing on the day of the *Quirinalia* the sacrifice they had not offered at the proper time of the *Fornacalia*. It is evident that this particular regulation takes us back to very early times, when the whole population of the emerging city used to be convened at the *Fornacalia*; otherwise, the chance of redemption offered to the *stulti* (Festus, p. 304 L, s.v. *Quirinalia*: . . . *stultorum feriae*) and the place reserved in the *curiae* for elements that were not well assimilated would make no sense at all. The conclusion is that, from the beginning, the members of the *curiae* or *Quirites* were recruited from the whole Roman people, without any division to weaken the strictness of this principle.[18]

These two facts help us in assessing the significance of another piece of evidence that is decisive and often misunderstood. Preserved by Aulus Gellius,[19] it goes back to Laelius Felix the jurist. Although he follows the traditional view in assigning criteria of census requirements and topographical division to the vote of the *comitia centuriata* and *tributa* respectively, he makes the extraordinary statement that the *suffragium* of the *comitia curiata* corresponds to the criterion of the *genera hominum*. Even if, at the time of Hadrian, the *comitia curiata* already belonged to a distant and mysterious past, it is still possible that this statement stems from a well-informed source. Whatever one might think about this possibility, the statement as such certainly does not allow the assumption that the *curiate* organization was structured primarily according to the gentilitial element. It is true that, as late as the classical period, the *comitia curiata* made decisions in matters of *adrogatio* and perhaps of *gentis enuptio*, and that the *comitia calata* (whose connections with the previous assembly, although unclear, are nevertheless certain) assisted at the *detestatio sacrorum* and at the *testamenti factio*. But all this simply attests to the fact that, in these two forms, the assembly dealt with matters of private law that affected the system and interaction of families and were therefore important to the community.[20] Furthermore, it is helpful to connect the formula *genera hominum* with a passage of the *Roman Antiquities* in which Dionysius of Halicarnassus characterizes the pre-

18. H. Last, *JRS* 35 (1945): 32f.; Heurgon, *Rise* (1973): 111f.
19. Aul. Gell. *Noctes Atticae* 15.27.5: *Item in eodem libro* [*sc. in libro Laelii Felicis ad Q. Mucium*] *scriptum est: cum ex generibus hominum suffragium feratur, curiata comitia esse, cum ex censu et aetate, centuriata, cum ex regionibus et locis, tributa*; L. Grieve, "Livy 40.51.9 and the Centuriate Assembly," *CQ* 35 (1985): 417–29.
20. J. Gaudemet, *Institutions* (1967): 275.

Servian tribes as "gentilitial" (*genikos*).²¹ It invites us to conclude that membership in these tribes and in the *curiae* of which they consisted was determined by birth and conditioned by kinship relations just as much in the *gentes* as in lesser family groups.

2

In sum, there are strong reasons to emphasize the unifying character of the curiate organization, which divided the whole body of *Quirites* into identical sections,²² all of which reached beyond family groups. Nevertheless, some inequalities did appear within this population. The birth of the patriciate was closely connected with such differentiation, which we can distinguish in several areas.

To begin with, archaeological evidence is helpful in understanding the broader outlines of the matter.²³ On the site of Rome, as in the rest of Latium, funerary material from periods I and II (which cover the time from c. 1000 to 700) is homogeneous in its similarity and poverty. It thus suggests an undifferentiated society in which crafts were practiced within an *oikos* economy and the family group. This situation changes completely, however, in periods III and IVA, which, in traditional chronology, correspond to the era of the Latin and Sabine kings. Henceforth, the necropoles reflect a society in the process of advanced differentiation. Certain tombs illustrate a tendency to accumulate valuable and prestigious possessions (objects from Etruria and the Greek world, chariots, and so on) and accordingly testify to the existence of a number of family groups that were strong and dynamic enough to monopolize a good part of the riches available at the time. The appearance of chamber tombs (such as tomb 95 in phase IVA or tomb 126 on the Esquiline in period IVB, 640–580) and the existence of a veritable hypogeum (tomb 125,

21. Dion. Hal. *Ant. Rom.* 4.14.2.
22. De Martino, *Cost.* I² (1972): 108; Piéri, *RD* 59 (1981): 585.
23. C. Ampolo, *DArch* 4/5 (1970–71): 46–49; G. Bergonzi and A. M. Bietti Sestieri, *DArch*, n.s., 2 (1980): 59f.; A. M. Bietti Sestieri, ibid., 91–92; A. Bedini and F. Cordano, ibid., 112f.; G. Bartoloni and M. Cataldi Dini, ibid., 146–48. These articles were read at a colloquium held in Rome in 1977 on the subject of *La formazione della città nel Lazio*. On the eighth century as the century in which the aristocracies of southern Etruria came into being, cf. M. Torelli, *DArch* 8 (1974–75): 41.

phase IVA) must certainly be explained by the aspirations of their owners to demonstrate the cohesion and permanence of these families.

Passing from the field of archaeology to that of onomastic studies, we become aware of important evidence that fits directly with the previous observations. The evolution resulting in the adoption of a hereditary patronymic—in other words, the emergence of the *nomen gentile*—had been accomplished at Rome by the beginning of the seventh century. This new practice cannot be separated from the claims of solidarity and permanence already mentioned. Henceforth, the *nomen gentile* was the element that identified as such the members of the emerging aristocracy.[24]

Everything indicates that the first nucleus of the patriciate should be sought among those groups whose vigor and will to power are evinced in the archaeological and onomastic evidence. The obligation to belong to the patriciate, still imposed in the classical period on the three major *flamines*,[25] necessarily takes us back to the Rome of the *curiae*. Proof is available in their connection with the archaic triad that later, under the Etruscan kings, must have been superseded by the Capitoline triad. On the other hand, it is precisely the case of the *flamen Dialis* that remains inexplicable in every reconstruction that proposes a republican origin for the patriciate and that recognizes in it the aristocracy of the consuls and their descendants.[26] Although this priest enjoyed the privileges of the *sella curulis*, a lictor and a guaranteed seat in the Senate,[27] we should not forget that he was precluded from holding any magistracy by the very fact that he might not look on a *classis procincta* properly drawn up outside the *pomerium*.[28] The principle guiding the selection of the major *flamonia* must, therefore, be much older; obviously it is inseparably connected with the appearance of the divisions that arose in a previously homogeneous society.

---

24. G. Colonna, *SE* 45 (1977): 184–86; L. R. Ménager, *SDHI* 46 (1980): 181.
25. Cic. *Dom*. 38: *Ita* [if adoptions similar to that of Clodius were to multiply] *populus Romanus brevi tempore . . . neque flamines nec salios habebit*; Paul. Fest. p. 137 L, s.v. *maiores flamines*; see further chapter VIII below at n. 1.
26. A. Magdelain, "*Auspicia*" (1964): 454–73; Ranouil, *Patriciat* (1975): 11–43.
27. Livy 1.20.2 (*sella curulis*); Plut. *Quaest. Rom*. 113, and Paul. Fest. p. 82 L, s. v. *flaminius lictor*; Livy 27.8.8 (on the right of the *Dialis* to take a seat in the Senate).
28. Aul. Gell. *Noctes Atticae* 10.15.4.

In Livy 27.8.1–3 the necessity of patrician rank is equally attested for the *curio maximus*; according to Livy, this priesthood was opened to the *plebs* only in 209, almost a century after the *lex Ogulnia*. Such a lag is not surprising, since in the city that emerged from the *exaequatio* this priesthood was obviously quite insignificant, although there remained for its holder the obligation of announcing the day of the *Fornacalia* each year.

Finally, we should mention the Salian priesthood, which even in the last century of the Republic remained closed to the *plebs*.[29] However, although later it declined in importance, in the beginnings of the *Urbs* this office must have been intimately connected with its military activities. This is amply attested by the rituals performed by the *Salii* throughout the month of March, whose purpose it was to mobilize Roman energies at the approach of the campaigning season. Furthermore, we know from Servius that they were *in tutela Iovis, Martis, Quirini*.[30] This is a decisive reason for placing the apex of their college under the Latino-Sabine kings and for assuming that the Salians enjoyed the same high esteem at that time as the major *flamonia*.

We cannot discuss the cases of the augurs and the pontiffs in depth here. But there are reasons to believe that, as in the previous cases, these priesthoods were monopolized by the patriciate for the benefit of its members at precisely the time when its claims were recognized as legitimate.[31]

In conclusion, the importance of, and the conditions imposed upon, the major *flamonia*, the *curio maximus*, and the Salian priests imply the existence of a patriciate even before the Etruscan kings. As is suggested by etymology, the patriciate appears to have been a senatorial aristocracy that owed its name to the fact that its members were descended from the *patres*, or senators. Along with Momigliano,[32] I am even inclined to think that the adjective *patricius* originally reflected the aspirations of certain family groups to secure for themselves hereditary membership in the Senate. I therefore believe that this term originally referred more to lineages[33] than to individ-

29. Cf. above at n. 25.   30. Servius on *Aen.* 8.663.
31. Richard, *Origines* (1978): 247.
32. Momigliano, *JRS* 53 (1963): 118.
33. Livy 3.27.1: *magistratum equitum dicit L. Tarquitium patriciae gentis*; 3.33.9: *apud P. Sestium, patriciae gentis virum*.

uals, and that later the idea of filiation tended to be overshadowed by claims of vocation and privilege.

Furthermore, although we know very little about the details, it is likely that the *interregnum* (which certainly was not an invention of the *respublica libera*) helped to increase the number of aristocratic families and their prestige.[34] We should remember that in Rome the king alone had the power to confer nobility. In other words, the *lectio senatus* allowed him to fulfill the aspirations of the *gentes* who had helped place him on the throne. Finally, we must add to the religious and political domains on which the emerging patriciate left its mark that of military activity, restricted here to the cavalry. The most ancient Roman *equitatus* was divided into three *centuriae inauguratae* named *Ramnes*, *Tities*, and *Luceres*. These centuries conferred a status similar to that of a *"milizia sacra"*[35] on their members, who were recruited among an elite and tended to form a functional and hereditary aristocracy.

It is clear then that the patriciate, which in the course of the fifth century closed its ranks and monopolized power, in its earliest stages goes back to the time of the Latino-Sabine kings. Various indications allow us to perceive the emergence in early Rome of an economically powerful elite that was not only rich in land and clients, but also highly ambitious. It therefore claimed the privilege of perpetuating itself in the Senate, of monopolizing several priesthoods, and, at least for certain of its members, of specializing in the *equitatus*. With the first conquests of the *Urbs*, this division within the population was marked even more strongly. This explains why these lineages obtained from the kings recognition of their claims—in other words, a special status. Thus the earliest patriciate emerged as the product of a natural selection that is mostly reflected in the political, religious, and military domains.[36]

Although it sought to be hereditary and exclusive, this patriciate was nonetheless an open aristocracy. Tradition has, in fact, retained the memory of individual or collective *adlectiones* that infused new blood into it.[37] The example of the *gentes Albanae* is important here,

---

34. Momigliano, *JRS* 53 (1963): 118 n. 1; Richard, *Origines* (1978): 235–38.
35. Livy 1.36.3 and 1.43.9; P. De Francisci, *Primordia* (1959): 524; V. Ilari, *RISG* 15 (1971): 143.
36. Richard, *Origines* (1978): 263.
37. Sabines of Titus Tatius: Dion. Hal. *Ant. Rom.* 2.47.1 (by means of an *adlectio*

because it illustrates the extent and strength of the ties of solidarity uniting the aristocracies of various Latin towns among themselves and making such instances of "osmosis" possible.[38]

The existence of such a patriciate does not, however, imply an equally early date for the existence of the *plebs*—at least if it is properly understood as a clearly established order with a precise function in the Roman community. Before the moment when, during and after the first secession, it gave itself an organization, the *plebs* can be defined only negatively, as the total of the non-noble families, the mass of *Quirites*.

3

Whatever one thinks about the exact conditions under which Etruscan domination was established in the *Urbs*, it seems, as I have proposed elsewhere, that this important change occurred at a time when the curiate organization was undergoing a crisis. Several factors must have contributed to it, among them the aggressiveness and desire for power of the patriciate, the policy of deportation, which, according to the annalists, was experimentally adopted in the case of the inhabitants of Alba before it became standard practice in the reign of Ancus Marcius,[39] and the extension of the ties of *clientela* made possible by such a policy.

At any rate, it is significant that the policies of Tarquin the Elder focused on precisely those three areas in which the tendencies of the patriciate to hereditariness and the monopolization of offices and privileges were most clearly visible. Ancient testimony actually mentions that this king promoted new senators, increased the number and differentiated the function of the equestrian centuries, and, as is

---

into the Senate), and 2.62.2; Plut. *Rom.* 20.1; *Num.* 2.5. Numa Pompilius: Dion. Hal. *Ant. Rom.* 4.3.4. Tarquin the Elder: Dion. Hal. *Ant. Rom.* 3.41.4 (integrated into the patriciate and admitted to the Senate), and 4.3.4; Dio 2.9.1; Zon. 7.8. *Gentes Albanae*: Livy 1.30.2; Dion. Hal. *Ant. Rom.* 3.29.7.

38. C. Ampolo, *DArch* 9/10 (1976–77): 333–45.

39. Cf. the case of the populations of Politorium, Tellenae, Medullia, and Ficana: Cic. *De re pub.* 2.33; Livy 1.33.1–2 and 5; Dion. Hal. *Ant. Rom.* 3.37.4; 3.38.2–3; 3.43.2; Zon. 7.7.

implied by various indications, tried to broaden the recruiting basis of the augural and—beyond any doubt—the pontifical college.[40]

Still, it seems that these remedies did not solve the problem, since, according to unanimous tradition, Servius Tullius comprehensively reorganized Roman society by introducing new structures in the administrative and military system: these were the local tribes, which replaced the "gentilitial" tribes of pre-Etruscan times, and the centuries. Without entering here into the details of an endless controversy,[41] I consider it certain that the division into tribes extended to the *ager*.[42] Certainly, in theory at least, the possibility cannot be excluded that the *ager* was divided among the four tribes later known as the *urbanae*, in a solution similar to, but not as sophisticated as, that which later at Athens allowed Cleisthenes, through the combination of *trittyes*, to create the new tribes destined to replace the previously existing ones. Such a system would, however, have perpetuated the preponderance of the urban element at the very time when the *classis* was composed of peasant-soldiers.

Also, insofar as gentilitial interests focused on the countryside as their preferred territory, any effort to neutralize them had to include a new organization of the areas outside the city. Strong ties of solidarity, allegiance, and dependence had developed to the advantage of the patrician families within the framework of the genetic tribes and the *curiae*. In order to weaken these ties, it was necessary to create an undifferentiated "civic space," both inside and outside Rome; for the new organization of the citizen body and some of the new civic functions, domicile was to be the decisive criterion. Since it was situated in a privileged position in the middle of the rural tribes grouped in a circle around it, the leading role of the *Urbs* as the focus of community activities was naturally confirmed.[43] As for the *ager*, because new bonds now united its inhabitants with the citizen

---

40. Richard, *Origines* (1978): 319–47 (where the evidence on the reforms of the first Tarquin is cited and discussed); L. R. Ménager, *MEFR* 88 (1976): 477–84.

41. Clearly summarized by Thomsen, *Serv. Tullius* (1980): 115–43.

42. Dion. Hal. *Ant. Rom.* 4.15.1; contra: ibid., 4.14.1–2; Paul. Fest. p. 506 L, s.v. *urbanas tribus; Vir. ill.* 7.7. The case of *Pap. Ox.* XVII, 2088, lines 10–14 is less clear. Cf. Richard, *RD* 62 (1983): 187ff.

43. C. Ampolo, *MEFR* 92 (1980): 567–76: according to the archaeological evidence, all the elements characteristic of the ancient city existed in the *Urbs* by the second half of the seventh century.

body, it maintained its function as an integral part of the community. The measures initiated by Servius Tullius attest to his intention of restraining the control the patriciate was able to exercise in the rural area through its extensive *clientelae*. This program calls to mind the reforms of Cleisthenes and his attempts to weaken the influence of the old Athenian families. The similarity of objectives is sufficient to explain the similarity of methods.

The intentions behind the creation of the *exercitus centuriatus* were closely related to those underlying the tribal reform. The infantry formation of 4,000 (?) men called a *classis* was, in fact, a phalanx borrowed by Rome from Etruria. As for those *infra classem* whose memory has equally been preserved for us, I do not think that they stood completely outside the military organization.[44] Certainly modern scholars are often inclined to take as analogous the dichotomy between the *classis* and the *infra classem* on the one hand, and the divergence between *adsidui* and *proletarii* on the other—the latter, moreover, being attributed to Servius in Cicero's *De re publica* (2.40). No doubt, etymology leads us to consider rural inhabitants the *adsidui* whom Cicero identifies with the *locupletes*, and in the Greek world the hoplites were essentially peasant soldiers. Nevertheless, those who were "beneath the *classis*" are not necessarily to be confused with the *proletarii* who were considered unworthy of bearing arms.[45] Rather, it could be significant that in 479 at the battle of Plataea, Pausanias led an army of 5,000 Spartiates, each accompanied by 7 light-armed helots.[46] There is no comparable positive evidence for Rome, but the hypothesis that contingents of light-armed infantry were recruited from among those who could not afford to procure their own panoply should be seriously considered (cf. Dion. Hal. *Ant. Rom.* 6.10.2). After all, the vulnerability of a phalanx at its flanks and rear is well known.

It has been remarked countless times that in the Greek world the development of the phalanx was intimately connected with the emer-

---

44. Guarino, *Riv.* (1975): 116; J.-C. Richard, *RPh* 51 (1977): 234; Thomsen, *Serv. Tullius* (1980): 182.
45. Aul. Gell. *Noctes Atticae* 16.10.11: *nisi in tumultu maximo scribebantur, quia familia pecuniaque his aut tenuis aut nulla esset.*
46. Herod. 9.10 and 28.

gence of egalitarian structures in the community,[47] since identical responsibilities fell on each hoplite-citizen in battle. Also, a heavy infantry division of 4,000 men could not be recruited exclusively from the patrician families,[48] whose clients, moreover, were not capable of procuring their own armaments. To focus on the most important aspect, the *classis* was made up for the most part of rural landowners who did well enough to be able to acquire the equipment necessary for a hoplite; they formed a large group of equals in which each member was interchangeable with his *commilitones*. This experience of homogeneity made the soldiers increasingly conscious of a solidarity that could not be limited to military activity. The same experience, in my opinion, must have been an important factor in the evolution of the word *populus*, which although etymologically predestined solely for military usage,[49] ended up designating the entire citizen body.

As for the reforms of the *equitatus* implemented by Servius Tullius, only hypotheses are possible. For electoral purposes, in the classical period, the equestrian centuries called the *sex suffragia* formed a group clearly separated from the other twelve. It is reasonable, therefore, to assume that Servius Tullius confined himself to doubling the centuries of *Ramnes*, *Tities*, and *Luceres*. Since they were different from the *classis*, and no doubt ranged above it,[50] the six centuries thus established continued to recruit their members by *turmae*—that is, from the pre-Servian tribes. The privileges granted to their members (*aes equestre, aes hordearium*) were based on the fact that they belonged to an equestrian aristocracy[51] in which, as we have seen, the patriciate played at least a predominant role.

The innovations associated with the reign of the sixth king are doubly significant. First, they do not all betray a desire for a radical break with a still recent past. Thus in the traditional model of the

---

47. M. Detienne, in *Problèmes de la guerre en Grèce ancienne*, edited by J.-P. Vernant (Paris and The Hague, 1968): 141.
48. Contra: Momigliano, "Patrizi e plebei" (1967): 216; id., *Contr. IV* (1969): 446f.
49. Fest. p. 224 L, s.v. *pilumnoe poploe*. Despite Ernout and Meillet, *Dictionnaire*[4] (1967): 552 (s.v. *populus*), *populor, -ari* is certainly a derivative of this word.
50. Cf. Alföldi, e.g., *Historia* 17 (1968): 454. On the Servian *equitatus*, cf. Cic. *De re pub.* 2.39; Livy 1.43.8–9; Dion. Hal. *Ant. Rom.* 4.18.1.
51. Nicolet, *Ordre équestre* I (1966): 35.

Servian "constitution," the *equitatus* is found in a place of honor, whereas the recruitment of the *turmae* still seems to follow the rules of heredity.[52] It therefore retains the primacy it derived from its ties with the patriciate. At the same time, such continuity demonstrates how cohesive, united, deeply rooted, and, most important, powerful the patriciate was by then.

Nevertheless, the more essential aspect lies elsewhere. According to a happy formulation of Momigliano's, the reforms of Servius Tullius constituted "an attempt to stop the separation of the orders."[53] Because of their structure and traditions, the equestrian centuries not only belonged to the past, but soon lost their value on the battlefield. The phalanx, on the other hand, became at the same time the spearhead of the Roman army and the flower of the civic community. Without going so far as to say that it remained closed to the patrician families, I am convinced that it was essentially recruited outside this nobility and its clients, from among the rural inhabitants who were wealthy enough to arm themselves at their own expense, and who, by that very fact, were bound together in a community of equals over which the patriciate had no control.

Moreover, the *exercitus centuriatus* cannot be separated from the *census*. A tradition that is coherent despite some anachronisms suggests that the *census* should be identified *ab origine* with an inventory establishing the economic worth of all those involved.[54] This is no doubt correct, even if the exact methods of estimation are unknown to us. Even though there remain some dark areas, a comparison with the Solonian system of census classes and the evidence of the annalistic tradition lead us to believe that the *census* played some role in the recruitment of the equestrian centuries,[55] which was equally influenced by the criterion of the *genera hominum*. However, the way this solemn ritual was performed in the classical period allows us to state with confidence that it was more directly connected with the organization of the phalanx.[56]

To be sure, the *census* created and emphasized hierarchy, since a

52. Guarino, *Riv.* (1975): 120, 296.
53. Momigliano, *JRS* 53 (1963): 120.
54. Cic. *De re pub.* 2.39–40; Livy 1.42.4–43.9; Dion. Hal. *Ant. Rom.* 4.16.1–19.4 and 7.59.2–10.
55. Cic. *De re pub.* 2.39; Dion. Hal. *Ant. Rom.* 4.18.1.
56. Piéri, *Cens* (1968): 58–75; Thomsen, *Serv. Tullius* (1980): 202–11.

tripartite division into *equites, classis,* and *infra classem* was introduced in Servian Rome.⁵⁷ But the *census* also defined the axis that constituted the grades of citizenship. If, solely on the basis of his fortune, a patrician could be part of the *classis* together with nonpatrician *commilitones,* then the *census* was egalitarian and fair, favoring no one. Although the patriciate was older than the sixth reign, its members were not for that reason privileged in the *census.* The lemma *Procum patricium* (Festus, p. 290 L) does not prove the contrary, since the *discriptio classium* whose authority is cited there is in all probability a later invention.⁵⁸ In other words, all the initiatives undertaken by Servius Tullius in the area that interests us seem to have been dictated by the desire to prevent the gap that already existed between the nobility and the rest of the population from expanding, and firmly to reunite a community that was in the process of falling apart.

Servius's efforts were not crowned with success. This is proved by the fact that the harshest blows the patriciate had to endure under the Etruscan monarchy were dealt it by his successor, Tarquin the Proud.⁵⁹ Although the tradition about this king is usually condemned as a fiction combining various elements borrowed from the stereotypical Greek image of the tyrant, it deserves to be examined more closely. What we can discern of his policies absolutely allows us to compare the reign of Tarquin the Proud with the tyrannical regimes that flourished in various cities of Magna Graecia and Sicily throughout the sixth century. Of course, we have to eliminate the stark colors and sensational details that have been grafted on to a number of valuable and authentic facts by the annalistic tradition, which was bound by the preconceived idea that the people rose up in a mass in 509 against a hated despot. It is then possible to recognize with reasonable certitude that Tarquinius's actions aimed at thoroughly mixing the Roman population. Hence his struggle against

---

57. Momigliano, *JRS* 53 (1963): 120, who includes the *proletarii* among the *infra classem;* less convincingly, in my view, B. Cohen, *BAGB* (1975): 273, seems to accept the existence of the three following *ordines* in Servian Rome: *equites, pedites, proletarii.*

58. The tradition referring to the *patricius vicus* (Paul. Fest. p. 247 L, s.v. *patricius*) according to which Servius Tullius assigned residences to the patricians in the region named after them is equally doubtful.

59. Richard, *Origines* (1978): 416–27.

the patriciate and against those strong old traditions that, in the realm of religion, helped to maintain hereditary allegiances.[60] Finally, since the centuriate organization had ensured the primacy of the rural population in the community, his policies encouraged the development of commerce. It is not by accident that the number of Greek potsherds found in the subsoil of the *Urbs* rises astronomically for his reign.[61]

4

Whatever the circumstances that brought about the end of the monarchy at Rome, I see no reason to reject the tradition according to which the new *libera civitas* had to restore a Senate that had been decimated by Tarquin the Proud. Although it is divided between L. Iunius Brutus and P. Valerius Publicola, the best-attested tradition honors one of the first consuls for having created the *conscripti* whom, in its most certain form, it places in opposition to the *patres*.[62] The few scattered references according to which the expression *patres conscripti* served to designate all the senators cannot prevail against this fact.[63]

Already in antiquity several opinions were current on the social origins of the first *conscripti*. No doubt, Verrius Flaccus and Livy both thought that they were chosen from the elite of the *plebs*. It is in fact at their suggestion that Festus and Paulus Diaconus in his *epitoma* of Festus (Festus, p. 304 L, s.v. *qui patres*; Paul. Fest. p. 6 L, s.v. *adlecti*; id., p. 36 L, s.v. *conscripti*) use the expressions *ex plebe* and *ex equestri ordine* indistinctly, whereas Livy himself (2.1.10) specifies that this *adlectio*, whose beneficiaries belonged to the equestrian order, was essential in order to maintain harmony between the two orders. Di-

---

60. Dion. Hal. *Ant. Rom.* 4.43.2.
61. J. C. Meyer, *Analecta Rom. inst. Danici* 9 (1980): 56–58, whose conclusions are more rigorous and, accordingly, more indicative than those of his predecessors.
62. Livy 2.1.10–11; Fest. p. 304 L, s.v. *qui patres*; Dion. Hal. *Ant. Rom.* 2.47.1, who to the *patres* or senators whom Romulus created at the very beginning opposes the *conscripti* later chosen by the same king.
63. Dion. Hal. *Ant. Rom.* 2.12.3 (from the first reign); Isid. *Orig.* 9.4.11; Lyd. *Mag.* 1.16, p. 20–21 W. There remain the testimonies of Plut. *Pub.* 11.2, and Servius Auct. on *Aen.* 1.426, who do not call the new senators of the first year of the Republic *conscripti* but *patres conscripti*.

onysius of Halicarnassus, on the other hand, has preserved another version for us (*Ant. Rom.* 5.13.2) according to which the new senators of the first year of the Republic came from the *plebs* but had to be admitted to the patriciate before being allowed to take their seats in the *curia*.

Neither of these traditions is satisfactory. In elevating the *conscripti* to the rank of patricians, the latter makes the mistake of reducing the distinction between old and new senators to a simple difference of degree. On the other hand, the former is open to criticism precisely because it emphasizes that the *conscripti* originated from a *plebs* that was still far from being a political entity. In addition, even if one were to accept the hypothesis that a dualism existed from the beginning or at least before 509, it would still be incredible that, after this date, more than half the senators should have been plebeians.[64] Had this indeed been the case, one would have great difficulty in understanding why the Conflict of the Orders erupted in the first years of the fifth century.

In fact, the *conscripti* cannot be defined except in negative terms—that is, as non-*patres*. They were created for the purpose of restoring to its former size a Senate that tradition simply describes as decimated.[65] No doubt the methods of accomplishing such a return to normalcy have mostly escaped the annalists. I believe that it is necessary to distinguish among several possibilities. On the one hand, there may have been families that now regained the place among the *patres* they had lost under Tarquin the Proud (whereas the descendants of the senators created recently by Tarquin the Elder were perhaps relegated to the rank of second-class patricians: Livy 1.35.6: *centum in patres legit qui deinde minorum gentium sunt appellati*). On the other hand, contrary to those *patres* whose hereditary right to sit in the *curia* was then reaffirmed, the *conscripti* proper were no doubt senators selected on the basis of individual virtue whose names were placed on a list, hence the name *conscripti*.

It is not surprising that the patriciate took advantage of the events of 509 in order to reaffirm its primacy on the same basis as previ-

---

64. That is, 164 out of 300, according to Festus, p. 304 L, s.v. *qui patres*.
65. On the purge of the Senate by Tarquin the Proud, cf. Livy 1.49.2–6; Dio 2.11.2–3. According to Dion. Hal. *Ant. Rom.* 4.42.4, this king himself filled the vacancies he had created.

ously. However, there remains the problem of the presence in the *fasti consulares* of *gentilicia* that are known to have been exclusively plebeian in the classical period.[66] All the solutions that have been proposed lack consistency and convincing proof; sooner or later, they all run into insurmountable difficulties. Only one recent hypothesis, that of Momigliano, has opened a new direction for discussion. It invites us to consider these names as those of *conscripti* whom the *patres* admitted to the Senate as their associates in handling the power.[67]

In support of this theory, we consider it highly significant that the disputed *gentilicia* form three distinct groups in the *fasti consulares* of the years 509–451. The first group corresponds to the years 502–497, which saw the clouds gathering on the horizon of the *libera civitas*. The second partially comprises the years 493–486, during which Rome was straining to normalize the situation brought about by the first secession. Finally, the third coincides with the period of agitation begun in 462 by the *rogatio Terentilia* and the Decemvirate. These coincidences[68] alone exclude the possibility that the names under discussion could have been those of families whom we would automatically assume to have been patrician at that period. On the other hand, it is equally out of the question that at such a remote date these could have been "plebeian" *gentilicia*. Because it avoids both these problems, Momigliano's hypothesis gains plausibility in my opinion.

As for the patriciate, it is clear that, in the first years of the Republic, it did not remain isolated and self-sufficient, but opened itself up to new elements. The welcome given to Attius Clausus[69] in 504 proves this sufficiently. Under these conditions, some *conscripti* might have been admitted into this group—all the more so since pa-

---

66. On this very important problem, cf. A. Schaefer, *Jahrb. f. class. Philol.* 113 (1876): 569ff.; A. Bernardi, *RIL* 79 (1945–46): 3ff., 15ff.; Richard, *Origines* (1978): 519–21.

67. Momigliano, *Contr.* IV (1969): 448f.; id., "Patrizi e plebei" (1967): 218, and "Origins of the Republic" (1969): 25f. But I refuse to agree with Momigliano that the *conscripti* were a creation of the regal period, even though I subscribe to the rest of his theory on the *conscripti*.

68. The only remaining cases are those of T. Numicius Priscus, *cos.* 469, and M. Genucius, *cos.* 445.

69. Livy 2.16.5; Dion. Hal. *Ant. Rom.* 5.40.5; Plut. *Pub.* 21.10; Suet. *Tib.* 1.2; Servius on *Aen.* 7.706.

trician families kept dying out. But the tightening of the patriciate noticeable in the *ager* (see section 5 below) was accompanied by a tendency to reserve for its members the charisma of *imperium* and *auspicia*. This tendency resulted in an attempt at monopolizing power and closing the ranks of the patriciate. When L. Mamilius from Tusculum received Roman citizenship in 458 (Livy 3.29.6), he no longer found open access into the nobility, which was striving to become a closed caste. Nevertheless, due to heavy pressure exerted by the *plebs*, the patricians, trying to avoid irreparable consequences, were clever enough to join to themselves some *conscripti* whom the plebeians would consider less hostile.

In the course of this development, the patriciate may have acquired a new source of legitimacy, which expressed itself in the administration of the *imperium* and the *auspicia*, as suggested by M. Humbert.[70] But this leads us too far away from the beginnings of the *libera civitas*. Quite naturally, for several decades most *patres* were not *consulares* (ex-consuls) but men who, on the basis of their birth into the right kind of family, could expect to become consuls some day. Had the patriciate consisted only of the descendants of former consuls, it would obviously have been so restricted in manpower at the time of the first secession that the Conflict of the Orders could not but have been very unequal. The lists assembled by P. C. Ranouil, however, have established that by 443 the patriciate had definitely become a closed caste, and that by then it was made up of all the lineages of which at least one member had held the highest magistracy.[71]

Since, on the other hand, the *conscripti* were unable to transmit the seat they held in the Senate to their descendants, they formed a second-class nobility, the actual influence and power of which was markedly restricted by the jealously guarded hereditary privileges

---

70. Cf. above at n. 26. See, too, M. Humbert's review of Richard, *Origines* (1978), in *RD* 60 (1982): 447ff., and id., *Institutions politiques et sociales de l'antiquité* (Paris, 1984): 198ff.

71. Ranouil, *Patriciat* (1975): 45, 61, dates this closure after 433. For Palmer, *Arch. Comm.* (1970): 248f., membership in the patriciate, which was implied by an ancestor's having held a magistracy with *imperium*, was not fixed *ne varietur* until 367. Finally, in a perspective that is admittedly different, since in his eyes the *patres* are defined as senators, Angelini, *Patriziato* (1979): 150–53, 160–85, has developed a hypothesis according to which it was in the years around 445 that the rank of patrician was recognized as a necessary condition for holding the highest office and for later on taking one's seat in the Senate.

and charisma of the *patres*. A split was therefore bound to appear among the members of the republican Senate when the *adlecti* of 509 realized that the expected collaboration with the patriciate was nothing but a bait. Even if it is possible that some of them eventually found a place in this elite, such promotions were extremely rare. I believe that for the great majority of *conscripti* there was no other solution but to embrace the cause of the *plebs* once it had taken its determined stance against the patriciate. In other words, the phenomenon that modern scholars, after G. De Sanctis, sometimes define as "*serrata del patriziato*,"[72] cannot be separated from the fact that from the beginning of the fifth century, an increasing number of *conscripti* were waiting for their chance to assume a more active role in politics and government.

5

Even if their number increased under the Etruscan kings, craftsmen, traders, and laborers enjoyed only a relatively low status in Rome during the sixth century. Consequently, the *plebs* cannot be described as having consisted mostly of the urban element of the population when it appeared on the historical scene with the first *secessio*. In addition, the consistent evidence provided by the annalistic tradition (on the founding of temples)[73] and by archaeology (on the amounts of imported Greek pottery)[74] forces us to envisage a city that was still prospering and open to external influence after 509, rather than to make the mistake of assuming that it was completely thrown back on the level of austere self-sufficiency.[75] It would therefore clearly be wrong to seek the active and leading elements of the plebeian revolution in the urban milieu[76] (where, at any rate, the *difficultas annonae* was much more severe than in the *ager*).

72. De Sanctis, *Storia* I^3 (1980): 241.
73. Cf. the dedication of temples to Saturn (497), Mercury (495), Ceres, Liber and Libera (493), and Castor (484): R. Bloch, *REL* 37 (1959): 124.
74. See J. C. Meyer, *Analecta Rom. inst. Danici* 9 (1980): 57–58, 64–65, whose lists demonstrate continuation of such imports, although at a much lower level than in the preceding period.
75. A theory defended by De Martino, *Cost.* I^2 (1972): 215–20.
76. Guarino, *Riv.* (1975): 167. On the other hand, B. Combet-Farnoux, *Mercure* (1980): 25, 51, emphasizes that the cult devoted to Mercury, god of the *mercatura*,

In the final form given it by the annalists, the tradition on the causes of the crisis that provoked the first secession[77] confirms our opinion. Reduced to its essential elements, it can be summarized as follows: as soon as the danger of a return of Tarquin the Proud had disappeared, the age of iron took the place of the golden age, and the reign of *aequum ius ac modestum* was succeeded by arbitrariness and violence. The large mass of farmers living on the *ager*, who had sustained the incessant wars with great personal and material sacrifices, now found themselves cornered by debt, despoiled of their possessions, and reduced to the status of *nexi*.

Although it shows some of the obvious characteristics of post-Gracchan annalistic historiography, the basic authenticity of this presentation of the elementary facts should not be doubted for at least two reasons. In the first place the *adsidui*—i.e., the owners of a plot of land that they had in permanent occupation—are confused in the annalistic tradition with that group of citizen-soldiers from whom not only the *classis* but, in my view, also the contingents of the *infra classem* were recruited. Second, the permanence of the dangers that pressed on the young Republic both from the North and the South meant that the difficulties of the rural population were almost endemic.

Under these conditions, C. Appleton's[78] analysis of the debt problem remains essentially valid. In the framework of a premonetary economy, debt was bound to be a serious problem for the most vulnerable of the *adsidui*. They had no alternative but to seek their salvation in the *nexum* by arranging a contractual loan of livestock or seed from one of the patricians who were better equipped to survive rough times. However, such loans were made under the harsh law of the *fenus unciarium*, a term that must be understood as expressing a monthly interest equal to one-twelfth of the borrowed "capital"—

---

does not have plebeian character; that a member of the *plebs*, M. Laetorius, allegedly played a role in the dedication of his temple must be attributed to late annalistic tradition.

77. Sall. *Hist.* 1.11 Maurenbrecher; Livy 2.23.1–31.6; Dion. Hal. *Ant. Rom.* 5.63.1–67.3; 5.70.1–5; 6.22.1–29.1; 6.34.1–44.3; Dio 4.17.1–8; Zon. 7.13–14. The most complete analysis of this tradition is still to be found in Schwegler, *Röm. Geschichte* II (1856): 203–24.

78. C. Appleton, *RD* 43 (1919): 467ff.; cf. E. Will, "La Grèce archaïque" (1965): 63, on debt in kind in archaic Greece; Finley, *Soc.* (1981): 150ff.

that is to say, an annual interest equal to the capital.[79] In short, the remedy was no less menacing than the original evil.

To be sure, the *nexum* in principle was placed under the protection of *fides*.[80] However, this notion is ambivalent enough to explain why it could cover behavior ranging from paternalism to pure and simple exploitation. Thus, if it is true that the bond created by the *nexum* not only preceded but was in fact independent of an eventual default of "payment," and that the *fenerator* therefore had the right to seize the person of the *nexus* whenever he desired it, it is clear that the latter was not guaranteed the necessary time to collect the harvest or to wait for the offspring of his herds and flocks, which would save him. In other words, it depended on the creditor alone whether or not the debtor was able to preserve or regain his liberty. Both the unrestrained desire for power and gain that we perceive as characteristic of the patriciate at that time,[81] and what we learn from comparison with the crisis for which Solon had to find a remedy, strongly confirm the testimony of the annalistic tradition, even in its darkest aspects.[82]

Thus all the conditions necessary for an explosion in the rural milieu were there. Whatever the cost of armor, I do not think that these difficulties primarily affected the hoplites. On the contrary, those peasant soldiers who were beleaguered by the *nexum* served in light-armed contingents that supported the *classis*. In fact, it very much looks as if Rome, in order to be able to repel the incessant threats

---

79. Appleton, *RD* 43 (1919): 520–21; Noailles, *Fas* (1948): 134; H. Zehnacker, "*Unciarium fenus*," in *Mélanges P. Wuilleumier* (Paris, 1980): 353–62.

80. J. Imbert, "*Fides et nexum*" (1953): 339ff.

81. It is obvious, e.g., in the creation, right after the battle at Lake Regillus, of ten new *tribus rusticae* with gentilitial names on the lands taken from the Latins: Humbert, *Municipium* (1978): 73–76 (who opts for eleven tribes). Cf. also Gagé, *Enquêtes* (1977): 185–213, especially 196–200; J. Ellul, *Index* 3 (1972): 155–67 (in whose view the creation of the first rustic tribes in 495 corresponded to the patricians' desire to make sure that their families would, by means of their *clientelae*, be in a position to impose their will on the urban tribes and their population); and Ferenczy, *Patr. State* (1976): 19. In any case, the annexation by the patriciate of the lands taken from the Latins (the tribes that were then created bear the names of patrician families) implies that the *classici* and the *infra classem* had no share in the fruits of victory. Combined with a tendency to distribute the spoils unequally (Richard, *Origines* [1978]: 495), this indicates that discontent could have spread rapidly among the rural population.

82. See chapter VII, part 3 below.

from the outside, resorted to giving them an important place in the army that was sent to war every year. The description Dionysius of Halicarnassus (*Ant. Rom.* 6.10.2) gives us of the Roman army at the battle of Lake Regillus seems to contain some indications that are useful in this context. The *psiloi* whose presence at the side of the *equitatus* and of the phalanx he mentions obviously correspond to the *infra classem*. I am also tempted to compare their function, *mutatis mutandis*, to that which Aristotle[83] attributes to the light infantry of the Greek cities. Since, unlike the hoplites, these soldiers were recruited from among the poor citizens, Aristotle considered them to tend toward democracy. Of course, the first secession cannot be described as a democratic movement; moreover, in Rome the *classici* supported the actions of the *infra classem*.[84]

But the hypothesis that the initiative that threatened the unity of the city originated with the *infra classem* undoubtedly deserves our serious consideration. The picture drawn of the situation in the years around 495 by the ancient sources is deceivingly simplistic. If the crisis had become so general as to interfere even with the recruitment of the *classis*, Rome necessarily would have found itself in a position of dangerous inferiority against its enemies. That it was able to maintain and later even to increase its power throughout the fifth century proves that this was not the case.

Thus the *plebs* entered history in the guise of the foot soldiers who seceded in 494–93. We therefore have to accept Varro's statement that the first *tribuni plebis* were military tribunes[85] who had assumed the leadership of the movement. As is natural in the perspective of a *secessio* of *armati*, the credentials of these tribunes made them the exception that proves the rule: their successors, lacking the *imperium*, had nothing to do with military affairs. They were obliged to render

83. Arist. *Pol.* 6.7. 1321a13ff.
84. Or they took control of them so that they would not degenerate: cf. Guarino, *Riv.* (1975): 313.
85. Varro, *Ling.* 5.81: *Tribuni plebei, quod ex tribunis militum primum tribuni facti qui plebem defenderent in secessione Crustumerina*; cf. also Zon. 7.15. What we can discern of the military character of the organization of the *plebs* assumed in 494–93 (Mommsen, *Röm. Staatsrecht* II³ [1887]: 273; Binder, *Plebs* [1909]: 378; Pais, *Ricerche* III [1918]: 263, 307; Altheim, *Lex sacr.* [1940]: 33–38) invites us to relate this evidence to the first secession (Richard, *Origines* [1978]: 545; Capogrossi Colognesi, *Istituzioni* [1978]: 270) and not to the second, despite Livy 3.51.2, and Dion. Hal. *Ant. Rom.* 11.43.6.

assistance to any plebeian who called on them, and such assistance required their personal intervention. More precisely, the *intercessio* was the material support necessary for the exercise of the *auxilium*; whenever the tribune intervened on behalf of a plebeian who asked for his assistance, he had to throw himself between the suppliant and the lictor who was charged with taking this person into custody. On the other hand, the *intercessio* was of no use against the *imperium*, whether *domi* or *militiae*, beyond the first milestone.[86] This limitation of the tribunician power and the ties that attached its holders to the very soil of Rome (they were not allowed to leave the *Urbs* even for one whole day)[87] must be understood correctly. Far from providing proof that the essential elements of the *plebs* were to be found in the city, these particular restrictions were due to the very purpose of the tribunate: since it exerted itself against the *imperium* of the magistrates[88] in the event of litigation between debtor and creditor, but also in matters of *dilectus*, the *auxilii latio*, even if it mostly benefited people living in the countryside, nevertheless naturally had to be enacted in the city.

6

In conclusion, the patricio-plebeian dualism was definitely the result of a long development. Of the factors that caused this division, some carry us back to the eighth and seventh centuries, others to the first years of the fifth. The history of the patriciate thus begins at an earlier date than that of the *plebs*. Unless we assume, against any likelihood, that *populus* originally designated the patriciate, the formula *populus plebsque* makes no sense for the regal period.[89] As for the Conflict of the Orders, it was born out of a reaction of self-defense on the part of a large number of despairing rurals who revolted

86. Mommsen, *Röm. Staatsrecht* I³ (1887): 66–70; Magdelain, *Imperium* (1968): 45 n. 4.
87. Dion. Hal. *Ant. Rom.* 8.87.6; Aul. Gell. *Noctes Atticae* 3.2.11, and 13.12.9; Macr. *Sat.* 1.3.8; Richard, *Origines* (1978): 554–56; Guarino, *Riv.* (1975): 167–68.
88. Livy 2.33.1: *ut plebi sui magistratus essent sacrosancti quibus auxilii latio adversus consules esset.*
89. Mommsen, *Röm. Staatsrecht* III.1 (1887): 6 with n. 4; Richard, *Origines* (1978): 129–30. Contra: Momigliano, "Patrizi e plebei" (1967): 212–13.

against a nobility whose appetite for power, felt equally in the political domain,[90] disported itself without restraint to the detriment of the unprotected peasants, whose personal liberty was annihilated *de facto*, if not legally. The insistence of the patrician families on exclusiveness had the result of throwing into the arms of the *plebs* the *conscripti* who, in the years to come, would expand the struggle into larger horizons.

90. From the 490s the development that caused the patriciate to close its ranks tended to become irreversible.

RICHARD E. MITCHELL

V

The Definition of *patres* and *plebs*: An End to the Struggle of the Orders

1. *The Problem and the Thesis*

Who were the original Roman *patres*, and how and when were they distinguished from the plebeians?[1] The debate on these questions is both long and complex, and the answers depend on the explanation of Rome's original social, political, and religious structures and institutions. The ancient tradition describes some of the exclusive posi-

---

1. This essay is distilled from a larger project and presented here to stimulate criticism and correction. I have already benefited a great deal from the comments of C. G. Starr, A. Momigliano, E. S. Gruen, K. Raaflaub, R. Holloway, R. Palmer, A. Ward, R. Rowland, and R. Saller—many of whom have long suffered my ramblings on the topic. My Illinois colleagues were also eager to save me from error, as I learned from the reflections of D. Queller, T. Krueger, and F. Jaher. Unfortunately none of the aforementioned can be blamed for what remains. I refer less frequently than I could to such basic reference works as those of Mommsen, Willems, Wissowa, Broughton, and Ogilvie, from which I mined material and so shamelessly borrowed, because they could easily be cited on virtually every point. Readers should

tions, powers, and privileges of both patricians and plebeians within the system, and sometimes in the process preserves an office, formula, or term of a supposedly reliable and authentic nature. However, these authentic pieces of information have been subjected to etymological speculation, arbitrarily placed in chronological sequence, and explained by excessive rationalization. Terms such as *patres, conscripti, interrex, patrum auctoritas, maiores* and *minores gentes, curiae, leges, plebiscita,* and a wide variety of legal and religious materials have been used in attempts to identify patricians and plebeians, but although such information is the basis for nearly all attempts to unravel the mysteries of early Roman society, scholars disagree on its reliability.[2] An even greater barrier to consensus is the acceptance by these same scholars of the single most pervasive preconception offered by our sources—namely, that patricians waged a political struggle to defend their privileges against plebeian encroachment.[3] Our sources, in fact, did not know what, if anything, distinguished *patres* from *plebs* politically, and by the time Romans began to comment upon their past centuries after the origins of the Republic, they unconsciously twisted the authentic information they did have into evidence of a struggle between distinct orders.[4] Political conflicts

---

assume a reference to Broughton for all dated republican events; much of the argument advanced herein is the direct result of going gleaning in his volumes. A reference to a work does not necessarily mean agreement, but merely that it is a convenient or adequate collection of ancient and modern literature. Both ancient and modern authors are often lumped together to characterize the nature of the evidence and the debate, but I trust without severe distortion of the original.

  2. Richard, *Origines* (1978), passim, recently presented a complete review of the ancient tradition and the modern scholarship (see also chapter IV above).

  3. None of the other papers in this volume is an exception. Those essays most important to my own offering are those of Richard (chapter IV) and Linderski (chapter VIII), but all the other papers share a common trait in attempting to explain the Conflict of the Orders in traditional fashions. I cannot argue here the many problems raised by my paper or write another essay on the struggle per se in the notes. Suffice it to say that if my thesis is correct, even in part, the very struggle itself must be reexamined.

  4. See Cornell, chapter II above at n. 63, on the nature and existence of authentic and reliable evidence bearing on early Rome. I cannot support Frier, *Annales* (1979): 83ff., 95, and 154, or Raaflaub (chapter I above at n. 41). Both underestimate the religious and legal nature of the surviving evidence by misinterpreting its undifferentiated religious and secular nature. Like our sources, modern scholars have failed to see the Conflict of the Orders as the questionable ingredient added to the tradition: cf. R. Mitchell, "Historical Development" (1984).

between stereotypes were a central theme of the developed story, but the struggle found in our ancient sources has a different form and significance than the struggle portrayed by modern scholars. The latter assume the struggle began in 494 B.C. with the creation of the plebeian tribunes and ended in 287 B.C. with the *lex Hortensia*.[5] However, in our sources the struggle began with Romulus's creation of patricians and plebeians and surfaced several times during the monarchy. Tribunes were created, says Livy, because patricians acted the same way toward plebeians as the tyrannical Tarquins had acted toward patricians.[6] The patrician-plebeian struggle that began with Romulus was not unlike the conflicts between king and patricians or *equites* and senators (or those of *populares* and *novi homines* with *optimates* and *nobiles*) that characterized the late republican tradition. The patrician-plebeian struggle continued, but its contestants were redefined. We cannot be certain when, if ever, the struggle ended.[7]

Thus, while a struggle between contending political forces is a constant in both ancient and modern Roman history, there is no consistent depiction of either patricians or plebeians as those who struggled. For example, we not only have the obvious examples of the "plebeian" names for kings, consuls, and priests, and "plebeian" associations with many of the early architectural and topographical features of early Rome, but we also know of countless "patricians" who supported the plebeian cause by sponsoring or voting for changes that benefited it.[8] Some plebeians also supported patricians,

---

5. This has been the near-unanimous opinion of scholars (cf. chapter I above at nn. 2, 6, and 7, and chapter VII below passim, with references to the literature).

6. Livy refers to the multitude, *plebs*, and *exercitus* that favored Romulus (1.15.8–16.8), and contrasts their alliance with the suspicious *patres*, who as *interreges* were one hundred times worse for the *plebs* than a single ruler. The *patres* also early engaged in factional disputes (1.17). Such examples can be multiplied. For the creation of the tribunate, see Livy 2.21–23 and Ogilvie, *Comm.* (1965): 243ff., for the entire story.

7. For additional argument, see Mitchell, "Historical Development" (1984): 194f. Cf. Brunt, *Conflicts* (1971): 72f., and Mitchell, "Aristocracy" (1974): 45; also chapter II above at nn. 61f.; but I cannot support Guarino's early identification of the *plebs* or the attempts by Develin (chapter XI) and Ungern-Sternberg (chapter XII) to date the end of the struggle to the second Punic War. They know the "traditional" date does not have support in the sources, but too much faith is placed in fragments of Sallust and Livy.

8. Note the treatment by Raaflaub, chapter VII below at n. 25, and especially part 6, with notes and references; Ranouil, *Patriciat* (1975): 64ff.; I. Shatzman, *CQ*

even in their claims to plebeian offices. The groups assumed to be patrician and plebeian were not politically monolithic and they did not always support their "orders," even though the orders were supposedly pitted against each other.

None of these difficulties have stopped modern historians from postulating a political battleground over which specific contestants struggled, just as our sources were not deterred from interpreting every feature of internal Roman history as the consequence of the political conflict waged between two clearly, but inconsistently, labeled groups. Earlier modern writers were skeptical about Rome's earliest history and gradually questioned specific features of the tradition in the attempt to salvage the overall outline. The tendency has been to emphasize the actual historical pattern of the struggle, while showing that details (and characters) were interpolated. The process must be reversed. Certain pieces of specific information have a greater chance of being historically reliable given the method and nature of the material preserved, but their reliability depends upon placing them within an entirely different historical context, outside the traditional Conflict of the Orders.[9]

This essay will demonstrate that the authentic evidence for a distinction between *patres* and *plebs* was religious and legal in nature, and will show that, if the *patres* are defined religiously, they must be removed from the context of the political struggle. The historical drama may unfold as a conflict between contesting political, religious, or economic groups, but these groups were not the *patres* and the *plebs*. These terms refer to identifiable, not always mutually exclusive, groups in Roman history—groups that were not in conflict with each other.

Suppose that the original regal Senate was composed primarily of priests, that priests were the *patres*, who were automatically senators by virtue of their priesthoods; that, initially, their heirs automatically succeeded to their priesthoods and thereby to their Senate seats; and that because the *patres* held their positions for life, they were the

---

23 (1973): 65ff.; and Richard, chapter IV above, part 1, with additional citations. I, too, find little value in the work of Ferenczy, *Patr. State* (1976); cf. chapter XI below, n. 60.

9. I am merely following the suggestion of A. Momigliano, *JRS* 53 (1963): 95, "that working hypotheses are indispensable to any subject."

ones who gave their approval (*patrum auctoritas*) to those public measures found to be in keeping with traditional behavior (*mos maiorum*). Once the *patres* are viewed in the technical sense as priests, we can see the religious nature of the office of *interrex* and the overall religious character of the Senate in general.[10] Let us review both the ancient tradition and its various interpretations in order to establish the nature of the problem.

2. Tradition and Interpretation

According to tradition, Romulus created the original Senate by selecting one hundred fathers (*patres*) from the most prominent clans, the *maiores gentes*, to serve as his senatorial advisors. The descendants of these *patres* were patricians. Subsequent additions to the senatorial aristocracy were made from the Latins, Sabines, and Etruscans, who were considered to have originally been plebeians or equestrians and often were equated with the members of the *minores gentes*. L. Junius Brutus and P. Valerius Publicola are also credited with filling out the Senate in the first year of the Republic by selecting either equestrians or the best plebeians to become senators. Despite confusion and inconsistency in the tradition, presumably senatorial membership made all such senators patricians.[11] However,

---

10. Others have noted the religious nature and importance of certain pieces of information, but have reached different conclusions; cf. Raaflaub, chapter VII below, part 5, where skepticism about the material is followed by a political interpretation of the acceptable religious evidence; Develin, chapter XI below at nn. 33f. notes the religious importance of such material, then disregards it. I want to stress, in contrast, the fundamental fact of the underlying religious importance and nature of much of Roman "political" activity.

11. In general, see Richard, *Origines* (1978), especially 232ff., 419ff., 448ff., 478ff., 519ff., 531ff., and chapter IV above; and Ogilvie, *Comm.* (1965): 61ff. The confusion in the traditions on *maiores* and *minores gentes*, *conscripti*, and the origins of the Senate is considerable. Tarquinius Priscus is credited with creating the *minores* (Cic. *De re pub.* 2.20.35; Livy 1.35.6; Dion. Hal. *Ant. Rom.* 3.67.1), but they are not seen as *patres*, although they are patricians. The *maior gens Claudia* arrived in Rome long after Romulus (Livy 2.16.4; Dion. Hal. *Ant. Rom.* 5.40.3). The *minores* are also seen as republican in origin, created by Brutus (Tac. *Ann.* 11.25) or by Valerius (Festus, p. 304 L, where the actual number of additions [164] to the Senate is reported). Broughton, *Magistrates* I (1951): 1, calls them *conscripti*, which is misleading. Whatever reliable material existed, it was made part of the story that attempted to account for the development of the Senate over a period of time (cf. Luce, *Livy* [1977]: 240ff.).

Livy says the new senators were called *conscripti*. The description of the combined Senate membership as *patres et conscripti* implies a distinction between those *qui patres qui conscripti estis*. In other words, the *patres* were the original senators, and the *conscripti* were those added by enrollment. The problem is to determine who the original senators were and to establish the bases upon which their membership rested.

Fortunately, the association of the *patres* with the Senate is not the only information we have about their origin. Ancient sources tell us that in early Rome only patricians were priests, magistrates, and judges. For example, we are specifically told that, even during the greater part of the Republic, the positions of *rex sacrorum, maiores flamines, curio maximus*, and several priesthoods were held only by patricians, that only senatorial *patres* could become *interreges*, and that only the *patres* in the Senate could give their *auctoritas* to public measures.[12]

Predictably, Romulus is also credited with creating the society and institutions in which such privileges were exercised. Those who monopolized positions and powers are assumed to have been leaders of *gentes*. Very little is known about the *gens*, but presumably several *gentes* constituted a *curia*. Romulus divided the population into thirty *curiae*, and in turn placed ten *curiae* in each of three archaic tribes. The *curia* was certainly the earliest fundamental unit in Roman society; the term *curia* was used when referring to a group of people, to a building in which members met, dined, or worshipped, and also to the Senate, which met *in curiam* and whose members were divided into *decuriae*. Furthermore, an undated law (*lex Ovinia*) called for senators to be selected *curiatim*, by *curiae*, and the theoretical number of senators was certainly based upon the thirty *curiae*, however unlikely the Senate was to have been 300 strong. The *curiae* had their own officials and priests, and in their sacred and secular functions apparently acted in a public, not a private, capacity. The assembly of *curiae*, the *comitia curiata*, voted on the *imperium* of the kings, just as it later voted on the *imperium* of republican magistrates (*lex curiata de imperio*). Modern scholarship does not support the view that only patricians originally belonged to *gentes* and *curiae*, but there is a widespread belief that the patrician *gentes* were those that

---

12. Cicero, *De domo* 38, is standard. See chapter IX below at n. 1 and chapter IV above at nn. 25ff. for additional ancient evidence and modern opinion.

emerged from the *curiae* in possession of both religious and political monopolies. The *curiae*, then, are currently viewed as the bases for Rome's earliest religious, political, and even military system, and, correspondingly, the patricians are seen as those who dominated the system.[13]

Dramatic reforms were made by Servius Tullius, who introduced a system based upon the military unit of the century. To determine a citizen's privileges and responsibilities within the system, Servius introduced the census; to make the census more manageable, he introduced the territorial tribes, which by the middle of the third century, had grown to thirty-five. Property (wealth), not birth, determined one's position within the Servian system. When the Republic began, the assembly of centuries, the *comitia centuriata*, elected magistrates with *imperium* and passed legislation, and the *comitia curiata* was reduced to a secondary role of merely confirming the *imperium* of magistrates and deciding essentially religious and legal questions.[14] The Servian system not only replaced the *curia* as the fundamental

---

13. A. Momigliano discusses the *gens* (in Fustel de Coulanges, *City* [1980]: ix–xxiii) and *curia* (*JRS* 53 [1963]: 108ff., and "Origins of the Republic" [1969]: 22ff.) and offers reconstructions. Palmer, *Arch. Comm.* (1970), especially 131ff. and 178ff., has collected the evidence on the *curiae* and offers a provocative thesis. Despite the interpretations offered recently by C. M. Stibbe, H. S. Versnel and others on the *Lapis Satricanus* (see Bibliography), we have not heard the last word on this important document, and hardly the first word on it from anthropologists: we have much to learn from the works of L. Gernet, M. Detienne, J.-P. Vernant, F. Bourriot, and D. Roussel, to say nothing of M. Gluckman and others (see, e.g., M. Gluckman, *The Judicial Process among the Barotse of Northern Rhodesia* [Manchester, 1955], and *The Ideas in Barotse Jurisprudence* [Manchester, 1972]). E. H. Winter, in *Anthropological Approaches to the Study of Religion*, edited by M. Banton (New York, 1966): 173, notes that "Sir Henry Maine drew a distinction between societies based upon kinship and those based upon territoriality. In its day this was a useful dichotomy but that day has passed, even though some anthropologists appear to be unaware of the fact. . . . [The problem is rather one] of showing how kinship principles are utilized to structure territorial groups." We Romanists, to use John Crook's words, "are too easily content with yesterday's anthropology" (*CR*, n.s., 25 [1975]: 66). Though comparative evidence may not prove useful, at least we ought not to hang on to nineteenth-century comparisons (cf. chapter XI below before n. 9).

14. See E. S. Staveley, *Historia* 5 (1956): 74ff., and Thomsen, *Serv. Tullius* (1980). I believe the *lex curiata de imperio* to have been republican in origin (cf. Ogilvie, *Comm.* [1965]: 733) and military in nature (cf. G. V. Sumner, *JRS* 60 [1970]: 75); cf. also R. Develin, *Mnemosyne*, 4th ser., 30 (1977): 49ff. As to *imperium*, I believe it was always confined to command and was applicable only in the military, not the urban, sphere (cf. Daube, *Law* [1969]: 2f.).

unit of Roman organization, it threatened the control of the patrician *gentes* over Roman society, or so many have assumed. In consequence, the aristocracy expelled the Tarquins because they changed the essential gentilitial structure of Roman society and admitted parvenus into the inner circle of the aristocracy.

The *patres*-patricians are identified as the king's senatorial advisors, who, once the Republic was created, monopolized the most essential secular and sacred positions and, even after they lost their monopoly, retained exclusive control over many of the aforementioned positions and privileges. Thus, since the struggle between patricians and plebeians is depicted as taking place over political and economic reforms, the aforementioned monopolies retained by *patres* and patricians after the struggle ended are considered vestiges of their once total control and examples of the original bases of aristocratic status.[15]

The other protagonists in the struggle, the plebeians, are normally defined negatively, simply as nonpatricians or as the clients of the *patres*, and sometimes they are equated with the army.[16] We do know that plebeians were citizens, that there were plebeian *gentes*, and that the *plebs* presumably were members of the *curiae*. Our sources often use "plebeian" both for destitute citizens of the later Republic and for those who struggled against the patricians in the earlier period. The fundamental distinction between the two orders is often seen as economic: a clash between haves and have-nots. According to this interpretation, during the first 200 years of the Republic, beginning with the creation of the tribunate in 494 B.C., plebeians persisted in their fight against the long-established aristocracy in an effort to obtain offices and priesthoods for ambitious plebeians and to win both economic and political reforms as well as personal freedom for the masses. Supposedly, the poorer plebeians supported the political changes desired by their richer leaders, who reciprocated by championing economic reforms on their behalf. Modern scholars commonly describe this Struggle of the Orders as

---

15. Cf. A. Momigliano, *JRS* 53 (1963): 118; Richard, *Origines* (1978): 312ff., 425, and Raaflaub, chapter VII below at nn. 54f., where aristocratic oppression is stressed. I cannot accept the insistence upon "constitutional" conflicts (see Develin, chapter XI below, part 2).

16. Livy 1.16.8; 2.23; cf. chapter VII below, part 4.

the central feature of Rome's internal historical development from 494 to 287 B.C., when passage of the *lex Hortensia* permitted plebeians to legislate for the entire population unimpeded by the *auctoritas* of the *patres*. Once the plebeian struggle with the patriciate ended, a joint patrician-plebeian aristocracy emerged, and the original distinctions between the two orders were less important or apparent.[17]

However, the limited "documentary" evidence does not support the equation of plebeians, or have-nots, with the politically powerless.[18] Roman kings belonged to *gentes* identified as plebeian; various hills and archaic topographical and architectural features of early Rome have plebeian names; and, finally, the early consular *fasti* contain the names of several magistrates who belonged to *gentes* later considered plebeian. To understate the case, not everyone agrees on the significance of this evidence. Some argue that the plebeian names were interpolations or were the names of those who belonged to patrician families that later died out or underwent *transitio' ad plebem*.[19] Others assume that the early prominence of plebeians was the direct result of a union between king and commons against the barons, and that there indeed had been "plebeian" aristocrats under the kings. Still others argue that neither plebeians nor patricians were differentiated during the monarchy, and that "discrimination was not practiced against the plebeians at least until the middle of the fifth century"[20]—thus the presence of so-called plebeian names in the *fasti*. According to this argument, after the expulsion of the Tarquins, a religious and political monopoly was gradually established by *gentes* who came to consider themselves patricians and who attempted to limit aristocratic status to themselves in an initial act of self-consciousness when, by a law of the Twelve Tables, they prohibited intermarriage between themselves and plebeians. Thus the immediate repeal of the prohibition clearly demonstrates that the patrician *gentes* had been merely temporarily successful in establish-

---

17. Typical are R. T. Ridley, *Latomus* 27 (1968): 554; Shatzman, *Wealth* (1975): 11; P. A. Brunt, *JRS* 72 (1982): 1ff., and Mitchell, "Aristocracy" (1974): 28ff.

18. Contrast: Ogilvie, *Early Rome* (1976): 58f.; Brunt, *Conflicts* (1971): 72; and Raaflaub, chapter VII below.

19. Cf. Palmer, *Arch. Comm.* (1970): 245; Richard, *Origines* (1978): 519f. (note Drummond's criticism of Richard, *JRS* 72 [1982]: 179); chapter VII, part 6 below; I. Shatzman, *CQ* 23 (1973): 65ff., 75ff.; and Ranouil, *Patriciat* (1975): 64ff.

20. Ogilvie, *Comm.* (1965): 237.

ing a reactionary government dominated by a select group of *gentes* only recently identified. The argument supporting the late emergence of the patricians (and plebeians for that matter) permits the admission of these first "plebeians" to the ranks of the aristocracy because such concepts as patrician and plebeian were not fully developed at the time. Nearly every modern solution to the problem of identification is an attempt to account for the presence of plebeian names on the consular *fasti* in such a fashion as to preserve the essential truth that patricians in early Roman history insisted upon their monopoly of religious and political positions and powers in the face of plebeian demands for equity.[21]

In fact, descendants of "patrician" houses did not monopolize the magistracies of the early Republic, and it is impossible to label as patrician those *gentes* whose members exercised *imperium et auspicium*.[22] Only extremely arbitrary interpretations distinguish "patrician" from "plebeian" consuls in Roman history, and in most instances such arbitrariness is compounded by the eventual necessity of postulating separate patrician and plebeian branches of the same *gens* or assuming that certain patricians transferred to the plebeians. Seeking the definition of the *patres* in the political sphere alone fails to establish that certain patrician *gentes* monopolized the Senate, the consulship, or other "political" offices. However, if we return to the religious bases for aristocratic status, we can show that certain *gentes* monopolized certain religious positions that in time became increasingly secular.

3. Priests, patres, *and the Senate*

Since religion and politics were undifferentiated during the regal period, it is reasonable to assume that the regal Senate was composed of priests, or officials with religious authority. Moreover, religious advisors are particularly appropriate to the kings of the Etrus-

21. Cf. chapter IV above at nn. 66f.
22. Cf. chapter VII below, part 5 and notes; chapter XI at nn. 3ff.; and Ranouil, *Patriciat* (1975): 32 and, especially, 45f., 58f., who closes the patriciate in 433 B.C. when the Folian *gens* obtained the military tribunate. Confusion over patrician and plebeian identification is common (note Mommsen and Münzer on the Veturii—see I. Shatzman, *CQ* 23 [1973]: 65ff., for discussion); there is also the problem of the

can period, since they were notorious for their *disciplina*.²³ Doubtless, kings selected advisors from priestly families because traditionally among Etruscans knowledge of rule, rituals, ceremonies, and procedures was transmitted within a family from generation to generation. A similar pattern of inherited priestly positions is clear from the Roman examples. Religious authority has long been recognized as "the first and easiest to monopolize because it implied some special knowledge and some leisure and required that respectability aristocrats always have," and, moreover, "religious authority was indeed what the Roman patricians traditionally tried to keep for themselves."²⁴ Those positions and powers that indicate most clearly who the *patres* were are the very ones they monopolized the longest—certain priesthoods and the *patrum auctoritas*—and all can be shown to be essentially religious in nature.

If senators were priests, this explains the frequency with which the Senate took an interest in the religious life and obligations of the state.²⁵ The Senate regularly considered religious matters before proceeding to political affairs, and often engaged in religious undertakings and observations: the *auspicia* belonged to the *patres* in the Senate; prodigies were reported to the Senate; and the consuls asked the *patres* for priestly advice; the Senate frequently consulted pontiffs, augurs, and *decemviri sacris faciundis* about portents, and the Senate was generally guided by priestly advice. In fact, the Senate often acted like a religious college, meeting in *templa*, and a veil of secrecy existed over the Senate proceedings; senators did not talk about *arcanum sanctumve*, just as priests did not utter their religious secrets publicly or otherwise make them known to the uninitiated.²⁶ In other words, the Senate had a sacred quality—precisely that

---

tribune Sulpicius Rufus and the tribune and *septemvir epulo* Cornelius Dolabella, both of whom appear patrician (see D. R. Shackleton Bailey, *Studies* [1976]: 29f., 131f.; P. A. Brunt *JRS* 72 [1982]: 14).

23. Torelli, *Elogia* (1976): 105ff., and E. Rawson, "Caesar, Etruria and the *Disciplina Etrusca*," *JRS* 68 (1978): 132ff., have admirable presentations of the ancient material and modern scholarship.

24. A. Momigliano, *JRS* 53 (1963): 118.

25. Cicero, *De domo* 1; *Har. resp.* 13; *Ad Att.* 4.2.4, are suggestive but inconclusive. The two speeches are loaded with references to religious and senatorial activities.

26. Willems, *Sénat* II (1885): 299ff.; but E. Rawson, *CQ* 21 (1971): 158ff., is skeptical about much of the religious material. Gellius, *Noctes Atticae* 14.7, reports that

demanded by the traditional role of the republican Senate and precisely that emphasized in this essay. The Senate's authority was religious and moral; it did not legislate or govern directly by law but by emphasizing adherence to ancestral tradition (*mos maiorum*).[27] The Senate's will was not compelling, but its *consulta* were virtually binding because of the *auctoritas* of its members. Priests were too important to such a body not to be members.

In other words, the priests in the Senate were a distinct group set apart by their religious functions, although it has been commonplace to see the religious importance of the *patres* (and patricians) as a consequence of the political power and influence of the *gens*, or as a mere survival of what once had been a more complete monopoly of all secular and sacred positions. Consequently, the explanation for the acquisition of certain positions and powers by specific *gentes* has been essentially political: certain prominent families "usurped" these rights or "extracted" them from the kings. The *patres* alone had the right to veto laws and elections by withholding their *auctoritas*, and they also secured the right to select and to become *interreges*. Still others maintain that the *patres* were distinguished from other senators by their inherited *sacra*, their religious functions. This difficulty can be resolved by abandoning the overwhelmingly political explanations in order to accommodate the acceptable details of the tradition. For example, let us examine Momigliano's assumption that "the first legal definition of the patrician group among the senators" was their right to become *interreges*.[28]

4. Interrex *and* patrum auctoritas

The existence of the title *interrex* (as well as *rex sacrorum*) not only shows that a *rex* once ruled but that the Romans did not fear the

---

the Senate met in *templa* (cf. Mommsen, *Röm. Staatsrecht* III. 2 [1888]: 925ff.), which having been inaugurated by augurs gave senatorial *consulta* a certain potency (cf. Macrob. *Sat.* 3.11.6; Livy 34.44.5; 55.4–8). Livy 23.22.9 reports on the arcane secrets.

27. Macrob. *Sat.* 3.8.9: *mos est inquit institutum patrium pertinens ad religiones caerimoniasque maiorum.*

28. A. Momigliano, *JRS* 53 (1963): 117f. n. 93. Cf. Ogilvie, *Comm.* (1965): 236, 147.

title. Both the *interrex* and *interregnum* are intimately associated with the Senate, and the implication is that senators filled the position and controlled the procedure. Not all senators could become *interreges*, but the reason was not political.[29] Political interpretation of their position as one based upon a right they had usurped or extracted from the kings overlooks an important feature of those who occupied the position: they were priests. If the *patres* monopolized the position of *interrex*, it might follow that they did so at a time when they could still be inter-kings, but they did not have to usurp the right. The list of republican *interreges* reads like a who's who of Roman aristocrats, including members of all the known *maiores* and *minores gentes*. Momigliano does not indicate why only certain *gentes* were eligible, although he apparently assumes that the office reflected their status. We know of approximately 150 *gentes* that belonged to the Roman political establishment at one time or another, but the *interreges* apparently came from no more than approximately 10 percent of that total.[30] Livy implies that the *maiores gentes*, those originally selected by Romulus, chose the *interreges*, and that the position rotated among them until a new consul was chosen.[31] Livy's simple implication disguises the fact that members of the *maiores* (and *minores*) *gentes* monopolized certain priesthoods, that the priests were automatically members of the Senate, and that the *interreges* were selected from the priests. The following discussion of those who became *interreges* after the second Punic War will make the equation clear.

Roman historical information is unreliable for any period, but reports of events prior to the second Punic War are particularly vulnerable to the inclusion of extraneous material and the omission of biographical details about particular individuals. Our information about those who became *interreges* after the war may be more reliable simply because we have more biographical detail about them. On the other hand, the number of *interreges* dramatically decreased after the second Punic War, which can mean either that the number of earlier examples should arouse suspicion or that the great increase in the

---

29. For the *interrex* cf. Richard, *Origines* (1978): 234ff., passim; Palmer, *Arch. Comm.* (1970): 145, 300ff.
30. Palmer, *Arch. Comm.* (1970): 300ff., gives dates and names of *interreges*.
31. Livy 1.17 presents the procedure (cf. Ogilvie, *Comm.* [1965]: 87f., 409f.). See also Jahn, *Interregnum* (1970), especially 55ff.; Momigliano, *JRS* 53 (1963): 11ff.

number of curule magistrates reduced the need for an *interrex*. Of the more than fifty *interreges*, only nine are known after 200 B.C., but M. Valerius Messalla Niger was *interrex* on three of those occasions. Q. Caecilius Metellus Pius Scipio Nasica (consul 52 B.C.) and Servius Sulpicius Rufus (consul 51 B.C.) alone belong to non-*maiores gentes*, but Caecilius was born a Cornelius and adopted by the man he succeeded in the pontifical college in 63 B.C.[32] Four of the *interreges*, in fact, held major priesthoods at the time of their selection as *interrex*, and most significant of all, M. Aemilius Lepidus (consul 46 B.C.), was *only* pontiff at the time of his selection. His curule aedileship is simply speculation based upon the fact that *interreges* were presumed to have been curule magistrates prior to their selection. Two others were priests, but no specific date is known for their entry into their colleges.[33] Only Servius Sulpicius Rufus is not specifically attested to have been a priest. However, the lack of specific information does not rule out the possibility that all were priests at the time they were selected as *interreges*. Servius, for example, numbered many priests among his ancestors and *gentiles*, and, more to the point, he served as the second *interrex* in 52 B.C., when Pompey was declared the sole consul. In 52 B.C. unique occurrences were not unusual. A pontifical office for Servius might be conjectured on the basis of the following: he was an old-fashioned jurisconsult, one who knew the sacred law, and legal wisdom was characteristic of pontiffs.[34] However, we are specifically told that a relative of Servius's, P. Sulp[icius] Q. f. Ruf[us], was a pontiff: supposedly a unique coin from Sinope has established

---

32. More importantly, Caecilius was tribune in 59 B.C., prior to becoming *interrex* in 53 B.C., and presumably was "plebeian." Cf. R. Syme, "Ten Tribunes," *JRS* 53 (1963): 56; Shackleton Bailey, *Studies* (1976): 92ff., 106ff. The problem is resolved if we look at *interreges* as priests rather than as patricians and if we see adrogation as the adoption method whereby public *sacra* were transmitted by inheritance.

33. Palmer, *Arch. Comm.* (1970): 300ff., omits L. Aemilius Paullus (*interrex* 162 B.C.). The information can be found in Broughton, *Magistrates* (1951), for the years 162, 82, 77, 55, 53, and 52 B.C. M. Aemilius Lepidus (consul 46 B.C.) was probably the direct pontifical successor of Aemilius Lepidus Livianus (consul 77 B.C.) between 69 and 60 B.C. The identification of Appius Claudius Pulcher, *interrex* 77 B.C., is a problem because it could be either the father (consul 79 B.C.) or son (consul 54 B.C.). The former died abroad and a return to Rome before his death is required for his *interregnum* (and then back to Macedonia), but no suppositions are needed for his son. Moreover, the son was augur (before 63 B.C.) and nothing prohibited his father holding the same priesthood.

34. See Schulz, *History* (1946): 40ff., cf. 6ff., for the importance of priests to the development of Roman legal science.

the fact. Servius could still have been a member of any one of a number of priesthoods.[35]

Only a priest could be an *interrex* precisely because of the religious nature of the auspices and the fact that *auspicium* returned to the *patres* when no magistrate was in position to exercise it.[36] Moreover, it should be equally apparent that the *patrum auctoritas* was not a political veto but the collective religious sanction voted by the priestly senators—the *patres*. Their approval satisfied ancestral custom and secured divine favor. Even requiring the *patres* to give their approval prior to a *comitia* vote was nothing more than the *patres* giving their *auctoritas* in the fashion of favorable auspices. What else was the *praerogativa* vote in the *comitia*? There are equally strong indications that the *princeps senatus* was also a priest. To be called upon to speak first in the Senate was hardly an honor to be given to anyone but a priest, particularly early in the history of the state when divine guidance was perhaps more eagerly, routinely, and honestly sought.[37] If *patres* were technically those priests with automatic seats in the Senate who gave their approval (*patrum auctoritas*) to those public measures found to be in keeping with the *mos* of the *maiores*, then the traditional "political" distinctions between *patres* and *plebs*, as well as the historicity of their conflict, are placed very much in doubt. This interpretation gains support from another of Momigliano's assumptions that "the same *patres* who monopolized the right to appoint the *interrex* may also have acquired the right to be succeeded automatically by their sons in the Senate—thence the name *patricii*."[38]

5. *Inherited Senatorial Positions and* toga praetexta

Unfortunately, no evidence of automatic succession to senatorial seats has been produced, and it has been thought that none existed. In

---

35. Broughton, *Magistrates* II (1951): 236, but note p. 292 and supplement p. 61f. for some confusion in the filiation of the pontiff.
36. See A. Magdelain, "*Auspicia*" (1964), for a political interpretation.
37. Cf. Mommsen, *Röm. Staatsrecht* III.2 (1888): 975 n. 2 (contrast 868 n. 4). Cf. Broughton, *Magistrates* II (1951): 130 n. 1, for the outline of the controversy over the question of the *princeps senatus* after Sulla.
38. Momigliano, *JRS* 53 (1963): 117f. and n. 93. Cf. Palmer, *Arch. Comm.* (1970): 268; and chapter XI below at n. 40.

fact, evidence exists that permits a reconciliation of the reliable details of the tradition. Proof of automatic, inherited senatorial membership, so often postulated by modern scholars, comes from the period of the second Punic War, in the context of the story about Gaius Valerius Flaccus, who was forced by the *pontifex maximus*, Publius Licinius Dives Crassus, to become the priest of Jupiter (*flamen Dialis*). Valerius is a classical example of how the priesthood made the man. With all the fire of a recent convert, he put aside his previous roguish ways and, in his attention to his priestly duties, became a model for all to follow. He also sought to reinstate a custom that the conduct of previous *flamines* had caused to lapse: by virtue of his office, he exercised the right to enter the Senate. Publius Licinius, a praetor, removed him, but Valerius appealed to the plebeian tribunes on the grounds that an old custom granted the *flamen* a Senate seat, a privilege acquired together with the curule chair and the *toga praetexta*.[39]

The praetor considered Valerius's demand anachronistic, based upon old annalistic information rather than upon recent practice, which indicated that no *flamen* had exercised such a privilege within the memory of the fathers or grandfathers. But the tribunes stated that, although previous *flamines* had been at fault in permitting the right to slip, the privilege should not be denied Valerius, and the *flamen* was introduced to the Senate. Although Valerius may have owed his seat more to his own merit than to any right of the office, he nevertheless clearly received what was legally his by virtue of his priesthood. Surely other priests could also lay claim to Senate seats. To illustrate, I shall concentrate on several points raised by Valerius's example and by his statement that he was entitled not only to a Senate seat and a curule chair but also to the right to wear the *toga praetexta*.

The *toga praetexta* was the characteristic garb of curule magistrates, certain priests, and other less well-known officials; it was also characteristically worn by certain boys from twelve to seventeen years of age—the toga worn before they donned the *toga virilis*. Originally the *toga praetexta* must have been a sign of distinction: Etruscan kings wore the toga and doubtless established the prece-

---

39. Livy 27.8.4–10; cf. Palmer, *Arch. Comm.* (1970): 268, cf. 274f.; Richard, *Origines* (1978): 240ff.

dent for those who were their secular and sacred heirs.[40] Clearly the *toga praetexta* was reserved as a symbol of honor, worn only by the sons of priests and magistrates, and indicating that as their sons they were entitled to certain privileges and rights precisely because of their kinship. One of these was the privilege of accompanying their fathers into the Senate house. Gellius preserves an extremely important story of Marcus Cato's about Lucius Papirius, who was given the honorific nickname "*Praetextatus*" because, after accompanying his father to the Senate, Lucius refused to divulge the nature of the senatorial debate to his mother.[41] Supposedly the Papirius in the story was the last *praetextatus* permitted to attend Senate meetings. He is thought to have been the censor of 272 B.C., who died in office and is not known to have held any other position. However, against the view that Papirius, the censor of 272 B.C., was the *Praetextatus* in question or that he was the last son of a senator permitted to attend Senate meetings, we have Polybius's criticism of those writers who presented too "dramatic a picture of the gloomy appearance of the Senate at the beginning of the Second Punic War, while in the same breath they tell us that fathers brought their sons from the age of twelve upwards to the Senate house and that they attended the debate and did not divulge a word of it even to their nearest relatives."[42] Possibly the admission of some *praetextati* to the Senate stopped during the Samnite Wars, but the sons of other senators continued to attend and, more importantly, the *toga praetexta* symbolized their right both to attend and to automatically succeed to the Senate seat on their fathers' demise. Sons of senators were permitted to attend Senate meetings in order to introduce them to the proceedings of the *curia*, because Senate membership was their hereditary right. The right also imposed certain obligations upon those who enjoyed it.

40. L. B. Warren, "Roman Triumphs and Etruscan Kings: The Changing Face of the Triumph," *JRS* 60 (1970): 60ff.; cf. Livy 1.8.3; 7.1.5; 27.37.13; 34.7.2; 45.40.8; Cic. *Pro Sestio* 69.144; Macrob. *Sat.* 1.6.12–14. Palmer, *Religion* (1974): 7ff., 13, 25f., has interesting observations; as does Wiseman, *Clio's Cosmetics* (1979): 127. Note J. Briscoe, *Comm.* (1973): 85.
41. Gell. *Noctes Atticae* 1.23; cf. Macrob. *Sat.* 1.6.19ff.
42. Polyb. 3.20.3. The translation is by I. Scott-Kilvert (Harmondsworth, England, 1970). See Walbank, *Comm.* I (1957): 332f., for criticism and references.

6. Common Religious Obligations of Priests and patres

The identification of priests with *patres* is confirmed by the fact that they were both set apart from the rest of society by a unique marriage ceremony, *confarreatio*, used only by patricians.[43] The *confarreatio* ceremony was assumed to be the oldest form of marriage and, by historical times, was generally confined to certain archaic priesthoods. In the archaic and more conservative priesthoods, succession required an unpolluted heir and adherence to certain rules governing marriage and personal conduct. Some priests had to be children of a *confarreatio* marriage and themselves had to marry by the *confarreatio* ceremony. Marriage by *confarreatio* meant that a wife came under her husband's *manus* and occupied the position of priestess within the cult. In some cases, the position of the wife/priestess was so important and the marriage vow by *confarreatio* so indissoluble that priests were forced to resign if their wives died.[44] Usually the children of priests and priestesses served as their attendants. Macrobius reports that Mercury was called Camillus because he was "the attendant of the gods" and notes that *camillus* and *camilla* were attendants of the *flamines* and *flaminicae* selected from the *nobiles et investes* youth, who had to be *patrimi et matrimi*, or youths whose parents were still both alive. As Servius explained the meaning of this requirement, children who were *patrimi et matrimi* had parents who had been married by *confarreatio*.[45] Thus, attendants of priests were children of *confarreatio* marriages whose parents were both alive. Of course, if at all possible, such acolytes were the priests' own children, but failing that, the criteria for selecting attendants shows that the choice was

---

43. Linderski, chapter VIII below, presents the essential ancient and modern testimony.

44. Corbett, *Marriage* (1930): 71ff., presents most of the testimony. Watson, *Law* (1970): 32, recognizes the realities: "Even if this form was not restricted to the aristocracy by law, it was in fact." Cf. G. Williams, "Some Aspects of Roman Marriage Ceremonies and Ideals," *JRS* 48 (1958): 23f., for interesting points about *univira*, the religious nature of which must be further analyzed.

45. Macrob. *Sat.* 3.8.7; to which add Gell. *Noctes Atticae* 1.12; Festus, p. 821 L; Livy 37.3.6. Servius, on *Georg.* 1.31, is often dismissed. See Linderski, chapter VIII below at nn. 20f., for details. One can begin the search for Greek parallels with L. Robert, "AMPHITHALEIS," *Harv. Stud. Class. Philol.* Suppl. 1 (1940): 509ff., and the connection between *paides amphithaleis* and those who were *patrimi et matrimi* (cf. Gordon, ed., *Myth* [1981]: 156.).

made from others who were *patrimi et matrimi*. If no natural child qualified, or no adoption by adrogation occurred, then other *praetextati, pueri et puellae* who were *patrimi et matrimi* were selected as acolytes. The priestly attendants were initiated into religious rituals, ceremonies, and mysteries and were required to marry by *confarreatio* if they wished to become priests. Presumably, death of a parent could impede the automatic succession of a son (or selection of a daughter) if death occurred before the child's marriage. Once married by *confarreatio*, the youth was free to take up the religious position as part of his inheritance. More than one candidate for a vacancy might exist and over the years the traditional practice of selecting a successor by the cooptation of new members by old was more and more restricted and altered by some combination of cooptation and election.

We know of several examples where either specific *gentes* monopolized specific cults or inauguration to a priestly position was required of particular individuals. The examples come from those priesthoods identified as patrician monopolies. They include the poorly documented *Luperci, Salii, Fetiales*, as well as the most archaic and most persistent religious sodality in Rome, the Arval Brethren, whose imperial inscriptions tell us a great deal about their priesthood. For example, within the Arval Brethren were *pueri praetextati patrimi et matrimi senatorum filii*—attendants who were sons of senators and whose parents were alive. The attendants were treated in the fashion of priests' sons, not simply as assistants.[46] Singling out *praetextati*, senators' sons, for religious instruction and training paralleled republican practices. Moreover, it reaffirms the connection between senators and priests, and establishes the fact that *praetextati* in the Senate continued to enjoy the prospect of an inherited position in the *curia*. The republican Senate, like the imperial *curia* and *decuria*, definitely had a religious component among its members, and the young sons of senators were welcomed into the body as a matter of course.[47] Since

46. G. Henzen, *Acta Fratrum Arvalium* (Berlin, 1874, repr. 1967): 12ff., 42ff. Cf. Momigliano, *JRS* 53 (1963): 99ff., 115ff., esp. 118f.; most recently, R. Syme, *Some Arval Brethren* (Oxford, 1980).

47. Note *ILS* no. 6121 (*CIL* IX, no. 338); Mommsen, *Röm. Staatsrecht* I³ (1887): 476·n. 2 (cf. id., *Inscriptiones regni Neapolitani Latinae*, no. 635); Willems, *Sénat* I (1878): 143f. *Praetextati* are also found in Thamugadi (*CIL* VIII, no. 2403), but I have made little effort to search out other *praetextati* in *decuriae* of the Empire and

the *praetextati* so often mentioned were sons of senators (both secular and sacred) then those who automatically succeeded to priesthoods held by their fathers also succeeded to their Senate seats, which were automatically held by certain priests.

7. *Succession to Priestly Office*

Although the taboos associated with the more conservative archaic religious positions restricted the politically ambitious members who held them,[48] tradition still demanded that they remain in the control of specific families. For example, the selection of a successor to Servius Cornelius Lentulus, *flamen Dialis* under Augustus and Tiberius, followed the traditional practice of nominating three patrician sons of parents married by *confarreatio*, one of whom would be made *flamen*. The latter, in turn, had to be married by the same archaic ceremony. Tacitus informs us that this form of marriage was out of favor, difficult, and avoided, probably because the wife of a *flamen* passed from her father's *potestas* to her husband's. Tiberius modified the rule to permit the *flaminica* to be under her husband's control only in her religious duties; otherwise she retained the normal position of women. Doubtless this refers to her right to inherit and to own property generally. Also, divorce was virtually impossible for such priests, as it was for all those married by *confarreatio*. Such restrictions explain why, when Augustus made Servius Cornelius *flamen* in 11 B.C., he was the first to hold the priesthood since Lucius Cornelius Merula, consul in 87 B.C. Moreover, since he was succeeded by his own son, the priesthood appears to have been traditionally associated with the Cornelian *gens*, which filled a large percentage of the known republican *flamonia*. Thus, the *flamen Dialis* who demanded his seat in the Senate as a right of office based his claim on a priesthood normally passed from father to son or to des-

---

offer these to elicit response. Augustus, *Res gestae* 5.25, mentions priests in the Senate, and he encouraged senators to bring their sons to the *curia* (Suet. *Div. Aug.* 38.2), although they were older than *praetextati*.

48. Wissowa, *Religion* (1912): 71, 501ff.; Linderski, chapter VIII below at nn. 2ff. and passim.

ignated heir. That sons did not always succeed fathers was in part due to obvious disadvantages certain priesthoods imposed upon their holders. In fact, some priesthoods were considered such political liabilities that ambitious aristocrats certainly ignored traditional religious practices in order to escape the responsibility.[49] However, there were other reasons for the failure of sons to succeed fathers. The political climate determined that Cornelius Merula would be succeeded by Gaius Julius Caesar. Interestingly enough, Caesar—a patrician—married a Cornelia prior to his father's death, although some assume not before 84 B.C. Although Sulla forced Caesar to resign (or never permitted him to take up) the priesthood, Caesar may have felt entitled to such an inheritance. When Caesar was nominated as a *flamen* he was only thirteen years old and could not have been expected to assume the priesthood without years of training. We are not certain what the required age was for such a priesthood, but Caesar was only seventeen years old when Sulla returned; doubtless this was the reason he could be dismissed from his religious office. As a suggestion of how complicated and yet predictable priestly succession could be, it should be noted that Cornelia was forced to give up her inheritance, legacies, and dowries; conceivably she carried the key to the Cornelian flaminate. Similarly, when Caesar was made pontiff in 73 B.C., he succeeded C. Aurelius Cotta, kinsman of Caesar's mother. Normally such selections are explained politically, but there were probably religious reasons that dictated the decisions, as well as religious requirements that had to be met.[50]

There were certainly other cases where no son existed, where the son had not married by *confarreatio*, where the father had died before the son's marriage, or where the son was prohibited from suc-

---

49. For restrictions placed on the *flamen*, see Gell. *Noctes Atticae* 10.15; Tac. *Ann.* 3.58, 59, 71, and 4.16 for sons succeeding fathers in a priesthood. Cf. Lewis, *Priests* (1955): 74f., and nos. 18 and 33 (pp. 30, 33) for discussion. Linderski, chapter VIII below, n. 4, has presented the essentials.

50. On Caesar's flaminate, see Linderski, chapter VIII below at nn. 37ff., with notes. Suet. *Div. Iul.* 1, and Plut. *Caesar* 1, emphasize Cornelia's dowry and ancestry. L. R. Taylor, "Caesar's Early Career," *CP* 36 (1941): 113ff., presents the important information and describes the difficulties surrounding Caesar's flaminate; cf. Taylor's other articles for additional details: "The Election of the *pontifex maximus* in the Late Republic," *CP* 37 (1942): 421ff.; "Caesar's Colleagues in the Pontifical College," *AJP* 63 (1942): 385ff.; "The Rise of Julius Caesar," *G&R* 4 (1957): 10ff. E. Badian,

ceeding for a wide range of reasons. Quintus Fabius Maximus, for example, had been an augur for sixty-two years, but his own son predeceased him so his successor, in 203 B.C., was his grandson, who died in 196 B.C. Livy says the latter died a youth, before he had held a magistracy: in other words, he was too young to be succeeded by his own son.[51] The example of the Fabii is one illustration of why we cannot always count on a priest being succeeded by his immediate descendant even in the advantageous priesthoods.

However, the large number of examples of members of the same *gens* succeeding to priesthoods held by fathers or kinsmen suggests that for a considerable period such succession must have been viewed as an obligation. For what other reason would a *pontifex maximus* be empowered "to take" priests and priestesses to fill vacancies?[52] The *flamen Dialis* was not the only archaic priesthood filled by members of the same *gens* by means of forced inauguration. In 180 B.C. the *pontifex maximus*, Gaius Servilius, fined the *duumvir navalis*, Lucius Cornelius Dolabella, and threatened him with court action if he refused to resign his secular office in order to be inaugurated *rex sacrorum*. Cornelius eventually relented, but a thunderstorm, presumably, interrupted the inauguration (Livy 40.42.10), and religious scruple prevented his taking the office. Had he become *rex*, he would have succeeded Gnaeus Cornelius Dolabella.[53] Gaius Valerius Flaccus, Lucius Cornelius Dolabella, and Servius Cornelius Lentulus were forced to assume their respective religious positions although all

---

"Caesar's *cursus* and the Intervals Between Offices," *JRS* 49 (1959): 81ff., makes the point that Caesar, as a patrician, may have been exempt from the restrictions of the *lex annalis*. Caesar's early career must be viewed again in the light of his patrician (= priestly) status. F. Münzer, *RE* 10. 477, thinks the *maiores* flaminates may have been a monopoly of the Julian *gens* (note Sextus Caesar, *flamen Quirinalis*, reported in Cic. *Har. resp.* 12). The entire problem of "patrician" priesthoods is compounded when seen in political terms (cf. Linderski, chapter VIII below, n. 48, on the question of "plebeian" *flamines Martiales*).

51. Livy 30.26.7–10; 33.42.6 (cf. Plut. *Fabius* 1.5; 24.4). Note that Q. Fulvius became *triumvir epulo, tum praetextatus* (Livy 40.42.7).

52. Gell. *Noctes Atticae* 1.12.15. See Linderski, chapter VIII below at n. 41, for discussion and bibliography.

53. Livy 40.42.8–10. Botsford, *Assemblies* (1909): 327f., insists that the *pontifex maximus* had judicial authority over those under his supervision. However, many of the examples concern creating such an authority—unless some persons were obligated to take religious positions. See n. 66 below for bibliography on the *pontifices*.

were reluctant to do so. Clearly, they were the legitimate and obvious heirs to such positions, which they viewed as liabilities—hindrances to their public, or secular, ambitions.

On the other hand, not all religious positions were considered impediments to personal and political secular activity. The aristocracy eagerly sought some priesthoods, and in time these same priesthoods became virtually magisterial and were filled, in part, by elections. The impression remains, however, that even such offices were often inherited, even though they were viewed as too important to be allowed to remain the monopoly of a particular *gens*.

We have a glimmer of the situation in Cicero's words, however biased and subjective they may be. He maintains that Pompey's augural position was properly his son's inheritance. Also, when lamenting the death of Quintus Hortensius, who had coopted him into the augurate, Cicero said that he considered Hortensius as a father: *ex quo augurum institutis in parentis eum loco colere debebam*.[54] Cicero replaced Publius Licinius Crassus, who had fallen at Carrhae in 53 B.C., but Publius probably succeeded Lucius Licinius Lucullus (consul 74 B.C.) in 56 B.C., who in turn probably succeeded Lucius Licinius Crassus (consul 95 B.C.), who died in 91 B.C.[55] We are further informed of a M. Licinius Crassus (consul 30 B.C.), who was an augur, conceivably after Cicero's death in 43 B.C., and also of M. Licinius Crassus Frugi, who was perhaps his successor.

Of course, the most celebrated case of the right to succeed to a desirable priesthood is certainly that of Cn. Domitius, tribune of 104 B.C., who passed a bill to fill vacancies in the pontifical college by popular vote, presumably because he had not been coopted to fill the position held by his father. The story is confused and complicated, and the debate over the issue somewhat misleading, but that Gnaeus claimed the right to succeed to his father's pontifical position is not at issue. Livy's summary actually states that Gnaeus Domitius was selected *pontifex maximus* in 103 B.C. as a result of his law, and it is entirely possible that he had automatically succeeded his father as *pontiff* sometime after the latter's last appearance in history in 114 B.C.[56] The law of Domitius may not have been the popular mea-

54. Cic. *Brut.* 1.1; *Phil.* 2.2.4; 13.5.12.
55. Cf. Shatzman, *Wealth* (1975): 274f.
56. Broughton, *Magistrates* I (1951): 556; cf. 565 for references to ancient sources. As a sample of the debate, see E. Badian, "Sulla's Augurate," *Arethusa* 1

sure many believe it to be, since the voting was restricted to seventeen tribes, and archaic tradition may be more a factor in the measure than we have perceived.

Quite clearly, religious custom demanded that priesthoods be filled by traditional *gentiles*, and, as Martha Lewis has recognized, even during the Empire religious honors long continued "to be built up in noble houses, and sons strove for their deceased father's priesthoods, as they had done in the Republic."[57] In fact, Octavian was among those who considered the priesthoods part of his inheritance from Julius Caesar, just as Sextus Pompey's coins show that he actually laid claim to his father's priesthood.[58] Yet, to say they strove for the priesthoods is not the same as to say they claimed them as an inheritance, which was clearly so often the case. The evidence suggests that such claims were made by those who considered themselves automatically the heirs to such priesthoods, and this fact helps to explain another feature of the *patres*.

8. Maiores *and* minores

Valerius, the reluctant *flamen*, and Cornelius, the *flamen Dialis* under Tiberius, were only two of several members of their respective *gentes* who were important priests, many of whom were *maiores flamines*. Since both the Valeria and the Cornelia were *maiores gentes*, the conclusion might well be that among the criteria for selection as a *maior flamen* was membership in a *maior gens*. In fact, both the *maiores* and *minores gentes*[59] may have acquired their original characterization as

---

(1968): 30, 42 n. 22. But it helps to know that Cn. Domitius was *pontifex* (consul 162 B.C.) and L. Domitius Cn.f. was senator in 129 B.C. and could very well have been a missing priest in the link of four consecutive *pontifices* (see Broughton, *Magistrates*, suppl. 23).

57. Lewis, *Priests* (1955): 18 nn. 56, 94ff. Cf. ibid., 106 n. 3, for examples of priests who succeeded to their positions on the demise of a relative or held the same priesthood as a kinsman.

58. The key to Octavian's inheritance may be his use of the *lex curiata* (App. *Bell. civ.* 3.94; Dio 46.47.5) I think it unlikely that Octavian became pontiff in 47 B.C., succeeding L. Domitius Ahenobarbus, since Cn. Domitius was pontiff about 45 B.C. Octavian's succession to Julius Caesar's pontificate was achieved by adrogation. See Broughton, *Magistrates* II (1951): 292, 314.

59. See Richard, *Origines* (1978): 319ff.; Ranouil, *Patriciat* (1975): 125ff.; and chapter VII below at nn. 123f.

maiores and *minores* because they monopolized the *maiora* and *minora flamonia* respectively. Of the nearly two dozen known *flamines*, two-thirds came from *maiores gentes*, and the others (including the *minor flamen Carmentalis*, Popillius) all belonged to old, established Roman *gentes* that may well have been either *maiores* or *minores gentes*. Where automatic succession was impossible, prohibited, or altered by subsequent changes in procedure, the college's existing membership may have coopted according to agnate kinship or from other appropriate *maiores* or *minores gentes*, or some combination of cooptation and election may have used a preliminary list of eligible candidates drawn up from the *gentes*. Such an explanation absolves us of any necessity to follow one of the several unconvincing arguments that the *maiores* were earlier than the *minores*, that the former were patricians and the latter were plebeians, or that they were composed of different ethnic groups. In sum, *maiores* and *minores gentes* were the *gentes* originally associated with the *maiores* and *minores flamines* (or similar distinguished religious corporations) because they monopolized the priesthoods.[60]

The fact that certain priesthoods were dominated by a single family or *gens* and succession was normally hereditary is clearly demonstrated by a perusal of Broughton's "Index of Careers."[61] The evidence is so strong that often it is possible to postulate an otherwise unattested priesthood for a certain member of a *gens* in order to bridge the gap between two known holders of the position. In other words, though there is evidence that certain religious positions and powers remained the monopoly of a particular group of *gentes*— most of whom are usually thought to have been patrician—there is no comparable evidence that these same *gentes* maintained control of essentially political and secular positions. Conclusions drawn from examples of those priests who succeeded to positions held by their

60. Ogilvie, *Comm.* (1965): 147, believes that the only known *minor gens*, *Papiria*, was added because "the expanding city required an enlarged religious establishment." Palmer, *Arch. Comm.* (1970): 244, defines "a *gens minor* as a patrician family whose sons were selected to an imperial magistracy after 444 and held the chief pontificate." The only other non-*maiores* or *minores gentes* to obtain flaminates were the Julia, Quinctilia, Sulpicia, and Veturia (on the latter see I. Shatzman, *CQ* 23 [1973]: 65ff.). See Cic. *Ad fam.* 9.21 (cf. Livy 8.37); Festus, p. 137 L and 144 L; Gaius, *Inst.* 1.115.

61. Broughton, *Magistrates* II (1951): 524ff., plus the supplement.

fathers (or gentilitial kinsmen) have misled many scholars into claiming that the aristocratic monopoly over such priesthoods is evidence of the *gens'* political clout, but such claims disregard the religious requirements for succession and completely ignore the rights and duties of the heir and the extent to which training and expertise were required of priests.[62] The *patres* were conceived in religion and finally retained only the initial features of their origin. To attempt to define them in political terms, originally or ultimately, is to strip them of their roots. Religious office and power determined who the *patres* were from the beginning: they were the automatic members of the republican Senate, just as they were the (only) members of the regal council of advisors.

Modern historians have customarily stressed the religious obligations and practices that dominated every aspect of Roman life, but they have failed to give a place of honor to Roman priests. Religious positions were prized by aristocrats, who often mentioned them first among their honors.[63] Although scholars have commonly emphasized that the major priesthoods were held by those who were politically successful and that the political elite dominated the religious offices to further their secular power, some priests were politically successful *because* they were priests, and the entire "problem of the 'pollution' of Roman religion with Roman politics is almost entirely one of our making."[64] Religious prestige allowed some priests to acquire political influence because, as priests, they already monopolized one of the most significant features of early Roman society—the law. Priests were the only known jurists in early Roman society; in fact, the pontifical college in particular is considered the "cradle

---

62. Willems, *Sénat* II (1885): 302; Frier, *Annales* (1979): 95f. D. E. Hahm, *TAPA* 94 (1963): 73ff., is typical of political interpretation: "A priesthood was normally bestowed, not as reward for meritorious service, but as a form of patronage to promising young men who were aspiring to political office" (84). Hahm points to the succession of kinsmen without realizing the religious requirements (83f., especially n. 35). Unfortunately, political interpretations of Roman religion and priesthoods are standard even in my own work (e.g., in my "Aristocracy" [1974]: 38f. and notes).

63. Cf. Lewis, *Priests* (1955): 18f.

64. M. Beard, *JRS* 71 (1981): 204 (rev. of J. H. W. G. Liebeschuetz, *Continuity and Change in Roman Religion* [Oxford, 1979]). Note also chapter X below for religious interpretation of a law in the Twelve Tables, and R. Develin, *Journ. of Rel. Hist.* 10 (1978): 3ff.

of the science of private law," but sacred and public law were also under priestly control and were not originally distinct categories.[65]

9. Pontifices

Early in Rome's history, the *pontifices* may have been less important than other priests, but they expanded and developed their power and influence step by step with the development of the Republic. Their *auctoritas* ultimately lay in their control of the essentially undifferentiated religious and legal material, which they not only wrote, collected, and preserved, but also changed by means of interpretation. Their importance was the result of their expertise in, and monopoly of, legal secrets, procedures, and rituals, and of determining the proper times to undertake private and public measures through setting up the calendar, which they also controlled. Because of the nature of their specialized knowledge, pontiffs gradually became more magisterial and administrative than priestly.[66]

Since it is inconceivable that such priests were not automatically senators, we must change the usual view that "ordinarily" the *pontifex maximus* was a member of the Senate, who "usually had been a curule magistrate,"[67] to one stressing the *pontifices*' automatic senatorial membership based on their importance to the system. Senators and priests, in particular the pontiffs, shared a common con-

---

65. See Schulz, *History* (1946): esp. 6ff.

66. The original nature of the *pontifices* (in contrast to that of the *rex sacrorum* and *flamines*) has long been disputed. Essentially, it is a question of the political power of the *pontifex* and the archaic religious practices of the other priests. Mommsen changed his mind, but no explanation of the legal significance of the *pontifices* is satisfactory. Fowler, *Experience* (1911): 270ff., may be the best; but Schulz, *History* (1946): 11ff., stresses the prior political success of those who became pontiffs; and De Sanctis, *Storia* I² (1956): 297ff., sees them as involved in political power struggles. All too often pontiffs and politics have been lumped together (cf. L. R. Taylor, *Party Politics in the Age of Caesar* [Berkeley and Los Angeles, 1949]: 76ff., 90ff., and, earlier, Jörs, *Privatr.* [1927]: 65f.; A. H. J. Greenidge, *Engl. Hist. Rev.* 20 [1905]: 10ff., and *Publ. Life* [1901]: 87f., 185f.). Despite Mommsen (cf. *Röm. Staatsrecht* II.1³ [1887]: 20ff.), the secular political and legal powers and jurisdiction of the pontiff may have been discarded (cf. J. Bleicken, *Hermes* 85 [1957]: 345ff.) in favor of a simple administrator (as Mercklin, *Cooptation* [1848]: 85ff., long ago advocated). Ogilvie, *Comm.* (1965): 100f., characterizes the debate.

67. Frier, *Annales* (1979): 96.

cern for *ius*, *mos*, and *fas*.⁶⁸ Moreover, until the reforms of Gaius Gracchus, the Senate remained the sole source of *iudices* because, for a considerable time, the only legal authorities in the state were senatorial priests.⁶⁹

However, the publication of the *legis actiones* in 304 B.C. made law and legal procedure public knowledge, and in 287 B.C. the *lex Hortensia* opened market days for legal business.⁷⁰ Although gradually private and public law became distinct from sacred law, still some priests continued to exercise a certain amount of influence over private and public affairs. In fact the increased legal activity required of the *pontifices* following the publication of the *legis actiones* may have resulted in the increase in the membership of the pontifical (and augural) college in 300 B.C. Their importance to the workings of state and society meant that such priestly positions continued to be monopolized by the aristocracy, which recognized the political significance of the priesthoods.

10. Fetials and Legates

The presence of priests in the Senate and their importance in public activities also help to identify many senators whose official positions are unspecified. Some senators were known only to have been priests; still others *might* have been priests.⁷¹ Some *gentes*, or families within a *gens*, that had held strictly religious positions emerge in time as political *novi homines*. Their late political emergence may belie their

---

68. Schulz, *History* (1946): 15ff.
69. The latest word on the *lex repetundarum*, the *lex Acilia*, and Gaius Gracchus is A. N. Sherwin-White, "The Lex Repetundarum and the Political Ideas of Gaius Gracchus," *JRS* 72 (1982): 18ff. See now my article on Roman law and Roman priests in the *Illinois Law Review*, 1984, no. 3, 541–60.
70. On the *lex Hortensia* and market days, see Macrob. *Sat.* 1.16.30, and Mitchell, "Historical Development" (1984): 197f. for discussion, and 193ff. for criticism of the view that the *lex Hortensia* ended the struggle and was even part of it (contrast chapter XI below, at n. 30, and chapter XII, part 3, for more traditional interpretations).
71. For example, P. Volumnius was *minor* pontiff before 69 B.C. and *iudex* in 66 (see Gruen, *Last Generation* [1974]: 195 n. 124, for the evidence and for reservations); but even more significant, because it was before the change in the composition of *iudices* in 70 B.C., C. Sulpicius Galba, pontiff before 73, was rejected as *iudex* in 70 B.C. (Cic. *Verr.* 2.1.18) and presumably was senatorial (cf. Broughton, *Magis-*

long religious prominence within the community: they may well have belonged to a hidden religious aristocracy, imperfectly recorded and poorly understood by our sources.[72] For example, perhaps the shadowy fetials were never actually an independent priesthood but were senatorial priests assigned diplomatic functions. If fetials originally were senators, this would explain the parallel fetial and senatorial function in "international relations" and account for the continuity between fetials and later senatorial legates.

Of the twenty patrician fetials, only four were customarily chosen to serve in an embassy. The principal emissary was called the *pater patratus*, a designation that went with the assignment, not a title borne for life. The possible meanings of the title include "one who is made father" or "the father accomplisher," but the best translation is "the father of the fatherhood." In this sense, the *pater patratus* was the spokesman for the *patres* in the Senate—the priest selected for that particular diplomatic mission.[73]

In the Greek world, diplomatic missions commonly employed *kerykes* and *presbeis*. The latter were quite comparable to Roman senators, both terms referring to the institutional affiliation and advanced age of their holders. Fetials were equivalent to the *kerykes*, who were professional messengers of the gods and made full use of

---

trates II [1951]: 136 n. 4; note the attempts to give him a qualifying position [other than pontifical] before 70 B.C.). Broughton, *Magistrates* II; Taylor, *Voting Distr.* (1960); Gruen, *Last Generation;* and Shatzman, *Wealth* (1975), have all appended lists of senators, many of whom lack "qualifying" positions. The number of unknown priests is equally large. We must also add the observation of L. R. Taylor and R. T. Scott, *TAPA* 100 (1969): 553ff., on the persons "known to have participated in senatorial *relationes* before they held curule office": all were public priests. They all were therefore *senatores pedarii*.

72. Again, a few examples suffice: Taylor, *Voting Distr.* (1960): 203, cites the example of an L. Claudius, *rex sacrorum* (cf. Broughton, *Magistrates* II [1951], suppl. p. 15); see P. A. Brunt, *JRS* 72 (1982): 16, for a pontiff named M. Pinarius Natta (Cic. *De domo* 118). The Pinarii had traditional associations with the cult and worship of Hercules (cf. Livy 1.7.3ff.). Q. Fabius Pictor, the annalist, was perhaps a priest (Livy 22.57.5 reports his religious mission to Delphi) and his son (see Frier, *Annales* [1979]: 231) was *flamen Quirinalis*. Was the father a *flamen* or a *minor* pontiff? He was certainly an important senator (Frier, *Annales*, 234ff.). C. Papirius was pontiff when called upon by the consul to write the terms of surrender for the Faliscans in 241 B.C. Presumably he was a senator.

73. Livy 1.24; Ogilvie, *Comm.* (1965): 110f. and 127ff. Note also the Papirius mentioned in the previous note, a pontiff who was author of surrender terms in 241 B.C.

priestly symbols and trappings. In Greece, too, diplomacy gradually became more secular and political, but the heralds remained essentially religious figures and retained their religious protections. More important for the Roman parallel, the position of herald was an inherited one, transmitted within specific families in both Sparta and Athens. As professionals, they knew the sacred law associated with their priesthood, and, in fact, as Douglas M. MacDowell points out, "most sacred laws had no remembered origin and were just ancestral traditions," known only to the experts, perhaps not even to all members of the college.[74] Similarly, Ogilvie observes that in Rome "it may well have been that the [fetial] traditions . . . were kept alive in patrician families from which the fetials were hereditarily chosen or through archaic ceremonies."[75] In other words, fetial priests were hereditary experts in and caretakers of legal-religious formulae, rituals, and ceremonies dealing with a wide variety of concerns broadly related to foreign policy, warfare, and diplomacy. Broken treaties, military defeats, and disasters resulting from confrontation with foreigners generally all required religious propitiation. The right words had to be uttered lest calamity strike again. The religious emphasis placed upon fetial procedure was not a precautionary or a "solely psychological" measure, but contained precise elements designed to obligate the other side to action and, at the same time, to influence the outcome by proper appeal to the gods.[76] All such concerns were shared by priests and senators, so we should not doubt that the two were synonymous in the persons of the senatorial *patres*.

However, Ogilvie points out that the late republican interest in fetials and their legal-religious procedures was a consequence of the publication of the pontifical records and that, if early fetial records had existed, "they would have been, like the chants of the Salii, utterly incomprehensible." What appear in the literature as fetial practices, formulae, rituals, and ceremonies are merely "archaizing reconstructions."[77] At most, fetials may have retained some role in treaty making and their formulae may have been "translations" from the original.

74. D. M. MacDowell, *Law* (1978): 192.
75. Ogilvie, *Comm.* (1965): 128.
76. Cf. Harris, *War* (1979): 171.
77. Ogilvie, *Comm.* (1965): 128, cf. 110. Ogilvie (ibid., 110ff., 127ff.) presents an extensive survey of the religious and legal questions and the modern opinion.

In sum, the dominant modern opinion is that fetials began to disappear during the third century B.C. and that both their presence and their practices in later periods were the result of antiquarian resuscitation. For example, it is argued that the archaic procedure fetials used for declaring war must have originated when Rome's enemies were her neighbors, who also employed fetials. Fetial *ius* mandated a three-stage procedure with a thirty-day interval between the initial stage and the declaration of war. Presumably, Rome could only use such a procedure when her enemy (and enemy territory) was close at hand. Once Rome's empire (and wars) were far afield, the several stages of fetial procedure, with set intervals of time between, gave way to a single-stage procedure. The change began after 281 B.C., when the fetial procedure became "too burdensome," and consequently declaring war was taken over by senatorial legates "empowered by the Senate and the people in advance to act . . . on their own authority without reference to Rome."[78]

I fail to see the merit in distinguishing fetials from legates, since they both originated in the Senate and they technically performed the same functions. W. V. Harris thinks the change was from "formal correctness in all elaborate procedures [by fetials] . . . to a concern for the appearance of virtuous behavior toward other states [by the legates]."[79] Such a postulation is unnecessary. The legates who declared war on Philip V of Macedon in 200 B.C. were selected by the consul P. Sulpicius Galba, at the direction of the fetials, from persons outside the Senate. The youthful M. Aemilius Lepidus (consul 187 B.C.) was chosen to issue the ultimatum to Philip, and it has been suggested that "a non-senator was sent as a compromise between religious scruples . . . and the dignity of the Senate."[80] Certainly the implication is that the function would normally have fallen to sena-

78. Ogilvie, *Comm.* (1965): 128. Harris, *War* (1979): 166f., expresses similar views. Harris's discussion of censorial and fetial prayers and their place in Roman expansion (118ff., 167ff., 265f.) has considerable merit.
79. Harris, *War* (1979): 173.
80. Walbank, *Comm.* II (1967): 543, on Polyb. 16.34.2. Cf. Briscoe, *Comm.* (1973): 77. Livy 31.8.3 suggests that Aemilius was not a senator, but he may have been a priest. His entry into the pontifical college is less clear than presumed: one Sulpicius Galba became pontiff in 203 and another in 202 B.C., and Lepidus supposedly was selected to replace the former Sulpicius in 199 B.C. The priestly succession during this period of Roman history is far from certain, and Aemilius may well have been a pontiff prior to becoming a legate in 201 B.C. I have less faith in the information of this period than Frier (*Annales* [1979]: 247 n. 56 goes too far).

tors (= fetials). Moreover, recent research has clearly indicated that faith in the continued use of a revised or modified fetial procedure by legates is unwarranted. Although the procedure for declaring war shows very little consistency,[81] the fact remains that both the fetial law and Roman private law are associated with the *legis actio per condictionem*, and both "have common roots far back in Roman legal history."[82] The *legis actio per condictionem*—the last *legis actio* to appear—is perhaps not much earlier than the late third century. The publication of the *legis actiones*, the secret monopoly of the *pontifices*, in 304 B.C. meant that all procedures, including those employed by fetials, became public knowledge, subject to continuous alteration, "translation" (to use Ogilvie's word), or interpretation, to be more precise. The fetials' association with formulae of civil law action demonstrates again the originally undifferentiated nature of both Roman secular and sacred law, as well as public and private life. The formulae, rituals, and procedures once controlled by the priests often were the starting point for a differentiated private law. Publication of the fetials' religious procedure probably resulted in their gradual replacement by legates, their secular heirs, who could now make use of newer formulae created by the senatorial jurisconsults for the particular occasion.[83]

Thus, by the late Republic, the number of priests in the Senate declined. Not all priests lost their seats in the *curia*.[84] Some, like the *pontifices*, remained senators, but as a consequence of the increased secularization and publication of their expertise, their powers and influences were more politicized. Other, more archaic priests, such as the fetials, gradually disappeared because their taboo-ridden life required the maintenance of ancient rituals and archaic standards and practices, including the requirement that priests be from specific families (or *gentes*).[85]

81. Rich, *War* (1976): 73ff.
82. Ogilvie, *Comm.* (1965): 127.
83. Kaser, *Priv. Law* (1968): 337f., for the development and dating of the *legis actio*. That Roman private law and procedure found their way into international relations, just as features of domestic patronage influenced the development of foreign *clientelae*, can be deduced from the *recuperatores* procedure (see Kelly, *Studies* [1976]: 40ff., for discussion and modern opinions).
84. L. R. Taylor and R. T. Scott, *TAPA* 100 (1969): 553ff., have pointed to senatorial priests who may have been *pedarii*. See n. 69 above.
85. G. Wissowa, *Religion* (1912): 71, 501 n. 2, notes that many flaminates were unfilled in the late Republic.

11. Changes in the Senate Membership

In the last 200 years of the Republic, dramatic changes occurred both in the process of selecting senators and in the identification of those eligible for Senate membership. Many priesthoods are nothing more than shadows to us. Although they had greater "significance in a primitive state," they declined or never achieved "the political importance or prestige of the major colleges."[86] Nevertheless, these priesthoods were once monopolized by "the same families who appropriated the right to appoint the *interrex*"[87]—families who constituted the original senatorial *patres*, senators by hereditary right who automatically qualified for their seats in the *curia*. Many priests held their positions for life. Eventually, some priests may have become back-benchers, *pedarii*, or were included among those who had only the right to speak in the Senate. In general, the trend was away from a Senate composed essentially of members who automatically succeeded to seats occupied by their ancestral or priestly predecessors and toward a membership composed of elected officials and distinguished citizens from the political and secular world. The trend from one to the other can only be highlighted.

12. Patres et conscripti

Although the change is not clearly evident from our sources, we know that republican senators were collectively referred to as *patres conscripti*, because persons not descended from the original, or automatic, members of the council were added to the Senate, and this "involved a change from automatic membership to some form of selection."[88] The *patres conscripti* were not originally a single group of "enrolled fathers," but consisted of two groups, *patres et conscripti*.[89] The *patres* were priests who were automatically senators; all other senators were *conscripti*.

This interpretation directly opposes the frequent attempts to

---

86. M. W. H. Lewis, *Priests* (1955): 111.
87. Momigliano, *JRS* 53 (1963): 118.
88. Ogilvie, *Comm.* (1965): 236.
89. For differing interpretations of *conscripti*, see Richard, *Origines* (1978): 478ff., 521ff.; Raaflaub, chapter VII below at nn. 116ff.

equate the *patres* (or patricians) in the Senate with those who very early in the Republic obtained curule magistracies that endowed their families with *imperium et auspicium*, which presumably made the families patrician and qualified the curule magistrate for Senate membership.[90] We frequently hear of distinctions between those who were curule senators, *pedarii*, and others,[91] but there is also clear evidence that curule magistrates could be *praeteriti*.[92] In one sense *praeteriti* were those members of the Senate who were subsequently passed over or omitted from a later list of senators. In another sense they were those who were eligible for Senate membership but were never enrolled as senators. Regardless, we know that curule magistrates had to await enrollment. However, Valerius, the *flamen Dialis*, demanded and received his rightful seat without reference to a senatorial *lectio*; the story states clearly that his *flamen* predecessors had not been senators because they were too indolent to take up the position, but their conduct did not preclude Valerius's resumption of the privilege.[93] In other words, curule magistrates were enrolled in the Senate; their selection could be delayed, or they could be passed over. Priests were not enrolled; they were automatically senators. The former were *conscripti*; the latter were *patres*.

By the late Republic the distinction between *patres* and *conscripti* virtually disappeared as the number of priests in the Senate declined. In the beginning, the number of priests acceptable as potential members of the Senate had been sufficient to fill a large percentage of seats. In addition to the thirty or sixty *curiones*, the number of pontiffs was increased from the original three to nine by 300 B.C., as was the number of augurs. There were also first *duumviri*, then *decemviri sacris faciundis*, and three *maiores* and twelve *minores flamines*. The original minimum was fifty, the final tally more than 100 even before we consider the several archaic priesthoods that remained exclusively patrician—the *rex sacrorum*, two groups of twelve Salian

---

90. Cf. Ranouil, *Patriciat* (1975): 32, 45f., 58f. Nearly all essays in this volume offer a version of this thesis.

91. In particular, see the discussion and excellent review of the problem of *senatores pedarii* and the changes in the Senate membership contained in L. R. Taylor and R. T. Scott, *TAPA* 100 (1969): 529ff., esp. 548ff. To which add Palmer, *Arch. Comm.* (1970): 253ff., especially 257f., 263ff.

92. Festus, p. 290 L; cf. Livy 33.44.5; 38.28.2; 27.11.22; Gell. *Noctes Atticae* 3.18.1 as indications of the evidence.

93. Livy 27.8.10.

priests, Fabian and Quinctilian *Luperci*, twelve Arval Brethren, and twenty fetials, plus countless other possibilities.[94] In other words, before the end of the fourth century, at least a third of the Senate seats may have been filled by those who automatically became senators because of their priesthoods. Even during the second Punic War, as Valerius's example shows, some positions in the Senate were still automatically filled by priests, although their number was declining. At the same time, we find a corresponding increase in the number of magistrates who became virtually ex-officio members of the Senate and the routine admission of plebeian officials. Possibly, Senate membership gradually increased to accommodate more members, but it is even more likely that those archaic priests who were restricted by taboos from full participation in the ever-increasing secular life of both the state and the Senate gradually lost their right to an automatic seat.[95] The change is reflected in the tendency for the *patres* and *conscripti* to become the *patres conscripti*, and can be elucidated by the development of the procedure for filling the Senate.

13. Censors and the Senate

A highly rhetorical passage from Festus tells us that before the undated *lex Ovinia* was passed both kings and republican magistrates had traditionally selected friends for membership in the Senate, passing over more worthy men until the Ovinian plebiscite made it law that censors were to select senators by *curiae* from the very best

---

94. On priests, see Dion. Hal. 2.63–74; Varro, *Ling.* 5.83–87, and Zon. 7.11, who specifically says the original *duumviri s. f.* were senators (cf. Dion. Hal. 4.62). Cic. *Ad fam.* 6.18.1 refers to Caesar's intention to add *haruspices* to the Senate, but E. Rawson, *JRS* 68 (1978): 144, thinks the reference to more than one "rhetorical." We also know of the dispute, involving Aemilianus, concerning the question of exemption for augurs from service as *iudices*, which implies they were senators at the time (Cic. *Brut.* 31.117). Palmer, *Arch. Comm.* (1970): 206ff., argues that *curiones* were regal senators; note ibid., 152 n. 2, on "priestly" *tribuni celerum* (cf. 267), and the debate over *epulones* and whether they were "plebeian" or "patrician" (cf. F. Münzer, *RE* 4.1290; Willems, *Sénat* I [1878]: 444ff.; and the discussion on Cic. *Har. resp.* 21 by J. O. Lenaghan, *A Commentary on Cicero's Oration de Haruspicum Responso* (The Hague and Paris, 1969): 112f.

95. I again offer Valerius Flaccus, *flamen*, as a single example. In 199 B.C. his brother had to take the oath for him when he was elected aedile (Livy 31.50.7–10). See Briscoe, *Comm.* (1973): 164, for additional bibliography.

men (*optimum*) from all ranks (*ordines*). Thereafter those passed over or removed from the Senate suffered shame.⁹⁶ Appius Claudius Caecus, censor in 312 B.C., undertook a *lectio* of the Senate, and although he omitted no living senators, he was accused of enrolling freedmen's sons, passing over more worthy men. We cannot say if the *lex Ovinia* enabled Caecus to undertake his *lectio* or if the law was passed as a consequence of his activities—an attempt to establish less subjective criteria for Senate membership.⁹⁷ By the second Punic War, the choice of persons to fill vacancies became more specific and was made according to obvious political and secular criteria.

Following the disaster at Cannae there were 177 vacancies in the Senate, so M. Fabius Buteo was made dictator and given authority to fill the *curia*. The emergency required an ex-censor who could make full use of previous senatorial (and censorial) records. Although Fabius omitted no living senators, he did follow specific criteria that may not have been fully employed previously. He did not select senators on an individual basis: he merely published the previous censors' list and filled the remaining vacancies by following the principle *ut ordo ordini, non homo homini praelatus videretur*. Fabius's *ordines* were curule magistrates who had held office since the last census and thus had not yet been enrolled, plebeian officials (and *quaestores*), and decorated soldiers. Instead of simply identifying the worthy individuals in the *curiae* and selecting them for the Senate, Fabius selected the new senators according to rank, by distinctions. Some such men would have been senators before,⁹⁸ but now the Senate was on its way to becoming an institution composed essentially of ex-officio members, whose political and secular contributions to the

---

96. Willems, *Sénat* I (1878): 153ff., has an extensive discussion of the *lex Ovinia* (= Festus, p. 290 L). Cf. Palmer, *Arch. Comm.* (1970): 255 n. 1, where *optimum* is translated as "wealthy," and especially 263ff.; Richard, *Origines* (1978): 97, 211, 241; chapter XI below at nn. 42ff.

97. Appius Claudius Caecus may well be one of the first authentic individuals in Roman history. Ferenczy, *Patr. State* (1976): 120ff. (152ff. for the *lex Ovinia*) presents the evidence and the discussion of his illustrative career, but my reaction to Ferenczy's own thesis is similar to Develin's (chapter XI below, especially n. 60). Dating the *lex Ovinia* after 287 B.C. is based upon the common interpretation that the *lex Hortensia* permitted the *plebs* unrestricted power to legislate.

98. The story is found in Livy 23.23, but note 22.49.16–18 for the indication that military tribunes were senatorial material. Festus, p. 198 L, clearly shows there was an *ordo sacerdotum* from which Senate members could be selected (cf. Richard, *Origines* [1978]: 240, 247).

state were recognized and whose positions were obtained as a result of popular election. The assumption is that birth and inheritance were no longer sufficient to obtain Senate membership.

However, it is impossible to believe that first consuls, then military tribunes, and finally censors possessed the same powers as kings to select senatorial advisors. The first censors were not the successful, influential, and powerful aristocrats the later ones were. As late as the second Punic War, not all censors were consular, and a censor's authority was inferior to both the consuls' and the praetors'.[99] The Romans never would have permitted censors to acquire the power and influence so often credited to them. In fact, the number of vacant seats to be filled in any given census period was too large to be left to the complete discretion of the censors. They must have always been constrained to follow previous membership lists and to select the *conscripti* from among identifiable aristocratic groups; from magistrates, plebeian officials, and distinguished soldiers; and from the descendants of all the aforementioned once their families became senatorial. But more important, before the Senate routinely included plebeian officials and was composed of essentially ex-officio members, a certain percentage of seats must have been filled automatically because the number of annual vacancies was much larger than the number of annual magistrates.

Statistical evidence obtained from republican material is notoriously unreliable, but even very rough estimates are better than none. Let us assume a Senate of 300 members. Various authorities who divine ancient population statistics and various life tables suggest that at the very minimum ten senators a year would die. However, since the senators were also military aristocrats and peace seldom broke out, the number was normally at least twice that figure.[100] For ex-

99. For examples, see Broughton, *Magistrates* I (1951), for the years 318, 312, 272, 265, and 209 B.C. E. Schmähling, *Die Sittenaufsicht der Censoren* (Stuttgart, 1938), and Suolahti, *Censors* (1963), collect most of the material on the Roman censors and census, but their analysis is wanting. Suolahti (24f.) believes the increased prestige of the censors was related to the disappearance of the dictator, thereby replacing one mystery with another. Cic. *De leg.* 3.12.27, states an ideal situation.

100. For general discussion, see Willems, *Sénat* I (1878): 165f., 303ff.; Taylor, *Voting Distr.* (1960): 175, who both present some figures. Among the attempts to determine mortality rates, see Gomme, *Population* (1933): 75ff.; A. H. M. Jones, *Athenian Democracy* (Oxford, 1969): 161ff.; K. Hopkins, *Conquerors and Slaves* (Cambridge, 1978): 21, 34f.; but Brunt, *Manpower* (1971): 132ff., has the best summary.

ample, the Senate was full in 220 B.C., when L. Aemilius Papus and C. Flaminius were censors, but in addition to eighty senatorial casualties at Cannae, natural attrition and earlier battles had taken a severe toll, resulting in ninety-seven additional vacancies between 219 and 217 B.C. Even in "normal" times, the number of vacant seats to be filled in any given census period must have been several dozen, and the implication from such statistical evidence is that censors would have had too much power if additions to the Senate's membership were more or less totally under their control. Sulla's Senate of 600 was filled by the automatic entry of the twenty yearly quaestors, and, by implication, before the second century at least ten replacements a year were needed to fill out the Senate of 300 members.[101] Many vacancies must have been filled automatically before it was customary for all ex-officials (including plebeians) to be acceptable members. Priests were more likely candidates for Senate seats, especially in light of their legal expertise and the importance of religion to public activity. There is reason to believe that plebeian officials had always been regular members of the state machinery, but apparently they were not very important (or very devisive) prior to the second century.[102]

For comparative information, consult H. A. Coale and P. Demeny, *Regional Model Life Tables and Stable Populations* (Princeton, 1966), on which see now B. Frier, "Roman Life Expectancy: Ulpian's Evidence," *Harv. Stud. Class. Philol.* 86 (1982): 213ff., for an overly complicated, but thorough, analysis of demographic information. I have generally made calculations based upon age specific death rates (see Frier, tables 2–5 for examples) for those thirty years of age and by reducing the sample size from 1,000 to 300. Rough estimates based upon life expectancy (see Hopkins and Brunt, cited above) supply the same result. For an excellent introduction to demography, T. H. Hollingsworth, *Historical Demography* (Ithaca, N.Y., 1969), has a discussion of ancient demographic analysis. Note especially 202ff. for the "Upper Classes" literature. See chapter I above at nn. 112ff. for additional discussion and bibliography (see especially at n. 123 on the size of the Senate).

101. In addition to increasing the quaestorships (Tac. *Ann.* 11.22; *CIL* I.^{2} 2, no. 587) and the number of senators (see R. Syme, "Caesar, the Senate and Italy," *PBSR* 14 [1938]: 22ff.), Sulla also increased the number of priests (Livy *Epit.* 89), which may have been connected with enlarging the Senate. The implication from Dio 37.46.4 that Sulla's system would have created more than 600 senators is unreliable (cf. Broughton, *Magistrates* II [1951]: 179 [on 61 B.C.], for the questionable censorship).

102. In a future publication I shall argue that plebeian officials were normal, not revolutionary in origin. Concerning their entry into the Senate, a considerable debate exists. A *lex Atinia* is the key. Cf. Broughton, *Magistrates* I (1951): 458f., for

Once plebeian officials and distinguished soldiers were added to the pool of candidates from whom senators were selected, the number was adequate to maintain the Senate at a constant level. Perhaps as a consequence of having more than the necessary number of potential senators, censors obtained some discretionary authority in selecting from the eligible candidates. Livy mentioned that censors passed over senators who had not been curule magistrates,[103] but even curule magistrates could be omitted from the list of senators for criminal acts, for misconduct, and for "moral" reasons. This was more the result of the original "moral" and religious character of the senators than it was a function of the censor's power. However, many priests, even those who strayed from the straight and narrow, held their positions for life and must have remained *patres*, beyond the censor's authority. Later censors gave black marks to senators and demoted them and could even remove them from the *curia* for certain offences. Sulla took even that authority from them when he increased the Senate membership and made the quaestorship the qualifying position. Although it was the introduction of the plebeian officials to the Senate that resulted in the greatest decline in the number of Senate seats automatically held by descendants and successors, a transformation in the composition of the Senate might have begun as early as the *lex Ovinia*: an essentially religious body was turning into a political one. Fewer sons succeeded automatically to their father's seats and, therefore, fewer *praetextati* appeared in the Senate: plebeian officials did not wear the *toga praetexta* nor, presumably, did their sons.[104] Both censors and tribunes, with their intimate association with the military levy and the census, were more characteristic of the new Senate and its increased political, military,

---

dating the law to 149 B.C., but Mommsen, *Röm. Staatsrecht* III.2 (1888): 862f., thought it belonged after Gaius Gracchus, a position supported by L. R. Taylor and R. T. Scott, *TAPA* 100 (1969): 531. However, cf. Develin, *CQ* 28 (1978): 141ff. and chapter XI below at nn. 42; cf. also chapter XII below at n. 10. I do not see plebeian officials added as a consequence of their success in a conflict.

103. On *praeteriti*, examples from Livy 9.30.2; 27.11.12; 34.44.5; 38.28.2; 39.47.9; and 40.51.2. Mommsen, *Röm. Staatsrecht* II.1³ (1887): 418ff., on *nota*, and his discussions of censors and *lectio* (II.1: 332ff.), and senators and Senate (III.2: 833ff.), remain indispensable.

104. See nn. 39ff. above. To which add L. R. Taylor and R. T. Scott, *TAPA* 100 (1969): 550f. and 556f.

and international concerns,[105] while priests remained associated with the old Senate's religious orientation. Archaic priests were more and more restricted and uncomfortable as the Senate became a political body given to secular deliberations and practices.

Consequently, *patres* gave way to *conscripti*. Not all priests lost their Senate seats, but the process of selecting those who remained changed, reflecting the changing nature of both the Senate and the priestly colleges. Augurates and pontificates, for example, became too influential politically to remain the monopolies of a narrow religious aristocracy.[106] Not only was the number of priests in these more politically important colleges increased, vacancies were filled by a vote of seventeen of the thirty-five tribes.[107] The earliest reliable evidence for the process is Cicero's reference to a law proposed (but rejected) by C. Licinius Crassus in 145 B.C. to change the cooptation of priests to *populi beneficium*, presumably election.[108] Some assume that these *comitia sacerdotum* were used to fill the most important priestly vacancies more than a century earlier.[109] Yet Cn. Domitius Ahenobarbus, tribune in 104 B.C., carried a measure that made the selection of pontiffs, augurs, *decemviri sacris faciundis*, and *epulones* subject to the vote of seventeen tribes.[110] Religious reasons prevented direct popular election, but a solution was found by having only part of the *pop-*

105. Development of this argument must await my future publication on *plebs* and tribunes.

106. However, the major priesthoods tended to be filled by younger relatives of previous (or existing) members; cf. D. E. Hahm, *TAPA* 94 (1963): 83ff.

107. Wissowa, *Religion* (1912): 70f., and Altheim, *Religion* (1938): 331, have interpreted election as the reason for decay of the entire religious system. The traditional political interpretation (and chronology) is found in chapter XII below at n. 60 (cf. chapter VIII at n. 43 for procedural discussion).

108. Cic. *Amic.* 25.96; cf. Botsford, *Assemblies* (1909): 391.

109. On the basis of Livy, Botsford, *Assemblies* (1909): 341f., proposes earlier elections of the *pontifex maximus* by seventeen tribes, a view reinforced by Cicero's judgment (*Leg. agr.* 2.7.16). Cf. L. R. Taylor, *Roman Voting Assemblies* (Ann Arbor, Mich., 1966): 82. Livy is too inconsistent in his use of language and too loose in his description of procedure to be relied upon. The use of seventeen tribes always has seemed to me to be a religious obligation—there were that many original tribes.

110. Broughton, *Magistrates* I (1951): 559, presents the ancient testimony, although the *epulones* remain poorly understood. They wore a *toga praetexta* like the pontiffs (Livy 33.42.1) whom they replaced (Cic. *De orat.* 3 [19]: 73). The debate over whether they were patrician, plebeian, or both might be settled if the *toga praetexta* of the *epulones* is significant. Cf. D. R. Shackleton Bailey, *Studies* (1976): 29f., for discussion.

ulus vote on the priests. The procedure is unclear, but obviously the prominent families did not lose their grip on the priesthoods as a consequence of the election process. Possibly the nomination of those who were finally elected by a vote of the tribes remained the prerogative of the priests. *Comitia* continued to play a role in the choice of priests during the Empire, but both the Senate and the religious colleges appear to have nominated persons voted upon to fill vacancies. Lewis believes that "Augustus allowed the priests to continue the republican practice of nominating candidates for the tribes to elect," because it gave "the appearance of free elections."[111] Such procedures were attempts to maintain traditional religious practices. We are seldom informed about either the nature of such traditional practices or about changes they underwent, and it is in the interest of obtaining some appreciation of modifications in custom that I offer the following speculation, which stresses and stretches a point raised by the story of C. Valerius Flaccus. As *flamen*, Valerius demanded a right no *flamen Dialis* in two generations had exercised: *nec patrum nec avorum memoria Dialem quemquam id ius usurpasse.*[112] Does *id ius usurpasse* have a technical, legal significance? Many stories concerning Appius Claudius Caecus were told to illustrate a legal or constitutional point. Caecus and his scribe Cn. Flavius were closely connected with Roman legal development. Flavius published the *legis actiones* and the *fasti*, previously the secret possessions of the pontiffs, and Caecus wrote a work *De usurpationibus*. *Usurpatio* means "to make use of," "to take," or "have possession and thereby the use of something," and can refer to customary possession or privilege, even to something obtained illegally. Caecus returned the flute players to Rome and permitted them their traditional use of the Capitoline temple; he took the cult of Hercules and its funds out of private hands and placed them under public control; and it is entirely possible that *usurpatio* is the point of all these stories primarily concerned with the right of possession and use.[113] Did Caecus attempt to

---

111. Lewis, *Priests* (1955): 16. See L. R. Taylor and R. T. Scott, *TAPA* 100 (1969): 559f., for some imperial practices pertaining to senatorial membership. We need a new study of cooptation (cf. Livy 4.4.7, and Mommsen's denial [*Röm. Staatsrecht* III.1 (1887): 30 n. 1] that the *patres* could coopt families).

112. Livy 27.8.9.

113. Broughton, *Magistrates* I (1951): 160ff., 168, has complete references to Appius's career and Flavius's publication. Flavius may have been a *minor* pontiff (cf.

define priestly rights of possession? Did the Pinarii and Potitii, families in control of Hercules' cult, lose their traditional Senate seats together with their monopoly of the cult? Papirius Praetextatus (censor of 272 B.C.) was a youth during Caecus's censorship; does his story reflect changes in the process of filling Senate vacancies?[114] We are told that Caecus opposed the *lex Ogulnia* (300 B.C.), which increased the number of members in the pontifical and augural colleges by adding plebeian members. Few scholars are comfortable with the depiction of the reactionary Claudii constantly pitted against plebeians desiring change.[115] Perhaps Caecus did not oppose "plebeian" priests but was against increasing the number of priests who automatically became senators or opposed changing the criteria for the priesthood: new members were not required to marry by *confarreatio*. Finally, the question of marriage brings us full circle, back to the law in the Twelve Tables that prohibited intermarriage between the orders, often cited as the strongest evidence of hostility and separation between patricians and plebeians.

14. The Prohibition Against Intermarriage

Presumably, unlike citizenship, the right to intermarriage with patricians did not extend to the lower classes: "there was no legal bar as such," says Ogilvie, "but sentiment and religion . . . formed an adequate obstacle." Ogilvie discounts other plebeian demands made at the time, but says the connubial law "is likely to be historical and to-

---

Livy 22.57.3; Gell. *Noctes Atticae* 1.15.9). L. H. Jeffery and A. Morpurgo-Davies, *Kadmos* 9 (1970): 118ff., present a possible Greek parallel, dealing with the hereditary position of a scribe who was the "recorder in public affairs both sacred and secular" (125). R. E. A. Palmer, *Historia* 14 (1965): 293ff., has an important contribution on the censor; Ferenczy, *Patr. State* (1976): 120ff., discusses most points. Concerning the *usurpatio* (cf. Pomponius, *Dig.* 1.2.2.36; Ferenczy, *Patr. State*, 212ff.), it may be significant that Varro, *Rust.* 2, *praef.* 1, says that the year was divided *ut nonis modo diebus urbanas res usurparent*. I am not certain that technical legal language is not preserved here (see Mitchell, "Historical Development" [1984]: 195ff., for methodological discussion).

114. On Papirius Praetextatus, see above at n. 41.

115. The Ogulnii have a close association with religious matters (Münzer, *Adelsparteien* [1920]: 87f.). Wiseman, *Clio's Cosmetics* (1979): 104ff., presents the latest unconvincing discussion of the antiplebeian Claudian character.

gether with the name Canuleius to have been preserved in the *Annales*, as the only authentic notice of 445."[116] In other words, within the space of five years intermarriage was declared illegal and then legal. We tend to forget that the *lex Canuleia de conubio* was part of a single tradition, unknown to Dionysius of Halicarnassus, who supposedly did not report the removal of the prohibition because it was too technical for his Greek audience. In truth, as it stands, the tradition is hardly intelligible to anyone. First, the repeal is likely to have been inserted in the tradition because of the political interpretation of the presumed prohibition against intermarriage in the Twelve Tables.[117] However, a perfectly reasonable religious principle was at work in such a prohibition: priests were forbidden to marry simply anyone. Plebeians were prohibited from marrying *patres*, not patricians. *Pater* is a legal, precise, and technical term; patrician smacks of politics and rhetoric. Religious custom demanded that a *pater* marry by *confarreatio*, a ceremony reserved to priests. The prohibition was probably contained in the eleventh table, where another suggested provision dealt with intercalation, a concern of the *pontifex maximus*.[118] If it was repealed, it is tempting to see it in the same context as the *lex Ogulnia*, which permitted plebeians to hold major priesthoods.

116. Ogilvie, *Comm.* (1965): 527. Heurgon, *Rise* (1973): 172, has a brief, but excellent, discussion and appreciation of the earlier literature. Linderski, chapter VIII below at nn. 23 ff., 51ff., has an excellent review of the problem and scholarship. Cf. chapter III above.
117. Raaflaub, chapter VII below at nn. 68ff., Linderski, chapter VIII below, and Eder, chapter IX below, present political interpretations of the Twelve Tables, despite recognition of their religious aspects.
118. The conclusion formulated by Toher (chapter X, part 5, below) can be applied to the entire body of law. There is too little appreciation of certain problems concerning the Twelve Tables. First, we know very little about the original arrangement of the laws (the prohibition against intermarriage is an exception), and even less about the degree to which it was changed by priestly or judicial interpretation. Finally, there is the problem of completely extraneous material being considered part of the original Twelve Tables because of inability to distinguish layers of legal development. For example, the law that established a hearing before a praetor on *nundinae* (Gell. *Noctes Atticae* 20.1.45–49 = Table 3) clearly incorporates both a later magistrate, the praetor (first in 366 B.C.), and a later rule established by the *lex Hortensia* (287 B.C.). The confusion has led inevitably to the political conclusion that the law was changed in 287 B.C. once plebeians won the right to legislate uninhibited by making *nundinae* days on which *comitia* could not be held: the *patres* giveth and the *patres* taketh away (see A. K. Michels, *The Calendar of the Roman Republic* [Princeton, 1967]: 103–06).

Both laws referred to the question of eligibility for religious offices based upon essentially religious and personal criteria: marriage ceremonies, personal practices, and traditional behavior had been used to restrict the access of some persons to religious positions based upon the assumption that pollution would result from the failure to adhere to ancestral forms.

15. Conclusion

My primary methodological assumption has been that the original Roman documentary evidence was essentially religious and legal in nature and was both older and more reliable than the narrative accounts in which it is often contained. The narrative accounts presumed the permanent existence of a pervasive conflict between *patres* and *plebs* and consequently made use of the reliable religious and legal details as evidence for the presumed struggle. My historiographical assumption has been that the struggle between *patres* and *plebs* itself is a fabrication, and if it is removed, the individual pieces of evidence can be seen in their original religious and legal context. I have not attempted either to describe what actually happened or to deny the existence of other possible conflicts within Roman society over a broad range of political and economic issues. Instead, my purpose has been both to show that there was no struggle between those known as *patres* and *plebs*, and to preserve the evidence that permits a reliable identification of the *patres*.

To the extent that *patres* were a reliably identifiable entity, they were priests and not political aristocrats determined to create and to sustain a secular monopoly. Accordingly, I argue not only that priests and senators shared a variety of distinctive traits, but also that *patres* and priests had many characteristics in common. Conversely, neither political accomplishments nor political criteria can explain the origins of the *patres* and their identification with the Senate. Well into the middle of the Republic, some priesthoods remained entitled to Senate seats automatically. Thus, the senatorial *patres* were those priests in the Senate who gave their collective religious sanction (*auctoritas*) to public measures and who were selected to be *interreges*. Secular magistrates who became senators were *conscripti*.

In other words, the answers to the questions of who the original

Roman *patres* were and how they were distinguished from other citizens are found in their identification as priests and in the religious obligations required of those who were, and those who would become, *patres*. Marriage by *confarreatio* was not devised to keep out the *plebs*, but to guarantee religious purity and traditional practices. The law in the Twelve Tables prohibiting intermarriage can no longer serve as the cornerstone of the edifice of the Conflict of the Orders, but must be seen as an essentially religious rule designed to guard against pollution. In reality, much of the evidence used to buttress the story of the Conflict of the Orders has precisely this same kind of religious and legal significance—in contrast to its often contrived political explanation. Consequently, the struggle itself must be called into question and the historical development of Rome reexamined in light of the religious and legal material that now no longer serves as the foundation of a preconceived political account.

ARNALDO MOMIGLIANO

VI

The Rise of the *plebs* in the Archaic Age of Rome

1

The Roman historical tradition tells us about a revolution in Rome around 500 B.C. The revolution was occasioned by the rape of Lucretia and resulted in the expulsion of the Etruscan kings and the appointment in their place of two annual consuls. Tradition further records that the consuls were elected by the people, assembled in the *comitia centuriata*. But eligibility for the consulship was confined to the members of certain privileged *gentes*, the so-called patricians, who also monopolized the priestly offices and had special powers in the Senate that distinguished them from the other senators, who belonged to nonpatrician *gentes*.

A lecture given at the University of Turin on April 19, 1967, as part of the "Lezioni Augusto Rostagni" of the academic year 1966–67; first published in *RSI* 79 (1967): 297ff., repr. in Momigliano, *Contr. IV* (1969): 437ff.; translated by T. J. Cornell. For some additional remarks by the author on recent scholarship, see Author's Appendix; for a brief survey of sources and literature, see Editor's Appendix.

The tradition in its present form dates back to the second half of the first century B.C.—the period in which Diodorus, Dionysius of Halicarnassus, and Livy, our direct sources, were writing. But there is no doubt that the general lines of the tradition were already to be found in Fabius Pictor and the other Roman historians who first put together an ordered account of Rome's past at the end of the third century B.C. These historians, who wrote in Greek, were preceded in their turn by Greek historians of Italy such as Timaeus, who took an interest in the rapid development of Roman power in the first half of the third century. Before the third century there are only vague traces of the tradition; in fact at that point we lose track of it altogether.

It is perfectly possible that some authentic record of the transition from monarchy to republic was preserved in the chronicle of the Roman *pontifices*, which was undoubtedly in existence before 400 B.C. It is also likely that episodes of Roman history such as the fall of the monarchy were recorded by Greek historians of Italy during the fifth century; and it is reasonable to suppose that local historians of Cumae, the Greek colony nearest to Rome, wrote about events in Latium around 500 B.C., because a local tyrant, Aristodemus, took part in them. We know moreover that Antiochus, the greatest Syracusan historian of the fifth century, was interested in Rome. The trouble is that, whereas our knowledge of Timaeus is vague, in the case of these older Roman and non-Roman sources the only thing we can be certain of is that they once existed; we know nothing of what they actually had to say about archaic Rome.

One of the greatest difficulties facing anyone who attempts a critical reconstruction of early Roman history is precisely this empty space of more than two centuries between the overthrow of Tarquin and the earliest historians of Rome.

In the fourth and third centuries B.C., Rome was transformed from the first city of Latium into the overlord of central and southern Italy, Sardinia, and Sicily. Victories over Pyrrhus and Carthage made Rome the most important military power in the Mediterranean. Roman influence had begun to spread in Spain and Greece, and the city emerged as the natural rival of the great monarchies of Macedonia, Egypt, and Syria. The development of Rome's military and political power was naturally accompanied by rapid changes not only in its juridical and governmental institutions, but also in its social structure. Certain basic events in this process of change were remembered by the tradition, for example the admission of plebeians to the consulship in 366 B.C., and the abolition of debt-bondage—or at least of that form of debt-bondage known as *nexum*—in 326 B.C. But it is clear that in the third century B.C. no one had any clear idea of what Roman society had been like in the first half of the fifth century. This is not to say that the records of that society had all been lost; in fact certain basic documents were still preserved—and indeed continued to survive at least until the time of Caesar. These documents included the law of Servius Tullius regulating the federal Latin cult of Diana on the Aventine, the treaty of c. 493 B.C. between Rome and the Latins (the so called *Foedus Cassianum*), and the plebiscite of 456 B.C., known as the *Lex Icilia de Aventino*, which concerned the plebeian occupation of the Aventine. Above all the Romans preserved the full text of the most important legal document of the archaic period, the compilation known as the Twelve Tables, which dated from the middle of the fifth century B.C. But the Roman historians were not trained in the practice of critically examining archival documents, which would have made it possible for them to reconstruct the conditions of a society that was so different from their own. It was far easier for them to assume that the *plebs* and the patriciate of 500 B.C. were much the same as the *plebs* and the patriciate of 200 B.C., and easier to interpret relations between Rome and the other Latin cities in the light of subsequent events that had led to the total subordination of Latium to Rome. Nor should we forget that for the greater part of our information on archaic Rome we depend not on Fabius Pictor, Cincius Alimentus, or Cato the Censor, the oldest historians, but on Diodorus, Dionysius of Halicarnassus, and Livy, historians who were still further removed from the events of the archaic period and who obtained most of their material from annalists of the age of the Gracchi and the civil wars. For these annalists the struggles between the patricians and the plebeians in the fifth century naturally appeared to be the same as the conflicts of the time of Gaius Gracchus and Sulla; their sympathies went respectively either to the *plebs* or to the patricians of the fifth century according to whether they sympathised with Gaius Gracchus or with his opponents, with the *populares* or with the *optimates* of the first century B.C.

A corrective to such simplifications was to some extent provided by antiquarians of the second and first centuries B.C., who applied philological diligence and juristic curiosity to the study of ancient documents—in particular the Twelve Tables—and took account of what had changed in the political and juridical organization of Rome. But it is a fundamental, indeed elementary, fact about the classical world that historians did not as a rule study antiquarians, and antiquarians did not study historians, except in matters of detail. Historians usually remained indifferent to the discoveries of antiquarians, and antiquarians such as Varro never saw it as their job to make the historians sit up and listen, as they could have done had they wished.

It is therefore left to us modern historians to attempt to go beyond the conventional reconstructions the Roman historians have given us. Today we know that even if the Rome of c. 500 B.C. had consuls, senators, patricians, plebeians, *comitia*, praetors, and clients, just as in the third or second century, even so the political, institutional and social realities represented by these terms in the fifth century B.C. *must* have been different from those of two or three centuries later.

The problem is certainly not new. It is one that has exercised Roman historians since the time of Niebuhr and has been tackled by eminent lawyers and historians from our university here in Turin; it is enough to mention the names of Gaetano De Sanctis and Giovanni Pacchioni. But in the past thirty or forty years, three factors have made a much more decisive contribution than previously to the problem of archaic Rome. The first is the enormous advance in our knowledge of other Italian societies contemporary with archaic Rome: the Etruscans, Osco-Umbrians, Celts, and Greeks of southern Italy and Sicily are today much better known than they were when Gaetano De Sanctis held his chair in this university. It is not solely a matter of archaeological discoveries; rather, the most important advances are probably those that have resulted from a more rigorous interpretation of Etruscan and Osco-Umbrian epigraphic texts, and from analysis of literary texts bearing on the various peoples of Italy. The second factor, however, is strictly archaeological. I refer to the fact that excavations have once again been undertaken in Rome and the surrounding region in an effort to elucidate the history of the archaic period. The resumption of excavations has moreover been accompanied by the systematic publication, by the Swedish archaeologist E. Gjerstad, of all the archaeological material that has accumulated in the museums and storerooms of Rome since the time of Giacomo Boni and before, and that no one had taken the trouble to publish until now.

Finally, the third factor is the ever-widening scope of comparative studies. This factor, too, is not entirely new. We are well aware of the amount of attention P. Bonfante gave to the comparative study of juridical institutions. But the improved knowledge of the ancient Near East, the decipherment of Hittite and Mycenaean, the more profound and articulated analysis of material from primitive societies in Africa, America, and Oceania, and above all the application of more refined techniques of comparison have created a new situation, of which we are only now beginning to take full account.

It is therefore natural today to reexamine the archaic civilization of Rome with new eyes. It is indeed hard to resist the appeal of what is emerging from the continual discoveries in or near Rome. In 1957 F. Castagnoli unearthed the federal Latin sanctuary of Lavinium; in 1964 the sensational discovery of a sanctuary in the Etruscan town of Pyrgi, with two dedications in Etruscan and one in Phoenician to the Carthaginian goddess Astarte, confirmed the close collaboration between Etruscans and Carthaginians that is attested in literary sources. At Veii during the Second World War excavations revealed some statuettes of Aeneas carrying Anchises, clear traces of a cult of Aeneas in the fifth century B.C.; and the existence of a cult of Aeneas in the environs of Rome was confirmed in 1956, when Marguerita Guarducci published an archaic dedication to Lar Aeneas. We already knew from literary sources that the Greek cult of Castor and Pollux—protectors of the aristocratic cavalry—had reached Rome around 500 B.C.; but now we can refer to a curious inscription, discovered at Lavinium and dating back to the fifth century B.C., that records a dedication to Castor and Pollux in a mixture of Greek and Latin. A few years ago, in Rome, American excavations of the Regia under Frank Brown demonstrated that the building was reconstructed de novo around 500 B.C. in order to accommodate the *rex sacrificulus*, the priest who took the place of the king in some of his religious functions, a substitution that was necessitated by the fall of the monarchy. In addition there have been innumerable minor discoveries, of limited significance in themselves but together forming a completely new chapter in the story. Recent finds at Veii include an offering made by Aulus Vibenna, the Etruscan hero of the age of

Servius Tullius, formerly known only from a confused pictorial tradition and late literary reports. At Rome at least three Etruscan inscriptions on vases confirm the penetration of Etruscan language and culture during the regal age. At Praeneste, modern Palestrina, the archaic tomb known conventionally as the Tomba Bernardini is probably to be attributed to a member of the princely clan of the Veturii; a branch of this clan was established at Rome around 500 B.C., and may even have migrated from Praeneste at this very time, in much the same way as the Claudii migrated from Sabinum to Rome around 504 B.C.

We are now beginning to reap the fruits of these researches. After S. Mazzarino's pioneering work, *Dalla monarchia allo stato repubblicano* (published in 1945), we now have the studies of A. Alföldi, whose recent book *Early Rome and the Latins* (1965) attempts to reconstruct the whole of archaic Roman history. But already in 1939 the remarkably perceptive Swedish scholar K. Hanell had proposed a new account of the early constitutional development of Rome, the effect of which was to lower the date of the beginning of the Republic and to make it coincide with the Decemvirate. Following Hanell's lead, E. Gjerstad interpreted the archaeological material as if it ought to prove that Rome was founded in c. 575 B.C. and that the Republic began in c. 450. Another basic trend in recent studies is represented by the work of the French scholar G. Dumézil, who in an uninterrupted series of studies over the past thirty years has propounded a picture of archaic Rome as heir to the tripartite system of Indo-European castes. In Rome as in archaic India there would have been well-defined categories of priests (brahmins), warriors, and peasants; the archaic Roman tribes, the Ramnes, Tities, and Luceres, would have corresponded to this tripartite functional division.

All this is well known, and I am calling attention to it only in order to emphasize a strange fact that is worth a moment's reflection. If there is one aspect of our tradition on archaic Rome that stands out, it is the struggle between the patricians and the plebeians. During my early childhood, at any rate, one of the first things we learned about Roman history, after the murder of Remus, was the reconciliation of the patricians and the *plebs* by Menenius Agrippa. The secessions of the *plebs*, the patrician arrogance of Appius Claudius, and the compromises of the Decemvirate are among the best-loved stories of Roman history for modern readers, just as they were for the Romans themselves. Now it is surely rather odd that the struggles between the patricians and the plebeians should have been overlooked by historians in the past thirty years. The last original work known to me is F. Altheim's *Lex sacrata* of 1940; less important for our purposes are juridical studies like that of A. Dell'Oro, *La formazione dello stato patrizio-plebeo* (1950).

In part this is a direct consequence of the predominant role of archaeological research in the study of archaic Rome. By their very nature social struggles in primitive conditions leave no traces that can be easily recognized by archaeological means. Tombs, houses, and temples can sometimes enable us to infer or confirm social differences, but they rarely define social relations, and are even less able to document class struggles. But it would be too simple to explain this conspicuous omission in contemporary studies solely by reference to archaeology. The prestige of the two most distinguished modern interpreters of archaic Roman society, G. Dumézil and A. Alföldi, may contribute further to the explanation. Dumézil's theory was born in the thirties, in an age of rapidly growing interest in the world of the primitive Aryans. There is no vulgar racism in the original and profound work of Dumézil, but it was typical of the period in which his ideas took root that Indo-European society was seen as a rigidly hierarchical structure in which economic and social conflicts were attenuated to the point of being passed over altogether. The case of A. Alföldi is more complex. A Hungarian of Jewish origin, Alföldi fled his country after the communist takeover. Before and since his exile, Alföldi has pursued the image of a primitive Roman society still rooted in the customs and social traditions of the nomadic horsemen of the steppes. In Alföldi's opinion, the descendants of these nomads were, on the one hand, Iranians and Latins, and on the other Turks and Hungarians. Alföldi has often hinted at a common inheritance of primitive political institutions between Latins and Turks, and promises a book full of surprises on this issue (*Die Struktur des voretruskischen Römerstaates* [Heidelberg, 1974]). Alföldi thus shares with Dumézil a belief in a static social structure belonging to a primitive epoch, and like him seeks nostalgically to reconstruct it—rather than to pursue the Romans in their unique social development, with its own internal conflicts of ideas and interests.

No corrective to these predominantly Western ideas has so far been forthcoming from Soviet scholars, as a casual observer might have been led to expect. In fact the contribution of Soviet writers to our understanding of archaic Roman society has been virtually nil. Lack of direct contact with the new (or for that matter with the old) archaeological material has naturally made it more difficult for Soviet scholars to write important works on this topic. But the principal reason is that Soviet historians are mainly interested in societies that were clearly based on slavery or feudalism. Consequently they have written important works on the society of the Roman Empire and the early Middle Ages. But a period like early Rome, with institutions poorly defined in terms of the prevalent schematism, has hitherto left Soviet historians cold and indifferent. Whether things are changing at this moment I am not in a position to say.

2

For our part we need to ask what are the implications of certain terminological contrasts in our sources on archaic Rome. Already in the surviving fragments of the Twelve Tables we find oppositions such as patricians and plebeians, patrons and clients, *assidui* and *proletarii*. Outside the Twelve Tables, but in documents that for various reasons can be traced back to the archaic period, we find other antithetical pairs: *classici* and *infra classem, populus* and *plebs, populus* and *equites, patres* and *conscripti*.

We can begin with the contrast *patres* and *conscripti*, which indicates two groups of senators: the collective expression *patres conscripti* defined the Senate. There is no doubt that, in the formula *patres conscripti, conscripti* is not an adjective qualifying *patres*, but rather a term antithetical to *patres*. An official formula, which probably served as a summons to the senators, is preserved in Festus and Livy, and runs: *qui patres, qui conscripti* (Livy 2.1.11; Festus, p. 304 L). We know who the *patres* were. They were members of the Senate who belonged to privileged clans—clans that precisely because they gave their heads of families (*patres*) to the Senate, were designated patrician. The members of these patrician clans also had privileges outside the Senate—for example, access to the magistracies and priesthoods. But their privileges were emphasized even more conspicuously in the Senate in contrast to the non-*patres*, the *conscripti*;

only the *patres* had the right to elect the *interrex* when there were no curule magistrates to hold the *comitia*, and only the *patres* could give their assent (known consequently as *auctoritas patrum*) to the resolutions of the *comitia*. There are several reasons for thinking that this distinction between *patres* and *conscripti* in the Senate goes back to the monarchic period. A monarchical origin for the distinction would be the best explanation of the fact that under the Republic only the *patres* could nominate the *interrex*, itself clearly a relic of the monarchy. It is also hard to imagine that the patrician clans, having gained control of the state after overthrowing the kings, would have taken the trouble to enlarge the Senate and to admit members from outside their own circle. In any case, whatever the origin of the distinction between *patres* and *conscripti*, it would be interesting to know who the *conscripti* were.

The usual interpretation is that the *conscripti* were plebeians, registered together with the *patres* on the roll of the Senate, and hence *con-scripti*; but precisely because they were plebeians, the *conscripti* were second-class senators.

This explanation seems satisfactory at first sight. But even as it stands it is open to certain objections. For example, it is hard to understand why, if some of the senators were plebeians, there is no mention in the tradition of conflicts in the Senate between patricians and plebeians from the very beginning of the Republic. But the most serious defect of the traditional view becomes clear as soon as we ask who the plebeians were. We then begin to see that the problem of identifying the *conscripti* is closely connected with the problem of identifying the plebeians.

There are two possible approaches to the problem of characterizing the *plebs*, and, as we shall soon see, the two end up by converging. The first line of approach is indicated by an analysis of the formula *populus plebesque*. The formula is undoubtedly archaic; it is found in sacral language—for example, in the formula of the *carmina Marciana* "*praetor is qui ius populo plebeique dabit summum*" (Livy 25.12.10). It is still used by Cicero in *Pro Murena* 1.1: "*ut ea res . . . populo plebique Romanae bene atque feliciter eveniret.*" It seems that the formula does not correspond to the distinction between the *comitia centuriata* and the *concilium plebis*. Now we know what the *populus* was in the archaic age: it was the army, and more particularly the infantry. An alternative title for the dictator was *magister populi*, i.e., commander of the infantry, in contrast to his deputy, the *magister equitum* (the commander of the cavalry). In one of the most ancient documents in the Latin language, the *Carmen Saliare*, the *populus* is designated "*pilumnus*"—that is, carrying the *pilum*, the weapon of the infantry. Finally, the verb *populor*, as is well known, is used to signify the action of an army, and means "to lay waste." It must therefore be considered very probable that, in the formula *populus plebesque*, the word *plebes* served to indicate those who were outside the *populus*—that is, the army of infantry.

Confirmation that the *plebs* was outside the *populus*—the people in arms—comes from a brief consideration of the structure of the plebeian institutions. When the plebeians set up their own organization in the first decades of the Republic, they took the institutions of the *populus* as their model; but they did so in a manner characteristic of people who seek to imitate institutions from which they are themselves excluded. The ten plebeian tribunes corresponded to the six legionary tribunes; the *concilia* or *comitia* of the *plebs* were modelled on the *comitia centuriata* that constituted the assembly of the army. But the plebeian tribunes were not the same as the legionary tribunes; and the *concilia plebis* were not the same as the *comitia centuriata*. Yet nothing would have been simpler for the plebeians than to use the *comitia centuriata*, or to transform the legionary tribunes into revolutionary leaders, if it were true, as the conventional view maintains, that the patricians constituted the cavalry and the plebeians formed the infantry.

It could be objected that the tradition continually refers to the refusal of the plebeians to perform military service, and that it would be difficult to understand how the patricians on their own were able to man the infantry if the plebeians were outside the infantry/*populus*. The two objections are of unequal weight and must be examined separately. It is true that tradition records the refusal of the plebeians to serve in the army; and I certainly do not mean to exclude the possibility that the plebeians could be called up in an emergency. We know that in Rome, as in the majority of ancient city-states, regular military service in the phalanx or the legion was reserved for specially privileged groups—usually identical with the possessing classes. But in times of crisis every able-bodied man was liable to be called up. The exclusion of the *plebs* from the *populus*—that is, we may now assume, from the legion—does not in itself imply that the *plebs* never took part in warfare. Now that this point has been clarified, we may turn our attention to an aspect of the tradition concerning the plebeian secession. There is no mention in our sources of an actual civil war, or even a single battle, between patricians and plebeians. The plebeians refused to obey the patricians, but they did not do battle with them. Unless human nature has changed since the fifth century B.C., the only possible explanation of this fact is that the *plebs* were able to cause serious embarrassment to the patricians by their disobedience, but were not adequately equipped to confront them in battle. Apart from this, the usual theory that equates the patricians with the cavalry—in opposition to the plebeian infantry—has no factual basis, as I believe I have demonstrated in an article in the *Journal of Roman Studies* (56 [1966]: 16–24). It is sufficient to pose a simple question: given that the cavalry in the archaic period numbered precisely 10 percent of the infantry and was very inefficient from a tactical point of view (the archaic horseman had no stirrups), would 300 or 600 mounted patricians have been able to dominate a solid legion of 3,000 or 6,000 plebeians? The answer is obvious.

Let us now turn to the second possible objection to our hypothesis that the plebeians were originally outside the legion. The objection, let us remember, is that the patricians on their own would not have been sufficiently numerous to provide the 3,000 or 6,000 troops of the archaic Roman legion. It is indeed extremely improbable, if not impossible, that the patricians could ever have put together 3,000 able-bodied males from their own ranks. We have no valid figures for the size of the Roman patriciate in the archaic age. Roman antiquarians of the late Republic seem to have reached the conclusion that there were some 130 patrician clans, and modern historians such as Mommsen have given similar estimates. Each clan naturally comprised one or more families; but we have no idea how many families there were altogether, nor do we know anything about the birth rate among the Roman aristocracy. Nevertheless it is clearly improbable that a hundred or so clans could have manned the Roman infantry as well as the cavalry. But the answer to the objection is very simple. The patricians had clients under their control, and everything we know for certain about archaic Rome and other archaic societies in Italy tends to show that clients provided an armed following for their patrons.

We all remember the story of the Fabii, who, attended only by their clients, went out to fight the Etruscans and died heroically at the River Cremera in 476 B.C. The story as we have it bears traces of imitation of the tale of Leonidas and his 300 Spartans at Thermopylae. But the basic historicity of the episode is beyond question. It is confirmed by the almost total disappearance of the Fabii from the consular *fasti* for many years after 476, whereas before the battle of the Cremera they had virtually monopolized the consulship. Another archaic story whose authenticity is beyond doubt is that of the Claudii, who came to Rome from their Sabine homeland in c. 504 B.C. accompanied by an army of clients. In Etruria the archaic condition of dependence of clients on their patrons survived much longer than at Rome. Indeed the Roman tradition preserves a record of Etruscan aristocrats who in time of war travelled around their estates mobilizing their clients. Moreover in Etruria, where there is no evidence that the plebeians ever achieved equality with the aristocracy, as they did at Rome, a strong infantry force could never have been organized if the clients had not manned the phalanx at the command of their patrons.

Obviously we should not visualize the clients of archaic Rome as an urban clientele coming together each morning to greet their master and to receive hand-outs, as they did in the late Republic and early Empire. We know all too little about the structure of ancient clientship, and many of the obligations of patrons and clients described by Dionysius of Halicarnassus are of dubious authenticity. But it seems to me beyond question that the archaic client was obliged to ransom his patron if he were taken prisoner and was also expected to contribute to the dowry of his patron's daughter, if the patron should chance to fall on hard times. These rules presuppose that the client might be a person of some means. In fact it would be hard to see how the patricians could have maintained their hold on the state for any length of time with a clientele of have-nots. The clients must have represented a relatively prosperous group, and must at least have possessed the means to obtain the costly heavy armor that was required for service in the legion. The mutual assistance of patrons and clients would undoubtedly have enabled the former to extend their private estates and to lease substantial tracts of *ager publicus* at a nominal rent; but it would also have given the clients an opportunity to improve their own position as small proprietors under the wing of the patriciate.

In this way we can begin to form a picture of an archaic society that was much more complex than is usually admitted. We have suggested that the plebeians should be differentiated from the *populus*, and that the *populus* included clients as well as the patricians themselves. We have seen that there is no reason to confine the patricians to the cavalry; rather, their power ought to have been based on control of the infantry. Consequently we should visualize the plebeians as artisans, laborers, merchants, and smallholders too poor to qualify for legionary service and in any case lacking the protection of a patrician patron who could have made their qualification possible. Now there are several reasons for thinking that those who served in the legion were originally called *classici*, and that those who were excluded from the legion or "class" were defined as *infra classem*. The obvious conclusion would therefore seem to be that the plebeians were originally identical with the *infra classem*.

If we now turn to the *conscripti*, we can see that obviously they cannot in origin have been plebeians. They must have represented another group of families connected with the patriciate (without whose assistance they could not have entered the Senate), but not to be confused with the bulk of the clients. For want of any other word we may use the term *conscripti* to indicate the social group that provided senators in addition to the *patres*. If we accept the idea of a group of *conscripti* who were neither patricians nor plebeians, we can perhaps at last resolve one of the oldest and most difficult problems raised by the republican *fasti*—the list of consuls from the beginning of the Republic. As is well known, tradition is unanimous in asserting that plebeians were first admitted to the consulship in 366 B.C. And yet a simple examination of the names of the consuls who held office in the period between 509 and 445 B.C. reveals the names of persons belonging to plebeian *gentes*, for example the Cassii, Volumnii, Sempronii, Minucii, and Genucii. Notoriously, those who maintain that the *fasti* were to a large extent interpolated in the last centuries of the Republic avail themselves of these same plebeian names in order to support their contention. But the interpolation hypothesis is open to various objections, one of which is that if plebeian names were inserted into the lists in the last centuries of the Republic, we should expect them to be the names of the plebeian *gentes* that were most important during the late Republic—the *gentes*, that is to say, who had an interest in projecting their current importance back into the past, and who had the means to tamper with the lists of the *fasti* and to interpolate them. Alternatively it has been suggested, in spite of what the tradition says, that plebeians were in fact admitted to the consulship in the first half of the fifth century, and that the proof lies precisely in the *fasti*. But it is not easy to understand how the tradition could have erred on such a fundamental point. It is also very hard to explain how there could have been plebeian consuls in the very period of the most bitter struggles between patricians and plebeians. Both the interpolation theory, and the view that the plebeian names are to be accepted as genuinely plebeian, encounter serious difficulties. A third and less improbable explanation, which found favor with G. De Sanctis, is that the fifth-century Cassii, Volumnii, Sempronii, and so on, were members of patrician clans that became extinct, and were not related to the plebeian *gentes* that later bore those names. But it must be conceded that this third explanation appears to be born of necessity; it postulates the existence of otherwise unknown patrician clans in order to maintain harmony between the *fasti* and the annalistic tradition. My view is that between the patricians and plebeians there was an intermediate group of *conscripti* from which senators were chosen. It does not seem unlikely that this same group of *conscripti* provided the few nonpatrician consuls during the first half of the fifth century. They were nonpatricians, but also nonplebeians, if considered from the point of view of contemporaries.

3

If we accept the above reconstruction of the social and political structure of Rome at the beginning of the Republic, a reconstruction that is admittedly hypothetical, we are faced with the problem of explaining how the *plebs* gradually came to absorb intermediate groups like the clients and the *conscripti*; how plebeians came to be admitted into the *classis*, or legion; and how the *plebs* became virtually identical with the *populus*—even if the *populus* continued to include patricians as part of the army. Resolving the problem would be tantamount to explaining the revolution that after some 150 years transformed the patrician state into a state governed by a mixed patrician-plebeian aristocracy.

Two difficulties stand in the way of our understanding of this revolution. The first is that like many other revolutions, this one too ended in compromise. An assessment based on the concluding events of 366 B.C. would involve the risk of misunderstanding the character of the plebeian movement of a century earlier. The second difficulty is the more serious: it is that we have almost no idea of the effect of the continuous warfare of the fifth century B.C. on the structure of Roman society. These problems of interpretation can be illustrated by a single concrete example. One of the most remarkable features of the first years of the fifth century is the proliferation of large temples in Rome. The temple of Jupiter Capitolinus of 509 B.C. was followed by those of Saturn (497 B.C.), Mercury (495 B.C.), Ceres (493 B.C.), and Castor (484 B.C.). We shall presently have to consider one of these temples as an expression of the religious needs of the early republican age. But it is clear that these constructions also represent an exceptional investment of capital and labor. Temples could only be built by specialized craftsmen, and, to judge from our knowledge of the Greek world, teams of specialized craftsmen moved from place to place as and when work became available. The construction of a number of temples in Rome must therefore imply either that groups of craftsmen migrated to Rome or that local workshops grew up in the city. In either case, and both are possible, Rome was infected by a new political and economic ferment. But if the provenance of the craftsmen is not precisely known, an even more obscure question is the source of the immense capital sums required to complete the construction of the temples. The period of the late sixth and early fifth centuries seems to have been one of considerable building activity in the religious sphere both in and around Rome. The Portonaccio temple at Veii, the temple of Poggio Casetta at Volsinii, and the temples at Ardea, Satricum, and Lanuvium seem to belong to this period; and we are only now beginning to see the systematic exploration of the archaic temples of Latium and southern Etruria. One has the impression that those responsible for the construction of the Roman temples were working in parallel with the neighboring cities, and perhaps competing with them for prestige. The phenomenon lasted for a couple of decades and then suddenly came to an end; for at least half a century afterwards, our tradition, which is meticulous in recording matters of this kind, knows of no further temple building in Rome. Should we ascribe the suspension of temple building to a diminution of religious sentiment, or to an economic recession caused by the increasingly difficult wars against the Aequi and Volsci? And what were the economic consequences of this suspension of activity in the field of public works? We can pose the questions, but we have no way of answering them.

Within the very narrow confines of our knowledge, one fact emerges as beyond dispute: the extraordinary strength of the plebeian organization. In the space of a few decades the plebeians created their own popular assembly in opposition to the *comitia centuriata*; they instituted their own magistrates, ten tribunes and two aediles, who were both more numerous and more effective than the patrician magistrates; and they founded their own religious center, the temple of Ceres, Liber, and Libera, which in its triadic form emulated the Capitoline triad of Jupiter, Juno, and Minerva. In the temple of Ceres the *plebs* established an archive, something the patricians seem not to have had. The intervention of the tribunes became formalized in precise juridical acts, which in part resembled the interventions of the consuls and in part went beyond them; even if their powers did not exceed those of the consuls, they certainly went beyond what the consuls actually did. The plebiscites of the plebeian assemblies acquired a de facto legal authority. Moreover processes of religious exclusion, which had the effect of lynch law, were used to paralyze the laws of the patrician state.

The success of the *plebs* in purely administrative terms is confirmed by the fact that the patricians were themselves forced to recognize the glaring omissions in the patrician state that had been revealed by the plebeians. The patrician state had no officials comparable to the plebeian aediles to look after its temples, markets, and archives. Consequently, at the time of the final compromise in 366 B.C., not only were the plebeian aediles recognized as state functionaries along with the tribunes of the *plebs*, but in addition two new aediles were created in imitation of them. It appears moreover that from as early as 449 B.C. *senatus consulta* had been deposited in the plebeian temple of Ceres, which was the only organized archive in Rome.

We do not know where the plebeians might have found the ideas and the effective means to bring about this process of organization, which to all appearances has no parallel among the other indigenous communities of ancient Italy, and is only with difficulty to be compared to the development of democracy in Sicily and in Athens. But certain indications nevertheless point in the direction of Greece both in the matter of religious ideas and in that of economic relationships. The temple of Ceres, Liber, and Libera was erected, so tradition maintains, in accordance with an instruction of the Sibylline oracles, which had been imported from Greek Cumae and were written in Greek. The temple itself was decorated by Greek artists whose names were recorded on the temple in a Greek inscription. The cult was Greek, and in later times at least it was run by Greek priestesses who were brought from Naples and Velia and were given Roman citizenship. On the economic side we know that the plebeians were sometimes obliged, in times of shortage, to have recourse to imported grain from Magna Graecia and Sicily. All of this is suggestive, even if none of it can be taken as proof. The Roman *plebs* was oriented toward the Greek world, whereas the patriciate was traditionally linked with Etruria. Even in the fourth century, the Fabii and other aristocrats were still sent to Caere to learn Etruscan; and we now know, thanks to the discovery of a silver bowl from the Tomba Bernardini, that the Veturii of Rome had Etruscan-speaking relatives in nearby Praeneste. The plebeians must have included craftsmen and merchants who spoke Greek and had visited Greek cities in the course of their work; Greek artists, we know, worked in Rome on the plebeian temple of Ceres, whereas Etruscan artists had decorated the temple of Capitoline Jupiter. It would be absurd to make a schematic equation of the opposition between *plebs* and patriciate and an opposition between Greek and Etruscan culture. Even if we were tempted in that direction, we should be contradicted by the fact that at that very time Rome was penetrated by the cult of Castor and Pollux, a cult that was both Greek and unequivocally aristocratic.

The foregoing remarks are perhaps sufficient to clarify, if not actually to explain, why the humble *plebs* became a formidable attraction to those who were not patricians. Dissatisfied clients and *conscripti* with grievances against the *patres* must have begun to wonder if it might not be worth joining the *plebs*. The plebeians offered them the opportunity to satisfy their ambitions, and provided new ties of political solidarity and the attraction of an alternative culture with a

Greek orientation. They afforded examples of administrative efficiency. In the difficult years of the wars against the Volsci and Aequi, in which the Roman territory undoubtedly contracted, it is likely enough that some of the old ties of *clientela* were enervated, and on the other hand that the patricians, forced onto the defensive, became less generous with their assistance and consequently began to lose clients.

We do not know when the process of polarization of Roman society between patricians and plebeians was concluded—if it is correct to speak of a conclusion. It may be that when the Twelve Tables introduced the short-lived ban on intermarriage between patricians and plebeians, the process was already complete. But that is neither certain nor even probable. There is no reason to assume that, when the Twelve Tables prescribed "*ne conubium patribus cum plebe esset*" (Livy 4.4.5; cf. Cic. *De re pub.* 2.37), they meant to preclude all marriages between patricians and nonpatricians. It is possible that in the Twelve Tables *plebes* still had the restricted meaning that we have attempted to establish in the earlier part of this paper. It is hard to believe that the son of a patrician senator would not have been able to marry the daughter of a conscript senator and vice versa. But it nevertheless remains certain that the Twelve Tables represent the most impressive body of evidence for the reorientation of Roman culture away from the Etruscan sphere and toward the Greek sphere in the fifth century. Whatever the truth of the story that the Romans sent ambassadors to Greece to study Greek laws, the codification of the Twelve Tables is an imitation of the Greek codes. Scholars have repeatedly pointed out the Greek influences on the language of the Twelve Tables, in respect not only of vocabulary but also of syntax. Precisely because the Twelve Tables were compiled in response to plebeian pressure (plebeians were included in the second Decemvirate, which I consider authentic), the codification finds its place in that political and cultural plebeian movement of the fifth century whose main developments we have attempted to trace. Another essential consequence of the plebeian movement was the gradual admission of plebeians into the legions. Unfortunately the details of this process are no longer detectable in our tradition, which is very poorly informed about the evolution of the army in the early centuries of the Republic. If, as seems certain, the army was originally identical with the *classis*, and excluded those who were *infra classem*, it follows that there must have been a long and complex evolution between this original phase and the later system described in detail in our sources, which divided the army into five census classes with different kinds of armor and weapons. The penetration of the *plebs* into the legion must have coincided with the subdivision of the *classis* into several classes and at the same time with the at least partial intermingling of plebeians and clients.

The movement slowed down in the second half of the fifth century, and in the end the richer and by now more respectable elements of the *plebs* made common cause with the patricians and obtained full political equality in return. If it is true, as we have tried to suggest, that nonpatrician senators and clients of the patricians were becoming identified with the *plebs*, the fact provides an additional explanation of the gradual emasculation of the plebeian movement in the fourth century. Other causes are to be found in the new territorial expansion of Rome, which made it easier for the patricians to provide colonial allotments for the plebeians. With the increase in its size, the *plebs* lost coherence.

All this provides material for further research on a topic no less important than the one we have sought to tackle—but perhaps of less human interest. For the rise of the Roman *plebs*, its orientation toward Greek culture, and the break it represented in the social and political structures of archaic Italy still engage us as ancient events of our culture.

Author's Appendix (1984)

My paper of 1967 has played its honorable part in the discussion on early Rome in the past fifteen years. It would be foolish to bring it up to date or to defend it from criticisms. Any serious contribution to scholarship bears the mark of the time, space, and circumstances in which it was produced. On the other hand, there is no point in reiterating one's own ideas: *dite la vostra che ho detto la mia*. I shall only observe that my paper implied two different conclusions: (1) that patricians and plebeians did not correspond to cavalry and infantry; (2) that the *conscripti* of the early Senate, together with the early legionaries, were provided by clients of the patricians. The theory that the patricians were horsemen was in those years around 1965 almost identifiable with the interpretation of archaic Rome by A. Alföldi. This brought me into discussions with him, for instance in *Historia* 18 (1969): 385–88 (now in Momigliano, *Contr. V* [1975]: 635–39), and in *RSI* 89 (1977): 160–62 (now in *Contr. VI*. II [1980]: 682–85); cf. Alföldi, *Frühgeschichte* (1976) and bibl. there quoted. See also V. Ilari, *RISG* 78 (1971): 117–65; and F. De Martino, *PP* 191 (1980): 143–60.

Far more complex is the interpretation of the evidence on *patres/conscripti*, *populus/plebs*, *adsidui/proletarii*. My later utterances on this question are to be found in my paper in *Labeo* 23 (1977): 7–15 (now in *Contr. VI*. II [1980]: 476–85) and in my chapter of the forthcoming second edition of *CAH* VII, a first draft of which is to be found in my *Settimo Contributo* (1984): 379–436. On this second thesis there is plenty of new and important work in different directions that has to be examined carefully. See, above all, L. R. Ménager, *RIDA* 19 (1972): 367–97; P. C. Ranouil, *Patriciat* (1975); A Guarino, *Riv.* (1975); D. Kienast, *Bonner Jahrb.* 175 (1975): 83–112; L. Zusi, *Critica storica* 6 (1975): 177–230; I. Hahn, *Oikumene* 1 (1976): 47–75; G. Mancuso, *Ann. sem. giur. di Palermo* 36 (1976): 253–88; J. Gagé, *Enquêtes* (1977); J.-C. Richard, *Origines* (1978); P. Angelini, *Patriziato* (1979); F. De Martino, "Clienti" (1980); V. Mannino, *Auctoritas patrum* (1979); J. Martinez-Pinna Nieto, *Ejército* (1981); S. Tondo, *Profilo* (1981); E. Ferenczy, *Oikumene* 3 (1982): 193–202; P. M. Martin, *Royauté* (1982), cf. my review in *RSI* 95 (1983): 521–23; A. Heuss, *Gedanken und Vermutungen zur frühen römischen Regierungsgewalt*, Nachr. Akad. Göttingen, 1982, no. 10; J.-C. Richard, *RD* 61 (1983): 181–94; T. Cornell, "Failure of the Plebs" (1983): 101–20.

Editor's Appendix

This is the paper that most clearly and comprehensively outlines the author's views on the rise of the plebeians and the social structure of Rome at the beginning of the Conflict of the Orders. The author discussed some of the same and related problems in a number of other articles: *JRS* 53 (1963): 95ff.; 56 (1966): 16ff.; "Patrizi e plebei" (1967); "Origins of the Republic" (1969); *Historia* 18 (1969): 385ff.; *Labeo* 23 (1977): 7ff. Among these, the "Interim Report on the Origins of Rome" (*JRS* 53 [1963]), contains ample references to ancient sources and modern research. The following brief selection of references is intended to provide at least a minimum of documentation to the reader of this volume. For general literature on archaic Rome, see Momigliano, *JRS* 53 (1963): 95 n. 5, and for an update the Author's Appendix above, which also lists his most recent contributions. Most of the views of this paper are discussed in great detail in Richard, *Origines* (1978).

Early sources on archaic Rome: For the pontifical chronicles: R. Besnier, "Archives" (1953): 1ff.; B. W. Frier, *Annales* (1979). For Aristodemus of Cumae: Dion. Hal. 5.36; Livy 2.14; Festus, p. 487 L.; cf. Alföldi, *Early Rome* (1965): 56ff. For Timaeus: Momigliano, "Timeo, Fabio Pittore e il primo censimento di Servio Tullio," in *Miscellanea di Studi Alessandrini in memoria di A. Rostagni* (Turin, 1963): 180ff. Early documents: for the law of Servius Tullius, cf. Dion. Hal. 4.26; for the *foedus Cassianum*: Cic. Pro Balbo 23.53; for the *lex Icilia de Aventino*: Livy 3.31; Dion. Hal. 10.32. Annalistic historiography and antiquarians: cf. E. Badian, "Early Historians" (1966); E. Gabba, "Tradizione letteraria" (1967): 133ff.; E. Rawson, *JRS* 62 (1972): 33ff.; *Latomus* 35 (1976): 689ff.; D. Timpe, in *ANRW* I.2 (1972): 928ff.; Frier, *Annales*.

Comparative studies: for Italian societies contemporary with archaic Rome, cf. Momigliano, *JRS* 53 (1963): 114ff. Use of anthropological evidence: ibid., 113f., and "Patrizi e plebei" (1967): 202f.

New archaeological evidence: for a thorough reexamination of the evidence, see E. Gjerstad, *Early Rome* (1953–73); for a recent summary, see the contributions in *DArch*, n.s., 2 (1980) on "La formazione della città nel Lazio." For the dedications to Astarte in Pyrgi: M. Pallottino et al., *Arch. class.* 16 (1964): 58ff. For the statuettes of Aeneas found at Veii: G. Q. Giglioli, *Bull. museo imp.* 12 (1941): 3ff.; for the dedication to Lar Aeneas: M. Guarducci, *Bull. del museo della civiltà romana* 19 (1956–58): 1ff.; cf. now the exhibition catalogue *Enea nel Lazio* (Rome, 1983). For the cult of Castor and Pollux at Rome: Livy 2.20.12; 42.5; at Lavinium: F. Castagnoli, *Lavinium* I (1972): 106f., 112. For the excavations of the Regia, see F. E. Brown, "Regia" (1967): 45ff., and now the summary of F. Coarelli, *Foro* (1983): 56ff. For the dedication by Aulus Vibenna found at Veii: L. Pareti, *SE* 5 (1931): 154ff.; M. Pallottino, *SE* 13 (1939): 455; G. Radke, *RE* VIIIA. 2 (1958): 2454ff. Vases with Etruscan inscriptions found in Rome:

M. Pallottino, *BCAR* 69 (1941): 101ff.; *SE* 22 (1952–53): 309. Tomba Bernardini in Praeneste: C. D. Curtis, *Mem. Am. Acad. Rome* 3 (1919): 9ff.

Works on archaic Rome mentioned in the text: K. Hanell, "Das traditionelle Anfangsjahr der römischen Republik," in *Dragma M. P. Nilsson dedicatum* (Lund, Sweden, 1939): 256ff.; id., *Amt* (1946); Gjerstad, *Early Rome*; on both see Momigliano, *JRS* 53 (1963): 101ff. G. Dumézil, *Jupiter, Mars, Quirinus* (Turin, 1955); *L'Idéologie tripartite des Indo-Européens*, Coll. Latomus 31 (Brussels, 1958); furthermore id., *Arch. Rel.* (1970), and *Camillus* (1980); on Dumézil see Momigliano, *JRS* 53 (1963): 113f., and *History and Theory* 23 (1984): 312ff.; cf. now the papers in *Opus* 2. 2 (1983) on "Aspetti dell'opera di Georges Dumézil."

Archaic terminology: for *patres/conscripti*, see Momigliano, "Patrizi e plebei" (1967): 204ff.; and "Origins of the Republic" (1969): 24ff.; for a recent detailed discussion: Richard, *Origines*, 478ff. *Populus plebesque*: Momigliano, "Patrizi e plebei," 212ff.; and "Origins of the Republic," 24ff.; cf. recently Richard, *Origines*, 110ff.

Patrician clans and their clients: for arguments against the theory that equates the patricians with the cavalry, cf. the literature mentioned in the Author's Appendix above, and Momigliano, *JRS* 56 (1966): 16ff.; *Historia* 18 (1969): 385ff. For ancient calculations of the number of patrician clans: Festus, p. 304 L.; Plut. *Popl.* 11; cf. Th. Mommsen, *RhM* 16 (1861): 32ff.; Ranouil, *Patriciat* (1975): 183ff. Fabii at the Cremera: Livy 2.50; in the consular *fasti*: Broughton, *Magistrates* I (1951): 1ff. Arrival of the Claudii in Rome: Livy 2.16.5; Dion. Hal. 5.40.5; Plut. *Popl.* 21; cf. Alföldi, *Early Rome*, 159ff.; C. Ampolo, *DArch* 4/5 (1970–71): 37ff. For the obligations of patrons and clients: Dion. Hal. 2.9–10; cf. now the detailed discussion by N. Rouland, *Clientèle* (1979): 33ff. Clients in Etruscan armies: Momigliano, "Origins of the Republic" (1969): 27; A. M. Snodgrass, *JHS* 85 (1965): 116ff.; H. H. Scullard, *Etr. Cities* (1967): 224f., 238; C. Saulnier, *Armée* (1980), chapter 5. For a recent discussion of the role of the clients in the Roman army, see Richard, *Origines*, 376ff. *Classici/infra classem*: Festus, p. 100 L.; Gellius, *Noctes Atticae* 6.13; cf. E. Meyer, *Staat* (1964): 54 with n. 22; Richard, *Origines*, 364ff.; id. *RPh* 51 (1977): 229ff.

The rise of the plebeians: For the absorption of the *conscripti* and *cli-*

entes into the *plebs*, cf. Momigliano, "Patrizi e plebei," 217ff., and "Origins of the Republic," 28ff. For the strength of the plebeian organization: id., "Patrizi e plebei," 217ff.; F. Altheim, *Lex sacr.* (1940); id., *Röm. Geschichte* II (1953): 170ff. Archives: Livy 3.55.13; cf. C. Dziatzko, *RE* II (1896): 560; G. De Sanctis, *RFIC* 10 (1932): 433ff.; H. Le Bonniec, *Cérès* (1958): 355ff. Lynching: J. Bleicken, *ZRG* 76 (1959): 351ff. Temple building in and around Rome: A. Andrén, *Architectural Terracottas from Etrusco-Italic Temples*, 2 vols. (Lund, Sweden, 1939–40). For the compromise of 366: Livy 6.42.13f.; cf. K. von Fritz, *Historia* 1 (1950): 13ff. Plebeians in the second Decemvirate: Livy 3.35.11; Dion. Hal. 10.58.4; cf. Ogilvie, *Comm.* (1965): 461f. For the development of the Roman army, see now D. Kienast, *Bonner Jahrb.* 175 (1975): 83ff.; Saulnier, *Armée*.

Greek influences in archaic Rome: cf. Momigliano, *JRS* 53 (1963): 120f.; id., "Patrizi e plebei," 216f., and "Origins of the Republic," 31f. For the Sibylline oracles and the temple of Ceres: Dion. Hal. 6.17. Greek artists: Pliny, *Nat. Hist.* 35.12.154. Greek priestesses from Naples and Velia: Cic. *Pro Balbo* 24.55; Festus, p. 268 L. Grain imports from Magna Graecia and Sicily: Momigliano, *Contr. IV*: 331ff. Knowledge of Etruscan among Fabii: Livy 9.36.3; Val. Max. 4.3.9. Roman ambassadors to study Greek laws: Livy 3.32, with Ogilvie, *Comm.*, 449f. For the Greek contribution to the Twelve Tables: F. Wieacker, "XII Tafeln" (1967): 330ff.

KURT A. RAAFLAUB

VII

From Protection and Defense to Offense and Participation: Stages in the Conflict of the Orders

1

If we keep to the traditional dates, the Conflict of the Orders broke out at Rome in 494 B.C. with the first *secessio plebis*, and it ended in 287 with the *lex Hortensia*, which made the decrees of the plebeian assembly binding for the whole community. In the context of social conflicts, such chronological limits usually have more symbolic than real value. The problems that led to social conflicts and the eruption of the *secessio* must have been building up over a long time.[1] And the

---

1. This is usually overlooked; it is indicated, for example, by the time span separating the early symptoms of an agrarian crisis depicted in Hesiod's *Works and Days* from the fully developed crisis in the time of Solon: cf. Austin and Vidal-Naquet, *Econ.* (1977): 58ff.; E. Will, "Aux origines du régime foncier grecque: Homère, Hésiode et l'arrière-plan mycénien," *REA* 59 (1957): 5ff.; id., "La Grèce archaïque" (1965): 62ff.

VII. Stages in the Conflict of the Orders   199

very nature of the compromise that brought about the last major achievement of the plebeians in 287 ensured that tensions would continue between the new governing class (the patricio-plebeian nobility) and all those who did not share their wealth and power.[2] Artificial as these chronological limits are, therefore, they still enclose a time span of more than two hundred years. Even for archaic societies, which, from the perspective of recent more hectic times, developed rather slowly, this is a very long time. And there are indications that it was a time full of dramatic events and significant changes, internally and externally. In fact, there seem to have been so many and such fundamental changes that any label designed to cover the whole period, although it may be necessary and justified from certain points of view and for practical purposes, is nevertheless bound to be misleading because it creates the unwarranted impression of unity and homogeneity.

Such a "unitarian view," with its concomitant tendency toward artificial homogenization, is common in modern works on the early Roman Republic. It is caused partly by the scarcity of contemporary sources, partly by a similar tendency prevailing in the reconstruction of the ancient historians, and partly by a lack of awareness of, and familiarity with, the specific character and problems of archaic societies. The inherent danger becomes obvious when we look at the corresponding period in Greece. Owing to the preservation of more numerous, more diverse and, most importantly, more contemporary sources we are somewhat better informed about developments in archaic Athens especially, where we would very much hesitate to describe the years between roughly 700 and 480 or 450 B.C. as one coherent and unified period.[3] We are used to making sharp distinctions not only between long but even between rather short periods within those two and a half centuries. We have learned to recognize the interdependence of external and internal developments and to place each single event and change in its proper context of historical causation and contemporary circumstances. Nobody would deny, for example, that the constitutional changes brought about by Cleisthenes

---

2. Cf. chapter XII below.
3. Although that, too, can be done profitably for specific purposes; see, e.g., A. Heuss, *A&A* 2 (1946): 26ff., and, recently, id., "Archaische Politik" (1981).

in c. 507 or by Ephialtes in 462 were the results of specific and unique political constellations. Most of what was demanded, proposed, and achieved at that time could not have been demanded, proposed, and achieved fifty years earlier. Similarly, the farmers who provided the bulk of the hoplite army (the *zeugitai*, corresponding to the Roman *adsidui* or *classici*) were only given access to the archonship in the middle of the fifth century, when this office had been devalued and democracy was fundamentally changing the political landscape; and wealthy nonaristocratic citizens did not gain a share in true political leadership until considerably later. We understand why neither of these groups could foster such ambitions in the sixth century, although their respective property classes had been politically acknowledged and integrated by the administrative reforms of Solon.

There is no apparent reason why the same principles should not be applied to the history of archaic Rome. The scarcity and problematic nature of our sources are not decisive obstacles. Even if we approach them most critically, there are enough indications to enable us to distinguish several different stages and to perceive the specific character not only of these stages but also of the changes and circumstances marking their beginning and end. This, however, is not done consciously enough in modern scholarship. If the Conflict of the Orders is not presented as one unified and homogeneous period, it is usually still understood as such. It is divided into sections mainly for practical reasons, and the lines of division tend to follow the highlights of the conflict or other crucial events, such as the decemviral legislation, the Gallic disaster, and the Licinio-Sextian laws. Even those who emphasize changes in plebeian strategy or distinguish between an earlier stage of unsuccessful plebeian fighting and a later stage of plebeian success and achievement still generally presuppose uniformity of content and objectives from beginning to end.

It certainly is not sufficiently accepted among scholars dealing with archaic Rome that the struggles of the middle of the fourth century cannot possibly have been the same as, or even similar to, those of a hundred years earlier. Changes in Rome's external position and within the groups opposed to each other must have fundamentally altered the conditions and methods of fighting and solving internal conflicts. In short, in a changing world each generation had its own problems and objectives, and the Conflict of the Orders must therefore have consisted of a sequence of conflicts of diverse character and complexity. It is the purpose of this paper to present some observations that may help to bring out the fundamental differences between the early and the late stages and thereby to reach a more differentiated understanding of the conflict as a whole.[4]

2

The first step toward overcoming the prevailing rather static view is to understand fully how much it is rooted in the concept of the Conflict of the Orders that was developed by generations of Roman historians in the last two centuries of the Republic. In chapter I it was suggested that the situation and developments of the late fourth and early third centuries acted as a screen for the earliest Roman historians. They knew there was something behind it, that the picture they saw was the result of a long evolution, but they had no idea where this evolution had started and what ways and detours it had taken. Their reconstruction was therefore bound to be linear and simplistic. Since, in addition, it was beyond their imagining that earlier conditions might have been totally different from those familiar to them, they did not hesitate to assume that most of those familiar concepts had either existed from the beginning or had been introduced very early.

A good example for this kind of thinking is the *leges Valeriae de provocatione*. The only authentic one was passed in 300 B.C., toward the end of the conflict. But for the annalists—at least for the latest ones[5]—it was natural to assume, and needed neither documentation nor justification, that laws of such fundamental importance for re-

---

4. I hope mainly to stimulate discussion. Since the emphasis lies in the presentation of possibilities and potential avenues of better understanding, the documentation has deliberately been kept to a minimum. For an attempt similar to mine, see now T. J. Cornell, "Failure of the Plebs" (1983).

5. I am aware of the problems connected with generalizations such as "the annalists." I use this one as a convenient formula for all that we know about the annalistic tradition, mostly of course through the interpretation of Livy and Dionysius of Halicarnassus.

publican freedom had been issued in the very first year of the Republic and reinstated after the tyranny of the second Decemvirate.[6]

In a similar process of anachronistic reconstruction, the familiar principle of *lectio senatus* was assumed to have been valid all through Roman history. Romulus, it was believed, had formed the first Senate by selecting the hundred most worthy *patres*. Some of his successors had added more and brought the number up to three hundred. Many senators had lost their lives in the cruel years of Tarquinius Superbus's reign; others had been expelled with or soon after the family of the "tyrant." The depleted senatorial ranks were filled in the first year of the Republic by promoting the best of the equestrian order. This last bit of information all too obviously reveals its origin in the time of, or after, Sulla, and the creation of the Senate by Romulus is a typical part of a Greek foundation legend.[7] But the whole concept of *lectio senatus* belongs in the middle or late Republic. It presupposes the existence not only of a large nonsenatorial but otherwise equally wealthy and prestigious upper class of *equites* out of which new senators could be recruited whenever needed, but also of a group of ambitious men within this class of *equites* who, like the *homines novi* of later centuries, strove for admission to high office.

The late republican annalists quite naturally assumed that there had been such groups at the beginning of the Republic and even earlier. Logically, therefore, from their point of view the Conflict of the Orders must from early on have been dominated by two separate aspects: the mainly economic and social demands of the lower classes and the primarily political demands of the upper classes. It should be noted, however, that the nonpolitical factors are given clear precedence in time. Livy does not mention plebeian aspirations to high office before the discussions about plebeian participation in the de-

---

6. Livy 2.8.2; 3.55.4 (both with Ogilvie's comm.); 10.9.3–6 (300 B.C.). Cf., e.g., J. Bleicken, *ZRG* 76 (1959): 345f., 357 with n. 67; Elster, *Studien* (1976): 120ff. Debate over this will probably never end; inter alios, R. Develin, *Mnemosyne*, 4th ser., 31 (1978): 45ff., and chapter XI below at n. 28ff., strongly disagrees with me; but see my suggestion in chapter I above (end of appendix).

7. For the sources, see O'Brien Moore, "Senatus," *RE* suppl. 6 (1935): 663ff.; A. Magdelain, *"Auspicia"* (1964): 471 n. 1; E. S. Staveley, *Historia* 32 (1983): 24 n. 1. For the time of Sulla, see Ogilvie, *Comm.* (1965): 236; for the foundation legends, see T. J. Cornell, "Foundation of Rome" (1978): 131ff.

cemviral college in 454 and plebeian access to the consulship in 445.[8] He does not recognize as plebeian those persons in the earliest consular *fasti* about whose allegedly nonpatrician status modern scholars have been conducting such a long and sophisticated debate.[9] He does not know of any socially prominent plebeian families in the first decades of the Republic (the plebeian leaders in those turbulent years are certainly not portrayed as such), and the Senate is for him practically synonymous with "the patricians."

All this certainly needs to be explained. But it seems more important in the present context that already in the second great confrontation, still very early in the Conflict of the Orders, Livy puts the struggle for plebeian participation in political leadership on center stage. From then on the socioeconomic and the political aspects of the struggle are equally prominent. Their combination in a comprehensive program finally gives the plebeian cause enough momentum for the first major breakthrough in 367. It is repeated successfully thereafter, and the conflict comes to an end when those separate demands are finally all satisfied.[10]

The annalists clearly assumed development and change in the conflict. But since, in their view, all the main elements had been introduced within the first fifty years,[11] and since the nonrecurrent problems (such as the codification of law and the abolition of the intermarriage ban) were settled early and rather quickly, they could only elaborate on the gradual intensification of the struggle and on the adoption of increasingly refined tactics by the plebeians. In other words, they expressed change by using criteria of quantity and intensity rather than quality and objectives. In their reconstruction, therefore, the character of the conflict basically remains the same, if not from the very beginning, at least from the middle of the fifth century to the end.

Historically, however, it is highly unlikely, and should make us

8. See, on the one hand, Livy 3.31.7f.; 32.6f., on the other, 4.1.2f., and, generally, 4.1–7.
9. Any senator and any consul of the early decades of the Republic naturally was a patrician to him, even if he was low-born (2.32.8); cf. Cic. *Brut.* 62; Palmer, *Arch. Comm.* (1970): 290ff.
10. Cf. especially the political analysis of Ferenczy, *Patr. State* (1976): 45ff.
11. Cf. Cornell, chapter II above at n. 59; id., "Tradizione storiografica" (1980): 32f.; Ungern-Sternberg, chapter XII below at n. 73.

very suspicious, that for more than 150 years the plebeians supposedly fought for the very goals they finally achieved in the late fourth and early third centuries.[12] Further, if in the time of the Decemvirate some plebeians were already so eager to reach positions of leadership, and if the plebeian organization was, as it seems, powerful enough to wrest various fundamental concessions from the patricians, then we should greatly wonder why, according to Livy's own admission, the first plebeian in fact only reached such a position more than forty years later.[13]

Nevertheless, many modern historians have adopted the annalists' view. In particular, they take it for granted that there always existed a class of wealthy and noble plebeians who were able and willing, even desperately eager, to compete for admission to high office and leadership, and that the Conflict of the Orders therefore had a socioeconomic and a specifically political component from the beginning. F. Heichelheim and C. Yeo, for example, write:

> The biggest fiction created by the annalistic tradition is that of the absolute and exclusive domination of the state by the patrician minority after the fall of the Tarquins. This fiction has become, both to the staunchest conservative defenders of the tradition and to its most radical skeptics, almost an unquestioned article of faith. . . . [In an] anachronistic and untrustworthy . . . portrayal of Roman society in the first two decades of the Republic . . . the annalists . . . represent the government of Rome as the exclusive mo-

---

12. To be precise, it is not the existence of certain economic and social problems plaguing a society over many decades in varying intensity that causes such suspicion (for that we have instructive analogies in archaic Greece: cf. n. 1), but rather the assumption that an acute social conflict was fought violently and almost continuously over such an extended period, over the same issues, and by two classes that each possessed its typical structure and composition from the very beginning. Long-term continuity and little change in some areas is, of course, easily compatible with fundamental change and the emergence of new factors in others.

13. Livy 5.12.8–11 (with Ogilvie's *Comm.*, for the year 400 B.C.); 6.37.8. Modern scholars have discovered three "plebeian" consular tribunes before then, the earliest in 422 (Heurgon, *Rise* [1973]: 174), but they were not recognized as such by Livy (or by Licinius Macer); they pose many difficult problems (cf. Pinsent, *Mil. Trib.* [1975]: 36ff.; Ranouil, *Patriciat* [1975]: 97ff.), and even if they were authentic plebeians, this would only modify, not invalidate, my statement. For a possible explanation of the difficulty, see now Cornell, "Failure of the Plebs" (1983): 112f.; for my answer to Bickerman's argument, see below n. 112.

nopoly of fifty or sixty patrician families in a period of war and uprising in Latium, internal unrest and confusion, with Sabine and Volscan tribesmen moving in to fill the power vacuum left by the Etruscans, while the Tarquins struggled to restore the monarchy. It would have been practically impossible under these conditions for the patricians to maintain their control of the government without the support, co-operation, and partnership of some of the rich and powerful families of the plebeian class.[14]

And in his basically very sensible sketch P. A. Brunt remarks that "the distinction [between patricians and plebeians] was one of birth, not wealth; the conflict of the orders is unintelligible unless there were rich plebeians . . . ; the rich plebeians, who desired to gain a share in political power, from time to time made themselves the champions of their oppressed brethren."[15]

The existence of a nonpatrician aristocracy must necessarily be assumed by all those who explain the "closure of the patriciate" in the 480s as the successful attempt to monopolize power by one part only of a much broader group of aristocratic families; according to this hypothesis those who did not belong to this elite or "inner circle" ended up among the plebeians and, of course, concentrated their efforts on regaining access to political office and decision making.[16] It is one of the objectives of this paper to challenge such views. In deliberate contrast to them, I would suggest that the early development and the specific character of the Roman Conflict of the Orders are only intelligible if there was at the outset no substantial nonpatrician, but otherwise comparable, rich and noble upper class.[17]

I propose to distinguish the following stages, which I purposely

14. F. M. Heichelheim and C. A. Yeo, *A History of the Roman People* (Englewood Cliffs, N.J., 1962): 83; only slightly modified in the 2nd ed. (1984): 55.
15. Brunt, *Conflicts* (1971): 47 (accepted, e.g., by Finley, *Econ.* [1973]: 45f.). The same view, e.g., in G. E. M. de Ste. Croix, *Class Struggle* (1981): 332ff.; J. Martin, *Soc. Hist.* 4 (1979): 295ff. (see chapter I, n. 92 above); Ungern-Sternberg, chapter XII below, part 1.
16. See, e.g., G. De Sanctis, *Storia* I² (1956): 219ff.; the discussion in Heurgon, *Rise* (1973): 165f.; Poma, *Studi* (1974): 69ff.; A. Magdelain, "*Auspicia*" (1964): 458ff., especially 462ff.; J. Cels Saint-Hilaire and C. Feuvrier-Prévotat, *Dial. d'hist. anc.* 5 (1979): 121ff.; E. S. Staveley, *Historia* 32 (1983), especially 40ff.
17. For a detailed discussion, see part 6 below.

describe in a rough (and probably too schematic) sketch.[18] At the beginning, it was a conflict between aristocracy and nonaristocracy. As in many archaic *polis* societies at this stage of their development, this was largely identical with a conflict between a group of powerful and wealthy clans with their dependents and followers on the one hand and a large part of the unattached economic middle and lower classes on the other. In a first phase, the plebeians almost exclusively fought for defensive goals: for protection, security, and fairness against the overwhelming economic, social, jurisdictional, and political power of the patricians and their magistrates. Economic grievances such as the debt problem and the shortage of land and food on the one hand and dissatisfaction with magisterial arbitrariness and the demand for codification of law on the other were the dominant issues. For the plebeians to compete for office was not only impossible, it was unthinkable. This phase extended well beyond the decemviral legislation.

Toward the end of this first phase there gradually emerged a plebeian elite of increasingly wealthy and influential families of various origins. In a second phase, which roughly covered the last third of the fifth century and the years down to the conquest of Veii and the Gallic disaster, these families had reached an economic and social status that enabled them to aim at overcoming the social barriers that the patricians had institutionalized in the intermarriage ban of the Twelve Tables. In the difficult wars at the end of this period, which necessitated a larger involvement of plebeians on all levels in the army, they successfully demonstrated their abilities in military leadership. In a third phase, therefore, beginning with the aftermath of the sack of Rome, the patrician monopoly of political and religious power and leadership was openly challenged for the first time by a plebeian upper class whose members had all the necessary

---

18. See the similar attempt by Cornell, "Failure of the Plebs" (1983): 101ff. That our reconstruction, like that of our ancient predecessors, should turn out to be too schematic and far too linear is almost inevitable once we base it only on those few facts that can be accepted as authentic (see part 3 below and chapter I, part 2 above) rather than on the detailed narrative of the literary sources. Historical development is never linear, of course, but we can only use straight lines to bridge all the gaps between the points of reasonable certainty provided by that authentic information. The danger of oversimplification can be at least partially balanced by taking into account all conceivable variables that fit between those "points of certainty."

qualifications to compete for the consulship except patrician status. Also in this phase, owing to a combination of internal and external factors, some of the old economic grievances of the plebeian lower classes for the first time found at least partial redress. In the fourth stage, which was intrinsically connected with the beginning of Roman expansion against the Latins and Samnites, the economic problems were solved step by step, and the plebeians, including their political offices and institutions, were fully integrated into a new social and political organism that was solid and cohesive enough to succeed in the great tasks of the third century.

What we read in Livy and Dionysius is, of course, the result of a series of reinterpretations and dramatizations based on the contemporary experiences of authors writing between the time of the Gracchi and Octavian's rise to power.[19] It is likely, however, that the core of the traditions on which those later elaborations were based, which was put together by the earliest annalists, was in all important respects directly influenced by this last phase. In other words, the last phase provided the model for the entire conflict. To this phase belong many elements that were pushed further and further back as the tradition developed, ending up in improbable or even impossible contexts.[20] Even though there is much confusion in our sources, and controversies abound among modern scholars on every piece of information recorded by them, the main issues, the general trend, and the results of this last stage are sufficiently clear.[21] There can be little doubt that plebeian access to political and religious offices was a main focus in this period. If it is correct that it could only be a main focus in the fourth century, we are faced with a discrepancy. The problem of regular political participation of the plebeian elite was

---

19. For examples, see Peppe, *Esecuzione* (1981): 55ff., especially 68ff., on debt, *concordia*, and the first *secessio*; Ungern-Sternberg, chapter III above, on the Decemvirate.

20. Obvious examples are the *leges de plebiscitis* and *de provocatione* (cf. Elster, *Studien* [1976]: 75ff., 120ff.) and the agitation for agrarian legislation (at least in the forms in which it is described; cf. Ed. Meyer, *GdA* III² [1937]: 477 n. 1; E. Gabba, *Athenaeum*, n. s., 42 [1964]: 29ff.; Ogilvie, *Comm.* [1965]: 340f.). Even the presentation of the debt problem in the early fifth century seems to be strongly influenced by fourth-century traditions (see Peppe, *Esecuzione* [1981]: 40ff., 99ff.).

21. Cf. Scullard, *History*⁴ (1980): 115ff.; Ferenczy, *Patr. State* (1976), part 2; chapter XI below.

solved, if not without resistance, nevertheless with steady progress and relatively quickly, with a first breakthrough in 367 and a decisive victory in 342.[22] But the grievances of the lowerclass plebeians were only taken care of more than a hundred years after they had caused the outbreak of the conflict early in the fifth century, and even then rather hesitantly: only in 326 or 313 was the *nexum* (debt-bondage) finally abolished.[23] It would seem, then, that in some of their very earliest and most serious objectives the plebeians were unsuccessful for a very long time.

We can only dissolve this discrepancy and answer many related questions if we are sufficiently able to understand the situation in Rome in the early fifth century, the nature of the opposition between plebeians and patricians, the composition of the patriciate and the character of its rule and power, the grievances and objectives of the plebeians, the *secessio plebis* and its results, and so on. By focusing on some of these aspects and on the characteristics of the first stage of the conflict, it should be possible to bring out how fundamentally different it was and how little it had in common with the last stages in the fourth century.

In order to avoid misunderstandings, it seems advisable to define briefly the position taken in this paper on several much debated problems. First, for practical reasons, I accept the traditional chronology.[24] Second, with a few exceptions, I also accept the evidence of

22. The *leges Genuciae*; cf. Ferenczy, *Patr. State* (1976): 45ff. (with literature cited in the notes).

23. The first relief measures for the debt problem (which had been aggravated by the Gallic disaster) were included in the Licinio-Sextian laws. They were followed by others: listed (with sources) in T. Frank, *Economic Survey* I (1933): 27ff.; Peppe, *Esecuzione* (1981): 98f., cf. 93ff. passim; see also F. Altheim, *Röm. Geschichte* II (1953): 361ff.; Ferenczy, *Patr. State* (1976): 49ff.; Starr, *Beginnings* (1980): 45f. For the *lex Poetilia Papiria*, cf. G. MacCormack, *Labeo* 19 (1973): 306ff.; Kaser, *Privatr.* I² (1971): 167 with n. 12.; Peppe, *Esecuzione*, 183ff. For the later period, see Brunt, *Conflicts* (1971): 56f. The distribution of land had begun after the conquest of Veii and was continued after the Gallic disaster with Roman participation in Latin colonies: Frank, *Economic Survey* I: 32f.; E. T. Salmon, *Phoenix* 7 (1953): 93ff., 123ff.; 9 (1955): 63ff.; and id., *Colon.* (1970): 40ff.

24. Cf. Heurgon, *Rise* (1973): 158ff., and the literature cited in chapter I above, n. 17. It should be pointed out, however, that the traditional date for the beginning of the Conflict of the Orders is less certain than that of the beginning of the Republic: cf. Ed. Meyer, *Kl. Schr.* I² (1924): 353ff.; A. Momigliano, *Contr. IV* (1969): 294ff.

the consular *fasti* with their allegedly nonpatrician names. Rather than simply eliminate them, we have to find a satisfactory explanation for their presence in the *fasti*.[25] Third, I believe that the hoplite phalanx and the centuriate system, together with a rough division of the population into appropriate property groups of *equites, classis*, and *infra classem*, had indeed been introduced in Rome by the sixth century. But, whatever its political functions under the kings, this system was adapted to the needs of a regular voting assembly only in the early years of the Republic. And the well-known complicated five-class system emerged after several changes only in the fourth or early third century.[26] Fourth, I agree with the view that, whereas the patrician aristocracy emerged and existed as such during the monarchy, it reached the full extent of its power and exclusiveness only after the expulsion of the king, and the plebeians became a socially and politically defined group only in the first decades of the Republic; in fact, the two "orders" were formed as such not only at roughly the same time, but most probably in a process of mutual reaction to each other.[27] Finally, however great the Rome of the Tarquins was, it was certainly not a major industrial city and probably not a major trading center in the early fifth century. The nonagricultural element can only have represented a small fraction of the total population. On the other hand, even together with their clients and other dependents, the patrician *gentes* counted for well

---

25. See in general Heurgon, *Rise* (1973): 160f.; Bengtson, *Grundriss*[2] (1970): 43f.; Altheim, *Röm. Geschichte* II (1953): 146ff.; Scullard, *History*[4] (1980): 407ff.; Ogilvie, *Comm.* (1965): 309ff. (with literature); Ranouil, *Patriciat* (1975): 61ff.; Richard, *Origines* (1978): 442ff.; I. Shatzman, *CQ* 23 (1973): 64ff., and the discussion in E. Meyer, *Staat*[3] (1964): 43ff. with literature in nn. 15f. on pp. 485f.; R. T. Ridley, *Athenaeum* 58 (1980): 264ff. The question of whether there was, in the first decades of the Republic, a single or a double magistracy and what its title was (see Heurgon, *Rise*, 161ff.; Meyer, *Staat*, 37ff.; E. S. Staveley, *Historia* 5 [1956]: 74ff.; Poma, *Studi* [1974]: 53ff., all with rich bibliographical notes) does not seem to affect my argument; but the introduction of the *tribuni militum consulari potestate* in the second half of the fifth century does: see n. 133 below.

26. A. Momigliano, *JRS* 53 (1963): 119f.; D. Kienast, *BJ* 175 (1975): 83ff.; Richard, *Origines* (1978): 351ff., especially 359ff., and *RPh* 51 (1977): 229ff.; Saulnier, *Armée* (1980) 89ff., 121ff. On the voting assembly, see n. 67 below. For recent discussions of "orders," see L. Zusi, *Critica storica* 12 (1975): 7ff.

27. Cf. Richard, *Origines* (1978): xi, xix, 189ff., 262ff., 465; id., "Population romaine" (1980): 43ff., and chapter IV, after n. 38 and in part 5, above. For further discussion, see below at n. 126.

under half, and probably even less than a quarter of the population. The great majority of the Romans were independent small farmers.[28]

3

Let us now turn to the causes and content of the earliest phase of the Conflict of the Orders. There cannot be much doubt that it broke out in the context of a severe agrarian crisis, which seems soon to have broadened into a general economic crisis.[29] Although the criteria for determining the extent and effects both of this crisis and of Rome's widely assumed power and economic prosperity during the sixth century need some thorough rethinking,[30] there are strong indications of severe economic difficulties in the fifth century. Famines, caused by bad harvests due to weather, pestilence, or enemy action, were, it seems, recorded in the annals of the *pontifices*. Grain needed to be imported, and the Sibylline books recommended the dedication of a temple to Ceres, Liber, and Libera.[31] That debt was wide-

---

28. Cf. H. S. Jones and H. Last in *CAH* VII (1928): 464ff.; F. Wieacker, "XII Tafeln" (1967): 306ff. The only available criterion for trade is imported Attic pottery; see below at n. 40. Typically, there is no discussion of pottery (or, for that matter, of any other products) *exported* from Rome; see Ryberg, *Arch. Record* (1940): 202ff. See further chapter I above at nn. 112ff. and 126.

29. Frank, *Economic Survey* I (1933): 5ff.; id., *Econ.* (1920): 13ff.; R. Bloch, *REL* 37 (1959): 118ff.; id., *Origins* (1960): 96ff.; F. Wieacker, "XII Tafeln" (1967): 310; Richard, *Origines* (1978): 502ff.; Peppe, *Esecuzione* (1981): 85ff.; F. De Martino, *Econ.* I (1979): 13ff.; J. C. Meyer, *Anal. Rom. inst. Dan.* 9 (1980): 47ff. For the causes of the agrarian crisis, cf. the discussions mentioned in n. 42 below.

30. See my remarks in chapter I above at nn. 31ff. Since G. Pasquali published his famous article on "La grande Roma dei Tarquini" in 1936, the discussion for the most part has been between extremes. For many it has become something like an article of faith to defend the grandeur and power of Rome in the sixth century. As A. Alföldi's example shows, those who dare to doubt this can expect a rather hostile reaction. Certainly not all of Alföldi's views can be accepted, but on this particular question I find what he writes (*Early Rome* [1965]: 318ff.; *Frühgeschichte* [1976]: 111ff.) reasonable and stimulating. Instead of flatly rejecting his arguments, we should use them as a starting point for a systematic reassessment of Rome's economic situation in the sixth and fifth centuries. A methodologically sound and comprehensive investigation of the economic background of the Conflict of the Orders remains an urgent desideratum.

31. Annals: Cato *Origines* fr. 77 P (Gell. *Noctes Atticae* 2.28.6). Temple of Ceres: Dion. Hal. 6.7.12ff.; 94.3; Tac. *Ann.* 2.49. The dates of temple dedications are generally believed to be trustworthy; this one has been challenged: Alföldi, *Early Rome*

spread among the plebeians and that the fate of failing debtors could be rough is supported by the detailed regulations on this issue in the Twelve Tables.[32] Unlike the dramatic stories woven around them by the later historians,[33] the bare facts are most probably authentic in both these cases. We cannot say as much about the demand for distribution of land to the poor. On general grounds, it is not improbable, but the form in which this issue is presented in our sources is totally anachronistic.[34] We do not have any independent evidence for it, and we do not know if it aimed at the estates of the aristocrats or only at *ager publicus* (if there was *ager publicus* at all).

The frequent allusions to the disastrous effects of wars and military service on the plebeians' economic situation are historically quite plausible if we disregard anachronistic elaboration and mis-

---

(1965): 92ff.; *Frühgeschichte* (1976): 126ff., with literature cited. Import of grain: Ogilvie, *Comm.* (1965): 256f., with list of passages; cf. the excellent discussion of A. Momigliano, *SDHI* 2 (1936): 373ff. = *Contr. IV* (1969): 331ff.; less convincing: E. Bayer, *ANRW* I.1 (1972): 320ff.; F. De Martino, *BIDR* 80 (1977): 13; cf. also H. Le Bonniec, *Cérès* (1958): 244ff. For the epidemics, see Peppe, *Esecuzione* (1981): 87 n. 5.

32. Twelve Tables, III.1–6; cf. Watson, *XII Tables* (1975): 111ff.; Kaser, *Privatr.* I² (1971): 166ff. (with literature cited in notes); Peppe, *Esecuzione* (1981): 111ff. More generally, see Richard, *Origines* (1978): 492ff.; F. Wieacker, "XII Tafeln" (1967): 306ff.; D. Kienast, *BJ* 175 (1975): 98f.

33. Livy (cf. Ogilvie, *Comm.* [1965]: 296ff.) and Dionysius both play on the theme, but both with little, if any, sound or contemporary information. Peppe, *Esecuzione* (1981): 40ff., 99ff., gives detailed references and discussion. He shows plausibly that Livy's famous episode in 2.23 (495–94) is based on a similar one in 6.14 (385), and Dionysius used the debt problem as his leitmotiv, largely expanding it and freely exploiting Greek analogies so that his narrative contains elements of which the Roman tradition knows nothing and that plainly contradict it.

34. Solonian Athens provides a good example for the combination of large-scale indebtedness, food shortage, and the demand for the distribution of land. For Rome, Ogilvie, *Comm.* (1965): 340, on Livy 2.41.3, lists the passages mentioning agitation to distribute *ager publicus*. The *rogatio agraria* of Spurius Cassius (Livy 2.41) is the best-known case; cf. Ogilvie, *Comm.*, 337ff.; E. Gabba, *Athenaeum*, n. s., 42 (1964): 29ff. Beloch, *Röm. Geschichte* (1926): 189ff., 323ff., moves Sp. Cassius and everything connected with his name down to the years after the Gallic disaster. In recent years credulity has taken over again: F. D'Ippolito, *Labeo* 21 (1975): 197ff.; F. De Martino, *Econ.* I (1979): 13ff.; J. Gagé, *Latomus* 38 (1979): 838ff.; and D. Capanelli, "Spurio Cassio" (1981), all basically argue for the reliability of the story. Peppe, *Esecuzione* (1981): 87 n. 5, is reasonably cautious. Richard, *Origines* (1978): 495, refers to the parallels in several cities of *Magna Graecia*. On the problems of land tenure in early Rome, see now L. Capogrossi Colognesi, *Terra* (1981); id., "Régime de la terre" (1979), and *BIDR* 83 (1980): 29ff.

takes and accept that plebeians were enrolled in the hoplite army.[35] In Athens at the end of the sixth century, a hoplite's equipment was worth thirty sheep, or more than one-seventh of the total annual harvest of a farmer who qualified as a hoplite—no small amount of dead capital.[36] The losses of crops, livestock, goods, and lives caused by the frequent incursions of hostile neighbors were probably worse. The historical facts hidden in the heroic legends and in the stories of incessant wars against Veii, Latin neighbors, and various mountain tribes, and the fate of many cities that fell to the Samnites and Volscans in the fifth century tell us enough about the precarious situation of Rome at that time.[37] Those farmers who lived a rather marginal existence even in normal times—certainly a large number—naturally bore the brunt of this multiple crisis. Under these specific conditions, the problem of debt and personal dependence, the most common plague of archaic and hierarchically structured societies, was bound to reach catastrophic dimensions. It threatened internal equilibrium and caused growing discontent and finally violent confrontation.

So much for the agrarian crisis. Since the plebeian movement was led by the farmer-hoplites,[38] these factors are crucial in our context. Their impact on Roman society was directly connected with the fact that after the expulsion of the king and the battle of Aricia, Rome and Latium were no longer part of the wider "Etruscan World," and that Rome was seriously threatened on all sides.[39] In addition, based on archaeological finds, the amount of imported Attic figured pottery dropped steeply in the first and again in the second quarter of

35. See nn. 79–81 below.
36. D. Kienast, *BJ* 175 (1975): 98f., with Meiggs and Lewis, *Gr. Hist. Inscr.* (1969), no. 14, lines 9ff., and Plut. *Sol.* 23.3.
37. For the mountain tribes and their conquests, see Altheim, *Röm. Geschichte* II (1953): 257ff.; Alföldi, *Early Rome* (1965): 334f., 365ff.; E. Manni, *Athenaeum* 17 (1939): 233ff.; Heurgon, *Rise* (1973): 178ff.; J. Poucet, *ANRW* I.1 (1972): 115ff. For the struggle against the Latins: Heurgon, *Rise*, 176ff.; against Veii and other Etruscans: Alföldi, *Early Rome*, 288ff.; Saulnier, *Armée* (1980), ch. 7; for the Fabii at the Cremera: Saulnier, ibid., and *BAGB* (1972): 283ff.; for the legend of Coriolanus: Altheim, *Röm. Geschichte* II: 259; Ogilvie, *Comm.* (1965): 314ff. (with literature cited); Ampolo, *DArch* 4/5 (1970–71): 43f.
38. See below at nn. 83ff.
39. G. Devoto, *Studii clasice* 6 (1964): 17ff., sees these changes mirrored in the linguistic development; but see the cautionary remarks by Peppe, *Esecuzione* (1981): 89 n. 9.

the fifth century; around midcentury it practically ceased to exist. The historiographical sources, which in these matters seem to be reliably informed, tell us that in 484, after a period of intensive activity, temple building came to an end for half a century. These two aspects feature prominently in modern discussions of the "crisis of the fifth century" and cause much confusion.[40] If studied in isolation, they seem to indicate that importing of fancy pottery and building of expensive temples continued well beyond the traditional date of the first *secessio*, and that the crisis reached its peak only in the middle of the century. Accordingly, some scholars deny a causal connection between the crisis and the outbreak of the Conflict of the Orders, or they accept such a connection only with modifications.[41] This conclusion, however, seems unwarranted. For these two indicators represent not the whole crisis but only partial aspects of it. They show that by the end of the first quarter, the crisis had seriously begun to affect not just agriculture but other sectors of the economy and society as well. In particular, it seems that the upper classes—whose wealth was based on landed property and on the well-being of their clients and tenants and expressed in costly imported goods and service to the community, including public building—began to suffer too.

This in turn must have added to the pressure on the dependent and the small independent farmers. The political changes brought about by the elimination of monarchy must already have caused a change in attitude, which we cannot reliably extract from our sources. The comparison with Greece may be helpful here. In fact, except for the impact of constant warfare, the symptoms of the crisis were remarkably similar in both areas, including the existence of at least two clearly distinguished statuses of personal dependence caused by, and expressed in, debt.[42] We can add the codification of law, which

---

40. Cf. the literature cited in n. 29 above; for a recent careful discussion of the archaeological evidence, see J. C. Meyer (as in n. 29) who also addresses the question of whether Attic figured vases are representative of the entire volume of trade. For the temples: Bloch, *Origins* (1960): 98f.

41. Cf. e.g., Bloch, *Origins* (1960): 96ff.; Peppe, *Esecuzione* (1981): 85ff., 136ff. (with careful discussion).

42. For Rome (*nexi* and *addicti, iudicati*), cf. Watson, *XII Tables* (1975): 111ff.; G. MacCormack, *ZRG* 84 (1967): 350ff.; Peppe, *Esecuzione* (1981). For Athens, cf. Will, "La Grèce archaïque" (1965): 63ff.; Austin and Vidal-Naquet, *Econ.* (1977):

everywhere was provoked at least partly by the demand for more justice, fairness, and equality before the law, and that means by widespread dissatisfaction with traditional aristocratic jurisdiction.[43] This brings up a decisive aspect: the nature of aristocratic rule. Its deficiencies are criticized with increasing bitterness in the second books of the *Iliad* and *Odyssey*, by Hesiod, and then by Solon, Theognis, Xenophanes, and other poets.[44] Solon's statements are most revealing: he establishes a direct link between the crisis and the abounding debt problem as one of its main manifestations on the one hand, and the danger of internal strife, civil war, and the seizure of power by a tyrant on the other. And he unambiguously blames the nobles for the crisis and its effects:

> Unjust, too, are the thoughts of the leaders: looming before us / countless sorrows appear, born of their arrogant pride . . . / . . . Having amassed their wealth by their unrighteous deeds . . . / . . . Neither the city's store nor the possession of gods / do they hold in awe, but plunder and steal all things from all quarters; / Dike's exalted law they rashly hold in contempt.[45]

In addition, Solon specifically mentions that some of the debt-slaves he had brought back to Athens had been sold justly, but others unjustly.[46]

No doubt greed, arbitrariness, and abuse of power by the ruling aristocracy were an important factor in the conflict Solon had been appointed to resolve.[47] They may even have been its most immediate cause. Debt, obligations, and personal dependence had always existed (M. I. Finley has shown that in archaic societies it was quite normal for large segments of the population to be tied in this way to the

---

58ff., especially 60; Rhodes, *Comm. Ath. Pol.* (1981): 90ff. (the same authors deal with the causes of the crisis). For both: Finley, *Soc.* (1981): 156ff.; Lintott, *Revol.* (1982): 43ff., 70ff.; de Ste. Croix, *Class Struggle* (1981): 162ff.

43. Cf. most prominently Hesiod *Works and Days* 27ff.; 202ff.; 213ff.; 267ff.; 286ff.; 298ff.; further, Homer *Il.* 16.384ff.; *Od.* 19.109ff., and Solon fr. 3.7f.; 24.18ff. D. For further discussion, see n. 69 below.

44. See the literature cited in chapter I above, n. 88.

45. Fr. 3.7ff. D (transl. J. Willis).

46. Fr. 24.9f. D: *dikaios*; *ekdikos*.

47. Cf. especially Spahn, *Mittelschicht* (1977): 121ff.

aristocratic clans),[48] but like the bonds of *clientela*, these relationships were to some extent protected by customary law and religious sanctions. The creditor had power, but also responsibilities; the debtor had obligations, but also rights.[49] Debt-bondage became objectionable only when it abounded or was mishandled, when the customary behavior and safeguards were neglected. This may have happened on a large scale in the last thirty years before Solon's archonship. C. G. Starr has argued plausibly[50] that the "Solonian crisis" may have been provoked not so much by a long-term gradual deterioration of the economic situation that happened to reach the critical stage just at that time, but rather by the increasingly fierce competition among groups of aristocratic families. Striving to secure for themselves as much power and influence as possible, even trying to monopolize such power in one form of "tyranny" or another, they unscrupulously mobilized all available economic and social resources and exploited their dependents. As a result, the debt problem in all its forms reached disastrous dimensions, and the hatred of the victims turned against their cruel masters.[51]

On the other hand, the careful analysis of P. Spahn has recently confirmed what many had assumed before him.[52] Not all Athenians were involved in this confrontation. There seems to have been a large group economically, socially, and politically in the middle. These were people who were not affected and dissatisfied enough to take sides, but who may have feared the consequences of a violent conflict and therefore supported a compromise and the election of a mediator. Since the aristocracy were not strong enough to defend all their privileges and to ignore the growing resistance, Solon was able not only to codify the law extensively and to introduce some major political reforms, but to enforce a rather radical solution for the main grievances: he cancelled existing debts and abolished the institution of debt-bondage. Although not all the wishes of the discontented were fulfilled and the principle of aristocratic leadership re-

---

48. Finley, *Soc.* (1981): 116ff., 150ff.
49. Cf. Richard, *Origines* (1978): 497; Peppe, *Esecuzione* (1981): 111ff.
50. Starr, *Growth* (1977): 46ff., 52f.; cf. id., *Origins* (1961): 313ff., 358; also, Gernet, *Anthropology* (1981): 279ff., especially 286f.
51. Cf. Raaflaub, *Entdeckung* (1985), ch. 2.3.
52. Spahn, *Mittelschicht* (1977), especially 135ff., 150ff.; cf. Eder, chapter IX below at n. 51.

mained unchallenged for a long time, there can be little doubt that the aristocracy suffered heavy losses in all three areas: economically, socially, and politically.[53]

Returning to Rome, there obviously is a possible analogy. It is a reasonable assumption that the strong monarchy had tended to restrict the power and ambitions of the patrician *gentes*.[54] When it fell, a fierce competition for influence and leadership must have broken out among those *gentes*.[55] Such strife and rivalry between individual *gentes* or various groups of families from one or several cities were widespread in Etruria and Latium in the sixth and fifth centuries just as in the Greek world. They are reflected, for example, in the famous paintings of the François tomb in Vulci; in the stories about the dislocation of whole clans from one city to another, in particular to and from Rome; in the hierarchical differentiation within the senatorial aristocracy; and, possibly, in the disappearance from the consular *fasti* of several previously prominent families, some of which, according to our legendary tradition, were involved in attempts at establishing a "tyranny."[56] At any rate, what Starr has suggested for Athens must indeed have happened here: the traditional paternalistic way of handling social, economic, and political relations, es-

---

53. Here my assessment (see also chapter I above at n. 88) differs from that of Eder (chapter IX below, passim). Detailed discussion would be necessary but is not possible here (see, in part, the appendix at the end of this chapter). On Solon's reforms: Aristotle, *Ath. Pol.* 5ff., with Plut. *Sol.* 14ff. For discussion, see the corresponding passages in Day and Chambers, *Ath. Pol.* (1962); Levi, *Comm. Ath. Pol.* I (1968); Manfredini and Piccirilli, *Plut. Sol.* (1977); and most recently and thoroughly, Rhodes, *Comm. Ath. Pol.* (1981), all citing more literature. In addition, see, e.g., Ehrenberg, *Solon* (1968): 62ff.; Spahn, *Mittelschicht* (1977): 139ff.

54. Cf. A. Momigliano, *JRS* 53 (1963): 118ff.; Richard, *Origines* (1978): 312ff., 347ff., 425ff.; valuable suggestions also in Cels Saint-Hilaire and Feuvrier-Prévotat, *Dial. d'hist. anc.* 5 (1979): 115f., 120.

55. Cf. recently Cels Saint-Hilaire and Feuvrier-Prévotat, *Dial. d'hist. anc.* 5 (1979): 110, 121; Magdelain, "*Auspicia*" (1964), especially 462ff.

56. On the François tomb, see Alföldi, *Early Rome* (1965): 221ff., with literature cited; on the migration of clans and its explanation by factional strife, see Ampolo, *DArch* 4/5 (1970–71): 37ff., and the literature cited in nn. 120f. below; on differentiation within the aristocracy, see the previous note; on the *fasti*, see below at nn. 103ff. According to Cornell, chapter II above after n. 22, attempts at establishing a tyranny would belong to the "structural facts" reliably recorded in the annalistic tradition. Given the prominence of this theme in late republican politics, I have my doubts. It would certainly be a mistake to see such factional strife in terms similar to those reconstructed on a prosopographical basis for the middle and late Republic by F. Münzer, M. Gelzer, and others. Following Cornelius, *Untersuchungen* (1940): 113ff., De Martino, *Cost.* I² (1972): 303 and passim, does precisely that.

pecially those of dependence between high and low, must have suffered when the patricians needed to mobilize additional resources. More than all the other factors contributing to the misery of many plebeians, the increasingly oppressive rule of the aristocracy may have created the psychological conditions necessary for a violent confrontation.[57]

If, however, we look for quick, radical solutions of the kind Solon had applied in a similar crisis, we are disappointed. There was no cancellation of debts or abolition of debt-bondage; not even, it seems, a significant improvement of the plight of the debtors.[58] Nor was the aristocratic monopoly of power institutionally restricted; the codification of law took place only after more than forty years and another round of intensive civil strife. There was no mediator, no real compromise, no third position; no truly political concept emerged that at least tried to overcome the deep rift in the community.[59] Instead, there occurred a massive revolt of the plebeians against the patricians, which resulted in a long-term split and an "institutionalized revolution."[60] That the community did not completely break apart and that no civil war broke out[61] was probably owing as

---

57. Cf. Momigliano, *JRS* 53 (1963): 121; Richard, *Origines* (1978): 494ff. Ferenczy, *Patr. State* (1976): 20 (with literature cited in n. 43), 31, probably goes too far. The extraordinary series of temples built within the first twenty years of the Republic might well be an indication of such competition among groups of patrician *gentes*. For varying interpretations, see, e.g., R. Bloch, *Origins* (1960): 98f.; Ogilvie, *Comm.* (1965): 293; Momigliano, "Origins of the Republic" (1969): 33f.; Richard, *Origines* (1978): 502; Poma, *Studi* (1974): 45ff.

58. Cf. Eder, chapter IX below at n. 61. However, the detailed regulations in the Twelve Tables (III.1–6) of the acceptable procedures in dealing with failing debtors might well have been seen as a significant improvement; cf., e.g., Altheim, *Röm. Geschichte* II (1953): 230f.; Wolff, *Law* (1951): 57f. For other aspects, see the detailed discussion by Peppe, *Esecuzione* (1981): 111–35, especially 116f.

59. For the importance of a "third position" in archaic Greek legislation and mediation of social conflicts, cf. C. Meier, *Pol.* (1980): 6ff., and index, s.v. "Dritte Position."

60. Cf. Mommsen, *Röm. Staatsrecht* II.1³ (1887): 281 (the plebeian organization as "permanent revolution"); J. Bleicken, *ZRG* 76 (1959): 347; see also Cornell's similar view in "The Failure of the Plebs" (1983): 118.

61. Civil war seems to have occurred in several *poleis* of the Aegean and Ionia in the late seventh and early sixth centuries: see A. R. Burn, *The Lyric Age of Greece* (1967): 214f., 218ff.; A. W. Lintott, *Revol.* (1982): 55f. Momigliano, *Contr. IV* (1969): 445f., "Patrizi e plebei" (1967): 215, and "Origins of the Republic" (1969): 27f., explains the absence of actual fighting in Rome by the very low social status of the *plebs*, outside the *populus* and the army. For arguments against this view, see below at nn. 78ff. I have argued in chapter I above, at n. 86, that external pressure effected

much to external pressure as to preexisting strong internal ties, especially of a religious nature. At any rate, plebeians obviously could not achieve anything before they took the extreme step of organizing a military strike, literally leaving the city and establishing their own antipatrician organization and strike force.

The results of the first *secessio* were indeed dramatic and revealing. Following a solemn old ritual known to several Italian tribes, the plebeians formed a sacred band. They chose leaders and swore an oath of absolute allegiance to them. Such sacred bands are known to have existed, for example, among the Volscans and Samnites in situations of special emergency. The oath and the dire ritual obliged the members never to abandon their ranks and their leaders and to sacrifice their lives for the common cause. Those who broke this oath were killed immediately.[62] Whatever the plans the plebeians were considering on that hill outside of Rome, and whatever the agreement that induced them to return,[63] they retained their sacred organization. Their leaders, the tribunes, whose title was probably chosen by analogy to an existing high office in the army, may well have originally been the officers who led them in their mutiny. Afterwards they were probably selected on the basis of relative economic and social status and, more importantly, their qualities of leadership. They had only one duty: to protect their fellow plebeians against abuse of power by the patricians and their magistrates. Later, perhaps much later than our sources imply, the organization was formalized and extended. Originally everything must have been informal, based on despair, determination, solidarity, and the sacred oath.[64] Whoever suffered injury by the patricians called for the help

---

discipline and cohesion within both the aristocracy and the entire community, despite serious disagreements. We have to keep in mind that this was not fifth-century Greece, where "democrats" (who are not to be confused with "lower classes" anyway) could count on the support of Athens; this was a world entirely dominated by aristocracies.

62. Cf. Altheim, *Lex sacr.* (1940); id., *Röm. Geschichte* II (1953): 179ff.; De Martino, *Cost.* I² (1972): 340ff.

63. The authenticity of the details in Livy's report (2.31.7ff.) is, of course, highly questionable; cf. Ogilvie, *Comm.* (1965): 309ff., and the literature listed there.

64. On the origins and primary duties of the tribunes, see E. Meyer, *Staat*³ (1964): 43ff., with literature cited; Momigliano, *Contr. IV* (1969): 294ff.; L. Zusi, *Critica storica* 12 (1975): 202ff.; Richard, *Origines* (1978): 559ff. On the lack of formality: Richard, *Origines* 559ff.; Momigliano, *Contr. IV* (1969): 315; J. Bleicken, *Republik* (1980): 23f.

of the tribunes. They stepped in between the patrician and his victim, protected only by the sacred oath. Everything depended on the willingness of the plebeians to protect or avenge their tribunes.[65] It seems they did. Very likely, the trials conducted, according to Livy, by tribunes in the *concilium plebis* against patrician magistrates, who were condemned and put to death after a formal procedure, conceal a brutal reality: the lynching by avenging plebeians of those who had violated the *sacrosanctitas* of the tribunes.[66]

The purpose of the plebeian organization, then, was purely defensive and protective. It was political only insofar as it interfered with the hitherto unlimited power of the patrician magistrates. Typically, we do not hear anything about an attempt to elect plebeian consuls or to change the voting structure in the assembly in favor of the plebeians. Nor were the principles that determined nomination and election over and above the vote ever adapted in order to curtail effectively the de facto control of the ruling aristocracy.[67] I suggest that at that time it did not even occur to the plebeians to challenge the principle of exclusive patrician leadership in the community as a whole.

An analysis of the circumstances that led to the codification of law at Rome, and of the contents of the Twelve Tables, allows a similar conclusion. Whatever the objectives of the patricians,[68] from the point of view of the plebeians, just as we learn from Hesiod and Solon for

---

65. For the origins of *auxilium* and *provocatio*, see J. Bleicken, *ZRG* 76 (1959): 324ff.; *RE* 23,2 (1959): 2444ff.; E. S. Staveley, *Historia* 3 (1954–55): 412ff.; A. W. Lintott, *ANRW* I.2 (1972): 226f.; W. Kunkel, *Kriminalverfahren* (1962): 24ff.

66. Cf. Altheim, *Röm. Geschichte* II (1953): 207ff.; J. Bleicken, *ZRG* 76 (1959): 351ff.; Kunkel, *Kriminalverfahren* (1962): 31; De Martino, *Cost.* I² (1972): 362f.

67. The centuriate system was probably adapted to the needs of a voting and electing assembly in the first years of the Republic: see E. S. Staveley, *Historia* 5 (1956): 82ff.; *Voting* (1972): 123ff.; and *Historia* 32 (1983): 43f., with literature cited in n. 60; A. Magdelain, "*Auspicia*" (1964): 117ff.; U. Hall, *Historia* 13 (1964): 270f.; Thomsen, *Serv. Tullius* (1980): 157f., with literature cited in nn. 47f.; cf. also Zusi, *Critica storica* 12 (1975): 218f. At that time, such an assembly became indispensable. Whether it was a result of the first plebeian uprising and, as such, a major plebeian success (as maintained by J. Bleicken, *Lex* [1975]: 79, n. 7, and *Republik* [1980]: 24f., 121f.; cf. also E. Ferenczy, *Labeo* 22 [1976]: 364) is a different question; I doubt it very much. Even if so, the presiding magistrate kept a decisive amount of procedural control over nomination and vote: E. Meyer, *Staat*³ (1964): 192ff.; De Martino, *Cost.* I² (1972): 295f.

68. See Eder, chapter IX below, and my preliminary comments on his contribution in part A of the appendix to this article.

archaic Greece,⁶⁹ the goals must have been protection against patrician arbitrariness and abuse of power, especially jurisdictional power, by fixing and publishing the existing norms. They may well have hoped that thereby the power of the magistrates, most of all the *coercitio*, would be defined and limited. To some extent such hopes were justified, and there clearly was more equality before the law thereafter.⁷⁰ But, as far as I can see, not one regulation in the Twelve Tables gave the plebeians a greater share in political power.⁷¹ The ten men who were entrusted to put the law code together were naturally all patricians. Not only is the second Decemvirate, in which plebeians were allegedly represented, an obvious fiction,⁷² but I would even suggest that participation in such an office still by far exceeded the realistic expectation of the plebeian leaders. Further, the all-important *formulae*, which were decisive for any proper legal procedure, were not published but remained under the well-guarded control of the *pontifices* for another 150 years.⁷³ We might suspect patrician cunning here. More likely, due to the religious connotations, this again was an area where plebeians could not, and did not yet, think of control themselves.

At this point, we have to face two questions. First, why were the patricians, unlike their fellow aristocrats in Athens, able to resist the plebeian demands so successfully? Why could they survive the crisis of the *secessio* (and many more years of plebeian assault) without major losses? Second, if the patricians were indeed so powerful and persistent, why did the plebeians get as far as they did? To be sure, they did not initially gain any of those concessions that Solon had secured for their Athenian fellow sufferers. Nevertheless, it was a remarkable achievement, unparalleled in the ancient world, that they succeeded in organizing themselves tightly and permanently and in using their antipatrician strike force so effectively that it not only provided them with the protection most urgently needed at the be-

69. Cf. n. 43 above.
70. Cf. W. Kunkel, *Introd.* (1973): 24ff.; H. F. Jolowicz and B. Nicholas, *Law* (1972): 109f.; F. Wieacker, "XII Tafeln" (1967): 314ff.; id., *RIDA*, 3rd ser., 3 (1956): 471ff.; De Martino, *Cost.* I² (1972): 310f.; Bleicken, *Lex* (1975): 90ff.; *Rep.* (1980): 25, 122f.; Guarino, *Riv.* (1975): 204ff., 319ff. See also Zusi, *Critica storica* 12 (1975): 219ff.
71. Kunkel, *Introd.* (1973): 24; Guarino, *Riv.* (1975): 210f.; Eder, chapter IX below. For a different view, see Ferenczy, *Patr. State* (1976): 33f.
72. Cf. chapter III above, with literature cited in nn. 7–9.
73. Kunkel, *Introd.* (1973): 30; Jolowicz and Nicholas, *Law* (1972): 91.

ginning, but was eventually formally acknowledged by the patricians and became the foundation for plebeian gains that reached far beyond the initial goals.

4

Let us begin with the second question. The plebeians could count on two factors: their solidarity and their importance for the community. Although the patricians were inferior in numbers, all the other factors that counted, especially wealth, prestige, social, political, and religious power, were heavily, if not exclusively, concentrated on their side.[74] The awe-inspiring superiority of such early aristocrats is impressively described in the second book of the *Iliad* and visible in the form, size, and contents of some tombs of the seventh and sixth centuries in Latium and Etruria.[75] Since the odds were clearly against the plebeians, therefore, and since there was no mediator and no readiness to compromise on the other side, they seem to have developed a strong sense of solidarity. As in Athens, probably not all plebeians were equally and directly affected by the crisis.[76] Certainly not all were *nexi* or in debt. But most of them must have joined the movement. Its success depended on determination, cohesion, and large numbers. A small group might have been able to terrorize the city for a while, but not to survive for long. Further, despite the concentration of wealth on the patrician side, we should not underestimate the collective economic importance of the plebeians for the community; after all, being for the most part small and middle farmers, they represented the majority of the food producers, which counted even more in a predominantly agrarian economy and in time of frequent food shortage. Finally, we would—maybe wrongly—expect that even under normal conditions even the toughest aristocracy would hesitate to alienate the vast majority of the population completely.[77] In this case, the conditions were not normal. The com-

---

74. Cf. n. 90 below.
75. Cf. Ampolo, *DArch* 4/5 (1970–71): 50ff.
76. For Athens, see above at nn. 44ff.
77. However, the testimonia from archaic Greece (cf. the literature cited in chapter I above, n. 88, esp. Donlan, Raaflaub) show a pronounced lack of concern on the side of the aristocrats for the needs and troubles of the lower classes; they obviously felt secure in their traditional and hitherto unchallenged superiority.

munity was forced to fight for survival more than once in those very years when the plebeian movement was formed and successfully brought into action. In the age of hoplite warfare, the number of available soldiers was a decisive factor. Our sources maintain that the plebeians were part of the army.[78] This made them indispensable. It gave them leverage.

Undoubtedly, the annalistic reports are anachronistic in many details. For example, we should not pay much attention to the frequent stories about draft refusals, which are something quite different from the military strike or mutiny (*secessio*). They fit into the situation of the second century B.C., when Roman and allied farmers were forced to fight neverending and senseless wars abroad for which they could easily and convincingly put the blame on the ambition, greed, and incompetence of the aristocracy; but they do not fit in the situation of the fifth century, when the Romans were defending their fields and families.[79] Equally anachronistic is the idea that the consuls levied armies (presumably from a much larger pool of available and qualified soldiers) for specific and extended campaigns, and that long absences from home and field during these campaigns caused economic hardship for the citizen-soldiers. Such views, hardly questioned by modern scholars, reflect much later situations; they are incompatible with the realities of a fifth-century *polis* that was surrounded by enemies, could count on only a limited number of hoplites, and had to expect the short, but intensive and possibly frequent, fighting characteristic of assaults and raids by mountain tribes and of hoplite battles between neighboring *poleis*.[80]

Apart from such elaborations, however, our sources must be right: a considerable number of plebeians were part of the hoplite army

---

78. It is Livy's unquestioned assumption; cf., e.g., 2.23ff.; 32.

79. Draft refusals: Livy 2.27.10f.; 28.5ff. (with Ogilvie's comm. on 28.7); 28.8–29.4; 43.1ff.; 55.1ff. (with Ogilvie's comm. on 55.4); 3.10.10ff.; 16.5ff.; 20.1ff.; 25.9ff.; 30.1ff., etc. These reports are taken seriously by most scholars: e.g., Altheim, *Röm. Geschichte* II (1953): 211; De Martino, *Cost.* I² (1972): 338; Bleicken, *ZRG* 76 (1959): 348f.; Guarino, *Riv.* (1975): 180ff. De Ste. Croix, *Class Struggle* (1981): 335, even defines the *secessio* as a "strike against conscription."

80. See chapter I above, n. 122. One should keep in mind that Veii was superior in territory and manpower. For the realities of warfare between Greek *poleis*, see J. de Romilly, "Guerre et paix entre cités," in *Problèmes de la guerre en Grèce ancienne*, edited by J.-P. Vernant (Paris, 1968): 207ff. See also Siewert, *Kleisthenes* (1982), parts 3 and 4, for important aspects.

and shared with the patricians responsibility for the survival of the whole community.[81] This basic fact made all the difference; it changed them from nobodies to somebodies.[82] In exceptional situations, they could even stage a *secessio*, a demonstration of their indispensability.

But *secessio* was not a tool for everyday politics. Another factor might be as important. Despite frequent refutations, there still is a surprising amount of support for the opinion that it was one of the main purposes of the so-called "Servian constitution" to integrate the immigrant nonfarming population into the citizen body and to make its wealth and manpower available for the hoplite army.[83] Both a look at later Roman values and judgments and a comparison with contemporary Greece prove that this view must be wrong. Equally wrong is the related assumption that the early republican plebeians (and, accordingly, the plebeian hoplites) were mostly "petty craftsmen, traders and workers, in the city."[84] In archaic societies of this type, the ability to possess land and to fight in the phalanx were privileges. They were intimately connected with each other and with the emerging notion of citizenship. Farmer and fighter, these were

---

81. This is agreed upon by most scholars. It has been denied recently by Momigliano: *Contr. IV* (1969): 444ff.; "Patrizi e plebei" (1967): 212ff., and "Origins of the Republic" (1969): 25ff. Contra: Richard, *Origines* (1978): 372ff., 395f., 540f. For further discussion, see Zusi, *Critica storica* 12 (1975): 191f.

82. Cf. De Martino, *Cost* I² (1972): 187ff. That participation in the hoplite phalanx had considerable consequences for self-confidence, social prestige, status, and, eventually, for the political rights of the nonaristocrats involved is generally accepted. The precise nature of such consequences and their (inter)relationship with other factors contributing to economic, social, and political change, have been frequently, if not always competently, debated. The whole complex of problems deserves a comprehensive reexamination. At present, see especially A. M. Snodgrass, *JHS* 85 (1965): 110ff.; for Greece: M. Detienne, "La phalange" (1968): 119ff.; P. Cartledge, *JHS* 97 (1977): 11ff.; J. Salmon, *JHS* 97 (1977): 84ff.; A. J. Holladay, *JHS* 102 (1982): 97, 99ff.; for Rome: M. P. Nilsson, *JRS* 19 (1929): 1ff.; Altheim, *Röm. Geschichte* II (1953): 153ff.; D. Kienast, *BJ* 175 (1975): 97ff., and C. Saulnier, *Armée* (1980), chs. 4 and 5; for Etruria: M. Torelli, "Rome et l'Etrurie" (1979): 258ff.

83. E.g., H. Last, *JRS* 35 (1945): 38ff.; L. R. Ménager, *RIDA*, 3rd ser., 19 (1972): 382ff.; Rouland, *Clientèle* (1979): 58f. Contra: Richard, *Origines* (1978): 351ff., especially 372ff.

84. Ogilvie, *Comm.* (1965): 294. Similarly Ménager, *RIDA*, 3rd ser., 19 (1972): 367ff., especially 373ff. Momigliano, *Contr. IV* (1969): 448, and "Patrizi e plebei" (1967): 27, describes the *plebs* in similar words, without, however, giving them a share in the hoplite army.

the two most reputable functions in the community, and both carried strong religious connotations.[85] Crafts and trade were important, but they never enjoyed high social reputation either in Greece or in Rome, where down to the late Republic the army was recruited only among the farming population.[86] Undoubtedly, therefore, the early Roman hoplites were all farmers. For the plebeians among them, the very fact that they were farmers and hoplites was the precondition for their eventual acceptance by the patricians and their full social and political integration.[87] That they vigorously supported the plebeian movement gave it that indispensable minimum of respectability that in turn made it possible for the patricians to cope reasonably with it, and finally to acknowledge it.[88] Had the plebeians consisted only of poor farmers, herdsmen, day laborers, craftsmen, and traders,[89] their movement would have been crushed at the first opportunity.

85. J.-P. Vernant, *Mythe et pensée chez les Grecs* II (Paris, 1971): 16ff.; M. Detienne, *Crise* (1963): 32ff., 52ff.
86. J. Hasebroek, *Wirtsch.* (1931): 260ff.; A. Aymard, *Études d'histoire ancienne* (Paris, 1967): 316ff.; Vernant, *Mythe et pensée chez les Grecs* II: 16ff.; C. Mossé, *The Ancient World at Work* (New York, 1969): 25ff.; M. M. Austin and P. Vidal-Naquet, *Econ.* (1977): 11ff.; Finley, *Econ.* (1973): 40ff., 60, 80f., and often; F. Gschnitzer, *Sozialgeschichte* (1981): 60f., 126ff. Especially for Rome, see further F. M. de Robertis, *Lavoro e lavoratori nel mondo romano* (Bari, 1963), and D. Nörr, "Zur sozialen und rechtlichen Bewertung der freien Arbeit in Rom," *ZRG* 82 (1965): 67ff. (both repr. in one vol., New York, 1979). Cf. especially Cato *De agr. praef.* 2, 4; Cic. *De off.* 1.150f.; Dion. Hal. 2.28.1; 9.25.2. Hoplites and *adsidui*: Richard, *Origines* (1978): 372ff., and "Population romaine" (1980): 57. For the fundamental importance of Tiberius Gracchus's agrarian reforms under military aspects, see D. Earl, *Tiberius Gracchus*, Coll. Latomus 66 (Brussels, 1963): 30ff.; E. Badian, "Tiberius Gracchus and the Beginning of the Roman Revolution," *ANRW* I.1 (1972): 680ff.
87. Cf. to some extent Spahn, *Mittelschicht* (1977): 41.
88. Eder, chapter IX below at n. 51, assesses the role of the hoplites differently. I can only express my disagreement here. What he writes at nn. 54ff., 58, about status and involvement of the independent farmers seems to me applicable to the hoplites as well.
89. This is Momigliano's definition of the *plebs* ("Patrizi e plebei" [1967]: 27; *Contr. IV* [1969]: 448). It is accepted by T. J. Cornell, "Failure of the Plebs" (1983): 118, who speaks of "the most impoverished and underprivileged group in society." It remains a mystery how this miserable bunch of people without economic power and social prestige could have had the social and political impact described by these authors—namely, of being able to develop a political organization far superior to that of the patricians, and soon to become attractive enough to cause the defection of *clientes* and *conscripti* (semi-aristocrats) from the patricians: Momigliano, "Patrizi e plebei," 217; "Origins of the Republic" (1969): 29ff.; and *Contr. IV*: 450ff.; Cor-

5

That leads us to the other question. Why, despite the plebeian revolt, were the patricians able to maintain their power and privileges for such a long time? Here we have to look at the character and structure of this aristocracy. There are all the well-known factors, typical for archaic aristocracies:[90] wealth in land, animals, and especially horses; an impressive genealogical background, social eminence, and various forms of dependence by which other members of the community were tied to them; close relations with the aristocracies of other *poleis*, with whom gift-exchange and intermarriage were frequently practiced; religious prerogatives and priesthoods of special cults, and a monopoly in jurisdiction, political office, military leadership, and membership in the council. In Rome, however, most of these qualities were developed more distinctly and formalized more rigidly than elsewhere; they were given a unique religious connotation, and they strongly emphasized authority and superiority. For example, the patricians had their own marriage rites;[91] their exclusiveness was underlined by the ban on intermarriage, which was not just morally condemned as in Theognidean Megara, but even-

---

nell, "Failure of the Plebs," 109. To be sure, once the plebeian organization was in place and had proved its efficiency, it could attract others. But the mystery is its creation by that particular group of people. Momigliano seeks the explanation in Greek influence (see chapter I above at nn. 97ff., especially 100f.); Cornell in addition stresses the revolutionary impetus ("Failure," 118). Both seem to me labels rather than real explanations; both would have contributed but cannot have been solely responsible for the achievement. In particular, the leaders of revolutionary movements usually do not belong to the class described by Momigliano and Cornell.

90. There is, to my knowledge, no modern comprehensive study of archaic aristocracy. For Rome, scholars have traditionally focused on the one hand on the late republican situation and on political aspects of the organization of power—Gelzer, *Nobility* (1969); Münzer, *Adelsparteien* (1920); Meier, *Res publica amissa* (1966): 24ff.—and on the other hand on the question of the origins of the patriciate and of the patricio-plebeian dichotomy—see, recently, Richard, *Origines* (1978), and Ranouil, *Patriciat* (1975). From the point of view of social history, there are only introductory surveys: e.g., G. Alföldy, *Römische Sozialgeschichte* (Wiesbaden, 1975): chap. 1; Bleicken, *Verfassung* (1975): 40ff. For Greece, see, e.g., Hasebroek, *Wirtsch.* (1931); Gernet, *Anthropology* (1981): 279ff.; Finley, *Odysseus*² (1977); M. T. W. Arnheim, *Aristocracy in Greek Society* (London, 1977: disappointing); Adkins, *Merit* (1960); Donlan, *Ideal* (1980); Gschnitzer, *Sozialgeschichte* (1981): 38ff., 60ff.

91. See chapter VIII below.

tually fixed by law;[92] the *clientela* system was developed on a large scale and formalized with strong sanctions;[93] the monopoly of jurisdiction was supported by a strictly formalized procedure, which was again founded on religion; the leading office was elevated by *imperium* and endowed with sacred and priestly functions; and the priests played an important role in the public life of the community.[94]

The list of such characteristics could be extended, but only one more needs to be mentioned. The nomination and election of candidates and the procedure in voting and legislation were regulated in a rigid way that left all the initiative and the final decision in the hands of the presiding magistrate. The aristocracy therefore maintained tight control over the assembly; most probably it was also favored by the system of group voting.[95] This gives us an important clue. The political structures were adapted to the new timocratic principles that were necessitated by the introduction of the hoplite army, without serious political losses for the aristocracy. Here again is a striking difference to the case of Athens.[96] And again, we should not see it as the result of cunning and manipulation, but rather as the lasting expression of the natural and generally accepted weight of aristocratic authority.

Although some of these elements of patrician superiority and control may have received their final form only in the first half of the fifth century, the general picture is clear enough. In its institutions and organization, this aristocracy must have appeared more powerful, and its rule far more oppressive, than its equivalent in Athens.[97] Furthermore, in Athens and elsewhere in Greece, the ruling aristocracies were unable to resist the demands of the discontented because they lacked cohesion and discipline. Largely due to the absence of external pressure, factionalism and rivalries abounded and in many cases led to the establishment of tyrannies. At Rome, on the con-

---

92. Twelve Tables, XI.1 (Cic. *De re pub.* 2.36.61–37.63). Theognis 183ff.; 193ff.; 31f.; 101ff., et al.; cf. Donlan, *Ideal* (1980): 80ff.

93. Twelve Tables, VIII.21 (Servius, on *Aen.* 6.609); for literature see chapter I above, n. 86.

94. See Mitchell, chapter V above. For a preliminary assessment of Mitchell's contribution, see part B of the appendix to this essay.

95. Cf. the literature mentioned in n. 67 above, and Bleicken, *Verfassung* (1975): 96ff.; *Ordnung* (1972): 64ff.

96. See Raaflaub, *HZ* 238 (1984): 557ff.

97. How much of that (not only in organization and institutions, but in outlook and self-understanding) was due to Etruscan influence, we cannot know.

trary, the deadly combination of external (enemy) and internal (plebeian) pressure forced the patricians to close their ranks, to limit and formalize their competition and to develop an extraordinary collective ethos and discipline, cohesion, and community-oriented value system.[98] They could not do without the plebeians, but they rarely gave them a chance to exploit internal dissension, and they never made more than the absolute minimum of concessions. In addition, owing probably less to the Etruscan background than to the precarious external and internal situation, and in marked contrast to the Greek *poleis*, the patrician state learned to rely on a strong and independent magistracy backed by the cumulative power and prestige of the *patres* in the Senate and eventually endowed with all the power needed to enforce obedience.[99] The patricians did not, therefore, lack the instruments to resist the plebeian demands.

Accordingly, this revolt was not, as in Athens, directed against aristocratic arbitrariness and oppression in general,[100] but specifically against the almost unlimited power of the magistrates and its abuse in support of patrician interests.[101] To form a sacred band and to charge its leaders with the task of preventing such abuse of power was the only way open to the *plebs*. Like all archaic communities, the patrician state did not, of course, provide its dissatisfied nonaristocratic members with political representation or a forum to voice their grievances.[102] Traditionally, the nonaristocrats were mute. They could only act.

6

This brings up the last point, the composition of the aristocracy. Four of the Roman kings and three of the seven hills bear names that

---

98. For all this, see chapter I above, after n. 83.
99. According to A. Heuss, *ZRG* 64 (1944): 57ff., especially 119ff., the comprehensive *imperium* of the highest magistracy, reaching far beyond the military sphere and permeating every area of communal life, was the patricians' reaction to continuous plebeian unrest. The older view (supported by Mommsen) that the republican magistracy simply carried on the full regal power still has its supporters: E. Meyer, *Staat*³ (1964): 37f.
100. Cf. Spahn, *Mittelschicht* (1977): 121ff.
101. Cf. especially Heuss, *ZRG* 64 (1944): 119f., 124ff.
102. The Thersites episode in *Iliad* 2.212ff. gives a good example.

were later considered to be plebeian.[103] And there are those bothersome nonpatrician names in the first years of the consular *fasti*. Accordingly, it has been maintained frequently not only that plebeians had access to the consulship in the first decade after 509, but that in earlier times the patrician nobility was not yet clearly defined and plebeian families were able to play a significant role in the leadership.[104] Since this was no longer the case after about 487, it was necessary to assume that the patricians had by drastic action established their exclusive control of the consulship and political power. Evidence for what G. De Sanctis called the *"serrata del patriziato,"*[105] was found in the ascendance of the Fabii in the *fasti* after 487, the disappearance of Etruscan names from the *fasti* at the same time, and the almost complete absence of "plebeian" consuls for the next twenty-five years. I do not want to discuss the so-called "plebeian" names in the *fasti* in detail. After all, more appear between 461 and 452. Some of them are obviously not historical. There must have been a considerable rate of attrition due to death, impoverishment, and emigration.[106] And who knows what else happened to those families in the dramatic, insecure, and dark years of the early Republic? How can we be sure that some hundred years later, plebeian consuls, of whose origin and background we know little, were direct descendants of their namesakes in archaic Rome, and that those, therefore, were plebeians as well?[107]

At any rate, it is more the underlying concept of aristocracy I am concerned with. As it is usually understood, the "closure of the patriciate" implies that at a certain point in the early Republic a group of families monopolized power and established themselves as a ruling aristocracy, thereby excluding other families that had hitherto

---

103. Cf. H. Jordan, *Die Könige im alten Italien* (Berlin, 1887): 17ff.; id., *Topographie der Stadt Rom im Altertum* I. 1 (Berlin, 1878): 187ff.; C. Hülsen, "I veri fondatori di Roma," *Atti pont. accad. rom. arch.*, 3rd ser., 2 (1924): 83ff.; more recently: H. Last, *JRS* 35 (1945): 30f.; Heurgon, *Rise* (1973): 111.

104. See for this whole passage the summary by Heurgon, *Rise* (1973): 165f., and the discussion by De Martino, *Cost.* I² (1972): 225ff.

105. De Sanctis, *Storia* I² (1956): 228f.

106. See n. 120 below.

107. Cf. the important observations of Momigliano, *Contr. IV* (1969): 448f., and in "Patrizi e plebei" (1967): 217f.; I. Shatzman, *CQ* 23 (1973): 65ff., especially 75ff.; Ranouil, *Patriciat* (1975): 64f. C. Ampolo, *DArch* 4/5 (1970–71): 41 n. 11, reminds us that in several cases the same *nomen gentile* is attested in other cities besides Rome.

shared this power and were therefore qualified for leadership.[108] That means they must have been equal or comparable to the patricians in every respect but one: they were not patricians. However, since they had been able to hold office and *imperium* before, this cannot have been a decisive obstacle.[109] If it was really turned into such later, it was by an artificial political move.[110] It seems to me that the very presence of such an ousted and frustrated elite among the plebeians could not have failed to change the character and direction of the Conflict of the Orders rather fundamentally soon after its beginning. In combination with a mostly plebeian hoplite army that year after year demonstrated its indispensable contribution to the survival of the community[111] and a highly motivated and efficient plebeian strike force, the presence of leaders whose families had traditionally been qualified for communal leadership would make it very difficult to explain the time gap of almost a whole century between the outbreak of the conflict and the election of the first "real" plebeian to the office of consular tribune.[112]

Moreover, this would be a unique case among ancient aristocracies. Of course, uniqueness is not in itself a decisive negative argu-

108. See the literature cited in n. 16 above.

109. In other words, if there was "plebeian" access to the magistracy before 487, such eminent patrician privileges as *interregnum, patrum auctoritas*, and, most of all, the ability to take *auspicia* would either have to be considered recent patrician usurpations of rights originally available to all who were qualified for, and worthy of, high office, or, if they were old patrician privileges, the *serrata del patriziato* was in reality a split within the patriciate, by which the victorious group deprived another group of its patrician status, and thereby of those privileges too. In either case, the limitation of those rights to the "true patricians" would have happened so late that it would seem almost impossible to justify the intermarriage ban and the prohibition of plebeians from high office with the danger of "tainted blood" and the "contamination of the auspices." See Linderski, chapter VII below after n. 54.

110. For a brief discussion of A. Magdelain's explanation of the formation of the patriciate ("*Auspicia*" [1964]: 450ff.) and of the partially similar views of E. S. Staveley (*Historia* 32 [1983]: 24ff.) see parts C and D of the appendix to this article.

111. Another marked difference from Athens, where the political activation and integration of the class of farmer-hoplites was delayed for a whole century, at least partly because it did not have to, and could not, prove itself indispensable; cf. C. Meier, *Pol.* (1980): 66f.; Spahn, *Mittelschicht* (1977): 76ff.

112. Cf. n. 13 above. In an admirable article, E. J. Bickerman, *RFIC* 97 (1969): 408, finds this time gap quite "natural" and reminds us "that the first Labour prime minister in England was appointed in 1924, almost sixty years after the enfranchising of the workers by the electoral reform of 1867." I do not feel competent to discuss this in detail, but I think in this case the comparison would be much more com-

ment, especially in dealing with a society that produced the unique plebeian organization. But it should make us doubly cautious. In fact, I do not know of any example in the Greek and Etruscan world[113] where a large group of families was permanently able to exclude another sizable (and, in some scholars' view, even larger) group of similar families from participation in power and leadership. We know of severe factional strife, of successful attempts by one or several clans to monopolize power for a certain time.[114] In very large *poleis*, such as Attica, there may have been distinctions at times between a dominant central aristocracy and marginal ones in remote areas.[115] But all these were struggles within an aristocratic upper class that despite a wide range of variations was quite homogeneous in its appearance, its economic and social status, its values and outlook. Those who at a given time succeeded in securing the power for themselves could hardly think of denying the "aristocratic quality" to those whom they had temporarily ousted. Because, then, it fundamentally disagrees with the concept and reality of archaic *polis*-aristocracies, the view that plebeians were permanently excluded by the "closure of the patriciate" from sharing powers and privileges they had previously enjoyed seems to me highly problematical.

Momigliano has suggested that the nonpatricians in the *fasti* were not plebeians but *conscripti*, whom he defines as a category of families "between patricians and plebeians," a noble elite of patrician clients. They only joined the plebeians at the end of a long process and

---

pelling if the individual elements were more closely comparable—that is, e.g., if the Labour party had been founded in 1867 as well; if the unions' and then the party's leaders had been socially prominent and acceptable to wide groups beyond the workers' unions; if there had not been a powerful third element in the Liberal party; and if electoral behavior in a nation in the era before television could be presumed to be similar to that in a small city-state; or if, on the other hand, the *plebs* had indeed included only the lowest classes and not also the majority of the independent farmers; if the plebeians had only been enfranchised after the *secessio*; if they had not had their tight organization with its oath of absolute allegiance toward their leaders, etc.

113. Nor do any of Bickerman's medieval examples (ibid., 402ff.) fit into this pattern.

114. The Bacchiadae in Corinth provide an instructive example; cf. E. Will, *Korinthiaka* (Paris, 1955): 295ff. A close comparison might yield interesting results.

115. See, e.g., C. Hignett, *A History of the Athenian Constitution* (Oxford, 1952): 102ff.; W. G. Forrest, *Emergence* (1966): 156ff. Contra: Spahn, *Mittelschicht* (1977): 131f.

many years after the outbreak of the Conflict of the Orders, when it had become clear beyond any doubt that the patricians' insistence on exclusiveness permanently robbed the *conscripti* of their chances of fulfilling their political ambitions. This is a striking suggestion, worth serious consideration.[116] However, I would like to go even further.

Archaic aristocracies developed gradually, over a long period of time.[117] They tended to be exclusive from early on, but there was still some vertical and much horizontal mobility. Although its composition changed with time, and differences existed in wealth and prestige, in my opinion there was in every community only one aristocratic upper class. In the course of the archaic crisis, for several reasons, the rule of this aristocracy was increasingly challenged. It responded by developing a strict aristocratic code that justified its claim to power with the nobleman's inherited qualities and natural superiority. Efforts were made to transform the aristocracy into a closed caste by prohibiting and morally condemning intermarriage and other close contacts with "low-born" people.

This is what we find in Greece down to the sixth century, and I suggest that the situation in Rome was not radically different. There was one aristocracy, the *patres* or *patricii*. It had emerged through internal differentiation and, once established, strengthened its position through personal and trade connections with neighboring com-

---

116. Momigliano, "Origins of the Republic" (1969): 24ff.; *Contr. IV* (1969): 443ff., 448f., and "Patrizi e plebei" (1967): 204ff., 217f.; cf. Richard, *Origines* (1978): 478ff., 519ff., especially 531ff. For recent discussions of the *conscripti*, see Zusi, *Critica storica* 12 (1975): 186ff. Momigliano's suggestions are summarized by T. J. Cornell, "Failure of the Plebs" (1983): 102ff., who goes on to show how this model can be used for a better explanation of the Conflict of the Orders as a whole (108ff.). Serious further discussion along the lines proposed by Cornell and myself (in the present paper) might indeed lead to a truly new and much more satisfactory understanding of the whole complex of problems.

117. Here, too, what is urgently needed is a comprehensive and systematic study that includes all ancient societies and incorporates the results of recent anthropological work. For valuable contributions in partial areas, see, e.g., for Greece, Starr, *Origins* (1961); id., *Growth* (1977); Donlan, *Ideal* (1980); id., *CW* 75 (1981–82): 137ff.; Gschnitzer, *Sozialgeschichte* (1981): 38ff., 56f., 60ff.; for Rome, Ampolo, *DArch* 4/5 (1970–71), especially 46ff.; id., "Stadtwerdung Roms" (1982): 321; J. Cels Saint-Hilaire and C. Feuvrier-Prévotat, *Dial. d'hist. anc.* 5 (1979): 105ff.; for Etruria, M. Torelli, "Rome et l'Etrurie" (1979): 251ff.; B. d'Agostino, *Annales* 32 (1977): 3ff. Richard, *Origines* (1978) is, despite the title, as much a work on the origins of the patriciate.

munities and far beyond.¹¹⁸ During the period of the formation of the city, there was an extraordinary amount of social mobility; accordingly, the number of *gentes* belonging to the aristocracy changed considerably in the course of time.¹¹⁹ Some became poor and lost their status, some died out, some emigrated or were expelled.¹²⁰ Others immigrated from neighboring areas: Latins, Sabines, Etruscans. Because of the traditional "international" relations among aristocracies, they naturally joined the ranks of the Roman patriciate.¹²¹ Others rose in status, promoted by the kings or as protégés of leading clans.¹²² There certainly were among the *gentes* differences in

118. Cf. Ampolo, *DArch* 4/5 (1970–71): 37ff., especially 46ff., 62ff. His conclusions seem to have been confirmed by the most recent excavations in many places in *Latium Vetus*: Cornell, *Arch. Rep.* (1979–80): especially 75ff.; cf. also the historical conspectus on the emergence of the city in Latium in *DArch*, n.s., 2 (1980), and M. Torelli, "Roma arcaica" (1980): 6ff.; J.-C. Richard, "Population romaine" (1980): 45ff. Contrary to his own belief (280), Guarino's explanation of the difference between patricians and plebeians (*Riv.* [1975]: 69ff., 279ff.) does not seem to be fully compatible with this archaeological evidence.

119. Cf. Torelli "Rome et l'Etrurie" (1979): 261f., and "Roma arcaica" (1980): 11f.; Linderski, chapter VIII below at n. 26.

120. Expulsion: e.g., the Tarquins (the whole *nomen*, not just the family of the last king; cf. F. Schachermeyr, *RE* 4A, 2 [1932]: 2365ff.). The other *gentes* (some with Etruscan, some with non-Etruscan names) that disappear from the *fasti* around 487 B.C. may well have suffered the same fate, or they may have decided, in reaction to the factional strife within the Roman aristocracy, to leave Rome voluntarily. This may also be the historical core of the Coriolanus saga: Ampolo, *DArch* 4/5 (1970–71): 43f. For other examples, see H. S. Versnel, "Historical Implications" (1980): 130f. Poverty: in archaic societies wealth and nobility are so intimately connected with each other that the loss of one must have led to the loss of the other. An impoverished patrician was hardly likely to be accepted as an equal by his former peers. The complaints of Theognis (especially 667ff.; 173ff.; 419f.; 267ff.; 683ff.; cf. Donlan, *Ideal* [1980]: 80ff.) and the loss of Spartiate status by those who could no longer pay for the common meals (Xen. *Lak. pol.* 10.7; Aristot. *Pol.* 2.1271a26ff.; cf. G. Busolt and H. Swoboda, *Griechische Staatskunde* II² [Munich, 1926]: 659) may serve as analogies; cf. Gschnitzer, *Sozialgeschichte* (1981): 40f. For the whole question of loss of status, cf. now Ranouil, *Patriciat* (1975): 144ff. For the shrinking numbers of the patrician *gentes*, cf. n. 131 below.

121. E.g., the Tarquinii, the Claudii (cf. J. Poucet, *ANRW* I.1 [1972]: 48ff.; Ampolo, *DArch* 4/5 [1970–71]: 37ff., with sources), the Veturii (Shatzman, *CQ* 23 [1973]: 65ff.); other examples in Versnel, "Historical Implications" (1980): 130f.; Richard, "Population romaine" (1980): 36. Cf. for Etruria the important observations of M. Torelli, "Griechen und Etrusker" (1974): 261f.; Ampolo, *DArch* 9/10 (1976–77): 333ff. More generally: Mommsen, *Röm. Forschungen* I (1864): 69ff.; Münzer, *Adelsparteien* (1920): 46ff.

122. Neither was difficult to imagine for the Roman historians, for whom the entrance of new families into the larger senatorial elite (although not into the nobility) was a common phenomenon. For modern historians the possibility is more

prestige, tradition, wealth, and size. Accordingly, there were differences in influence. Such differences may even have been expressed institutionally (for example through the distinction of hereditary and *ad personam* membership in the Senate)[123] or in terminology (such as the distinction between *maiores* and *minores gentes*);[124] some families that could claim the supreme distinction of having repeatedly held "the magistracy" with *imperium* and *auspicia* may have emerged as an inner elite.[125] But they all were aristocrats and as such patricians, sharing most of the well-known social, religious, and political prerogatives.

The events leading to the expulsion of the king may then have emphasized old or created new internal distinctions. Owing to the ensuing free competition, the effects of wars and increasing external pressure, changes in and dissension about politics, and many other factors, there may have been more fluctuation than ever in the early years of the Republic.[126] But there still was only one aristocracy, the

---

difficult to accept. No doubt cases of "internal promotion" decreased in frequency the more the patriciate was established as a distinct and self-consciously exclusive group. See Altheim, *Röm. Geschichte* II (1953): 170ff., especially 174, 176f. (with examples), and Linderski, chapter VIII below at nn. 20ff., 27ff. The possibility is also accepted by Magdelain, "*Auspicia*" (1964): 460f.; J. Cels Saint-Hilaire and C. Feuvrier-Prévotat, *Dial. d'hist. anc.* 5 (1979): 110f. It should further be noted that Odysseus's fictitious life story (*Od.* 14.199ff.) is based on various possibilities of vertical mobility (especially 202–12; 229–39). Cf. the important remarks by Gschnitzer, *Sozialgeschichte* (1981): 40 (on "Homeric Society"): "Was den vornehmen Mann ausmacht, ist ... in erster Linie das Vermögen, nicht die Abkunft. ... Wer reich wird, kommt auch zu Ansehen. Freilich wird es unter den gegebenen wirtschaftlichen Verhältnissen Neureiche nur selten gegeben haben; der meiste Reichtum wird ererbter Reichtum gewesen, also mit vornehmer Abstammung zusammengefallen sein; daneben kommt vor allem erbeuteter Reichtum in Betracht, der Normalfall des Emporkömmlings ist der tüchtige Kriegsmann."

123. If such a distinction really existed; it has been proposed to explain the difference between *patres* and *conscripti:* cf. the discussion in Richard, *Origines* (1978): 478ff., 521ff.

124. For their interpretation see Richard, *Origines* (1978): 319ff.; Ranouil, *Patriciat* (1975): 125ff.

125. But see my discussion of the "legal criterion" stressed by A. Magdelain, "*Auspicia*" (1964): 427ff., and his pupil Ranouil (*Patriciat* [1975], especially 11ff.), in the appendix to this article (part C).

126. See n. 120 above. The need for an *adlectio senatus* after the expulsion of the Tarquins (sources and discussion: Richard, *Origines* [1978]: 481f.) was obvious for the Roman historians who assumed a fixed number of 300 senators from early on (cf. O'Brien Moore, *RE* suppl. 6 [1935]: 663ff., 672ff.). Despite the obvious correlation of this figure with other triple divisions in early Roman society (cf. Altheim,

patricians. Then the growing unrest among the lower classes climaxed in the *secessio*, and the plebeians created their sacred organization. Under permanent external pressure, the patricians had already begun to discipline themselves. The plebeian revolt accelerated this process and created a strong sense of solidarity. Now the patricians closed their ranks, emphasized their exclusiveness, and insisted on their prerogatives even more than before. The strict polarization between plebeians and patricians was the consequence of the emerging plebeian organization. There was indeed a *"serrata del patriziato,"* but not in the sense that nonpatrician members of the aristocracy were excluded.[127] Rather, the aristocracy was fixed as it was, membership was frozen, no one else was admitted thereafter—neither immigrant nobles from other communities nor upstarts in Rome itself.[128]

There was, therefore, no plebeian aristocracy at the beginning of the Conflict of the Orders. That does not mean, however, that there

---

Röm. Geschichte II [1953]: 72), I wonder whether it was not fixed on that level only much later. Not only has Palmer (*Arch. Comm.* [1970]: 5ff.) shattered the credibility of such figures, but in the sixth and early fifth centuries the number of available patricians probably was far too small (cf. chapter I above at n. 123; O'Brien Moore, loc. cit. 665f.). Moreover, one ought to know more generally when and for what purposes council membership was fixed at a precise number. Except for very small councils such as the Spartan *gerousia*, I should think that such restrictions were rare and necessitated mostly by the desire for even representation and/or by the existence of a pool of candidates that by far exceeded a practical size of the council. The formation of the patricio-plebeian aristocracy after 367 provides an example for the relatively fast change from an extremely open situation with much fluctuation after a major turning point in social and constitutional development to a closed aristocracy with extremely limited access, or none at all; cf. Bleicken, *Republik* (1980): 28.

127. For a different explanation of the *"serrata,"* see Cornell, "Failure of the Plebs" (1983): 109ff. For a brief discussion of E. S. Staveley's recent contribution on "The Nature and Aims of the Patriciate" (*Historia* 32 [1983]: 24ff.), see part D of the appendix to this essay.

128. For a similar process in Etruscan cities, cf. M. Torelli, *PP* 26 (1971): 61: "Mentre nei secc. VIII e VII la struttura gentilizia della società, ancora caratterizzata da notevole fluidità, permetteva forme di integrazione ed assimilazione di elementi stranieri, nella prima metà del VI sec. a.C. . . . la compagine sociale etrusca, ormai nettamente solidificata e strutturata per grandi *gentes*, respinge e marginalizza i gruppi esterni." It seems to me that it is less difficult to see why the patricians tried to close themselves off and succeeded in doing so than to explain why this situation prevailed for such a long time. This question is related to the same problem concerning the patrician-plebeian nobility, and to a third one, why Rome remained an aristocracy through the end of the Republic.

were only poor plebeians. Quite the contrary, many of them qualified as hoplites; some may even have owned substantial property. But none of them could match that blend of wealth, social prestige, power (through *gens* and *clientela*), nobility of descent, religious charisma and "know-how," connections, lifestyle, and experience in leadership that characterized the old patrician families, and that were quickly adopted even by those who had successfully penetrated the patrician ranks more recently. Accordingly, there was nobody among the plebeians who qualified for, or could even think of aiming at, the highest magistracy. But there certainly were numerous men, experienced soldiers and proud farmers, who were able, determined, and charismatic enough to stand up to patrician arbitrariness, to lead the plebeians into a mutiny or strike, and to organize the plebeian counterforce as tribunes. This helps to explain the character of the plebeian struggle and its purely defensive and protective goals in the first stage. The plebeians could only turn to offense and aim at more social equality and political participation when an elite emerged among them that possessed the necessary economic resources, was socially acceptable and able to distinguish itself militarily, and was numerous enough to challenge the patrician monopoly of power.

The formation of this elite and the changes in Rome's external situation were the decisive preconditions for the different character of the struggle and for the plebeian successes in the fourth century. It certainly was a long and complex process, based on continued immigration (a few years later Attus Clausus would have found himself a plebeian)[129] and internal differentiation. It was facilitated by the closure of the patriciate, which blocked the previously natural integration of new *gentes* into the existing aristocracy. Members of the families of former plebeian tribunes who had successfully performed their protective duties may indeed have been elected frequently and emerged as plebeian *patroni*, acquiring a growing *clientela* of their own.[130] There probably were many more factors. Loss of status by some patrician *gentes* due to impoverishment, disgrace, or other causes should not be excluded for this early stage. The patriciate

---

129. As indeed happened in 458 to L. Mamilius from Tusculum: Livy 3.29.6, with Münzer, *Adelsparteien* (1920): 66f.
130. Cf. Ed. Meyer, *Kl. Schr.* I² (1924): 351.

must have been shrinking anyway owing to losses in wars and natural extinction.[131] In short, in the course of this process, it became thinkable to overcome the intermarriage ban,[132] to give plebeians a share in military leadership,[133] and finally to elect plebeians to the highest political and religious offices. More than that, it became necessary.

7

This second, transitional stage had its own problems and character. It was marked by continuing economic difficulties, the continuation of the struggle to survive, and, later, after the first expansive moves, new challenges, successes, and setbacks of a magnitude that called for the concentration and cooperation of all the forces available in Roman society: the conquest of Veii and the defeat by the Gauls. Not only were more plebeians—and less wealthy ones—called on to serve in the army,[134] the emergence of a plebeian elite and its ambitions must have deeply changed the nature of the conflict. It became more complex and diverse. With the changes on both sides in Roman society and Rome's external situation, not only did new demands come up, but new possibilities were found to cope with old grievances. Apart from Roman participation in several colonies founded by the

131. Ranouil, *Patriciat* (1975): 183ff., counts 43 patrician *gentes*, 12 of which disappeared before 450. In 366, only 21–23 were left. Cf. Mommsen, *Röm. Forschungen* I (1864): 69ff., especially 107ff.

132. Probably much later than Livy indicates (4.1ff.: 445 B.C.); cf., e.g., J. Bayet, *Tite-Live* IV (Paris, 1965): 129; Linderski, chapter VII below, n. 54. The traditional date is usually accepted in scholarship; cf. Ogilvie, *Comm.* (1965): 527f. with literature cited. For new interpretations of the intermarriage ban, see Linderski at nn. 23ff. and Cornell, "Failure of the Plebs" (1983): 110.

133. This may have been facilitated considerably by the introduction of the office of *tribuni militum consulari potestate*. As J. Linderski suggested in 1981 in a hitherto unpublished part of his paper, this office provided both a larger number of magistracies and "junior positions" without independent *imperium* and *auspicia*. Since the *fasti* listed names without distinctions of office, the annalists interpreted them as holders of equal *potestas* and then confused presumed effect with purpose. For the discussion about this office cf. Heurgon, *Rise* (1973): 173ff.; E. S. Staveley, *JRS* 43 (1953): 30ff.; J. Bayet, loc. cit., 132ff.; De Martino, *Cost.* I² (1972): 317ff.; Ranouil, *Patriciat* (1975): 20ff.; J. Pinsent, *Mil. Trib.* (1975); L. Zusi, *Critica storica* 12 (1975): 225ff.; Cornell, "Failure of the Plebs" (1983): 111ff.

134. Cf. D. Kienast, *BJ* 175 (1975): 100ff.; C. Saulnier, *Armée* (1980): 121ff.

Latin League in the course of the fifth century,[135] the conquest of Veii provided the first opportunity for large-scale land distribution to Roman citizens.[136] Or, rather, for the first time it became inevitable that territorial gains be distributed among poor fellow citizens instead of leaving them primarily to the collective exploitation of a few patrician *gentes*.[137] On the other hand, the sack of Rome may indeed, as Livy claims, have pushed debt up to intolerable and hitherto unknown levels, so that, in the context of the changes mentioned before, remedy could no longer be postponed.[138]

At any rate, once we have adjusted our thinking to the idea that the Conflict of the Orders went through several fundamentally different stages, we should reconsider the possible plebeian objectives of each of them. Even concerning the same issue, what was thinkable, desirable, and possible in the fourth century, may have differed considerably from a hundred years before. The debt problem again offers an example. Despite the model provided by Solon,[139] the abolition of the *nexum*, as it was realized by the *lex Poetilia* in the last quarter of the fourth century, may not have been a goal of the plebeians at the time of the first *secessio*. In view of the firmly entrenched power and the generally accepted authority of the patriciate, we should consider the possibility that all that the plebeians could think of and realistically hope for was redress within the existing system (i.e., a reduction of arbitrariness and abuse and a definition of rights and procedures), not a radical change of the system.[140]

Appendix

In order to facilitate future discussion, I briefly summarize here my reasons for disagreeing with some of the views expressed in this volume by W. Eder and R. E. Mitchell, and with the hypotheses con-

135. E. T. Salmon, *Colon.* (1970): 40ff.
136. Livy 6.5.8.
137. For the earlier solutions: G. Tibiletti, *Athenaeum* 26 (1948): 173ff.; Alföldi, *Early Rome* (1965): 310ff., 314ff.
138. Livy 6.11.9; 31.2; 32.1; 34.2. Cf. Peppe, *Esecuzione* (1981), especially 93ff.
139. See chapter I at nn. 94ff. on the problems connected with Greek models and Greek influence.
140. Such a possibility gains support from Peppe's examination of the sources on the debt problem in the fifth century; see *Esecuzione*, chs. 2 and 3 (1981).

cerning the formation of the patriciate proposed by A. Magdelain in 1964 and E. S. Staveley in 1983. Similar statements as regards the contributions to this volume by T. J. Cornell and R. Develin are contained in the appendix to chapter I above. I wish to emphasize that these statements represent my initial reaction in a necessarily very condensed form; I hope that a more detailed discussion of our main points of disagreement will be possible elsewhere.

A. In his analysis of the political significance of the codification of law in archaic Greece and Rome, W. Eder (chapter IX below) strongly emphasizes something almost universally overlooked in recent scholarship—namely, that codification must "be regarded as a measure to ensure aristocratic predominance; it was an attempt to stabilize the political and economic status quo that was being seriously threatened by social unrest" (after n. 2; see also n. 60). He is aware that one of the purposes of providing "the opportunity to appeal to a defined and published body of law" must have been "to prevent further unrest that might be caused by an arbitrary use of customary law." But Eder's main objective is clearly to demonstrate that the codification primarily served the interests of the ruling class; it was designed to strengthen equality, homogeneity, and uniform behavior among the aristocrats, to prevent accumulation of power in only few hands, and to protect existing property arrangements. Though I find Eder's contribution extremely valuable and his demonstration of these particular aspects generally convincing, I disagree with a number of his assessments and think he has tipped the scales too far in the other direction. Since he cannot find in our sources any explicit demand for codification expressed by the lower classes (at n. 33), he denies that such demands and widespread dissatisfaction were a major factor in realizing it. He emphasizes that political, economic, social, and jurisdictional aspects cannot be strictly separated in archaic societies (after n. 3); therefore, since the codification failed substantially to improve the lower classes' political and economic situation (at nn. 36f., 39ff., 49f., and passim) he denies that they profited significantly at all (before n. 20). Here I disagree. First, though for Rome we have no contemporary evidence illuminating the historical background of the Twelve Tables, for Greece we do have explicit testimony of dissatisfaction with aristocratic arbitrariness in jurisdiction and in general. Hesiod called for "straight decisions"; Solon, in a stronger position, not only complained but acted: he codified the law and introduced significant reforms. Without denying leadership and superiority to the aristocracy, he explicitly created "equal law for high and low." I find it easy to accept that in his codification Solon was reacting comprehensively to grievances he himself, Hesiod, and probably many others before them had heard. Second, if the codification intended to limit aristocratic arbitrariness, and if it was at least partially successful in doing so, then the lower classes profited (in Athens probably more than in Rome). Once customary law was no longer automatically respected and handled responsibly by those in power, once arbitrariness had become a major problem, regulation meant improvement, as Eder himself points out. Such basic improvement may or may not have been accompanied by political innovation or economic changes (here I see a much bigger difference between Athens and Rome than Eder does). Because it defined the norms of aristocratic behavior and rule, such regulation transcended individual sectors of community life. It seems wrong, therefore, to interpret lack of institutional or economic improvement as a general indication that the lower classes failed to make substantial gains. All this certainly needs more discussion, but at present I suggest that we accept Eder's emphasis on the upper classes' objectives without denying a very substantial element of lower class involvement and gain.

B. Although I disagree with a number of R. Mitchell's assumptions, analytical methods, and conclusions, I find his contribution (chapter V above) highly stimulating; it certainly deserves careful consideration and detailed discussion. Debate would have to focus on the one hand on the source basis and the individual supporting arguments (which I cannot do here, although there certainly are weak spots: for example, with respect to hereditary succession in the Senate), on the other hand on the thesis as such and its historical implications. I just want to emphasize two points.

First, Mitchell's elimination of the Conflict of the Orders is not absolute. He contests a long-term conflict between patricians and plebeians (which he sees not as social orders but as groups defined by legal and religious criteria). But he admits the possibility of other kinds of conflicts over economic, social, and political issues. I find it difficult to accept, however, that the later Roman authors should have been so completely wrong in identifying the opposing groups. For if originally there was no *social* distinction between *patres* and *plebei*, how could *plebs* have acquired the meaning of "lower class, rabble" that is so pervasive in the later Republic? Mitchell thinks about the meaning and etymology of *pater* and *patricius* but not about that of *plebs* (see the discussion in Richard, *Origines* [1978]: 103–34).

Second, Mitchell is successful, in my view, in demonstrating that the religious prerogatives of the patricians were much more pervasive and important than is generally assumed, but he is unsuccessful in establishing the absolute priority of the religious aspects. I agree that the political and religious spheres cannot be strictly separated in archaic societies; but he replaces what he sees as a predominantly political interpretation by an exclusively religious one, which again distorts the picture. He claims that the *patres* were priests and qua priests were influential, powerful, and maintained a hereditary claim to membership in the Senate. Unfortunately, he fails to explain how this priestly caste of patricians came into existence—when and how those *gentes* succeeded in monopolizing the priesthoods. The answer (which can only be based on comparative and anthropological study) must, I think, be that in the course of early social and economic differentiation the emerging "upper class" took control of the increasingly complex religious "apparatus" of the community simply because these crucially important functions could naturally only be held by its most eminent members.

Aristocratic predominance in archaic societies, I suggest, rests on a complex set of economic, social, religious, military, jurisdictional, and political prerogatives; all these aspects were interconnected and all of them were part of the exclusive status of the aristocrat: he was wealthy and (or therefore) socially eminent and conspicuous, well trained and well educated, "best in council and war," leader in battle and "politics," judge and priest (or at least holder of a special relationship to the gods). Although one or the other of these aspects could become more important than others at times, it would be wrong to isolate it or give it an absolute value. I should therefore say: because the patricians were the leading class economically and socially, they monopolized the priesthoods (which in some cases originally belonged to gentile cults anyway) *and* were the advisors of the king and later the senators (whether hereditarily or not) *and* tried to monopolize the magistracy, and so on. Priesthood, in other words, was not a primary, absolute function, but a secondary, derived one.

Although priestly functions certainly were more important politically, Rome was no more a theocracy or an oligarchy of priests than the Greek cities were. The contrary view would have to be demonstrated much more comprehensively and cogently than has been done (possibly such a thesis might argue Etruscan influence, but not even for Etruria has the argument for a theocracy been convincingly stated, let alone proved).

Once established, the pattern suggested above developed dynamics of its own. The control of certain priesthoods added to the prestige of certain families; it was one of the mechanisms of internal differentiation within the aristocracy. The same is true for control of law and jurisdiction. What is made obvious by Mitchell's study is the lack of a comprehensive analysis of the connection between religion and politics in archaic Rome as well as Greece; this is another urgent desideratum.

C. In dealing with the question of the formation of the patriciate, I explained why I find it difficult to accept the traditional view of the "*serrata del patriziato*" as a split in an existing aristocracy by which one group monopolized power and privileges while the others were ousted radically and permanently from a position they had shared before (see above at nn. 108ff. and n. 109). In an unusually stimulating and helpful article discussing the origins of the patriciate ("*Auspicia ad patres redeunt*" [1964]), A. Magdelain seems to be aware of this very problem. Accordingly, he characterizes claims to monopolization of *auspicia*, *gens*, and nobility by the patricians as skillful propaganda (464f.). In his view, the vehicle this small group of families used to separate itself from the bulk of the aristocracy as an exclusive inner elite was a strictly legal one—the distinction of having obtained the supreme magistracy with *imperium* and *auspicia* and with the regal charisma of standing under Jupiter's own protection. This legal criterion was then supported by propagandistic claims such as the monopolization of certain distinctions and characteristics and the retrojection of patrician status to the time of Romulus (470f.).

I have four basic objections. First, insofar as Magdelain's solution attributes an absolute value to a legal criterion, it is strictly legalistic. I find it uncertain whether that is appropriate for the archaic period; at least it is a problem that should be properly addressed. Second, whatever the value of this "legal criterion," in my opinion, it must have been secondary, not primary, just like the religious criterion stressed with unjustified absoluteness by Mitchell. In other words, the "legal criterion" did not "make" the patriciate, but rather the emerging patriciate used it as an additional strong argument to emphasize its power, superiority, and exclusiveness. In addition, it may have promoted differentiation within the closed ranks of the patriciate. Thus it must have been obvious to all that only the highest-ranking senators, the former magistrates and holders of *auspicia*, could become *interreges*. Third, for the arguments used by the emerging patriciate to justify its claims, Magdelain relies heavily on the literary sources. He does not discuss whether this is methodologically legitimate, and he seems unaware of the fact that these arguments were largely inspired by the claims and self-representation of late republican *nobiles*, *equites*, and *novi homines*. Fourth, Magdelain's concept is purely theoretical; its practical sides are not explored. The thesis that in the first century of the Republic "un petit groupe de familles accapare la magistrature supérieure, au nom d'une prédestination du sang, et abaisse au-dessous de cette caste nouvelle toutes les autres familles aristocratiques qui . . . sont exclus du patriciat et doivent accepter la qualification plébéienne" (464) remains unexplained. How could these few families do it? Why were their claims and propaganda successful? Why did the others accept their demotion from a position of real or potential equality to one of clear inferiority? And how do these various and sizable groups of aristocrats fit into the limited population of archaic Rome? In short, although I find Magdelain's discussion of *interregnum* and *auspicia* splendid and appreciate his many valuable suggestions, I cannot accept his explanation of the formation of the patriciate. I suggest, however, that most of his evidence and arguments could be used to illustrate an emerging differentiation within the patriciate (see above at n. 123).

D. On the other hand, unfortunately, I find E. S. Staveley's 1983 contribution on "The Nature and Aims of the Patriciate" mostly mistaken. Staveley starts from the observation that, although frequently assumed in modern scholarship, a split within a preexisting senatorial aristocracy is "inherently improbable." He then examines the meaning of *patricius*, which he understands as an "artificial creation fashioned by a self-appointed elite to give itself a titular identity" (33), and the patrician prerogatives, which he finds to have been at least partially "redesigned to operate within a totally different constitutional framework" at the beginning of the Republic. He concludes that the patriciate was created in the fifth century (40) when "an entirely new caste" of patrician families closed itself off by excluding a number of previously prominent members of the aristocratic elite. They did so, however, not as self-motivated and power-hungry "appropriators or usurpers but rather as the prime movers in the establishment of an entirely new constitutional framework" (41), which replaced the "military-style provisional government" (43) of the very first years of the Republic after the major upheaval in the mid-480s and Sp. Cassius's attempt to establish a tyranny. Their objective to create a civil government with strong constitutional safeguards enjoyed widespread popular support and marked the return to the pre-Etruscan principles of the Latin monarchy (48). As is visible especially on pp. 47–50, this is an entirely speculative reconstruction based on an arbitrary use of the literary sources (cf. 53 as opposed to 56) and exaggerates not only "devotion to the old Latin ideal" and anti-Etruscan sentiments (49) but also the idealistic, unselfish objectives (49–50) and propagandistic sophistication (33) of the "patrician movement"; it operates with an anachronistic view of the opposition between "military" and "civil" in Roman society and with a completely unrealistic idea of archaic *polis*-aristocracies (cf. especially 50). Moreover, Staveley assumes a "closure" of the patriciate against one part of the aristocracy and continuing access of plebeians to office, resulting in a patricio-plebeian aristocracy (50–53) that had already after the Decemvirate stifled the attempts of an emerging class of nouveaux riches to gain access to office (52–53). In this rather complicated scheme, elements traditionally assumed to have been characteristic of the fourth century are moved far back into the fifth, and a conflict over office tenure between patricians and plebeians before the Decemvirate is denied. There is no place, therefore, for the traditional kind of Conflict of the Orders, but neither are the social and economic demands of the lower classes ever mentioned in Staveley's paper. In conclusion, the patricians' attitudes and actions as portrayed by Staveley are so completely contradicted both by those of the later Roman nobility and those of contemporary Greek aristocracies that they cannot be accepted as historically plausible.

JERZY LINDERSKI

VIII

Religious Aspects of the Conflict of the Orders: The Case of *confarreatio*

The Conflict of the Orders touched upon all facets of life, public and private, in early Rome. The role *religio* played in this conflict offers itself as an ideal testing ground for the various methodologies and approaches devised to penetrate behind the fictional scheme of our literary sources. Institutions have their own life, and their structure can reveal much about their past. One such institutional structure was prominent in the Conflict of the Orders: that of marriage, or, more exactly, intermarriage between patricians and plebeians.

Cicero complains that if every patrician followed the example of Clodius and got himself adopted into a plebeian family, the consequences would be disastrous: very soon the Roman people would have neither the *rex sacrorum* nor the *flamines* nor the Salii; it would lose half of the other priests, and, finally, as the interrex had to be nominated by the patricians and had to be a patrician himself, the auspices too would perish.¹ The *flamines* attract attention. They will now lead us from the bright day of Cicero into the mist and fog of archaic Roman history.

The *flamines maiores* and the *rex sacrorum* form a special case, in that their status, unlike that of other priests, was inseparably connected with a particular form of marriage, the marriage *per confarreationem*.² In order to be eligible for the priesthood, they had to be born *ex farreatis* and had themselves to live in a marriage concluded *per confarreationem*.³ Marriage was, in fact, an inseparable part of their *sacerdotium*: upon the death of the *flaminica* the *flamen Dialis* was obliged to resign his priesthood, and, needless to say, he was not allowed to divorce his wife.⁴ As the *regina sacrorum* and the *flaminica*

1. Cic. *Dom.* 38.: *Ita populus Romanus brevi tempore neque regem sacrorum neque flamines nec Salios habebit, nec ex parte dimidia reliquos sacerdotes neque auctores centuriatorum et curiatorum comitiorum, auspicia populi Romani, si magistratus patricii creati non sint, intereant necesse est, cum interrex nullus sit, quem et ipsum patricium esse et a patriciis prodi necesse est.* Cf. R. G. Nisbet, *M. Tulli Ciceronis de domo sua ad pontifices oratio* (Oxford, 1939): ad loc.

2. The basic text is Gaius, *Inst.* 1.112: *Farreo in manum conveniunt per quoddam genus sacrificii, quod Iovi Farreo fit: in quo farreus panis adhibetur, unde etiam confarreatio dicitur; conplura praeterea huius iuris ordinandi gratia cum certis et sollemnibus verbis praesentibus decem testibus aguntur et fiunt. Quod ius etiam nostris temporibus in usu est: nam flamines maiores, id est Diales, Martiales, Quirinales, item reges sacrorum, nisi ex farreatis nati non leguntur; ac ne ipsi quidem sine confarreatione sacerdotium habere possunt* (cf. the commentary by M. David and H. L. W. Nelson, *Studia Gaiana* 3 [Leiden, 1954]: 132–33, citing further literature). Ulp. *Regulae* 9.1 does not contain any new information, but Servius Auctus, on *Aen.* 4 .103, 339, 374, and especially on *Georg.* 1.31 (ed. G. Thilo), is of importance: *tribus enim modis apud veteres nuptiae fiebant: . . . farre, cum per pontificem maximum et Dialem flaminem per fruges et molam salsam coniungebantur, unde confarreatio appellabatur.* Of modern literature, see A. Rossbach, *Untersuchungen über die römische Ehe* (Stuttgart, 1853): 95ff., 361ff.; R. Leonhard, "Confarreatio," *RE* 4 (1900): 862–64; G. Wissowa, *Religion* (1912): 118–19, 387, 506; P. E. Corbett, *Marriage* (1930): 73ff.; M. Kaser, *Privatr.* I² (1971): 76–77; A. Watson, *The Law of Persons in the Later Roman Republic* (Oxford, 1967): 23–24.

3. On the basis of Gaius, S. Brassloff, "Die Erneuerung des Flaminates," in *Studi in onore di P. Bonfante* II (Milan, 1930): 363–79, especially 372ff., argues that the *flamines* and *reges sacrorum* had to be married *per confarreationem* before they assumed their priesthood. But in practice they may have been required to undergo this ceremony in the period between their *captio* (*lectio* or *nominatio*) and *inauguratio*. Cf. below at nn. 37ff.

4. Gell. 10.15.22–24: *Matrimonium flaminis nisi morte dirimi ius non est. Uxorem si amisit, flamonio decedit* (from Fabius Pictor through the intermediary of Ateius Capito and Masurius Sabinus, cf. R. Peter, *Quaestionum pontificalium specimen* [Strassburg, 1886]: 15–16, 20–21; G. Rowoldt, *Librorum pontificiorum Romanorum de*

(in historical times this term was used almost exclusively with reference to the wife of the *flamen Dialis*)[5] fully participated in the priesthood of their husbands,[6] it is very probable that they, too, had to be born *ex farreatis*. The *flamines maiores* and the *rex sacrorum* had to be patricians, and this brings us to the heart of our problem.

So far the facts: this was the situation that obtained in the last centuries of the Republic. On this meager basis far-reaching and far-fetched theories have been erected concerning the origin of the differentiation between patricians and plebeians. The facts we have can be arranged in a number of combinations, the final result being largely predetermined by our first move. Probability must be the final judge.

We can assume that *confarreatio* was the original form of Roman marriage and that it was restricted to patricians. Now Roman tradition is unanimous that there was a time when all magistracies and all priesthoods were a patrician preserve. As confarreate birth and confarreate marriage were formal requirements for the patrician *flamines*, we can surmise that at one time a similar requirement existed for all or most patrician priesthoods, and perhaps for patrician magistracies as well. Now the following development took place: the magistracies and priesthoods were gradually thrown open to plebeians, but *confarreatio* remained an exclusively patrician ceremony. As a result it was dropped as a requirement for those priesthoods to which the plebeians were admitted. It lost its political importance, and as it was a cumbersome and personally uncomfortable form of

---

caerimoniis sacrificiorum reliquiae [Halle, 1906]: 27–28; L. Strzelecki, *C. Atei Capitonis fragmenta* [Wroclaw, 1960]: 17); Plut. *Quaest. Rom.* 50 (from Ateius Capito, probably through Iuba, cf. Peter 20ff.; Strzelecki 18–19, and in greater detail, id., *De Ateio Capitone nuptialium caerimoniarum interprete* [Wroclaw, 1947]: 23ff.; but see also H. J. Rose, *The Roman Questions of Plutarch* [Oxford, 1924]: 20ff., who vigorously protests against overestimating Plutarch's use of Iuba). For other sources, see J. Marquardt, *Staatsverwaltung* III[2] (1885): 328–29. Servius Auctus, on *Aen.* 4.29, causes difficulty, for his statement runs counter to that of Gellius and Plutarch: *sane caerimoniis veterum flaminicam nisi unum virum habere non licet . . . nec flamini aliam ducere licebat uxorem, nisi post mortem flaminicae uxoris*. This is either inaccurate, represents relaxation of the original custom, or refers only to the *flamen Martialis* and *Quirinalis*, whose *castus* were less *multiplices* than those of the *flamen Dialis* (Servius Auctus, on *Aen.* 8.552).

5. Wissowa, *Religion* (1912): 506 n. 5; *TLL* s.v. *flaminica*.
6. Marquardt, *Staatsverwaltung* III[2] (1885): 322, 331–32.

marriage, it fell into desuetude. The twin requirements of patrician and confarreate birth survived as a relic of the past only with respect to the *flamines maiores* and the *rex sacrorum*, the priesthoods that were important in ritual but quite secondary in politics.[7]

This interpretation has two points in its favor: logic and simplicity. Yet history need not be simple or logical, and if we scrutinize the traditional theory more closely we shall easily discover two weak points: (a) we do not know for certain whether marriage by *confarreatio* was *always* restricted to patricians; (b) we do not know for certain whether *confarreatio* was ever required for any priesthoods other than the major *flamonia* and the *rex sacrorum*.

And so we arrive at the starting point of a rival theory developed some fifty years ago by Pierre Noailles[8] and Paul Koschaker.[9] They observed that our sources speak of *confarreatio* almost exclusively in connection with the major *flamonia*.[10] As Noailles put it, ancient sources restrict *confarreatio* to the "recruitment of the priestly caste of major flamines."[11] Hence the conclusion: the rite of *confarreatio* was introduced in order to limit the selection of the *flamines* to a small circle of certain privileged families. Thus the rite of *confarreatio* in conjunction with the institution of the *interregnum* played a major, perhaps decisive, role in the formation of a hereditary nobility, the future patriciate.

This is a captivating theory, but before we are seduced by it, let

---

7. Cf. above all Mommsen, *Röm. Staatsrecht* III.1 (1887): 33–36, 78–80. Very characteristic of Mommsen's way of thinking is the following argument (p. 79): "Auch zeigt uns das Recht zwei gleichberechtigte Eheformen, die bürgerliche in der Gestalt des religiösen Ehebündnisses durch Confarreation und die Consensualehe der Halbfreien. Dass jene nur bei den Patriciern begegnende dem Plebejer von Rechtswegen versagt war, wird allerdings nicht ausdrücklich überliefert, ist aber darum nicht weniger sicher."

8. P. Noailles, "Les rites nuptiaux gentilices et la *confarreatio*," *RD* 15 (1936): 401–17; "Les *dii nuptiales*," *RD* 16 (1937): 549–50; "Les tabous du mariage dans le droit primitif des Romains," in id., *Fas* (1948): 12–13 (originally published in *Annales Sociologiques*, series C, fasc. 2 [1937]: 6–34); "Junon déesse matrimoniale des Romains," in *Fas*, 29–43 (originally published in *Festschrift P. Koschaker* I [Weimar, 1939]: 386–400).

9. P. Koschaker, "Le mariage dans l'ancien droit romain," *RD* 16 (1937): 746–49; "Die Eheformen bei den Indogermanen," in *Zeitschr. für ausländ. und intern. Privatrecht* 11, suppl. vol. (1937): 77ff.

10. This is especially true of Servius Auctus, on *Aen.* 4.103, 339, 374.

11. Noailles, *Fas* (1948): 32.

us examine it in some detail. Not everybody has been convinced: Max Kaser in his celebrated *Das römische Privatrecht* described it as a "doubtful" and "artificial construction."[12] But an "artificial construction" need not be false, and in fact in his earlier and equally celebrated work *Das altrömische ius*, Kaser provided some support for the ideas of Noailles and Koschaker.[13] For Mommsen *confarreatio* was the original form of marriage; he says that there may have been a time when sacrally concluded marriage was regarded as the only valid form of marriage, particularly with respect to the legal position of children.[14] On the other hand according to Noailles and Koschaker *confarreatio* was not the oldest but rather the most recent form of *manus* marriage.[15] This is the heart and backbone of their theory, and it may indeed perplex the casual reader, for *confarreatio* has at first sight a truly archaic appearance. Yet as Kaser[16] points out very perceptively, it is *confarreatio* itself that is perplexing. From a legal point of view it is an oddity: a sacral ceremony with consequences in civil law. The legal result of *confarreatio*, i.e., of a sacral act, is the acquisition of *manus* over the wife by her husband, i.e., a civil act; it is further striking that the sources do not mention the participation in the ceremony of the previous holder of the *manus*, the father of the bride, although it was his *potestas* that was being transferred to the husband. Hence one can surmise that in fact *confarreatio* originally consisted of two separate acts: (1) the religious act that established the sacrally valid marriage, in itself a remarkable thing, for in Rome marriage was primarily a matter-of-fact arrangement—one that was naturally accompanied by religious ceremonies, but that was in no way established or validated by any religious act; (2) a civil act that transferred the *manus*. What was the character of that civil act? Kaser conjectures that originally *manus* could be established or transferred only by *coemptio*. We have to remember that we do not know the wording of the ritual formulas recited at the *confarreatio*, but they may well have contained elements taken over from the legal for-

12. Kaser, *Privatr.* I² (1971): 77 n. 14.
13. Kaser, *Ius* (1949): 342–45. Recently the ideas of Noailles and Koschaker have been endorsed by Richard, *Origines* (1978): 240–44. For an inspiring discussion, see also C. W. Westrup, *Recherches* (1943): 14ff.
14. Mommsen, *Röm. Staatsrecht* III.1 (1887): 34, cf. 79–80.
15. Cf. especially Noailles, *Fas* (1948): 12.
16. Kaser, *Ius* (1949): 343–44, cf. 316–21.

mula of *coemptio*.[17] Altogether the reconstruction of Noailles is quite appealing: we would have an old and primitive legal institution, the marriage by purchase, upon which at a later stage a sacral ritual was grafted. In historical times this sacral ritual overshadowed, at least in our sources (and perhaps in real practice as well), the legal side of the transaction. We may say that this theory seems to make sense of the complex double nature of *confarreatio* as a sacral and civil institution. Legally it is an impeccable construction, but let us inquire whether it gives better insight into the social history of archaic Rome.

Let us turn again to Mommsen.[18] With respect to the dichotomy between patricians and plebeians, he postulates two stages in the legal position of marriage. There was a later stage (immediately before the *lex Canuleia*) when, because of the lack of *conubium* between patricians and plebeians, for the legal validity of marriage not only the husband but the wife, too, had to be patrician. This may have been preceded by a still earlier stage during which not only the patriciate birth of both parents but *confarreatio* as well were the necessary prerequisites for the validity of marriage. Only children born of such marriages would inherit the social position of their fathers. Thus from the very beginning of the city *confarreatio* was, according to Mommsen and his followers, a patrician form of marriage; it did not play any role in the formation of the aristocracy.

To this basically static view, the new theory introduces social and sacral dynamism. We replace the original idea of a patriciate existing since time immemorial with the concept of aristocracy *in statu nascendi*. And we discover that religious institutions may have played an important role in the process of the social definition of that class. Yet we have to beware of a new schematism.

---

17. The phrase *certa et sollemnia verba* (Gaius 1.112, cf. *certa verba*, Ulp. *Reg.* 9.1) points to a set and unchangeable formula. Yet we do not know who pronounced the *certa verba*: the marrying parties or the priests? Nor do we know what these words represented: the consensus of the parties to conclude marriage, the formula of *coemptio*, or perhaps a prayer? All these solutions have been proposed at one time or another; Westrup, *Recherches* (1943): 11 n. 6, and Kaser, *Privatr.* I² (1971): 77 n. 12, prefer, perhaps wisely, to leave the matter *sub iudice*. Yet we have to remember that Gaius gives only a summary; as he himself says, *complura praeterea . . . aguntur et fiunt*—many various acts accompanied by many solemn words. The expression of the consensus of the parties, the transference of *manus* (cf. the discussion by E. Volterra, "La *conventio in manum* e il matrimonio romano," *RISG* 12 [1968]: 205ff.), and the *precationes*—all these acts will not have been missing. The marriage ceremony was a long-drawn-out and elaborate affair (cf. Marquardt, *Privatleben*² [1886]: 42ff.).

18. Mommsen, *Röm. Staatsrecht* III.1 (1887): 34.

First we have to look more closely at the ritual of *confarreatio*. That this complicated and plainly archaic ritual was conceived and introduced simply as a matter of political expediency defies imagination. But there are two distinct elements in the ritual of *confarreatio*: private and official. Some of the ceremonies were performed by the groom and the bride, the central act being the consumption and offering of a cake of *far*, a coarse wheat.[19] This gave the name to the whole ceremony and was plainly its most archaic layer. But what strikes the observer is the official element: the participation of the *flamen Dialis* and *pontifex maximus*.[20] Now Roman marriage was a pri-

19. Gaius 1.112 says that *farreus panis* (cf. Paul. *Epit. Festi* 65 L., *farreum libum*) was used at the sacrifice *quod Iovi Farreo* [*farreo:* Marquardt, *Privatleben*[2] (1886): 50 n. 3] *fit*. To be sure, we are not told expressly that it was the groom and the bride who performed the sacrifice, although many scholars assume this without further discussion (cf., e.g., Kaser, *Privatr*. I[2] [1971]: 77 n. 11). The text of Servius Auctus, on *Aen*. 4.374, attracts attention: *in confarreatione* the *nubentes* sat together *velatis capitibus* on two *sellae iugatae*. It is important to note that not only the bride, but also the groom was veiled; consequently this *velatio* is to be distinguished from the veiling of the bride with the *flammeum*. In all books on the *res nuptiales* I have consulted, and even in the otherwise very competent dissertation by H. Freier (see below) these two acts are commonly confused (but cf. Marquardt, *Privatleben*, 50). At the *velatio capitis* only the back of the head was veiled, the face was uncovered; this was the normal attire of the *sacrificantes ritu Romano* (see H. Freier, *Caput velare* [Tübingen, 1963]: 102ff., especially 132–33). On the other hand the *flammeum* covered the face of the bride; *obnubere* was the terminus technicus for this ceremony (cf. the passages collected by Freier, 129–30). Hence we can assume that the bride and groom were engaged in some sort of sacrifice; and indeed Gaius mentions the sacrifice of *panis farreus* and Servius Auctus (loc. cit.) the sacrifice of an *ovis*. On monumental representations either the face of the bride is covered or only the back of her head (Rossbach, *Die römische Ehe* [see n. 2 above]: 376–79; id., *Römische Hochzeits- und Ehedenkmäler* [Leipzig, 1871]: 16, 44, 96, 120, 153). This has caused some perplexity (cf. Marquardt, *Privatleben*, 45 n. 3; Freier 133). Now we have the explanation: the bride is represented either as *sacrificans* or as *nupta*. Thus Servius and monumental representations explain each other.

20. Servius Auctus, on *Georg*. 1.31, is normally adduced as the only authority attesting the participation at the *confarreatio* of the *flamen Dialis* and *pontifex maximus*, but his information goes back (through unknown intermediaries) to a very good source, Ateius Capito's *De pontificio iure*. L. Strzelecki, in *Lanx Satura N. Terzaghi oblata* (Genoa, 1963): 321–24, has ingeniously and convincingly ascribed to Ateius Capito the gloss *confarreatis nuptiis* of *Gloss. Abol.* CO 102 (*Gloss. Lat.* 3 [Paris, 1926]: 113). Its wording is almost identical with that of Servius: *multis modis nuptiae fiunt . . . farre, cum per pontificem maximum e(t) Diale(m) flaminem per fruges et molam salsam coniunguntur, ex quibus nuptiis patrimi et matrimi nascuntur*. See also W. (= L.) Strzelecki, *C. Atei Capitonis fragmenta* (Leipzig, 1967): xxvi-xxviii and 30 (fr. 6a); F. Bona, *Contributo allo studio della composizione del "De verborum significatu" di Verrio Flacco* (Milan, 1964): 90–91 n. 143. Incidentally the passage in question shows that the original

vate and family affair: there is no obvious or necessary ritual connection between the offering and sharing[21] of the cake of *far* by the groom and bride and the presence of the highest priests of the state. The participation of the state priests reveals itself as an overtly political and chronologically posterior element. Thus the historic *confarreatio* was composed of four separate intersecting components: sacral and civil, private and official. As the most primitive elements we can safely isolate the *manus* marriage by *coemptio* and the religious ceremony of the sharing and offering of *far*. These two institutions existed side by side, the ceremony of *far* being clearly outside the realm of *ius*: it was the procedure of *coemptio* that produced *manus*. The *coemptio* was not restricted to any particular class, nor should we imagine that this primitive *confarreatio* was classbound. In the ritual itself there is nothing that is patrician or aristocratic. The participation of the *flamen Dialis* and the *pontifex maximus*[22] profoundly altered the character of *confarreatio*. It transformed what had been a private institution into an institution of the state. This transformation was probably also responsible for that blending of sacral and civil elements that is so perplexing to us today.

The *confarreatio* now became a class institution and an instrument of class policy. It is obvious that the priest of Jupiter and the chief

---

meaning of *patrimi et matrimi* was "the children born of confarreate parents"; the meaning "the children whose parents are still alive" appears to be a later development. Richard in his instructive discussion (*Origines* [1978]: 241–42) unfortunately missed the studies of Strzelecki.

21. According to Wissowa, *Religion* (1912): 387 n. 3, the sharing of *far* is not directly attested; it has, however, been postulated by a number of scholars, see, e.g., A. Dieterich, *Eine Mithrasliturgie*³ (Leipzig and Berlin, 1923): 121–22; P. De Francisci, *Primordia* (1959): 286; cf. Kaser, *Privatr.* I² (1971): 77. But in fact Dion. Hal. *Ant. Rom.* 2.25 speaks expressly of the κοινωνία τοῦ φαρρός, the sharing of *far* (cf. Westrup, *Recherches* [1943]: 12). Thus there is no reason to amalgamate the sacrifices mentioned by Gaius 1.112 and Servius Auctus, on *Georg.* 1.31 (= Ateius Capito, fr. suppl. 6a Strzelecki), and ascribe them either to the *nubentes* or the priests. Most probably we here deal with two separate sacrificial acts: the offering and testing of *libum farreum* by the groom and the bride, and the sacrifice of the *fruges* and *mola salsa* performed by the *flamen Dialis* and *pontifex maximus*.

22. De Francisci, *Primordia* (1959): 286–87, conjectures that the ceremony took place before the *pontifex maximus* and only later, "in seguito allo sviluppo delle credenze religiose," was transformed into a *genus sacrificii* performed in the presence of the *flamen Dialis*. This is unwarranted for it is hardly likely that the *pontifex* predated the *flamen*.

pontiff were not able to participate in each and every marriage ceremony. Thus their participation was by necessity limited to a narrow group of select families. These families formed the nucleus of a hereditary aristocracy.

I submit that this reconstruction makes better sense of *confarreatio* as a social institution than other theories, for it finds ample parallels in other epochs and other social systems. For the purpose of promoting coherence within a social group and for keeping strangers away, there is no better means than the introduction of marriage restrictions, first customary, then religious, and, finally, restrictions enshrined in law.[23]

The Twelve Tables form a watershed in this respect. They testify to an attempt by the patricians to form a closed caste. The argument is very straightforward here. We have to treat the prohibition of intermarriage between patricians and plebeians contained in one of

23. One can juxtapose this development with the innovations enacted by the marriage laws of Augustus (the denomination *lex de maritandis ordinibus* is in itself very telling) and with further changes and restrictions introduced in the course of the Empire. Cf. R. Astolfi, *La lex Iulia et Papia* (Padua, 1970): 16–56 ("I divieti matrimoniali"). In feudal Europe there was virtually no intermarriage between gentry and peasants, and examples can be adduced from three parts of the world as disparate geographically, chronologically, and politically as ancient and medieval China, medieval France, and early modern Russia for a tendency among the nobility to contract marriages within their own ranks and to reach outside only for the purpose of concluding alliances with rich or powerful upstarts; see, e.g., the recent studies by P. Buckley Ebrey, *The Aristocratic Families of Early Imperial China* (Cambridge, 1978); G. Duby, "Lineage, Nobility, and Chivalry in the Region of Macôn during the Twelfth Century," in *Family and Society: Selections from the Annales*, edited by R. Forster and O. Ranum (Baltimore, 1976): 16–40; R. O. Crummey, *Aristocrats and Servitors: The Boyar Elite in Russia, 1613–1689* (Princeton, 1983). But for direct parallels we have to go, as in so many other cases, from Rome to India, with its legal and religious prohibitions of intermarriage between the castes (*jāti*) and its ideal of the purity of the three upper classes (*varna*); see J. H. Hutton, *Caste in India*[4] (Oxford, 1963); P. Kolenda, *Caste in Contemporary India* (Menlo Park, Calif., 1978). G. Dumézil, *Mariages Indo-Européens* (Paris, 1979), is, as always, stimulating, unreliable, and replete with errors of fact and logic. He maintains (p. 48) that only patricians could serve as witnesses at the confarreate marriage, whereas Gaius 1.112 (whom Dumézil quotes on the same and preceding pages) speaks only of ten witnesses without specifying their status. And as far as logic is concerned it is inadmissable to juxtapose the *usurpatio trinoctii* in Rome and the *trirātra* in India (p. 52). The function of the former was purely legal: to break the *usus* and prevent the acquisition of *manus* by the husband; to achieve this goal it had to be repeated each year. On the other hand the function of the *trirātra* was ritual, not legal: it was a three-night period of continence following immediately upon the marriage ceremony.

the two last tables as a decemviral innovation. Such is the tenor of the sources, above all of Cicero: the decemvirs added two tables of unjust laws, among which was one that most cruelly prohibited intermarriage between plebeians and patricians.[24] This does not sound like a report of a codification of the existing law. This interpretation—now supported by a number of eminent scholars[25]—fits smoothly into what is the most probable model of social development after the beginning of the Republic.

As is well known, plebeian names crop up in the *fasti* and in the Senate; they are prominent among the kings and appear in Roman topography.[26] If the patriciate was not yet a closed caste, this should not surprise us. Obviously there was movement in and out: some families lost their position as a result of feuds and infighting—the relatives of the Tarquinii for instance; others may simply have died out, so that their plebeian namesakes in the later Republic had in fact nothing but the name in common with them. Yet some of those plebeian families, for instance the plebeian Claudii, would have been the junior or less fortunate branches of the original *gens*. They were left out when the patriciate was coalescing into a closed caste. Thus in a sense both the patriciate and the *plebs* were the product of division and polarization within the gentilitial society. Newcomers and descendants of *liberti* swelled the numbers of the *plebs*, but new families were also accepted into the ranks of the aristocracy, as the example of the Claudii demonstrates. This example also shows that there existed a close relationship between the aristocracy of Rome and the aristocracies of other Italian communities, especially the Latins and Sabines. The case of intermarriage between the Roman Horatii and the Alban Curiatii points to the existence of *conubium*, the right to conclude valid marriages, between Rome and at least some Latin communities. The aristocrats tended to conclude marriage alliances with the aristocracies of the neighboring commu-

24. Cic. *De re pub.* 2.63 (*FIRA* I: 70).
25. H. Last, *JRS* 35 (1945): 31–33; F. de Visscher, *RIDA* 1 (1952): 401–22; A. Alföldi, "Struktur des Römerstaates" (1967): 233–34; A. Watson, *XII Tables* (1975): 20ff. Of recent scholars Gjerstad and Kienast reject this interpretation (at least by implication), but to my mind they produce no valid argument: E. Gjerstad, *Early Rome* V (1973): 186–87 (the prohibition of intermarriage dates from the sixth century); D. Kienast, *BJ* 175 (1975): 98.
26. Cf. Richard, chapter IV above, at nn. 12ff., with further literature cited.

nities, and at the same time they attempted to cut themselves off from the nonaristocratic classes in their own cities.[27]

Thus we would postulate at first a natural tendency within any aristocracy to limit marriage as far as possible to its own class—that class being originally a social group, not yet a strictly defined legal entity. Then would come the introduction of ceremonial and religious marriage sanctified by the presence of the highest priests;[28] people married in this way were marked as belonging to the highest aristocracy. And as the last step came the attempt by the decemvirs to sever by law all marriage ties between patricians and plebeians. If this was an innovation, legal prohibition of intermarriage could not have existed before the Twelve Tables, whatever the social practice.

The extant testimonies concerning the Twelve Tables contain only two references to marriage regulations. One is the prohibition of intermarriage ascribed to the second, tyrannical board of decemvirs. The other is the report of Gaius, commonly attributed to table VI, referring to the *usurpatio trinoctii* in connection with the marriage by *usus*.[29] There is no mention of *confarreatio*, and our task is to fit this form of marriage into the system of the Twelve Tables.

A reminder is in order: the Twelve Tables did not treat of marriage as such, but rather of the *conventio in manum*—that is, of the methods of acquiring or avoiding *manus* in connection with marriage. But if the decemvirs treated of *usus*—as the definition goes "a formless acquisition of marital power over the wife through an uninterrupted cohabitation . . . of one year with the intention of living as husband and wife"[30]—they would certainly also have treated of *coemptio*, the acquisition of *manus* over the wife through a fictitious sale. Alan Watson[31] points out that the Twelve Tables may, in fact, have contained a reference to all three ways in which *manus* was cre-

---

27. F. De Visscher, *RIDA* 1 (1952): 412ff. For a similar tendency among the aristocrats of Gaul, see Caes. *De bello Gallico* 1.3.5; 1.8.6–7.

28. It is difficult to decide when this process began. J.-C. Richard (chapter IV above, part 2) thinks of the pre-Etruscan regal period; A. Alföldi, "Struktur des Römerstaates" (1967): 232–33, and Noailles, *Fas* (1948): 12–13, 31–32, argue for the early years of the Republic.

29. Gaius 1.111 (*FIRA* I: 44).

30. A. Berger, *Encyclopedic Dictionary of Roman Law*, Trans. Amer. Philos. Soc. 43, no. 2 (Philadelphia, 1953), s.v. *usus*, p. 755.

31. Watson, *XII Tables* (1975): 9–19.

ated. He argues that the list *usu, farreo* (*farre*), *coemptione*, found in four later authors,[32] in all probability derived from the Twelve Tables. This is an interesting and on the whole convincing proposition, but it creates new problems. Was *confarreatio* limited to patricians? If by *confarreatio* we understand the official ceremony in which the participation of the *flamen Dialis* and the *pontifex maximus* was indispensable, it is obvious that for all practical purposes it had to be.

We have already considered the possibility of the existence of private *confarreatio*, sacred rites and offerings requiring no presence of the official priests. This type of *confarreatio* would, of course, have been available to plebeians, but the important question is this: could this kind of ceremony be thought of as creating *manus*? Unfortunately this question is better left *sub iudice*, especially as extrajuridical sources are not especially helpful either. No importance can, of course, be attached to a notice in the *Historia Augusta* (*Alex. Sev.* 22.3), a corrupt notice at that,[33] that the *ius confarreationis* abolished by Elagabalus was restored by the Emperor Alexander Severus, but a *cursus honorum* recording a *sacerdos confarreationum et diffareationum* attracts attention.[34] The *sacerdos* in question, M. Aurelius Papirius Dionysius, was a *iurisperitus* and a high equestrian official under Marcus Aurelius and Commodus, hence not a patrician. In his capacity as *iurisperitus*, he was *adsumptus* as a *sexagenarius* into the imperial council, and subsequently was appointed, as H.-G. Pflaum puts it, to "un sacerdoce fort ancien." The task of this priest was to apply "tous les vieux précepts qui ordonnaient que certains fonctions du culte officiel ne pussent être revêtues que par des patriciens mariés selon le rituel de la *confarreatio*."[35] But far from being an ancient *sacerdotium*, this is a priesthood of which we know nothing; and, secondly, it was the traditional duty of the pontiffs to explain the sacral law. Hence it is very unlikely that we have here a patrician form of marriage or one that required the presence of the *flamen Dialis* or chief pontiff. Most probably the inscription uses the term *confar-*

32. Gaius 1.110; Boethius, on Cic. *Top.* 3.14; Arnobius, *Adv. gent.* 4.20; Servius Auctus, on *Georg.* 1.31.
33. Cf. E. Hohl in his edition in app. crit. ad loc.
34. *CIL* 10.6662 = *ILS* 1455.
35. H.-G. Pflaum, *Les Carrières procuratoriennes équestres sous le Haut-Empire romain* (Paris, 1960): 473–74.

reatio in an untechnical and general sense (as Apuleius also employs the word)[36] to denote simply marriage ceremonies without any allusion to the legal aspects of marriage, and in particular without any allusion to the creation of *manus*. The inscription in question was found at Antium and was set up by the *Antiates public(e)* to honor Aurelius Papirius. This offers a clue. I would suggest that the *sacerdotium confarreationum et diffareationum* was a municipal priesthood to which the Antiates hastened to appoint the distinguished *iurisperitus* after he achieved the signal honor of being invited to join the *consilium principis* at Rome.

In this connection a curious event in the life of Julius Caesar arouses interest. Under the domination of Marius and Cinna, he was selected to become *flamen Dialis*: *destinatus* is the term Suetonius uses,[37] Velleius has *creatus*.[38] Now the selection of the *flamen Dialis* was a complicated process:[39] three candidates were nominated (*nominati*) by the college of pontiffs,[40] and then one of them was *captus* by the *pontifex maximus*.[41] As the third stage an augur performed the *inau-*

36. *Met.* 5.26; 10.29.
37. Suet. *Caes.* 1: *Annum agens sextum decimum patrem amisit* [to enter into the discussion concerning the date of Caesar's birth is beyond the scope of this study]; *sequentibus consulibus flamen Dialis destinatus* [possibly early in 86; M. Leone (see n. 39 below) opts for 84] *dimissa Cossutia, quae familia equestri sed admodum dives praetextato desponsata fuerat, Corneliam Cinnae quater consulis filiam duxit uxorem . . . neque ut repudiaret compelli a dictatore Sulla ullo modo potuit. Quare et sacerdotio et uxoris dote et gentiliciis hereditatibus multatus diversarum partium habebatur.*
38. Vell. 2.41: *paene puer a Mario Cinnaque flamen Dialis creatus victoria Sullae, qui omnia ab iis acta fecerat irrita, amisisset id sacerdotium.*
39. Cf. M. Leone, "Il problema del flaminato di Cesare," in *Studi di storia antica offerti a Eugenio Manni* (Rome, 1973): 193–212, with ample literature cited.
40. Tac. *Ann.* 4.16.2. Cf. Livy 40.42.8–11 (referring to the *rex sacrorum*), where in the phrase *secundo loco inauguratus* we have to read *nominatus*, as proposed by J. Rubino, *Untersuchungen über römische Verfassung und Geschichte* (Kassel, 1839): 243 n. 1, and now generally accepted.
41. Livy 27.8.4–5; Gell. 1.12.15 (who erroneously extends the procedure of *captio* to the augurs and pontiffs). Tac. *Ann.* 4.16.2 uses the term *legere* (cf. Gaius 1.112), and Livy 29.38.6 has *creatus inauguratusque*, where *creatus* clearly takes the place of *captus*. Gaius 1.113 says that *praeterea exeunt liberi virilis sexus de parentis potestate, si flamines Diales inaugurentur et feminini sexus, si virgines Vestales capiantur* (see also Ulp. *Reg.* 10.5; cf. Servius, on *Aen.* 7.303). On this basis some scholars have denied the existence of the procedure of *captio* with respect to the *flamines*, most eloquently P. Catalano, *Contributi allo studio del diritto augurale* I (Turin, 1960): 215–20, and Guizzi, *Vesta* (1968): 30–66. This is unjustified for Gaius is interested in *patria potestas*, and not in *inauguratio* or *captio*. For the Vestals the *captio* was the last stage in the process of their ordination; for the *flamines* the last stage was the *inauguratio*. It was

guratio of the new *flamen*.⁴² Suetonius's *destinatus* probably refers to the stage of *nominatio*,⁴³ whereas Velleius's *creatus* seems to denote the *captio*.⁴⁴ At that time Caesar was engaged to Cossutia, the daughter of a rich *eques*, but he now broke this engagement and married the patrician⁴⁵ Cornelia, daughter of Cinna. The religious explanation (leaving the political one aside) is simple: as the *flaminica* had to be married by *confarreatio* and presumably had also to be born *ex farreatis*, Cossutia was apparently not eligible for this function;⁴⁶ her parents had almost certainly not been married by *confarreatio*. But on the other hand, there is no reason to suppose that a plebeian woman was at that time not capable of concluding confarreate marriage with a patrician; Caesar's mother Aurelia belonged to a plebeian *gens*, yet for Caesar to be eligible for the *flamonium* she had to have

---

only the *inauguratio* that transformed into a *flamen* the person who was *captus* (cf. S. Brassloff, "Die rechtliche Bedeutung der Inauguration beim Flaminat," *Hermes* 48 [1913]: 458–63). Consequently for the Vestals it was *captio* that caused consequences in civil law, for the flamens only *inauguratio*.

42. See Catalano, *Contributi allo studio del diritto augurale* I: 212.

43. This is borne out by Suetonius's usage at *Cal.* 12: *Deinde augur in locum fratris sui Drusi destinatus, priusquam inauguraretur, ad pontificatum traductus est*. The four stages in the ordination of an augur, at least in the practice of the late Republic, were *nominatio* by the members of the college, election (i.e., *creatio*) by the *comitia* of the seventeen tribes, *cooptatio* by the college, and, finally, *inauguratio* (*Rhet. ad Herennium* 1.20; Cic. *Phil.* 2.4; *Brut.* 1.1; *Leg. agr.* 2.18). Under the Empire the *comitia* of the seventeen tribes ceased to function, and as Caligula was certainly the sole candidate, his *nominatio* meant de facto also *cooptatio*. Thus structurally *destinatio* took the place of republican *nominatio*, the essence of which was the establishment of a binding and exclusive list of candidates. This is also the role of *destinatio* in the *Tabula Hebana*; cf. R. Frei-Stolba, *Untersuchungen zu den Wahlen in der römischen Kaiserzeit* (Zurich, 1967): 120–29.

44. According to L. R. Taylor, *CP* 36 (1941): 114–16, Caesar was *nominatus*, but he was not *captus* by the *pontifex maximus*. This is of course quite possible, but in trying to explain Velleius's *creatus*, it is important to note that the *captio* of the *flamines* structurally corresponded to the *creatio* of other priests. This *creatio* was originally achieved through *cooptatio* by the members of the college, but after the *lex Domitia* the priests were *creati* by popular election, the *cooptatio* remaining as a purely formal element.

45. There is no reason to follow Mommsen, *Röm. Forschungen* I (1864): 113–14, in denying patrician status to the Cornelii Cinnae. That Cinna was consul in 86 together with the patrician Valerius Flaccus (cf. Broughton, *Magistrates* II [1951]: 53) finds an easy explanation in the turbulent character of the times, in which many other irregularities occurred.

46. Cf. G. De Sanctis, "La data della nascita di G. Cesare," *RFIC* 62 (1934): 550–51.

been married to Caesar's father by *confarreatio*. Annia, the wife of Cinna⁴⁷ and mother of Cornelia, was also a plebeian.

Yet ultimately Caesar was not *inauguratus*, and it might not appear impossible to argue that Sulla adduced the lack of confarreate marriage between Caesar's parents (and the parents of his wife) as the formal obstacle to Caesar's flaminate. This argument is only seemingly valid. We know from Macrobius⁴⁸ that the *flamen Martialis*, L. Cornelius Lentulus Niger (praetor by 61), was married to a Publicia; Publicii were a plebeian family, and hence it follows that at least the *flamines Martiales* (and, no doubt, *Quirinales*) were not obliged to marry patrician women. This is consistent with the generally less stringent regulations governing these priesthoods⁴⁹ and also conclusively shows the possibility of confarreate marriage between patrician men and plebeian women. Thus only the *flamen Dialis* would be required to marry the *patricia* born *ex farreatis*.

In Caesar's time we would thus have had confarreate marriages between patricians and between patrician men and plebeian women; whether there existed marriages of this kind between plebeian men and patrician women is difficult to say, but appears rather unlikely.⁵⁰ But we can safely conclude that plebeians did not practice *confarreatio* among themselves; this seems to follow from Cicero, *Pro Flacco* 84. Cicero there mentions only two forms of marriage *cum manu*: *usus* and *coemptio*. The parties in question were a freedwoman and an *ingenuus* (of libertine origin), hence technically plebeians. As Cicero is at pains to enumerate every legal possibility, it seems reasonable to assume that in this case the *confarreatio* was not a legal possibility.⁵¹ Whether this conclusion is valid also with respect to the plebeian nobility is another question; but here we enter the realm of surmises, not facts.

If *confarreatio* originally served the goal of delimiting the patrician class, informal marriage without *manus* may have had an altogether

---

47. Vell. 2.41.2.
48. Macr. *Sat.* 3.13.10. This disproves the contention of L. R. Taylor, *CP* 36 (1941): 115 (who missed the text of Macrobius, although later she dealt with it in an erudite article), that Caesar's parents could not have been married *per confarreationem* inasmuch as Caesar's mother was a plebeian.
49. Servius Auctus, on *Aen.* 8.552.
50. Westrup, *Recherches* (1943): 55ff.
51. Cf. A. Watson, *Law of Persons* (see n. 2 above): 23–24.

different purpose. We cannot here go into various theories concerning marriage by *usus*, but important for our subject is the institution of *trinoctium*. If each year the wife stayed away from the marital house for three consecutive nights, the acquisition of *manus* by her husband was interrupted, and as a result she remained under the *potestas* of her father or, if she was *sui iuris*, under the control of her agnatic guardians. The rule of the *trinoctium* is sometimes represented as an innovation introduced by the Twelve Tables, yet in the text of Gaius (1.111) there is nothing to suggest this interpretation. Most probably we are dealing here with the codification of a customary practice, which we may surmise had its roots in religion: the wife would stay away from the *sacra* of her husband and thus reaffirm her membership in her agnatic clan. Kaser remarks very sensibly that as *trinoctium* was a device to interrupt the acquisition of *manus*, it must be substantially later than the concept of *manus* marriage. He confesses, however, that the social circumstances in which a need for the institution of *trinoctium* arose are as enigmatic as ever.[52]

Now marriage without *manus* may have been in the interest of the father of the wife and of her agnates, but the cooperation of the husband was necessary too. Here the studies of the Danish scholar C. W. Westrup offer an attractive idea.[53] He conjectures that the *trinoctium* was primarily a device invented to safeguard the patrician woman from falling by *usus* under the *manus* of her plebeian husband in mixed marriages. The story reported by Livy (10.23) under the year 295 illustrates the tendency of patricians to avoid *manus* when marrying their daughters into plebeian families. Verginia, a patrician married to a plebeian, L. Volumnius, the consul of 296, was prevented by other patrician matrons from sacrificing in the *sacellum* of Pudicitia Patricia because she *e patribus enupsisset*. Now Verginia must have been married without *manus*, for if the *conventio in manum* had taken place, she would have suffered the *capitis diminutio minima*—would have become a member of the new family *in filiae loco* and a full participant in the *sacra* of the Volumnii. In this situation she would hardly have been described as a *patricia*.

To sum up: we have (not counting *coemptio*) two opposite forms of

52. Kaser, *Ius* (1949): 319–20; id., *Privatr.* I² (1971): 79–80; Watson, *XII Tables* (1975): 16–18.
53. Westrup, *Recherches* (1943): 55ff., especially 64–65.

marriage, both of them of political and religious significance: the *confarreatio*, which was surrounded by a religious aura and which a nucleus of patrician families used as an instrument to build up a closed caste; and the informal marriage without *manus*, which served the purpose of cementing alliances of presumably weaker patrician families with rich plebeians. In this perspective the prohibition of intermarriage enacted by the decemvirs reveals itself as an attempt by patrician purists and hardliners to gain undisputed ascendancy not only by fending off the plebeians, but also by weakening those of their patrician rivals who relied for their political survival on marriage alliances with plebeian families.

Reaction was inevitable. Our sources attribute the repeal of the decemviral rule to the *lex Canuleia*, a plebiscite commonly dated to 445. The Canuleian law raises a host of problems. We cannot here go into the tangled question of tribal legislation before the *lex Hortensia* or the legal validity of plebiscites. Suffice it to say that it appears highly unlikely that a plebiscite can at that early period have had the force of law. But the fact itself, the removal of the ban on intermarriages, is indisputable. The date, 445 B.C., may derive (as Ogilvie thinks)[54] from information going back to the *Annales*, yet even this is far from certain.

What attracts one's attention is that the sources, Livy primarily, but also Cicero, speak in one breath of *conubium* and auspices. This reflects a late republican doctrine, of course, but there may be a grain of truth in it. To counter the agitation of Canuleius, Livy reports (4.6.2–3), the patricians argued that the decemvirs had abolished the *conubium* (*conubium diremisse*) in order to prevent the auspices from being thrown into confusion by uncertain offspring (*ne incerta*

---

54. Ogilvie, *Comm.* (1965): 527ff. To propose any specific date would be pure guesswork. One can suspect, however, that the lifting of the ban on intermarriage would have occurred before the first appearance (or at least frequent appearance) of plebeians among consular tribunes, i.e., before the end of the fifth century. Mitchell, chapter V, part 14 above, connects the lifting of the ban with the changes caused by the *lex Ogulnia* of 300, which opened the major priesthoods to plebeians. But we should rather say that before the Ogulnian law all priests had to be born of parents married by the ceremony of *confarreatio*, and hence had to have at least patrician fathers; by admitting the plebeians to the major priesthoods (above all the colleges of pontiffs and augurs) the *lex Ogulnia* abolished this requirement, which remained in force only with respect to the major *flamines* and the "king of sacrifices."

prole auspicia turbarentur; cf. 4.2.5 *conluvio gentium, perturbatio auspiciorum publicorum privatorumque*). This they justified by the fact that no plebeian possessed the auspices (*quod nemo plebeius auspicia haberet*). "The argument is fallacious," says Ogilvie in his commentary,[55] "for in law *origo sequitur patrem*." Yes, of course, in the developed law—but apparently not in the law of the Twelve Tables. In the marriage by *confarreatio*, the status of the bride seems to have been of legal and religious importance, and the decemvirs would simply have extended this rule to other marriages as well. If the *patres* succeeded in establishing the rule that purity of blood was a necessary requirement for the holding of certain priesthoods, it was a natural and logical step to argue that mixed marriages would ultimately lead to total contamination of the auspices used by the magistrates, for in the end there would be nobody of pure patrician blood. The argument is not fallacious—it is only perverse, for it attempts to present a patent innovation as a hallowed rule of great antiquity.

The decemviral attempt to redefine the concept of *conubium* is, in fact, no more striking or unusual than the Augustan laws *de maritandis ordinibus*. Despite a compromise on this front, the patriciate was able not only to survive undiluted but to maintain a dominant position, because it had established itself as a religious entity. The confarreate marriage, a relic of the power struggle in the distant past, remained a patrician preserve down to imperial times.[56]

---

55. Ogilvie, *Comm.* (1965): 532 on 4.2.5. On p. 537 (on 4.12) he corrects his argument and points out that "it is only children born of *iustae nuptiae* . . . that take the status of the father." And the patrician doctrine denied the possibility of *iustae nuptiae* between patricians and plebeians.

56. This reconstruction differs substantially from that proposed by Mitchell (chapter V above). I cannot find any compelling evidence for his identification of priests and *patres* or for his contention that all priests automatically qualified as senators. As far as we know, this may have been the case with respect to the *flamen Dialis*, but from this isolated case no safe inferences can be drawn concerning other priests. In any case Cicero *Ad Att.* 4.2.3–4 (missed or disregarded by Mitchell) shows clearly that not all pontiffs were members of the Senate. On the other hand differences between the reconstruction proposed in this paper and the ideas presented by Raaflaub (chapter VII above) are more apparent than real. As Raaflaub points out (part 6) "the closure of the patriciate" need not be imagined as the wholesale ousting of the vanquished in the political struggle from the ranks of the aristocracy, but rather as the building of fences to keep the upstarts out. The ritual of *confarreatio* was one of those fences.

WALTER EDER

IX

The Political Significance of the Codification of Law in Archaic Societies: An Unconventional Hypothesis

1. *The Problem*

In a book that deals with the Conflict of the Orders in archaic Rome, why should we discuss again the old question of the political significance of the codification of law? Has it not already found an answer? The Twelve Tables, the famous collection of Roman law codified about 450 B.C., have always been regarded as a good example of the political success of a hitherto excluded and oppressed social group. As H. H. Scullard states in the latest edition of his outstanding *His-*

The following text is the largely extended version of a lecture given in the winter of 1981–82 at Brown University, Providence, R.I., at the annual meeting of the American Philological Association in San Francisco, and at the Center for Hellenic Studies in Washington, D.C. I would like to express my gratitude to all discussants for criticism and encouragement. Above all, I have to thank C. Fornara, E. S. Gruen, B. M. W. Knox, J. Linderski, T. Martin, and K. Raaflaub. They should not be blamed for errors left in the text. This article represents only a rough sketch of the topic's

tory of the Roman World, "the plebs had won a great victory."[1] And what is supposed to be true for the Roman *plebs* seems to be equally true for the *demos* of Solonian Athens and, more generally, for the lower classes all over the archaic Greek world. Thus F. Gschnitzer expresses a widely accepted view in stating that the numerous codifications of law that are attested for the archaic period had been wrested from the governing class in more or less bloody unrest.[2] Indeed, modern scholars quite commonly assume that both the reforms and laws of Solon and the Twelve Tables were prompted by strong political pressures; these are usually connected with the beginning of the process in which increasingly broad groups of citizens came to share political responsibility.

It is not the purpose of the present article to support this almost generally accepted interpretation with new arguments. On the contrary, it is my intention to focus on a different aspect of the political role that the codification of customary law undoubtedly played in the archaic period. In my opinion, it must primarily be regarded as a measure to ensure aristocratic predominance; it was an attempt to stabilize the political and economic status quo, which was being seriously threatened by social unrest.

I suggest that the archaic law codes had the following three main purposes. First, they were designed to stop the unpredictable development of customary law and political behavior, which under the increasing pressure of the discontented were about to change to the detriment of those in power. Second, they were supposed to provide appeal to a defined and published body of law. On the one hand, this could help to prevent further unrest that might be caused by an arbitrary use of customary law; on the other hand, it could secure or at least encourage uniform behavior on the part of the members of the

---

main outlines and is part of a larger research project. The notes have therefore been kept as short as possible and are not too numerous. I hope to present a more detailed treatment of archaic codifications of law in Greece and Rome in the near future. I want to say special thanks to my wife Gabriele for her great help in translating the text into English, and also to E. Badian and the editor, who both did much more than just refine the language.

1. Scullard, *History*[4] (1980): 89.
2. Gschnitzer, *Sozialgeschichte* (1981): 75: "die grosse Welle der Rechtskodifikationen [wird] dem herrschenden Stand in der Regel durch mehr oder weniger blutige Unruhen abgerungen."

upper class who still held and would continue to hold the positions of judges and officials in the future. Third, a legal basis for existing property arrangements was thus to be created in order to render ineffective any demand for cancellation of debts or distribution of land. Considering the outstanding importance attributed to landed property in ancient societies, this aspect seems to deserve special attention.

The codification of law thus does not really appear as a concession to the many, but rather as a reaction of the few aiming at preserving their political influence as completely as possible. This was to be achieved by legally securing the economic basis of power and by insisting on homogeneous behavior on the part of the aristocracy, since the inconsiderate behavior of individuals could well endanger the order as a whole. Actually, we learn from the sources that for several generations to come, in Rome as well as in Greece, political power remained with those who had belonged to the governing class before the laws were codified. It seems justifiable, therefore, to doubt the political success allegedly gained by the *plebs*. Moreover, as far as the economic demands of the lower classes are concerned, it is indeed surprising and difficult to understand that neither the Twelve Tables nor the laws of Draco actually fulfilled these. The laws of Solon did so only partly and insufficiently.[3] Nevertheless, once codification was put into effect, such demands, which had been brought up for so many years, were no longer heard. Who after all benefited from those codifications? It seems as if we have to look for new answers.

It must be emphasized here that for the period we are concerned with it is hardly possible to clearly separate economic and political aspects. In archaic societies a person's political influence depended on his economic resources; at the same time, opportunities to increase one's wealth through war booty, jurisdiction, trade with other *poleis*, and so forth, were directly related to a person's social and political status. Economic and political claims are therefore interrelated. Accordingly, our attention must focus equally on the economic aspects of the crises contemporary to, and somehow connected with, the codifications, and on the political implications of the law codes.

3. See n. 37 below, and cf. n. 43.

I am, of course, fully aware that the interpretation offered in this paper cannot be more than a hypothetical reconstruction, since neither the space nor the evidence available allow us to draw definite and completely satisfactory conclusions. Moreover, to emphasize this hypothesis involves the risk of being suspected of a one-sided argument. It is therefore especially important to explain clearly the individual methodological steps taken in the following discussion.

First, as always when investigating archaic times that are poor in written evidence, we have to establish carefully what sources exist, what problems are connected with them, and what methods are available to extract a maximum of reliable information from them. Second, we have to define the term "codification" and establish how it is associated with its contemporary political background—that is, the relationship between codification and political crisis. In the next part, we shall be concerned with the role played by the aristocracy before, during, and after the process of codification, and we shall consider the different political and social conditions in Athens and Rome. In the fourth part, we shall investigate both how codification affected the certainty of law, and how law and political power influenced each other. In these four parts, we shall mostly deal with problems of codification as a whole; we shall look at it primarily under the general aspect of its significance to the historical development of archaic societies. In the final part, however, we shall take a closer look at some important individual regulations in order to check their compatibility with our hypothesis. In accordance with the concerns of the present volume, methodological questions and theoretical reflections will be emphasized. Obviously, this essay cannot replace a detailed and comprehensive examination and interpretation of the sources, but it can illustrate the fact that, by asking different questions, we may find different answers without necessarily pressing and violating the sources.

2. *Sources and Methods*

The evidence for the codification of law in archaic times is scarce, widely scattered, and of extremely uneven value. A written law code has been preserved neither from the time of Solon nor from that of the Twelve Tables. The only well-preserved example was found in the town of Gortyn on Crete. Unfortunately, however, the fragmentary tradition about the history of Crete does not enable us reliably to determine the date of origin of these early laws, whose extant version dates to the fifth century B.C., nor does it allow us to distinguish the original parts from later additions with any certainty.[4]

Some other codifications are only known to us through the name of the lawgiver. Although we may also know the place where he acted, and in some rare cases even something about the contents of his laws, all this remains vague and unreliable in many respects. For ancient authors tended to cast their accounts of archaic Greek lawgivers in a somewhat legendary pattern that usually includes three stages: (a) the community has plunged into a deep crisis (*anomia*); (b) an arbitrator is elected in order to end the crisis by means of a codification of law; (c) the general situation is stabilized by the high quality of those laws (*eunomia*).[5] The genesis of the Twelve Tables has been described in terms of the same threefold pattern, although in Rome we find a group of ten lawgivers, the *decemviri*, whereas the Greeks preferred a single arbitrator, the *aisymnetes*.

This more or less schematic view of the transition from *anomia* to *eunomia* must deeply have influenced the presentation and interpretation of facts in our sources. Differences in the preconditions and consequences of the various codifications of law may have been levelled, and unjustified comparisons may accordingly have been drawn among them. Thus the historical value of the literary sources is considerably diminished. And there are additional causes of error that increase the general uncertainty. For example, the earliest literary reports on archaic lawgiving were written more than 200 years after the act of codification. Furthermore, both the laws of Solon and the Twelve Tables were used by later generations as actual political arguments in their struggles over the constitution. In accordance with the more refined political understanding of the times that produced our sources, the old law codes were lifted to the rank of constitutions, and the lawgivers were declared authorities that could be referred to in order to find support in contemporary political quar-

---

4. See R. F. Willetts, *Law Code* (1967); id., *Aristocratic Society in Ancient Crete* (London, 1955): 3f., 105f., 152f.; M. Lemosse, *RIDA*, 3rd ser., 4 (1957): 131–37.
5. For the sources and the problem of evaluation, see F. E. Adcock, *Cambr. Hist. Journ.* 2 (1927): 95ff.; A. Szegedy-Maszak, *GRBS* 19 (1978): 199ff.

rels.⁶ The contents of the old laws could easily be falsified by adding new paragraphs, and if one attempted to buttress one's own political intentions by quoting a suitable statement by a famous forerunner, there existed few restraints—unless it was possible to check such an assertion against the documentary evidence available to contemporaries.⁷ Historians and classical philologists widely disagree about the chances of such a correction, however, for in Athens as well as in Rome a major disaster occurred between the time of the codification and its first appearance in literary sources: the destruction of Athens by the Persians and the sack of Rome by the Gauls may well have caused the destruction of all the monuments and documents connected with codification. With the disappearance of all the written records, one might presume, there was nothing to limit the imagination of later authors and commentators.⁸

For most of the tradition this may be true, but it cannot be postulated to the same extent for the field of law. For laws and their application are not so closely tied to written texts. Doubtless, laws had existed even before the invention of the alphabet. The facts that the regulations of the Spartan *rhetra* were not fixed in writing and that Roman pupils were obliged to memorize the text of the Twelve Tables both indicate clearly that there existed a very strong oral tradition.⁹

---

6. On later changes in the tradition about Solon, see, for example, E. Ruschenbusch, *Historia* 7 (1958) 398ff.; S. S. Markianos, *Hellenica* 32 (1980): 255ff. For political influence on the rewriting of early Roman history, see E. Gabba, *Athenaeum*, n. s., 39 (1961): 98ff.; K. M. Girardet, "Entstehung des Tribunats" (1977): 179ff.; L. Perelli, *Quad. di storia* 5, no. 10 (1979): 285ff.; see also chapter III above.

7. But apparently nobody was interested in doing so. The skepticism concerning the life and writings of Solon (cf. M. R. Lefkowitz, *The Lives of the Greek Poets* [Baltimore, 1981]: 40–49) seems to be justified in view of the unreliable traditions about events even of the fifth century. Thus, according to K. Meister, *Die Ungeschichtlichkeit des Kalliasfriedens und deren historische Folgen*, Palingenesia 18 (Wiesbaden, 1982), the peace of Kallias (allegedly of 449) was faked in the fourth century by Isocrates, and inter alia, the authenticity of the "Themistocles Decree" and the "Oath of Plataea" have been convincingly contested as well: cf. C. Habicht, *Hermes* 89 (1961): 1ff.

8. For early Roman history see the extremely skeptical view of J. Bleicken, *Lex* (1975): 75 n. 4. Cornell, chapter II above; Tondo, *Profilo* (1981), especially 3ff.; and others show more confidence in the sources.

9. Plut. *Lyc.* 13.1; Cic. *De leg.* 2.4.9. On the so-called "unwritten laws," see G. Cerri, *Legislazione orale e tragedia greca: Studi sull'Antigone di Sofocle e sulle Supplici di Euripide*, Forma, materiali e ideologia del mondo antico 13 (Naples, 1979). Unfortunately, the English vocabulary does not provide different words for *lex* and *ius*,

This was a characteristic that epic poetry and law had in common. It may have contributed to the fact that law, like the contents of the *epos*, developed and changed more slowly than the economic and social conditions of a given society. Moreover, the normative character of law has a stabilizing and even retarding effect. That is why legal texts were less endangered by accidental destruction or unscrupulous falsification than, for instance, the historical texts of the annalistic tradition. This again is a feature common to law and religion, which are hardly separable in their early stages. Accordingly, the reconstruction of the history of law, as of the history of religion, is facilitated by a remarkable constancy of religious cults and customs, which sometimes last for centuries. As a matter of fact, therefore, the historian of law seems to be in a relatively good position, especially in regard to the dark centuries of archaic Greece and Rome.

Yet in trying to separate authentic regulations from later additions and to arrange and interpret the often mysterious fragments of early laws, the historian cannot afford to neglect the results obtained by other disciplines, such as philology, etymology, anthropology, linguistics, and especially archaeology. Although D. M. Lewis is right in thinking that "one cannot write political history from pots"[10] and that the value of archaeological finds is sometimes exaggerated, it is, on the other hand, hardly possible now to write political, economic, and social history without those pots and stones. This is especially true in view of the significant changes in approach and methodology that are occurring in some fields of archaeology. Most of all, there seems to be an increasing interest in the material culture of antiquity, and geography and topography are being rediscovered as useful targets of investigation.[11] Following up such investigations, this might be a fruitful moment for historians and philologists to engage more deeply in the study of the ancient geographers—above all, Pliny, Strabo, and Pausanias.

---

nomos and *dike*. Terminology, therefore, cannot be as distinct as it is in most languages (*loi/droit*, *legge/diritto*, *Gesetz/Recht*, etc.), for "law" has to be used to describe both "the unwritten code of commonly accepted social behavior" and "the single legal regulation."

10. D. M. Lewis, in *Classical Contributions: Studies in Honour of M. F. McGregor*, edited by G. S. Shrimpton and D. J. McCargar (Locust Valley, N.Y., 1981): 73 n. 9.

11. See, e.g., S. C. Humphreys, *Anthropology* (1978): 109ff., and some of her other essays in the same volume. See, too, D. Clarke, "Archaeology: The Loss of

It does not therefore seem to be too difficult to collect a considerable amount of material, scattered as it may be. Rather, the real problem is how to cope with such a collection of fragmentary sources and how to find methodological tools enabling us to draw a convincing and sensible picture. For it is very doubtful indeed that by merely accumulating and combining a summary of sometimes highly hypothetical "facts," we can produce a reliable picture of those fascinating but dark ages of ancient history.

For this task of arranging, evaluating, and interpreting our material, the "comparative approach"[12] may be helpful—if, that is, we understand "comparative" in a very broad sense. We have to juxtapose and compare individual laws as well as the social structures and political systems of different and perhaps even distant communities. However, the historian of law especially cannot help but emphasize the danger inherent in this approach.[13] For the temptation to explain Greek and Roman history through examples and alleged parallels from distant India or Ireland may be particularly strong when either the appropriate evidence or a sound methodology or even both are missing. Obviously, the comparative approach should only be applied and can only produce useful results when it can be based on solid foundations. Further, it is vital to realize that "to compare" also means to bring out the differences, and above all that "explorations in foreign climes may often tell us what to look for, but never what to find."[14] On the basis of these general reflections, we can now formulate some methodological principles for dealing with the sources.

First, sources should be evaluated according to the "principle of

---

Innocence," *Antiquity* 47 (1973): 6–18. On "social ecology" and the project "Ancient Greek Cities," see S. C. Bakhuizen, *AC* 44 (1975): 211–18. For a summary of the most recent work in Italy, see Cornell, *Archaeol. Reports* (1979–80): 71–88, and chapter II above. One has to add: *Enea nel Lazio: Archeologia e mito* (1981), the catalogue of an exhibition in Rome, 1981–82. On new questions of methods of archaeology, see now the periodical *Hephaistos*, whose first issue appeared in 1979.

12. See chapter I part 3 above.

13. The different points of view are properly collected by E. Ferenczy, *Klio* 61 (1979): 25–31; also very useful are the remarks in the same issue of P. Blaho, 44–47, and T. Giaro, 97–100. The viewpoint of an ancient historian is formulated by H. Galsterer, *Critica storica* 17 (1980): 185ff.

14. F. W. Maitland, *Township and Borough* (Cambridge, 1898): 24 (quoted by A. Watson, *XII Tables* [1975]: 7 n. 14).

concentric circles." That means on the one hand that we ought to seek an explanation for a given historical phenomenon primarily in the very area where it actually occurred. For example, we should not consider Greek influence on the Twelve Tables or on the development of Roman magistracies a primary factor as long as we can find satisfactory answers to our questions in Rome itself or in its immediate neighborhood. On the other hand, the farther removed a source is from the object of investigation, the less useful it will be for purposes of comparative research. The "principle of concentric circles" implies, therefore, that the chances of detecting mutual contacts and influences are especially good in those areas where the imaginary circles of influence, centered in the areas under comparison, touch or overlap each other. Accordingly, in trying to assess the influence of Greek or even Athenian laws on Rome, we should focus our attention on the cities of Magna Graecia.[15]

Second, comparative studies always have to take into consideration a certain "*mimesis* effect." In the present case, one might be tempted to presuppose comparable political structures in Athens at the time of Solon and Rome at the time of the Twelve Tables simply because codification of law took place in both cities. Such a conclusion would be justified only within narrow limits, however, if at all. For we have to keep in mind that (for example) existing patterns of political behavior can be transferred by means of imitation (*mimesis*) from one society to others that have not yet reached the same stage of social, economic, and political development.[16] Comparable events and phenomena may, but need not necessarily, be traced back to comparable underlying social structures. In each case of such a *mimesis* phenomenon, it is therefore highly important to find out why it appears at that specific moment of history in those specific societies.[17]

---

15. From archaic times on, there were strong connections between Greece and Magna Graecia on the one side and Magna Graecia and Rome on the other. See the contributions in *La Magna Grecia e Roma nell'età arcaica: Atti del VIII convegno di studi sulla Magna Grecia* (Naples, 1969), and in *Locri Epizefirii: Atti del XVI convegno di studi sulla Magna Grecia* (Naples, 1977). It may be just a coincidence that we find the Dioscuri fighting for Locri as well as for Rome (see J. Heurgon in *La Magna Grecia e Roma*, 22, and M. Gigante in *Locri Epizefirii*, 632). See, furthermore, C. Ampolo, *PP* 29 (1974): 382–88 (Rome and Sicily); E. Bayer, *ANRW* I.1 (1972): 323f.

16. This point is stressed in regard to tyranny by M. Pallottino, "Magna Grecia" (1969): 46 ("diffusione mimetica del fenomeno della tirannia"), and has been emphasized in regard to codification of law by E. Badian in private communication.

17. See chapter I above at nn. 108ff.

Third, in comparing or combining different kinds of evidence (for example, archaeological and philological sources) one has to observe the "principle of partial confirmation." According to this principle, if a statement in a literary source is confirmed by evidence from a related field of research (such as archaeology), we are only entitled to assume that other statements of the literary source may also be correct if the given items are comparable. For example, archaeological evidence suggests the existence in the sixth century B.C. of two Roman temples that can plausibly be connected with the temples of Mater Matuta and Fortuna, which, according to our literary sources, were built by Servius Tullius.[18] The same literary sources mention a third temple, built by the same king and dedicated to Diana. Inasmuch as such a temple would constitute a "comparable item," it is probable that it indeed existed, even though archaeological proof is missing so far. Accepting such circumstantial evidence, we may cautiously draw one further conclusion—namely, that a Roman king, perhaps named Servius Tullius, tried to establish some closer connection with the Latins by favoring their federal goddess, Diana.[19] To say more would be pure speculation; the agreement of literary and archaeological evidence cannot be stretched too far; the fact that the erection of temples is confirmed by such an agreement does not justify any further conclusions concerning the credibility of Livy's and Dionysius's reports on the reign of Servius Tullius.

It is the purpose of such methodological reflections to make us aware of possible dangers inherent in the comparative approach; they should help to avoid misinterpretation and abuse of the sources. In the present case, another potential source of error lies in the very hypothesis that forms the starting point of our investigation— namely, that the early codifications of law were effected above all in

---

18. Dion. Hal. 4.27.7; Liv. 10.46.14; Ovid, *Fasti* 6.569ff.; 773ff. (on the temple of Fortuna). Liv. 5.19.6; Ovid *Fasti* 6.475ff. (on the sanctuary of Mater Matuta). On the archaeological evidence, see T. Hölscher, *RM* 85 (1978): 320ff.; M. Pallottino, *CRAI* (1977): 216ff.; Cornell, *Arch. Reports* (1979–80): 84f., and chapter II above at n. 42. For a detailed discussion of the literary and archaeological evidence, see Thomsen, *Serv. Tullius* (1980): 260–78.

19. Dion. Hal. 4.26.4; Liv. 1.45; Strabo 4.1.5. On the goddess Diana in archaic Rome and the political intentions of Servius Tullius, see R. Bloch, "Religion romaine" (1980): 355ff.; Thomsen, *Serv. Tullius* (1980): 291–314 (emphasizing relations with the Latins); J. Cels Saint-Hilaire and C. Feuvrier-Prévotat, *Dial. d'hist. anc.* 5 (1979): 116–18 (on the sanctuary as a means of internal integration in Rome itself).

order to strengthen the position of the ruling aristocracies. It is a legitimate and often useful approach to start the search for historical truth with a hypothesis, although in doing that one is easily blamed for operating with preconceived ideas and neglecting the objective and profound analysis of all the available sources. Especially in the field of social and economic history, a well-known ideological battlefield, such suspicions can hardly be avoided. But they can be shown to be unjustified if the hypothesis is, in fact, derived from the analysis of those very sources that form the basis of our investigation.

Our hypothesis is developed directly from the following observation. Both in Athens and in Rome our sources indicate a striking contradiction between the alleged demands of the lower classes and the final gains granted them by codification. Since the supposed goals do not seem to be causally related to the final results, there thus appears to be a "logical break" in the historical development that upsets the "normal" experience of the historian. In other words, the historical process as it is presented by our sources and usually understood by modern historians is not compatible with reflections based on common sense.[20] Although nobody will consider common sense a stronger argument than any conclusion based on a careful interpretation of the sources, such a striking violation of expectations based on historical common sense should force us to rethink the problem and even to look for unconventional explanations.

It is the main purpose of this paper to stimulate discussion. Therefore the Twelve Tables and the laws of Solon will primarily serve as examples that allow us briefly to sketch the main questions, to propose some answers, and to demonstrate why such a new interpretation of old problems is both necessary and useful.

3. Codification and Crisis

Livy describes the Twelve Tables as "the source of all public and private law" (*fons omnis publici privatique iuris*: 3.34.6). That is rather exaggerated, as ancient codification never claimed to be the only

20. "There can be hardly any doubt that this 'appeal to common sense' will always play an important part in historical criticism and that even the best authorities must sometimes be rejected if what they say is plainly contrary to the common

source of law. In fact, in striking distinction to modern law codes, the ancient codes do not represent a legal system providing rules and measures for handling any conceivable or predictable event in society and law. The *horror vacui* seems to have been unknown to ancient lawgivers. It is hardly possible, therefore, to find any attempt in the codes to classify laws according to their subject matter: civil law, criminal law, and regulations concerning legal procedures are mixed with religious laws and rules that regulate the moral life of citizens.[21]

Further, and again in contrast to modern law, in antiquity law and religion were closely connected.[22] As a consequence, written codes as well as orally fixed regulations were mainly based on traditional and customary law, because religious conservatism would prevent innovations. We might plausibly assume, therefore, that the main task of ancient lawgivers, especially in archaic times, consisted of collecting the existing rules and laws. So the codification of law offered little room for the inclusion of new regulations and was hardly a suitable vehicle for fulfilling new demands.

There are, however, slight indications that early codification was more than a mere recording of customary law. New conditions, both political and social, required new provisions. But what does "new" mean? Most of the few regulations that appear to be new in the law codes can be explained either as a reaction to an urgent contemporary problem[23] or as the record of changing social behavior, which was not yet common to the community as a whole, but nevertheless existed and cannot be considered an invention of the lawgiver.[24]

---

sense." Thus K. von Fritz, *Schriften* (1976): 117, but he did not forget to add: "Yet unlimited and uncritical application of the principle may lead and often has led to serious errors."

21. On the incompleteness of ancient codifications as opposed to modern ones, see V. Korosec, "Le problème de la codification dans le domaine du droit hittite," *RIDA* 4 (1957): 93ff. Considering the close connection between codification and crisis, one may ask whether in most cases the codification was not realized too fast and hastily; thus F. Pringsheim, ibid., 310.

22. Cf. chapters V (Mitchell), passim, and VIII (Linderski) above. On the role of the *auctoritas patrum* and the *ius auspicii* as an "Ausdruck sakraler Macht" of the patricians in the Struggle of the Orders, see Bleicken, *Lex* (1975): 296–304.

23. As the *seisachtheia* in Athens, for instance, and possibly the prohibition of the export of grain by Solon (see below at n. 74).

24. See below on the *usus auctoritas* sentence (at nn. 83f.), on the intermarriage between patricians and plebeians (at nn. 48, 80), and on the sumptuary laws in Rome (n. 79).

From this point of view, discussion of whether we are dealing with "codification" or "creation" of law hardly seems useful. Codification of law is at the same time creation of law because customary and new regulations are inseparably intertwined in it: in its written form, customary law acquires a new quality, and new regulations have to fit into the existing social "climate" in order to be accepted. Ancient peoples never created laws to keep them in stock and wait until they might be needed. Each law, every regulation of practice, was intimately connected with the actual conditions and problems of the time of its origin. Accordingly, the difference between the *rogatio* of a special and single law and the collection of a law code should be seen not so much in the number and volume of regulations involved, but rather in the amount of unrest and disturbance in a given society, which then provoked the formalization of rules. As a general assumption we may say, the more disturbances, the more laws.[25]

It cannot be mere accident, therefore, that in all the cases where we know enough about contemporary conditions, codification as the most comprehensive act of legislation coincided with serious social unrest that threatened the very existence of the whole community. Thus the laws of Draco have been connected quite convincingly with the murderous consequences of the Cylonian affair.[26] Solon draws an impressive picture of the dangerous situation in Attica, which he tried to calm by restoring *eunomia*.[27] *Eunomia* was likewise effected in Sparta by the *rhetra* of Lycurgus, bringing to an end a period of turmoil and unrest.[28] Similarly, Rome at the time of the Twelve Tables was greatly shaken by the Conflict of the Orders.

Codification thus appears as a remedy introduced to secure peace and cure a deep political crisis.[29] Presumably, the positive political

---

25. As pointed out by Bleicken, *Lex* (1975): 387ff., the increasing mass of laws in the late Roman Republic is closely connected with the political crisis ("die Jurifizierung von *mos*"). Cf. the complaints by Isocrates and Plato about lawgiving in fourth-century Athens.

26. M. Gagarin, *Drakon* (1981): 21, 104.

'27. Solon fr. 4W = 3D. 30–39 (= Dem. 19.255).

28. Cf. Herodot. 1.65f.; Thuc. 1.18.1; Plut. *Lyc.* 2.6f.; on Sparta, see now K. Bringmann, *Gymnasium* 87 (1980): 467ff.

29. In the sixth century the political situation seems to have been unstable even in Crete. At least the people of Dreros had to put a law into force forbidding a second tenure of the highest office (*kosmos*) before an interval of ten years had passed (see R. Meiggs and D. Lewis, *Gr. Hist. Inscr.* [1969], no. 2; Fornara, *Archaic Times*²

IX. Significance of the Codification of Law   275

effects of codification were understood early. Accordingly, the leading groups may not have waited until demands for codification were actually voiced by the politically disadvantaged, but rather have initiated codification precisely when they realized that the political *status quo* was threatened. Codification thus tended to become an object of *mimesis*. Whether or not such *mimesis* actually occurred in Greece, in the case of the Twelve Tables we have strong indications that it did. For the idea of shaping law into a codified form is genuinely Greek, not Roman. We know of a considerable number of codifications in the Greek world, but in non-Greek Italy, Rome provides the only example. Moreover, although there was no lack of severe crises in Roman history, the next comprehensive codification of law occurred about a thousand years later, characteristically enough not in Rome but in Constantinople, executed by Greek and Syrian jurists.[30] Since codification of law does not, therefore, seem to have been considered an appropriate tool in Roman legal thinking, the question of why the law of the Twelve Tables occurred precisely at that moment in Roman history is even more important.

If it was indeed caused by *mimesis*, or Greek influence, we should not think of it as a simple transfer of Solonian law to Rome, an adaptation of a law code from Magna Graecia, or the result of the personal assistance of a Greek named Hermodorus in the act of codification.[31] Rather, we should emphasize a different point: this procedure, although alien to Roman thinking, may have been adopted precisely

---

[1983], no. 11). Dreros obviously was facing a problem quite familiar to archaic cities: uninterrupted holding of power by magistrates often ended in tyranny. The law code of Gortyn, which in its original form dates to the sixth century as well, may have been provoked by similar quarrels.

30. The explanation for such stability of Roman law may be found in the methods used to further develop the law. Whereas in Athens all legislation was enacted by the assembly, in Rome law was primarily adapted to changing conditions by the praetors. In their annual edict they announced their principles of jurisdiction; since those were usually accepted by the succeeding magistrates as a basis for their own conduct of office, the praetorian edict came to embody continuity of law and procedure. Only in the late Republic, when legislation by the popular assembly increased in volume, did the idea of a comprehensive collection and revision of the mass of existing laws occur, but neither Sulla nor Caesar and Augustus, who thought of it, realized such a project.

31. For these problems, see F. Wieacker, "Solon und die XII Tafeln" (1971): 757ff.; P. Siewert, *Chiron* 8 (1978): 331ff.; M. Ducos, *Influence* (1978); and chapter X below at nn. 2ff.

because it could promote social peace, or was at least considered a stabilizing factor.[32]

Moreover, whatever we think of the possibility of *"mimesis,"* if there really was a close connection between codification and crisis, the analysis of the crisis itself should provide important clues for our understanding of the codification in question. Its purpose might become clearer if we could answer the following questions: (1) Who demanded codification and who actually accomplished it? (2) What had been the real menace to the "system" and what precisely would have been preserved or improved by codification?

The answer to the first question is quite astonishing. In Athens we cannot trace any explicit demand for codification, either in Draco's or in Solon's time.[33] In Rome, however, such a demand is attested in the sources, but it appears rather late and is pursued inconsistently.[34] Thus there is reason to suspect that we are confronted here with a later invention—just as in the case of the second Decemvirate.[35] Yet, although a convincing demand for codification is not traceable, the laws were codified. This was done by members of the upper classes, probably the *eupatridae* in Athens and certainly the *patricii* in Rome. We need not wonder about that—who else should have done the job? But we should keep this fact in mind when asking for the reasons that brought about codification as a measure to cope with political crisis.

In order to find an answer to the second question, we have to look at the character of the crisis and the situation of the communities

---

32. Momigliano's suggestion (*Contr. IV* [1969]: 451f.) that the plebeians were looking south to the Greeks, and the patricians north to the Etruscans, seems too simple. At least in the case of the Twelve Tables, the patricians were inspired by the Greeks in the south as well.

33. A comprehensive evaluation of the sources is presented by W. Donlan, *Historia* 22 (1973): 145ff. We do not hear of any explicit demand for codification or even for political participation. What the *demos* wanted was that its betters should govern more responsibly. The arbitrariness of the aristocratic judges was perceived as oppressive; therefore it had to be restricted. However, there is a long way from such appeals to the judges as they are voiced by Hesiod and Solon to the idea of defining binding norms of behavior in written form.

34. Dion. Hal. 10.1, 15, 17, 35, 41, 50–52; Livy 3.9.5; 10.5; 25.4; 31.7; 32.6f. The codification as an alleged result of intermittent and scattered efforts of the *tribuni plebis* can hardly be linked with the original demand eleven years earlier (462 B.C.), *ut quinque viri creentur legibus de imperio consulari scribendis* (Livy 3.9.5).

35. See chapter III above.

involved. Conditions may have differed between the various Greek *poleis* and Rome, but in each case the sources speak of a striking deterioration in the economic situation of large parts of the population. Impoverishment and debt-bondage were the main consequences and, one may suppose, also the primary reason for measures to relieve the situation. The astonishing fact, however, is that the codifications were not very effective in tackling or curing those problems. They were not taken care of at all by Draco and the Twelve Tables,[36] and only partially and superficially by Solon; in neither case were the real causes of the economic emergency abolished.[37]

This brings us back to the question of what kind of threat the system had to cope with. At first glance, neither the economic or social status nor the political leadership of the leading groups were directly threatened by the fact that the lower classes were suffering from economic hardship. Indirectly, however, the discontent of so many people, who were impoverished and often treated unjustly, was a menace that was not to be underestimated. A member of the aristocracy, or even an outsider, might assemble a following among the discontented and exploit it for his personal ends. This might either lead to tyranny, which more than once threatened and finally occurred in Athens, or cause the ruling aristocracy serious difficulties in other ways, as was the case with the "negative power" of the tribunes of the *plebs* in Rome.[38] Even if he could not take over the gov-

---

36. In Rome the codification had no economic effects for the poor: the land was not distributed, the debts were not cancelled, and debt-slavery was now even fixed by law (Twelve Tables, III.1–6; see below at n. 61). The *plebs* did not obtain access to the high magistracies or priesthoods. In Athens land was not distributed either, but the debts were cancelled. Yet the causes of the growing distress were not eliminated or even mentioned. Interest rates presumably were not fixed. Political and religious functions were kept in the hands of the *eupatridae* and the rich. See also below at nn. 39ff. The Twelve Tables are still quoted here according to *FIRA* I: 23ff., which follows Schoell. For a new reconstruction, see M. Lauria, *Ius Romanum* I.1 (Naples, 1963), and the review by F. Wieacker, *Jura* 16 (1965): 269–83.

37. This is not to deny that both the *seisachtheia* and the abolition of debt-slavery brought great relief to many Athenians. But this may not have been the primary goal of the aristocracy in making such concessions to the *demos*. In the present context, I am mostly interested in the primary concerns of, and advantages for, the aristocracy; see also below at nn. 74f.

38. See chapter IV above at nn. 38 and 87; on the negative definition of the *plebs* and the power their tribunes directed against the consuls (*adversus consules*, Livy 2.33.1), see below at n. 77.

ernment himself, such a person might nonetheless severely disturb the aristocracy's control of political power. Thus in both cases it was primarily the monopoly of political power still held by the governing aristocracy as a whole that was really in danger and had to be maintained, because loss of power could also lead to heavy loss of property.

Power and property could only be defended if the aristocracy acted as a homogeneous group. Thus it had to be the prime goal to develop a sense of unity by promoting a consistent code of conduct and by strengthening political consensus within the group. All the members of the group should be offered equal or at least similar political opportunities. Ideally, the aristocracy should form a monolithic bloc. Such solidarity was needed to prevent any single member from reaching a position of political superiority that might endanger the cohesion and influence of the group, as well as to strengthen resistance to political and economic demands raised from outside the governing group. The former goal was most urgent in Athens, the latter in Rome. Consequently, we should expect that each measure introduced in such a situation would primarily aim at securing the endangered consensus within the aristocracy.

Aristocracy, crisis, and legislation were, therefore, closely related to one another. For the political crisis of those times was above all a crisis of aristocratic government, and the codification of law was undertaken to resolve the crisis. In order further to support this conclusion, two other aspects need to be examined: first, the role, outlook, and self-understanding of the aristocracy in general at the time of the codification; second, the possibility that the aristocracy had a strong interest in stopping the evolution of customary law and, at the same time, in binding its own members by creating a code of written law.

4. *Codification and Aristocracy*

The first question is to what extent the aristocracy actually was in control at the time of the codification. The evidence of our sources is clear: in Athens political power, although endangered by the *hybris* of the mighty,[39] was firmly held by the aristocracy. In Rome, if we can

---

39. Cf. Solon, fr. 13W = 1D. 11,16; 4W = 3D. 8,34; 36W = 24D. 14.

believe Cicero, the power of the patrician Senate was at its height at the time of the Twelve Tables.[40] Moreover, even if we are willing to consider unrest and pressure from below a threat to those in power, the consequences of the codification in both cities force us to doubt the seriousness of such a threat. For, although the lower classes achieved only relatively small gains, the dangerous tensions seem to have been alleviated for a long time. Not until about eighty years later did the struggle break out again in Rome. In Athens, too, the *demos* remained quiet for about the same period; accordingly, the aristocratic groups again indulged in their traditional political fights. As usual, their rivalries took no notice of the needs of the *demos*. Even later, after the reforms of Cleisthenes, who allegedly took the *demos* into his *hetaireia*, the aristocracy continued to determine political issues for another fifty years.[41] In Rome we find the same pattern: the patricians exclusively continued to hold the highest magistracies and priesthoods;[42] thus jurisdiction and the development of law remained in their hands. In both places "the men with good fathers" (*eupatridae* and *patricii*) and the "well born" (*eugeneis*) stayed among themselves.

These political developments indicate at least that the political influence of the aristocracy had soon been reestablished after the codification, if it needed to be reestablished at all. For neither the political power of the aristocracy nor the economic substance on which it rested had been seriously affected by codification; there is no indication that allows us to assume any form of wider political participation by the *demos* or the *plebs*.[43] Nevertheless the people and their leaders kept quiet.

40. Cic. *De re pub.* 2.36.61.
41. Herod. 5.66.2; Arist. *Ath. Pol.* 20ff., 25. On the continuity of aristocratic power after Cleisthenes' reforms, see J. Martin, *Chiron* 4 (1974): 5ff.
42. See Livy 6.35–42, and the brilliant discussion by K. von Fritz, *Historia* 1 (1950): 3ff. On the *lex Ogulnia*, see Livy 10.6–9.
43. In Solon's work we do not find any hint of the alleged Council of 400 (Arist. *Ath. Pol.* 8.4; Plut. *Sol.* 19.1) or of other constitutional measures in favor of the lower classes. The common picture of Solon as a political reformer is based on Solon fr. 5W = 5D. 1–4 (*geras* is left to the *demos*); a law of Chios (Meiggs and Lewis, *Gr. Hist. Inscr.* [1969], no. 8; Fornara, *Archaic Times*[2] [1983], no. 19), where a *boule demosie* is mentioned; and the archaeological evidence of the Athenian Agora (see H. Thompson, *Hesperia* 6 [1937]: 117ff.; *Hesperia* suppl. 4 [1940]: 8ff.; and id., in *The Athenian Agora* XIV [1972]: 25–29). However, *geras* did not necessarily have a political meaning in the sense of "influence"; it was comparable to *time* and therefore fitted well into the aristocratic meaning of *eunomia*, which was not linked to any

In view of the differences between Athens and Rome, it might be objected that comparison, and, based on it, a general statement about the lawgivers' intentions, is questionable. Three differences especially must be considered in the context of our topic: (1) the setting of the codification within the historical process; (2) the political role of the aristocracy in Athens and Rome at the time of the codification and its aftermath; (3) the specific character and place of the struggle that led to the codification within the crisis as a whole. A few remarks are necessary on each of these points.

First, the Twelve Tables were not only codified much later than the laws of Solon but also held a completely different position in the intellectual and legal development of the community. The laws of Solon stand in a formal, though short, tradition of codification that began with the written laws of Draco. Moreover, they can be seen as a stage in the seminal process of systematizing and secularizing the human environment that included the construction of the Olympic pantheon by Hesiod, regulation of social life on earth by the lawgivers, and speculation as to the origins and nature of the cosmos by the early Ionian philosophers. The Twelve Tables in Rome, by contrast, appear as an unprecedented and unique attempt to secularize law and environment.

Despite these discrepancies in intellectual tradition and absolute chronology, however, the relative chronology of events shows certain

---

form of constitution. The *boule demosie* of Chios may have been a council of the people or the council of a topographically determined *demos*, comparable to the Cleisthenic *demoi*. In Athens the archaeologists have uncovered two buildings of the second half of the sixth century (C = "primitive Bouleuterion"; F = "Prytanikon") that are situated exactly in the area of the Tholos and the old Bouleuterion of the fifth century. But some cautionary remarks are necessary: first, building C is far from providing room for 400 people (15 × 6.70 m); second, the connection of the early Athenian *boule* with a prytany system is questionable (cf. P. J. Rhodes, *The Athenian Boule* [Oxford, 1972]: 18, who however accepts the Solonian Council of the 400). The fact that buildings C and F are connected by a wall means nothing, therefore, not even if C is interpreted as an annex to the courtyard next to C, where the *boule* might have held its meetings. Third, the new find of a stele representing Aglauros (allegedly in situ) on the eastern slope of the Acropolis (S. J. Dontas, "The True Aglaurion," *Hesperia* 52 [1983]: 48–63) could give reason to rethink the question of the location of the early Agora. According to Pausanias 1.18.2–3 (cf. Herod. 8.53), the Prytaneion was near the cave of Aglauros (which is usually presumed to have been near the western corner of the Acropolis). On the political role of the Roman *comitiatus maximus* quoted in the Twelve Tables (IX.1–2), see below at n. 88.

common elements. For all the initiatives toward codification of law in archaic times are to be found at an early stage of a period of "class struggle" or "conflict of the orders." They seem to be the first comprehensive response of a ruling aristocracy challenged by a deep economic crisis tending to turn into a political crisis.

As for the second point, in regard to the place of codification within the constitutional development, comparability seems more doubtful. Whereas in Athens the laws of Solon were produced by an aristocratic society that long since had abolished kingship, in Rome the patricians had only recently freed themselves from royal supremacy. The two aristocracies were thus not facing identical problems.

During its long, independent, and unquestioned rule, the aristocracy in Athens had lost much of its cohesion. In Theognis, Alcaeus, Solon, and others we find much evidence that the Greek aristocracy in the seventh and sixth centuries was deeply divided. The reasons are not clear. They may be found in old local rivalries, or in power struggles such as the conflicts at Athens connected with the assassination of the followers of Cylon, or in controversies concerning appropriate aristocratic behavior, including the ways to accumulate wealth. In the latter case we would have to distinguish between those whose fortune was solely based on landed property, and those who had gained additional wealth by trade. Whatever the reasons, the aristocracy clearly was no longer a homogeneous group.[44]

In strong contrast, the Roman aristocracy had gained its independent role only recently, after the expulsion of the king. Thus aristocratic rule was still in its beginning, and the patricians had to define themselves as a political and social body with a capacity for leadership. Soon, however, they not only claimed the leadership but aimed at monopolizing it: already around 480 B.C., the patricians seem to have closed their ranks.[45] Obviously the *patres* tried to manage the community without taking the *plebs* much into consideration. The unsuccessful adventure of the *gens Fabia* in the 470s against the neighboring town of Veii can be interpreted as a deliberate attempt to return to an old-fashioned manner of warfare without involving

---

44. For the most recent evaluation of the sources, see I. Muñoz Valle, *Euphrosyne*, n. s., 8 (1977): 43ff.; W. Rösler, *Dichter und Gruppe* (1980); H. Patzer, "Arete-Kanon" (1981): 197ff.; G. Nagy, *Arethusa* 15 (1982): 109ff.; id., *Class. Ant.* 2 (1983): 82ff.

45. See Raaflaub, chapter VII above, part 6.

the hoplite army,[46] parts of which guaranteed the *sacrosanctitas* of the tribunes of the *plebs*.

The best proof of this *serrata del patriziato* is to be found in the Twelve Tables, in the legal prohibition of intermarriage between patricians and plebeians.[47] It has been pointed out convincingly that this prohibition was not invented by the *decemviri*, but represented legal recognition of a practice already followed by patrician purists.[48] At the same time the prohibition of intermarriage makes it clear that besides the ruling aristocracy there existed an economically strong and self-confident group that considered itself good enough to marry into patrician families. Those nonpatricians surely had no doubts about their own ability to take over leading positions in the government, and that was precisely what was to be prevented by the law against intermarriage.

We may conclude, therefore, that despite some different preconditions, the leading aristocracies in Athens and Rome pursued the same goal of unifying themselves and securing exclusive political authority. Hence, if, according to our hypothesis, this was precisely the purpose of the codification of law, we should find confirmation in both cities in the developments following this comprehensive effort. Yet again the differences prevail. In Athens there followed a time of severe troubles, caused by quarrels among several aristocratic factions that finally led to a special form of aristocratic rule—namely, tyranny. After its fall, political participation was gradually extended to parts of the nonaristocratic citizen body until its fullest realization in Periclean democracy. In Rome, on the other hand, neither a patrician nor a plebeian ever attained a tyrantlike position. But neither could ordinary Roman citizens ever participate in politics to the same extent as the Athenian *demos* of the fifth and fourth centuries. The Roman constitution remained aristocratic down to the late Republic, even though the composition of the leading class changed after the *leges Liciniae-Sextiae*.

These differences in constitutional development after codification are decisive. Only the Twelve Tables were successful in securing col-

---

46. Livy 2.48.5–50.11; cf. W. Eder, *Servitus publica* (Wiesbaden, 1980): 128, 154. For a different but not contradictory view, see C. Saulnier, *Armée* (1980): 140–50 (the Fabii protecting a border fortress attacked by the Veientes).
47. Cf. Livy 4.1.1–6.4; Cic. *De re pub.* 2.63.183; Florus 1.25.
48. See chapter VIII above at nn. 23ff.

lective aristocratic rule, for in Athens the tyranny of Peisistratus put an end to the other aristocrats' political ambitions. Yet there also exists a striking analogy: in neither city did codification fulfill any of the demands our sources connect with these times of trouble and unrest: political rights were not extended to the lower classes,[49] and their economic situation was at best partially improved.[50] Neither in Athens nor in Rome was the basically aristocratic character of the constitution changed, nor were the traditional patterns of political behavior disturbed or altered by the codification of law.

That brings us to the third point. Such continuity of aristocratic power in Athens and in Rome is the more astonishing since, despite superficial analogies, the social structure and the basic features of "class struggle" in the two cities differed considerably. To begin with the analogies, besides the self-confident aristocracy characterized before, we find in both cities a population of farmers and craftsmen who were suffering increasing impoverishment and, through debt-bondage, becoming more and more dependent on the great landowners. This population had no visible political rights; at the outset of the Conflict of the Orders it was not even organized politically.

According to our literary sources, society thus was rather schematically divided into patricians and plebeians, rich and poor, *esthloi* and *kakoi*. Between these two extremes we find a population of landowners who belonged to neither side, namely the hoplites. Their existence is widely attested by literary and archaeological evidence. Whereas in Athens they do not seem to have played a significant role in the conflict between rich and poor, there are indications of their involvement in Rome. But since their status required much more than a minimal fortune, in neither city can the hoplites have been very active in promoting demands for the abolition of debts and the distribution of land. Certainly, among the impoverished masses there may have been some former hoplites who could no longer afford their own armor; but since they had lost their former social and political status, they could no longer have been forceful fighters for political and economic improvements. Accordingly, the position of the hoplites, often mentioned by scholars as a leading force in the class struggle, should be assessed as follows: as long as they owned

49. See n. 43 above.
50. See n. 36 above.

sufficient property to keep their hoplite status, they had little reason to fight for the improvement of their own economic situation or that of others to whom they felt superior economically and hence politically. If, however, they had lost so much of their property that they could no longer serve their *polis* as hoplites, they were no longer capable of fighting efficiently for their own interests. Consequently, there remains little space for the active role of the hoplites—so highly stressed by our sources—in the fight for economic changes.[51]

Yet the question of who actually was involved in those social conflicts is more complicated. For apart from the stratified division between upper, "middle," and lower classes, there also existed hierarchical formations, hardly ever mentioned in the ancient sources, which can be compared to social pyramids. At the top of such a pyramid, we find an aristocratic family or group of families; at the bottom, the members of the *clientela* in Rome or the dependent farmers and craftsmen of the *oikos* in Greece. Due to this vertical division of society, it is extremely difficult to determine who profited from political, social, or economic measures. For the political and religious privileges of the aristocracy may have produced some positive effects for their nonaristocratic followers and dependents, and the economic and political achievements of those followers may also have proved advantageous to the aristocrat at the top of the pyramid.[52] These "overlapping interests" should remind us not to divide ancient societies too simply into those at the top and those at the bottom.[53]

---

51. In regard to the hoplites as a driving force for innovation, I agree with A. M. Snodgrass, *JHS* 85 (1965): 115 ("It remains difficult to see in the hoplite class a driving force for military and political innovation."); for a similar view, see F. Ducat, *Ann. fac. des lettr. et sc. humaines de Nice* 37 (1979): 11–15, and K. Bringmann, *Gymnasium* 88 (1981): 82–84, in a review of Spahn, *Mittelschicht* (1977). For the ephebic oath as a possibly pre-Solonian instrument used by the aristocracy to keep the hoplites obedient, see P. Siewert, "The Ephebic Oath in Fifth-Century Athens," *JHS* 97 (1977): 102–11.

52. See, for instance, Dion. Hal. 2.10: the Roman client had to assist his patron materially, too.

53. To see the adversaries in the class struggle simply as the rich and the poor (cf. J.-P. Vernant, *Eirene* 4 [1965]: 5ff.) is not satisfactory. Although in many cases this may be the point, it cannot be generalized. For even long after the census classes had been introduced some important privileges of those who were aristocrats by birth remained intact (cf. the *phylobasileis*, the *exegetai, rex sacrorum, interrex*, and the quarrels about the *auspicia* in Rome). It is noteworthy, however, how much significance Thucydides (1.13ff.) attributes to wealth as a factor in the general political development of early Greece.

IX. Significance of the Codification of Law   285

But the social situation was even more complicated. There existed another part of the population, consisting of many groups of differing economic character. These groups were situated neither at the top nor at the bottom of the social pyramids, but lived outside and in between them.[54] Their "in between" position affected them in two ways. Though to some extent they were independent of aristocratic factions, nevertheless, owing to the domination of the aristocracy, they remained without protection and were always in danger of being treated as people who stood outside the law and, so to speak, outside the community or state. In both Athens and Rome there is evidence of such people, who had either immigrated recently or lived there independently for a long time.[55] Although because of their independent and precarious position we might expect them to have played a considerable role in the social conflicts, they seem to have been a decisive factor only in Rome: many of the plebeians, who formed a "conspiratorial" organization by means of a *lex sacrata* under the guidance of an elected tribune of the *plebs*, must have belonged to this large group of people who were not bound to a *patronus* by the religious ties of *clientela*.[56] It is above all the existence of such an "organization" that demonstrates the striking differences between Rome and Athens. In Athens, there was no comparable organization of the hoplite-citizens that might have effectively been able to challenge the leadership claimed by the *eupatridae*. Solon certainly was no tribune of the *plebs*.

Such basic differences in the consciousness of the two "middle classes" were far more important than the differences in the style and sequence of the conflicts. Whereas the hoplite-*zeugites* in Athens in the early sixth century left hardly any historical mark, in Rome the new military discipline that was necessary for the hoplite phalanx also made an impact in the political field. Such a difference in the behavior of two social groups whose economic and military situations were quite comparable may be explained by the different origins and functions of the hoplite phalanx in the two cities. In Athens

---

54. See K.-W. Welwei, *Polis* (1983): 50.
55. On such independent people, see W. Peremans, "Droit de cité" (1972): 122ff.; K.-W. Welwei, *Gymnasium* 88 (1981): 7-13; J. Cels Saint-Hilaire and C. Feuvrier-Prévotat, *Dial. d'hist. anc.* 5 (1979): 109f., 117ff.
56. See D. Kienast, *BJ* 175 (1975): 96ff. ("eine nicht ganz kleine Zahl von begüterten klientelfreien Bauern": 97).

the phalanx was created by the aristocracy and operated in an environment that was dominated by the aristocracy;[57] in Rome it gained its importance under the Etruscan kings. Here it was profitable for both the king and the hoplites to increase the military, and consequently political, role of this broad and economically important group.[58] That they formed some kind of an alliance against the aristocracy also explains the amazingly unified group behavior of the plebeian hoplites after the king had been expelled by the aristocracy. The hoplites, who were not bound to aristocratic *patroni*, were now deprived of their royal *patronus* and threatened by the sometimes arbitrary actions of the Roman patricians. When the government was taken over by the patricians, numerous members of the Roman community who previously had felt connected with the state through the person of the king now suddenly found themselves unprotected and standing somewhat outside that community.

Obviously the Roman hoplites had developed a strong sense of being part of their *polis* long before the codification of law. In Athens, on the contrary, such a sense of belonging to the *polis* is visible only many years after the codification of Solon—namely, at the time of Cleisthenes. Thus, although we should not underestimate the remarkable differences in the preconditions and the way the conflict was handled, we still find a striking parallel: in both cities the hoplites seem to have derived no immediate economic or political profit from the codification of law. Accordingly, such potential consequences of the codification probably were not affected by the mode and intensity of the hoplites' involvement in the struggle of the orders.

5. *Codification, State, and Certainty of Law*

We now have to deal with a rather fundamental objection to our hypothesis. The aristocrats, it might be observed, could not have been

---

57. For the archaeological evidence, see T. Hölscher, *Griechische Historienbilder des 5. und 4. Jh. v. Chr.*, Beitr. zur Archäol. 6 (Würzburg, 1973), especially 31ff. (aristocrats are represented as hoplites); cf. also J. Salmon, *JHS* 97 (1977): 84ff.; F. Ducat, *Ann. fac. des lettr. et sc. humaines de Nice* 37 (1979): 11–15; Th. Schwertfeger, "Der Schild des Archilochos," *Chiron* 12 (1982): 253ff.

58. For Etruscan influence on Roman hoplite warfare, see Saulnier, *Armée* (1980): 89–120; on the role of Servius Tullius, see Thomsen, *Serv. Tullius* (1980):

truly interested in the publication of customary law, since it was bound to eliminate their absolute control over the law. Moreover, the possibility of arbitrary jurisdiction was useful for their own purposes. The certainty and equality before the law that were created by a written code would finally lead to the aristocrats' loss of power and to the development of more democratic, or at least timocratic, forms of constitution.

This objection is, however, based on arguments that are hampered by serious methodological weaknesses. First, conclusions about the lawgivers' intentions are usually drawn from consequences of the fixation of law that manifested themselves only three generations later; in particular, the inclusion of broad strata of society in the process of political decision making cannot be seen as an immediate effect of the codification. Second, there is a tendency to overestimate the effectiveness of a written code in creating legal certainty.

Undoubtedly, the binding and visible regulation of social life may have had a great influence on the development of the state in the political sense and on the emergence of political responsibility. The idea that the rules and forms of communal life were not unchangeable, as they were given by tradition and divine law, must have spread quickly, although at the time of the codification itself only few people would have been aware of it. This important experience, perhaps even deepened by other factors,[59] may have greatly affected the formation of the concept of citizenship; it may have helped to objectify political behavior by reducing the use of violence; and it may generally have contributed to the emergence of more intensive and complex forms of political interaction. Such political consequences, however, appeared in individual city-states only many years after the codification. More importantly, such long-term political changes contrast strikingly with the period directly following the

---

144–211; J. Cels Saint-Hilaire and C. Feuvrier-Prévotat, *Dial. d'hist. anc.* 5 (1979): 110–21 ("L'obligation du service militaire pour . . . les 'plébéiens' . . . semble découler logiquement de leur entrée dans la clientèle du roi Servius Tullius: les forces de celui-ci paraissent de la sorte considérablement accrues": 119).

59. Such as the search for a "constitution" for a newly founded colony, the rise of a tyrant who levelled the political difference between aristocracy and *demos*, or the efforts made by the population as a whole to defend their community against external enemies. On the impact of the Twelve Tables on citizenship, see F. de Visscher, "*Ius Quiritium*" (1955): 244ff.

codification, where we observe an unbroken continuity of the economic and political status quo. It is better, therefore, to seek the causes of long-term economic improvements and of the extension of political participation in the very time at which these changes actually occurred, and not to assume a causal relationship between codification and "democratization."

It is more difficult to refute the other objection—namely, that codification was detrimental to the aristocracy because, by making the laws generally accessible, it excluded arbitrary jurisdiction. Conversely, because it guaranteed equality and certainty of law, codification is supposed to have been advantageous to the lower classes. But "fixed law" need not necessarily mean "just law," as is shown by many historical examples. In the same way, arbitrary behavior cannot be totally excluded by the installation of a law code. Once a code existed, however, arbitrary actions by a judge would become more obvious and thus more liable to be censured by society. To restrict arbitrary actions was also to the advantage of the aristocracy because it contributed to uniform treatment of comparable cases, helped to enforce unified standards of social conduct, and thereby increased the homogeneity of the social group the judges came from. Moreover, if the number of arbitrary decisions increased, precedents were bound to lose their value as guidelines for future decisions. Consequently, even the outcomes of legal quarrels among the aristocracy would become unpredictable. Legal uncertainty could thus not but hurt the aristocrats themselves. Finally, reducing the frequency of arbitrary and "crooked" decisions[60] would help to avoid social unrest and discontent among the middle and lower classes who had no share in judicial offices. This supports our assumption that the codification of law was a measure to ensure the political power of the leading social group. For the individual aristocratic judge would find it much more difficult now to form a personal following by favoring those he wanted obligated to himself, thereby endangering the unity of the whole group. However, for the common thief, who was to be sentenced to death according to Draco's harsh law, the codified certainty with which he could expect this radical punishment was no improvement. Nor was it an advantage for the failing Roman debtor that he now could read from the

60. Cf. Hesiod *Works and Days* 221, 250; Solon fr. 4W = 3D. 36.

Twelve Tables (if he could read at all) that he was to be sold *trans Tiberim* or even executed.⁶¹

Extreme though they are, these examples demonstrate that the reduction of arbitrary judgment did not necessarily favor only one side, but could be advantageous to both sides in the Conflict of the Orders. In trying to determine who in fact benefited most from codification, it will be useful to examine briefly the theoretical concepts of "certainty of law" and "equality before the law." Certainty of law is generally understood as the predictability of legal consequences; equality before the law as equal opportunity for every citizen to attain justice as a plaintiff or as a defendant. Certainty of law in the sense of predictability has little to do with codification, however, as it is neither bound to nor derived from a written text,⁶² but it has a lot to do with the fact that an individual can rely on the functioning of the legal system, and that common opinion corresponds to his personal evaluation of social conduct. Certainty of law thus largely depends on those who actually influence public opinion, who usually dispense the law, and who, in the case of doubt, develop the law further by interpreting it. At the time of the codification, and even long thereafter, this was done by the members of the upper class, who alone were trained and experienced in the handling of legal matters.⁶³ So, in form as well as in content, certainty of law even after the codification in many ways depended on the aristocratic judges.

Equality before the law is closely related to, and even part of, the complex concept of certainty of law. It mostly depends on the existing social structure and on the strength of those forces that are supposed to guarantee its legal institutions. As long as the communal or "state" authorities were still challenged by the powerful *gentes*, the

---

61. On Draco's severe laws, see Xen. *Oecon.* 14.4f.; Arist. *Pol.* 1274 b 15ff.; Plut. *Sol.* 17. On Rome: Twelve Tables, III.5 (= Gell. *Noctes Atticae* 20.1.46f.), 6 (= Gell. 20.1.48–52). For a different interpretation of *partis secanto*, see V. Londres da Nobrega, ZRG 76 (1959): 499–507 (the debtor was not to be killed, but his belongings distributed).

62. On this and the following, see M. Corsale, *La certezza di diritto* (Milan, 1970): 30ff.

63. For the *exegetes* even in the fifth century, see H. Bloch, "The Exegetes of Athens and the Prytaneion Decree," *AJP* 74 (1953): 407–18. On the role of the priests in developing the law, see Noailles, *Droit* (1949), and Mitchell, chapter V above passim.

"state" was not yet able to guarantee law and justice and fully to provide equal rights for every citizen, rich or poor. The fragments of criminal law show the weakness of public authority at the time of the codification both in Rome and Athens. The "state," whatever that means in speaking of archaic times, could declare the offender an outlaw (*sacer* or *atimos*) and leave the person to the mercy of his foes, but it could not provide legal protection. For example, a person convicted of unintentional homicide had no choice but to go into exile, because the state was unable to protect him if he stayed at home. The significant role that self-help played in early criminal law (and probably also in procedural and civil law), and the remarkable power gap between the leading aristocracy and the less influential groups in society make it improbable that, even after the codification, equality before the law really existed.[64] Despite the written code, the rich and powerful enjoyed many more opportunities to enforce their rights and to protect themselves from the demands of others.[65]

In other words, even the codification of law did not substantially change the supremacy of the strongest in society. Since, however, it made it more difficult for the aristocrats to rule as they pleased, why should they have been interested in codification at all? This process of aristocratic self-binding raises another important question concerning the sociology of law. Without even looking at the content of individual regulations, we have to find out why, and in what ways, the act of codification was in itself already highly profitable to the rule of the aristocracy.

The answer to this question is closely connected with the general problem of the interdependence of law and political power.[66] In that

---

64. On the weakness of the "state" and the extent of self-help in early Greece and Rome, see, e.g., E. Ruschenbusch, *Historia* 9 (1960): especially 149; K. Latte, *Kleine Schriften* (Munich, 1968): 252ff., 268ff.; E. Weisz, in *Zur griechischen Rechtsgeschichte*, WdF 45 (Darmstadt, 1968): 315ff.; U. E. Paoli, "La notion de *prorrhesis* en droit attique," *RIDA* 3 (1956): 135–42; W. Kunkel, *Kriminalverfahren* (1962); id., "Ein direktes Zeugnis für den privaten Mordprozess im altrömischen Recht," *ZRG* 84 (1967): 382ff. = id., *Kleine Schriften* (Weimar, 1974): 111ff. For recently found evidence of a private "execution company" in Italy, see F. De Martino, *Labeo* 21 (1975): 211ff. See also n. 91 below.

65. Cf. Plut. *Sol.* 5.6; Livy 3.37.

66. For a discussion of the problem of law and power, see, e.g., Th. Geiger, *Vorstudien zu einer Soziologie des Rechts*² (1970): 337–81; W. Abendroth, B. Blanke, and U. K. Preuss, eds., *Ordnungsmacht? Über das Verhältnis von Legalität, Konsens und Herrschaft* (1981).

context the concept of certainty of law plays a prominent role. The effect of law on the stabilization of power can be described schematically by distinguishing several steps. First, the exercise of power is provided with a framework of law—that is, those who hold the power oblige themselves to follow certain rules. Thus in an important field the behavior of the ruling class becomes predictable for everybody. As a consequence, in the eyes of those who are not qualified to administer the law, the codification of law acquires an absolute and positive quality precisely because it creates certainty in the sense of predictability. Thus codified law is generally accepted, objectified, and disconnected from its origins; it is now a suitable instrument to legitimize in turn the very power that brought it into existence, thus providing more room for the formation and exercise of power. Within this conceptual framework, therefore, codification is to be seen as a measure to secure the existing distribution of power, since it ensures the consent of the subjects to their rulers.

This argument might provoke two serious objections. On the one hand, its ideological premises may appear unrelated to the subject matter. On the other hand, it raises the question of whether, at the moment of codification, the upper classes were actually conscious of the long-term effects of such intricate mechanisms for securing their power.

The first objection is difficult to counter because it is directed against a complex and rather rigid hypothesis that is vulnerable precisely because it is merely a hypothesis. I can only emphasize here what was said above about the importance and value of a working hypothesis.

At first sight, the second objection seems to be easier to deal with since it does not actually affect the theoretical problem. According to the theory presented above, it is an objective consequence of every codification or act of lawgiving that the power of the ruling elite is secured. This result thus does not depend on the intention of the lawmaker, who does not need to understand the historical process induced by his own actions in order to achieve it.

Yet it is the aim of our investigation to elucidate the lawgiver's immediate intentions and the purpose of the individual codifications. Unintentional consequences should therefore not be taken into consideration here. Moreover, since long-term consequences were not necessarily planned or foreseen at the very moment of codification, we are not entitled to use such consequences as evidence of the actual intentions of the lawgivers. Consequently, the fact that the fixation of customary law in the long run proved to be detrimental to aristocratic supremacy cannot be used as an objection to our assumption that the aristocracy initiated the codification in order to support its own interests in the Conflict of the Orders.

6. *Codification and Political Interests*

So far, our discussion has focused on methodology and on the preconditions, circumstances, and consequences of codification. We now have to take a closer look at some specific regulations in the laws of Solon and the Twelve Tables. Naturally, it is not the purpose of this paper to present a minute examination of every text and fragment available, but rather to examine a selection of passages that are of particular importance to our question.

According to our hypothesis, it was the purpose of archaic codifications to secure the political and economic status quo for a ruling class that was especially concerned with its own group interests. We therefore have to assume that the success of the group as a whole was given priority over the gain or loss of individual aristocrats.[67] Moreover, since the Athenian nobles had to avert the threat of tyranny, whereas the Roman patricians were trying to control an already existing counterforce (the tribunate of the *plebs*), the goals pursued by the two aristocracies in codifying the law could have been similar, but hardly identical.

In Athens at the time of Draco, the situation was tense in two respects. There was a widening gap between the rich and the poor, who were probably identical with aristocrats and nonaristocrats, and a split within the aristocracy itself. Draco's measures sought to meet the dangers that arose from the impoverishment of large parts of society by applying the brutal logic of the powerful: deterrence should be effected through severe penalties for any crime that might endanger the existing order. The underlying causes of the general

---

67. Hence the alleged impoverishment of some aristocrats after the reforms of Solon cannot be taken as an indication of the anti-aristocratic tendency of Solon's codification in general; cf. Arist. *Ath. Pol.* 13.3.

deterioration of the situation were not taken into consideration, but the discord among the aristocracy was taken seriously. By legally restricting the possibilities of *vendetta*, Draco tried to prevent a further weakening of aristocratic strength and unity.[68]

Certainly the same goal must have induced Solon to include this law in his own code. In addition, some other laws ascribed to Solon reveal the same tendency to strengthen the homogeneity of the aristocratic group. Thus the sumptuary laws can be interpreted as an attempt to reduce the opportunity for aristocratic clans to gain political influence through ostentatious expenditure.[69] Other laws served the same purpose by distributing chances to gain political power and influence more equally among the aristocracy, by preventing armed uprisings, and by keeping individual aristocrats from assembling too many followers. In this context the "law concerning *stasis*"[70] makes a lot of sense: the very fact that it required every citizen to take sides in the case of an internal conflict (*stasis*) made the success of any armed uprising doubtful. For an aristocrat aiming at tyranny now had to reckon with an "institutionalized military opposition" that presumably would be larger than any *hetaireia* he might have assembled himself.[71] The law was successful; as the career of Peisistratus shows, thereafter tyranny could only be established in any durable form by relying on outside military forces.

---

68. Under Draco's law, a crop thief was to be punished by death (Plut. *Sol.* 17.2); the same was true in Rome (Twelve Tables, VIII.9 = Plin. *Nat. Hist.* 18.3.12). Theft of crops in times of crisis and starvation seems to have been a frequent crime in both areas: see Livy 2.34, where a patrician is complaining about plebeian thieves. On the *vendetta*, see M. Gagarin, *Drakon* (1981).

69. Cic. *De leg.* 2.25.63–26.66; cf. 2.23.59, and Plut. *Sol.* 21.5. I do not think that sumptuary laws in archaic times (and later) should be considered concessions to the feelings of the poor. I agree with J. K. Davies, *Athenian Propertied Families 600–300 B.C.* (Oxford, 1971): xviiff., and S. C. Humphreys, *JHS* 100 (1980): 110ff., that luxuriousness and especially funerary expenditures were a way of getting acknowledged by the aristocratic society. Sumptuary laws that prevented the wealthiest and most powerful families from increasing their advantage over the rest of the aristocracy should therefore be considered a means of securing equality among aristocrats. On the funerary restrictions, see now Toher, chapter X below. See also n. 79 below.

70. Arist. *Ath. Pol.* 8.5; Gell. *Noctes Atticae* 2.12.1; cf. Cic. *Att.* 10.1.2; Plut. *Sol.* 20.1; id., *Mor.* 550c; Diog. Laert. 1.58.

71. For a different view, see, e.g., Ruschenbusch, SOLONOS NOMOI (1966): 83; J. A. Goldstein, "Solon's Law for an Activist Citizenry," *Historia* 21 (1972): 538ff.; B. Manville, "Solon's Law of *stasis* and *atimia* in Archaic Athens," *TAPA* 110 (1980): 213ff.

Further laws pursuing the same political goal are found in the area of economic legislation. The law on property[72] not only excluded the accumulation of land in the hands of only a few families, but also made it impossible to gather a large number of dependent peasants who could be used as instruments in political struggles. By restricting the number and types of immigrants, the "law concerning metics"[73] made it more difficult to gain a strong "*clientela*" by inviting in foreigners, who could be of some value in an armed political conflict. Moreover, the groups that were allowed to immigrate were mostly people who would settle in Athens rather than in the surrounding countryside, which was directly controlled by the aristocracy. Even the *seisachtheia*[74] had a double political effect. On the one hand, it immediately relieved a distressing situation and appeased dangerous and widespread discontent. On the other hand, it broke up those strong, concrete forms of personal dependence that could create or increase political disparity among the aristocracy. By abolishing debt-bondage, the aristocracy abandoned a source of income that was increasingly considered not only unjust by those enslaved and their families, but also unfair by those aristocrats who were deprived of seasonal laborers and, perhaps, craftsmen, because land and labor force were more and more concentrated in the hands of the wealthiest. By restoring an economic situation that may have existed before the *hybris* and greed of the most powerful prevailed,[75] the *seisachtheia* brought back sound conditions for aristocratic rule.

As a further significant consequence of the liberation of the peasantry, land may have again become available for acquisition. Those aristocrats willing to turn to trade and business may have profited from these conditions. Since the causes of impoverishment had not been removed, and since it was no longer possible to collect loans on the certainty of the borrower's person, many small farmers had no

---

72. Arist. *Pol.* 1266b14ff. L. Piccirilli, in *Scritti storico-epigrafici in memoria di Marcello Zambelli*, edited by L. Gasperini (Rome, 1978): 321–24, has pointed out that the law about dowry is not to be seen as a sumptuary law; rather, it was intended to protect landed property by prohibiting the splitting of land by marriage.
73. Plut. *Sol.* 24.4; cf. 22. On the impact on "citizenship," see Whitehead, *Metic* (1977): 140ff.; J. K. Davies, *CJ* 73 (1977–78): 115.
74. Solon fr. 36W = 24D (= Arist. *Ath. Pol.* 12.4); cf. Arist. *Ath. Pol.* 2.2; 6.1; Diod. 1.79.4; Plut. *Sol.* 13–15.
75. Cf. Solon fr. 4W = 3D. 7ff.; 13W = 1D. 7ff.; 15W = 4D; 36W = 24D. 9f.

choice but to sell their property in case of misfortune. So the liberation of the peasantry and the alienability of land could provide manpower for manufacturing endeavors and land for large olive plantations. Whether or not Solon intended this, in view of the economic situation in Athens in the early sixth century, it cannot be excluded that people were fully aware of the potential consequences of these measures.[76]

As has already been pointed out, in Rome conditions were different; the problem was not to avert the threat of a tyranny in an already chaotic situation but to prevent a well-organized *plebs* and its leaders from interfering with the power of the patrician magistrates.[77] The main goal was to reintegrate the *plebs* into an order of community and state that was exclusively defined by the patricians themselves. For it was not the *plebs* that wanted to build up a state within the state, but the patricians who excluded it by insisting on forming the state according to their own ideals.[78] To secure the ho-

---

76. For aspects of Solon's activity that may have favored the established order, i.e., the "rich," see T. C. W. Stinton, "Solon fragment 25," *JHS* 96 (1976): 159–62 (on fr. 25D = 37W. 7–10). I disagree with W. Peremans, "Droit de cité" (1972): 124, who speaks of "l'industrialisation du pays" by Solon's economic measures, but we should not underrate the active export of Athenian pottery; see J. M. Cook, "Athenian Workshops around 700," *BSA* 42 (1947): 139–55, and, for the increase at the end of the seventh century, B. L. Bailey, "The Export of the Black-Figure Ware," *JHS* 60 (1940): 60ff.; Sealey, *History* (1976): 110. Furthermore, the export of oil required not only olive trees but workmen for the production of the oil and the oil amphoras for packing and shipping. Thus the suggestion by R. M. Cook, "Archaic Greek Trade: Three Conjectures," *JHS* 99 (1979): 152ff., that the Corinthian *diolkos* was constructed about 600 B.C. not primarily in regard to Corinthian shipping but to get tolls from non-Corinthian ships (perhaps, I would add, in view of growing Athenian exports) fits in well with an attempt at emphasizing the economic motives of Solon's reforms.

77. For the most recent discussion of the "plebejische Lynchjustiz gegen die Widersacher der plebejischen Einrichtungen," see Bleicken, *Lex* (1975): 92 and 201ff.

78. Mommsen's statement (*Röm. Staatsrecht* II³ [1887]: 280) about the plebeian *Gemeinde in der Gemeinde* has been quoted almost everywhere. But it seems reasonable to remember three points: first, the *secessio plebis* was not supported by all non-patricians, at least not by most of the clients; second, the plebeians obviously left their families at home; and third, the plebeians clearly demonstrated their devotion to a unified Rome by swearing that the violator of a tribune should be *sacer Iovi*, i.e., to the god of the "patrician state." The efforts of the plebeians, therefore, seem to have been aimed at reintegrating themselves into a community in which they had already enjoyed some protection in the times of the Etruscan kings (see above at n. 58).

mogeneity of the patricians and the economic status quo were only secondary goals.

Nevertheless, those secondary goals were pursued effectively. As in Athens we find in Rome "sumptuary laws" that were supposed to guarantee equality and unity among the aristocratic class.[79] Moreover, in the prohibition of intermarriage between the orders, we find a rigid separation of nonpatricians and patricians. It has been demonstrated convincingly that such an attempt to cut the relationships between some patricians and plebeians was not only directed against the *plebs* but chiefly intended to exclude those patrician families whose political and economic existence depended on marriage connections with plebeian families.[80] Accordingly, one may suppose that the removal of the ban on intermarriage by the *lex Canuleia* five years later was not so much sought by the plebeians as by those patricians already linked to plebeian families. This fits in well with J. Linderski's interpretation of the *trinoctium* of the Twelve Tables as a measure to prevent patrician women from falling into the *manus* of a plebeian,[81] and with the hypothesis that the Twelve Tables were primarily an instrument designed to preserve power for those who already held it.

As far as the economic measures are concerned, the "*usus auctoritas* sentence" seems to be of special importance. It says that everything that had been held in unchallenged possession by a citizen for at least one year (or two years in the case of land) was to become his full property.[82] Since, on the one hand, it was most likely the patricians who generously endowed the *gens Claudia* with land; since, on the other hand, the same patricians refused to distribute land to the plebeians; and since, moreover, it was probably the landowning aris-

---

79. Twelve Tables, X.2–10 (= Cic. *De leg.* 2.23.59–25.64). For the purpose of regulations concerning luxuriousness and consumption at Rome in general, see Bleicken, *Lex* (1975): 170; M. Bonamente, "Leggi suntuarie" (1980): 67ff. The interpretation of the funeral regulations as a concession to the poor faces the additional difficulty that, according to a suggestion founded on archaeological evidence, the Twelve Tables merely codified a limit on expenses that had been in existence for a long time; cf. Cornell, *Archaeol. Rep.* (1979–80): 83, but see now Toher, chapter X below at nn. 68ff.

80. See chapter VIII above before n. 54.

81. Ibid. at n. 53.

82. Twelve Tables, VI.3 (= Cic. *Top.* 4.23; cf. Cic. *Caec.* 19.54; Gai. *Inst.* 2.42).

tocracy that profited most from the increase in conquered land,[83] it is surely not exaggerated to see the "*usus auctoritas* rule" as a means of fixing and protecting by law property conditions that were already de facto indisputable.[84] Even land that was only occupied, not owned, was thus safe from distribution.

The main goal of the patricians—namely, to keep pressure by the *plebs* and its leaders under control—is also visible in the *leges Valeriae-Horatiae of* 449.[85] Why did the plebeians need to secure the reinstallation of the tribunate by another *secessio* and to have the *sacrosanctitas* of the tribunes confirmed in a new law? There is only one logical answer: the patricians had tried to use the Twelve Tables to abolish the tribunate. The moment was well chosen, since for at least one year there had been no tribunes.[86] Of course, the tribunate could not really be abolished by law, because it had no legal existence. However, by fixing the laws and the legal procedures, by regulating the penalties, and by introducing the right of appeal to the *comitiatus maximus*, the codification had in fact rendered useless the hated *ius auxilii* of the tribunes. It cannot be regarded as an advantage for the *plebs* that henceforth capital punishment could only be inflicted by the *comitiatus maximus* (probably the centuriate assembly).[87] The failing plebeian debtor, for example, lacked such protection, because his penalty was specifically defined by the Twelve Tables. Moreover, the legally fixed rights of the creditor against the debtor made it impossible for the tribune of the *plebs* to intervene; any application of his *ius intercedendi* would have violated written law.

---

83. Dion. Hal. 5.40.3–5; Livy 2.16.3–6; Plut. *Publ.* 21 (on the distribution of land to the *gens Claudia*). For the patrician occupation of conquered land, see chapter IV above at n. 81; J. Cels Saint-Hilaire and C. Feuvrier-Prévotat, *Dial. d'hist. anc.* 5 (1979): 119, 127.

84. On this argument, see M. Horvat, "Réflexions sur l'usucapion et l'auctoritas," *RIDA* 3 (1956): 258ff., 330f.; G. Diosdi, *Ownership* (1970): 85ff., 91ff. M. Horvat's suggestion, *RIDA* 4 (1957): 290, seems plausible: "La codification était pour la classe privilégiée une forte arme contre les éventuelles pressions ultérieures des plébéiens."

85. Dion. Hal. 11.15; Livy 3.55. For a recent discussion of contents and meaning of the *leges Valeriae-Horatiae*, see Elster, *Studien* (1976): 48–60.

86. See Cic. *De re pub.* 2.37.62 (he even speaks of more than two years *non oppositis tribunis plebis*).

87. Twelve Tables, IX.1–2 (= Cic. *De leg.* 3.4.11; 19.44). On the identification with the *comitia centuriata*, see Cic. *Sest.* 65, and *De re pub.* 2.36.61.

Those who profited were again the patricians: as they probably held a majority in the *comitiatus maximus*, they were no longer subject to the lynch law of the tribunes of the *plebs*.[88]

Furthermore, another attempt was made to destroy the unity of the plebeian movement by strengthening the personal ties between patron and client. The sentence "If patron shall have defrauded client, he must be solemnly forfeited" (*patronus si clientem fraudem fecerit, sacer esto*)[89] enforced the obligation of the *patronus*. It was something like an amnesty law, for it guaranteed the care and benevolence of the patrician patron even toward those clients who had cooperated politically with the *plebs*. Such a guarantee might have further weakened the plebeian front, which was not uniform anyway. The legally fixed separation between *assidui* and *proletarii*,[90] and the importance attributed to self-help in the Twelve Tables, may have had the same effect.[91] If so, such measures might indeed have helped to weaken the "revolutionary impetus" of the *plebs*, which in turn could explain why the decades after the introduction of the Twelve Tables were so surprisingly peaceful.

Finally, this interpretation might also resolve another difficult

---

88. On the lynch law of the plebeian *concilia* led by their tribunes, see n. 77 above. Who held the majority in the *comitiatus maximus* depended on the number as well as the organization of the centuries. If we accept the full number of 193 centuries, the votes of the rich—*equites* and the first class (mostly patricians or their dependents, I suppose)—would prevail. But even if we agree with D. Kienast, *BJ* 175 (1975): 83ff., who plausibly thinks of 12 centuries of *equites* (109 n. 78) and 40 centuries of hoplites (93) at the time of the Twelve Tables, the majority seems to be clear; since most of the *equites* were patricians and only the group votes were counted, only 15 of the 40 hoplite centuries had to be dominated by patricians or their clients in order to win the majority of the votes.

89. Twelve Tables, VIII.21 (= Servius, on *Aen.* 6.609 [transl. E. H. Warmington]; cf. Dion. Hal. 2.10). On *clientela* in archaic Rome, see F. De Martino, "Clienti" (1980): 679ff.

90. Twelve Tables, I.4 (= Gell. 16.10.5; cf. 16.10.8).

91. See also n. 64 above. Self-help in its broader sense also comprised the regulations that made the result of a lawsuit dependent on the wealth and the power of those involved in it. Thus the plaintiff might already fail at the stage of the *in ius vocatio* (Twelve Tables, I.1–3; cf. 6–7), the *manus iniectio* (III.2), or the *talio* (cf. VIII.2) if the opponent possessed a *clientela* strong enough to protect himself from being forced into court or from being molested by the plaintiff (cf. II.3). The trial might also fail to come about if, for instance, the *proletarius* was not able to provide a carriage for his sick opponent (I.3), pay the deposit (*sacramentum*, see II.1a = Gai. *Inst.* 4.14), or find a solvent *vindex*. For the necessity in Greece of paying a certain sum in order to have a judgment made, see *Iliad* 18.507f.

problem—namely, the fact that the *legis actiones*, those important formulas needed to initiate any legal procedure, as well as the calendar of court days, were published only about 150 years later, in the so-called *ius Flavianum*.[92] How are we to assess the achievement of the plebeians if they knew their rights but were not able to use them without the help of the patricians? That they indeed depended on such help does not contradict our sources but disproves modern interpretations that claim the Twelve Tables as a great success of the *plebs*.

7. Conclusion

At the beginning of this essay I formulated the hypothesis that the codifications of law in archaic times primarily served the purpose of securing aristocratic predominance. The laws of Solon and the Twelve Tables have been used as examples, allowing us to investigate the historical background of those codifications, to examine the social and political aspects of power, to look at the specific situation in which the laws were given, and to compare all this with the immediate consequences of the codification. Although conditions in Athens and Rome differed to a certain extent, we have been able to establish a comparable pattern. First, the laws were always codified in the initial phases of a severe crisis, but nowhere was the codification explicitly demanded by the lower classes. Second, the act of lawgiving was in both cases performed by the old governing class, the aristocracy. With very few exceptions, such as the abolition of debt-slavery in Athens, there seem to have been no serious breaks in social development; if changes in political life and style occurred at all, they do not seem to have been a direct consequence of the codification. Thus the act of lawgiving seems to have stopped, or at least retarded, the political crisis at a significant point of its development, and certainly not to the detriment of the aristocrats, who in Athens as well as in Rome went on to determine the course of politics for several generations.

92. On the *ius Flavianum*, see Livy 9.46.5–6; cf. Cic. *Mur.* 11.25; *Att.* 6.1.8; Plin. *Nat. Hist.* 33.1.17; Macr. *Sat.* 1.15.9. On its significance, see Ferenczy, *Patr. State* (1976): 189f.

In the last part of the paper, the overall function and purpose of the archaic law codes was compared with some individual regulations. As far as I can see, not a single regulation positively attested for the laws of Solon or the Twelve Tables contradicts the results of the previous examination. And it seems that several measures that previously were explained only inadequately[93] can be reinterpreted more plausibly on the basis of our hypothesis. In conclusion, there indeed are substantial indications that it was an immediate aim of the codification to secure the homogeneity of the aristocratic group in Athens and to defend aristocratic prerogatives against a non-patrician but powerful "side-force" (*Nebeninstanz*), the *tribunus plebis*, in Rome.

93. For instance the law on *stasis* in Athens, the sumptuary laws, and even the rather puzzling sequence of laws at Rome in the years 451–50, 449, and 445.

MARK TOHER

X

The Tenth Table and the Conflict of the Orders

1

There is good reason to believe that by the middle of the fifth century B.C., Rome was approaching the point of violent social conflict. Power and wealth had been concentrated in the control of a few great aristocratic families for generations, and a large segment of the Roman community was effectively excluded from any opportunity of participating in the important political and religious offices of the community. As in Athens in the early sixth century B.C., there was the demand for agrarian reform and for the cancellation of

---

I am in debt to Alan Boegehold for his comments and advice on a number of ideas contained in this paper; to Robert Develin, who, in the spirit of the cooperative nature of this volume, provided constructive and useful criticism of an earlier draft; and, most of all, to Kurt Raaflaub, who, from the very beginning, provided encouragement and guidance in the development of its thesis.

debts; furthermore, there was discontent with the aristocratic monopoly of jurisdiction. The narrative in the second and third books of Livy may be inaccurate at specific points, but the general picture is clear and trustworthy. The measure taken to alleviate this tension, the institution of the Decemvirate with autonomous power to codify a set of laws for Rome, had its closest analogies in the Greek world and seems to have been Greek in its concept and purpose.[1]

The product of the Decemvirate's work was the Twelve Tables, and the tenth table contains obvious evidence of Greek influence. The issue of Greek influence on the Twelve Tables is a topic whose origins go back to antiquity.[2] Cicero presumed that the laws of Solon were used almost word for word in the composition of the tenth table;[3] but it is quite likely that this was his own deduction from a comparison of the two documents.[4] It is also quite likely that the tradition that there were embassies to Athens and the Greek cities of Magna Graecia to study their laws evolved at about the same time and was based on the ideas of Cicero.[5]

It is reasonable to assume that in such constructions the evidence of the tenth table played a decisive role,[6] just as it still does in modern speculation. The analogies are indeed striking, and when placed in the context of Greek funerary practice, the funerary regulations of this table appear, if not purely Greek, at least alien to the Italic tradition. They prohibited a corpse from being buried or cremated within the city; the funeral pyre was to be smoothed only with an axe; in order to remove *lamentatio*, only ten flute players were allowed at a funeral; the women in the procession were to wear no more than three mourning shawls and only one small purple tunic;[7]

---

1. F. Wieacker, "XII Tafeln" (1967): 332.
2. See most recently P. Siewert, *Chiron* 8 (1978): 331–34; M. Ducos, *Influence* (1978); C. Ciulei "Einfluss" (1969): 21ff.
3. Cic. *De leg.* 2.59.
4. E. Ruschenbusch, *Historia* 12 (1963): 25–53; P. Siewert, *Chiron* 8 (1978): 332–38; E. Rawson, *JRS* 62 (1972): 38.
5. Livy 3.31.8 and Dion. Hal. 10.51.5; cf. also Siewert, *Chiron* 8 (1978): 338–44, and Ogilvie, *Comm.* (1965): 449–50. E. Norden, *Aus altrömischen Priesterbüchern* (Leipzig, 1939): 255–57, argues that both the vocabulary and syntax of the tables reflect the style of the Greek law codes; cf. also J. Delz, *MH* 23 (1966): 73.
6. Most of the regulations of the tenth table are to be found in Cic. *De leg.* 2.59–61. Other relevant ancient authorities are cited in the notes.
7. Cf. Festus, p. 274 M, and Nonius, p. 371, who cites the authority of Varro. Although it has been supposed that these garments were to go on the corpse, more

they were not to lacerate their cheeks as a sign of mourning[8] nor raise a funeral lamentation (*lessum*);[9] no bones were to be taken from the corpse in order to hold a second funeral; anointing with oil by slaves or any kind of passing of the cup (*circumpotatio*) was prohibited; costly sprinklings (presumably with wine),[10] long garlands, and boxes of incense were also prohibited (although, if the deceased had won a garland, this could be placed in the grave);[11] the table prohibited the pouring of a myrrh drink on the corpse,[12] and no gold was to be placed on the pyre unless it had been in the teeth of the deceased; no new grave mound or pyre was to be built within sixty feet of the structure of another man without the consent of that man; and the entrance of a tomb or the grave mound itself could not be acquired by *usucapio* or the right of long usage.

Scholars who discuss the Greek tradition of funeral legislation have placed it within the category of sumptuary laws that are credited to most of the archaic Greek lawgivers. S. Mazzarino provides the most elaborate presentation of this theory.[13] He finds political significance in the numerous statements in the Greek lyric poets concerning the influx of luxury into the Greek cities of Ionia from Lydia. The fragment of Xenophanes (cf. Athenaeus 12.526a) concerning the *habrosynē* of the Colophonian aristocracy is his strongest evidence.[14] Mazzarino interprets archaic sumptuary legislation as

---

likely the *recinia* and the *tunicula* refer to the dress of the mourning women; cf. Wieacker, "XII Tafeln" (1967): 346–47.

8. Festus, p. 273 M.

9. The meaning of this term is unclear: see *OLD* ad loc. and Cic. *De leg.* 2.59. Cf. Cic. *Tusc.* 2.55; Plin. *Nat. Hist.* 11.157; Servius, on *Aen.* 12.606, for other discussions of the term.

10. Pliny, *Nat. Hist.* 14.88, credits Numa with such a regulation: *Numae regis Postumia lex est: "vino rogum ne respargito."* It is not clear whether such a regulation was incorporated in the tenth table. This passage may be taken as a salutary warning against presuming too readily that the regulations of the tenth table were not paralleled or actually existent in earlier unwritten customs and rituals.

11. Cf. Cic. *De leg.* 2.60; Pliny, *Nat. Hist.* 21.7.

12. The evidence for this is to be found in Festus, p. 154 M. It is to be noted that most authoritative editions of the Twelve Tables (see, e.g., K. G. Bruns and O. Gradenwitz, *Fontes Iuris Romani Antiqui*[7] [Tübingen, 1909]) ignore the important fact that the authority for this piece of the tenth table is Varro in the first book of his *Antiquitates*.

13. Mazzarino, *Fra oriente e occidente* (Florence, 1947): 193–94 and 214–16.

14. The interpretation and even the text of this fragment is not very clear; cf. C. Bowra, "Xenophanes, Fragment 3," *CQ* 35 (1941): 121ff. For the text, see M. L. West, *Iambi et Elegi Graeci* II (Oxford, 1972): 166, fr. 3.

one of the important aspects of the crisis of the aristocracies in Greece leading to the installation of autonomous lawgivers and tyrants.[15] E. Will has followed Mazzarino in attributing political significance to this archaic Greek sumptuary legislation. In his work on Corinth, Will accepts and restates Mazzarino's position in his analysis of the laws of the Cypselids.[16] More recently, H. Pleket has repeated the idea in his work on the archaic tyrants.[17]

More significant for the issue of the tenth table is the fact that scholars have categorized the funerary laws of Solon and other Greek lawgivers with this class of sumptuary legislation. The best statement of the idea can be found in M. Nilsson's work on Greek religion.[18] The most recent comprehensive studies of burials at Athens still accept this idea with regard to the archaic legislation of Solon and later laws.[19] The implications of such an interpretation of

---

15. Mazzarino, *Fra oriente e occidente*, 193: "Questa 'legislazione suntuaria' è, del resto, uno dei primi aspetti che la crisi delle aristocrazie, e la conseguente instaurazione di regimi 'nomotetici' o 'esimnetici' o addirittura 'tirannici,' presenta nel mondo greco."

16. Will, *Korinthiaka* (Paris, 1955): 513–14: "Il a montré aussi que les tyrans, nomothètes, aisymnètes qui ont marqué de leur personnalité et de leur oeuvre la crise de la société aristocratique à la fin du VIIe s. et au VIe ont tous été amenés à prendre position contre cette expression la plus voyante du déséquilibre social de la cité archaïque.... Mazzarino a montré qu'il ne s'agissait point là de mesures superficielles.... mais bien d'un aspect fondamental de la lutte pour l'*isonomie*: cet effort visant à établir des relations sociales fondées en justice grâce à des lois valables pour tous, cet effort qui travaillait le monde grec entier ne pouvait tolérer qu'une catégorie de citoyens affirmât par son ostentation sa volonté de maintenir l'inégalité."

17. Pleket, "The Archaic Tyrannis," *Talanta* 1 (1969): 49f.; "the nobility should be persuaded that in a society which tended toward isonomy, in which everyone had equal legal rights, the exuberance of the exclusive, aristrocratic 'society life' was undesirable.... The tyrant prevented the aristocracy from vaunting their riches (anti-luxury laws) and from passing their exclusive, aristocratic culture in an equally exclusive manner onto their children."

18. Nilsson, *Geschichte der Griech. Religion* I^3 (Munich, 1967): 714. That the state was so concerned about the restriction of funerals and their conduct is to be explained by the fact "dass die Einschränkung des verschwenderischen Bestattungsluxus einen Bestandteil des demokratischen Vorstosses gegen den Adel bildete; dieser liebte es, bei der Bestattung seiner Toten eine Schaustellung seines Reichtums zu geben, die das ärmere Volk als einen sinnlosen Aufwand betrachten musste." A more elaborate and recent presentation of this view of Greek funerary legislation can be found in M. Alexiou, *The Ritual Lament in Greek Tradition* (Cambridge, 1974): 14–23.

19. R. Stupperich, *Staatsbegräbnis* (1977): 73: "die Begrenzung des Teilnehmerkreises kann an sich in der archaischen Gesellschaft Athens nur einen begrenzten Kreis treffen, mächtige Adelsfamilien, zu deren Begräbnissen eine grosse Zahl von

Greek funerary laws for an analysis of the purpose of the tenth table are clear. Rome of the mid–fifth century B.C. was in the midst of social upheaval, and the codification of law is seen as a response to this problem. Having as it does so many affinities to Greek legislation, the tenth table ought naturally to be interpreted in the same way as the Greek laws have been: as an attempt to restrict aristocratic display and offensive expenditure in order to promote isonomy and to prevent unrest among the nonaristocrats. Such an explanation of the contents of the tenth table was presented as long ago as 1905 by O. Lenel. It has been emphasized recently by F. Wieacker, who concludes that the regulations of the tenth table were aimed at suppressing the offense caused by the patricians' overly luxurious lifestyle, which, at a time when the young Republic was increasingly suffering from war and economic distress, was bound to provoke the plebeians and to keep the flame of social conflict burning.[20] A similar explanation has been accepted by D. van Berchem, by G. Colonna in his discussion of the tomb material of archaic Latium,[21] and, with emphasis on aristocratic self-interest, by W. Eder in his contribution to this volume on the meaning of the codification of law in archaic Graeco-Roman society.[22]

As will be seen in part two of this paper, the tenth table finds its context in the Greek tradition of funerary legislation. Given the scholarly interpretation of the Greek tradition, it becomes clear that the tenth table could have great relevance to the Conflict of the Orders in archaic Rome. The question, indeed, is whether the tenth table was instituted to curb the display of wealth and prestige by the

---

Anhängern und Abhängigen kamen." Cf. S. C. Humphreys, *Family* (1982): 79–129, whose study indicates that the tombs of the archaic cemeteries in Athens demonstrate less of a sense of familial importance than one might expect to have been the case if they were seen as displays of wealth and power by aristocratic clans.

20. Wieacker, "XII Tafeln" (1967): 313. See also O. Lenel, *ZRG* 26 (1905): 516–17: "Auf der einen Seite ist die starke Einwirkung der nahen und zeitweise herrschenden Etrusker in Erwägung zu ziehen, die bei den Alten wegen ihrer Üppigkeit berüchtigt waren. Wäre es irgendwie erstaunlich, wenn innerhalb des römischen Patriziats gelegentlich die Neigung sich geltend gemacht hätte, bei der Ehrung der Toten es dem etruskischen Prunke gleichzutun? . . . Es war sehr natürlich, dass die Plebejer an pomphaften patrizischen Leichenbegängnissen Anstoss nahmen, und es war gut patrizische Politik, wenn man diesen Anstoss beseitigte."

21. D. van Berchem, "Rome et le monde grec" (1966): 745f.; G. Colonna, *PP* 32 (1977): 159; cf. M. Torelli, "Roma arcaica" (1980): 14.

22. Chapter IX above at nn. 69 and 79.

aristocratic families of Rome, and whether it therefore provides evidence of intended isonomy on the part of the Decemvirate.

It is the thesis of this paper that ancient funerary and sumptuary laws must be seen as related, but clearly different, categories. Their function and purpose were not necessarily identical. Practically all the political explanations of funerary legislation mentioned above are unwarranted and unsupported by any ancient evidence. A close examination of the content, context, and circumstances of all the relevant funerary laws in the Graeco-Roman world reveals that they had little, if anything, to do with political considerations. Such legislation, therefore, was neither the result of specific demands by the lower classes nor of attempts by the ruling aristocracy to discipline itself in order to avoid discontent and revolution. In short, the funerary laws have no direct relevance to the Conflict of the Orders.

By analyzing one limited phenomenon both in the Greek and Roman world, this paper provides an example of the useful results that can be gained by applying the "comparative approach" to the history of the archaic period.[23] Part two of this paper will establish the Greek context of the tenth table; part three will examine the only ancient evidence that discusses the purpose and function of such legislation in any detail; part four will consider the circumstances surrounding the individual Greek funeral regulations in order to determine whether any political considerations were factors in their enactment; and, finally, part five will return to a consideration of the tenth table itself, and its significance for the Conflict of the Orders.

2

An examination of the ancient Greek funerary laws, which extend over a wide geographical and chronological span, provides a context for the provisions of the tenth table.

Solon[24] prohibited excessive wailing and would not allow women

---

23. Cf. Raaflaub, chapter I part 3 above.
24. Plut. *Sol.* 21.5–7; Cic. *De leg.* 2.59; Demosth. 43.62 = E. Ruschenbusch, SO-LONOS NOMOI (1966), F. 109, who doubts that this passage of Demosthenes reflects a law of Solon. This, however, is not essential to the issue under consideration here. There is no reason to doubt that there was such a law as that quoted by Demosthenes operative in Athens in his own time at least.

to wear more than three *himatia* or carry with them a reed mat of more than a cubit's length while they were in mourning; women were not to lacerate themselves in mourning, and no meat or drink was to be brought to the grave if it exceeded one obol in value; there was to be no wailing outside the tomb of "another" (presumably a person not belonging to the family); there was to be no sacrifice of an ox at the grave, and neither could one add more than three *himatia* to the grave; it was forbidden to visit another's grave unless there was a funeral. Demosthenes attributed to Solon regulations decreeing that funeral processions had to take place before sunrise on the day after the laying out of the corpse (*prothesis*), and no women under the age of sixty were either to accompany the corpse into the tomb or to be present when it was brought out of the tomb unless they were at least a daughter or a first cousin of the deceased; in the funeral procession men were to precede the corpse and women to follow behind.

Lycurgus[25] is supposed to have removed all superstition about death in Sparta by allowing burial within the city and erection of memorials to the dead near sanctuaries; furthermore, he allowed the corpse to be wrapped only in a single crimson garment and olive leaves, and no one was to have his name inscribed unless he had died in battle. The period of mourning was limited to twelve days.

There was a law attributed to Pittakos[26] that prohibited persons not of the deceased's family from attending a funeral.

A law at Athens, which Cicero dates to some time after (*post aliquanto*) Solon,[27] regulated the form of the tomb or burial monument. The sepulcher could be no greater than what ten men working for three days could build, and the tomb was not to be decorated with herms or *opus tectorium*, a kind of stucco or plasterwork. The law allowed no private funeral orations at the graveside.

A late fifth-century inscription from Ceos[28] states that the corpse is to be covered by only three or fewer coverlets, the total value of which is not to exceed one hundred drachmae. The corpse is to be carried out on a plain bier with only the head uncovered; only three measures of wine and one of oil can be brought to the tomb, and the

---

25. Plut. *Lyc.* 27.1.   26. Cic. *De leg.* 2.66.   27. Cic. *De leg* 2.64–65.
28. Dittenberger, *Syll.*⁴ (1960): 1218; a partial translation can be found in D. C. Kurtz and J. Boardman, *Burial Customs* (1971): 200–201.

vessels are to be taken back home after the ceremony; the funeral is to proceed in silence to the tomb, and the corpse is to be covered during the procession; preliminary sacrifice is to be conducted according to ancestral custom, and the bier and coverlets are to be brought back from the tomb; women attending the funeral are not to leave the tomb before the men (the reading of this line is uncertain, and it may state that the women were to leave before the men who, presumably, would stay behind to raise the funeral mound).[29] The inscription also provides instructions for the rites of purification of the house and the participants after the period of mourning.

Another inscription, that of the Delphic phratry of the Labyadai,[30] dated to c. 400 B.C., does not allow material worth more than thirty-five drachmae, whether bought or made at home, to be placed in the tomb; there is to be a thick grey upper garment (presumably for the corpse), and a *stroma* (spread) is to be placed under the corpse along with one pillow; the corpse is to be kept covered and carried out in silence; the bier is not to be put down at any turns, nor is there to be loud lamentation outside the house before the procession reaches the tomb; there is to be no expiation sacrifice before the lid of the tomb is closed, and there is to be no lamentation for the deceased either on the day after the funeral or on the tenth day after or a year after. A fine of fifty drachmae is provided for the transgression of certain of these rules.

Cicero says that in reaction to the growing lavishness of funerals at Athens, Demetrios of Phaleron[31] instituted a law providing that funeral processions must take place before dawn; he also strictly regulated the form of grave monuments, allowing nothing other than a *columella* (of no more than three cubits height), a *mensa*, or a *labellum*,[32] and he instituted a magistrate to enforce his law.

29. Humphreys, *Family* (1982): 85 n. 3.
30. F. Solmsen and E. Fränkel, *Inscriptiones Graecae ad inlustrandos dialectos selectae*[4] (Leipzig, 1930; repr. Stuttgart, 1966), no. 49 C.
31. Cic. *De leg.* 2.66.
32. The meaning of *columella* as a "small ornamental column serving as a tombstone" and of *mensa* as a "table for offerings to the dead" seems to be tolerably clear. *Labellum* is more complicated. It seems to mean a bowl or a basin. The archaeological evidence is of no aid. Cf. J. Twele, *AJA* 74 (1970): 204, for an unconvincing explanation of the three terms; cf. also Kurtz and Boardman, *Burial Customs* (1971): 166–69.

A law of the city of Gambreion in Asia Minor,[33] dated to the third century B.C., stated what color garment those in mourning should wear and required that the funeral rites be completed within three months. The period of mourning was limited to four months for men and five for women.[34]

In light of this evidence, it is obvious that the tenth table stands in the Greek tradition. The number of mourning shawls, the prohibition of ritual laceration, the restriction on wailing and on use of wine at the graveside, all find parallels in the various Greek laws. The expression of amounts of material in maximum terms and the emphasis on the restriction of the conduct of the mourners (especially the women) are also in accord with the Greek attitude toward such activity.

The Greek nature of the tenth table becomes even more obvious when one considers that such funerary regulations were alien to the Italic tradition. Etruscan funerary practice remained lavish until well into the third century B.C.[35] Although some scholars have specu-

33. Dittenberger, *Syll.*¹ (1960): 1219.
34. There is some evidence for three other laws relating to funeral legislation in Greece: Charondas of Catana (Stob. 44.40 = IV p. 152 of Hense's ed.) is credited with the sentiment that it was proper to honor the dead not with tears and lamentation but with good memory and a yearly offering from the harvest, for wailing and excessive grief were not pleasing to the chthonic deities; at Syracuse, there was a law that put an end to costly funerals (Diod. 11.38.2); Plutarch (*Sol.* 21.7) states that most of the prohibitions found in the laws of Solon were operative in his day among the Boeotians. This list does not include the evidence from Lys. 1.14; Ael. *VH* 5.14; Plut. *Quaest. Gr.* 296 F 24, all of which seem to refer only to custom and not to any law. *IG* IV. 1607 and *IG* V.2,4 deal with rites of purification and expiation, and they seem to relate to funerary practice, but they are not of the order of the items cited as laws above. It is impossible to determine if *Syll.*¹ 1220 concerns funerary restrictions (cf. Dittenberger's n. 1). The evidence that is supposed to be found in an archaic epigram from Troizen (cf. P. Legrand, *BCH* 24 [1900]: 179ff.; A. Wilhelm, *BCH* 29 [1905]: 416) has been excluded. There is no good reason to interpret *ephameron* in the last line of the epigram as meaning that the tumulus was built "within one day." It is better to take the term in its more usual sense of lasting for only a short time; cf. M. Toher and R. Renehan, "An Epigram from Troizen," *CP* 79 (1984): 212–14. For contrary views, cf. O. Reverdin, *La religion de la cité platonicienne* (Paris, 1945): 112; W. Peek, *Griechische Grabgedichte* (Berlin, 1960): 8. Finally, an inscription from Thasos mentions regulations regarding the conduct of women at a funeral, but J. Pouilloux, *Recherches sur l'histoire et les cultes de Thasos* (Paris, 1954): 371–78, is probably correct in believing that the *agathoi* referred to are men who have died in a certain battle. Hence the law related only to the conduct of the *public* funeral in that one instance.
35. F. Wieacker, "XII Tafeln" (1967): 333.

lated that such funerary regulation came to Rome by way of Etruria,[36] it is better to agree with Wieacker that, if anything, the tenth table was written in reaction to lavish Etruscan funeral practices.[37] The latest archaeological evidence indicates that lavish burials in Latium ceased almost a century before the traditional date of the expulsion of Tarquin from Rome.[38] There is also no evidence that any other non-Greek communities in Italy engaged in such regulation of funerals. Even at Rome itself, similar legislation does not occur for almost four hundred years after the Twelve Tables, not until 81 B.C. and the *lex Cornelia*.

3

Discussion of the motivation for such funerary legislation appears in only two ancient texts, the second book of *De legibus* of Cicero and the *Nomoi* of Plato.

The relevance of the second book of *De legibus* is obvious, for it provides us with the contents of the tenth table. The inspiration for Cicero's work was Plato's *Nomoi*, which also contains evidence relevant to the issue of funerary regulation and practice, since much of Plato's ideal legislation had precedent in practice. Plato will not allow wailing outside of the house (960a1–2); he, too, places restrictions on the size of the tomb, which are expressed in the same terms as those used in the law dated by Cicero to some time after Solon (958e6–7); furthermore, like the law of the Labyadai, Plato places limits on expenditure (959d2–6). Unlike Cicero, Plato never cites the authority of practice in his discussion, but the insight he provides is significant since he was not as interested in presenting the Greek

---

36. C. Ciulei, "Einfluss" (1969): 38–40, following O. Lenel, *ZRG* 26 (1905): 516–17.

37. Wieacker, "XII Tafeln" (1967): 333–34; cf. id., *RIDA* 3 (1956): 474–75, where he points out the fact that many of the items mentioned in the tenth table appear in Etruscan wall-paintings. But this is not strong evidence that there is Etruscan influence on the tenth table, or that the tenth table is a reaction to Etruscan influence, for many of the items in the tenth table are also mentioned in Greek funerary laws. Such a theory also cannot account for the lack of archaeological evidence from tombs in Latium after the mid–sixth century B.C.

38. Cornell, *Arch. Reports* (1979–80): 76.

attitude toward such matters as he was in presenting an ideal system of law in which funerary regulation played a role.

Although he attempts to base his reasoning for such funerary regulation in practice, Cicero admits that in at least one instance the meaning of a regulation in the tenth table was obscure to even the earliest interpreters (*De leg.* 2.59). Obviously the evidence in *De legibus* must be used with caution when discussing the Conflict of the Orders and the state of affairs in archaic Rome. Cicero and preceding generations had been witness to a growing spectacle of funerals and funeral games. More than once in *De legibus* he states that funerals and tombs at Rome had become lavish and immoderately costly in his time (2.62, 66). The spectacular funeral games of Julius Caesar for his father (who had died twenty years before) were a notorious example of the political purpose of such occasions.[39] It is clear that Cicero's attitude toward the issue was affected by contemporary events. But although he may apply a certain amount of philosophical piety that might seem out of place in archaic Rome, he does cite almost all of his sources in discussing the issue. If at times his interpretation of events or practice can be questioned, his facts cannot.

Given the nature of their attitudes and their contexts, neither the writings of Plato nor those of Cicero can be taken as final authority on the motivation behind such funerary legislation. But they are the only extant discussions of the issue, and they can be revealing as much for what they do not say as for what they do. For Cicero, the first and obvious explanation of funeral austerity is religious. Extravagant expenditure in such affairs was not in keeping with religious practice. In justifying his own proposed law, Cicero says, "The rule that 'piety shall be brought, but riches left behind' means that uprightness is pleasing to the gods, but that great expenditure is to be avoided" (*De leg.* 2.25).[40] This is the attitude of Cicero throughout the second book of *De legibus*. He says that "it is in accordance with nature that differences in wealth should cease at death" (59). In death, material possessions cease to have significance, and extrava-

---

39. For the funeral games of Caesar, cf. Dio Cass. 37.8 and Pliny, *Nat. Hist.* 33.53; for other funeral games of the republican period, cf. Livy 23.30.15; 31.50.4; 39.46.2; 41.28.11.

40. All translations are taken from the edition of C. Keyes in the Loeb Classical Library, with some minor modifications.

gance in mourning is offensive to the gods of the underworld (62). This last idea is similar to that attributed to Charondas by Stobaeus.[41]

Not entirely divorced from the religious motivation is that of ancestral practice. According to Cicero (who again quotes his own law), the rites of the ancestors are to be followed closely, for they were close to the gods: "Next, 'the preservation of the rites of the family and of our ancestors' means preserving the religious rites, which, we can almost say, were handed down to us by the gods themselves, since ancient times were closest to the gods" (*De leg.* 2.27; cf. 2.40). Plato, in a similar way, states that prudent funeral rites are best: those that neither exceed accustomed pomp nor fall short of what the ancestors paid to their parents (*Nom.* 717d7–e1). Plato decrees that the laying out of the corpse should conform to custom, *nomos*, except where the state curbs excess (959e5–7).

For Cicero, the surest test of a law is its conformity to nature, and the regulations in the tenth table do just this (*De leg.* 2.61). A similar sentiment about the appropriateness of funeral rites that accord with nature is found in Xenophon's account of the burial of Cyrus, who insisted on being simply united with the earth, which brought forth so much that was good for men (*Cyr.* 8.7.25). Numa Pompilius is supposed to have had a similar burial (*De leg.* 2.56).

In addition to the reasons set out above, Plato presents an elevated philosophical rationalization for austerity in funeral practice: moderation in burial is only reasonable, since in death the soul, the real essence of man, has departed; to spend lavishly on a carcass of flesh is to be wasteful over a soulless altar to the gods of the underworld (*Nom.* 959c2–8). The value of this rationalization is not that it in any way reflects archaic Greek thought. Rather, it is valuable as the account of an original thinker, who, when faced with the necessity of justifying funeral austerity, presents no political motivation for such practice.

But this is not to deny that pragmatic considerations are revealed in each of these accounts. Cicero demonstrates a sense of equality in his account. He says that the pathway to the gods must be open to all and that poverty should be no hindrance:

---

41. See n. 34 above.

For indeed, since we desire that poverty shall be equal to riches even among men, why should we exclude it from the presence of the gods by adding costliness to our rites, especially since nothing would be less pleasing to the god himself than that the pathway to his favor and to his worship should not be open to all alike? (*De leg.* 2.25).

Though equality among men is a desirable condition generally, its absence before the gods is especially displeasing. The context of the statement and, indeed, of the whole second book of *De legibus* indicates that Cicero does not feel that the need for any kind of political or social equality was a motivating factor; rather such secular inequality is the implied status quo. In *De re publica*, Cicero approves of such inequality among men socially and politically, otherwise there can be no gradation of *dignitas* (1.43). Thus it is important simply on the basis of religious scruple that such inequality of material wealth should cease to be a consideration in the worship of the gods and in funerary practice (*De leg.* 2.59).

Evidence from Plato indicates that yet another consideration in the restriction of the size of tombs and burial plots may have been the land available for cultivation and habitation. In the *Nomoi*, Plato forbids the placing of tombs on land that has been cultivated. Tombs are to be placed only in those areas suitable for this purpose (958e1), and the dead are not to deprive the living of land suitable for the production of food (958d6–e6).[42] Such a consideration would explain why the need for funeral legislation was recurrent in some states. It is not unreasonable to see the provision of the *post aliquanto* law cited in Cicero as being motivated by the lack of space in the Kerameikos, something that may have been a problem even in the archaic period.[43] Although it is not entirely clear from the description that Cicero gives of Demetrios of Phaleron's law (*De leg.* 2.66), it is possible that his restrictions were intended, in part, to alleviate crowded conditions in the cemetery of Athens. Cicero says that even in his own time there was a problem of extravagant funerals at Rome

---

42. Paraphrased by Cicero in *De leg.* 2.67.
43. Kurtz and Boardman, *Burial Customs* (1971): 80–81.

(*De leg.* 2.66), and in one of the *Philippics* he proposes that the curule aedile's edict regarding funerals be suspended and that Servius Sulpicius Rufus, in return for his service to the state, be granted a burial plot of thirty-foot radius in a public place on the Esquiline (9.17). This limitation would seem to imply that thirty feet was a substantial interment in this period in Rome. All of this indicates that space must have become a factor in the ancestral cemeteries over the course of time. For it seems that once a plot of land had been consecrated for burial, it could not be used for another purpose.[44]

Another practical consideration in the institution of funeral legislation was the reduction of public disruption. Cicero says that a limit on the crowd at a funeral is necessary, for a crowd only increases the grief (*De leg.* 2.65). Needless to say, Cicero's own era must have exaggerated this aspect of the issue,[45] but his attitude is not completely anachronistic. The regulation of Pittakos allowed only family members to attend a funeral (*De leg.* 2.66); and the law of the Labyadai prohibited funeral processions from stopping or putting the bier down and enjoined that the funeral train proceed in silence.[46] Both Demetrios and the law attributed to Solon by Demosthenes ordered that the funeral procession take place before sunrise.[47] All of this had the effect, if not the intent, of reducing the public disruption that a funeral could cause.[48]

Plato makes another observation that is interesting in this context. He states that gold and silver are not suitable to be presented as votive offerings, for they cause envy (*Nom.* 955e8 56a2: *epiphthonon*). It is possible to argue that this envy should be interpreted in a political sense—that is, that it was engendered by lavish display of wealth and could then lead to social unrest. It seems more likely, however, that in both Cicero and Plato the context and other evi-

---

44. Plato, *Nom.* 955e6–8; Cic. *De leg.* 2.45 and 58.
45. For other examples of funerals being disruptive, cf. Horace, *Sat.* 1.62.42 and *Epist.* 2.2.74.
46. Solmsen and Fränkel, *Inscr. Graec. Inlust. Dial.* (as in n. 30), no. 49 C 33–35.
47. Cic. *De leg.* 2.66; Demosth. 43.62.
48. A probable cause for limitation of the size of funerals can also be found in the fact that extravagant mourning at funerals and even the administration of funerals by non–family members was often used in court cases as evidence of a claim to the estate of the deceased. Cf. Humphreys, *Family* (1982): 83–84; Alexiou, *Ritual Lament* (as in n. 18): 20f., and B. Garland, "Gynaikonomoi: An Investigation of Greek Censors of Women" (diss., Johns Hopkins University, 1981): 75–76.

dence of their discussion do not allow such an interpretation. Each writer provides evidence of a variety of considerations for funeral austerity, but there is nothing to indicate that political factors entered into their thinking on this issue in any way. The envy mentioned by Plato can easily be interpreted in the sense of the religious attitude expressed in Cicero: all considerations of material wealth should cease before the gods (*De leg.* 2.25), and anything that could engender envy was inappropriate to the rite for that reason. Certainly the attitude of Plato, founded as it is on the consideration of the purity of the soul (*Nom.* 959c1–d3), would have tended toward a philosophical and religious context for the envy rather than a political one.

It is not likely that Plato or Cicero, each in his own way an acute observer of political affairs, would have been unaware of a political motive for such funeral legislation, had one existed. Yet it might be argued that the very nature of the theoretical treatise on which each was engaged precluded the presentation of any such crude motive and that such regulation had to be appropriately couched in a more august religious and ancestral tradition, even though the baser truth was known to each.

It is unlikely, however, that either author was so circumspect. Plato implies that the practical consideration of restricted space was a factor in the limiting of burial plots and tombs. It would not have been improper for Plato to cite any political benefits of restricted funerary practice had he believed there were any. Cicero does not deny the pragmatic utility of religious rites. He speculates that the provision prohibiting funeral pyres within the city stems from the fear of fire (*De leg.* 2.58). Although he believes that augury is, ultimately, divine, he agrees with Atticus that in the archaic period it was a useful tool for quelling political crises (*De leg.* 2.33). In the third book of *De legibus*, Cicero is quite pragmatic in his analysis of the institution of the tribunate. In response to his brother's passionate criticism, Cicero points out that it had become necessary to institute the office, for some freedom had to be given to the *plebs* (3.24). In the case of his own burial, Cicero indicated that the restrictions on expenditure in his own time were of no great concern and he feared no penalty (*Att.* 12.35; 12.36.1).

Plato's *Nomoi* and Cicero's *De legibus* provide a good deal of material for speculation about the motivation behind such funerary legislation, but in no place do they provide good evidence that, either in their own time or in the archaic period, political factors entered into the issue. The predominant considerations were religious scruple and ancestral precedent.

4

Superficial study of the major Greek laws relating to funerary practice reveals a remarkable similarity in attitude despite the different places and eras in which these laws were enacted. This alone should be strong evidence that funerary legislation transcended the local political and social context of each law. Analysis of these circumstances where they are well enough known to us indicates that political reform and isonomy are nowhere evident as a motivation for such regulations.

Nothing of value can be said about the laws of Lycurgus or the supposed law of Charondas of Catana. Whether either of these two reformers ever existed has been questioned.[49] Certainly the reforms attributed to Lycurgus were part of a larger cultural metamorphosis that Sparta underwent in the eighth and seventh centuries B.C. Charondas, who is supposed to have expressed the notion that it is better to honor the dead with good memory than with displays of tears and grief, is said to have been of the "middle class", *tōn mesōn politōn*, according to Aristotle (*Pol.* 1296a21). But it is clear that Aristotle had no evidence at hand to indicate such a social classification for Charondas. It was simply his belief that all such reformers, since they were not proponents of extreme positions in politics, could not have been members of the opposed classes that maintained such positions.[50] Since nothing at all is known of the circum-

---

49. On Lycurgus, cf. P. Cartledge, *Sparta and Lakonia* (London, 1979): 131ff.; A. Toynbee, *Some Problems of Greek History* (Oxford, 1969): 274–83; P. Oliva, *Sparta and Her Social Problems* (Amsterdam and Prague, 1971): 63–70. On Charondas, cf. K. J. Beloch, *Griechische Geschichte* I.2² (Strassburg, 1914): 257.

50. A. Santoni, "Aristotele, Solone e l'*Athenaion Politeia*," *ASNP*, 3rd ser., 9 (1979): 959–84, especially 966ff. On the two lawgivers, Zaleukos and Charondas, see the articles of M. Mühl, *Klio* 22 (1929): 104–24, 431–63; and T. Dunbabin, *The Western Greeks* (Oxford, 1948): 68–75.

stances surrounding the supposed statement or even the date of Charondas's activity, it would seem unreasonable to presume that his attitude stemmed from a period of social unrest, or that the short statement in Stobaeus had a political motivation.

The circumstances surrounding the law of Pittakos are also unknown to us. Although his laws were the product of a period of unrest in Mytilene, there is no evidence, despite the assumptions of some scholars, that he was a "democratic" reformer.[51]

The law limiting expenditure on funerals at Syracuse has no indication of date as mentioned in Diodorus (11.38.2), and there is no good reason to relate it to the time of Gelon.[52] Since the context of the passage shows that Gelon was adamant that the law should apply to his own funeral, it is unlikely that Diodorus would have referred to it simply as a law passed by the Syracusans if, in fact, it had been instituted by Gelon himself. Nothing else is known about this law.

There is no information at all about the circumstances surrounding the composition of the three inscriptions from Ceos, Delphi, and Gambreion. It is hardly likely, however, that a phratry would have had a political motivation or isonomic intent in establishing funeral regulations like those operative among the Labyadai. E. Norden is probably correct in his assessment that these laws were copies of older regulations, dating to times much earlier than the stones themselves.[53] If anything, such legislation would have been instituted against a phratry in the archaic period as part of a reformer's program to break the grip of the phratries on the religious functions of the archaic community.[54]

A bit more can and should be said about the supposed late archaic Athenian law that Cicero dates to some time after Solon. The scholarship on this issue is instructive in regard to methodology, and it must be discussed in detail. Cicero says that after Solon the need for restriction on extravagant burials recurred:

---

51. D. Page, *Sappho and Alcaeus* (Oxford, 1955): 172–79; F. Romer, "The *Aisymnēteia*: A Problem in Aristotle's Historic Method," *AJP* 103 (1982): 25–46.
52. E. Freeman, *History of Sicily* II (Oxford, 1891): 215–16; L. Ziehen, in I. de Prott and L. Ziehen, *Leges Graecorum sacrae e titulis collectae* II (Leipzig, 1906): 261 n. 9, dates the law to Diocles.
53. Norden, *Aus altrömischen Priesterbüchern* (as in n. 5): 255–56.
54. F. Jacoby, "*Genesia*: A forgotten festival of the dead," *CQ* 38 (1944): 73f.

But somewhat later, on account of the enormous size of the tombs we now see in the Kerameikos, it was provided by law that no one should build a tomb that required more than three days' work for ten men. Nor was it permitted to adorn a tomb with stucco-work or plaster, nor to place upon it herm pillars, as they are called. Speeches in praise of the deceased were also forbidden except at public funerals, and then allowed to be made only by orators officially appointed for that purpose. The gathering of large numbers of men and women was also forbidden, in order to limit the cries of mourning; for a crowd only increases the grief (*De leg.* 2.64–65).

Despite the large bibliography on this passage,[55] the vague nature of the *whole* passage is all too often overlooked.

The first problem arises with exactly what the passage entails. Does it refer to one law or to a number of laws from different eras between Solon and Demetrios? It seems that Cicero implies that it is one law, although this cannot be demonstrated conclusively. If this passage is citing regulations from a number of different laws, then nothing significant can be said about a date or a context for the regulations. If, however, the passage does refer to a single law, then a secure *terminus post quem* exists in the reference to public funeral orations, which were probably not occurring at Athens before 480 B.C.[56] But for many scholars the abrupt disappearance of grand archaic Attic grave stelai at the end of the sixth century B.C. proves too tempting, and this law has been dated by different scholars to the

---

55. R. Stupperich, *Staatsbegräbnis* (1977): 71–85; J. Kleine, *Untersuchungen zur Chronologie der attischen Kunst von Peisistratos bis Themistokles*, Istamb. Mitt., suppl. 8 (1973): 61–65; Kurtz and Boardman, *Burial Customs* (1971): 89f.; V. Zinserling, *Wiss. Zeitschr. F. Schiller Univ. Jena*, Gesellsch. u. sprachwiss. Reihe 14, no. 1 (1965): 29–34; G. Richter, *The Archaic Gravestones of Attica* (Greenwich, Conn., 1961): 38–39; *AJA* 49 (1945): 152; ead., *Archaic Attic Gravestones* (Cambridge, Mass., 1944): 91 n. 21 with bibliography; H. Moebius, *Die Ornamente der griechischen Grabstelen klassischer und nachklassischer Zeit* (Munich, 1968): 101 and 113; F. Eckstein, "Die attischen Grabmälergesetze," *Jahrb. Deutsch. Archäol. Inst.* 73 (1958): 18–29; id., review of C. Karouzos, *Aristodikos*, in *Götting. Gelehrte Anz.* 216 (1964): 167–70.

56. Which accepts W. Kierdorf, *Erlebnis und Darstellung der Perserkriege*, Hypomnemata 16 (Göttingen, 1966): 83–95; cf. also F. Jacoby, *JHS* 64 (1944): 37–66. E. Vanderpool, "Three Prize Vases," *Archaiologikon Deltion* 24a (1969): 1–5, has dated certain inscribed prizes from the Athenian state funeral games to c. 480 B.C. on the letter style.

eras of Solon, Peisistratus, Cleisthenes, and Themistocles. It is obvious that those who present such dates assume a priori that such a law must have been the work of a political reformer or tyrant or a "democratic" politician. That so many different candidates have been nominated would seem to indicate the futility of the whole enterprise.

Even in the best of circumstances, dating by archaeological evidence must allow for a margin of error greater than the chronological accuracy desired by the scholars trying to date this law. G. Richter finally had to abandon her attempt to date the law to the time of Peisistratus when, as she said, the evidence of new finds and scholarship had made the issue "an open question."[57] Any conclusions about the law's date derived from the evidence of Attic grave stelai (or lack thereof) must be open to serious question since very little of our evidence is found in situ.[58] More damaging for the archaeological argument is the fact that nothing mentioned in this law can be found to correspond securely with any archaic evidence. The architectural terms that Cicero uses are obscure, and any attempt to date the law by the disappearance of archaeological material assumes that the law would have been strictly enforced and obeyed, something that is unlikely.[59] To assume that this law was the work of a "democratic" reformer and then to attempt to date it is both methodologically flawed and futile.

Any attempt to say anything specific based on this passage is further undermined by Cicero's claim that he had seen such grand tombs at Athens (*quas in Ceramico videmus*). It is not likely that after the depredations of Philip V and Sulla there would have been much original material to see in the Kerameikos dating to such an early period. Jacoby has shown that the account of Pausanias, written in the second century A.D., was probably based on *Peri Mnatōn* of

---

57. Richter, *Archaic Attic Gravestones* (as in n. 55 above): 38–39.
58. Kurtz and Boardman, *Burial Customs* (1971): 84.
59. Even the movers and supporters of such legislation did not obey it themselves. Plutarch, *Sulla* 35, says that Sulla ignored his own law in the case of his wife's funeral. Cicero seems to have had little regard for the law of his own time concerning funerals; see *Att.* 12.35 and 36.1; Gelon (Diod. 11.38.2) had a moderate funeral but his tomb was noteworthy (*axiologon*). This last case highlights a fact that is significant. Most funeral legislation was directed against the conduct of the funeral, not at the size and cost of the tomb or memorial. Cf. also Kurtz and Boardman, *Burial Customs* (1971): 121f.

Diodorus of Athens, which is dated to the third century B.C.[60] Some material may have been restored in the cemetery[61] but it is hardly likely that any private graves of the late sixth and early fifth centuries B.C. would have been restored.

It is quite obvious that this whole passage of Cicero's was not written with the scholarly accuracy that modern standards demand. And since this is the case, very little can be said about it or based on it. To speculate about the mover and circumstances of this law quoted in Cicero may be interesting but it cannot be enlightening.

Lacking evidence to the contrary, a political motive can be plausibly maintained for the funerary legislation of Solon, and it may well have had the isonomic and democratizing effect that Nilsson and others have argued that it was intended to have.[62] But it must be remembered that Solon was credited with a number of laws that can have had no relation to the economic and political problems of his time. Among them were regulations regarding cult and ritual practice, along with an injunction against pederasty.[63] As in the cases of the treatises of Plato and Cicero, it is important to note that none of our ancient sources mentions a political motivation for Solon's funerary legislation. Aristotle's *Athenaion Politeia*, which provides most of our information about Solon's political and economic "reforms," does not even mention his funeral legislation. This is an important omission since it is obvious that a primary concern of the author of this tract was to trace the isonomic development of Athens.

Graves became lavish again at Athens in the fourth century B.C., and Cicero says that it was to curb this extravagance that Demetrios of Phaleron instituted his law regulating funeral practices (*De leg.* 2.66). Of all Greek funerary legislation, the circumstances surrounding Demetrios's enactment are the best known, yet there is nothing to indicate that it had any political purpose. As suggested above, the Kerameikos must have become crowded by this late date, and this may have been a consideration. Two scholars have suggested that Demetrios was acting out of Peripatetic repugnance against such funeral extravagance.[64] Evidence for this idea can be found in Dio-

60. F. Jacoby, *JHS* 44 (1944): 40 n. 2, 54.
61. As Pausanias seems to imply, 1.29.11; cf. also Jacoby, *JHS* 44 (1944): 40 n. 2.
62. Cf. n. 18 above.
63. Cf. Ruschenbusch, SOLONOS NOMOI (1966): F. 81 and 74 a–e.
64. E. Bayer, *Demetrios Phalereus, der Athener* (Darmstadt, 1969): 61ff.; W. Ferguson, *Hellenistic Athens* (London, 1911): 42; id., *Klio* 11 (1911): 269.

genes Laertius (5.53.61), who, in recording the supposed wills of Theophrastus and Strato, shows that a major concern of the Peripatetics was that their funerals be neither too mean nor too lavish.⁶⁵

This argument can be concluded as follows: to explain the occurrence and nature of Greek funerary legislation by local political issues has remained an attractive and plausible hypothesis because so much of this legislation was supposed to originate with tyrants and lawgivers who acted in periods of social unrest. But there is almost no evidence to support this hypothesis. The circumstances surrounding most of the early enactments are obscure and unknown, and none of the enactments of the classical period provide any evidence that isonomic motivation was a factor. The most persuasive case for such a hypothesis, the legislation of Solon, is, at the same time, the archetypal example of the Greek lawgiver whose name was invoked by antagonists in later political conflicts,⁶⁶ and who, over the course of time, came to be credited with all kinds of regulations that seemed of ancient ancestry in the community. It is obvious that the ancient sources never viewed the issue of funerary legislation as politically motivated. Funerary restrictions and tendencies toward it were probably as ancient as any regulations found in a Greek community, and they probably originated from a tendency to austerity that was common to Greek religious practice. Therefore, either the legal reformers were codifying what was, more or less, already the practice, or they were credited with laws that were not of their invention. Such an explanation can better deal with the anomaly that only one supposedly "democratic" reformer can plausibly be shown to have instituted such funerary legislation, and Solon's case cannot explain other, later cases of funerary restriction that were in no way related to economic and political difficulties.

5

Although it is not completely clear on first consideration, it seems that we have a relatively complete idea of what the contents of the tenth table were as it related to funerary restriction.⁶⁷ At *De leg.* 2.60

---

65. Cf. also Humphreys, *Family* (1982): 118f.
66. Cf. E. Ruschenbusch, *Historia* 7 (1958): 399–408.
67. There is only one part of the extant table not provided by Cicero, and that

Cicero says that the contents of the tenth table are in accordance with nature, which is the measure (*norma*) of law. The remaining material is according to custom. The sense of *reliqua* seems to imply that all other practices concerning funerals are other than those based in the law of the tenth table, and thus it would seem that Cicero has provided us with a reasonably complete picture of the substance of the tenth table as it related to funerals. It is improbable that Cicero would have neglected to mention other restrictions in the tenth table, especially if they related to the limiting of expenditures on funerals. We may not be able to assert that we have all the contents of the tenth table, but it does seem that we are not ignorant of any substantive regulations regarding the cost and lavishness of funerals.

If this is the case, then the tenth table takes on an anomalous aspect as a set of regulations motivated by the intent of limiting aristocratic display of wealth and prestige.

The latest finds of archaeological excavations indicate that lavish burials had ceased in Latium by c. 580 B.C. One could speculate with Cornell and others[68] that this demonstrates that the tenth table was only codifying what had been the practice at Rome for over a century before the Decemvirate. The tradition that such a prohibition went back to the time of Numa Pompilius would seem to lend credence to this theory.[69] Yet it must be remembered that most of the restrictions in the tenth table were not of a type that, if transgressed, would have left material evidence in the graves. This aspect of the issue is important since there was no prohibition against the building of monumental tombs or memorials, and this certainly would have been (and was) a means by which great families could demonstrate their wealth and prestige. Moreover, most of the funeral gifts found in the more lavish burials of eighth- and seventh-century Latium (especially various kinds of pottery, bronze vessels and weapons, and jewelry made of different materials) are not mentioned at all in the

---

comes from the first book of Varro's *Antiquitates* (cf. Festus, p. 154 M). It is clear that Varro discussed the tenth table both here and in the first book of his *De gente populi Romani*. The passage of the first book of the *Antiquitates* about the pouring of a myrrh drink on the corpse would seem to be part of, or related to, the prohibition of *sumptuosa respersio* mentioned by Cicero.

68. T. J. Cornell, *Archaeological Reports* (1979–80): 76, 83; G. Colonna, *PP* 32 (1977): 131ff.

69. Plut. *Numa* 12.1–2 and Pliny, *Nat. Hist.* 14.88.

tenth table. In fact, the scope of the restrictions in the tenth table leaves a great deal of room for display of wealth, yet the archaeological evidence attests that this was not the practice in Rome and Latium for over a century before the Decemvirate. If the tenth table was meant to limit the disruptive display of wealth at aristocratic funerals, it would not have been very effective, and, more importantly, it does not seem that there was such a problem at Rome in the mid–fifth century B.C. in any case.

As noted above, unlike the Greek tradition, which demonstrates a remarkably uniform and widespread practice of funerary regulation, the Roman tradition has little else other than the tenth table in this regard. Sulla instituted legislation in 81 B.C. that limited the expense of funerals,[70] and Cicero refers to a *poena legis* for too large a funeral monument.[71] This, along with two statements in Ovid and Cicero,[72] constitutes all the evidence for funeral legislation at Rome until the time of Augustus. It is not surprising that there should be funerary legislation at Rome dating from the first century B.C., but it is significant that there is no indication of any funerary regulation for almost four hundred years after the Twelve Tables.

Yet Rome had no lack of sumptuary legislation from the third century B.C. on. These were laws regarding clothing, food, and possessions, however, and they had no relation to funeral practice.[73] It is because this distinction between funerary regulation and strict sumptuary legislation has not been made that scholars have seen funerary regulation as part of a political program exercised against the aristocracy.[74] In the Greek tradition most of the archaic legal reformers and codifiers of law were credited with such sumptuary legislation, but there is nothing in the Twelve Tables that even remotely approaches what could be called sumptuary legislation in this sense. If

70. Plut. *Sulla* 35.3.
71. Cic. *Att.* 12.35. For speculation as to what law Cicero is referring to here, cf. R. Tyrrell and L. Purser, *The Correspondence of M. Tullius Cicero* V (London, 1897): dlxxvii, and D. Shackleton Bailey, *Cicero's Letters to Atticus* V (Cambridge, 1966): comm. on letter 274.
72. Ov. *Fasti* 6.663–64; Cic. *Phil.* 9.17.
73. B. Kübler, s.v. *sumptus*, *RE* IVA. 1: 901–8.
74. Cf., e.g., M. Bonamente, "Leggi suntuarie" (1980): 67ff., who opens her discussion by citing the tenth table as the earliest example of Roman sumptuary legislation. She simply assumes, without argument, that the tenth table is a form of sumptuary legislation, and discusses the table no further.

the tenth table were part of a program that, for whatever reasons, was intended to limit the disruptive and offensive display of aristocratic wealth, it is strange that there is no other evidence of such intent in either this or the other tables. When one considers the Roman attitude as demonstrated in later periods, it is hardly likely that such material, if it were in the Twelve Tables, would have been overlooked or forgotten. Three writers of much later periods provide summaries of Roman sumptuary legislation.[75] Two of these writers, Macrobius and Tertullian, wrote in the context of outrage at lavish display and indulgence. Yet none of these accounts contains any reference to funeral regulation or expenditure. Meager though the evidence is, it seems that the Roman tradition saw sumptuary legislation in a separate category from funeral regulation. During the Republic, the Romans were concerned frequently with the former, but very rarely, and only at the very beginning and at the very end, with the latter.

This paper has been concerned with demonstrating how the comparative method can present a better understanding of one supposed product of the Conflict of the Orders. Its purpose has been to show that the regulations in the tenth table are not a product of social disruption in archaic Rome and that the issue is much more complex and intricate. To attempt to explain why the tenth table was instituted would require another essay of similar length. Nevertheless, this paper can best conclude by suggesting a few factors that would seem to better explain the material in the tenth table in terms of primitive religious practices.

Studies of other primitive societies reveal that the practice of a second burial (such practice is implied in the tenth table by the prohibition against gathering bones for a second funeral and mentioned explicitly by Cicero, *De leg.* 2.60) can be a complex social and religious phenomenon, which can serve in some societies as the termination of mourning and the fulfillment of the death rite. In other primitive societies, funerals and secondary burials become occasions for regenerating exchange ties among members of the society, in some cases taking on a function similar to that of potlatch.[76] Thus the

---

75. Tertullian, *Apol.* 6.1–6; Gellius, *Noctes Atticae* 2.24; Macrob. *Sat.* 3.17.
76. S. C. Humphreys, "Death and Time," in ead. and H. King, eds., *Mortality* (1981): 268, summarizing the theory of R. Hertz concerning the secondary burial

whole complex of primary and secondary burials provides an opportunity for reaffirming social relationships through exchange. In at least one society, the whole process of primary and secondary burial can place a severe strain on the resources of the community members, and it is not difficult to understand why restriction might be imposed.[77]

The whole question of the disappearance of elaborate burials in Latium during the sixth century B.C. might be better understood by comparison with the disappearance of elaborate burials in England during the eighth century A.D. In the latter case, it is quite clear that the resources that would have been expended at funerals were dedicated instead to the new churches that were being built.[78] It is probably not simple coincidence that at the same time that the burials in Latium become less elaborate, public sanctuaries appeared in the region.[79] Such an idea is far more reasonable than the supposed "economic depression" that scholars have invented to explain this phenomenon.[80]

The practice of funerary restriction through law finds no parallel in other primitive societies, and this may be a function of the fact that, outside of the Graeco-Roman tradition, the practice of codification of law is rare at such an early stage. It is clear that Graeco-Roman religion found lavishness in religious rites repulsive, and it is significant that most of the funerary laws discussed in this paper concentrate on the conduct of the funeral itself; the restrictions regulate what material can be present at the funeral, how the mourners

---

marking the completion of the death rite; on the secondary burial as a form of exchange, cf. the articles by D. DeCoppet, "The Life-Giving Death," and A. Strathern, "Death as Exchange," in the same volume.

77. D. Miles, "Socio-Economic Aspects of Secondary Burial," *Oceania* 35 (1965): 161–74.

78. P. Rahtz, "Artefacts of Christian Death," in Humphreys and King, eds., *Mortality* (1981): 118.

79. G. Colonna, *PP* 32 (1977): 157f., notes the simultaneous occurrence of less elaborate burials during the sixth century B.C. and the development of public sanctuaries such as that of Sant'Omobono in Rome, but he fails to draw any correlation between the two.

80. On the too easily accepted assumption that tombs and their contents accurately reflect the prevailing economic conditions or the status and wealth of their occupants, cf. the comments of M. Torelli, *DArch* 4 (1970): 81f., and Humphreys, *Family* (1982): 172f.

are to conduct themselves, and how long the period of mourning is to last. These are the same elements of the funerary rite that are elaborately developed and regulated by ritual and tradition in other primitive societies. Clearly such matters would have had strong precedent in custom and practice in Greek and Roman communities long before the introduction of written law. To that extent, these laws would seem to be codifying known and accepted practice. Such an idea better explains the somewhat piecemeal approach toward regulation reflected even in the complete laws.

The anomaly of the existence of such regulations in the Twelve Tables also cannot be conclusively resolved in this paper. As has been demonstrated, the whole practice of funerary regulation, although common among the Greeks, seems to have been quite alien to the Italic tradition. The fact that three temples of Greek origin (those to Ceres, Mercury, and Apollo) were founded at Rome in the period before and around the time of the Decemvirate would seem to point to the factor of general Greek religious influence at Rome in this period.[81] In a similar vein, both the institution of the Decemvirate and the act of codification of law were Greek concepts. It took the Romans almost four centuries before they engaged in such funeral regulation again. Certainly, then, the tenth table must have been a factor of this Greek influence at Rome. We can assume, however, that there were compelling reasons in Rome of the mid–fifth century to submit to this particular kind of foreign influence. To put it simply, the Roman patricians would hardly have incorporated a whole table into their law code simply because it was "fashionable" in the Greek world to regulate funerary practice. However, little more can be said beyond that, and it does seem that a proper understanding of the tenth table would entail a long comparative study of primitive societies and their funerary rituals. The significance of the tenth table is more complicated than the simple equation of restriction with isonomy, and almost certainly the tenth table has nothing to do with the Conflict of the Orders and the complaints of the plebeians about the extravagant and oppressive rule of the patricians.

81. Cf. E. Bayer, *ANRW* I.1 (1972): 326–28, and Momigliano, *Contr.* V (1975): 328–31, on the foundation dates of these temples.

ROBERT DEVELIN

XI

The Integration of Plebeians into the Political Order After 366 B.C.

In 367 the Licinian-Sextian rogations were passed in full, identifying the issues that were to dominate patrician-plebeian politics for a considerable time.[1] They dealt with debt, possession of public land, and the reinstating of the consulship as the chief annual magistracy, with one consul to be plebeian. It was also secured that half of the *decemviri sacris faciundis* should be plebeian.[2] These hard-won concessions were only the beginning of a process that saw reinforcement of rights gained and further encroachment on patrician preserves, leading to

---

1. Sources in Broughton, *Magistrates* I (1951): 109. References to work of my own "elsewhere" indicate more detailed discussion in Develin, *Practice* (1985).
2. Livy 6.42.2. More on priesthoods below. Doubt as to whether the law of 367 did require one consul to be plebeian, as expressed by K. von Fritz, *Historia* 1 (1950): 3ff., can be met by an acceptance of what is subsequently in the text of Livy and a consideration of the nature of public law (on which see below).

relatively full, but never complete, plebeian participation in the constitutional order. This process was a long one. Sallust (*Hist.* fr. 11 Maurenbrecher) could end a very generalized discussion of discord between *patres* and *plebs* with the opinion that an end came only with the second Punic War, which ushered in an era of concord lasting until the destruction of Carthage.[3] But it was not until 172 that there were two plebeian consuls, not until 131 that the censorship followed suit, and certain patrician prerogatives survived the crumbling Republic.

Awareness of the difference between the orders persisted, but as time went on the odds were stacked against the patricians, whose numbers could at best remain constant, while those of the plebeians grew. Losses in war and the need to hold an extraordinary *lectio* in 216 to fill 177 vacant places in the Senate[4] would only have emphasized the numerical dominance of plebeians in the Senate. And as the number of praetors increased, more of these plebeian senators would have held *imperium*: between 197 and 180 plebeians held over 60 percent of the praetorships.[5] Such factors made the reservation of one consulship each year for a patrician anomalous and in the circumstances, it was hardly surprising that eventually two plebeians should form the consular college; though the *fasti* record the latter fact, Livy makes no remark. It would naturally take longer with the censorship.[6] In the religiously sensitive times of the Hannibalic War, the displeasure of the gods prevented a plebeian suffect joining the regularly elected plebeian consul,[7] but reality eventually won over tradition.

And yet, if we accept details in the historical tradition, these possibilities had been envisaged at a much earlier stage. Already in 342 a plebiscite could allow for two plebeian consuls, and by 339 it may have been established that both censors could be plebeian.[8] So we may be alerted to the fact that at least some plebeian politicians were pressing for the recognition that patricians had no god-given right

---

3. On this see Ungern-Sternberg's interpretation, chapter XII below at nn. 75ff., but cf. n. 59 below.
4. Livy 23.22f.; this represented over half the Senate.
5. Develin, *Patterns* (1979): 47; the trend continued.
6. On which see Develin, *Antichthon* 14 (1980): 84ff.
7. Develin, *Journ. of Rel. Hist.* 10 (1978): 14ff.
8. Livy 7.42.2; 8.12.16. On both matters, see below part 2.

to any sort of major monopoly. And yet we shall see that in some respects patricians were to maintain a special position.

This is not the place for full-scale discussion. Rather we may aim to consider the bases of plebeian successes and patrician reactions, to understand the nature of the issues and the political system in which they were advanced. The treatment is organized under three headings: Information, Constitution, Politics. There is nothing new in this, and my stance may be called old-fashioned: the fundamental necessity is attention to the information we possess and the establishment of sensible criteria that will allow its maximum utilization. This is not to say that the conclusions of such an approach will be conventional. Comparative elements from antiquity may be admitted with caution. Let me say at once, however, that I am wary of the importation into the study of Roman politics of purported insights derived from the social sciences. Excessive zeal for sociological input can have dangerous results, and even a more balanced application may try to dress up as scientific method, which it strictly is not, the educated imagination that has long been evident and must be allowed in the examination of foggy antiquity.

1. Information

Our major source for the two centuries after 366 is, of course, Livy.[9] Polybius has little to offer on political matters at Rome, and there is not much else in the way of independent additions that serves to elucidate rather than confuse, issues. It is to be hoped that Luce's recent excellent treatment of Livy will help to turn the tide against the hypercritical emphasis on that historian's perceived shortcomings. Livy was alive to the sort of distortive practices to be found in his predecessors and in family records. He lets us know this as he ends book 8.

> I think the record has been vitiated by funeral eulogies and false subscriptions on busts, as each family appropriates to itself the

---

9. Other contributions to this volume have dealt with the historical tradition, but I am concerned only to put my own views and that too only as they relate to the material dealt with in this paper. Let me merely say that I am in general sympathy

fame of achievements and magistracies won, with deceptive misrepresentations; as a result of this, confusion has certainly affected the deeds of individuals and public records of events. Nor is there available any writer contemporary with those times to provide a sufficiently reliable authority by which to take a stand. (8.40.4)

Such awareness did not necessarily make Livy immune to misrepresentations, but it does provide a starting point for an assessment of the information provided by him.

However we choose to view Livy, specific items stand to be judged on their own merits and with regard to the means by which accurate record may have survived. And here I may introduce a parallel of sorts from the history of Athens. There it has long been orthodox to believe[10] that accounts given by individual Atthidographers, prominently Androtion, especially concerning matters of more remote antiquity, could be informed by political tendency; that the work of Solon, to take a central example, could be reconstructed according to the committed imagination of historian, pamphleteer, or determined politician. Distortion of fact could therefore have influenced the surviving account in the Aristotelian *Constitution of the Athenians*, an offshoot, if you will, of the *Atthis*. We may also observe this sort of thinking in discussions of Roman historiography, applied a fortiori, I suppose, to the earliest times, but nonetheless visible in our period. Livy, it is said, was the dupe of his predecessors, who reconstructed early Roman history to suit their contemporary interests, or in the light of later conditions. As it is asked how anyone could know, say, the early history of the Areiopagos or what exactly Solon did, so the record of fourth-century Rome is questioned.

The parallel is real: in both cases history began to be written at a relatively late stage and dealt with matters already of considerable antiquity. Just what could the writers find out, and why should we suppose that they were disinclined to invent and distort, coming as

---

with the remarks of Cornell in chapter II above and rather skeptical about the views presented by Raaflaub in chapter I, especially part 2, above, and by Ungern-Sternberg in chapter III. Detailed discussion is not possible here, but, given the state of much current opinion, there is perhaps a need for points to be repeated in any case.

10. See most recently the discussion by P. J. Rhodes, *Comm. Ath. Pol.* (1981): 15ff., with an attempt at balance.

they did from the upper, political levels of society? Well, the reaction in the Athenian area has begun. The capacity of the Atthidographer to invent for political reasons has been properly questioned[11] and the survival of genuine and documentary evidence vigorously defended.[12] There are signs that the long overdue reassessment of information surviving on our Roman period is in train. It has been remarkable to see how much is confidently stated about early Roman historians based upon the scanty remains of their work.

Fact must always be distinguished from interpretation. The Atthidographers, so far as we can see, agreed for the most part on fact.[13] This left ample opportunity for differences of interpretation, be they informed by political or historical considerations. It is not necessary to invent facts to put a slant on history. So in the literary genre that was history by Livy's time, authors did not need to distort basic data, at least to any great degree, in order to mold the same events into different shapes. Thus, even if one wishes to believe in an anti-Claudian tradition,[14] one need not as a consequence disbelieve the facts of Claudian activity as presented. It is indeed equally possible (some of us would say more likely) that the Claudii were indeed individualists capable of acting in an outrageous or unconventional manner.[15] I find it difficult to believe that actions have been invented wholesale simply to discredit a family. Similarly, I have said that the invention of early Valerian laws on *provocatio* by Valerius Antias would be as implausible as it was unnecessary.[16] In a continuing historical tradition—a point that will bear repeating—outright inventions would be unlikely to find a permanent place.[17] On the other

11. P. Harding, *Historia* 26 (1977): 148ff.; Develin, *Athenaeum*, n. s., 62 (1984): 295ff.
12. R. S. Stroud, "State Documents" (1978): 20ff.
13. F. Jacoby, *Atthis* (1949): 119ff.
14. See, most recently, T. P. Wiseman, *Clio's Cosmetics* (1979): 57ff.
15. The tale of Claudii behaving in an untoward manner continues into what must be regarded as historical times, despite Wiseman's emphasis on rhetorical overlay (again, interpretation or presentation is different from fact), with the consuls of 249 (Broughton, Magistrates I [1951]: 214) and 185 (Livy 39.32.5ff.), the father-in-law of Tib. Gracchus, and the infamous tribune who was Cicero's bête noire—and this is to follow only one branch of the *gens*.
16. Develin, *Mnemosyne* 31 (1978): 48ff.
17. On the Athenian side, cf. Develin, *Athenaeum*, n. s., 62 (1984): 295ff. Perhaps I should state that I am not eliminating altogether the possibility of invented details finding their way into surviving histories. I am simply providing reasons for a more positive approach to the evidence in general. The essential method demands that,

hand, a family such as the Claudii could not deny actions everyone knew their ancestors had taken, though they might be able to obscure them or put a different construction on them.

Our job, then, is to be careful in identifying elements of interpretation apart from the bare bones of fact and then to ask questions first about the fact. A particular problem with the Conflict of the Orders, of course, is that it would be likely to be drawn in colors influenced by later events. The terms used and the presentation of the issues might not precisely reflect what was actually the case.[18] But so much should be obvious and with due caution it ought to be possible to trace events with a large degree of probability. Negative ideas need not dominate and it is not fundamentalist (a popular and misused term) to be willing to accept, after proper consideration, what intelligent Romans believed.

We may briefly consider the channels by which information may have survived. Family records (a broad term) would be one, and at least they could provide information, if it were needed, for the reconstruction of the *fasti*. In most respects we must surely accept the list of magistrates, despite some problems, such as the dictator years.[19] Too many families had a stake in the matter to allow falsifications to thrive in great number. Naturally, families would also recall achievements and actions of their ancestors, though, as Livy saw, not always accurately, and their memories could be selective and rosy. But then one family's memories would cross with another's and so on, allowing a composite picture to be built up, not necessarily balanced, but controlled to some degree.

One finds folk memory invoked most often as a means of casting doubt as to fact, and indeed, at a general level, there would have been anecdotes and even sagas surviving in the mouths of folk. We may try to appreciate what the nature of these survivals may have been. Stories that did continue to be told (compare perhaps the story of Kylon's conspiracy in Athens) ipso facto maintained appeal and even relevance and could have incidentally provided clues to antique

---

although wider concepts may be borne in mind, each item stands to be judged in itself. Though scholarly consensus is too much to hope for, the general lines of a credible history can surely be sketched.

18. For an example of this, see below at n. 60 on Maenius and the events of 314.

19. On which see now the thorough and revealing article of A. Drummond, *Historia* 27 (1978): 550ff. Livy at any rate was not taken in by this fiction.

institutions. Whether the parallel is useful, I leave to the reader to decide, but many of the traditional ballads of Great Britain, which, though initially written, survived orally, dealt with evidently historical events and in their own right reflected social and economic conditions. Though initially people at large might receive news of the major internal and external events by word of mouth, from the sixteenth to the nineteenth century in England occurrences and issues of note could be cast in the form of songs and issued on broadside sheets. Even when newspapers existed, they were beyond the resources of the lower classes, for whom broadsides were a substitute. And not a few of these songs survived in oral circulation well beyond the time of their immediate relevance. Such accounts were by their nature embellished and popularized. One can well imagine, then, a stock of stories (or songs) existing at the general level, but for the historians tales kept alive among the political aristocracy, conscious of its past, would probably have been more important. This approximates to what I call institutionalized memory, given that the aristocracy could be called a continuing institution. But there is a much more concrete sense in which the term may be used.

One important area where one must, I think, have confidence in the record is legislation. Whether or not there were archival documents, and whatever was included in the pontifical chronicle, laws provided the living, continuing basis for constitutional, institutional, social, and economic activities. Functioning law was *mos* and took its place with nonstatutory *mos* in the canon of behavior.[20] Important legislation could be remembered without reference to statutes themselves and would be embedded in the consciousness of those participating in a continuing system. Laws might also reveal the origin or eventual solidification of a practice; it is clear that recollection of "firsts" was a dominant feature and a successful vehicle: the first plebeian consul, censor, dictator, praetor, pontifex maximus, the first proconsul, and so on. Here, I repeat, we are surely on firm ground, though each item of legislation yet requires examination in its own right.

As for fact, then, it is not at all difficult to believe that essential data were accurately retained in record or memory, and the despair

20. Texts on this are many; see the collection by H. Rech, *Mos maiorum* (1936): 14ff., 40ff. In his *Timaeus* (11.38) Cicero, translating Plato's *nomos*, writes *veteri legi morique parendum est*.

of those who believe that proper historical investigation is hardly possible before the third Samnite War, or even later, is entirely unwarranted. As for interpretations, those of an ancient historian, though presented in a manner generally alien to modern historical methods, may be judged in the same way as any such interpretations, with due attention to the author's aims, concerns, and preconceptions, conscious and unconscious influences from later events, and so on. There is a challenge here that is well worth taking up.

2. Constitution

The political struggles of the plebeians would be resolved ultimately through constitutional channels and in constitutional enactments. It is vital, therefore, that we have a proper understanding of the workings of the system, the concepts it involved, and the practicalities it had to recognize.

The *comitia centuriata* that elected magistrates with *imperium*—consuls, praetors, and censors[21]—were heavily stacked in favor of the upper class. In fact, until the reform of the second half of the third century, the second-class votes were in theory, and probably most often in practice, unnecessary to achieve an electoral result.[22] The prerogative vote, being religiously sanctioned, gave an almost compulsory lead to the votes of subsequent centuries.[23] This vote was exercised by the centuries of *equites*, eighteen in all, including the senators in the *sex suffragia*, until, perhaps as a concomitant of the reform, it was given to a junior century of the first class chosen by lot, while the *equites* proper voted with the first class and the *sex suffragia* voted separately after it. Thus, though the patricians at the beginning of our period may have had a considerable influence on the voting, this would have been gradually eroded as plebeians began to dominate the senate numerically. As I have argued, however, the re-

---

21. Censors are controversial; I believe they had a limited *imperium*. See F. Cancelli, *Censores* (1957): 1ff., modified in *Labeo* 6 (1960): 225ff.; Versnel, *Triumphus* (1970): 338f.

22. On the matters treated in this paragraph, see Develin, *Athenaeum* 56 (1978): 346ff.; *RhM* 122 (1979): 155ff.

23. See below at nn. 33ff. on matters of religion.

form was not political, but military.²⁴ It must be recognized from the start that the vast majority of the voters who counted were wealthy plebeians, and herein must have lain a powerful weapon in favor of plebeian politicians. This would come into play also if a plebeian, such as Q. Publilius Philo as dictator in 339, used these *comitia* for legislative purposes.²⁵

And yet it is clear that this force could be negated. Although the law of 367 enjoined the election of one plebeian consul, in the 350s and 340s we find all-patrician colleges in some years. We are told on one occasion (Livy 7.18.3–10) that the plebeians deserted the *comitia* in great numbers, which we might have assumed in any case, but that cannot be the whole story, and this action was a consequence of measures already taken. There would have been a patrician reaction such that the presiding officer would refuse to countenance plebeian candidates. The patricians could have recourse to an interregnum (whether or not that meant greater control on electoral procedure,²⁶ interreges would be patrician) or a dictator might be used, with his overriding *imperium*, but the elections for 354 were conducted by the consuls (more properly, one of the consuls). One may suspect that some of the plebeians already admitted to the highest offices may have collaborated in this in an effort to protect their charmed position, but this cannot be pressed. At any rate we have sufficient background to understand the need to reassert plebeian rights to the consulship in 342 (Livy 7.42.2). Livy tells us that not all annalists included the laws of Genucius, and this particular measure is recorded as laying down that *both* consuls could be plebeians. Hence doubts in

---

24. The political explanation of N. Rouland, *Clientèle* (1979): 174ff., does not seem to me to make historical sense.

25. As is also relevant to what will be said later, I continue to believe, as I argued in *Athenaeum* 53 (1975): 302ff.; 55 (1977): 425ff., that there were never *comitia tributa populi*, but tribal assemblies were always plebeian, even if in the late Republic consuls could preside over them, this despite C. Nicolet, *Rome* I (1977): 341; the important text cited by Nicolet is *CIL* I² 2500, which may require some revision of my stated views on Frontinus, *De aquis* 2.129 (*Athenaeum* 53 [1975]: 315) and Cic. *Pro Planc.* 35 (*Antichthon* 12 [1978]: 47f.).

26. I do not believe that it did, thus agreeing with J. Jahn, *Interregnum* (1970): 50ff., against E. S. Staveley, *Historia* 3 (1954–55): 193ff. On the dictatorship, see R. Rilinger, *Wahlleiter* (1976): 16ff. and 24ff. Rilinger unfortunately accepts the probably erroneous view that the interrex named only one consul; on this see now E. S. Gruen, *CSCA* 11 (1978): 73f.

modern discussions.²⁷ It is not an argument against these terms that the impact of the law was not felt until 172; possibility does not mean likelihood, and tradition alone, with a perception of the importance of patricians to the state (see below), could have maintained one consulship for patricians. Perhaps Genucius's law was cast as it was to emphasize plebeian rights more strongly, or it represents an insistence that was not pressed by other plebeians and did not become reality. But this law and a concomitant ban on iteration within ten years (also perhaps the prohibition on cumulation of magistracies in a given year), which for a time was valid among plebeians, could have been aimed at assuring a continuing augmentation of plebeian representatives at the highest level, taking into account not only patrician colleges but the exclusivity of plebeian *gentes* who had already made it. Indeed, these laws were passed by a Genucius, a member of a family that had been one of the first to provide plebeian consuls, but which seems to have suffered after the failure of the consul of 362. Let us remark a point we shall discuss later—that it remained possible as late as the 290s for a patrician to press for an all-patrician college.

It will be well here to emphasize the fallible nature of this sort of legislation. Though plebiscites might be weaker than full *leges*, such status need not be invoked to explain why the Licinian law was not respected. For such laws contained nothing to say what would happen if their terms were not implemented.²⁸ The Roman account was aware of this; Livy says (7.21) that in the elections for 352, plebeian pressure led to the Senate telling the interrex to observe the *lex Licinia*. There was no necessity for this to happen and no legal recourse if it did not. The same also applied, as I have argued, to laws "guaranteeing" the right of *provocatio*, which needed to be reaffirmed in 300 for reasons now lost to us.²⁹ One simply has to envisage a situa-

27. Most recently J.-C. Richard, *Historia* 28 (1979): 65ff.
28. On this and the following, see Develin, *Mnemosyne* 31 (1978): 45ff.
29. I cannot accept the argument of R. A. Bauman, *Historia* 22 (1973): 34ff. He thinks that the law of 300 arose from an unfavorable attitude to the dictator's immunity to appeal on the part of the Valerii from 325 on. But the events of 325 do not seem recent enough to have been a factor, there is no reason to believe the dictatorship was a particular problem in this regard, and some more general difficulties in the final years of the century would provide a more immediate context. Why, in any case, should the Valerii have waited so long? It was more in the nature of Roman legislation to respond to contingent circumstances.

tion where magistrates were using or threatening summary jurisdiction without granting the right of appeal. This at least bears testimony to a considerable degree of tension continuing at Rome.

The argument on repeated legislation I have also applied to laws stating the full validity of plebiscites. Here, as with *provocatio*, we are dealing with full *leges*, not plebiscites. There was obviously a problem in making the principle stick. In 339 came the second law, but yet another emerged from the problems that led to the appointment of Q. Hortensius (whoever he was) as dictator in 287 or 286. Again we are unaware of the precise circumstances that made this necessary, but one thinks most naturally in terms of a refusal by patricians (or indeed others) to recognize the validity of specific plebiscites.[30] In 339 one may look to the Genucian plebiscite and more generally to laws dealing with plebeian rights to office, in 287/86 to recent attempts to alleviate economic distress and the possibility of similar future attempts.

Though more details will emerge in the next section, one may draw a picture of constitutional issues not easily solved. Some patricians at least endeavored to stymie or to minimize the advancement of plebeian interests. Short of exercising whatever influence they may have had,[31] they could do nothing directly to prevent the plebeian tribal assembly passing whatever measures the tribunes put before it, and similarly they had no means of controlling electoral results in this assembly (of which they were not members) once candidates were known. But statutory demands that plebeian votes should be binding on all were always susceptible to the patricians' ability to claim that the plebeian assembly did not represent or affect them. It took a long time for this issue to result in *mos*.

The tribal assembly had evidently long been used for the election of minor officials as well as for legislation. Small wonder that hard upon the creation of the curule aedileship, it was opened to the plebeians in alternate years, especially if the tribes did the voting.[32]

---

30. On 287/86, see G. Forni, *Athenaeum* 31 (1953): 200ff., and, with a different explanation, Ungern-Sternberg, chapter XII below at nn. 50f.

31. I am aware that I am skating over this issue, but I address it in *Practice* (1985). The word *clientela* will not appear in the body of my text, and I cannot see that understanding of it has been advanced by Rouland, *Clientèle* (1979).

32. Livy 7.1. I wonder if Livy's remark that the patricians were able to secure the aedileship for two of their own *gratia campestri* must mean centuriate election. Given

But the consulship represented the important victory, and other offices of *imperium* had eventually to fall to plebeians. The censorship came in 351 with the election, though not unchallenged, of C. Marcius Rutilus (Livy 7.22.7–10). But the censorship was relatively unimportant until the end of the century. Much more striking is Marcius's dictatorship in 356 (Livy 7.17.6), successful despite patrician obstruction. Presumably Marcius was nominated by the plebeian consul of the year. It was not until 336 that a plebeian praetor was chosen, despite an attempt to thwart this by the patrician consul of 337 (Livy 8.15.9); the Senate opted not to join this opposition. Until that time the consulship had been the main issue, but now plebeians had access to all other sorts of *imperium*, and the issue could not be fought. In terms of eligibility for office, then, the battle had been sooner won.

While giving due attention to the tale of plebeian advancement, one cannot, I think, properly understand the constitutional issues without looking at patrician prerogatives that were less easily stolen and at elements that went unchallenged. There were conceptual areas evidently understood by all, and at the end of this section we shall see vivid testimony to the fact.

The Roman constitution was replete with religious elements with which the patricians had a particular association.[33] In general, all executive, electoral, and legislative business was carried out with due consideration of heaven's favor. The very power concept of *imperium* was a religious one, strikingly illustrated in the nomination of a dictator. But all *potestas* was gained by a grant of *auspicium* through a *lex*

---

plebeian dominance of the *centuriata*, the point is not so important. Later aedilician elections were tribal. *Verecundia*, mentioned by Livy, seems a tame reason for the *patres* to concede the point to the *plebs*.

33. On other religious matters, see the contributions of Linderski, chapter VIII above, and Mitchell, chapter V above, the latter of which contains much interesting material, even if in the service of an erroneous thesis that ascribes invention of the political struggle to the annalists—a fabrication for which they had no need, so far as I can see—and imagines in the historical tradition a loss of memory as to the actual state of affairs that is beyond belief. The part of religious elements as a defining principle between patricians and plebeians is not to be doubted, but the elevation of the religious aspect to the extent of eliminating the political involves an argumentative process that begins with possibilities and modulates quickly into ever more confident expressions that, when stripped bare, are revealed as virtual *obiter dicta*. The process of counter-argument would be lengthy and is, I suggest, quite unnecessary.

curiata; the consul operating outside the city (and the dictator) held full *auspicia populi Romani*.[34] In 362 L. Genucius was the first plebeian, we are told, to hold *auspicia* in the field.[35] His failure is represented by Livy as provoking in the patrician Ap. Claudius the argument that plebeian holding of *auspicia* struck at the foundations of the state. Rhetoric aside, this must, I believe, be taken seriously. One cannot ignore the effect of patrician self-interest, but I have argued elsewhere[36] that religious matters were not viewed lightly, and indeed that manipulation of religion to political ends cannot be baldly assumed. When the possibility of an all-plebeian consular college arose in 215 (Livy 23.31.7–14), nervous ears and not necessarily political calculation could have created the clap of ominous thunder that negated the election. And by that time plebeian augurs were well established. We have mentioned that in 367 plebeians had been admitted to half of the places in the college of *decemviri sacris faciundis*, who concerned themselves largely with portents, but the pontifical and augural colleges, so intimately concerned with law and procedure, were not so opened up until 300, on the heels of the publication of the *legis actiones* and in circumstances to be mentioned in the next section.

Confirmed traditional ideas may have helped the patricians maintain a monopoly of these major priesthoods for so long, just as these explain their continuing retention of flaminates. This traditionalist thinking goes a long way toward explaining other phenomena. Never was the dominance of wealth in the centuriate assembly the subject of popular complaint;[37] Cicero (*De re pub.* 2.22.39) describes and defends the ideology. People at large were content to let others hold office and make decisions, and plebeian politicians had no interest in disrupting the system. The same principle may be transferred to tribal assemblies. Recent calculations of voter turnout in the late Republic[38] can perhaps be retrojected: relatively few would

---

34. I have argued for this in *Mnemosyne* 30 (1977): 49ff.

35. Livy 7.6.7ff. If this is correct, it has consequences for understanding the authority of plebeian military tribunes *consulari potestate*, none of whom can have held full military *imperium*; this can perhaps be tested, but not here.

36. See Develin, *Journ. of Rel. Hist.* 10 (1978): 3ff.

37. The proposal of C. Gracchus to revolutionize voting order in the *comitia centuriata* (Sall. *Ad Caes. sen.* 2.8) was not made law.

38. R. MacMullen, "How Many Romans Voted?," *Athenaeum* 58 (1980): 454ff.; cf. Nicolet, *Citizen* (1980): 291.

ever vote in regular circumstances, and so even *comitia tributa* would be dominated by the wealthy and city dwellers (though by the latter only in four tribes), unless, of course, there was an issue that dramatically affected the lower orders.

Within the system the patricians, who alone, they claimed, had *auspicia privata*, had a privileged religious position. The interregnum was always conducted by patricians; the *patres* guaranteed the continuity of *imperium* and the *auspicia*.[39] Also unchallenged as a constitutional necessity was the *auctoritas patrum*,[40] the sanction given by the patricians to the results of centuriate voting, although it was emended, a fact that lends itself to interpretation. In 339 one of Publilius Philo's measures had the *patrum auctoritas* placed before, rather than after (as previously), legislative votes. Later, on a particular occasion Curius Dentatus is reported to have forced the *patres* to give their *auctoritas* before an election, which presumes that the *lex Maenia* establishing this as a rule was not then in force.[41] The *patres*, it seems, were gradually compelled to show their hand before the vote; the fact that this was first required for legislation and that it was only much later extended to elections shows where the major concern resided. In 339 Philo attempted to make plebiscites binding on all, and it is no surprise to find him turning his attention also to the plebeian-dominated *centuriata*. Likewise the *lex Maenia* would fit well in the aftermath of the *lex Hortensia*. Yet there was no attempt to suggest that *patrum auctoritas* be dispensed with.

The perception that patricians did have a special place in the constitution may help explain why for so long one consulship and one censorship were reserved for a patrician and why the *princeps senatus* was always a patrician, a fact for which there is no other ready expla-

---

39. See P. Voci in *Studi in memoria di E. Albertario*, edited by V. Arangio-Ruiz et al., II (1953): 92f. On the *interregnum*, see E. S. Staveley, *Historia* 3 (1954–55): 193ff.; Jahn, *Interregnum* (1970); E. Friezer, *Mnemosyne* 12 (1959): 301ff.; A. Magdelain, "*Auspicia*" (1964): 427ff.

40. For the survival of this to the time of Cicero, see G. Branca, "Cic. *De Domo* 14.38 e *patrum auctoritas*," *Iura* 20 (1969): 49ff.

41. Philo: Livy 8.12.15; Dentatus: Cic. *Brutus* 14.55: *De vir. ill.* 34.3 (for doubts see Staveley, *Historia* 3 [1954–55]: 201 and n. 4; also G. V. Sumner, *The Orators in Cicero's Brutus: Prosopography and Chronology*, Phoenix, suppl. 11 [1973]: 28f.; G. Forni, *Athenaeum* 31 [1953]: 187ff.). On the *lex Maenia*, see Broughton, *Magistrates* I (1951): 193; if the law was passed by the consul of 338 (Staveley, loc. cit.) we should expect to have been told so.

nation. We have, it seems, to bear in mind this aspect of plebeian thinking, and conceptual awareness may help us to understand the two items with which I conclude this section.

Until perhaps the Hannibalic War, when pressures led to its rescinding, there was a rule that forbade senators from becoming tribunes.[42] Unfortunately we do not know from when this rule applied. We are told that plebeians had been chosen into the Senate by consuls and military tribunes before the Ovinian plebiscite of (perhaps) around 314 (Festus, p. 290 L), but again we cannot date the beginning of plebeian entry to the Senate. But, leaving aside any political explanation, what our rule seems to suggest is a belief in the separateness of various sorts of offices. Those thus banned from the tribunate would have entered the Senate, presumably after holding one of the full magistracies of the people; such an office once having been held, it was not felt proper that the sectional magistracy of the tribunate should follow. Some such concept provides a link with the second and more peculiar item.[43]

There was a law—so far as we know never rescinded and never contravened until 49—that forbade anyone with a father alive who had held curule office to hold plebeian office. This presumably dated from after 366, and, given that it restricted opportunities for rising political careers, it ought to be interpreted as embodying an accepted principle. Even when they could be held by plebeians, the full offices of state could be referred to as *patricii magistratus*, and within these the curule offices were a special group.[44] This is evidence for a continuing concept of the magistracies that shared in the *auspicia* as patrician by nature, and an idea that plebeians in these offices came into contact with something patrician; Cicero (*De domo* 14.38) could say "if patrician magistrates are not elected, the auspices of the Roman people must perish." The fact that the sons of men who had come into contact with the majesty of curule office were restricted by the law in question demonstrates the strength of the concepts involved. A qualitative difference between curule and

42. Develin, *CQ* 28 (1978): 141ff.
43. Develin, *Antichthon* 15 (1981): 111ff. I have indicated in this paper that, in my view, this regulation was not concerned with the matter of *patria potestas*, as is supposed by Ungern-Sternberg (chapter XII below at nn. 10f.).
44. Mommsen, *Röm. Staatsrecht* I³ (1887): 18 and n. 2, 402. See also G. Lobrano, *SDHI* 41 (1975): 245ff.

plebeian magistracies was accepted by plebeians and patricians alike without question, and the idea embedded in law would have emerged as the principles upon which the patrician-plebeian constitution would operate were worked out in the years after 366. Common ground could be established.

3. Politics

The questions that need consideration in this area are more readily delineated than answered, and it is by no means easy to separate patrician-plebeian struggles from general political practice. We need to ponder relationships between patricians and plebeians and, conversely, the degree of coherence that may have existed among plebeian politicians. We need to form some idea about the nature and extent of political problems. Then there is also the matter of the connection between the aspirations of plebeian politicians and the discontent evidenced at lower levels. We meet problems at every turn, and it is important to stress the limits of our evidence. We rarely have full data on careers such as might enable us to determine why and how certain plebeians came to prominence when they did. The vexed question of the origins of plebeian families, and whether these origins can yield explanations for particular elections or elucidate possible concerns, is simply stated here without further development. There are sufficient problems left to address.

Let me at once sound a warning on prosopographical "method" that deduces factions from *fasti* or behavior. I will not here go into the supposition of factions based on policy alternatives, of which the most prominent example is the work of F. Cassola on the third century in particular, except to notice the weakness of any attempt to identify patrician or plebeian policies in regard to external affairs.[45] Nor will I discuss in detail factional explanations that have been offered in the cases to be mentioned. It is, however, necessary to probe the use of the *fasti* in prosopography. I begin with the years immediately following 366.

---

45. See E. T. Salmon, *Samnium* (1967): 282.

The consular *fasti* for 366–61 and 360–56 were as follows:

(a)	366	L. Aemilius L. Sextius	(b)	360	M. Fabius C. Poetilius
	365	L. Genucius Q. Servilius		359	M. Popillius Cn. Manlius
	364	C. Sulpicius C. Licinius		358	C. Fabius C. Plautius
	363	Gn. Genucius L. Aemilius		357	C. Marcius Cn. Manlius
	362	Q. Servilius L. Genucius		356	M. Fabius M. Popillius
	361	C. Licinius C. Sulpicius			

The repeated names in each set are tempting fodder for factional speculation and can lead to statements such as that of A. J. Toynbee: "The peaceful revolution of 357 (364 or 363) B.C. had been made by a coalition between the aspiring upper layer of the plebs and an open-minded and prescient minority of the patriciate."[46] But the patricians prominent in the years 366 to 361 were not those who appear as connected with the plebeian cause earlier. M. Fabius Ambustus had married his daughter to C. Licinius Stolo, and by cooperating with Licinius and Sextius (so it is said) became popular with the *plebs*:[47] Fabii appear as consuls only from 360 on. So, too, with the Manlii, and the dictator Manlius is said to have claimed a close relationship in choosing Licinius as *magister equitum*. On the other hand, for example, L. Aemilius Mamercinus, *cos.* 366, was *magister equitum* to the dictator M. Furius Camillus, who was bitterly opposed to plebeian demands. One may suspect, therefore, that the patricians put forward as consuls men who would not indulge their plebeian colleagues. Of the other patrician consuls, Q. Servilius Ahala in 362 appointed Ap. Claudius dictator *consensu patriciorum* (Livy 7.6.12),

---

46. Toynbee, *Hannibal's Legacy* I (1965): 321 and n. 2; also, of course, F. Münzer, *Adelsparteien* (1920): 8ff.; cf. J. Heurgon, *Capoue préromaine* (1942): 247ff.

47. On this and what follows, see Livy 6.34ff.

and C. Sulpicius Peticus was to share in three all-patrician colleges, in 355, 353, and 351.

So the *fasti* are suspect evidence for patrician-plebeian collaboration, and it continues to be difficult to draw neat and meaningful factional lines. The plebeian families represented in the first six consulships failed to establish a pattern of continuing success at that level. The picture is one of patrician recalcitrance continuing into the 350s, despite a somewhat quieter period and the appearance of plebeians whose families would maintain success. One can easily see how some patricians may have seen virtue and reward in collaboration with plebeians, but the evidence does not allow us to identify them, and it would appear that when there were problems, loyalty to the order won out. All-patrician colleges in the 350s and 340s are stark evidence of attempted reaction by the patricians. The work of R. Rilinger[48] has shown a desire on the part of the patricians to avoid having plebeians conduct elections: when the possibility arose, they could resort to an interregnum or dictatorship. The account of Livy bears examination.

After a long interval, an interregnum was used in 356 to secure the election of two patricians.[49] Central to this was the major plebeian figure C. Marcius Rutilus, consul in 357 and the first plebeian dictator in 356, who was obstructed by the *patres* and avoided by them as president of the elections. When later he announced his candidature for the censorship of 351, he met patrician opposition (Livy 7.22.7–10). Despite possible attempts at cooperation between patricians and plebeians,[50] the problems continued. The interreges who oversaw the elections for 355 were the same men who had been consuls since 366. The consuls of 355 saw to the election of patrician successors, despite the absence of many voters (7.18.3–10) and, the *plebs* being distracted by debt problems, two patricians could again be chosen for 353 (7.19.5f.). More determined plebeian opposition eventually led to the *lex Licinia* being observed,[51] after a protracted struggle; but patrician success came again in 351, Livy claiming that

48. Rilinger, *Wahlleiter* (1976), especially 52.
49. Livy 7.17.10ff.; J. Jahn, *Interregnum* (1970): 64ff.
50. M. Popillius Laenas, who as consul in 356 would have nominated Marcius dictator, had as consul in 359 allayed a plebeian *seditio*; Cic. *Brut.* 14.56. Cf. Münzer, *Adelsparteien* (1920): 27ff., on these years.
51. Livy 7.21; Jahn, *Interregnum* (1970): 69f.

the *plebs* was better disposed due to debt relief.[52] The choice of a dictator to hold elections for 350, deliberately made, we are told, to prevent the Licinian law being observed, did not have the desired effect,[53] but the next year the same expedient was successful.[54] The *plebs* was not happy with this, and for the next three years plebeians were consuls. We next have patrician colleges in 345 and 343, with only a hint in Livy (7.28.9f.) of patrician machination.

Nothing of a factional nature can sensibly be made of the evidence. What we do see is the possibility that some plebeians at least might work with patricians to assuage popular anger, yet all plebeians might unite against patrician attempts to return to a monopoly of the consulship. The early iterations did tend to create a closed group of plebeian notables, such that it may have provoked the law of 342 prohibiting iteration within ten years. That plebeians were concerned with their own political activities as well is evidenced by the fact that the law of 358 against *ambitus* was concerned with the behavior of new men and was brought by a plebeian tribune who was at least of a consular house, if not consular himself (Livy 7.15.12).

The early years of the plebeian consulship, then, were marked particularly by attempts by the patricians to minimize the success of the plebeians and maximize their own, perhaps with a residual hope that their consular monopoly might be restored. For we must not assume that it was accepted that plebeian consuls were there to stay, even in a spasmodic fashion; that still had to be established as *mos*. It was in 342 that plebeian determination produced the definitive word on the matter. The patricians had been aided by what looks like an attempt at exclusivity on the part of a number of plebeian consular *gentes*. That, too, was henceforth to be moderated.

After 342, or more precisely after 340, we have a series of new names in the consulship, a process that eventually slowed and was for a time halted by the need for iterations,[55] to resume at the end of the century, after which the influx of new men took on a regular pattern.[56] It is difficult to assess whether or not various new plebeian

---

52. Livy 7.22.1ff.; Jahn, *Interregnum* (1970): 71.
53. Livy 7.22.10f.; Jahn, *Interregnum* (1970): 71.
54. Livy 7.24.11; Jahn, *Interregnum* (1970): 72.
55. That there was a need will be argued in Develin, *Practice* (1985).
56. Develin, *Patterns* (1979): 49ff.

consuls had any association with their colleagues or with others and whether or not we can thus explain their election. Intermarriage between the orders was, of course, a reality, and associations in general would grow up. But in the absence of specific evidence—and there is very little of that—conclusions are dangerous. Specific evidence we do have for the friendship of C. Fabricius Luscinus and Q. Aemilius Papus, consuls in 282 and 278 and censors in 275 (Cicero *De amic.* 11.39), and by this time in the third century we are entitled to assume a mixed nobility largely reconciled and with the advantage in association not always going necessarily to the plebeians.

This is not to suggest that the reconciliation of the orders came about quickly. Episodes arise that, however we decide to interpret them, are presented in terms of patrician-plebeian conflict. There is the dictatorship of Q. Publilius Philo in 339, critically presented by Livy (8.12.4–17), and we have seen how a patrician consul was prepared to oppose Philo's suit for the praetorship of 336 (Livy 8.15.9). In 327 the tribunes complained that it was the dictator's plebeian rank that led the augurs (still patrician of course) to declare him *vitio creatus*.[57] In the context of Ap. Claudius Caecus's censorship (312), we are told of the resumption of contention between patrician magistrates and tribunes after a period of quiet (Livy 9.33.3ff.). One may wonder if the Ovinian plebiscite, which probably preceded Caecus's censorship, came about because of plebeian discontent at methods of selection into the Senate (more on this period below). Caecus figures as the patrician representative in the contentious debate leading to plebeian access to the augurate and pontificate in 300 (Livy 10.6.4ff.) and again as a voice for patrician consular colleges in the 290s.[58] Then there was the sedition leading to the dictatorship of 287/86.

And so some individual patricians, at least, might set themselves against further encroachments by plebeians, or might seek to take advantage of critical situations to revive the memory of old prerogatives. Tensions were not easily resolved or forgotten. Yet the formation over time of a mixed political order would change the nature of

---

57. Livy 8.22.13ff.; Jahn, *Interregnum* (1970): 87ff.; Rilinger, *Wahlleiter* (1976): 20f., 52. It must not be assumed that I necessarily accept the tradition in these instances.

58. Livy 10.15.7ff.; Cic. *Brut.* 14.55; *De vir. ill.* 34.3. See also n. 41 above.

the dispute, and though provocative tribunes, such as C. Flaminius in 232, might always appear, their activities were not likely to be directed only against patricians.[59] Though the nature of conflict in the political arena might change, however, the terminology used to describe it need not. Indeed, the influence of later events may well have shaped the terms in which earlier ones were presented. It is with this in mind that we may look at an episode from the year 314 that we cannot afford to ignore.[60]

C. Maenius was made dictator to look into conspiracies in Campania, subsequently being instructed to turn his attention to Rome and any who had joined together against the *res publica*: "and coalitions [*coitiones*] made for the sake of gaining office were against the *res publica*." He widened the enquiry, and *nobiles homines* were indicted. Tribunes would not respond to their appeal. All the nobles, not only those charged, declared that such accusations could not apply to *nobiles*, for whom, trickery aside, the road to honors lay open, but rather to new men—such as the dictator and his *magister equitum*. When Maenius and his *magister equitum* abdicated, they were tried and acquitted, as was Publilius Philo, "hated by the nobility." The enquiry did not persist at the highest level, but went lower, until the

---

59. On Flaminius, see Develin, *AC* 45 (1976): 638ff.; *RhM* 122 (1979): 268ff. I might say here that the contention of Ungern-Sternberg, chapter XII below, that the Conflict of the Orders, if in altered form, continued until the Hannibalic War seems to me erroneous and starts from an overconfident reliance on Livy F 12, as I shall argue elsewhere. Once that fragment is set aside, all the other items mentioned can be otherwise interpreted.

60. Livy 9.26.5ff. Discussion will be found in Toynbee, *Hannibal's Legacy* I (1965): 320; Heurgon, *Capoue préromaine* (1942): 279; F. Cassola, *Gruppi politici* (1962): 127f.; Staveley, *Historia* 8 (1959): 427ff.; A. W. Lintott, *Historia* 21 (1972): 631; E. J. Phillips, *Athenaeum* 50 (1972): 343ff. Here, as elsewhere, I hesitate to refer to the work of E. Ferenczy (for this episode, *AAH* 13 [1965]: 395); his articles are synthesized in his *Patr. State* (1976), which not everyone seems to find as feeble and erroneous as for the most part I do. When it comes to the treatment of the period involving Ap. Claudius Caecus, which is central to his work, he imagines the dates of the offices Caecus held previous to his censorship and so is able to insert him into areas of contention such as that which concerns us here. Such involvement is not mentioned in our sources, which is at least noteworthy, given the attention that Caecus attracted. Ferenczy also indulges in the very worst sort of mechanical prosopography from the *fasti* in defiance of the ancient tradition. Hence his overall view of politics and factions is wrong. In a matter where I have strong views (to be detailed elsewhere), I fear I cannot be tolerant.

very *coitiones* and *factiones* that were the object of investigation put an end to it.

Political interpretations are imaginative. It is hard to know how far to strip away layers of interpretative embellishment. It is peculiar to find the patrician Folius classed along with his dictator, Maenius. What does seem to emerge is that the *nobiles* portrayed were patricians. The *fasti* before and after 314 suggest nothing explicitly about the workings of *coitiones*. We are in the middle of the period 321 to 308, for which we do not know of any new men, so that if there were *coitiones* on their part, they were prodigious failures. It is suggested that the *coitiones*, involving *viliora capita*, operated to the advantage of either new men or *nobiles*. Yet there is no indication that any convictions resulted, and the charges may have had no substance, the whole affair arising out of tensions inherent in the difficult external situation. But the era of patrician-plebeian struggle was not over and it may be possible (though not here) to salvage something from the episode, which is also within tempting range of the Ovinian plebiscite (probably) and the censorship of Ap. Claudius Caecus.

But, as I have intimated, attention must be paid to the terms used if we are to base any interpretation upon a sound footing and use this episode as evidence for anything of substance. What is involved is the stock opposition of new men and *nobiles*, an obvious caution in itself. On a strict reading, the *nobiles* in the Maenius affair must be patricians, as they are implicitly in the account of 304 (Livy 9.46.1ff.) and certainly in that of the elections for 296 (Livy 10.15.7ff.). But the problems over the election of C. Terentius Varro to the consulship of 216 are cast in the same terms,[61] although we cannot see it as a patrician-plebeian conflict. So we realize that we cannot rely on the words used in describing the events of 314 as a reliable index of the issues involved.

This does not mean, however, that there is no basis to the story, and neither is it unlikely that an investigation by a plebeian dictator, going beyond what was expected, excited latent tensions between patricians and plebeians. Moreover, the presentation of the issue is such that it moves us in the direction of other questions. One is the

---

61. Livy 22.33.9ff., on which see most recently E. S. Gruen, *CSCA* 11 (1978): 61ff. Similar to a degree is the description of Cato's path to the censorship: Livy 37.57.15; 39.41.1ff.

attitude of plebeian politicians who had achieved success and had the opportunity to create a political tradition for their families, and what implications this may have had for the influx of new men. Another concerns the relationship between the plebeian nobility and the *plebs* as a whole, since the *coitiones* of Maenius's time are said to have involved *viliora capita*, "commoners." To these matters we may turn briefly.

We are, I think, able to conclude that the plebeians fell in with the mechanisms that led to political success, and though new men could succeed, there were comprehensible forces at work that favored established families. The plebeian nobility, as it developed, could adopt the exclusive habits of their patrician counterparts, but the very nature of things prevented the same degree of exclusivity. New men came in steadily, and we can see chances for success without dependence on established families (again Flaminius is the classic case). Credentials could be established through regular military channels (consider the career of P. Decius Mus., *tr. mil.* 343, *cos.* 340) and/or through political channels; the tribunate, on which we are so miserably informed, offered a particular vehicle for plebeians, but it was not a great deal of use unless there were issues a tribune could take up. Many plebeians could be tribune, few could move up from there, and among those who did a few *gentes* only managed to maintain a consular record. From 299 to 200, thirty-five plebeian *gentes* produced consuls, of which seven supplied fifty-one.[62] This would result not only from the interests of the *gentes* concerned, but also from the general conservatism of the electorate.

But it has been well noted that political explanations need to go beyond examination of leaders alone.[63] We may ask here how far plebeian politicians found a natural constituency in the lower levels of society with their particular problems. Some have seen this association as vital to the plebeian politicians' success against the patricians.[64] We may bear in mind also, however, that plebeian politicians,

---

62. Cf. Develin, *Patterns* (1979): 49 (which erroneously says six). Given the dominance of these few *gentes* and the limited number of patrician consular *gentes*, there would be a natural coincidence of names in the *fasti* such as ought further to weaken the chances of factional reconstruction.

63. L. Stone, "Prosopography," *Daedalus* 100 (1971): 62ff.

64. See P. A. Brunt, *Conflicts* (1971): 55f. G. E. M. de Ste. Croix, *Class Struggle* (1981): 332ff., makes an attempt (unsuccessfully?) to make the Conflict of the Orders a class struggle.

who were in competition with one another for positions of authority, may have been rivals for the support of this constituency.

Debt and economic hardship run throughout the plebeian story. According to Livy (6.35), it was felt that the debt problem could only be solved by securing high office for plebeians. It remained a factor in plebeian discontent, and it is said to have distracted attention from patrician consular monopoly in 354/53 (Livy 7.19.5f.). Economic problems added to the volatility of the continuing situation, putting pressure on the *patres*; in 352 *quinqueviri mensarii* were chosen and did a good job.[65] As portrayed, debt problems certainly fed into the political situation, but we struggle to put it into perspective. At first sight it seems incredible that economic relief should cause pressure for a plebeian consulship to abate (Livy 7.22.1–3), but we should not be too ready to assume that, even if plebeian politicians could respond to these problems, their political demands were of overriding importance to people at large. We may recall that Livy tells us (6.39.2) that once the *plebs* approved the Licinian-Sextian rogations dealing with debt and the agrarian situation, but not that on the consulship. Some have and doubtless will disbelieve this, but it is a comprehensible index of what really concerned people at large.

There is no need here to discuss all the instances where these economic troubles again came to the fore.[66] But we do need to be aware of the possibilities. Plebeian politicians would have relied most upon the voters in the first-class centuries for elections to offices with *imperium*, and perhaps indeed for lower positions too—that is, upon men, like themselves, of high economic status. Yet it is comprehensible that they should have sought at least vocal support from the lower levels in times of political crisis, and that this should count for something. Yet there was a problem if the politicians were more closely associated with, and were indeed part of, the class of creditors. For nothing concerned the mass of people more than their economic well-being, and they would have had to be persuaded that politicians could have their interests at heart. In social terms it might be a great mistake to draw the line between patricians and the *plebs*

---

65. Livy 7.21.5ff. The three plebeians on the commission perhaps all became consul if C. Duillius is in fact K. Duillius, *cos.* 336.

66. See now C. G. Starr, *Beginnings* (1980): 42, on public land, and 46 on control of interest rates and the abolition of *nexum*.

as a whole, including the politicians, for the common man might rather have lumped all politicians together. From the other point of view, all politicians might have viewed the social turbulence that came with economic hardship as threatening to their common interests. Nevertheless, economic and political issues had gone hand in hand from the days when the patricians were the political masters, and it was from plebeians that the depressed elements might expect promises of relief. And politicians not associated with the existing establishment would be more credible sponsors of measures in aid of the poor. None of the plebeian *quinqueviri* of 352 was of a family yet consular. We might expect to find *viliora capita* in whatever political organizations new men fostered. And, what is more, genuine concern could be exhibited. Economic concerns formed at least part of the background to the final plebeian secession and the legislation of Hortensius in 287/86. M'. Curius Dentatus had to do with distributions of land, and we even have him with a band of young supporters prepared for action and attacking the Senate before the people.[67] The need for plebiscites to be binding on all may have had a direct connection with a popular desire that the plebeians control their own destiny. But again our sources do not help.

We have now come to an era when clearly enough the patrician-plebeian Senate was the focus of protest. If plebeian politicians fought patricians for political rights and in so doing associated themselves at times with the plight of their less fortunate brethren, with the establishment of the patrician-plebeian nobility grievances such as arose at the lower levels no longer bore the same significance. Richard Mitchell's thesis that there was no political Conflict of the Orders (chapter V above), that this was an invention of historiography, seems to me quite out of the question. Through Livy in particular we have the record of a comprehensible process wherein plebeians had to combat patrician opposition for some twenty-five years after the *lex Licinia* and then slowly and spasmodically worked their way into the system more fully, as conflict broke out occasionally and ever less appropriately. Conservatism was a potent force on all sides and had a role in determining the pace of change. The traditions of

---

67. Livy, *Per.* 11; Appian, *Samn.* 5. See G. Forni, *Athenaeum* 31 (1953): 193ff.; W. V. Harris, *War* (1979): 180.

aristocratic politics sat well with the plebeian aristocracy, for whom, having once gained a share in the orchard, there was little reason to upset the apple cart. Later problems were of a different order.

We move on another century before we find the next advance in the plebeian story. There will be those who struggle to find a factional explanation behind the fact that two plebeians were elected consul for 172, and they may construct a group of plebeians, perhaps new men, pressing for this. But Livy's silence on the matter is eloquent and needs no explanation.[68] Already for 179 the patrician consul had been born brother of his plebeian colleague. As a memory from the past, the patrician-plebeian conflict may have impinged upon the consciousness of politicians, but it was no longer a living issue with practical implications.

It may seem that this paper is out of place in a volume that promises new approaches. The point is that we have not yet exhausted the possibilities of the old. Whatever help we may be able to summon from comparative data or perspectives derived from other disciplines (and I repeat that I have seen little of value in that regard), we shall ultimately be reliant upon information pertaining solely to the events under study. We must engage in intense scrutiny of the literary evidence, identifying the conceptual framework of the language used and the intentions of the author, identifying factual and interpretative layers, trying to understand the legal and social framework. And let us, as our editor enjoins, keep our minds open, but concentrated, and above all think out the method we are to follow and make it clear to those who must suffer what we write.

68. For a recent attempt, see P. Botteri Pellizer, "Un silenzio politico (Livio 42, 9,8ss)," *Quaderni di storia* 7 (1978): 217ff.

JÜRGEN VON UNGERN-STERNBERG

XII

The End of the Conflict of the Orders

1

The traditional picture of the Conflict of the Orders is primarily determined by Livy's account of the prehistory of the first *secessio plebis*, the temporary emigration of the plebeians from Rome. There the impoverished plebeians, who have been driven from home and farm and are threatened by debt-bondage, confront the cruel and proud

---

This essay is a revised and expanded version of my inaugural lecture at the University of Basel (February 13, 1980), which was published in German as "Das Ende des Ständekampfes," in *Studien zur antiken Sozialgeschichte: Festschrift F. Vittinghoff* (Cologne and Vienna, 1980): 101ff. I would like to thank Iris Werthmüller, Mark Toher, and Kurt Raaflaub for the translation into English. Sections 1 and 4 have been added to the original text. Additional bibliographical references are indicated by square brackets. The translations are from the editions in the Loeb Classical Library.

patricians. In several attempts they try to find solutions for the debt problem. Several times the patricians, pressured by the assault of external enemies, make concessions, only to take them back as soon as victory is secured. Finally the plebeian army leaves the city in protest and occupies the *Mons Sacer* (or the Aventine); as a result of the ensuing negotiations, the tribunate of the *plebs* is established as an office explicitly charged with the protection of the plebeians. It quickly comes to symbolize the liberty of the people.

Modern scholars have come up with a much more differentiated view of the *plebs*. Certainly there were plebeians who were dispossessed, often heavily indebted, and threatened by the harsh customary law regulating debt and obligations. But in addition to *proletarii*, the Twelve Tables already know of *adsidui*, i.e., landowners. Since in the fifth century voting was reorganized according to property classes (the so-called Servian centuriate system), clearly there must have been many plebeians who owned substantial property. In addition, we have to expect that aristocratic families who migrated from other cities to Rome but were not accepted into the ranks of the patricians soon played a leading role among the plebeians.

Accordingly, the nature of the Conflict of the Orders is seen differently by modern scholars. On the plebeian side, it seems to have been fought by some kind of coalition. Whereas the majority were mostly interested in achieving some alleviation of the debt burden and in being allotted more and better farmland, the socially prominent plebeians aimed at equality with the patricians, both in matters of private law and in political and religious life. They demanded, therefore, that intermarriage of patricians and plebeians be officially permitted, and they wanted plebeians to be eligible for magistracies and priesthoods. They were the natural candidates for the plebeian offices (the tribunate and aedileship) and became powerful leaders of the separate plebeian community. Ultimately, both groups profited from this coalition, though not to the same extent and not at the same time. The wealthy and noble plebeians gained access to magistracies and priesthoods in the course of the fourth century, but the economic situation of the plebeian lower classes changed later and more slowly: after initial gains in the fourth century, lasting improvements were achieved only in the third century and probably only as a result of large-scale territorial expansion.

Such a view of the Conflict of the Orders helps to explain why it was occasionally fought in revolutionary forms but never became a revolution. For its goal never was to change social conditions radically or substantially to democratize political life at Rome. Certainly none of the participants thought of introducing the Athenian model of radical democracy. The prominent plebeian families considered themselves equal in social standing to the patrician *gentes*. Their prestige was based on the same economic and social foundations—namely, large-scale landed property and *clientelae*. Both groups together were developing a new, elaborate and imposing life style. Without major difficulties, therefore, they melted into a new social and political elite, the "nobility," already in the second half of the fourth century. Together they aimed at establishing against upstarts and newcomers the same kind of exclusiveness that previously the patricians had successfully maintained for such a long time.

On the basis of all this, it seems justified to a certain extent that modern scholars usually assume a sharp break around the years 300–287, a break that separates the early Republic as the period of the Conflict of the Orders from the classical Republic as the period of unchallenged rule by the nobility. Such precisely dated divisions between historical epochs are always problematical, however, and even more so when dealing with social conflicts: major questions tend to be obscured or forgotten. In particular, it remains unclear in most modern accounts, what the other, non-noble plebeians thought about all this. Did they, too, stop feeling opposed to the patricians? Even the most general considerations speak against such an assumption. It was hardly due to Roman conservatism alone that, just as before, year after year ten tribunes of the *plebs* and two plebeian aediles were elected—that is, that the organizational structures of the separate plebeian community continued to exist and to function. Further, we ought to wonder why precisely at that time, in 287 B.C., the *lex Hortensia* turned the decrees of the *plebs* (*plebiscita*) into laws (*leges*) that bound the whole citizen body (*populus*), including the patricians. Finally, it was again in that same period (300 B.C.) that the protection of the individual citizen against magisterial execution (*ius provocationis*) was recognized as a legal "right" by a *lex Valeria*. Why was that necessary? After all, the time was long gone when there were only patrician consuls to invoke martial law against the plebeians; now there were plebeian consuls, one every year, who could have prevented oppressive measures against their fellow plebeians.

In other words, previous analyses of the end of the Conflict of the Orders have been one-sided and insufficient. By focusing on the prominent families and leaders, the other plebeians were lost from sight. Accordingly, the problem of how the emergence of the patrician-plebeian nobility affected the plebeians in their entirety has largely been neglected.

2

There exists, however, an important reason for such a gap in present scholarship. Since books 11–20 of Livy's history are lost, we do not have any detailed account of the years 292–219 B.C., which are crucial in our context. Yet there are a few testimonia. At least in part, they are concerned with rather specific matters, which cannot easily be presented and require some detailed discussion. But, taken together, the results of such discussion will offer important clues and enable us to formulate an answer to our question.

More than a hundred years ago, P. Krüger edited and Th. Mommsen commented upon a fragment from the twentieth book of Livy's history, or more probably from an ancient summary of its content (*periocha*):

> Publius Cloelius,[1] a patrician, was the first to go against the ancient custom by marrying a wife within the seventh degree of relationship. On this account Marcus Rutilius, a plebeian, complained that his betrothed was taken from him by an unprecedented sort of marriage; he stirred up a riot of the people so severe that the senators in terror took refuge on the Capitol.[2]

Since its first edition, this fragment has often been quoted in works on Roman marriage law.[3] Nevertheless, its significance for the internal development of Rome in the third century B.C. has hardly been

---

1. The manuscript gives the plebeian *nomen gentile* Celius (Caelius or Coelius).
2. Fr. 12 W.; Krüger and Mommsen, "Anecdoton Livianum," *Hermes* 4 (1870): 371–76 = Mommsen, *Ges. Schr.* VII (1909): 163ff.
3. M. Kaser, *Privatr.* I² (1971): 316.

appreciated so far. It was referred to only by L. Lange,[4] who called it a "testimony for the tensions between the nobility and the people"; later it was also mentioned by J. M. Nap,[5] though he interpreted it in a rather problematic way. Perhaps violent actions of the plebeians against the patricians contrast all too much with the generally accepted view of the years between 241 and 219 B.C., the period covered by the lost twentieth book: "*sed ut mirandi causa iusta est, ita nulla est dubitandi*" (Mommsen, *Ges. Schr.* VII: 167).

First of all, it was natural that the antagonism between the orders was manifested precisely in questions of marriage. The ban on intermarriage in the Twelve Tables and the so-called *lex Canuleia* provide examples of this, and the story of the maiden from Ardea (Livy 4.9–10), despite its legendary nature, may reflect such antagonism as well.[6] Further, it is interesting to note that at a later time marriages between relatives within the fourth degree were permitted due to pressure caused by rivalries between the orders. According to Plutarch's account (*Quaest. Rom.* 6 = *Mor.* 265d–e), a poor man was accused on the ground that he had married his cousin, a rich heiress. But since he enjoyed greater popularity with the people than all the "politicians" (the formula οἱ πολιτευόμενοι probably includes all the senators, or at least the *nobiles*), the people dismissed the charge and permitted marriage between cousins by a special law.[7]

It is, however, remarkable that in the fragment of Livy the antagonism between plebeians and patricians shifts to one between the people and the Senate: all the *patres* are frightened and seek refuge

---

4. Lange, *Altertümer* II³ (1879): 152. His reference to Plutarch (*Pomp.* 30.4) is ingenious. There, in his futile struggle against the *lex Manilia*, Q. Lutatius Catulus urges the Senate "to seek out a mountain, as their forefathers had done, or a lofty rock, whither they might fly for refuge and preserve their freedom." However, Catulus may well refer to the *secessio plebis in montem sacrum* (as K.-H. Ziegler suggests in his translation in the Bibliothek der Alten Welt), which would be an ironic reversal of the former events. In any case, it is hardly appropriate to relate it to the successful defense of the Capitol against the Gauls, as do R. Flacelière and E. Chambry in the Coll. Budé ed.

5. Nap, *Republik* (1935): 90ff., 412ff.

6. Cf. Ogilvie, *Comm.* (1965): 546ff.; Nap, *Republik* (1935): 91ff., is very imaginative.

7. Cf. W. Kunkel, *RE* 14 (1930): 2266, s.v. *matrimonium*. E. Weiss, *ZRG* 29 (1908): 355, unsuccessfully attempts to connect Livy fr. 12 directly with Plut. *Quaest. Rom.* 6.

on the Capitol. Yet, since the end of the fourth century at the latest,[8] the leading plebeians who had attained the consulship or the praetorship ranked among the *patres* as well. Consequently, the people now perceived themselves to be as remote and alienated from them as from the patricians.[9]

A series of laws from the period between the first two Punic Wars can be connected with this observation:

A. In 209 the plebeian aedile C. Servilius Geminus was accused of illegally holding his aedileship as well as the preceding tribunate because it was discovered that his father of praetorian rank, who had been believed dead, was still held captive by the Gauls (Livy 27.21.10). When he was consul in 203 Servilius succeeded in freeing his father. The people decreed "that it should not be a ground for charges against Gaius Servilius that while his father, who had occupied a curule chair, was still alive—a fact of which he was unaware—he had been tribune of the *plebs* and plebeian aedile, contrary to provisions of the laws" (Livy 30.19.9). Obviously the sons of a father who had held a curule office were prohibited during his lifetime from holding an office of the separate plebeian community.[10] Such a restriction plainly presupposes a collision of interests between the representatives of the *plebs* and the Senate (including those plebeians who had reached political equality with the patricians); it attempts at least to prevent the father from exerting massive pressure on a plebeian magistrate by means of his *patria potestas*.[11]

B. Ateius Capito states: "For the tribune of the *plebs* also had the

---

8. J. Bleicken, *Lex* (1975): 378ff.

9. Accordingly, in Plutarch's narrative this is also the social dividing line.

10. A different interpretation by Mommsen, *Röm. Staatsrecht* I³ (1887): 487 n. 2, has been refuted by F. Münzer, *Adelsparteien* (1920): 137ff., and especially by A. Aymard, *REA* 45 (1943): 204ff. But, as Aymard points out (ibid., 209f.), Münzer's own doubts are equally unfounded. According to our (admittedly all too fragmentary) evidence, all the tribunes of the *plebs* and the plebeian aediles between 232 (for this date, see below) and 200 comply with this legal restriction. [Cf. now R. Develin, *Antichthon* 15 (1981): 111ff., and chapter XI above at n. 43, where, however, the law is dated earlier and interpreted differently.]

11. Cf. L. Lange, *Altertümer* II³ (1879): 152; Nap, *Republik* (1935): 412f.; A. Aymard, *REA* 45 (1943): 217ff. (who points out the danger of tribunician *intercessio* against colleagues who were eager to undertake reforms); G. De Sanctis, *Storia* IV.1² (1969): 524. [It is interesting to note in this context that C. Servilius's father carried out the *transitio ad plebem*, doubtless in order to raise the family's prestige; cf. Münzer. *Adelsparteien* (1920): 139; Bleicken, *Volkstribunat*² (1968): 95 with n. 1.]

right of convening the Senate although before the law of Atinius they were not senators" (Gellius, *Noctes Atticae* 14.8.2). According to the prevailing view, the Atinian law generally made the former tribunes regular members of the Senate.[12] Yet R. Develin[13] has established that such an interpretation is contradicted by the context in Gellius, where the tribunes before the *lex Atinia* are being compared with the *praefectus urbi Latinarum causa*—that is, with an official who, for reasons of age, may not be a senator. Consequently, before the *Atinium plebiscitum* the senators were generally prohibited from holding the tribunate. It corresponds with this observation that Zonaras (Cassius Dio) 7.15 mentions as the third stage in the relationship between the tribunate and the Senate that former tribunes could be admitted to the Senate (by no means all, and there obviously was no obligation to do so), whereas only in the fourth stage did senators themselves aspire to the tribunate.

R. Develin quite plausibly connects the Atinian law with the extraordinary *lectio senatus* in 216 B.C., after the battle of Cannae. The Senate, reduced in numbers by heavy casualties, was at that time replenished with numerous men who had not held any office before (Livy 23.23.6). They could hardly be debarred from candidacy for the tribunate. This date of the Atinian law, of course, cannot claim any certainty. For our purposes, however, it is sufficient to conclude that for a long time after the formation of the patrician-plebeian Senate, the tribunes, who were the plebeians' representatives par excellence, could not be members of this body while holding their office. Again the intention seems to have been to avoid the risk of a conflict of interests.

C. The *lex Claudia de nave senatorum* of 218 (?) was also aimed at imposing certain restrictions upon the Senate (Livy 21.63.3–4). Furthermore, the fact that senators' sons were included emphasizes to what extent the senatorial families were perceived as an order. Whether or not the *lex Claudia* indeed had the long-term effect of stabilizing or actually defining the *ordo senatorum*,[14] we cannot doubt

---

12. Mommsen, *Röm. Staatsrecht* III.2 (1888): 862; Bleicken, *Volkstribunat*² (1968): 23 n. 3.
13. R. Develin, *CQ* 28 (1978): 141ff., and chapter XI above at n. 42.
14. E. Meyer, *Staat*³ (1964): 96f.; Bleicken, *Lex* (1975): 172f.; id., *Verfassung* (1975): 50ff., 63ff. Roman laws usually did not aim at long-term effects; see below at

the accuracy of Livy's report that the law was passed against vehement opposition of the Senate. Apparently large sections of the citizen body were in favor of restricting the senators' economic activities, either in the interest of other businessmen[15] or on the principle of separating politics and business—or possibly even for both reasons.[16] At any rate, in this case, too, the gap between *plebs* and Senate is evident.[17]

According to Livy, C. Flaminius was the only senator to back the Claudian law. Although he thereby attracted the hostility of the *nobiles* (*invidiam apud nobilitatem*), at the same time he won the favor of the masses (*favorem apud plebem*) and, as a result, was elected consul for the second time (217).[18] But at that time the name of Flaminius was already associated with former vehement confrontations between Senate and people, especially the dispute about the *lex agraria* he had introduced in 232 when he was tribune of the *plebs*.[19]

Polybius accuses Flaminius of being "the originator of this popular policy that we must pronounce to have been, one may say, the first step in the demoralization of the populace, as well as the cause of the war with the Gauls that followed,"[20] a judgment that has often been

---

n. 53, but also Bleicken, *Lex*, 182f. [Th. Schleich, "Überlegungen zum Problem senatorischer Handelsaktivitäten," *Münstersche Beiträge zur ant. Handelsgeschichte* 3 (1984): 47ff.]

15. Z. Yavetz, *Athenaeum* 40 (1962): 325ff.; F. De Martino, *Cost.* II² (1973): 306ff.

16. Meier, *Res publica amissa* (1966): 123f., 313. [C. Nicolet, *Annales ESC* 35 (1980): 871ff. A. Guarino, *Labeo* 28 (1982): 7ff., connects the law with the crisis at the beginning of the second Punic War.]

17. The contemporary *lex Metilia de fullonibus* (220 or 217: T. R. S. Broughton, *Magistrates* I [1951]: 236, 244) cannot be considered here: that it was especially directed against senatorial display of luxury cannot be inferred from the sole reference to it in Pliny, *Nat. Hist.* 35.197f.; contra: Bleicken, *Volkstribunat*² (1968): 31f.; cf. Yavetz, *Athenaeum* 40 (1962): 340. [See further I. Sauerwein, *Leges sumpt.* (1970): 36ff.; G. Clemente, "Leggi sul lusso" (1981): 4f. A possible amendment of Fest. p. 470 L. to <*lege Fla*>*minia minus solvendi* has been considered but we can only speculate; cf. R. Develin, *RhM* 122 (1979): 269f.; more optimistically, C. Nicolet, *Historia* 28 (1979): 291f.]

18. D. Kienast, *Gnomon* 29 (1957): 108, and C. Meier, *Res publica amissa* (1966): 61 n. 192, doubt whether he was really the only senatorial supporter. The question is rather irrelevant; at least he was the only prominent senator to support the law. [For the following, cf. the very stimulating discussion by C. A. M. Triebel, *Ackergesetze* (1980): 17ff., 62ff.]

19. For the date, see Broughton, *Magistrates* I (1951): 225.

20. Polyb. 2.21.8; cf. 3.80.3.

interpreted as having been influenced by the tribunate of Ti. Sempronius Gracchus (133 B.C.). The very fact that Cicero repeatedly mentions Flaminius among the forerunners of the late Roman *populares* may have contributed to this view,[21] but recently K. Bringmann has shown it to be incorrect.[22] Polybius claims the greatest stability and balance for the Roman constitution in the time of Cannae and thereafter.[23] He only begins to consider the possibility of its degeneration in the period of Rome's undisputed supremacy after 168 (6.57). He therefore simply cannot have dated the change for the worse at Rome to the year 232. Consequently, here he reflects the opinion of his source, Fabius Pictor, whose unfavorable view of Flaminius is apparent in other parts of Polybius's narrative as well.[24] Probably it was motivated to a large extent by the fact that Q. Fabius Maximus, a member of Fabius Pictor's own *gens*, had been the project's principal opponent (Cicero, *Cato* 11). What we must understand, therefore, is what precisely it was in Flaminius's actions that made them so offensive to the Senate of the third century B.C. In answering this question, we have to distinguish between the actual conflict of the year 232 and the later judgment on the whole political activity and achievement of Flaminius.

It was the aim of the *lex agraria* to distribute the *ager Gallicus* south of Ariminum *viritim* (Cato, fr. 43 P). Polybius interprets this as a cause of the Gallic War of 225–22, since the adjoining Gauls felt threatened by the colonists and were therefore prompted to take preventive action. But such a view hardly seems credible. The citizen colony of Sena Gallica had been founded c. 283; the vast Latin fortress of Ariminum in 268. Why should the Gauls so much later consider Roman settlements even farther south a special threat?[25] Furthermore, this by no means could be considered an argument of

---

21. Cic. *Acad. prior.* 2.13; cf. id. *De inv.* 2.52; *De leg.* 3.20.
22. Bringmann, *A&A* 23 (1977): 30f. Ed. Meyer, *Kl. Schr.* I² (1924): 374, in particular, related Polybius's opinion to the political activity of Tiberius Gracchus; thus also G. A. Lehmann, "Polybius" (1974): 195 n. 1; and M. Caltabiano, *CISA* 4 (1976): 102ff. (with an interesting comparison between the traditions given by Polybius and Livy respectively).
23. Polyb. 3.2.6; 6.10.14, 58.1 et al.
24. Cf. Polyb. 2.33.7f.; 3.80.3. Cf. M. Gelzer, *Kl. Schr.* III (1964): 76ff. But doubtless such an assessment was quite in accordance with Polybius's own conviction; cf. K.-W. Welwei, *Historia* 15 (1966): 282ff.
25. Against Gelzer, *Kl. Schr.* III (1964): 72ff., cf. U. Hackl, *Chiron* 2 (1972): 154.

Flaminius's senatorial opponents in 232, nor does Polybius say so. In pursuing its policy of colonization, the Senate never showed any consideration for the feelings of the affected peoples or their neighbors.[26] Only in hindsight could anyone see an opportunity of putting the blame for the Gallic war on the detested Flaminius. On the other hand, the opposition cannot have been caused by a general unwillingness on the part of the senators to admit any further distribution of land because they wanted to seize and exploit the territory themselves by means of occupation.[27] For in the course of the third century numerous colonies, in some cases with extensive territories, were established on the Senate's initiative, especially in northern Italy; Placentia and Cremona were founded shortly afterwards, on the eve of the Hannibalic War.

Hence, as P. Fraccaro first noticed,[28] it must have been the unusual method of colonization—namely, by assigning land to individuals rather than by establishing a colony—that caused the Senate's resistance. The ancient tradition persistently points to this fact, as it emphasizes from Cato on[29] that the land was distributed individually (*viritim*). Such a procedure conflicted with the hitherto customary and successful principle of granting the distribution of land only in the organizational framework of defensive settlements that were spread all over Italy according to strategic requirements (*propugnacula imperii*: Cicero *Leg. agr.* 2.73).[30] Why, then, did Flaminius in-

26. Bleicken, *Volkstribunat*² (1968): 29.
27. Thus, e.g., Meyer, *Staat*³ (1964): 286. The attempt to relate the *lex de modo agrorum*, which is attested already in Cato (fr. 167 *ORF*⁴), to the *lex Flaminia* (Nap, *Republik* [1935]: 18ff.; C. Rienzi, *Archivio Giuridico* 191 [1976]: 38ff.; A. Valvo, *Miscellanea greca e romana* 5 [1977]: 179ff.) is completely unjustified. At best, following De Martino, *Cost.* II² (1973): 458, the law could for general reasons be dated to Flaminius's time. [Cf. D. Stockton, *The Gracchi* (Oxford, 1979): 211.]
28. P. Fraccaro, *Athenaeum* 7 (1919): 73ff. = id., *Opuscula* II (1957): 191ff.
29. Cato, fr. 43 P.; cf. Cic., *Brut.* 57; id. *Cato* 11; Val. Max. 5.4.5.
30. A. Heuss, *Röm. Geschichte*⁴ (1976): 80f. A different view is to be found in U. Hackl, *Chiron* 2 (1972): 148ff., 154f. Hackl thinks that the Senate opposed the establishment of new tribes, which might have been necessitated by the distribution of land to individuals (*Viritanassignation*). This corresponds with the view presented in this paper, insofar as in that case, too, the conflict would have centered upon the question of citizenship. [For a possible connection with the distribution of land by M'. Curius Dentatus in 290 (or only after the *lex Hortensia* in 287?), see A. J. Toynbee, *Hannibal's Legacy* I (1965): 377ff.; and Triebel, *Ackergesetze* (1980): 10ff. However, according to Plutarch, *Apophth. Rom.* 194E, its extent was (perhaps) moderate; cf. Bleicken, *Volkstribunat*² (1968): 21 n. 1.]

sist on a different method and thereby risk conflict with the Senate? Did he intend to ingratiate himself with the masses by handing over land without, as it seemed, formally asking in return for the military service traditionally expected from such colonists?[31] Whatever their formal status, however, in case of danger the colonists were certainly obliged, even forced, to fight. Did Flaminius try to avoid creating colonies as new urban centers in order to strengthen the rural complement of the Roman citizen body?[32] Such an interpretation, however, would seem to overlook the almost completely agrarian character of these colonies.

Once again, it was P. Fraccaro[33] who found the adequate explanation. Most of the colonies, especially the major ones that were located in strategically important places and in remoter areas, obtained Latin status (*ius Latii*).[34] Consequently, Roman citizens who moved to a colony automatically lost their former citizenship. For a long time, the colonists had willingly accepted this in return for the advantage of being provided with land. But now, owing to the large number of colonies founded in the previous decades, the shortage of land had been substantially reduced. On the other hand, Rome's rise to supremacy in Italy and, even more, its victory over Carthage in the first Punic War substantially increased the attractiveness of Roman citizenship. The *lex Flaminia agraria* made allowances for these changed conditions. In doing so, however, it had to violate the traditional methods of colonization, and it extended Roman citizenship to a region far from the political center at Rome. Both these aspects must have provided reason enough for the negative reaction of the Senate, which certainly did not intend to tolerate such a development.

Consequently, C. Flaminius could pursue his plan only *contra auctoritatem senatus*.[35] By doing this and succeeding through a plebiscite, he made it evident that the interests of Senate and people were far

---

31. A. H. Bernstein, *Tiberius Sempronius Gracchus: Tradition and Apostasy* (Ithaca, N. Y., and London, 1978): 177f.
32. Heuss, *Röm. Geschichte*[4] (1976): 81.
33. Fraccaro, *Opuscula* II (1957): 201ff.; contra: Meyer, *Staat*[3] (1964): 528 n. 3 (citing additional literature), on which see Fraccaro, ibid., 191 (introductory note to reprint ed.); Toynbee, *Hannibal's Legacy* I (1965): 311ff.
34. Cf. H. Galsterer, *Herrschaft* (1976): 59f.
35. Cic. *De Inv.* 2.52; *Cato* 11; *Acad. prior.* 2.13; and Val. Max. 5.4.5.

from identical. All through his political career, Flaminius acted according to the very principles he had set out with. During his first consulship (223), he did not allow himself to be denied his victory over the Insubres by a senatorial order referring to his improper election; he celebrated his triumph on the basis of a plebiscite when the Senate refused to give its permission.[36] As censor of the year 220, he built the Via Flaminia to Ariminum, a measure by which he emphasized and supported his earlier policy of agrarian settlement.[37] By building the Circus Flaminius and, at the same time, introducing the *Ludi Plebei*, he tried to accentuate the independence of the *plebs* as opposed to the *populus* (the entire citizen body) with its *Ludi Romani*. Typically, in their ceremonial setup, these two games closely corresponded to each other.[38]

36. See the evidence in F. Münzer, *RE* 6 (1909): 2498, s.v. Flaminius, no. 2. Bleicken, *Volkstribunat*² (1968): 30, is right in asserting that Q. Fabius Maximus, who unscrupulously exploited the opportunities offered by the *auguria* for his political aims (Cic. *Cato* 11), was responsible for nullifying Flaminius's consulship. [Contra: R. Develin, *Journ. of Rel. Hist.* 10 (1978): 13ff.] Whether Flaminius was *magister equitum* to Fabius in 221 need not be discussed here, because the tradition sometimes mentions Minucius instead of Fabius, as well as because the dictatorship ended with an abdication due to a bad omen; cf. Jahn, *Interregnum* (1970): 111ff. [Develin, *RhM* 122 (1979): 268ff., is opposed to any attempt "to ascribe a coherent and consistent policy to Flaminius" (277). He is right if one thereby tries to integrate Flaminius into a fixed faction, but he clearly underestimates Flaminius's relationship with the *plebs* (e.g., on p. 274, where the very fact that the people conferred a triumph on Flaminius is not assessed properly).]

37. However, the reform of the *comitia centuriata*, which must be dated between 241 and 218, can hardly be assigned to him. Neither date nor substance nor tendency of the reform is sufficiently clear; cf. U. Hackl, *Chiron* 2 (1972): 135ff. (with comprehensive bibliography). [Cf. now also R. Develin, *Athenaeum* 56 (1978): 346ff. For the via Flaminia, cf. T. P. Wiseman, *PBSR* 38 (1970): 138, 143; E. Herzig, *ANRW* II.1 (1974): 598ff.]

38. G. Wissowa, *Religion* (1912): 454. The introduction of the *Ludi Plebei* in the year 220 is not directly attested; the earliest evidence is for 216. But since the circus part of the *Ludi* occurred in the Circus Flaminius, it is safe to assume (following Mommsen, *Röm. Staatsrecht* II³ [1887]: 520) that their introduction coincided with the dedication of the Circus. For the significance of the games for the careers of the aediles who organized them, cf. H. H. Scullard, *Politics* (1973): 24f. It is noteworthy that according to Livy 3.54.15 the ten tribunes of the *plebs* were elected for the first time after the overthrow of the decemvirs in 449 B.C. *in pratis Flaminiis . . . quem nunc circum Flaminium appellant* (this contradicts 54.10, where the event is located on the Aventine). The name is a naive anticipation of the place's later name. A reference to the *ludi plebei* later held there seems quite probable (see Ogilvie's comm. ad loc.). The second time the *prata Flaminia* are mentioned (3.63.7), Livy again implicitly refers to Flaminius, but this time to his consulship; this happens in connec-

Furthermore, it may be safely assumed that Flaminius played an important role in enacting the laws (discussed at the beginning of this paper) that aimed at restricting senatorial influence. For the *lex Claudia de nave senatorum* his support is directly attested. Concerning the law that prohibited the son of any former curule magistrate from holding plebeian office as long as his father was alive, Flaminius's support is suggested by the fact that during his tribunate his own father had caused him considerable difficulties. Tradition maintains that this man even removed his son from the *rostra* during a popular assembly convened to discuss Flaminius's *lex agraria*. Thereby he created a classic conflict between the *patria potestas* on the one hand and the *maiestas* of the people, which was offended in the person of the tribune,[39] on the other.

Consequently, the judgment passed by Polybius/Fabius Pictor (2.21.8) for the year 232 can be explained by the fact that with his agrarian law Flaminius indeed introduced a policy that could be considered "the first step in the demoralization of the Roman people." Such a verdict from his enemies obviously would include the developments of the following fifteen years. It must comprise for ex-

---

tion with the triumph of the *"populares"* consuls L. Valerius Potitus and M. Horatius who were refused the honor by the Senate but nevertheless celebrated it *primum sine auctoritate senatus populi iussu* (63.11). W. K. Quinn-Schofield, *Latomus* 26 (1967): 677ff., blindly trusts the sources and is of little use; on the other hand, T. P. Wiseman, *PBSR* 42 (1974): 3ff.; 44 (1976): 44f., fails to prove that the *ludi circenses* never took place in the Circus Flaminius. [For additional measures by Flaminius in the religious sphere, cf. Triebel, *Ackergesetze* (1980): 18ff., whose reference to the cult of the *genius populi Romani* (21ff.) is very important; for the continuation of the building program in the second century, cf. ibid., 99ff.]

39. Cic. *De inv.* 2.52; Val. Max. 5.4.5; cf. A. Aymard, *REA* 45 (1943): 219ff. Valerius Maximus's statements can usually not be trusted. But as he incorporates the case into the chapter *"De pietate in parentes,"* we have reason to believe that there was no trial *maiestatis*; cf. Dion. Hal. 2.26.5 (without a name). R. A. Bauman, *Crimen* (1967): 31, 215, disagrees with this view. (It is hardly necessary to comment upon the thesis of R. Develin, *AC* 45 [1976]: 638ff., that there was no *lex Flaminia* at all, because the intervention of Flaminius's father caused the failure of the proposal.) The note in Cicero, *De re pub.* 2.60, that the testimony of his own father caused the downfall of the great *"popularis"* of the early republic, Sp. Cassius, is probably taken from Fabius Pictor. Later authors even construed a *iudicium domesticum* out of it (Livy 2.41.10). For the different versions, see Ogilvie, *Comm.* (1965): 337ff. [P. Botteri, "Figli pubblici e padri privati: *tribunicia potestas e patria potestas,*" in *La paura dei padri nella società antica e medievale*, edited by E. Pellizzer and N. Zorzetti (Bari, 1983): 47ff.]

ample all the irregularities surrounding the dictatorship of Q. Fabius Maximus and his *magister equitum*, M. Minucius Rufus, who not only was elected by the people contrary to custom, but finally was even appointed co-dictator on the motion of the tribune M. Metilius;[40] it would also include the agitation of the tribune Q. Baebius Herennius in 216 aimed at promoting the consular election of C. Terentius Varro:

> After that the consuls[41] had employed the arts of Fabius to prolong the war, when they could have ended it. The nobles had all made a compact to this effect; nor would his hearers see an end of the war until they had elected a true plebeian, a new man, to the consulship; for the plebeian nobles had already been admitted to the same rites as the others and had begun to look down on the *plebs* from the moment when they themselves had ceased to be looked down on by the patricians [*nam plebeios nobiles iam eisdem initiatos esse sacris et contemnere plebem ex quo contemni a patribus desierint coepisse*]. (Livy 22.34.7–8)

Although the speech in Livy's text is certainly colored by the propaganda of the late republican *populares*, it nevertheless precisely formulates the core of the problem.[42] Flaminius and his supporters had realized that the upstart plebeians were no longer willing to fight for specifically plebeian demands. Accordingly, they strove to keep the consciousness of separate plebeian identity alive among the plebeians (hence the *Ludi Plebei*). In this they were successful, as the incident concerning the bride of M. Rutilius illustrates (Livy, fr. 12). Moreover, they used the opportunities offered by the tribunate, even against the Senate's will. In doing so, they were above all anxious to prevent the nobility from exerting any influence on the plebeian magistracies.

---

40. F. W. Walbank, *Comm.* I (1957): 192f.; for the evidence see Broughton, *Magistrates* I (1951): 243.

41. This refers to the consul of 217, Cn. Servilius Geminus, and the *cos. suff.* M. Atilius Regulus.

42. A. Aymard, *REA* 45 (1943): 219 n. 2. For Varro, cf. G. Zecchini, *CISA* 4 (1976): 118ff. [Cf. also E. Gruen, *CSCA* 11 (1978): 61ff. Livy 31.6.4 unfortunately makes the tribune of the *plebs* Q. Baebius talk in the same way in the year 200; in this case it certainly is an annalistic invention: see W. Dahlheim, *Völkerrecht* (1968): 242 n. 23.]

3

We have no information about the social composition of C. Flaminius's following; we can only judge by his actions. Because of his *lex agraria* we might expect him to have enjoyed the support of the conservative rural class;[43] on the basis of the *lex Claudia*, backing by groups that were vitally interested in finance and commerce and formed the nucleus of the aspiring equestrian order (cf. n. 15) seems no less likely. Yet, taking into account the fact that Flaminius pursued a deliberately "plebeian" policy in opposition both to the patrician-plebeian nobility and to the Senate dominated by it, his consistent success over a period of fifteen years is only explicable if we reckon with a kind of coalition of both the rural and equestrian forces.

With good reason this reminds us of the coalition that had determined the course of the Conflict of the Orders, although then the alliance of socially prominent families and the plebeian masses[44] had been kept together by their common opposition to the patriciate, whereas it was now reinforced by the contrast to the patrician-plebeian nobility. Consequently, we have to ask whether Flaminius's policy represented a new beginning (at most reactivating "revolutionary" practices after more than half a century) or whether, though adapted to contemporary needs, it nevertheless continued the Conflict of the Orders. To answer this question, we have to take a closer look at the *lex Hortensia*, which is commonly supposed to have terminated the Conflict of the Orders.

According to the explicit testimony of Livy (*Per.* 11), the *secessio plebis* of about 287 occurred on account of the unsolved question of debts: *post graves et longas seditiones*.[45] We can still discern part of the

---

43. Cf. Bleicken, *Volkstribunat*² (1968): 32ff.

44. Still excellent on the subject: W. Hoffmann, *NJAB* 1 (1938): 82ff.; *RE* 21.1 (1951): 73ff.; cf. Toynbee, *Hannibal's Legacy* I (1965): 315ff. [See also F. Wieacker, *Labeo* 23 (1977): 66f., discussing A. Guarino, *Riv.* (1975); G. E. M. de Ste. Croix, *Class Struggle* (1981): 332ff. Raaflaub, chapter VII above, rightly emphasizes the need to differentiate between the conflict of the fifth and that of the fourth century; but this hardly bears upon the final phase around 300.]

45. Cf. August. *De Civ. D.* 3.17. The problem of debt is unjustifiably minimized by Bleicken, *Volkstribunat*² (1968): 20. [See, against Bleicken's view, G. Maddox, *Latomus* 42 (1983): 277ff. It is interesting to note that the recruitment of *proletarii* is well attested only for 281 (or 280?: Broughton, *Magistrates* I [1951]: 191) and not later on, even during the predicament of the second Punic War; cf. P. A. Brunt, *Manpower* (1971): 395 n. 6; Y. Shochat, *Recruitment and the Programme of Tiberius Gracchus*, Coll. Latomus 169 (Brussels, 1980): 27f.]

conflict in a fragment of Cassius Dio (fr. 37; cf. Zonaras 8.2); it tells us that the tribunes repeatedly tried to pass a law settling the question of debts, but failed because of the resistance not, as we should expect, of the patricians, but of the creditors, the wealthy and the powerful. The antagonism between the orders of patricians and plebeians had thus been converted into a social opposition of the poor and the rich. Consequently, the plebeians now had to enforce their demands upon the new establishment, the nobility.[46] And logically they relied on *homines novi* such as Sp. Carvilius Maximus, M'. Curius Dentatus, C. Fabricius Luscinus, and Ti. Coruncanius. These men substantially influenced Rome's politics and development between 290 and 270, but, characteristically, their families were hardly, if at all, integrated into the nobility.[47] It is particularly noteworthy that the dictator Q. Hortensius came from a family that had never distinguished itself at Rome,[48] and that he himself had not held the consulship. Evidently he reached the dictatorship as the acknowledged and trusted leader of the plebeians.[49] His appointment therefore already indicated the later compromise, the law proposed by and named after him. The *lex Hortensia*, which made plebiscites as binding and effective as the resolutions of the whole *populus*, was later regarded as one of the fundamental laws of the Roman constitution. It is not by chance that the jurists continued to mention it to Justinian's time, when plebiscites had long become obsolete.[50] That is pre-

---

46. L. Lange, *Altertümer* II³ (1879): 103ff., presents all the evidence; cf. further Hoffmann (as in n. 44) and Ferenczy, *Patr. State* (1976), who focuses too much on Ap. Claudius Caecus, though. One wonders whether the introduction of the *tresviri capitales* about 289 (Livy, *per.* 11) belongs to the same context and ought to be understood as a disciplinary measure of the nobility (Lange, *Altertümer*, 106). These officials used to be underestimated, cf. W. Kunkel, *Kriminalverfahren* (1962): 71ff.

47. The late reports are rather anecdotal, which does not imply, however, that these men only later became "Lieblingsgestalten des gemeinen Mannes" (thus wrongly F. Münzer, *RE* 6 [1909]: 1931, s.v. Fabricius, no. 9). Equally unfounded are Münzer's speculations (*Adelsparteien* [1920]: 61f.) concerning their social rank. [For Curius Dentatus's opposition to the Senate, see Cic. *Brutus* 55; *Vir. ill.* 30.10, and the isolated note in Appian *Samn.* 5. Cf. n. 30 above; G. Forni, *Athenaeum* 31 (1953): 170ff.]

48. For the very dubious tribune of 422, cf. Ogilvie, *Comm.* (1965): 597.

49. Cf. Mommsen, *Röm. Staatsrecht* II³ (1887): 146 with n. 2; Beloch, *Röm. Geschichte* (1926): 484f.

50. Laelius Felix in Gell. *Noctes Atticae* 15.27.4; Gaius 1.3; Pomp. *Dig.* 1.2.2.8; Iustin. *Inst.* 1.2.4.

cisely why it gained in hindsight an importance that it hardly deserved in the eyes of the parties involved. Its substance, "that an order of the *plebs* should be binding on all citizens" (*ut quod ea [= plebs] iussisset omnes Quirites teneret*),[51] originally was simply intended to enforce against the opposition of the nobility the *rogatio* concerning the annulment of debts that had failed repeatedly before. The same is true of the second regulation we happen to know of. By declaring the market days (*nundinae*) *dies fasti*, it aimed at eliminating another *gravamen* of the plebeians. According to Granius Licinianus (Macrobius, *Sat.* 1.16.30), this law made it possible for "lawsuits" to "take place on the *nundinae* when the peasants, taking advantage of the country holiday, came to Rome on business."[52]

As F. Wieacker[53] observes, Roman republican legislation was always prompted by specific needs and occasions (*stets Gelegenheitsgesetzgebung*). Thus it was the intention of the *lex Hortensia* to secure recognition for the specific demands of the *plebs* without risking the kind of protracted confrontation that had so far characterized each important stage of the Conflict of the Orders. This seemed all the more necessary in view of the fact that the patriciate had been strengthened by an alliance with the leading plebeian families. But at the same time the law certainly was not yet intended to promote the method of using plebiscites to settle questions that concerned the *populus*. Although our information is far from complete, it makes perfect sense that we perceive the use of that method only after 217—that is, in an entirely different situation (see below).[54]

---

51. Thus Plin. *Nat. Hist.* 16.37; the wording differs in other reports but the substance is the same.

52. *OCD*², 530. This has been the common interpretation since Lange, *Altertümer* II³ (1879): 113ff.: by declaring the *nundinae dies fasti non comitiales*, the plebeians would be prevented from participating in large numbers at the popular assemblies on market days. Such a view is, to say the least, too intricate. Lange is followed by Bleicken, *Volkstribunat*² (1968): 23 (and, more cautiously, *Lex* [1975]: 257f.); Heuss, *Röm. Geschichte*⁴ (1976): 35.

53. Wieacker, *Recht*² (1961): 68ff.; cf. the important discussion by Bleicken, *Lex* (1975): 178ff., 186: "Hinter dem generellen Volksgesetz der römischen Republik steht also keine normative Idee." Yet, Bleicken (ibid.) seems to take the (general) law too confidently as an "Objektivierung der Ordnung" of the *res publica*; cf. the review by C. Meier, *ZRG* 95 (1978): 378ff., especially 386ff. See also the useful observations in M. Elster, *Studien* (1976).

54. Cf. Bleicken, *Volkstribunat*² (1968): 20ff., 43ff.; C. Meier, *Res publica amissa* (1966): 122f. [D. Liebs has reminded me of the *lex Aquilia* of 286 B.C.(?) whose regu-

Accordingly, the modern view[55] that the *lex Hortensia* ended the Conflict of the Orders must be substantially modified. To be sure, the general acceptance of all future (!) plebiscites on the part of the nobility presupposes that the plebeians by then were well integrated into the community. The *lex Hortensia* was only practicable if the range of issues subject to plebiscite was relatively restricted and the extent of the demands fairly easy to anticipate—in other words, if they were not expected to threaten the system.[56] In addition, the very fact that the plebeian part of the nobility could be represented among the ten tribunes (and was therefore capable of controlling the college by means of *intercessio*) would have helped to make such an agreement possible. On the other hand, the antagonism between the orders was not abolished by the *lex Hortensia*, but actually institutionalized, as had been the case before when the tribunate of the *plebs* was acknowledged and the *provocatio* legalized.[57] The plebeian organization at least potentially retained its revolutionary character. Whether and to what extent the plebeians continued to see themselves in such terms is quite a different question. Their self-perception may have varied anyway, according to the general state of affairs.[58]

---

lations do not seem to have any connection with the Conflict of the Orders; cf. M. Kaser, *Privatr.* I² (1971): 161f., 619ff.; A. Völkl, "*Quanti ea lex erit in diebus triginta proximis:* Zum dritten Kapitel der *lex Aquilia*," *RIDA* 24 (1977): 461ff. The Anon. ad Bas. 60.3.1 and Theophilus *ad Autol.* 4.3.15, Byzantine scholars commenting on the *Institutiones* of Justinian state, though, that the law was enacted in a period of tensions between the *plebs* and the *patres*; quoted in G. Niccolini, *Fasti* (1934): 390f. The date is very controversial; cf. J. A. Crook, "Lex Aquilia," *Athenaeum* 62 (1984): 67ff.]

55. References will hardly be necessary, but the very inspiring presentation by Heuss, *Röm. Geschichte*³ (1976): 32f., is worth mentioning. See also the different view in Lange, *Altertümer* II³ (1879): 116ff.; W. Hoffmann, *RE* 21.1 (1951): 88ff.; Bleicken, *Volkstribunat*² (1968): 24ff.; Toynbee, *Hannibal's Legacy* I (1965): 348ff.

56. On this, though within a larger range, see C. Meier, *Res publica amissa* (1966): 45ff. ("monistische Gesellschaft" [53], in my view goes too far); id., *ZRG* 95 (1978): 385ff. [Ortega y Gasset's *Del imperio romano* is worth reading with regard to the tribunes.]

57. The legalization of *provocatio* against patrician as well as plebeian (!) magistrates by the *lex Valeria* (300 B.C.) clearly demonstrates the new confrontation between the nobility and the plebeians. It is further confirmed by the beginning of a conscious program of monumental representation and public building around this time: T. Hölscher, *RM* 85 (1978): 315ff.

58. With all due caution we may compare the function of the unions in our day (for example in the Federal Republic of Germany): they are an important element

Because Livy's second decade is lost, we have hardly any information on internal conditions at Rome during the following years. Yet there are several indications that this special plebeian self-consciousness persisted. It is indeed striking that as consuls and censors Carvilius and Curius as well as Fabricius and Coruncanius continued to shape Roman politics even after 287, and to have considerable influence until the late seventies. In about 254, the first plebeian became *pontifex maximus* (Livy, *Per.* 18). Although at first this could be understood as a continuation of the classical struggle of the upstart plebeians to gain access to the magistracies and priesthoods, both the person elected (Ti. Coruncanius) and the fact that popular election to this office was probably introduced at that time indicate an altered situation. For when the plebeians had become eligible for the colleges of the augurs and pontiffs in 300, the principle of cooptation had been left unchanged. Now, although in a modified form (through only seventeen tribes), the popular assembly was given the right to vote and decide.[59] Coruncanius was also the first jurist to admit an audience when he was giving legal advice. In doing this, he definitely broke an important monopoly hitherto maintained by the college of the pontiffs: he provided those interested with new ways to receive guidance in legal affairs and to be introduced to the methods of applying the law; thus he made an important part of the *arcana imperii* (or *Herrschaftswissen*) accessible to the public.[60]

Other indications of plebeian self-consciousness are to be found in the proceedings against the consul of 249, P. Claudius Pulcher, and

---

of the social system (which is symbolized by the *konzertierte Aktion*, the "coordinated management" of economy executed by representatives of the federal, state, and local governments, the German Federal Bank, the employer associations, and the trade unions) although potentially (at least in ideology and self-understanding) they oppose it. [P. Catalano, *Tribunato* (1971), especially 21ff., has valuable remarks on how modern phenomena such as trade unions, the general strike, etc., have been influenced by the ancient tradition on the Conflict of the Orders.]

59. The election is attested in 212 for the first time; it must have been introduced in the period covered by Livy's second decade (Mommsen, *Röm. Staatsrecht* II³ [1887]: 27). It probably should be connected with Ti. Coruncanius. To replace cooptation with popular election later became a typical issue of the *populares*: J. Martin, *Die Popularen in der Geschichte der späten Republik* (Freiburg i. Br., 1965): 210f.

60. *Dig.* I.2.2.35, 38; cf. F. Münzer, *RE* 4 (1901): 1664, s.v. Coruncanius, no. 3. [Cf. also F. D'Ippolito, *I giuristi e la città* (Naples, 1978): 27ff., with the critical remarks by D. Nörr, *ZRG* 97 (1980): 398f.; and R. A. Bauman, *Lawyers in Roman Republican Politics* (Munich, 1983).]

his sister Claudia. Claudius had lost his fleet at Drepana and for this reason was prosecuted for *perduellio* in the *comitia centuriata* by two tribunes of the *plebs*. The trial was called off due to a storm. But in a second proceeding in the *comitia tributa*, the tribunes succeeded in having Pulcher condemned and sentenced to a heavy fine.[61] R. A. Bauman[62] is probably right in assuming that Pulcher's case "may be noted as the earliest known instance where the *Rechenschaftsprozess* was pursued in the form of the *crimen maiestatis*." It is certain that in 246 Claudia was prosecuted *maiestatis* in the *comitia tributa* by the plebeian aediles C. Fundanius and Ti. Sempronius *novo more* (Suetonius *Tib.* 2.3), because she made insulting comments about the people. Ti. Sempronius spent the fine of 25,000 asses (Gellius 10.6.3) on the building of a temple of Libertas on the Aventine (Livy 24.16.19). Unfortunately we are not certain, although it seems quite probable, whether this sanctuary was identical with the temple of Jupiter Libertas (also situated on the Aventine).[63]

Thus the existence of a temple of Jupiter Libertas on the hill of the plebeians gains in significance. It has to be understood as a counter-foundation to the Capitoline temple of Jupiter, which had been consecrated, according to the tradition, at the beginning of the Republic. Obviously we find here the same attitude that led to the separation of the *Ludi Plebei* from the *Ludi Romani* of the *populus*.[64]

Chronologically as well as thematically, we thus again reach the period of C. Flaminius, which does not appear at all to be a fresh, revolutionary beginning. On the contrary, it proves to be traditional to a surprisingly great degree. Long before Flaminius, the *plebs* had managed to preserve its identity and independence against the patrician-plebeian Senate. It had even strengthened its importance in the existing order.[65] However, during the fifteen years of his po-

---

61. For the references see Broughton, *Magistrates* I (1951): 214f. [For a more skeptical view of the trials against Claudius and his sister, see Wiseman, *Clio's Cosmetics* (1979): 90f.]

62. Bauman, *Crimen* (1967): 27ff. J. Suolahti, "Claudia insons," *Arctos* 11 (1977): 133ff., is of little use.

63. For the evidence, see S. B. Platner, *A Topographical Dictionary of Ancient Rome* (London, 1929): 296f.

64. Wissowa, *Religion* (1912): 138f.; A. U. Stylow, *Libertas und Liberalitas: Untersuchungen zur innenpolitischen Propaganda der Römer* (Munich, 1972): 5f.

65. In this context the (obviously rather important) role played by the popular assembly both at the beginning and at the end of the first Punic War ought to be

litical activity, Flaminius was able to systematize the existing tendencies and to accentuate them in a novel way. He realized that the independence of the *plebs* necessarily implied an equal independence of the Senate and nobility, and he was anxious to keep both spheres as neatly separated as possible. The *lex Claudia* most clearly indicates this intention. Moreover, it reveals Flaminius's ability to make allowances for the growing differentiation in Roman economy and society, which had become obvious, for example, in the emergence of the equestrian order as the new leading class among the *plebs*. Yet the position of the Senate was by no means undermined; nor did Flaminius intend to create an insurmountable gulf between the orders. Like his more prominent supporters, he himself was a member of the Senate, and with his two consulates and the censorship, he even reached the highest rungs of the *cursus honorum*. But at the same time he intended to secure firmly, and therefore institutionally, the interests of the *plebs* in an aristocratic system of government. This goal was as much a consequence of the preceding Conflict of the Orders as it was an original conception of Flaminius's.

The altercations surrounding Flaminius's *lex agraria* were as decisive in forming his conception as they were for its vehement rejection by his opponents. By succeeding with his land bill, Flaminius acted in accordance with the *lex Hortensia* which enabled the *plebs* to realize its demands on its own, but he did so in the sphere of settlement policy, traditionally the Senate's domain. The Senate risked a confrontation and was defeated. It was precisely the Senate's action that (unintentionally) made explicit the persistent importance of the *lex Hortensia* for protecting plebeian interests. In addition, it became evident that the *lex Hortensia* provided an excellent instrument for successfully pursuing a policy even against the will of the Senate.[66]

Flaminius was, of course, no "revolutionary,"[67] though some riots

---

reconsidered; that may apply to the reform of the *comitia centuriata* as well. But these rather controversial problems cannot be discussed here. [Also, we ought not to forget the important speculations by R. von Ihering, *Scherz und Ernst in der Jurisprudenz*[13] (Leipzig, 1924): 175ff., especially 212ff., who emphasized the social and political importance of the *lex Papiria*. It can only vaguely be dated between 241 and 124: Broughton, *Magistrates* II (1951): 471.]

66. See Bleicken, *Volkstribunat*[2] (1968): 36.

67. Meier, *Res publica amissa* (1966): 124 n. 371; Heuss, *Röm. Geschichte*[4] (1976): 81 and 552.

may have occurred in 232.⁶⁸ He used the newly discovered opportunities moderately and, on the whole, only in order to adjust and reform the existing order. The *nobiles* perhaps grasped the situation more clearly; they certainly were more spiteful, stigmatizing his behavior as downright "demagogic." In a similar way, they tried to slander indiscriminately as demagogy or revolution each attempt at reform from 133 on—attempts at reform that offer interesting parallels to Flaminius's policy. As in 232, Ti. Gracchus took up the agrarian question first. After his early death, his brother Gaius pursued a policy that, *inter alia*, intended to assign independent spheres of influence to the Senate, the *plebs*, and the newly constituted *ordo equester*.⁶⁹

The catastrophes of Lake Trasimene and Cannae made it impossible to continue the policy of Flaminius and his supporters. However, it was the deadly threat of Hannibal rather than Flaminius's death, brought about by his own fault, that made the Senate and the people draw closer. Now the tribunes of the *plebs* began to propose plebiscites on the Senate's initiative; thus they became political agents of the state rather than of the *plebs*.⁷⁰ At this time there was no room for any conflict between the orders.

On the basis of this conclusion, it becomes possible to restore the relevance of two well-known pieces of testimony that are seldom fully appreciated.⁷¹ One is Polybius's remark that Rome's constitution had reached its best and most perfect form in the time of the Hannibalic War.⁷² Such a view is perfectly compatible with the fact that the evolution of Rome's mixed constitution ended for Polybius in 449 with the overthrow of the Decemvirate and the Valerio-Horatian

---

68. Cic. *De inv.* 2.52: *per seditionem*; Val Max. 5.4.5: *ac ne exercitu quidem adversus se conscripto . . . absterritus* (rather exaggerated).

69. Martin, *Popularen* (as in n. 59): 161ff.; Meier, *Res publica amissa* (1966): 131ff.; J. von Ungern-Sternberg, *Untersuchungen zum spätrepublikanischen Notstandsrecht*, Vestigia 11 (Munich, 1970): 48ff. For the consistency of the issues of Roman legislation, cf. F. Wieacker, *Recht²* (1961): 61ff. [On Cicero's judgments providing an example of the attitude of the *optimates* toward reform, see now L. Perelli, *Il movimento popolare nell' ultimo secolo della repubblica* (Bari, 1982): 25ff.]

70. Bleicken, *Volkstribunat²* (1968): 46ff.

71. See the explanation proposed by C. Meier, *RE* suppl. 8 (1956): 582, s.v. *Praerogativa centuria*.

72. Polyb. 6.11: καὶ κάλλιστον καὶ τέλειον ἐν τοῖς Ἀννιβαϊκοῖς καιροῖς. Cf. K. von Fritz, *The Theory of the Mixed Constitution in Antiquity* (New York, 1954): 467ff.

laws.[73] Polybius probably adopted this arrangement of Roman history from Fabius Pictor,[74] who offered little information on the further development of the Roman constitution, but, as was shown above, attributed principal importance to the confrontation between Flaminius and the Senate, which he described as the last fundamental conflict of interests.

On the other hand, Sallust's statement in the *prooemium* of his *Histories* (preserved by Augustine, *De civ. D.* 2.18 = fr. 11 M) has to be reconsidered: "The Romans enjoyed greater harmony and a purer state of society between the second and the third Punic Wars than at any other time."[75] Sallust emphasizes this observation once more after a short survey of the Conflict of the Orders: "it was only the second Punic War that put an end on both sides to discord and strife." There have been attempts to explain such an extreme shortening of Rome's "good times" by reference to Sallust's increasingly pessimistic conception of history.[76] However that may be,[77] at least it now becomes evident that even Sallust in his last work adopted Fabius Pictor's portrayal of early Rome. Characteristically, like Fabius Pictor and Polybius, on the one hand Sallust ends his report of factual developments with the overthrow of the Decemvirate; on the other hand, he stresses the importance of the second Punic War as the moment when the greatest internal consensus existed at Rome.

4

Is it justified, therefore, to conclude that the Conflict of the Orders ended with the second Punic War? Just as for the year 287 with the

---

73. Von Fritz, *Mixed Constitution*, 135f. The same view (following Polybius) is to be found in Cic. *De re pub.* bk 2. [J. L. Ferrary, *JRS* 74 (1984): 88ff., thinks that Polybius used Fabius Pictor or rather Cato.]

74. D. Timpe, *ANRW* I.2 (1972): 938f.

75. In his commentary on Liv. fr. 12 (*Ges. Schr.* VII [1909]: 166f.), Th. Mommsen already refers to Sallust.

76. Cf. F. Klingner, *Studien zur griechischen und römischen Literatur* (Zurich, 1964): 571ff. However, Sallust may really have acquired a new insight in this particular case: R. Syme, *Sallust* (Berkeley and Los Angeles, 1964): 182.

77. For the unity of Sallust's view of history, cf. K.-E. Petzold, "Der politische Standort des Sallust," *Chiron* 1 (1971): 233f., and especially K. Vretska, *Kommentar zu Sallust "De Catilinae coniuratione"* (Heidelberg, 1976): 206ff.

last *secessio plebis* and the *lex Hortensia*, good reasons can be claimed in support of so late a terminal date: for a considerable time there were no tribunes of the *plebs* who conceived and tried to realize independent policies against the will of the Senate; nor were there large groups of dissatisfied citizens whose support would have been indispensable for such policies. Rome was fighting for its existence against Carthage, then rapidly expanding its control over the entire Mediterranean world. All energies were therefore occupied, and there was enough booty to satisfy not only all justified but even many unjustified claims.[78]

Yet the *plebs* with its special cults and games and its political organization continued to exist as a separate entity.[79] There still were the tribunes with their special powers, such as the *ius auxilii*, which in daily life may well have played a more important role than is revealed by the tradition.[80] In a convincing philological analysis, R. Seager recently demonstrated that the plebeians continued to be aware of a marked distance between themselves and the Senate.[81] Equally, it could be suppressed temporarily but not forgotten that by its very nature the tribunate of the *plebs* was an office of opposition (*Oppositionsmagistratur*).[82]

There is yet another aspect. Whereas in this paper we have followed the contrast between the orders down to the years 217/16 with our interpretation of Flaminius's policy, L. R. Taylor focused her attention on the "forerunners of the Gracchi" whose activities began in the middle of the second century.[83] The chronological interval between them and Flaminius was hardly greater than that between the *lex Hortensia* and Flaminius. From such a perspective, the year 133 does not at all appear as a revolutionary new beginning. To a certain extent Ti. Gracchus was justified in referring to "good old law" when

78. K. Hopkins, *Conquerors and Slaves* (Cambridge, 1978); W. V. Harris, *War* (1971): J. A. North, "The Development of Roman Imperialism," *JRS* 71 (1981): 1ff.
79. Cf. Triebel, *Ackergesetze* (1980): 17ff., 62ff.
80. Bleicken, *Volkstribunat*² (1968): 78ff.
81. Seager, *CQ* 27 (1977): 377ff., especially 380ff., with testimonia from Plautus and Terence. Certainly Plut. *Quaest. Rom.* 6 = *Mor.* 265d–e, is to be dated after 200 too.
82. J. Bleicken, *Chiron* 11 (1981): 87ff., especially 98ff.; J. von Ungern-Sternberg, "Die beiden Fragen des Titus Annius Luscus," in *Sodalitas: Scritti in onore di A. Guarino* (Naples, 1984): 339ff.
83. Taylor, *JRS* 52 (1962): 19ff.

he relied on the powers of his office resulting from the *lex Hortensia* and tried to realize his agrarian reform against the will of the Senate. On the other hand, the Senate clearly violated the basic understanding of the compromise of 287, which essentially had endowed the *plebs* with the power of regulating independently those matters that were considered crucially important for the plebeians themselves. Consequently, when the late republican *populares* manifested in word and action their claim to be continuing the tradition of the Conflict of the Orders,[84] such claims seem justified to a much higher degree than modern scholars are usually prepared to admit.

It might not even be completely wrong to go one step further and to conclude that the Conflict of the Orders really ended only when the Empire was established and people and Senate ceased to be independent political forces. The history of the Roman Republic is characterized not by sharp breaks but by conservatism and gradual development; when new forms were created, the old ones were preserved in them as well. However, if the term "Conflict of the Orders" were to be expanded to cover so much more of republican history, it would change its nature: instead of characterizing a specific epoch, it would then describe a permanent antagonism within republican society and constitution. It is the purpose of this paper to present for discussion the question of whether the term "Conflict of the Orders" should remain reserved for the period down to 287 or, though gradually changing its content,[85] be extended to cover the years to 217/16 as well.

---

84. For C. Gracchus's retreat to the Aventine, see Cornell, chapter II above at n. 61; more broadly: W. Nippel, "Die *plebs urbana* und die Rolle der Gewalt in der späten römischen Republik," in *Vom Elend der Handarbeit*, edited by H. Mommsen and W. Schulze (Stuttgart, 1981): 70ff., especially 85f. Cf. also the orations of Memmius and Licinius Macer in Sall. *Jug.* 31, *Hist.* 3, 48 M.

85. Basically by analogy to the development of the Conflict of the Orders itself: cf. Raaflaub, chapter VII above.

Bibliography

The following bibliography is intended to provide a representative, although by no means complete, selection of scholarly writings on the early Roman Republic and the Conflict of the Orders. It lists (a) all the books and articles pertaining to the Conflict of the Orders mentioned in the contributions to this volume; (b) other literature referred to at least twice in one or more contributions; and (c) additional relevant literature on the Conflict of the Orders and contemporary Roman history, as well as on the immediately preceding and following periods. Reviews and, with a few exceptions, *lemmata* in lexica and encyclopedias are not included. Additional references may be found in, for example, Heurgon, *Rise* (1973): 261–312; Richard, *Origines* (1978): 601–26; Thomsen, *Servius Tullius* (1980): 319–38; K. Christ, ed., *Römische Geschichte: Eine Bibliographie* (Darmstadt, 1976); in the new edition of the *Cambridge Ancient History*; in many contributions to *ANRW* (for example, W. Kissel, in vol. II.30.2 [1982]: 899–997, and E. J. Phillips, in vol. II.30.2 [1982]: 998–1057, on recent research on Livy; R. Schilling, in vol. I.2 [1972]: 317–47, on religion), and, of course, in the annual bibliographical survey of *L'Année philologique*.

Short forms of titles used in the notes and elsewhere are given parenthetically following the entries.

Adcock, F. E. 1927. "Literary Tradition and Early Greek Code-Makers." *Cambr. Historical Journal* 2, 95–109.

———. 1957. "Consular Tribunes and their Successors." *JRS* 47, 9–14.

Adkins, A. W. H. 1960. *Merit and Responsibility: A Study in Greek Values.* Oxford. Repr. Chicago, 1975. (*Merit*)

Adrados, F. R. 1948. *El sistema gentilicio decimal de los indoeuropeos occidentales y los orígenes de Roma.* Manuales Emerita 7. Madrid.

Afzelius, A. 1942. *Die römische Eroberung Italiens 340–264 v. Chr.* Copenhagen. (*Eroberung*)

D'Agostino, B. 1977. "Grecs et 'indigènes' sur la côte tyrrhénienne au VIIe siècle: La Transmission des idéologies entre élites sociales." *Annales* 32, 3–20.

Alfisi, E. 1970. "Le fonti dei censimenti romani in Livio." *RIL* 104, 166–95.

Alföldi, A. 1952. *Der frührömische Reiteradel und seine Ehrenabzeichen.* Deutsche Beitr. zur Altertumswiss. 2. Baden-Baden. (*Reiteradel*)

———. 1960. "Rom und der Latinerbund um 500 v. Chr." *Gymnasium* 67, 193–96.

———. 1960. "Diana Nemorensis." *AJA* 64, 137–44.

———. 1961. "Il santuario federale di Diana sull' Aventino e il tempio di Ceres." *Studi e materiali di stor. delle relig.* 32, 21–39.

———. 1962. "*Ager Romanus antiquus.*" *Hermes* 90, 187–213.

———. 1963. "Die Etrusker in Latium und Rom." *Gymnasium* 70, 385–93.

———. 1965. *Early Rome and the Latins.* Ann Arbor. (*Early Rome*)

———. 1967. "Zur Struktur des Römerstaates im 5. Jh. v. Chr." In *Les Origines de la république romaine*, Entr. sur l'ant. class. 13, 223–78. Vandoeuvres-Geneva. ("Struktur des Römerstaates")

———. 1967. "Die Herrschaft der Reiterei in Griechenland und Rom nach dem Sturz der Könige." In *Gestalt und Geschichte: Festschrift für Karl Schefold*, Antike Kunst suppl. vol. 4, edited by M. Rohde-Liegle, H. A. Cahn, and H. C. Achermann, 13–47. Berne. ("Herrschaft der Reiterei")

———. 1968. "(*Centuria*) *procum patricium.*" *Historia* 17, 444–60.

———. 1976. *Römische Frühgeschichte: Kritik und Forschung seit 1964.* Heidelberg. (*Frühgeschichte*)

Altheim, F. 1931. *Griechische Götter im alten Rom.* Religionsgesch. Versuche und Vorarbeiten 22, no. 1. Giessen. (*Götter*)

———. 1938. *A History of Roman Religion.* Enlarged transl. of *Römische Religionsgeschichte.* Berlin-Leipzig, 1931–32. London. (*Religion*)

———. 1940. *Lex sacrata: Die Anfänge der plebeischen Organisation.* Albae Vigiliae 1. Amsterdam. (*Lex sacr.*)

———. 1941. "Patriziat und Plebs." *Die Welt als Geschichte*, 217–33.

———. 1950. "Diodors römische Annalen." *RhM* 93, 267–86.

———. 1951–53. *Römische Geschichte*. 2 vols. Frankfurt. (*Röm. Geschichte*)

Ampolo, C. 1970. "L'Artemide di Marsiglia e la Diana dell'Aventino." *PP* 25, 200–210.

———. 1970–71. "Su alcuni mutamenti sociali nel Lazio tra l'VIII e il V secolo." *DArch* 4/5, 37–68.

———. 1971. "Analogie e rapporti fra Atene e Roma arcaica: Osservazioni sulla *Regia*, sul *rex sacrorum* e sul culto di Vesta." *PP* 26, 443–60.

———. 1974. "*Servius rex primus signavit aes*." *PP* 29, 382–88.

———. 1975. "Gli Aquilii del V secolo a.C. e il problema dei fasti consolari più antichi." *PP* 30, 410–46.

———. 1976–77. "Demarato: Osservazioni sulla mobilità sociale arcaica." *DArch* 9/10, 333–45.

———. 1980. "Le condizioni materiali della produzione. Agricoltura e paesaggio agrario." *DArch*, n.s., 2, 15–46.

———. 1980. "Periodo IV B (640/30–580 a.C.)." *DArch*, n.s., 2, 165–92. Written in conjunction with G. Bartolini.

———. 1980. "Le origini di Roma e la 'cité antique'." *MEFR* 92, 567–75.

———. 1982. "Die endgültige Stadtwerdung Roms im 7. und 6. Jh.: Wann entstand die *civitas*?" In *Palast und Hütte: Beiträge zum Bauen und Wohnen im Altertum*, edited by D. Papenfuss and V. M. Strocka, 319–24. Berlin. ("Stadtwerdung Roms")

———. 1983. "La storiografia su Roma arcaica e i documenti." In *Tria Corda*, edited by E. Gabba, 9–26. Como. ("Storiografia e documenti")

———. 1983. "Servio Tullio e Dumézil (Osservazioni su Dumézil e le tradizioni e i documenti della storia romana del VII–VI secolo a.C.)." *Opus* 2, *Aspetti dell'opera di Georges Dumézil*, 391–400.

André, J. 1976. "Les Etymologies d'*adsiduus* et la critique textuelle." *RPh* 50, 22–23.

Andrén, A. 1960. "Dionysius of Halicarnassus on Roman Monuments." In *Hommages à L. Herrmann*, 88–104. Brussels.

Angelini, P. 1979. *Ricerche sul patriziato*. Milan. (*Patriziato*)

Appleton, C. 1919. "Contribution à l'histoire du prêt à intérêt à Rome: Le Taux du *fenus unciarium*." *RD* 43, 467–543.

Austin, M. M., and P. Vidal-Naquet. 1977. *Economic and Social History of Ancient Greece: An Introduction*. Berkeley and Los Angeles. (*Econ.*)

Aymard, A. 1943. "Liviana: A propos des Servilii Gemini." *REA* 45, 199–224.

Badian, E. 1966. "The Early Historians." In *Latin Historians*, edited by T. A. Dorey, 1–38. London. ("Early Historians")

Bakhuizen, S. C. 1975. "Social Ecology of the Ancient Greek World." *AC* 44, 211–18.

Balogh, E. 1948. "Cicero and the Greek Law." In *Scritti in onore di C. Ferrini*, edited by G. G. Archi, III: 1–27. Milan.

Balsdon, J. P. V. D. 1971. "Dionysius on Romulus: A Political Pamphlet?" *JRS* 61, 18–27.

Barbagallo, C. 1926. *Il problema delle origini di Roma da Vico a noi.* Milan. (*Problema*)

Bartošek, M. 1970. "Le classi sociali nella Roma antica." In *Etudes offertes à Jean Macqueron*, 43–88. Aix-en-Provence.

Basanoff, V. 1947–48. "Le Conflit entre *pater* et *eques* chez Tite-Live." *Annuaire de l'Ec. des Hautes Et. sect. sc. rel.*, 3–23.

———. 1950. "Tradition mythologique des annales, I–IV." *Latomus* 9, 13–26, 257–62, 263–64, 265–72.

Basile, M. 1978. "Analisi e valore della tradizione sulla *rogatio Cassia agraria* del 486 a.C." *Miscellanea greca e romana* 6, 277–98. Rome.

Bauman, R. A. 1966. "The Abdication of Collatinus." *Acta classica* 9, 129–41.

———. 1967. *The Crimen Maiestatis in the Roman Republic and Augustan Principate.* Johannesburg. (*Crimen*)

———. 1973. "The *lex Valeria de provocatione* of 300 B.C." *Historia* 22, 34–47.

Bayer, E. 1972. "Rom und die Westgriechen bis 280 v. Chr." *ANRW* I.1: 305–40.

Bayet, J. 1938. "Tite-Live et la précolonisation romaine." *RPh* 64, 97–119. Repr. in id., *Mélanges de littérature latine*, 351–75. Rome, 1967.

———. 1969. "L'organisation plébéienne et les *leges sacratae*." In Livy, *Histoire Romaine*, edited by J. Bayet, bk. III, 145–53. Paris.

Behrends, O. 1974. *Der Zwölftafelprozess: Zur Geschichte des römischen Obligationenrechts.* Göttingen. (*Zwölftafelprozess*)

———. 1974. "Das *nexum* im Manzipationsrecht oder die Ungeschichtlichkeit des Libraldarlehens." *RIDA* 21, 137–84.

Beloch, K. J. 1880. *Der italische Bund unter Roms Hegemonie: Staatsrechtliche und statistische Forschungen.* Leipzig. (*Ital. Bund*)

———. 1886. *Die Bevölkerung der griechisch-römischen Welt.* Leipzig. (*Bevölkerung*)

———. 1926. *Römische Geschichte bis zum Beginn der punischen Kriege*. Berlin-Leipzig. (*Röm. Geschichte*)

Bengtson, H. 1970. *Grundriss der römischen Geschichte mit Quellenkunde* I. *HdAW* III.5.1. Munich. 2nd ed. (*Grundriss*)

Berchem, D. van. 1935. "Il tempio di Cerere e l'ufficio dell'*annona* a Roma." *BCAR* 63, 91–95.

———. 1966. "Rome et le monde grec au VI^c siècle avant notre ère." In *Mélanges d'arch. et d'hist. offerts à A. Piganiol*, edited by R. Chevallier, II: 739–48. Paris. ("Rome et le monde grec")

———. 1980. "La Gérousie d'Ephèse." *MH* 37, 25–40.

Beretta, A. 1937. *L'esecuzione contro il debitore nel diritto romano ed il nexum*. Udine. (*Esecuzione*)

Beringer, W. 1961. "Soziale Entwicklung und Wertschätzung der Arbeit im Alten Rom (bis zur Zeit Ciceros)." *Studium Generale* 14, 135–51.

Bernardi, A. 1945–46. "Patrizi e plebei nella costituzione della primitiva repubblica romana." *RIL* 79, 3–14.

———. 1945–46. "Ancora sulla costituzione della primitiva repubblica romana." *RIL* 79, 15–26.

———. 1952. "Dagli ausiliari del *rex* ai magistrati della *res publica*." *Athenaeum* 30, 3–58.

Bertelli, L. 1972. "L'apologo di Menenio Agrippa: Incunabulo della *homonoia* a Roma?" *Index* 3, 224–34.

Besnier, R. 1934. "L'Etat économique de Rome au temps des rois." *RD* 13, 405–63.

———. 1950. "La Méthode de l'histoire économique et l'antiquité romaine." In *Conf. de l'Inst. de Droit Romain 1947*, 3–21. Paris.

———. 1953. "Les Archives privées, publiques et religieuses à Rome au temps des rois," in *Studi in memoria di E. Albertario*, edited by V. Arangio-Ruiz, II: 1–26. Milan. ("Archives")

———. 1955. "L'Etat économique de Rome de 509 à 264 av. J.-C." *RD* 33, 195–226.

Bianchini, M. 1972. "Sui rapporti fra *provocatio* ed *intercessio*." In *Studi in onore di G. Scherillo*, I: 93–110. Milan.

Bickerman, E. J. 1952. "*Origines gentium*." *CP* 47, 65–81.

———. 1969. "Some Reflections on Early Roman History." *RFIC* 97, 393–408.

Binder, J. 1909. *Die Plebs: Studien zur römischen Rechtsgeschichte*. Leipzig. (*Plebs*)

Biscardi, A. 1941–53. "*Auctoritas patrum.*" *BIDR* 48, 403–521; 57/58, 212–94.

Bitto, I. 1968. "*Tribus* e *propagatio civitatis* nei secoli IV e III a.C." *Epigraphica* 30, 20–58.

Blakeway, A. 1932–33. "Prolegomena to the Study of Greek Commerce with Italy, Sicily and France in the 8th and 7th Centuries B.C." *ABSA* 33, 170–208.

———. 1935. "Demaratus: A Study in Some Aspects of the Earliest Hellenisation of Latium and Etruria." *JRS* 25, 129–49.

Bleicken, J. 1957. "Oberpontifex und Pontifikalkollegium: Eine Studie zur römischen Sakralverfassung." *Hermes* 85, 345–66.

———. 1959. "Ursprung und Bedeutung der Provocation." *ZRG* 76, 324–77.

———. 1963. "Rom und Italien." In *Rom: Die römische Welt*. Propyläen Weltgeschichte, edited by G. Mann and A. Heuss, IV: 27–96. Berlin-Frankfurt-Vienna. ("Rom und Italien")

———. 1968. *Das Volkstribunat der klassischen Republik: Studien zu seiner Entwicklung zwischen 287 und 133 v. Chr.* Zetemata 13. Munich. 2nd ed. (*Volkstribunat*)

———. 1972. *Staatliche Ordnung und Freiheit in der römischen Republik.* Frankfurter Althistor. Studien 6. Kallmünz. (*Ordnung*)

———. 1975. *Lex publica: Gesetz und Recht in der römischen Republik.* Berlin. (*Lex*)

———. 1975. *Die Verfassung der römischen Republik: Grundlagen und Entwicklung.* Paderborn. (*Verfassung*)

———. 1980. *Geschichte der römischen Republik.* Munich-Vienna. (*Republik*)

———. 1981. "Das römische Volkstribunat: Versuch einer Analyse seiner politischen Funktion in republikanischer Zeit." *Chiron* 11, 87–108.

———. 1981. *Zum Begriff der römischen Amtsgewalt: auspicium–potestas–imperium.* Nachr. Akad. Göttingen, phil.-hist. Kl., no. 9.

Bloch, G. 1881. "Quelques mots sur la légende de Coriolan." *MEFR* 1, 215–25.

———. 1882. "Recherches sur quelques *gentes* patriciennes." *MEFR* 2, 241–76.

———. 1883. *Les Origines du Sénat romain.* Paris. (*Sénat*)

———. 1911–12. "La Plèbe romaine: Essai sur quelques théories récentes." *RH* 106, 241–75; 107, 1–42.

———. 1913. *La République romaine: Les conflits politiques et sociaux.* Paris (*Conflits*)

Bloch, R. 1954. "Une *lex sacra* de Lavinium et les origines de la triade agraire de l'Aventin." *CRAI*, 203–12.

———. 1959. "Rome de 509 à 475 environ av. J.-C." *REL* 37, 118–31.

———. 1960. *The Origins of Rome.* New York. (*Origins*)

———. 1960. *Les Prodiges dans l'antiquité classique.* Paris. (*Prodiges*)

———. 1960. "L'Origine du culte des Dioscures à Rome." *RPh* 34, 182–93.

———. 1961. "Le Départ des Etrusques de Rome selon l'annalistique et la dédicace du temple de Jupiter." *Rev. d'hist. des rel.* 159, 141–56. Cf. also *CRAI* (1961): 62–70.

———. 1965. *Tite-Live et les premiers siècles de Rome.* Paris. (*Tite-Live*)

———. 1980. "Recherches sur la religion romaine du VIe siècle et du début du Ve siècle av. J.-C." In *Recherches sur les religions de l'antiquité classique,* edited by R. Bloch, 347–81. Paris. ("Religion romaine")

Boddington, A. 1959. "The Original Nature of the Consular Tribunate." *Historia* 8, 356–64.

Boethius, A. 1945. "Maeniana: A Study of the Forum Romanum of the Fourth Century B.C." *Eranos* 43 (*Mélanges Löfstedt*), 89–110.

Bonamente, M. 1980. "Leggi suntuarie e loro motivazioni." In *Tra Grecia e Roma: Temi antichi e metodologie moderne,* edited by M. Pavan, 67–92. Rome. ("Leggi suntuarie")

Bonfante, G. 1970. "Le origini della repubblica romana." In *Studi in onore di G. Grosso,* IV: 465–84. Turin.

Botsford, G. W. 1909. *The Roman Assemblies from their Origin to the End of the Republic.* New York. (*Assemblies*)

Bredehorn, U. 1968. *Senatsakten in der republikanischen Annalistik.* Marburg. (*Senatsakten*)

Bréguet, E. 1978. "Récits d'histoire romaine chez Cicéron et Tite-Live." *MH* 35, 264–72.

Bremmer, J. 1982. "The *suodales* of Poplios Valesios." *ZPE* 47, 133–47.

Bringmann, K. 1977. "Weltherrschaft und innere Krise Roms im Spiegel der Geschichtsschreibung des zweiten und ersten Jh. v. Chr." *A&A* 23, 28–49.

———. 1980. "Die soziale und politische Verfassung Spartas: Ein Sonderfall der griechischen Verfassungsgeschichte?" *Gymnasium* 87, 467–84.

Briscoe, J. 1973. *A Commentary on Livy: Books XXXI-XXXIII.* Oxford. (*Comm.*)

Brisson, J.-P., ed. 1969. *Problèmes de la guerre à Rome*. Paris. (*Guerre à Rome*)

Broughton, T. R. S. 1951. *The Magistrates of the Roman Republic*. 2 vols. Cleveland. (*Magistrates*)

Brown, F. E. 1967. "New Soundings in the Regia: The Evidence for the Early Republic." In *Les Origines de la république romaine*, Entr. sur l'ant. class. 13, 45–60. Vandoeuvres-Geneva. ("Regia")

Bruhl, A. 1953. *Liber pater: Origine et expansion du culte dionysiaque à Rome et dans le monde romain*. Paris. (*Liber*)

Bruno, L. 1966. "*Libertas plebis* in Tito Livio." *GIF* 19, 107–30.

———. 1966. "*Crimen regni* e *superbia* in Tito Livio." *GIF* 19, 236–59.

Bruno, L., and M. Pinto. 1954. *La costituzione romana nella prima deca di Tito Livio*. Naples. (*Costituzione*)

Brunt, P. A. 1971. *Social Conflicts in the Roman Republic*. London and New York. (*Conflicts*)

———. 1971. *Italian Manpower 225 B.C.–A.D. 14*. Oxford. (*Manpower*)

———. 1980. "Cicero and Historiography." In *Philias Charin: Miscellanea di studi classici in onore di E. Manni*, I: 309–40. Rome. ("Cicero and Historiography")

———. 1982. "*Nobilitas* and *novitas*." *JRS* 72, 1–17.

Bruun, P. 1967. "The *foedus Gabinum*." *Arctos* 5, 51–66.

Bruwaene, M. van den. 1955. *La Société romaine*. Vol. I, *Les Origines et la formation*. Brussels. (*Société*)

Burck, E. 1940. "Altrom im Kriege." *Antike* 16, 206–26.

———. 1957. "Zum Rombild des Livius: Interpretationen zur zweiten Pentade." *Der Altsprachl. Unterricht*, 3rd ser., 2, 34–75 (= id., *Menschenbild* I: 321–53).

———. 1964 [1934]. *Die Erzählungskunst des T. Livius*. Berlin-Zurich. 2nd ed. 1st ed. 1934. (*Erzählungskunst*)

———. 1964. "Die Gestalt des Camillus." In id., ed., *WL*, 310–28. Repr. from "Aktuelle Probleme der Livius-Interpretation." In *Beihefte zum Gymnasium* 4, 22–46. Heidelberg, 1964.

———. 1966–81. *Vom Menschenbild in der römischen Literatur*. 2 vols. Heidelberg. (*Menschenbild*)

———. 1966. "Das Bild der Revolution bei römischen Historikern." *Gymnasium* 73, 86–109 (= id., *Menschenbild* II: 118–43).

———, ed. 1967. *Wege zu Livius*. WdF 132. Darmstadt. (*WL*)

———. 1968. "Die Frühgeschichte Roms bei Livius im Lichte der Denkmäler." *Gymnasium* 75, 74–110 (= id., *Menschenbild* II: 181–213).

Burdese, A. 1966. "Riflessioni sulla repressione penale romana in età arcaica." *BIDR* 69, 342–54.

Calderaro, F. 1952. *Nuovi discorsi sulla prima deca di Tito Livio: Studio filosofico, storico, politico.* Il pensiero filos., vol. 1, no. 9. Padua. (*Discorsi*)

Calonge, A. 1968. "El *pontifex maximus* y el problema de la distinción entre magistraturas y sacerdocios." *Ann. de hist. del derecho Español* 38, 5–29.

Caltabiano, M. 1976. "Motivi polemici nella tradizione storiografica relativa a C. Flaminio." *CISA* 4, 102–17.

Cancelli, F. 1957. *Studi sui* censores *e sull*'arbitratus *della* lex contractus. Milan. (*Censores*)

———. 1960. "Postilla sul potere dei *censores*." *Labeo* 6, 225–27.

Capanelli, D. 1981. "Appunti sulla *rogatio agraria* di Spurio Cassio." In *Legge e società nella repubblica romana*, edited by F. Serrao, I: 3–50. Naples. ("Spurio Cassio")

Capogrossi Colognesi, L. 1969–76. *La struttura della proprietà e la formazione dei* iura praediorum *nell'età repubblicana.* 2 vols. Milan. (*Proprietà*)

———. 1970. "Ancora sui poteri del *pater familias*." *BIDR* 73, 357–425.

———. 1971. "In margine al primo trattato tra Roma e Cartagine." In *Studi in onore di E. Volterra*, V: 171–89. Milan. ("Primo trattato")

———. 1978. *Storia delle istituzioni romane arcaiche.* Rome. (*Istituzioni*)

———. 1979. "Le Régime de la terre à l'époque républicaine." In *Terre et paysans dépendants dans les sociétés antiques, Coll. intern. de Besançon, 1974*, 313–88. Paris. ("Régime de la terre")

———. 1980. "Alcuni problemi di storia romana arcaica: *ager publicus, gentes* e clienti." *BIDR* 83, 29–65.

———. 1981. *La terra in Roma antica* I. Rome. (*Terra*)

Capozza, M. 1966. *Movimenti servili nel mondo romano.* Vol. I, *Dal 501 al 184.* Rome. (*Mov. serv.*)

———. 1973. *Roma fra monarchia e decemvirato nell'interpretazione di Eutropio.* Pubbl. Ist. Stor. Ant. Univ. Padova 10. Rome. (*Eutropio*)

Cartledge, P. 1977. "Hoplites and Heroes: Sparta's Contribution to the Technique of Ancient Warfare." *JHS* 97, 11–27.

Cassola, F. 1962. *I gruppi politici romani nel III secolo a.C.* Trieste. (*Gruppi politici*)

———. 1968. "La repubblica romana." In A. Bernardi, F. Cassola et al., *Nuove questioni di storia antica*, 283–374. Milan.

———. 1982. "Diodoro e la storia romana." *ANRW* II.30.1: 724–73.

Castagnoli, F. 1958. "Roma antica." In *Topografia e urbanistica di Roma*. Storia di Roma 22, 3–186. Bologna.

———. 1972–75. *Lavinium*. Vol. I, *Topografia generale: Fonti e storia delle ricerche*. Vol. II, *Le tredici are*. Rome. (*Lavinium*)

———. 1973–74. "Topografia romana e tradizione storiografica su Roma arcaica." *Arch. Class.* 25/26, 123–31.

———. 1974. "Topografia e urbanistica di Roma nel IV secolo a.C." *SR* 22, 425–43.

———. 1978. *Roma antica: Profilo urbanistico*. Rome. (*Roma*)

———. 1980. *Topografia di Roma antica*. Turin. (*Topografia*)

Catalano, P. 1971. *Tribunato e resistenza*. Turin. (*Tribunato*)

———. 1977. "A proposito dei concetti di 'rivoluzione' nella dottrina romanistica contemporanea (tra 'rivoluzione della plebe' e dittature rivoluzionarie)." *SDHI* 43, 440–55.

Cavaignac, E. 1949. "L'Evolution de l'organisation centuriate d'après les derniers travaux numismatiques." *RIDA* 2, 173–88.

Ceci, L. 1926. "Roma e gli Etruschi." *La cultura* 6, 1–6.

Cels Saint-Hilaire, J., and C. Feuvrier-Prévotat. 1979. "Guerres, échanges, pouvoir à Rome à l'époque archaïque." *Dial. d'hist. anc.* 5, 103–36.

Champeaux, J. 1983. *Fortuna: Recherches sur le culte de la fortune à Rome et dans le monde romain des origines à la mort de César*. Vol. I, *Fortuna dans la religion archaïque*. Paris. (*Fortuna*)

Chantraine, H. 1972. "Zur Entstehung der Freilassung mit Bürgerrechtserwerb in Rom." *ANRW* I.2: 59–67.

———. 1983. "Münzbild und Familiengeschichte in der römischen Republik." *Gymnasium* 90, 530–45.

Ciaceri, E. 1937. *Le origini di Roma: La monarchia e la prima fase dell'età repubblicana dal sec. VIII alla metà del sec. V a.C.* Milan. (*Origini*)

———. 1943. *L'opera di Livio e la moderna critica storica*. Quad. liviani: La figura e l'opera di Livio 2. Rome. (*Livio*)

Ciulei, C. 1944. "Die XII Tafeln und die römische Gesandtschaft nach Griechenland." *ZRG* 64, 350–54.

———. 1969. "Gab es einen Einfluss des griechischen Rechts in den Zwölftafeln?" In *Gesellschaft und Recht im griechisch-römischen Altertum*, edited by M. Andreev, II: 21–46. Akad. der Wiss. Berlin, Schriften Sekt. Altertumswiss. 52. Berlin. ("Einfluss")

Classen, C. J. 1965. "Die Königszeit im Spiegel der Literatur der römischen Republik." *Historia* 14, 385–403.

Clemente, G. 1981. "Le leggi sul lusso e la società romana tra III e II secolo a.C." In *Società romana e produzione schiavistica*, vol. III, *Modelli etici, diritto e trasformazioni sociali*, edited by A. Giardina and A. Schiavone, 1–14. Bari. ("Leggi sul lusso")

Clerici, L. 1943. *Economia e finanza dei romani dalle origini alla fine delle guerre sannitiche*. Bologna. (*Economia*)

Cloud, J. D. 1977. "The Date of Valerius Antias." *LCM* 2, 225–27.

Civiltà del Lazio Primitivo. 1976. Exhibition Catalogue. Rome.

Coarelli, F. 1974. *Guida archeologica di Roma*. Rome. (*Roma*)

———. 1982. "Lo sviluppo urbanistico della città nel primo periodo repubblicano." In *Roma repubblicana fra il 509 e il 207 a.C.*, edited by I. Dondero and P. Pensabene, 19–27. Rome. ("Sviluppo urbanistico")

———. 1983. *Il foro romano: Periodo arcaico*. Rome. (*Foro*)

Cohen, B. 1975. "La Notion d'*ordo* dans la Rome antique." *BAGB*, 259–82.

Coli, U. 1951. *Regnum* (= *SDHI* 17, 1–168). Rome. (*Regnum*)

———. 1953. "Sui limiti di durata delle magistrature romane." In *Studi in onore di V. Arangio-Ruiz*, IV: 395–418. Naples.

———. 1955. "Tribù e centurie dell'antica repubblica romana." *SDHI* 21, 181–222.

Colini, A. M. 1977. "L'area sacra di Sant'Omobono: Ambiente e storia dei tempi più antichi." *PP* 32, 7–19.

Colonna, G. 1964. "Aspetti culturali della Roma primitiva: Il periodo orientalizzante recente." *Archeol. Class.* 16, 1–12.

———. 1974. "Preistoria e protostoria di Roma e del Lazio." In *Popoli e civiltà dell'Italia antica*, II: 273–346. Rome. ("Preistoria e protostoria")

———. 1977. "Nome gentilizio e società." *SE* 45, 175–92.

———. 1977. "Un aspetto oscuro del Lazio antico: Le tombe del VI–V secolo a. C." *PP* 32, 131–65.

Colonna, G., M. Cristofani, and G. Garbini. 1966. "Bibliografia delle pubblicazioni più recenti sulle scoperte di Pyrgi." *Archeol. Class.* 18, 279–82.

Columba, G. M., P. Fraccaro et al. 1934. *Studi liviani*. Rome.

Combet-Farnoux, B. 1957. "Cumes, l'Etrurie et Rome à la fin du VIe siècle et au début du Ve siècle: Un aspect des premiers contacts de Rome avec l'hellénisme." *MEFR* 69, 7–44.

———. 1980. *Mercure romain: Le Culte public de Mercure et la fonction mercantile à Rome de la République archaïque à l'époque augustéenne.* BEFAR 238. Paris. (*Mercure*)

Corbett, P. E. 1930. *The Roman Law of Marriage.* Oxford. (*Marriage*)

Cornelius, F. 1940. *Untersuchungen zur frühen römischen Geschichte.* Munich. (*Untersuchungen*)

Cornell, T. J. 1975. "Aeneas and the Twins: The Development of the Roman Foundation Legend." *PCPhS* 21, 1–32.

———. 1976. "Etruscan Historiography." *ASNP* 6, 411–39.

———. 1978. "The Foundation of Rome in the Ancient Literary Tradition." In *Papers in Italian Archaeology*, edited by H. M. Blake, T. W. Potter, and D. B. Whitehouse, I: 131–40. Brit. Arch. Rep. suppl. ser. 41. Oxford. ("Foundation of Rome")

———. 1979–80. "Rome and *Latium Vetus*, 1974–1979." *Archaeological Reports*, 71–89.

———. 1980. "Alcune riflessioni sulla formazione della tradizione storiografica su Roma arcaica." In *Roma arcaica e le recenti scoperte archeologiche*, 19–44. Milan. ("Tradizione storiografica")

———. 1983. "The Failure of the Plebs." In *Tria Corda: Scritti in onore di A. Momigliano*, edited by E. Gabba, 101–20. Como. ("Failure of the Plebs")

Costanzi, V. 1929. "Sul divieto di connubio fra patrizi e plebei." In *Atti I congr. naz. di studi romani*, II: 171–77. Rome.

Crake, J. E. A. 1940. "The Annals of the Pontifex Maximus." *CP* 35, 375–86. In German in Pöschl, *Geschichtsschreibung*, 256–71.

Crawford, M. 1975. *Roman Republican Coinage.* 2 vols. Cambridge. (*Coinage*)

———. 1976. "The Early Roman Economy, 753–280 B.C." In *L'Italie préromaine et la Rome républicaine: Mélanges . . . J. Heurgon*, I: 197–207. Coll. Ec. Franç. de Rome 27. Paris. ("Roman Economy")

Crifò, G. 1960. *Ricerche sull'exilium: L'origine dell'istituto e gli elementi della sua evoluzione.* Milan. (*Ricerche*)

———. 1961. *Ricerche sull'*exilium *nel periodo repubblicano.* Milan. (*Exilium*)

———. 1963. "Alcune osservazioni in tema di *provocatio ad populum*." *SDHI* 29, 288–95.

———. 1972. "La legge delle XII tavole: osservazioni e problemi." *ANRW* I.2: 115–33.

Cristofani, M. 1974. "Diffusione dell'alfabeto e onomastica arcaica nell'Etruria interna settentrionale." In *Aspetti e problemi dell'Etruria interna: Atti dell'VIII conv. naz. di studi etruschi ed italici*, 307–24. Florence.

Dahlheim, W. 1968. *Struktur und Entwicklung des römischen Völkerrechts im 3. und 2. Jh. v. Chr.* Vestigia 8. Munich. (*Völkerrecht*)

Dal Cason, F. 1985. "La tradizione annalistica sulle piu antiche leggi agrarie: riflessioni e proposte." *Athenaeum* 63, 174–84.

Daube, D. 1969. *Roman Law: Linguistic, Social and Philosophical Aspects.* Edinburgh. (*Law*)

Davies, J. K. 1977–78. "Athenian Citizenship: The Descent Group and the Alternatives." *CJ* 73, 105–21.

Day, J., and M. Chambers. 1962. *Aristotle's History of Athenian Democracy.* Berkeley and Los Angeles. (*Ath. Pol.*)

De Francisci, P. 1944. "Dal *regnum* alla *res publica*." *SDHI* 10, 150–66.

———. 1953. "Per la storia dei *comitia centuriata*." In *Studi in onore di V. Arangio-Ruiz*, I: 1–32. Naples. ("*Comitia centuriata*")

———. 1956. "La communità sociale e politica romana primitiva." *SDHI* 22, 1–86.

———. 1959. *Primordia civitatis*. Rome. (*Primordia*)

Dell'Oro, A. 1950. *La formazione dello stato patrizio-plebeo.* Milan. (*Formazione*)

Delz, J. 1966. "Der griechische Einfluss auf die Zwölftafelgesetzgebung." *MH* 23, 69–83.

De Martino, F. 1953. "La *gens*, lo stato e le classi in Roma antica." In *Studi in onore di V. Arangio-Ruiz*, IV: 25–49 (= id., *Dir. e soc.*, 51–74). Naples. ("*Gens*")

———. 1972–75. *Storia della costituzione romana*. 6 vols. Naples. 2nd ed. (*Cost.*)

———. 1972. "Intorno all'origine della repubblica romana e delle magistrature." *ANRW* I.1: 217–49 (= id., *Dir. e soc.*, 88–129).

———. 1974. "Intorno all'origine della schiavitù a Roma." *Labeo* 20, 163–93 (= id., *Dir. e soc.*, 130–61).

———. 1975. "Riforme del IV secolo a.C." *BIDR* 78, 29–70 (= id., *Dir. e soc.*, 183–224).

———. 1977. "Territorio, popolazione ed ordinamento centuriato." *BIDR* 80, 1–22 (= id., *Dir. e soc.*, 162–82).

———. 1979. *Diritto e società nell'antica Roma: Scritti di diritto romano* I. Bibl. di storia ant. 6. Rome. (*Dir. e soc.*)

———. 1979. *Storia economica di Roma antica*. 2 vols. Florence. (*Econ.*)

———. 1979. "Produzione di cereali in Roma nell'età arcaica." *PP* 34, 241–53.

———. 1980. "Clienti e condizioni materiali in Roma arcaica." In *Philias charin: Miscellanea di studi classici in onore di E. Manni*, II: 679–705. Rome. ("Clienti")

———. 1980. "Sulla storia dell'*equitatus* romano." *PP* 35, 143–60.

De Sanctis, G. 1909–10. "La Légende historique des premiers siècles de Rome." *Journ. des Sav.* 7, 126–32, 205–14; 8, 310–19.

———. 1929. "Sul *foedus Cassianum*." In *Atti I congr. naz. di studi romani*, I: 231–39. Rome.

———. 1932. "La origine dell'edilità plebea." *RFIC* 60, 433–45.

———. 1933. "Le origini dell'ordinamento centuriato." *RFIC* 61, 289–98.

———. 1956–69. *Storia dei Romani*. 4 vols. Florence. 2nd ed. (*Storia*)

———. 1980. *Storia dei Romani* I. New edition by S. Accame. Florence. (*Storia* I³)

Detienne, M. 1963. *Crise agraire et attitude religieuse chez Hésiode*. Coll. Latomus 68. Brussels. (*Crise*)

———. 1968. "La Phalange: Problèmes et controverses." In *Problèmes de la guerre en Grèce ancienne*, edited by J.-P. Vernant, 119–42. Paris and The Hague. ("La Phalange")

Develin, R. 1975. "*Comitia tributa plebis*." *Athenaeum* 53, 302–37.

———. 1976. "C. Flaminius in 232 B.C." *AC* 45, 638–43.

———. 1977. "*Comitia tributa* again." *Athenaeum* 55, 425–26.

———. 1977. "*Lex curiata* and the Competence of Magistrates." *Mnemosyne*, 4th ser., 30, 49–65.

———. 1978. "*Provocatio* and Plebiscites: Early Roman Legislation and the Historical Tradition." *Mnemosyne*, 4th ser., 31, 45–60.

———. 1978. "Religion and Politics at Rome during the Third Century B.C." *Journal of Religious History* 10, 3–19.

———. 1978. "The Third Century Reform of the *comitia centuriata*." *Athenaeum* 56, 346–76.

———. 1978. "The Atinian Plebiscite, Tribunes, and the Senate." *CQ* 28, 141–44.

———. 1979. *Patterns in Office-Holding 366–49 B.C.* Coll. Latomus 161. Brussels. (*Patterns*)

———. 1979. "The Voting Position of the *Equites* after the Centuriate Reform." *RhM* 122, 155–61.

———. 1979. "The Political Position of C. Flaminius." *RhM* 122, 268–77.

———. 1980. "Patrician Censors 218–50 B.C." *Antichthon* 14, 84–87.

———. 1981. "A Peculiar Restriction on Candidacy for Plebeian Office." *Antichthon* 15, 111–17.

———. 1984. "The Constitution of Drakon." *Athenaeum*, n.s., 62, 295–307.

———. 1985. *The Practice of Politics at Rome 366–167 B.C.* Coll. Latomus 188. Brussels. (*Practice*)

Devijver, H. 1981. "Livius' boek der koningen en de archeologie: Legende versus archief?" *Kleio* 11, 149–201.

Devoto, G. 1964. "La crisi del latino nel V sec. a.C." *Studii clasice* 6, 17–23 (= id., *Scritti minori*, II: 362–68. Florence, 1968).

———. 1968. "Tre aspetti della romanità arcaica." *RSI* 80, 658–68.

———. 1972. "Storia politica e storia linguistica." *ANRW* I.2: 457–65.

Diósdi, G. 1970. *Ownership in Ancient and Preclassical Roman Law*. Budapest. (*Ownership*)

D'Ippolito, F. 1975. "La legge agraria di Spurio Cassio." *Labeo* 21, 197–210.

Dittenberger, W., ed. 1960. *Sylloge inscriptionum Graecarum*. 4 vols. Hildesheim. 4th ed. (= 3rd ed., 1915–24). (*Syll.*)

Dondero, I., and P. Pensabene, eds. 1982. *Roma repubblicana fra il 509 e il 207 a.C.* Rome.

Donlan, W. 1973. "The Tradition of Anti-Aristocratic Thought in Early Greek Poetry." *Historia* 22, 145–54.

———. 1980. *The Aristocratic Ideal in Ancient Greece: Attitudes of Superiority from Homer to the End of the Fifth Century B.C.* Lawrence, Kans. (*Ideal*)

———. 1981–82. "Reciprocities in Homer." *CW* 75, 137–75.

Drummond, A. 1978. "The Dictator Years." *Historia* 27, 550–72.

Ducat, F. 1979. "Quelques éléments pour une réflexion sur les nobles en Grèce archaïque." *Ann. fac. lettr. et sc. humaines de Nice* 37 (*L'Histoire dans ses variantes*), 11–15.

Ducos, M. 1978. *L'Influence grecque sur la loi des douze tables*. Paris. (*Influence*)

Dumézil, G. 1943. *Servius et la Fortune: Essai sur la fonction sociale de louange et de blâme et sur les éléments indoeuropéens du cens romain*. Paris. (*Servius*)

———. 1969. *Idées romaines*. Paris. (*Idées*)

———. 1970. *Archaic Roman Religion.* 2 vols. Chicago. French ed., Paris, 1966. (*Arch. Rel.*)

———. 1980. *Camillus: A Study of Indo-European Religion as Roman History.* Berkeley and Los Angeles. (*Camillus*)

Duval, N., and H. G. Pflaum, eds. 1977. *L'Onomastique latine.* Coll. intern. du C.N.R.S. 564. Paris.

Edlund, I. E. M. 1976. "Dionysios of Halikarnassos: Liberty and Democracy in Rome." *CB* 53, 27–31.

Ehrenberg, V. 1968. *From Solon to Socrates.* London. (*Solon*)

Ellul, J. 1972. "Réflexions sur la révolution, la plèbe et le tribunat de la plèbe." *Index* 3, 155–67.

Elster, M. 1976. *Studien zur Gesetzgebung der frühen römischen Republik: Gesetzesanhäufungen und -wiederholungen.* Frankfurt and Berne. (*Studien*)

Enea nel Lazio: Archeologia e mito. 1981. Exhibition catalogue. Rome.

Erasmus, H. J. 1962. *The Origins of Rome in Historiography from Petrarch to Perizonius.* Assen. (*Origins*)

Erb, N. 1963. *Kriegsursachen und Kriegsschuld in der ersten Pentade des T. Livius.* Zurich. (*Kriegsursachen*)

Ernout, A., and A. Meillet. 1967. *Dictionnaire étymologique de la langue latine.* Paris. 4th ed. (*Dictionnaire*)

Fadinger, V. 1969. *Die Begründung des Prinzipats: Quellenkritische und staatsrechtliche Untersuchungen zu Cassius Dio und der Parallelüberlieferung.* Berlin and Bonn. (*Prinzipat*)

Ferenczy, E. 1951. "Critique des sources de la politique extérieure romaine de 390 à 340 av. notre ère." *AAH* 1, 127–59.

———. 1965. "La Carrière d'Appius Claudius Caecus jusqu'à la censure." *AAH* 13, 379–404.

———. 1966. "The Rise of the Patrician-Plebeian State." *AAH* 14, 113–39.

———. 1967. "The Censorship of Appius Claudius Caecus." *AAH* 15, 27–61.

———. 1968. "Zur Vorgeschichte des zweiten römisch-punischen Vertrages." *AAH* 16, 209–13.

———. 1969. "Die römisch-punischen Verträge und die Protohistorie des commercium." *RIDA* 16, 259–82.

———. 1969. "Zur Verfassungsgeschichte der Frührepublik." In *Beiträge zur Alten Geschichte und deren Nachleben: Festschrift für F. Altheim,* edited by R. Stiehl and H. E. Stier, I: 136–50. Berlin. ("Verfassungsgeschichte")

———. 1970. "The Career of Appius Claudius Caecus after the Censorship." *AAH* 18, 71–103.

———. 1973. "Die Bevölkerung von minderem Recht Roms zur Zeit der Frührepublik." *AAH* 21, 153–60.

———. 1975. "Die erste Entwicklungsphase der Verfassung der römischen Republik: Vom Verfall der Monarchie bis zum Dezemvirat." *Ann. Univ. Budapest (sectio class.)* 3, 65–80.

———. 1975. "Zum Problem des *foedus Cassianum*." *RIDA* 22, 223–32.

———. 1976. *From the Patrician State to the Patricio-Plebeian State*. Amsterdam. (*Patr. State*)

———. 1976. "L'immigrazione della *gens Claudia* e l'origine delle tribù territoriali." *Labeo* 22, 362–64.

———. 1976. "*Uti legassit . . . ita ius esto*." *Oikumene* 1, 173–83.

———. 1978. "Eherecht und Gesellschaft in der Zeit der Zwölftafeln." *Oikumene* 2, 153–61.

———. 1978–79. "Clientela e schiavitù nella repubblica romana primitiva." *Index* 8, 167–72.

———. 1979. "Römische Rechtsgeschichte–antike Rechtsgeschichte." *Klio* 61, 25–31.

———. 1982. "Über die alte Klientel." *Oikumene* 3, 193–201.

———. 1983. "Römische Gesandtschaft im perikleischen Athen." *Oikumene* 4, 38–41.

Ferrary, J.-L. 1984. "L'Archéologie du *De Re Publica* (2,2,4–37,63): Cicéron entre Polybe et Platon." *JRS* 74, 87–98.

Ferri, S. 1960. "*Vei patria victa*." In *Hommage à L. Herrmann*, 350–58. Coll. Latomus 44. Brussels.

Ferron, J. 1972. "Un Traité d'alliance entre Caere et Carthage contemporain des derniers temps de la royauté étrusque à Rome ou l'évènement commémoré par la quasi-bilingue de Pyrgi." *ANRW* I.1: 189–216.

Finley, M. I. 1965. "La Servitude pour dettes." *RD* 43, 159–84. English in id., *Soc.*, 150–66.

———. 1965. "Myth, Memory and History." *History and Theory* 4, 281–302. Enlarged in id., *The Use and Abuse of History*, 11–33. London and New York, 1975.

———. 1973. *The Ancient Economy*. London and Berkeley. (*Econ.*)

———. 1977. *The World of Odysseus*. London. 2nd ed. (*Odysseus*)

———. 1981. *Economy and Society in Ancient Greece*. New York. (*Soc.*)

———. 1983. "The Ancient Historian and His Sources." In *Tria Corda: Scritti in onore di A. Momigliano*, edited by E. Gabba, 201–14. Como. ("*Ancient Historian*")

Flores, E. 1974. *Letteratura latina e ideologia del III–II sec. a.C.: Disegno storico-sociologico da Appio Claudio Cieco a Pacuvio*. Naples. (*Ideologia*)

La formazione della città nel Lazio. 1980. DArch, n.s., 2.

Fornara, C. W. 1983. *Archaic Times to the End of the Peloponnesian War*. Cambridge. 2nd ed. (*Archaic Times*)

———. 1983. *The Nature of History in Ancient Greece and Rome*. Berkeley and Los Angeles. (*History*)

Forni, G. 1953. "Manio Curio Dentato uomo democratico." *Athenaeum* 31, 170–239.

Forrest, W. G. 1966. *The Emergence of Greek Democracy*. London. (*Emergence*)

Fowler, W. W. 1911. *The Religious Experience of the Roman People from the Earliest Times to the Age of Augustus*. London. (*Experience*)

Fraccaro, P. 1919. "Lex Flaminia de agro Gallico et Piceno viritim dividundo." *Athenaeum* 7, 73–93 (= id., *Opuscula* II: 191–205).

———. 1931. "La storia dell'antichissimo esercito romano e l'età dell'ordinamento centuriato." In *Atti II congr. naz. di studi romani*, III: 91–97 (= id., *Opuscula* II: 287–92). Rome.

———. 1934. "Ancora sull'età dell'ordinamento centuriato." *Athenaeum* 22, 57–71 (= id., *Opuscula* II: 293–306).

———. 1952. "La storia romana arcaica." *RIL* 85, 85–118 (= id., *Opuscula* I: 1–23).

———. 1956–75. *Opuscula*. 4 vols. Pavia. (*Opuscula*)

———. 1975. *Della guerra presso i Romani* (= id., *Opuscula* IV). Pavia. (*Guerra*)

Franciosi, G. 1963. "Sui *decemviri stlitibus iudicandis*." *Labeo* 9, 163–202.

Frank, T. 1920. *An Economic History of Rome to the End of the Republic*. Baltimore. (*Econ.*)

———. 1930. "Roman Census Statistics from 508 to 225 B.C." *AJP* 51, 313–24.

———. 1931. *Some Economic Aspects of Rome's Early Law*. Proc. Am. Philos. Soc. 70. Philadelphia. (*Law*)

———. 1933. *An Economic Survey of Ancient Rome*. Vol. I, *Rome and Italy of the Republic*. Baltimore. Repr. New York, 1975. (*Economic Survey*)

Fraschetti, A. 1982. "Inquadramento storico e fonti." In *Roma repubblicana fra il 509 e il 270 a.C.*, edited by I. Dondero and P. Pensabene, 13–18. Rome. ("Inquadramento storico")

Fraser, A. D. 1955. "Two Metamorphoses of the *plebs*." *CB* 32, 13–20.

Frezza, P. 1946. "Intorno alla leggenda dei Fabi al Cremera." In *Scritti di diritto romano in onore di C. Ferrini*, edited by G. G. Archi, 295–306. Milan.

———. 1977. "Secessioni plebee e rivolte servili nella Roma antica." *Index* 7, 95–109 (= *SDHI* 45 [1979]: 310–27).

Frier, B. W. 1975. "Licinius Macer and the *consules suffecti* of 444 B.C." *TAPA* 105, 79–97.

———. 1979. *Libri annales pontificum maximorum: The Origins of the Annalistic Tradition*. Pap. and Monogr. of the American Academy in Rome 27. (*Annales*)

Friezer, E. 1959. "*Interregnum* and *patrum auctoritas*." *Mnemosyne*, 4th ser., 12, 301–29.

Fritz, K. von. 1950. "The Reorganization of the Roman Government in 366 B.C. and the so-called Licinio-Sextian Laws." *Historia* 1, 3–44 (= id., *Schriften*, 329–73).

———. 1953. "*Leges sacratae* and *plebei scita*." In *Studies . . . D. M. Robinson*, edited by G. E. Mylonas, II: 893–905 (= id., *Schriften*, 374–87). Saint Louis. ("*Leges sacratae*")

———. 1976. *Schriften zur griechischen und römischen Verfassungsgeschichte und Verfassungstheorie*. Berlin and New York. (*Schriften*)

Fustel de Coulanges, N. D. 1980. *The Ancient City: A Study on the Religion, Laws, and Institutions of Greece and Rome*. New ed. with a foreword by A. Momigliano and S. C. Humphreys. Baltimore. (*City*)

Gabba, E. 1960. "Studi su Dionigi da Alicarnasso: I, La costituzione di Romolo." *Athenaeum*, n.s., 38, 175–205.

———. 1961. "Studi su Dionigi da Alicarnasso: II, Il regno di Servio Tullio." *Athenaeum*, n.s., 39, 98–121.

———. 1964. "Studi su Dionigi da Alicarnasso: III, La proposta legge agraria di Spurio Cassio." *Athenaeum*, n.s., 42, 29–41.

———. 1964. "Un documento censorio in Dionigi d'Alicarnasso, 1,74,5." In *Synteleia V. Arangio-Ruiz*, edited by A. Guarino and L. Labruna, I: 486–93. Naples. ("Documento censorio")

———. 1966. "Dionigi d'Alicarnasso sul processo di Spurio Cassio." In *La storia del diritto nel quadro delle scienze storiche, Atti I congr. intern. della soc. ital. di stor. del dir.*, 143–53. Florence. ("Processo di Spurio Cassio")

———. 1967. "Considerazioni sulla tradizione letteraria sulle origini della Repubblica." In *Les Origines de la république romaine*, Entr. sur l'ant. class. 13, 133–74. Vandoeuvres-Geneva. ("Tradizione letteraria")

———. 1973. "Dionigi e la 'Storia di Roma arcaica'." In *Assoc. G. Budé: Actes du IXe congrès, Rome 1973*, I: 218–29. Paris. ("Dionigi e Roma arcaica")

———. 1974. "Storiografia greca e imperialismo romano (III–I sec. a.C.)." *RSI* 84, 652–742.

———. 1975. "Istituzioni militari e la colonizzazione in Roma mediorepubblicana (IV–III sec. a.C.)." *RFIC* 103, 144–54.

———. 1976. "Sulla valorizzazione politica della leggenda delle origini troiane di Roma." In *I canali della propaganda nel mondo antico*, edited by M. Sordi, 84–101. Milan.

———. 1982. "La 'storia di Roma arcaica' di Dionigi di Alicarnasso." *ANRW* II.30.1: 799–816.

———, ed. 1983. *Tria corda: Scritti in onore di A. Momigliano*. Como.

———. 1984. "The *collegia* of Numa: Problems of Method and Political Ideas." *JRS* 74, 81–86.

Gagarin, M. 1981. *Drakon and Early Athenian Homicide Law*. Yale Classical Monographs 3. New Haven. (*Drakon*)

Gagé, J. 1950–51. "*Frumentum Siculum*." *Bull. Fac. Lettr. Strasbourg* 29, 347–59 (cf. id., "Le *frumentum Siculum* dans l'histoire de Rome au Ve siècle av. J.-C." *CRAI* [1950]: 325).

———. 1955. *Apollon romain: Essai sur le culte d'Apollon et le développement du 'ritus Graecus' à Rome des origines à Auguste*. BEFAR 182. Paris. (*Apollon*)

———. 1955. "Les Traditions des Papirii et quelques-unes des origines de l'*equitatus* romain et latin." *RD* 33, 20–50, 165–94 (= id., *Enquêtes*, 219–77).

———. 1962. "Mercure et le centurion." *Cah. intern. de soc.* 35, 85–112 (= id., *Enquêtes*, 185–217).

———. 1970. "Les Rites anciens de lustration du *populus* et les attributs triomphaux des censeurs." *MEFR* 82, 43–71 (= id., *Enquêtes*, 338–66).

———. 1970. "La *plebs* et le *populus* et leurs encadrements respectifs dans la Rome de la première moitié du Ve siècle av. J.-C." *RH* 94, 5–30 (= id., *Enquêtes*, 313–37).

———. 1970. "Les Chevaliers romains et les grains de Cérès au Ve siècle av. J.-C.: A propos de l'épisode de Spurius Maelius." *Annales* 25, 287–311 (= id., *Enquêtes*, 278–312).

———. 1976. *La Chute des Tarquins et les débuts de la République romaine*. Paris. (*Débuts*)

———. 1977. *Enquêtes sur les structures sociales et religieuses de la Rome primitive*. Coll. Latomus 152. Brussels. (*Enquêtes*)

———. 1977. "Vindicius en face des licteurs consulaires." *RD* 55, 613–25.

———. 1978. "La *lex Aternia*, l'estimation des amends (*multae*) et le fonctionnement de la commission décemvirale de 451–449 av. J.-C." *AC* 47, 70–95.

———. 1978. "La *rogatio Terentilia* et le problème des cadres militaires plébéiens dans la première moitié du V^c siècle av. J.-C." *RH* 102, 289–311.

———. 1979. "*Rogatio Maecilia*: La Querelle agro-militaire autour de Bolae, en 416 av. J.-C. et la probable signification des projets agraires de Sp. Cassius, vers 486." *Latomus* 38, 838–61.

Gallo, F. 1952. "La riforma dei comizi centuriati." *SDHI* 18, 127–57.

Galsterer, H. 1976. *Herrschaft und Verwaltung im republikanischen Italien: Die Beziehungen Roms zu den italischen Gemeinden vom Latinerfrieden 338 v. Chr. bis zum Bundesgenossenkrieg 91 v. Chr.* Münchener Beitr. zur Papyrusforsch. und ant. Rechtsgesch. 68. Munich. (*Herrschaft*)

———. 1980. "Diritto e scienza giuridica in Grecia e Roma." *Critica storica* 17, 185–98.

Gantz, T. N. 1975. "The Tarquin Dynasty." *Historia* 24, 539–54.

Garzetti, A. 1947. "Appio Claudio Cieco nella storia politica del suo tempo." *Athenaeum* 25, 175–224.

Gatti, C. 1970. "Riflessioni sull'istituzione dello *stipendium* per i legionari romani." *Acme* 23, 131–35.

———. 1973. "A proposito degli *accensi* dell'ordinamento centuriato." *Athenaeum* 51, 377–82.

Gaudemet, J. 1967. *Institutions de l'antiquité*. Paris. (*Institutions*)

Geldner, H. 1972. *Lucretia und Verginia: Studien zur virtus der Frau in der griechischen und römischen Literatur*. Mainz. (*Lucretia*)

Gelzer, M. 1933. "Römische Politik bei Fabius Pictor." *Hermes* 68, 129–66 (= id., *Kl. Schr.* III: 51–92). Also in Pöschl, *Geschichtsschreibung*, 77–129.

———. 1934. "Der Anfang römischer Geschichtsschreibung." *Hermes* 69, 46–55 (= id., *Kl. Schr.* III: 93–103). Also in Pöschl, *Geschichtsschreibung*, 130–53.

———. 1935. "Die Glaubwürdigkeit der bei Livius überlieferten Senatsbeschlüsse über römische Truppenaufgebote." *Hermes* 70, 269–300 (= id., *Kl. Schr.* III: 220–55). Also in Pöschl, *Geschichtsschreibung*, 154–97.

———. 1954. "Nochmals über den Anfang der römischen Geschichtsschreibung." *Hermes* 82, 342–48 (= id., *Kl. Schr.* III: 104–110).

———. 1962–64. *Kleine Schriften*. 3 vols. Wiesbaden. (*Kl. Schr.*)

———. 1969. *The Roman Nobility*. Oxford. German ed., Stuttgart, 1912. (*Nobility*)

Gentili, B., and G. Cerri. 1983. "Caratteri e tendenze della storiografia romana arcaica." In id., *Storia e biografia nel pensiero antico*, 33–62. Rome and Bari.

Gernet, L. 1981. *The Anthropology of Ancient Greece*. Baltimore. French ed., Paris, 1968. (*Anthropology*)

Gervasio, M. 1942. "Tito Livio e la critica storica." *Iapigia* 13, 5–35.

I Galli e l'Italia. 1978. Exhibition Catalogue. Rome.

Giannelli, G. 1935. "Origine e sviluppi dell'ordinamento centuriato." *Atene e Roma* 37, 229–43.

Gierow, P. G. 1964–66. *The Iron Age Culture of Latium*. 2 vols. Lund, Sweden. (*Latium*)

———. 1979. *Relative and Absolute Chronology of the Iron Age Culture of Latium in the Light of Recent Discoveries*. Scr. Min. Reg. Soc. Hum. Litt. Lundensis 1977/78, 3. Lund, Sweden. (*Chronology*)

Gintowt, E. 1948–49. "Le Changement du caractère de la *tribus* romaine, attribué à Appius Claudius Caecus." *Eos* 43, 198–210.

Gioffredi, C. 1943–45. "*Rex, praetores* e *pontifices* nella evoluzione dal regno al regime consolare." *BCAR* 71, 129–35.

———. 1945. "Il fondamento della *tribunicia potestas* e i procedimenti normativi dell'ordine plebeo (*sacrosanctum, lex sacrata, sacramentum*)." *SDHI* 11, 37–64.

———. 1958. "Sulle attribuzioni sacrali dei magistrati romani." *Iura* 9, 22–49.

———. 1976. "Il frammento di Fabio Pittore in Gell. *N.A.* 10, 15, 1, e la tradizione antiquaria dei testi giuridico-sacrali." *BIDR*, 3rd ser., 18, 27–47.

Giovannini, A. 1983. "Volkstribunat und Volksgericht." *Chiron* 13, 545–66.

Girardet, K. M. 1977. "Ciceros Urteil über die Entstehung des Tribunats als Institution der römischen Verfassung (*rep.* 2, 57–59)." In *Bonner Festgabe Joh. Straub*, edited by A. Lippold and N. Himmelmann, 179–200. Bonn. ("Entstehung des Tribunats")

Giua, M. A. 1967. "La valutazione della monarchia a Roma in età repubblicana." *Studi class. e orient.* 16, 308–29.

Giuffrè, V. 1970. "*Plebei gentes non habent.*" *Labeo* 16, 329–44.

Gjerstad, E. 1953–73. *Early Rome*. 6 vols. Lund, Sweden. (*Early Rome*)

———. 1962. "Legends and Facts of Early Roman History." Scr. Min. R. Soc. Human. Litt. Lundensis 1960/61, 2. Lund. Repr. in German in Pöschl, *Geschichtsschreibung*, 367–458.

———. 1965. "Cultural History of Early Rome: Summary of Archaeological Evidence." *AArch* 36, 1–41.

———. 1966. "Trade Relations with Greece in Archaic Rome." In *Mélanges d'arch. et d'hist. offerts à A. Piganiol*, edited by R. Chevallier, II: 791–94. Paris. ("Trade Relations")

———. 1967. "The Origins of the Roman Republic." In *Les Origines de la république romaine*, Entr. sur l'ant. class. 13, 3–43. Vandoeuvres-Geneva.

———. 1967. "Discussions Concerning Early Rome. 3." *Historia* 16, 257–78.

———. 1970. "The Aventine Sanctuary of Diana." *AArch* 41, 99–107.

———. 1972. "Innenpolitische und militärische Organisation in frührömischer Zeit." *ANRW* I.1: 136–88.

Gladigow, B. 1972. "Die sakrale Funktion der Liktoren: Zum Problem von institutioneller Macht und sakraler Präsentation." *ANRW* I.1: 295–313.

Gnoli, G., and J. P. Vernant, eds. 1982. *La Mort, les morts dans les sociétés anciennes*. Cambridge. (*Mort*)

Goehler, J. 1939. *Rom und Italien: Die römische Bundesgenossenpolitik von den Anfängen bis zum Bundesgenossenkrieg*. Breslau. (*Rom*)

Gomme, A. W. 1933. *The Population of Athens in the Fifth and Fourth Centuries B.C.* Oxford. Repr. Chicago, 1967. (*Population*)

Gordon, R. L., ed. 1981. *Myth, Religion and Society*. Cambridge. (*Myth*)

Greenidge, A. H. J. 1901. *Roman Public Life*. London. (*Publ. Life*)

———. 1905. "The Authenticity of the Twelve Tables." *Engl. Hist. Rev.* 20, 1–21.

Groh, V. 1936. "*Potestas sacrosancta* dei tribuni della plebe." In *Studi in onore di S. Riccobono*, II: 1–9. Palermo.

Grosso, G. 1977. "Appunti sulla valutazione del tribunato della plebe nella tradizione storiografica conservatrice." *Index* 7, 157–61.

Gruen, E. S. 1974. *The Last Generation of the Roman Republic*. Berkeley and Los Angeles. (*Last Generation*)

———. 1978. "The Consular Elections for 216 B.C. and the Veracity of Livy." *CSCA* 11, 61–74.

Gschnitzer, F. 1968. "*Exercitus:* Zur Bezeichnung und Geschichte des Heeres im frühen Rom." In *Studien zur Sprachwissenschaft und Kulturkunde: Gedenkschrift W. Brandenstein,* edited by M. Mayrhofer, 181–90. Innsbruck.

———. 1981. *Griechische Sozialgeschichte von der mykenischen bis zum Ausgang der klassischen Zeit.* Wiesbaden. (*Sozialgeschichte*)

Guarino, A. 1973. *Le origini quiritarie: Raccolta di scritti romanistici.* Bibl. di Labeo 5. Naples. (*Origini*)

———. 1975. *La rivoluzione della plebe.* Naples. (*Riv.*)

———. 1975. *Storia del diritto romano.* Naples. 5th ed. (*Diritto*)

———. 1975. "La *perduellio* e la plebe." *Labeo* 21, 73–77.

———. 1975. "Genesi e ragion d'essere del patriziato." *Labeo* 21, 343–53.

———. 1982. "*Quaestus omnis patribus indecorus.*" *Labeo* 28, 7–16.

Guizzi, F. 1968. *Il sacerdozio di Vesta: Aspetti giuridici del sacerdozio romano.* Naples. (*Vesta*)

Günther, R. 1957–58. "Wirtschaftliche und soziale Differenzierung im ältesten Rom." *Wiss. Zeitschr. Univ. Leipzig* 7, 593–612.

———. 1959. "Die Entstehung der Schuldsklaverei im alten Rom." *AAH* 7, 231–249.

Habicht, C. 1961. "Falsche Urkunden zur Geschichte Athens im Zeitalter der Perserkriege." *Hermes* 89, 1–35.

Hackl, U. 1972. "Das Ende der römischen Tribusgründungen 241 v. Chr." *Chiron* 2, 135–70.

Haffter, H. 1964. "Rom und römische Ideologie bei Livius." *Gymnasium* 71, 236–50 (= E. Burck, ed., *WL,* 277–97).

Hahm, D. E. 1963. "Roman Nobility and the Three Major Priesthoods, 218–167 B.C." *TAPA* 94, 73–84.

Hahn, I. 1976. "The Plebeians and Clan Society." *Oikumene* 1, 47–75.

Hall, U. 1964. "Voting Procedures in Roman Assemblies." *Historia* 13, 267–306.

Hampl, F. 1958. "Das Problem der Datierung der ersten Verträge zwischen Rom und Karthago." *RhM* 101, 58–75.

———. 1979. "Das Problem des Aufstiegs Roms zur Weltmacht: Neue Bilanz unter methodisch-kritischen Aspekten." In id., *Geschichte als kritische Wissenschaft,* III: 48–119. Darmstadt.

Hanell, K. 1946. *Das altrömische eponyme Amt.* Lund, Sweden. (*Amt*)

———. 1956. "Zur Problematik der älteren römischen Geschichtsschreibung."

In *Histoire et historiens dans l'antiquité*, 147–70 (= Pöschl, *Geschichtsschreibung*, 292–311). Entretiens sur l'ant. class. 4. Vandoeuvres-Geneva.

———. 1967. "Probleme der römischen Fasti." In *Les Origines de la république romaine*, Entr. sur l'ant. class. 13, 175–91. Vandoeuvres-Geneva.

Harding, P. 1977. "*Atthis* and *politeia*." *Historia* 26, 148–60.

Hardy, E. G. 1913. "Some Notable *iudicia populi* on Capital Charges." *JRS* 3, 25–59.

Harris, W. V. 1971. *Rome in Etruria and Umbria*. Oxford. (*Etruria*)

———. 1979. *War and Imperialism in Republican Rome, 327–70 B.C.* Oxford. (*War*)

Hasebroek, J. 1931. *Griechische Wirtschafts- und Gesellschaftsgeschichte bis zur Perserzeit*. Tübingen. (*Wirtsch.*)

Hellegouarc'h, J. 1970. "Le Principat de Camille." *REL* 48, 112–32.

Heurgon, J. 1942. *Recherches sur l'histoire, la religion et la civilisation de Capoue préromaine des origines à la deuxième guerre punique*. Paris. (*Capoue préromaine*)

———. 1957. *Trois études sur le Ver sacrum*. Coll. Latomus 26. Brussels. (*Ver sacrum*)

———. 1966. "La Coupe d'Aulus Vibenna." In *Mélanges d'arch., d'épigr. et d'hist. offerts à J. Carcopino*, 515–28. Paris.

———. 1966. "The Inscriptions of Pyrgi." *JRS* 56, 1–15.

———. 1967. "Magistratures romaines et magistratures étrusques." In *Les Origines de la république romaine*, Entr. sur l'ant. class. 13, 97–127. Vandoeuvres-Geneva.

———. 1969. "La Magna Grecia e i santuari del Lazio." In *La Magna Grecia e Roma nell'età arcaica. Atti del VIII convegno di studi sulla Magna Grecia*, 9–31. Naples.

———. 1970. "Classes et ordres chez les Etrusques." In *Recherches sur les structures sociales dans l'antiquité classique*, edited by C. Nicolet, 29–41. Paris.

———. 1971. "L'Interprétation historique de l'historiographie latine de la République." *BAGB*, 219–30.

———. 1973. *The Rise of Rome to 264 B.C.* London. French ed., Paris, 1969. (*Rise*)

———. 1977. "Onomastique étrusque: la dénomination gentilice." In *L'Onomastique latine*, edited by N. Duval and H. G. Pflaum, 25–32. Paris.

Heuss, A. 1944. "Zur Entwicklung des Imperiums der römischen Oberbeamten." *ZRG* 64, 57–133.

———. 1946. "Die archaische Zeit Griechenlands als geschichtliche Epoche." *A&A* 2, 26–62 (= F. Gschnitzer, ed., *Zur griechischen Staatskunde*, 36–96. WdF 96. Darmstadt, 1969).

———. 1973. "Das Revolutionsproblem im Spiegel der antiken Geschichte." *HZ* 216, 1–69.

———. 1976. *Römische Geschichte*. Braunschweig. 4th ed. (*Röm. Geschichte*)

———. 1981. "Vom Anfang und Ende 'archaischer' Politik bei den Griechen." In *Gnomosyne: Menschliches Denken und Handeln in der frühgriechischen Literatur: Festschrift für W. Marg*, edited by G. Kurz, D. Müller, and W. Nicolai, 1–29. Munich. ("Archaische Politik")

———. 1982. *Gedanken und Vermutungen zur frühen römischen Regierungsgewalt*. Nachr. Akad. Göttingen, phil.-hist. Kl., no. 10.

Hill, H. 1952. *The Roman Middle Class in the Republican Period*. Oxford. (*Middle Class*)

———. 1961. "Dionysius of Halicarnassus and the Origins of Rome." *JHS* 51, 88–93.

Hirschfeld, O. 1913. "Zur Kamillus-Legende." In id., *Kleine Schriften*, 273–87. Berlin.

Hölscher, T. 1978. "Die Anfänge römischer Repräsentationskunst." *RM* 85, 315–57.

Hoffmann, W. 1934. *Rom und die griechische Welt im 4. Jahrhundert*. Philologus suppl. 27.1. Leipzig. (*Rom*)

———. 1938. "Die römische Plebs." *NJAB* 1, 82–98.

———. 1951. "*Plebs*." *RE* 21.1: 73–103.

Holladay, A. J. 1982. "Hoplites and Heresies." *JHS* 102, 94–103.

Holzapfel, L. 1897. "Il numero dei senatori durante il periodo dei re." *Riv. stor. ant.* 2, 52–64.

Horvat, M. 1957. "Quelques aspects politiques des codifications romaines." *RIDA*, 3rd ser., 4, 289–99.

Humbert, M. 1978. *Municipium et civitas sine suffragio: L'Organisation de la conquête jusqu'à la guerre sociale*. Coll. Ec. franç. de Rome 36. Paris. (*Municipium*)

Humphreys, S. C. 1967. "Archaeology and the Social and Economic History of Classical Greece." *PP* 22, 374–400 (= ead., *Anthropology*, 109–29).

———. 1978. *Anthropology and the Greeks*. London and Boston. (*Anthropology*)

———. 1980. "Family Tombs and Tomb Cult in Ancient Athens: Tradition or Traditionalism?" *JHS* 100, 96–126 (= ead., *Family*, 79–129).

———. 1982. *The Family, Women and Death: Comparative Studies*. London and Boston. (*Family*)

Humphreys, S. C., and H. King, eds. 1981. *Mortality and Immortality: The Anthropology and Archaeology of Death*. London and New York. (*Mortality*)

Ihne, W. 1866. "Über die Entstehung und die ältesten Befugnisse des römischen Volkstribunats." *RhM* 21, 161–79.

———. 1873. "Die Entwicklung der römischen Tributcomitien." *RhM* 28, 353–79.

Ilari, V. 1971. "I *celeres* e il problema dell'*equitatus* nell'età arcaica." *RISG* 15, 117–63.

Imbert, J. 1953. "*Fides et nexum.*" In *Studi in onore di V. Arangio-Ruiz*, I: 339–63. Naples. ("*Fides et nexum*")

Jacobs, K. 1937. *Gaius Flaminius*. Leiden. (*Flaminius*)

Jacoby, F. 1923–58. *Die Fragmente der griechischen Historiker*. 3 parts in 15 vols. Berlin and Leiden. Various reprints. (*FGrHist*)

———. 1944. "*Patrios Nomos:* State Burial in Athens and the Public Cemetery in the Kerameikos." *JHS* 64, 37–66.

———. 1949. *Atthis: The Local Chronicles of Ancient Athens*. Oxford. (*Atthis*)

Jahn, J. 1970. *Interregnum und Wahldiktatur*. Frankfurter Althistorische Stud. 3. Frankfurt. (*Interregnum*)

Jolowicz, H. F., and B. Nicholas. 1972. *Historical Introduction to the Study of Roman Law*. Cambridge. 3rd ed. (*Law*)

Jones, C. P. 1971. *Plutarch and Rome*. Oxford. (*Plutarch*)

Jones, H. S., and H. Last. 1928. "The Early Republic," and "The Making of a United State." *CAH* VII: 436–84, 519–46.

Jörs, P. 1927. *Geschichte und System des römischen Privatrechts*. Berlin. (*Privatr.*)

Kajanto, I. 1977. "On the Chronology of the *cognomen* in the Republican Period." In *L'Onomastique latine*, edited by N. Duval and H. G. Pflaum, 63–70. Paris.

Kaser, M. 1949. *Das altrömische ius: Studien zur Rechtsvorstellung und Rechtsgeschichte der Römer*. Göttingen. (*Ius*)

———. 1949. "Zur altrömischen Hausgewalt." *ZRG* 67, 474–97.

———. 1968. *Roman Private Law*. London. German ed., Munich, 1955. (*Priv. Law*)

———. 1971. *Das römische Privatrecht*. HdAW. X.3.3. 2 vols. Munich. 2nd ed. (*Privatr.*)

Kelly, J. M. 1976. *Studies in the Civil Judicature of the Roman Republic*. Oxford. (*Studies*)

Kienast, D. 1975. "Die politische Emanzipation der Plebs und die Entwicklung des Heerwesens im frühen Rom." *BJ* 175, 83–112.

Kierdorf, W. 1980. "Catos 'Origines' und die Anfänge der römischen Geschichtsschreibung." *Chiron* 10, 205–24.

Kissel, W. 1982. "Livius 1933–1978: Eine Gesamtbibliographie." *ANRW* II.30.2: 899–997.

Klotz, A. 1937. "Diodors römische Annalen." *RhM* 86, 206–224 (= Pöschl, *Geschichtsschreibung*, 201–21).

———. 1938. "Zu den Quellen der Archaiologia des Dionysios von Halikarnassos." *RhM* 87, 32–50.

———. 1938. "Livius' Darstellung des zweiten Samniterkrieges: Ein Beitrag zur Quellenkritik des IX. Buches des Livius." *Mnemosyne* 6, 83–102.

———. 1940–41. *Livius und seine Vorgänger*. In *Neue Wege zur Antike* II, nos. 9–11. Leipzig-Berlin. (*Livius*)

———. 1940. "L. Siccius Dentatus." *Klio* 33, 173–79.

Knoche, U. 1939. "Roms älteste Geschichtsschreibung." *NJAB* 2, 193–207 (= Pöschl, *Geschichtsschreibung*, 222–40).

———. 1939. "Das historische Geschehen in der Auffassung der älteren römischen Geschichtsschreiber." *NJAB* 2, 289–99 (= Pöschl, *Geschichtsschreibung*, 241–55).

Kornemann, E. 1905. "*Polis* und *Urbs*." *Klio* 5, 72–92.

———. 1911. "Die älteste Form der Pontifikalannalen." *Klio* 11, 245–57 (= Pöschl, *Geschichtsschreibung*, 59–76).

———. 1911. "Die Alliaschlacht und die ältesten Pontifikalannalen." *Klio* 11, 335–42.

———. 1912. *Der Priestercodex in der Regia und die Entstehung der altrömischen Pseudogeschichte*. Tübingen. (*Priestercodex*)

———. 1920. "Die Anfänge der römischen Republik." *Intern. Monatsschr. für Wiss., Kunst und Technik* 14, 481–502.

Kromayer, J., and G. Veith. 1928. *Heerwesen und Kriegführung der Griechen und Römer*. HdAW IV.3.2. Munich. (*Heerwesen*)

Kunkel, W. 1962. *Untersuchungen zur Entwicklung des römischen Kriminalverfahrens in vorsullanischer Zeit.* Abh. Bayer. Akad. 56. Munich. (*Kriminalverfahren*)

———. 1972. "Magistratische Gewalt und Senatsherrschaft." *ANRW* I.2: 3–22.

———. 1973. *An Introduction to Roman Legal and Constitutional History.* Oxford. 2nd ed. (*Introd.*)

Kurtz, D. C., and J. Boardman. 1971. *Greek Burial Customs.* London and Ithaca, N.Y. (*Burial Customs*)

Lacey, W. K. 1968. *The Family in Classical Greece.* London and Ithaca, N.Y. (*Family*)

Lambert, J. N. 1956. "Les Origines de Rome à la lumière du droit comparé." In *Studi in onore di P. De Francisci* I: 337–60. Milan.

———. 1956. "Le Patronat et la très ancienne succession romaine à la lumière de l'histoire comparée." *RD* 34, 479–512.

Le lamine di Pyrgi. 1970. Acc. naz. Lincei: Problemi attuali di scienza e di cultura, Quad. 147. Rome. (*Lamine di Pyrgi*)

Lange, L. 1876–79. *Römische Altertümer.* 3 vols. Berlin. 3rd ed. (*Altertümer*)

Last, H. 1945. "The Servian Reforms." *JRS* 35, 30–48.

Latte, K. 1931. "Beiträge zum griechischen Strafrecht I, II." *Hermes* 66, 30–48, 129–58 (= id., *Kleine Schriften zur Religion, Literatur und Sprache der Griechen und Römer*, 252–67, 268–93, Munich, 1968).

———. 1936. "The Origin of the Roman Quaestorship." *TAPA* 67, 24–33.

———. 1960. *Römische Religionsgeschichte.* HdAW V.4. Munich. (*Religionsgeschichte*)

Le Bonniec, H. 1958. *Le Culte de Cérès à Rome des origines à la fin de la République.* Paris. (*Cérès*)

Le Bras, G. 1959. "Capacité personnelle et structures sociales dans le très ancien droit de Rome." In *Droits de l'antiquité et sociologie juridique: Mélanges H. Lévy-Bruhl*, 417–29. Paris.

Lehmann, G. A. 1974. "Polybios und die ältere und zeitgenössische griechische Geschichtsschreibung: Einige Bemerkungen." In *Polybe*, 147–200. Entretiens sur l'ant. class. 20. Vandoeuvres-Geneva.

Lejay, P. 1920. "Appius Claudius Caecus." *RPh* 44, 92–141.

Lemosse, M. 1949. "Affranchissement, clientèle, droit de cité." *RIDA* 3, 37–68.

———. 1956. "L'Aspect primitif de la *fides*." In *Studi in onore di P. De Francisci*, 39–52. Milan.

———. 1957. "Les Lois de Gortyne et la notion de codification." *RIDA*, 3rd ser., 4, 131–37.

Levi, M. A. 1968. *Commento storico alla respublica Atheniensium di Aristotele*. 2 vols. Milan-Varese. (*Comm. Ath. Pol.*)

———. 1976. "Tradición y polémica sobre el tribunado de la plebe republicano." *Estudios de historia antigua* 21, 57–104.

Lewis, G. C. 1855. *An Inquiry into the Credibility of Early Roman History*. 2 vols. London. (*Credibility*)

Lewis, M. W. H. 1955. *The Official Priests of Rome under the Julio-Claudians*. Rome. (*Priests*)

Liebold, K. 1890. *Die Ansichten über die Entstehung und das Wesen der gentes patriciae in Rom seit der Zeit der Humanisten bis auf unsere Tage: Eine literar-historische Untersuchung*. Programm der Realschule zu Meerane. Meerane, Germany. (*Gentes patr.*)

Linderski, J. 1986. "The Augural Law." *ANRW* II.16.3: 2146–2312.

Lintott, A. W. 1968. *Violence in Republican Rome*. Oxford. (*Violence*)

———. 1970. "The Tradition of Violence in the Annals of the Early Roman Republic." *Historia* 19, 12–29.

———. 1972. "*Provocatio:* From the Struggle of the Orders to the Principate." *ANRW* I.2: 226–66.

———. 1972. "Imperial Expansion and Moral Decline in the Roman Republic." *Historia* 21, 626–38.

———. 1982. *Violence, Civil Strife and Revolution in the Classical City*. London and Baltimore. (*Revol.*)

Lipovsky, J. 1981. *A Historiographical Study of Livy, Books VI–X*. New York. (*Livy*)

Lobrano, G. 1972. "Fondamento e natura del potere tribunizio nella storiografia giuridica contemporanea." *Index* 3, 253–62.

———. 1974. "*Potestates, potestas, tribunicia potestas.*" In *Il problema del potere in Roma repubblicana*, 41–150. Sassari.

———. 1975. "*Plebei magistratus, patricii magistratus, magistratus populi Romani.*" *SDHI* 41, 245–77.

Lombardi, G. 1941. "Su alcuni concetti del diritto pubblico romano: *civitas, populus, res publica, status rei publicae*." *Archiv. giur.* 126, 192–211.

Lübtow, U. von. 1936. "Das altrömische *nexum* als Geiselschaft." *ZRG* 56, 239–55.

———. 1949. "Zum Nexumproblem." *ZRG* 67, 112–61.

———. 1952. "Die *lex curiata de imperio*." *ZRG* 69, 154–71.

———. 1955. *Das römische Volk: Sein Staat und sein Recht*. Frankfurt. (*Volk*)

Luce, T. J. 1971. "Design and Structure in Livy: 5.32–55." *TAPA* 102, 265–302.

———. 1977. *Livy: The Composition of His History*. Princeton. (*Livy*)

Lupinetti, M. Q. 1969. "Liv. 3.6.9, Dion. Hal. 6.95.3–4 e le origini dell'edilità plebea." *RISG* 13, 285–315.

Luzzatto, G. I. 1962. "Il passaggio dall'ordinamento gentilizio alla monarchia in Roma e l'influenza dell'ordinamento delle *gentes* nella costituzione romana durante la monarchia e la prima repubblica." Accad. naz. Lincei: Probl. att. di sc. e di cult. Quad. 54, 193–234.

MacCormack, G. 1967. "*Nexi, iudicati,* and *addicti* in Livy." *ZRG* 84, 350–55.

———. 1973. "The *lex Poetelia*." *Labeo* 19, 306–17.

MacDowell, D. M. 1978. *The Law in Classical Athens*. London and Ithaca, N.Y. (*Law*)

Maddox, G. 1983. "The Economic Causes of the *Lex Hortensia*," *Latomus* 42, 277–86.

Magdelain, A. 1962. "Cinq jours épagomènes à Rome?" *REL* 40, 201–27.

———. 1964. "*Auspicia ad patres redeunt*." In *Hommages à J. Bayet*, edited by M. Renard and R. Schilling, 427–73. Coll. Latomus 70. Brussels. ("*Auspicia*")

———. 1964. "Note sur la loi curiate et les auspices des magistrats." *RD* 42, 198–203.

———. 1968. *Recherches sur l'imperium: La Loi curiate et les auspices d'investiture*. Paris. (*Imperium*)

———. 1969. "*Praetor maximus* et *comitiatus maximus*." *Iura* 20, 257–84.

———. 1972. "Remarques sur la société romaine archaïque." *REL* 49, 103–27.

———. 1978. "Les *accensi* et le total des centuries." *Historia* 27, 492–95.

———. 1979. *La Loi à Rome: Histoire d'un concept*. Paris. (*Loi*)

———. 1979. "Le Suffrage universel à Rome au Ve siècle av. J.-C." *CRAI*, 698–713.

La Magna Grecia e Roma nell'età arcaica. 1969. Atti dell'VIII convegno di Studi sulla Magna Grecia, Taranto 1968. Naples.

Malcovati, E., ed. 1976. *Oratorum Romanorum fragmenta liberae rei publicae*. Turin. 4th ed. (*ORF*)

Mancuso, G. 1972. "Alle radici della storia del *senatus*: Contributo all'identificazione dei *patres* nell'età precittadina." *Ann. semin. giur. Palermo* 33, 169–335.

———. 1973. "*Patres minorum gentium*." *Ann. semin. giur. Palermo* 34, 397–421.

———. 1976. "*Patres conscripti:* Un ipotesi sulla composizione dell'antico senato romano." *Ann. semin. giur. Palermo* 36, 253–88.

Manfredini, A. D. 1976. "Tre leggi nel quadro della crisi del V secolo." *Labeo* 22, 198–231.

Manfredini, M., and L. Piccirilli. 1977. *Plutarco: La Vita di Solone*. Milan. (*Plut. Sol.*)

Manni, E. 1939. "Le tracce della conquista volsca nel Lazio." *Athenaeum* 17, 233–79.

———. 1970. "Diodoro e la storia arcaica di Roma." *Kokalos* 16, 60–73.

———. 1973. *Roma e l'Italia nel Mediterraneo antico*. Turin. (*Italia*)

Mannino, V. 1979. *L'auctoritas patrum*. Milan. (*Auctoritas patrum*)

Marchesi, C. 1942. *Livio e la verità storica*. Opusc. accad. ser. liviana 1. Padua. (*Livio*)

Marin, D. 1969. "Dionisio di Alicarnasso e il latino." In *Hommages à M. Renard*, edited by J. Bibauw, I: 595–608. Brussels.

Markale, J. 1959–60. "Rome et l'épopée celtique." *Cahiers du sud* 49, 331–56.

Markianos, S. S. 1980. "The 'Democratic Version' of the Solonian Constitution: Its Date and Origin." *Hellenica* 32, 255–66.

Marquardt, J. 1881–85. *Römische Staatsverwaltung*. 3 vols. Leipzig. 2nd ed. (*Staatsverwaltung*)

———. 1886. *Das Privatleben der Römer*. Leipzig. 2nd ed. (*Privatleben*)

Martin, J. 1974. "Von Kleisthenes zu Ephialtes: Zur Entstehung der athenischen Demokratie." *Chiron* 4, 5–42.

———. 1979. "Two Ancient Histories: A Comparative Study of Greece and Rome." *Soc. Hist.* 4, 285–98.

Martin, P. M. 1971. "La Propagande augustéenne dans les 'Antiquités romaines' de Denys d'Halicarnasse (livre I)." *REL* 49, 162–79.

———. 1982. *L'Idée de royauté à Rome*. Clermont-Ferrand. (*Royauté*)

Martinez-Pinna Nieto, J. 1981. *Los orígenes del ejército romano: Estudios de las formas pre-militares en su relación con las estructuras sociales de la Roma más primitiva*. Madrid. (*Ejército*)

———. 1982. "Tarquinio Prisco y Servio Tullio." *Archivo Español de Arqueología* 55, 35–61.

Mattingly, H. 1937. "The Property Qualifications of the Roman Classes." *JRS* 27, 99–107.

Mazzarino, S. 1947. *Dalla monarchia allo stato repubblicano*. Catania. (*Stato rep.*)

———. 1966. *Il pensiero storico classico*. 3 vols. Bari. (*Pensiero stor.*)

———. 1971. *Vico: L'annalistica e il diritto*. Naples. (*Vico*)

———. 1971. "Intorno ai rapporti fra annalistica e diritto: Problemi di esegesi e di critica testuale." In *Atti II congr. intern. di storia del diritto, Venezia 1967*, 441–66. Florence.

———. 1971–72. "Sul tribunato della plebe nella storiografia romana." *Helikon* 11/12, 99–119.

———. 1972. "Note sul tribunato della plebe nella storiografia romana." *Index* 3, 175–91.

Meier, C. 1966. *Res publica amissa: Eine Studie zu Verfassung und Geschichte der späten römischen Republik*. Wiesbaden. (*Res publica amissa*)

———. 1980. *Die Entstehung des Politischen bei den Griechen*. Frankfurt. (*Pol.*)

Meiggs, R., and D. Lewis. 1969. *A Selection of Greek Historical Inscriptions to the End of the Fifth Century B.C.* Oxford. (*Gr. Hist. Inscr.*)

Meloni, P. 1948. "Tre note nella storia del senato regio." *Ann. fac. lett. Cagliari* 15, 119–56.

Ménager, L. R. 1972. "Nature et mobiles de l'opposition entre la plèbe et le patriciat." *RIDA*, 3rd ser., 19, 367–97.

———. 1976. "Les Collèges sacerdotaux, les tribus et la formation primordiale de Rome." *MEFR* 88, 455–543.

———. 1980. "Systèmes onomastiques, structures familiales et classes sociales dans le monde gréco-romain." *SDHI* 46, 147–68.

Mercklin, L. 1848. *Die Cooptation der Römer*. Leipzig. (*Cooptation*)

Merlin, A. 1906. *L'Aventin dans l'antiquité*. Paris. (*Aventin*)

Messer, W. S. 1920. "Mutiny in the Roman Army: The Republic." *CP* 15, 158–75.

Meyer, Ed. 1884–1902. *Geschichte des Altertums*. 5 vols. Stuttgart. Important for archaic Rome: III^2, 1937; $IV.1^3$, 1939; V^4, 1958; all repr. Darmstadt, 1965–69. (*GdA*)

———. 1895. "Der Ursprung des Tribunats und die Gemeinde der vier Tribus." *Hermes* 30, 1–24 (= id., *Kl. Schr.* I: 333–61).

———. 1923. "Das römische Manipularheer, seine Entwicklung und seine Vorstufen." *Abh. preuss. Akad.*, phil.-hist. Kl. 1923, 3 (= id., *Kl. Schr.* II: 193–329).

———. 1924. *Kleine Schriften*. 2 vols. Halle. 2nd ed. (*Kl. Schr.*)

Meyer, E. 1952. "Zur Frühgeschichte Roms." *MH* 9, 176–81.

———. 1964. *Römischer Staat und Staatsgedanke*. Zurich. 3rd ed. (*Staat*)

———. 1972. "Die römische Annalistik im Lichte der Urkunden." *ANRW* I.2: 970–86.

Meyer, J. C. 1980. "Roman History in the Light of the Import of Attic Vases to Rome and Etruria in the 6th and 5th Centuries B.C." *Analecta Rom. Inst. Danici* 9, 47–68.

———. 1983. *Pre-Republican Rome*. Odense, Denmark. (*Rome*)

Michaelidès-Nouaros, G. 1977. "Quelques remarques sur le droit vivant à Rome aux époques préclassique et classique." *RD* 55, 329–57.

Michel, A. 1970. "Ordres et classes chez les historiens romains." In *Recherches sur les structures sociales dans l'antiquité classique*, edited by C. Nicolet, 243–57. Paris.

Mitchell, R. E. 1974. "The Aristocracy of the Roman Republic." In *The Rich, the Well-Born, and the Powerful: Elites and Upper Classes in History*, edited by F. C. Jaher, 27–63. Urbana, Chicago, and London. ("Aristocracy")

———. 1984. "Roman History, Roman Law, and Roman Priests: The Common Ground," *Univ. of Illinois Law Review*, 1984, no. 3, 541–60.

———. 1984. "Historical Development in Livy." In *Classical Texts and Their Traditions: Studies in Honor of C. R. Trahman*, edited by D. F. Bright and E. S. Ramage, 179–99. Chico, Calif. ("Historical Development")

Momigliano, A. 1931–33. "Ricerche sulle magistrature romane." *BCAR* 58, 29–42, 42–55; 59, 157–77; 60, 217–28, 228–32 (= id., *Contr. IV*: 273–327).

———. 1936. "Due punti di storia Romana arcaica." *SDHI* 2, 373–98 (= id., *Contr. IV*: 329–61).

———. 1938. "Studi sugli ordinamenti centuriati." *SDHI* 4, 509–20 (= id., *Contr. IV*: 363–75).

———. 1942. "Camillus and Concord." *CQ* 36, 111–20 (= id., *Contr. II*: 89–104).

———. 1955. *Contributo alla storia degli studi classici*. Rome. (*Contr. I*)

———. 1957. "Perizonius, Niebuhr, and the Character of Early Roman Tradition." *JRS* 47, 104–14 (= id., *Contr. II*: 69–87). In German in Pöschl, *Geschichtsschreibung*, 312–39.

———. 1960–84. *Secondo [Terzo, Quarto, Quinto, Sesto, Settimo] contributo alla storia degli studi classici e del mondo antico*. II, 1960; III (2 vols.), 1966; IV, 1969; V (2 vols.), 1975; VI (2 vols.), 1980; VII, 1984. Rome. (*Contr. II–VII*)

———. 1960. "Linee per una valutazione di Fabio Pittore." *RAL*, 8th ser., 15, 310–20 (= id., *Contr. III*: 55–68).

———. 1963. "An Interim Report on the Origins of Rome." *JRS* 53, 95–121 (= id., *Contr. III*: 545–98).

———. 1966. "*Procum patricium.*" *JRS* 56, 16–24 (= id., *Contr. IV*: 377–94).

———. 1967. "Osservazioni sulla distinzione fra patrizi e plebei." In *Les Origines de la république romaine*, 197–221 (= id., *Contr. IV*: 419–36). Vandoeuvres-Geneva. ("Patrizi e plebei")

———. 1967. "L'ascesa della plebe nella storia arcaica di Roma." *RSI* 79, 297–312 (= id., *Contr. IV*: 437–54; in the present volume, chapter VI).

———. 1968. "*Praetor maximus* e questioni affini." In *Studi in onore di G. Grosso*, I: 161–75 (= id., *Contr. IV*: 403–17). Turin.

———. 1969. "The Origins of the Roman Republic." In *Interpretation: Theory and Practice*, edited by C. Singleton, 1–34 (= "Le origini della repubblica romana." *RSI* 81, 5–43; id., *Contr. V*: 293–331). Baltimore. ("Origins of the Republic")

———. 1969. "Il *rex sacrorum* e l'origine della repubblica." In *Studi in onore di E. Volterra*, I: 357–64 (= id., *Contr. IV*: 395–402). Milan.

———. 1969. "Cavalry and Patriciate: An Answer to Professor A. Alföldi." *Historia* 18, 385–88 (= id., *Contr. V*: 635–39).

———. 1977. "Prolegomena a ogni futura metafisica sulla plebe romana." *Labeo* 23, 7–15 (= id., *Contr. VI. 2*: 477–86).

Mommsen, Th. 1861. "Die römischen Patriciergeschlechter." *RhM* 16, 321–60 (= id., *Röm. Forschungen* I: 69–127).

———. 1861. "Die patricischen Claudier." *Preuss. Akad. Wiss., Monatsber.*, 317–38 (= id., *Röm. Forschungen* I: 285–318).

———. 1864–79. *Römische Forschungen*. 2 vols. Berlin. (*Röm. Forschungen*)

———. 1864. "Die patricischen und die plebeischen Sonderrechte in den Bürger- und den Rathsversammlungen." In id., *Röm. Forschungen* I: 129–284.

———. 1870. "Die Erzählung von Cn. Marcius Coriolanus." *Hermes* 4, 1–26 (= id., *Röm. Forschungen* II: 113–52). Repr. in Pöschl, *Geschichtsschreibung*, 31–58.

———. 1871. "Sp. Cassius, M. Manlius, Sp. Maelius, die drei Demagogen der älteren republikanischen Zeit." *Hermes* 5, 228–80 (= id., *Röm. Forschungen* II: 153–220).

———. 1887–88. *Römisches Staatsrecht*. I³, II³, III.1, 1887; III.2, 1888. Leipzig. (*Röm. Staatsrecht*)

———. 1905–13. *Gesammelte Schriften*. 8 vols. Berlin. (*Ges. Schr.*)

Moscati, S., and M. Pallottino. 1966. "Rapporti tra Greci, Fenici, Etruschi ed altre popolazioni italiche alla luce delle nuove scoperte." Acc. Lincei: Problemi attuali di scienza e di cultura, Quad. 87, 3–16.

Müller-Karpe, H. 1962. *Zur Stadtwerdung Roms*. RM suppl. 8. Heidelberg. (*Stadtwerdung*)

Münzer, F. 1920. *Römische Adelsparteien und Adelsfamilien*. Stuttgart. Repr. Darmstadt, 1963. (*Adelsparteien*)

———. 1922. "Consulartribunen und Censoren." *Hermes* 57, 134–49.

Muñoz Valle, I. 1977. "La ideologia de la aristocracia griega antigua." *Euphrosyne*, n.s., 8, 43–56.

Musti, D. 1970. *Tendenze nella storiografia romana e greca su Roma arcaica: Studi su Livio e Dionigi di Alicarnasso*. Quad. Urbinati di cultura classica 10. Rome. (*Tendenze*)

Nagy, F. 1964. "Volksbegriffe im römischen Altertum: *populus* und *plebs*." In *Neue Beiträge zur Geschichte der Alten Welt* II: 69–74. Berlin.

Nagy, G. 1982. "Theognis of Megara: The Poet as Seer, Pilot and Revenant." *Arethusa* 15, 109–127.

———. 1983. "Poet and Tyrant: *Theognidea* 39–52, 1081–1082b." *Class. Ant.* 2, 82–91.

Nap, J. M. 1935. *Die römische Republik um das Jahr 225 v Chr.: Ihre damalige Politik, Gesetze und Legenden*. Leiden. (*Republik*)

Nenci, G. 1958. "Le relazioni con Marsiglia nella politica estera romana, dalle origini alla prima guerra punica." *Riv. di studi liguri* 24, 24–97.

Néraudau, J. P. 1980. "Jeunesse et politique à Rome au IVe siècle av. J.-C. (d'après Tite-Live III)." In *Mélanges de littérature et d'épigraphie latines, d'histoire ancienne et d'archéologie: Hommage à la mémoire de P. Wuilleumier*, 251–60. Paris. ("Jeunesse et politique")

Neumann, K. J. 1900. *Die Grundherrschaft der römischen Republik, die Bauernbefreiung und die Entstehung der servianischen Verfassung*. Strassburg. (*Grundherrschaft*)

Niccolini, G. 1895. "La legge di Publio Volerone." *ASNP* 11, 3–15.

———. 1924. "I tribuni della plebe e il processo capitale." *Atti soc. ligust. sc. lett.* 3, 1–20.

———. 1925. "Sui comizi romani." *Atti soc. ligust. sc. lett.* 4, 38–82.

———. 1928. "Le *leges sacratae*." *Historia* 2, 3–18.

———. 1929. "Origine e primo sviluppo del tribunato della plebe." *Historia* 3, 181–207.

———. 1932. *Il tribunato della plebe*. Milan. (*Tribunato*)

———. 1934. *I fasti dei tribuni della plebe*. Milan. (*Fasti*)

———. 1934. "Le lotte tra il patriziato e la plebe nell'opera di Livio." In *Studi liviani*, 81–109. Rome.

Nicholls, J. J. 1956. "The Reform of the *comitia centuriata*." *AJP* 77, 225–54.

———. 1967. "The Content of the *lex curiata*." *AJP* 88, 257–78.

Nicolet, C. 1966–74. *L'Ordre équestre à l'époque républicaine (312–43 av. J.-C.)*. 2 vols. Paris. (*Ordre équestre*)

———. 1977–78. *Rome et la conquête du monde méditerranéen, 264–27 av. J.-C.* Nouvelle Clio 8. 2 vols. Paris. (*Rome*)

———. 1977. "L'Onomastique des classes dirigeantes sous la République." In *L'Onomastique latine*, edited by N. Duval and H. G. Pflaum, 45–61. Paris.

———. 1980. *The World of the Citizen in Republican Rome*. London. French ed., Paris, 1976. (*Citizen*)

———. 1980. "Economie, société et institutions au 2ᵉ siècle av. J.-C. De la *lex Claudia* à l'*ager exceptus*." *Annales* 35, 871–94.

Niebuhr, B. G. 1828–42. *The History of Rome*. Translated by J. C. Hare and C. Thirlwall. 3 vols. Cambridge. German ed. 1826–30. (*Hist.*)

Nilsson, M. P. 1928. "Die Hoplitentaktik und das Staatswesen." *Klio* 22, 240–49.

———. 1929. "The Introduction of Hoplite Tactics at Rome: Its Date and Consequences." *JRS* 19, 1–11.

Noailles, P. 1940–41. "Nexum." *RD* 19/20, 205–74 (= id., *Fas*, 91–146).

———. 1948. *Fas et ius: Etudes de droit romain*. Paris. (*Fas*)

———. 1949. *Du droit sacré au droit civil*. Paris. (*Droit*)

Noè, E. 1979. "Ricerche su Dionigi d'Alicarnasso: La prima stasis a Roma e l'episodio di Coriolano." In *Ricerche di storiografia antica*, vol. I, *Ricerche di storiografia greca di età romana*, 21–116. Bibl. di studi ant. 22. Pisa.

Nörr, D. 1965. "Zur sozialen und rechtlichen Bewertung der freien Arbeit in Rom." *ZRG* 82, 67–105.

———. 1976. "Pomponius oder 'Zum Geschichtsverständnis der römischen Juristen.'" *ANRW* II.15: 497–604.

Oberziner, G. 1901. *Origine della plebe romana*. Leipzig. (*Plebe*)

———. 1912. *Patriziato e plebe nello svolgimento delle origini romane: Appunti critici*. Milan. (*Patriziato*)

Ogilvie, R. M. 1965. *A Commentary on Livy, Books 1–5*. Oxford. (*Comm*.)

———. 1969. "Some Cults of Early Rome." In *Hommages à M. Renard*, edited by J. Bibauw, II: 566–72. Coll. Latomus 102. Brussels.

———. 1976. *Early Rome and the Etruscans*. Glasgow. (*Early Rome*)

Olivesi, A. 1956. "Manius Curius Dentatus et le mouvement démocratique à Rome au début du IIIe siècle av. J.-C." *L'Information historique* 18, 85–90.

Oltramare, A. 1932. "Spurius Cassius et les origines de la démocratie romaine." *Bull. Soc. d'hist. et d'arch. de Genève* 5, 1–18.

Les Origines de la république romaine. 1967. Entretiens sur l'antiquité class. 13. Vandoeuvres-Geneva.

Pabst, W. 1969. *Quellenkritische Studien zur inneren römischen Geschichte der älteren Zeit bei T. Livius und Dionys von Halikarnass*. Innsbruck. (*Studien*)

———. 1973. "Die Ständekämpfe in Rom als Beispiel für einen politisch-sozialen Konflikt." *Der altsprachliche Unterricht* 16, 5–28.

Pagliaro, A. 1967. "*Proletarius*." *Helikon* 7, 395–401.

Pais, E. 1913–20. *Storia critica di Roma durante i primi cinque secoli*. 5 vols. Rome. (*Stor. crit*.)

———. 1915–21. *Ricerche sulla storia e sul diritto pubblico di Roma*. 4 vols. Rome. (*Ricerche*)

———. 1923. "Serie cronologica delle colonie romane e latine della età regio fino all'impero." *Accad. Linc. Mem.* 17, no. 8, 311–55.

———. 1926–28 [1898]. *Storia di Roma dalle origini all'inizio delle guerre puniche*. 5 vols. Rome. 3rd ed. First edition, 1898. (*Storia*)

Pallottino, M. 1960. "Le origini di Roma." *Arch. Class.* 12, 1–36.

———. 1963. "Fatti e leggende (moderne) sulla più antica storia di Roma." *SE* 31, 3–37.

———. 1965. "Nuova luce sulla storia di Roma arcaica dalle lamine d'oro di Pyrgi." *SR* 13, 1–13.

———. 1969. "La Magna Grecia e l'Etruria." In *La Magna Grecia e Roma nell'età arcaica*, 35–48. Naples. ("Magna Grecia")

———. 1972. "Le origini di Roma: Considerazioni critiche sulle scoperte e sulle discussioni più recenti." *ANRW* I.1: 22–47.

———. 1975. *The Etruscans*. London. Repr. Harmondsworth, England, 1978. Transl. from the 6th Ital. ed., 1968. (*Etruscans*)

———. 1977. "Servius Tullius à la lumière des nouvelles découvertes archéologiques et épigraphiques." *CRAI*, 216–35.

———. 1979. "Lo sviluppo socio-istituzionale di Roma arcaica alla luce di nuovi documenti epigrafici." *SR* 27, 1–14.

Palmer, R. E. A. 1965. "The Censors of 312 B.C. and the State Religion." *Historia* 14, 293–324.

———. 1970. *The Archaic Community of the Romans*. Cambridge. (*Arch. Comm.*)

———. 1974. *Roman Religion and Roman Empire: Five Essays*. Philadelphia. (*Religion*)

Pareti, L. 1934. "Le lotte contro gli Etruschi nell'opera liviana." In *Studi liviani*, 47–65. Rome.

———. 1959. "Sulla battaglia del lago Regillo." *SR* 7, 18–30.

Paribeni, E. 1959–60; 1968–69. "Ceramica d'importazione dell'area sacra di S. Omobono." *BCAR* 77, 109–24; 81, 7–15.

Pasquali, G. 1936. "La grande Roma dei Tarquini." *Nuova antologia* 16, 405–16 (= id., *Terze pagine stravaganti*, 1–24. Florence, 1942).

Patzer, H. 1981. "Der archaische Areté-Kanon im Corpus Theognideum." In *Gnomosyne: Festschrift W. Marg*, edited by G. Kurz, D. Müller, and W. Nicolai, 197–226. Munich. ("Areté-Kanon")

Pekáry, T. 1969. "Das Weihedatum des kapitolinischen Iupitertempels und Plinius n.h. 33, 19." *RM* 76, 307–12.

Pelling, X. 1980. "Plutarch's Adaptation of His Source-Material." *JHS* 100, 123–39.

Pena, M. J. 1981. "La dedicación y el dedicante del templo de Júpiter Capitolino." *Faventia* 3, 149–70.

Peppe, L. 1981. *Studi sull'esecuzione personale*, vol. I, *Debiti e debitori nei primi due secoli della repubblica romana*. Pubbl. dell'Ist. di diritto romano 60. Milan. (*Esecuzione*)

Perelli, L. 1979. "Note sul tribunato della plebe nella riflessione ciceroniana." *Quad. di storia* 5, no. 10, 285–303.

Peremans, W. 1933–34. "Over de romeinsche *plebs*." *Phil. Stud.* 5, 227–32.

———. 1934. "Notes sur l'histoire romaine avant l'invasion des Gaulois." *AC* 3, 209–21.

———. 1972. "Sur l'acquisition du droit de cité à Athènes au VIᵉ siècle av. J.-C." In *Antike und Universalgeschichte: Festschrift H. E. Stier*, edited by R. Stiehl and G. A. Lehmann, 122–30. Münster. ("Droit de cité")

Perl, G. 1964. "Der Anfang der römischen Geschichtsschreibung." *Forschungen und Fortschritte* 38, 185–89, 213–18.

Perrin, B. 1953. "La Consécration à Cérès." In *Studi in memoria di E. Albertario*, edited by V. Arangio-Ruiz, II: 385–417. Milan.

Peruzzi, E. 1970–73. *Origini di Roma*. 2 vols. Bologna. (*Origini*)

Peter, H. 1879. *Zur Kritik der Quellen der älteren römischen Geschichte*. Halle. (*Quellen*)

———. 1914. *Historicorum Romanorum reliquiae* I. Leipzig. 2nd ed. Repr. Stuttgart, 1967. (*HRR*)

Petzold, K.-E. 1972. "Die beiden ersten römisch-karthagischen Verträge und das *foedus Cassianum*." *ANRW* I.1: 364–411.

Phillips, E. J. 1972. "Roman Politics during the Second Samnite War." *Athenaeum* 50, 337–56.

———. 1982. "Current Research in Livy's First Decade: 1959–1979." *ANRW* II.30.2: 998–1057.

Piéri, G. 1968. *L'Histoire du cens jusqu'à la fin de la République romaine*. Paris. (*Cens*)

———. 1981. "Statut des personnes et organisation politique aux origines de Rome." *RD* 59, 583–92.

Piganiol, A. 1917. *Essai sur les origines de Rome*. BEFAR 110. Paris. (*Origines*)

———. 1919. "Les Attributions militaires et les attributions religieuses du tribunat de la plèbe." *Journ. des Savants* 17, 237–48 (= id., *Scripta varia*, II: 261–71. Brussels, 1973).

———. 1920. "Romains et Latins." *MEFR* 38, 285–316 (= id., *Scripta varia* II, 203–28).

———. 1933. "Un Document d'histoire sociale: La Constitution servienne." *Ann. d'hist. écon. et soc.* 5, 113–24.

———. 1974. *La Conquête romaine*. Paris. 6th ed. (*Conquête*)

Pinsent, J. 1959. "Antiquarianism, Fiction and History in the First Decade of Livy." *CJ* 55, 81–85.

———. 1975. *Military Tribunes and Plebeian Consuls: The Fasti from 444V to 342V*. Historia Einzelschr. 24. Wiesbaden. (*Mil. Trib.*)

Pollera, A. 1979. "La carestia del 439 a.C. e l'uccisione di Spurio Melio." *BIDR* 82, 141–68.

Poma, G. 1974. *Gli studi recenti sull'origine della repubblica romana*. Bologna. (*Studi*)

———. 1976–77. "La valutazione del decemvirato nel *De Republica* di Cicerone." *RSA* 6/7, 129–46.

———. 1978. "Le secessioni e il rito dell'infissione del *clavus*." *RSA* 8, 39–50.

———. 1984. *Tra legislatori e tiranni. Problemi storici e storiografici sull'età delle XII tavole*. Bologna.

Pöschl, V., ed. 1969. *Römische Geschichtsschreibung*. WdF 90. Darmstadt. (*Geschichtsschreibung*)

Poucet, J. 1968. "*Acta triumphalia* et *falsi triumphi*: Le Triomphe remporté sur les Samnites et les Nequinates par le consul Fulvius en 299 av. J.-C. et les *falsi triumphi* de la *gens Fulvia* à l'époque des guerres Samnites." In *Recueil commém. du Xe annivers. de la fac. de philos. et lettres, Kinshasa*, 205–19. Louvain.

———. 1972. "Les Sabins aux origines de Rome: Orientations et problèmes." *ANRW* I.1: 48–135.

———. 1975. "Une Nouvelle Histoire des origines et des premiers siècles de Rome." *AC* 44, 185–95.

———. 1978; 1979. "Le Latium protohistorique et archaïque à la lumière des decouvertes archéologiques récentes." *AC* 47, 566–601; 48, 177–220.

———. 1979. "Archéologie, tradition et histoire: Les Origines et les premiers siècles de Rome; La période urbaine et la civilisation archaïque." *Les Etud. class.* 47, 201–14, 347–63.

———. 1981. "Georges Dumézil et l'histoire de la Rome royale." *Cahiers pour un temps* 3, 187–215.

Prachner, G. 1967. *Untersuchungen zu Überlieferungsproblemen der frührömischen Sklaverei und Schuldknechtschaft*. Münster. (*Schuldknechtschaft*)

Ptaschnik, J. 1863. "Die Wahl der Volkstribunen vor der Rogation des Volero Publilius." *Zeitschr. für die österr. Gymnasien* 14, 627–38.

———. 1866. "Die Publilische Rogation 283 u.c." *Zeitschr. für die österr. Gymnasien* 17, 161–200.

———. 1881. "Das Stimmrecht der Patricier in den Tributcomitien." *Zeitschr. für die österr. Gymnasien* 32, 81–102.

Pugliese Carratelli, G. 1962. "Achei nell'Etruria e nel Lazio?" *PP* 17, 5–25.

———. 1965. "Intorno alle lamine di Pyrgi." *SE* 33, 221–35.

———. 1968. "Lazio, Roma e la Magna Grecia primo del secolo quarto a.C." *PP* 23, 321–47 (= *La Magna Grecia e Roma nell'età arcaica*, 49–81, Naples, 1969).

Pulgram, E. 1948. "The Origin of the Latin *nomen gentilicium*." *Harv. Stud. Class. Philol.* 58/59, 163–87.

Quinn-Schofield, W. K. 1967. "Observations upon the *Ludi Plebei*." *Latomus* 26, 677–85.

Raaflaub, K. A. 1981. "Politisches Denken und Handeln bei den Griechen." In *Propyläen Geschichte der Literatur*, edited by E. Wischer, I: 36–67. Berlin. ("Politisches Denken")

———. 1984. "Freiheit in Athen und Rom: Ein Beispiel divergierender politischer Begriffsentwicklung in der Antike." *HZ* 238, 529–67.

———. 1985. *Die Entdeckung der Freiheit: Zur historischen Semantik und Gesellschaftsgeschichte eines politischen Grundbegriffes der Griechen.* Vestigia 37. Munich. (*Entdeckung*)

Radke, G. 1969. "Die territoriale Politik des C. Flaminius." In *Beiträge zur Alten Geschichte und deren Nachleben: Festschrift für F. Altheim*, edited by R. Stiehl and H. E. Stier, 366–86. Berlin.

———. 1970. "Sprachliche und historische Beobachtungen zu den *leges XII tabularum*." In *Sein und Werden im Recht: Festgabe für U. von Lübtow*, edited by W. G. Becker and L. Schnorr von Carolsfeld, 223–46. Berlin.

———. 1975. "Grenzen der Information und des Interesses bei Livius (Beispiele aus dem 4. Jh. v. Chr.)." In *Werte der Antike*, edited by F. Hörmann, 72–99. Munich.

Rambaud, M. 1953. *Cicéron et l'histoire romaine.* Paris. (*Cicéron*)

Ranouil, P. C. 1975. *Recherches sur le patriciat: 509–366 av. J.-C.* Paris. (*Patriciat*)

Rawson, E. 1971. "Prodigy Lists and the Use of the *Annales Maximi*." *CQ* 21, 158–69.

———. 1972. "Cicero the Historian and Cicero the Antiquarian." *JRS* 62, 33–45.

———. 1976. "The First Latin Annalists." *Latomus* 35, 689–717.

Rech, H. 1936. *Mos maiorum: Wesen und Wirkung der Tradition in Rom.* Marburg. (*Mos maiorum*)

Rhode, G. 1932. *Die Bedeutung der Tempelgründungen im Staatsleben der Römer.* Marburg. (*Tempel*)

Rhodes, P. J. 1981. *A Commentary on the Aristotelian* Athenaion Politeia. Oxford. (*Comm. Ath. Pol.*)

Riccobono, S., et al., eds. 1968. *Fontes iuris Romani anteiustiniani.* 3 vols. Florence. 2nd ed. (*FIRA*)

Rich, J. W. 1976. *Declaring War in the Roman Republic in the Period of Transmarine Expansion.* Brussels. (*War*)

Richard, J.-C. 1968. "Sur quelques grands pontifes plébéiens." *Latomus* 27, 786–801.

———. 1977. "*Classis–infra classem.*" *RPh* 51, 229–36.

———. 1977. "Edilité plébéienne et édilité curule: A propos de Denys d'Halicarnasse, *Ant. Rom.* VI, 95, 4." *Athenaeum* 55, 428–34.

———. 1978. *Les Origines de la plèbe romaine: Essai sur la formation du dualisme patricio-plébéien.* Paris. (*Origines*)

———. 1978. "Sur les prétendus corporations numaïques: A propos de Plutarque, *Num.* 17, 3." *Klio* 60, 423–28.

———. 1978. "*Proletarius:* Quelques remarques sur l'organisation servienne." *AC* 47, 438–47.

———. 1979. "Sur le plébiscite *ut liceret consules ambos plebeios creari* (Tite-Live VII, 42, 2)." *Historia* 28, 65–75.

———. 1980. "La Population romaine à l'époque archaïque: Sa composition, son évolution, ses structures." In *Roma arcaica e le recenti scoperte archeologiche*, 35–64. Milan. ("Population romaine")

———. 1981. "Sur le droit de la plèbe à exercer la censure: A propos de Liv. 8,12,16." *Mnemosyne* 34, 127–35.

———. 1981. "Variations sur le thème de la citoyenneté à l'époque royale." *Ktema* 6, 89–103.

———. 1983. "L'Oeuvre de Servius Tullius: Essai de mise en point." *RD* 61, 181–93.

Ridley, R. T. 1968. "Notes on the Establishment of the Tribunate of the Plebs." *Latomus* 27, 535–54.

———. 1975. "The Enigma of Servius Tullius." *Klio* 57, 147–77.

———. 1980. "*Fastenkritik*: A Stocktaking." *Athenaeum* 58, 264–98.

———. 1983. "*Falsi triumphi, plures consulatus.*" *Latomus* 42, 372–82.

Riemann, H. 1969. "Beiträge zur römischen Topographie." *RM* 76, 103–21.

Rienzi, C. 1976. "Brevi appunti storico-esegetici sull'azione riformatrice di Gaio Flaminio." *Archivio giuridico* 191, 29–51.

Riis, R. J. 1967. "Art in Etruria and Latium during the First Half of the

Fifth Century B.C." In *Les Origines de la république romaine*, 65–92. Vandoeuvres-Geneva.

Rilinger, R. 1976. *Der Einfluss des Wahlleiters bei den römischen Konsulwahlen von 366 bis 50 v. Chr.* Vestigia 24. Munich. (*Wahlleiter*)

———. 1978. "Die Ausbildung von Amtswechsel und Amtsfristen als Problem zwischen Machtbesitz und Machtgebrauch in der Mittleren Republik (342–217 v. Chr.)." *Chiron* 8, 247–312.

Rix, H. 1972. "Zum Ursprung des römisch-mittelitalischen Gentilnamensystems." *ANRW* I. 2: 700–758.

Rösler, W. 1980. *Dichter und Gruppe: Eine Untersuchung zu den Bedingungen und zur historischen Funktion früher griechischer Lyrik am Beispiel Alkaios.* Munich. (*Dichter und Gruppe*)

Roma arcaica e le recenti scoperte archeologiche: Giornate di studio in onore di U. Coli, Firenze 1979. 1980. Milan.

Roma medio repubblicana: Aspetti culturali di Roma e del Lazio nei secoli IV e III a.C. 1973. Exhibition Catalogue. Rome.

Romanelli, P. 1965. "Certezze e ipotesi sulla origine di Roma." *SR* 13, 156–67.

Roos, A. G. 1940. *Comitia tributa, concilium plebis, leges, plebiscita.* Amsterdam. (*Com. Trib.*)

Rose, H. J. 1922. "Patricians and Plebeians at Rome." *JRS* 12, 106–33.

Rosenberg, A. 1911. *Untersuchungen zur römischen Zenturienverfassung.* Berlin. (*Zenturienverfassung*)

———. 1913. "Studien zur Entstehung der Plebs." *Hermes* 48, 359–77.

———. 1919. "Zur Geschichte des Latinerbundes." *Hermes* 54, 113–73.

———. 1920. "Die Entstehung des sogenannten *foedus Cassianum* und des latinischen Rechts." *Hermes* 55, 337–63.

Rouland, N. 1979. *Pouvoir politique et dépendance personnelle dans l'antiquité romaine: Genèse et rôle des rapports de clientèle.* Coll. Latomus 166. Brussels. (*Clientèle*)

Rudolph, H. 1939. "Das *imperium* der römischen Magistrate." *NJAB* 2, 145–64.

Ruschenbusch, E. 1958. "*Patrios politeia*: Theseus, Drakon, Solon und Kleisthenes in Publizistik und Geschichtsschreibung des 5. und 4. Jhdts. v. Chr." *Historia* 7, 398–424.

———. 1960. "*Phonos.* Zum Recht Drakons und seiner Bedeutung für das Werden des athenischen Staates." *Historia* 9, 129–54.

———. 1963. "Die Zwölftafeln und die römische Gesandtschaft nach Athen." *Historia* 12, 250–53.

———. 1966. *SOLONOS NOMOI: Die Fragmente des solonischen Gesetzeswerkes mit einer Text- und Überlieferungsgeschichte.* Historia Einzelschr. 9. Wiesbaden. (*SOLONOS NOMOI*)

Ryberg, I. S. 1940. *An Archaeological Record of Rome from the Seventh to the Second Century B.C.* London and Philadelphia. (*Arch. Record*)

Sabbatucci, D. 1951–52. "Sacer." *SMSR* 23, 91–101.

———. 1953–54. "Patrizi e plebei nello sviluppo della religione romana." *SMSR* 24/25, 76–92.

———. 1954. "L'edilità romana, magistratura e sacerdozio." *Mem. Acc. Lincei*, 8th ser., 6. 3, 255–333.

———. 1972. "La censura: Istituzione rivoluzionaria dell'antica Roma." *Index* 3, 192–202.

Ste. Croix, G. E. M. de. 1981. *The Class Struggle in the Ancient Greek World.* London and Ithaca, N.Y. (*Class Struggle*)

Sallmann, K. G. 1971. *Die Geographie des älteren Plinius in ihrem Verhältnis zu Varro: Versuch einer Quellenanalyse.* Berlin. (*Plinius*)

Salmon, E. T. 1953. "Rome and the Latins." *Phoenix* 7, 93–104, 123–35.

———. 1955. "Roman Expansion and Roman Colonization in Italy." *Phoenix* 9, 63–75.

———. 1963. "The *coloniae maritimae.*" *Athenaeum* 41, 3–38.

———. 1967. *Samnium and the Samnites.* Cambridge. (*Samnium*)

———. 1970. *Roman Colonization under the Republic.* London and Ithaca, N.Y. (*Colon.*)

———. 1982. *The Making of Roman Italy.* London and Ithaca, N.Y. (*Italy*)

Salmon, J. 1977. "Political Hoplites?" *JHS* 97, 84–101.

Santilli, A. 1981. "Le agitazioni agrarie dal 424 a.C. alla presa di Veii." In *Legge e società nella repubblica romana*, edited by F. Serrao, I: 281–306.

Sargenti, M. 1973. "Riflessioni sull'attribuzione dei poteri giurisdizionali a Roma nel passaggio dalla monarchia alla Repubblica." In *Studi G. Donatuti*, III: 1157–93. Milan.

Sauerwein, I. 1970. *Die leges sumptuariae als römische Massnahme gegen den Sittenverfall.* Hamburg. (*Leges sumpt.*)

Saulnier, C. 1972. "L'Histoire militaire de la Rome archaïque chez Denys d'Halicarnasse." *BAGB*, 283–95.

———. 1980. *L'Armée et la guerre dans le monde étrusco-romain, VIIIe–IVe siècles*. Paris. (*Armée*)

Scalais, R. 1941. "Anachronismes chez Tite-Live." *LEC* 10, 31–34.

Scevola, M. L. 1968. "Sulla prima guerra sannitica." *Aevum* 42, 291–97.

———. 1973. "Sulla più antica espansione territoriale romana in Campania." *RIL* 107, 1002–40.

———. 1975. "Consequenze della *deditio* di Roma a Porsenna." *RIL* 109, 3–27.

Schachermeyr, F. 1930. "Die gallische Katastrophe." *Klio* 23, 277–305.

Schaefer, A. 1876. "Zur Geschichte des römischen Consulates." *Jahrb. f. Class. Philologie* 113, 569–83.

Schilling, R. 1964. "Une Victime des vicissitudes politiques: La Diane latine." In *Hommages à Jean Bayet*, edited by M. Renard and R. Schilling, 650–67. Coll. Latomus 70. Brussels.

———. 1972. "La Situation des études relatives à la religion romaine de la République (1950–1970)." *ANRW* I. 2: 317–47.

Schmidt, J. 1886. "Die Einsetzung der römischen Volkstribunen." *Hermes* 21, 460–66.

Schönbauer, E. 1950. "Zwei Grundbegriffe der römischen Rechtsordnung: *nexus* und *mancipium*." *Anz. Österr. Akad. der Wiss.*, phil.-hist. Kl. 87, 323–65.

———. 1950. "*Mancipium* und *nexus*." *Iura* 1, 300–305.

———. 1953. "Die römische Centurien-Verfassung in neuer Quellenschau." *Historia* 2, 21–49.

Schroeder, W. A. 1971. *Marcus Porcius Cato: Das erste Buch der Origines: Ausgabe und Erklärung der Fragmente*. Beitr. zur klass. Philol. 41. Meisenheim, West Germany. (*Cato*)

Schulz, F. 1946. *History of Roman Legal Science*. Oxford. (*History*)

Schwartz, E. 1903. "Notae de Romanorum annalibus." *Rektoratsprogramm Göttingen*, 3–15 (= id., *Gesammelte Schriften*, II: 337–51. Berlin, 1956).

———. 1905. "Dionysios von Halikarnassos (Dionysios no. 113)." *RE* 5.1: 934–71.

Schwegler, A. 1856–67. *Römische Geschichte*. 3 vols. (I², 1867; II–III, 1856–58). Tübingen. (*Röm. Geschichte*)

Schwind, F. von. 1940. *Zur Frage der Publikation im römischen Recht, mit Ausblicken in das altgriechische und ptolemäische Rechtsgebiet*. Münch. Beitr. z. Papyrusforsch. und ant. Rechtsgesch. 31. Munich. (*Publikation*)

Scullard, H. H. 1967. *The Etruscan Cities and Rome.* London and Ithaca, N.Y. (*Etr. Cities*)
———. 1973. *Roman Politics 220–150 B.C.* Oxford. 2nd ed. (*Politics*)
———. 1980. *A History of the Roman World, 753–146 B.C.* London and New York. 4th ed. (*History*)
Seager, R. 1977. "*Populares* in Livy and the Livian Tradition." *CQ* 27, 377–90.
Sealey, R. 1959. "Consular Tribunes Once More." *Latomus* 18, 521–30.
———. 1976. *A History of the Greek City-States, 700–338 B.C.* Berkeley and Los Angeles. (*History*)
Sereni, E. 1955. *Comunità rurali nell'Italia antica.* Rome. (*Com. rurali*)
———. 1972. "Considerazioni di metodo su Stato, rivoluzione e schiavitù in Roma antica." *Index* 3, 203–11.
Serrao, F., ed. 1981. *Legge e società nella repubblica romana* I. Naples.
———. 1981. "Lotte per la terra e per la casa a Roma dal 485 al 441 a.C." In *Legge e società nella repubblica romana* I: 51–180. Naples.
Shackleton Bailey, D. R. 1976. *Two Studies in Roman Nomenclature.* Amer. Class. Stud. 3. University Park, Pennsylvania. (*Studies*)
Shatzman, I. 1973. "Patricians and Plebeians: The Case of the Veturii." *CQ* 23, 65–77.
———. 1975. *Senatorial Wealth and Roman Politics.* Brussels. (*Wealth*)
Sherwin-White, A. N. 1973. *The Roman Citizenship.* Oxford. 2nd ed. (*Citizenship*)
Siber, H. 1936. *Die plebejischen Magistraturen bis zur Lex Hortensia.* Leipz. Rechtswiss. Studien 100. Leipzig. (*Magistraturen*)
———. 1937. "Die ältesten römischen Volksversammlungen." *ZRG* 57, 233–71.
———. 1951. "*Plebs.*" *RE* 21.1: 103–87.
Siena, E. 1956. "La politica democratica di Quinto Publilio Filone." *SR* 4, 509–22.
Siewert, P. 1978. "Die angebliche Übernahme solonischer Gesetze in die Zwölftafeln. Ursprung und Ausgestaltung einer Legende." *Chiron* 8, 331–44.
———. 1982. *Die Trittyen Attikas und die Heeresreform des Kleisthenes.* Vestigia 33. Munich. (*Kleisthenes*)
Sigwart, G. 1906. "Römische Fasten und Annalen bei Diodor: Ein Beitrag

zur Kritik der älteren republikanischen Verfassungsgeschichte." *Klio* 6, 269–86, 341–79.

Snodgrass, A. M. 1965. "The Hoplite Reform and History." *JHS* 85, 110–22.

Solari, A. 1934. "Cincinnato e le lotte contro gli Equi e i Volsci secondo Livio." In G. M. Columba et al., *Studi liviani*, 67–80. Rome.

Soltau, W. 1880. *Über die Entstehung und Zusammensetzung der altrömischen Volksversammlungen*. Berlin. (*Volksvers.*)

———. 1882. "Die ursprüngliche Bedeutung und Competenz der *aediles plebis*." In *Histor. Untersuchungen A. Schaefer . . . gewidmet*, 98–147. Bonn.

———. 1885. "Die Gültigkeit der Plebiszite." *Berliner Stud. für class. Philol. und Archäol.* 2, 1–176.

———. 1909. *Die Anfänge der römischen Geschichtsschreibung*. Leipzig. (*Anfänge*)

———. 1911. "Reiter, Ritter und Ritterstand in Rom." *Zeitschr. für die österr. Gymnasien* 62, 385–404, 481–511, 577–90.

———. 1912. "Bot Diodors annalistische Quelle die Namen der ältesten Volkstribunen?" *Philologus* 71, 267–71.

———. 1913. "*Classis* und *classes* in Rom." *Philologus* 72, 358–72.

Sordi, M. 1960. *I rapporti romano-ceriti e l'origine della civitas sine suffragio*. Rome. (*Rapporti*)

———. 1965. "Sulla cronologia liviana del IV secolo." *Helikon* 5, 3–44.

———. 1969. *Roma e i Sanniti nel IV secolo a.C.* Bologna. (*Sanniti*)

———. 1972. "La *lex Maria de suffragiis ferendis* e il tribunato di C. Letorio nel 471 vulg. (storia e pseudostoria nell'annalistica romana)." *Athenaeum* 50, 132–41.

———. 1972. "La leggenda dei Dioscuri nella battaglia della Sagra e di Lago Regillo." *CISA* 1, 47–70.

———. 1976–77. "La leggenda di Arunte chiusino e la prima invasione gallica in Italia." *RSA* 6/7, 111–17.

Spahn, P. 1977. *Mittelschicht und Polisbildung*. Frankfurt, Berne, and Las Vegas. (*Mittelschicht*)

———. 1980. "*Oikos* und *polis*: Beobachtungen zum Prozess der Polisbildung bei Hesiod, Solon und Aischylos." *HZ* 231, 529–64.

Sprey, K. 1971. "Het ontstaan van de Romeinse Republiek." *Tijdschr. voor Geschiedenis* 84, 1–13.

Starr, C. G. 1961. *The Origins of Greek Civilization, 1100–650* B.C. New York. (*Origins*)

———. 1977. *The Economic and Social Growth of Early Greece, 800–500* B.C. New York. (*Growth*)

———. 1980. *The Beginnings of Imperial Rome: Rome in the Mid-Republic.* Ann Arbor, Mich. (*Beginnings*)

Staveley, E. S. 1953. "The Reform of the *comitia centuriata*." *AJP* 74, 1–33.

———. 1953. "The Significance of the Consular Tribunate." *JRS* 43, 30–36.

———. 1954–55. "The Conduct of Elections during an *interregnum*." *Historia* 3, 193–211.

———. 1954–55. "*Provocatio* during the Fifth and Fourth Centuries B.C." *Historia* 3, 412–28.

———. 1955. "Tribal Legislation before the *lex Hortensia*." *Athenaeum*, n.s., 33, 3–31.

———. 1956. "The Constitution of the Roman Republic, 1940–54." *Historia* 5, 74–119.

———. 1959. "The Political Aims of Appius Claudius Caecus." *Historia* 8, 410–23.

———. 1962. "Cicero and the *comitia centuriata*." *Historia* 11, 299–314.

———. 1972. *Greek and Roman Voting and Elections.* London and Ithaca, N.Y. (*Voting*)

———. 1983. "The Nature and Aims of the Patriciate." *Historia* 32, 24–57.

Stella-Maranca, F. 1901. *Il tribunato della plebe dalla lex Hortensia alla lex Cornelia.* Lanciano. Repr. Rome, 1967. (*Tribunato*)

Stibbe, C. M. et al. 1980. *Lapis Satricanus: Archaeological, Epigraphical, Linguistic and Historical Aspects of the New Inscription from Satricum*, Archeol. Stud. van het Nederl. Inst. te Rome, Scripta minora 5. The Hague. (*Lapis Satricanus*)

Stroud, R. S. 1978. "State Documents in Archaic Athens." In *Athens Comes of Age: From Solon to Salamis*, edited by W. A. P. Childs, 20–42. Princeton. ("State Documents")

Stupperich, R. 1977. *Staatsbegräbnis und Privatgrabmal im klassischen Athen.* 2 vols. Münster. (*Staatsbegräbnis*)

Stuveras, R. 1964; 1965. "La Vie politique au premier siècle de la République Romaine à travers la tradition littéraire." *MEFR* 76, 295–342; 77, 35–67.

Sumner, G. V. 1960. "Cicero on the *comitia centuriata: De re publica* II.22.39–40." *AJP* 81, 136–56.

———. 1970. "The Legion and the Centuriate Assembly." *JRS* 60, 67–78.

Suolahti, J. 1963. *The Roman Censors: A Study on Social Structure.* Ann. Acad. Scient. Fennicae B 117. Helsinki. (*Censors*)

Szegedy-Maszak, A. 1978. "Legends of the Greek Lawgivers." *GRBS* 19, 199–210.

Szemler, G. J. 1972. *The Priests of the Roman Republic: A Study of Interaction Between Priesthoods and Magistrates.* Brussels. (*Priests*)

Täubler, E. 1921. *Untersuchungen zur Geschichte des Decemvirats und der Zwölftafeln.* Berlin. (*Decemvirat*)

Tamborini, F. 1930. "La vita economica nella Roma degli ultimi re." *Athenaeum* 8, 299–328, 452–87.

Taylor, L. R. 1952–54. "The Four Urban Tribes and the Four Regions of Ancient Rome." *Rend. Pont. Acc. Rom. di Arch.* 27, 225–38.

———. 1957. "The Centuriate Assembly before and after the Reform." *AJP* 78, 337–54.

———. 1960. *The Voting Districts of the Roman Republic: The 35 Urban and Rural Tribes.* Papers and Monogr. Amer. Acad. Rome 20. Rome. (*Voting Distr.*)

———. 1962. "Forerunners of the Gracchi." *JRS* 52, 19–27.

Taylor, L. R., and R. T. Scott. 1969. "Seating Space in the Roman Senate and the *senatores pedarii*." *TAPA* 100, 529–82.

Thomas, C. G. 1977. "Literacy and the Codification of Law." *SDHI* 43, 455–58.

Thomsen, R. 1957–61. *Early Roman Coinage.* 3 vols. Copenhagen. (*Coinage*)

———. 1980. *King Servius Tullius: A Historical Synthesis.* Copenhagen. (*Serv. Tullius*)

Thormann, K. F. 1943. *Der doppelte Ursprung der mancipatio: Ein Beitrag zur Erforschung des frührömischen Rechtes unter Mitberücksichtigung des nexum.* Münch. Beitr. z. Papyrusforsch. 33. Munich. (*Mancipatio*)

Tibiletti, G. 1948; 1949. "Il possesso dell'*ager publicus* e la norme *de modo agrorum* sino ai Gracchi." *Athenaeum* 26, 173–236; 27, 3–41.

———. 1961. "Latini e Ceriti." In *Studi giuridici e sociali in memoria di E. Vanoni*. Pavia. 239–49.

Timpe, D. 1970–71. "Le Origini di Catone e la storiografia latina." *Atti Accad. patavina, cl. di sc. mor. lett. ed arti* 83, 1–33.

———. 1972. "Fabius Pictor und die Anfänge der römischen Historiographie." *ANRW* I.2: 928–69.

———. 1979. "Erwägungen zur jüngeren Annalistik." *A&A* 25, 97–119.

Tomulescu, D. 1977. "L'Existence du droit international public chez les Romains: Ses origines." *RIDA* 24, 423–37.

Tondo, S. 1981. *Profilo di storia costituzionale romana* I. Milan. (*Profilo*)

Torelli, M. 1971. "Contributo dell'archeologia alla storia sociale: L'Etruria e l'Apulia." *DArch* 5, 431–71.

———. 1974. "Beziehungen zwischen Griechen und Etruskern im 5. und 4. Jh. v. u. Z." In *Hellenische Poleis: Krise—Wandlung—Wirkung*, edited by E. C. Welskopf, II: 823–40. Berlin. ("Griechen und Etrusker")

———. 1974–75. "Tre studi di storia etrusca." *DArch* 8, 3–78.

———. 1976. *Elogia tarquiniensia*. Florence. (*Elogia*)

———. 1979. "Rome et l'Etrurie à l'époque archaïque." In *Terre et paysans dépendants dans les sociétés antiques*, 251–99. Paris. Ital. in *DArch* 8, 1974/75, 3–53. ("Rome et l'Etrurie")

———. 1980. "Roma arcaica: Archeologia e storia." In *Roma arcaica e le recenti scoperte archeologiche*, 1–17. Milan. ("Roma arcaica")

Toynbee, A. J. 1965. *Hannibal's Legacy: The Hannibalic War's Effects on Roman Life*. 2 vols. Oxford. (*Hannibal's Legacy*)

Tränkle, H. 1965. "Der Anfang des römischen Freistaats in der Darstellung des Livius." *Hermes* 93, 311–37.

Treptow, R. 1964. *Die Kunst der Reden in der ersten und dritten Dekade des livianischen Geschichtswerkes*. Kiel. (*Reden*)

Triebel, C. A. M. 1980. *Ackergesetze und politische Reformen: Eine Studie zur römischen Innenpolitik*. Bonn. (*Ackergesetze*)

Tsirkin, Y. B. 1983. "The Battle of Alalia." *Oikumene* 4, 209–21.

Ulf, C. 1982. *Das römische Lupercalienfest: Ein Modellfall für Methodenprobleme in der Altertumswissenschaft*. Impulse der Forschung 38. Darmstadt. (*Lupercalienfest*)

Ungern-Sternberg, J. von. 1975. *Capua im Zweiten Punischen Krieg: Untersuchungen zur römischen Annalistik*. Vestigia 23. Munich. (*Capua*)

———. 1982. "Weltreich und Krise: Äussere Bedingungen für den Niedergang der römischen Republik." *MH* 39, 254–71.

Urban, R. 1973. "Zur Entstehung des Volkstribunats." *Historia* 22, 761–64.

Valvo, A. 1975. "Le vicende del 44–43 a.C. nella tradizione di Livio e di Dionigi su Spurio Melio." *CISA* 3, 157–83.

———. 1977. "Il *modus agrorum* e la legge agraria di C. Flaminio Nepote." *Miscellanea greca e romana* 5, 179–224.

———. 1978. "Ottaviano e l'opinione pubblica di Roma in un passo liviano sulla *lex Pedia*." *CISA* 5, 111–16.

Venturini, C. 1981. "Il *plebiscitum de multa T. Menenio dicenda*." In *Legge e società nella repubblica romana*, edited by F. Serrao, I: 181–96. Naples.

Verdin, H. 1974. "La Fonction de l'histoire selon Denys d'Halicarnasse." *Anc. Soc.* 5, 289–307.

Vernant, J.-P. 1965. "Remarques sur la lutte de classe dans la Grèce ancienne." *Eirene* 4, 5–19.

Versnel, H. 1970. *Triumphus: An Inquiry into the Origin, Development and Meaning of the Roman Triumph.* Leiden. (*Triumphus*)

———. 1980. "Historical Implications [of the new inscription from Satricum]." In C. M. Stibbe et al., *Lapis Satricanus*, 95–150. The Hague. ("Historical Implications")

———. 1982. "Die neue Inschrift von Satricum in historischer Sicht." *Gymnasium* 89, 193–235.

Visscher, F. de. 1929. "La *lex Poetelia Papiria* et le régime des délits privés au V^c siècle de Rome." In *Mélanges P. Fournier*, 755–65. Paris.

———. 1952. "*Conubium* et *civitas*." *RIDA* 1, 401–22 (=id., *Etudes de droit romain public et privé*, III: 147–67. Milan, 1966).

———. 1955. "*Ius Quiritium, civitas romana* et nationalité moderne." In *Studi in onore di U. E. Paoli*, 239–51. Florence (=id., *Études* . . . III: 99–116). ("*Ius Quiritium*")

Vogt, J. 1973. *Römische Geschichte*, vol. I, *Die Römische Republik*. Munich. 6th ed.

Volkmann, H. 1948. "Valerius Antias (Valerius no. 98)." *RE* 7A.2: 2313–39.

Walbank, F. W. 1957–79. *A Historical Commentary on Polybius.* 3 vols. Oxford. (*Comm.*)

Walde, A., and J. B. Hofmann. 1938–56. *Lateinisches etymologisches Wörterbuch.* 3 vols. Heidelberg. 3rd ed. (Walde-Hofmann)

Waldstein, W. 1972. "Zum Fall der *dos Liciniae*." *Index* 3, 343–61.

Walsh, P. G. 1955. "Livy's Preface and the Distortion of History." *AJP* 76, 369–83. German in E. Burck, ed., *WL*, 181–99.

———. 1961. *Livy: His Historical Aims and Methods.* Cambridge. (*Livy*)

———. 1974. *Livy.* Greece & Rome: New Surveys in the Classics 8. Oxford. (*Survey Livy*)

Watson, A. 1970. *The Law of the Ancient Romans*. Dallas. (*Law*)

———. 1975. *Rome of the XII Tables: Persons and Property*. Princeton. (*XII Tables*)

Watson, G. R. 1958. "The Pay of the Roman Army: The Republic." *Historia* 7, 113–20.

Weisz, E. 1968. "Die grosse Inschrift von Gortyn und ihre Bestimmungen über Selbsthilfe und Prozess." In *Zur griechischen Rechtsgeschichte*, edited by E. Berneker, 315–49. WdF 45. Darmstadt. Greek in *Pragm. Akad. Athen.* 14, 1, 1–28. Athens, 1948.

Welwei K.-W. 1966. "Demokratie und Masse bei Polybios." *Historia* 15, 282–301.

———. 1981. "Adel und Demos in der frühen Polis." *Gymnasium* 88, 1–23.

———. 1983. *Die griechische Polis: Verfassung und Gesellschaft in archaischer und klassischer Zeit*. Stuttgart. (*Polis*)

Werner, R. 1963. *Der Beginn der römischen Republik*. Munich. (*Beginn*)

———. 1968. "Die Auseinandersetzungen der frührömischen Republik mit ihren Nachbarn in quellenkritischer Sicht." *Gymnasium* 75, 45–73. Critical comments by R. M. Ogilvie, ibid., 505–9, and R. Werner's reply, ibid., 509–19.

———. 1973. "Vom Stadtstaat zum Weltreich: Grundzüge der innenpolitischen und sozialen Entwicklung Roms." *Gymnasium* 80, 209–35, 437–56.

———. 1973. "Die phoinikisch-etruskischen Inschriften von Pyrgoi und die römische Geschichte im 4. Jh. v. Chr." *Grazer Beitr.* 1, 241–71.

Wesenberg, G. 1953. "Zur Frage der Kontinuität zwischen königlicher Gewalt und Beamtengewalt in Rom." *ZRG* 70, 58–92.

Westrup, C. W. 1943. *Recherches sur les formes antiques de marriage dans l'ancien droit romain*. Danske Vidensk. Selsk. Hist.-Filol. Medd. 30, no. 1. Copenhagen. (*Recherches*)

———. 1947. *Note sur la sponsio et le nexum dans l'ancien droit romain: Le Nouveau Fragment des Institutes de Gaius*. Danske Vidensk. Selsk. Hist.-Filol. Medd. 31, no. 2. Copenhagen. (*Sponsio*)

———. 1956. *Some Notes on the Roman Slave in Early Times: A Comparative Sociological Study*. Danske Vidensk. Selsk. Hist.-Filol. Medd. 36, no. 3. Copenhagen. (*Slave*)

Whitehead, D. 1977. *The Ideology of the Athenian Metic*. *PCPhS* suppl. 4. (*Metic*)

Wieacker, F. 1940. "Privatrechtsgesetzgebung und politische Grundordnung im römischen Freistaat." *Die Antike* 16, 176–205 (=id., *Recht* [1st ed., 1944], 38–85).

———. 1956. "Zwölftafelprobleme." *RIDA*, 3rd ser., 3, 459–91.

———. 1961. *Vom römischen Recht*. Stuttgart. 2nd ed. (*Recht*)

———. 1967. "Die XII Tafeln in ihrem Jahrhundert." In *Les Origines de la république romaine*, 291–359. Vandoeuvres-Geneva. ("XII Tafeln")

———. 1971. "Solon und die XII Tafeln." In *Studi in onore di E. Volterra*, III: 757–84. Milan. ("Solon und XII Tafeln")

———. 1977. "Sulla plebe antica." *Labeo* 23, 59–69.

Wiehemeyer, W. 1938. *Proben historischer Kritik aus Livius XXI–XLV*. Emsdetten, Germany. (*Kritik*)

Will, E. 1965. "La Grèce archaïque." In *2nd Intern. Conf. of Econ. Hist.*, vol. I, *Trade and Politics in the Ancient World*, 41–115. Paris. ("La Grèce archaïque")

Willems, G. P. H. 1878–85. *Le Sénat de la république romaine: Sa composition et ses attributions*. 2 vols. Paris. (*Sénat*)

Willetts, R. F. 1967. *The Law Code of Gortyn*. Kadmos suppl. 1. Berlin. (*Law Code*)

Wirszubski, Ch. 1950. *Libertas as a Political Idea at Rome during the Late Republic and Early Principate*. Cambridge. (*Libertas*)

Wiseman, T. P. 1974. "The Circus Flaminius." *PBSR* 42, 3–26.

———. 1974. "Legendary Genealogies in Late-Republican Rome." *G&R*, 2nd ser., 21, 153–64.

———. 1979. *Clio's Cosmetics: Three Studies in Greco-Roman Literature*. Leicester. (*Clio's Cosmetics*)

———. 1983. "The Credibility of the Roman Annalists." *LCM* 8, 20–22.

Wissowa, G. 1912. *Religion und Kultus der Römer*. HdAW V.4. Munich. 2nd ed. (*Religion*)

Wittek, P. 1922. "Die Zenturienordnung als Quelle zur älteren römischen Sozial- und Verfassungsgeschichte." *Vierteljahresschr. für Soz.- und Wirtschaftsgesch.* 16, 1–38.

Wolff, H. J. 1951. *Roman Law: An Historical Introduction*. Norman, Okla. (*Law*)

———. 1961. "*Interregnum* und *auctoritas patrum*." *BIDR* 64, 1–14.

Yavetz, Z. 1962. "The Policy of C. Flaminius and the *plebiscitum Claudianum*." *Athenaeum* 40, 325–44.

Zancan, L. 1935–36. "La teoria gentilizia e il concetto della cittadinanza romana." *Atti Ist. veneto di sc. lett. e arti* 95, 321–57.

———. 1939. *Il pensiero di Livio sulla storia romana.* Padua. (*Livio*)

Zecchini, G. 1976. "La figura di C. Terenzio Varrone nella tradizione storiografica." *CISA* 4, 118–30.

Ziegler, K.-H. 1972. "Das Völkerrecht der römischen Republik." *ANRW* I.2: 68–114.

Zohren, C. 1910. *Valerius Antias und Caesar.* Münster. (*Antias*)

Zusi, L. 1975. "Patriziato e plebe: Rassegna degli studi 1966–1971." *Critica storica* 12, 177–230.

Contributors

Timothy J. Cornell: Ph.D. 1972, University of London. Lecturer in ancient history, University College, London. Main interests: ancient historiography; the history and archaeology of early Rome and Latium; the history and culture of pre-Roman Italy; the social and economic history of the Roman Republic. Publications: *Early Roman History to 264 B.C.* (in preparation); ed. (with J. Matthews), *Atlas of the Roman World* (Oxford, 1982); three chapters in *Cambr. Anc. Hist.* VII² (forthcoming); several articles.

Robert Develin: Ph.D. 1973, University of Michigan. Senior lecturer in classics, University of Tasmania, Australia. Main interests: the political, social, and constitutional history of Athens to 323 B.C., and of republican Rome; ancient historiography. Main publications: *Patterns of Office-Holding 366–49 B.C.* (1979); *The Practice of Politics at Rome 366–167 B.C.* (1985); several articles.

Walter Eder: Ph.D. 1969, University of Munich, Germany. Professor of ancient history, Free University of Berlin. Main interests: Greek and Roman social, intellectual, and legal history. Main publications: *Das vorsullanische Repetundenverfahren* (1969); *Servitus publica: Untersuchungen zur Entstehung, Entwicklung und Funktion der öffentlichen Sklaverei in Rom* (1980); articles.

Jerzy Linderski: Ph.D. 1960, University of Cracow, Poland. Paddison professor of Latin, University of North Carolina at Chapel Hill. Main interests: Latin literature, epigraphy, and linguistics; social, constitutional, legal, and religious history of the Roman Republic and the early Empire. Main publications: *The Roman State and the Collegia: Studies in the History of Roman Associations in the Late Republican Period* (1961, in Polish); *Roman Electoral Assemblies from Sulla to Caesar* (1966, in Polish); *The Augural Law* (forthcoming); *The Death of Tiberius Gracchus* (in preparation); numerous articles.

Richard E. Mitchell: Ph.D. 1965, University of Cincinnati. Associate professor of history, University of Illinois at Urbana-Champaign. Main interests: social and political history of the Roman Republic, numismatics. Publications: *Patres and Plebs* (in preparation); several articles.

Arnaldo Momigliano: D.Litt. 1929, University of Turin, Italy. Professor emeritus of ancient history, University College, London, and Scuola Normale Superiore, Pisa; Alexander White professor, University of Chicago. Main interests: ancient historiography; all aspects of Greek and Roman history; history of the ancient world in general; the classical tradition; *Wissenschaftsgeschichte*. Main publications: *La composizione della storia di Tucidide* (1929); *Prime linee di storia della tradizione maccabaica* (1931, 1968); *Claudius, the Emperor and his Achievement* (1934, 1961, Italian: 1932); *Filippo il Macedone* (1934); *The Conflict between Paganism and Christianity in the Fourth Century* (ed., 1963); *Studies in Historiography* (1966); *The Development of Greek Biography* (1971); *Alien Wisdom* (1975); *Essays in Historiography* (1977); *La storiografia greca* (1982); *Problèmes d'historiographie ancienne et moderne* (1983); *New Paths of Classicism in the Nineteenth Century* (1983); *Sui Fondamenti della Storia Antica* (1984); contributions to *Cambridge Ancient History*, vols. X (1st ed.) and VII (2nd ed.); ed. of volumes on H. Usener and G. Dumézil (1983); numerous articles, mostly collected in *Contributo alla storia degli studi classici* (1955) and *Secondo [Terzo, Quarto, Quinto, Sesto, Settimo] contributo alla storia degli studi classici e del mondo antico* (1960–84).

Kurt A. Raaflaub: Ph.D. 1970, University of Basel, Switzerland. Professor of classics and history, Brown University, Providence, Rhode Island. Main interests: social, political, and intellectual history of Greece and Rome; history of political concepts and terminology. Main publications: *Dignitatis contentio: Studien zur Motivation und politischen Taktik im Bürgerkrieg zwischen Caesar und Pompeius* (1974); "Zum Freiheitsbegriff der Griechen: Materialien und Untersuchungen zur Bedeutungsentwicklung von *eleutheros/eleutheria* in der archaischen und klassischen Zeit" (1981); *Die Entdeckung der Freiheit: Zur historischen Semantik und Gesellschaftsgeschichte eines politischen Grundbegriffes der Griechen* (1985); several articles.

Jean-Claude Richard: Ph.D. 1976, Université de Paris-Sorbonne, France. Professor of Latin language and literature at the Sorbonne, Paris. Main interests: the cult of the emperor in the early Roman Empire; social, political, and legal history of archaic Rome; the Roman annalistic tradition and its survival in the Empire. Main publications: *Les Origines de la plèbe romaine: Essai sur la formation du dualisme* *patricio-plébéien* (1978); *Pseudo-Aurelius Victor: Origo gentis Romanae* (ed., transl., comm., 1984); numerous articles.

Mark Toher: Ph.D. 1984, Brown University. Assistant professor of classics, Union College, Schenectady, New York. Main interests: funeral regulations in archaic societies; historiography, literature, and politics in the Augustan era; ancient historiography. Publications: *The* Bios Kaisaros *of Nicolaus of Damascus* (in preparation); articles.

Jürgen von Ungern-Sternberg: Ph.D. 1968, University of Munich, Germany. Professor of ancient history, University of Basel, Switzerland. Main interests: historiography; social, political, and institutional history of the Roman Republic; *Wissenschaftsgeschichte*. Main publications: *Untersuchungen zum spätrepublikanischen Notstandsrecht: Senatusconsultum ultimum und hostis-Erklärung* (1970); *Capua im Zweiten Punischen Krieg: Untersuchungen zur römischen Annalistik* (1975); ed., Teubner Reprint Series; several articles.

Index of Subjects

Addicti, 213 n.42
Adlecti, adlectio, 113, 113 n.37, 114, 120, 124
Adrogatio, 109, 143 n.32, 148, 153 n.58
Adsidui, 42, 82, 116, 125, 182, 194, 200, 224 n.86, 298, 354
Aediles, aedileship, 190, 337, 337 n.32, 354–55, 358, 358 n.10, 364 n.38
Ager publicus, 19, 75, 186, 211, 211 n.34, 327
Ager Romanus, 24–25, 115, 125
Agrarian reform. See Distribution of land; Law: agrarian
Aisymnetes, 266
Ambitus, 345
Annales, annalists, 3, 10, 17, 23–24, 47, 121, 177, 195, 201–8, 222, 236 n.133, 335, 338 n.33. See also Tradition: annalistic
Annales Maximi, 3, 12, 12 n.26, 16 n.41, 53, 63 n.32, 86, 172, 176, 195, 210, 210 n.31, 260, 333
Anomia, 266
Anthropology, anthropological, 9, 28, 195, 231, 240, 268
Antiquarianism, antiquarians, 3, 9, 12 n.27, 17, 23–24, 52, 81, 84, 177–78, 185, 195
Archaeology, 8–10, 23, 27, 65–71, 110–11, 124, 178–81, 195–96, 212–23, 268, 271, 286 n.57, 310, 310 n.37, 319, 322–23
Archives, 63 n.32, 190, 197
Archon basileus, 38–39
Aristocracy, aristocrats, 7, 27, 30, 30 n.78, 31, 31 n.82, 35 n.92, 38–40, 43–45, 58, 66, 110 n.23, 111, 113–14, 117, 134, 137–38, 152, 155, 157–58, 166, 169, 173, 179, 185, 191, 205–6, 209, 214–17, 217 n.61, 219, 222, 225–27, 227–37, 238–43, 249, 251–54, 263–300, 322, 324, 333, 352, 354; *adulescentes nobiles*, 93, 93 n.47; Greek, 34 n.89, 213–16, 231, 243, 293, 301–6; Gallic: 254 n.27. See also Patricians
Army, Roman, 21, 39, 69–70, 113, 137, 183–84, 188, 192, 196–97, 206, 217 n.61, 222–24, 236
Artisans. See Craftsmen
Artists: Etruscan, 191; Greek, 191, 197
Arval Brethren. See Fratres Arvales
Assembly: Athenian (*Ecclesia*), 34; of Roman citizens, 82–83, 209, 219, 219 n.67. See also Comitia; Comitiatus maximus; Concilium plebis
Atimos, 290
Atthis, Atthidographers, 330–31
Auctoritas patrum. See Patrum auctoritas
Augurate, augurs, 112, 115, 140, 151–52, 164 n.94, 169, 171, 257 n.43, 315, 339, 346, 364 n.36, 371
Auspicium, auspicia, 123, 139–40, 144, 163, 229 n.109, 233, 236 n.133, 241–42, 260–61, 273 n.22, 284 n.53, 338–41
Auxilium, 128, 219 n.65, 297, 376

Ballads, English, 333
Bellum iustum, 86
Building, public, in archaic Rome, 13–14, 45, 325, 370 n.57
Burials. See Tombs

439

440 Index of Subjects

Calendar, 156
Camillus, camilla, 147
Capitoline temple. *See* Temples: of Jupiter Capitolinus
Capitoline triad, 111, 190
Captio, 245 n.3, 256 n.41, 257, 257 n.44
Carmen Saliare, 184
Carmina Marciana, 183
Castes, 252 n.23
Catilinarian conspiracy. *See* Sergius Catilina, L.
Cavalry, 113, 179, 185, 187, 193, 196. *See also Equites*; *Equitatus*
Censorship, censors, 164–71, 328, 334, 334 n.21, 338, 340, 344, 348
Census, 118–19, 136, 193; classes at Athens, 46; figures at Rome, 42, 72 n.55
Centuria, centuriae: equestrian, 114; *inauguratae*, 113; *praerogativa*, 144, 334
Centuriate assembly. *See Comitia*
Centuriate ("Servian") organization, 44 n.122, 70, 72, 116, 120, 136–37, 209, 219 n.67, 223, 298 n.88, 354. *See also Comitia: centuriata*
Centuries. *See Centuria*; Centuriate ("Servian") organization; *Comitia: centuriata*
Chronicle, pontifical. *See Annales Maximi*
Circus Flaminius, 364, 364 n.38
Citizenship, citizens, 22, 30, 30 n.78, 31, 31 n.82, 42–43, 106–7, 119, 171, 223, 287, 287 n.59, 294 n.72, 363. *See also* Population
City of Rome, size and early growth, 13 n.30, 24, 27, 65–67, 69, 110–11
City-state (*polis*), xv, 6–7, 26, 30, 40, 107, 206, 222, 225, 284, 286; Etruscan, 68–69, 234 n.128; Greek, 26, 29, 35, 222 n.80, 230, 241; in Italy, 27 n.67; Latin, 177; medieval Italian, 28
"Civic Space," 115
Clans, 34, 34 n.90, 66, 182, 196, 206, 293. *See also* Gens
Class struggle, 281, 349 n.64
Classici. *See Classis*
Classis, 25, 72, 115–17, 119, 125–27, 182, 187–88, 192–93, 196, 200, 209. *See also Infra classem*
Clientela, clientes, 33, 33 n.86, 34, 34 n.90, 45, 106, 113–14, 116–18, 126 n.81, 137, 161 n.83, 178, 182, 185–86, 188, 191–93, 196–97, 209, 213, 215, 224, 226, 230, 235, 284–85, 294, 295 n.78, 298, 298 n.91, 337 n.31, 355. *See also Patroni*
Closure of the patriciate. *See* Patricians: closure of the patriciate
Coemptio, 248–49, 249 n.17, 251, 254–55, 258–59

Coercitio, 220
Coinage, 74
Coitio, coitiones, 347–49
Colonies, colonization, 32, 36 n.93, 62, 236–37, 287 n.59, 362–63
Columella, 308, 308 n.32
Columna Minucia, 60
Comitia, 170, 172 n.118, 178, 183; *calata*, 109; *centuriata*, 25, 74, 135–36, 144, 175, 183–84, 190, 297, 297 n.87, 334–35, 337 n.32, 339–40, 364 n.37, 372, 373 n.65; *curiata*, 109, 135–36; *sacerdotum*, 169; *tributa*, 109, 257 n.43, 335 n.25, 337, 339–40, 372
Comitiatus maximus, 25, 279 n.43, 297–98, 298 n.88
Comparison of Rome with Greece. *See* Evidence: comparative
Concilium plebis, 19, 183–84, 190, 219, 298 n.88
Concordia ordinum, 207 n.19
Confarreatio, 26, 147, 148–50, 171–72, 174, 244–61
Conflict of the Orders, xv–xxiv, 26, 35 n.92, 38, 41, 46, 49, 67, 75, 78, 85 n.15, 91, 121, 123, 128–29, 131 nn.3–4, 132–33, 137–38, 144, 180–81, 194, 198–243, 281, 283, 289, 292, 305–6, 311, 324, 326, 332, 347 n.59, 348, 349 n.64, 351, 353–58, 367, 369–70, 373, 375, 377
Conscripti, 120–24, 129, 131, 134 n.11, 135, 162–64, 166, 169, 173, 182–83, 187–88, 191–92, 193–94, 196, 224 n.89, 230–31, 231 n.116, 233 n.123
Constitution. *See* History: constitutional
Consuls, consulship, 21, 25, 76, 78–81, 89, 120, 139, 166, 175, 178, 187, 203, 206, 219, 327–28, 334–35, 338–41, 345, 349–50
Conubium, 249, 253, 260–61. *See also* Intermarriage
Conventio in manum, 254
Cooptatio, 169, 170 n.111, 257 nn.43–44, 371, 371 n.59
Council, 233 n.126; Athenian (*Boule*), 34, 34 n.90; of 400, allegedly established by Solon, 279 n.43; *boule demosie* at Chios, 279 n.43; Spartan (*Gerousia*), 233 n.126
Crafts, 110
Craftsmen: Greek, 36, 294; Roman, 45, 124, 187, 189, 191, 223–24, 283–84
Creatio, 257 nn.43–44
Crimen maiestatis, 372
Crisis: in archaic Rome, 6 n.14, 7, 14, 67–68, 125, 190, 210–21, 281; in archaic Greek city-states, 26, 35–36, 39, 198 n.1, 213–16, 266, 304; in archaic

societies, 30, 30 n.77, 31, 264–65, 273 n.21, 276, 278, 299, 350
Cults: Greek, 36–37; Roman, 62; of the *plebs*, 376. *See also* Temples
"Cumaean Chronicle," 26
Curia, curiae, 27 n.65, 107–11, 115, 131, 135–37, 164–65; *Aculeia*, 108; *Faucia*, 108; *Titia*, 108
Curiate organization, 114
Curio, curiones, 163, 164 n.94; *maximus*, 108, 112, 135

Debt, debt-bondage, 18 n.44, 19, 28 n.71, 29 n.75, 31, 34 n.91, 36 n.93, 125–26, 177, 206, 207 nn.19–20, 208, 208 n.23, 210–17, 217 n.58, 221, 237, 237 n.140, 264, 277, 277 nn.36–37, 283, 288–89, 294, 297, 299, 301–2, 327, 344–45, 350, 353–54, 367–69. *See also* Nexum
Decemvirate, decemvirs, 49, 77–104, 122, 180, 192, 197, 200–204, 207 n.19, 243, 253–54, 260–61, 266, 282, 302, 374–75; second Decemvirate a fiction, 83–85, 220, 276
Decemviri sacris faciundis, 140, 163, 169, 327, 339
Decuria, decuriae, 135, 148
Demes, Cleisthenic, 79 n.43
Democracy, 191, 282, 287
Demography, 167 n.100. *See also* Population
Demos, Athenian, 263, 277 n.37, 279, 279 n.43, 282, 287 n.59
Destinatio, 257 n.43
Detestatio sacrorum, 109
Dictatorship, dictator, 183–84, 332, 335, 336 n.29, 338–39, 344–45, 347, 366
Dictator clavi fingendi causa, 25
Dignitas, 313
Dike, 267 n.9
Diplomacy, 158–61
Disciplina, Etruscan, 140
Discriptio classium, 119
Distribution of land, 208 n.23, 211, 211 n.34, 237, 264, 277 n.36, 283, 296–97, 297 n.83, 362, 362 n.30
Draft refusal, 80, 184, 222, 222 n.79
Duumviri, 163, 164 n.94

Economy, economic, 31, 137, 189–90, 204 n.12, 206–7, 210–22, 225, 230, 235, 236, 238–39, 264, 268, 272, 277–79, 281–84, 286, 289, 294, 295 n.76, 296, 305, 325, 337, 350–51, 354–55, 360, 373

Elections, 169, 169 n.107, 219, 226, 344, 371, 371 n.59
Epic poetry, 8, 268
Epigraphy, 12, 16; Etruscan, 178, 180, 195–96; Osco-Umbrian, 178
Epulo, epulones, 164 n.94, 169, 169 n.110
Equality: among aristocrats, 293, 296; before the law, 83, 85, 214, 220, 235, 239, 278, 287–90, 305–6, 312–13, 316, 320–21, 354
Equestrians. *See* Equites
Equites, 21, 45, 45 n.125, 119, 134, 182, 202, 209, 242, 334, 367, 373–74
Equitatus, 117–18, 127. *See also* Cavalry
Etruscan language, 191
Eugeneis, 279
Eunomia, 266, 274, 279 n.43
Eupatridae, 276, 277 n.36, 279, 285
Evidence: comparative, 24–46, 136 n.13, 179, 189, 195, 199–200, 213–16, 238–40, 252 n.23, 263–300, 301–26, 329, 352; documentary, 8, 267, 331, 333; linguistic, 27; onomastic, 27, 111. *See also* Archaeology
Exegetai, 284 n.53, 289 n.63
Exercitus, 132 n.6; *centuriatus*, 116. *See also* Army, Roman
Expansion: Roman, 6, 40, 62, 72 n.55, 176, 193, 207; Spartan, 32
Export: lack of, from archaic Rome, 45; of oil from Attica, 295 n.76. *See also* Importation

Faction, factionalism, 226, 230, 232 n.120, 282, 284, 293, 342–45, 347 n.60, 348, 352, 364 n.36
Familiae, families, 33, 33 n.86, 34, 34 n.90, 108–11; patrician, number of, 100–107; records of, 12
Famine, 12, 30–31, 59, 60 n.23, 68, 210
Farmers, 212, 223–24, 224 n.88, 229 n.111, 235, 283–84
Fas, 157
Fasti consulares, 8 n.19, 49, 56, 62, 84, 89, 106, 122, 138–39, 170, 186–88, 196, 203, 208–9, 216, 228, 230, 232 n.120, 236 n.133, 253, 328, 332, 342–44, 347 n.60, 348, 349 n.62
Fenus unciarium, 125–26
Fetiales, 148
Fides, 126
Flamen, flamines, flamonia, 111–13, 135, 145, 149–50, 150 n.49, 153–55, 161 n.85, 163, 244, 245 n.3; *Carmentalis*, 154; *Dialis*, 111, 145, 149–50, 151, 153,

Flamen (continued)
  163, 170, 245, 245 n.4, 246, 250–51, 251 n.22, 255–58, 261 n.56; *maiores*, 245–47; *Martialis*, 151 n.50, 246 n.4, 258; *Quirinalis*, 151 n.50, 158 n.72, 246 n.4, 258
Flaminica, 149, 245
Foedus Cassianum, 8 n.19, 177, 195
Formulae, 159, 161, 220
Fornacalia, 108–9, 112
François tomb, 216, 216 n.56
Fratres Arvales, 148
Freedom, 22, 354

Genera hominum, 109
Gens, gentes, 33, 33 n.86, 76, 106–10, 113, 135–39, 141–42, 148, 151–55, 157–58, 161, 170, 175, 187–88, 206, 209–10, 216, 217 n.57, 232–33, 235, 237, 240–41, 289, 336, 349, 349 n.62; *Albanae*, 113, 113 n.37, 114; *maiores*, 131, 134, 134 n.11, 142, 153–54, 233; *minores*, 131, 134, 134 n.11, 142, 153–54, 233; *patriciae*, 107; *Cassia*, 187–88; *Cispia*, 108; *Claudia*, 85 n.16, 88 n.30, 103, 134 n.11, 171, 180, 186, 196, 232 n.121, 253, 296, 297 n.83, 331, 331 n.15; *Cornelia*, 149–50, 153–54; *Cornelia Cinna*, 257 n.45; *Fabia*, 45, 45 n.124, 151, 164, 186, 191, 196–97, 212 n.37, 228, 281–82; *Folia*, 139 n.22; *Genucia*, 187; *Iulia*, 151 n.50, 154 n.60; *Minucia*, 187; *Papiria*, 154 n.60; *Pinaria*, 171; *Potitia*, 171; *Publicia*, 258; *Quinctilia*, 154 n.60, 164; *Sempronia*, 187–88; *Sulpicia*, 154 n.60; *Titia*, 108; *Valeria*, 45 n.124, 153–54, 336 n.29; *Veturia*, 139 n.22, 154 n.60, 180, 232 n.121; *Volumnia*, 187–88. *See also* Clans
Gentilitial names, 66, 107–8, 111, 126 n.81, 228 n.107
Gentis enuptio, 109
Gentilis, gentiles, 45, 153
Grain. *See* Importation: of food (grain)

Haruspex, 164 n.94
Helots, 32, 116
Hippeis, 44
Historians: Greek, 17, 41, 51, 330–32; Roman, 1–3, 12 n.27, 16–23, 52–76, 77–104, 199, 201–8, 211, 211 n.33, 213, 232 n.122, 233 n.126, 330–34, 338 n.33; ancient, methods of, 8, 16–22; modern, methods of, xvii–xix, 5, 9, 24, 38, 173, 178–82, 242, 244, 265–72, 287–89, 342–43, 352. *See also Annales*, annalists; Tradition, annalistic
History, constitutional, 4 n.7, 4 n.9, 180, 282, 334–42, 374–75; legal, 4, 6, 333
Hoplites, 34 n.91, 43, 44 n.122, 45, 46, 70–71, 200, 212, 222–24, 224 n.86, 224 n.88, 226, 229, 229 n.111, 235, 281–86, 286 n.58, 298 n.88; number of, in classical Athens, 44, 44 n.120; in early Republican Rome, 42–45, 44 n.122, 70, 70 n.50, 116–17; phalanx, 29 n.75, 37, 118, 127, 184, 186, 209, 223, 223 n.82, 285–86
Hypercriticism, 10, 47, 47 n.128, 63–68, 329

Iliad, 214, 221
Immigration, immigrants, 45, 223, 235, 285, 294
Imperium, 123, 123 n.71, 127–28, 135–36, 136 n.14, 139, 163, 226, 227 n.99, 229, 233, 236 n.133, 241, 328, 334–35, 339 n.35, 340, 350
Importation: of food (grain), 13 n.30, 36, 36 n.95, 191, 197, 210, 210 n.31; of Greek (Attic) pottery, 124, 210 n.28, 212–13, 213 n.40
Impoverishment, 277, 283, 292–95
Inauguratio, 245 n.3, 256–57, 257 n.43
Influence: of Etruscans on archaic Rome, 286 n.58; of Greeks on archaic Rome, 29 n.75, 32, 36, 36 n.95, 37–38, 92, 107, 191–92, 197, 202, 224 n.89, 237, 237 n.139, 270, 275–76, 302–26
Infra classem, 25, 70, 116, 119, 119 n.57, 125, 127, 182, 187, 192, 196, 209
Inscriptions. *See* Epigraphy
Intercessio, 128, 219, 297, 358 n.11, 370
Intermarriage: in archaic societies, 225, 231, 253–54; between patricians and plebeians, 244, 346, 354; banned between patricians and plebeians, 82–85, 138, 171–74, 192, 203, 206, 229 n.109, 231, 236 n.132, 252–53, 260–61, 282, 296, 357. *See also Conubium*
Interregnum, interrex, 113, 131, 132 n.6, 134–35, 141–43, 162, 173, 183, 229 n.109, 242, 244–45, 247, 284 n.53, 335–36, 340, 344
Isonomia. See Equality
Iteration, 336, 345

Iudex, iudices, 135, 157 n.70, 164 n.94
Iudicati, 213 n.42
Ius, 157, 267 n.9
Ius auxilii. See Auxilium
Ius Flavianum, 299, 299 n.92
Ius intercedendi. See Intercessio
Ius Latii, 363
Ius provocationis. See Provocatio

Judges. *See Iudex*
Jurisdiction, 31, 37, 214, 225–26, 241, 264, 275 n.30, 279, 287–89, 302
Jurists, 81, 155–56, 275, 371

Kings: Greek, 38–39; Etruscan at Rome, 31 n.79, 32, 40, 88, 114–20, 286, 295 n.78; Roman, 2, 48, 65, 113, 137–38, 141–42, 164, 166, 183, 227, 232, 240, 243, 253; Roman, fall of, 2, 30, 38, 97, 121–24, 138, 175–76, 179, 233, 310. *See also* Tarquins; Tullius, Servius

Labellum, 308, 308 n.32
Laborers, 124, 187, 223–24, 294, 295 n.76
Lapis Satricanus, 15 n.37, 136 n.13
Law, 8 n.19, 51, 82–83, 132, 155–61, 170–71, 214–15, 226, 241, 248, 252, 262–300, 333, 369; agrarian, 88 n.29, 350, 377; certainty of, 265, 286–92; codification of, 36, 36 n.95, 37, 86, 203, 206, 213–15, 217, 219–20, 238–39, 253, 262–300, 302, 305, 325; funerary, 41, 41 n.110, 82, 296 n.79, 301–26; modern, 273; sumptuary, 41, 82, 293, 293 n.69, 294 n.72, 296, 296 n.79, 300, 303–6, 323–24. *See also Lex*
Lawgivers, 266, 273, 280, 287, 291–92, 303–4, 321
Leadership, aristocratic, 31–34, 39, 216–17, 281–82
Lectio: of priests, 245 n.3; *senatus*, 113, 163, 164–71, 202, 233 n.126, 328, 359
Legati, 157–61
Legends, Roman, 17, 62, 202, 212
Legions, 184–87, 192
Legis actio, 157, 161, 161 n.83, 170, 299, 339
Legislation. *See* Law
Lessum, 303
Levy, 80. *See also* Draft refusal
Lex, leges, 131, 267 n.9, 336–37, 355; *Acilia*, 157 n.69; *agrariae*, 207; *annalis*, 151 n.50; *Atinia*, 167 n.102; *Canuleia de conubio*, 172, 249, 260, 296, 357; *Claudia de nave senatorum*, 359–60, 365, 367, 373; *Cornelia*, 310; *curiata de imperio*, 135, 136 n.14, 153 n.58, 338–39; *Domitia*, 257 n.44; *Flaminia agraria*, 360–65, 365 n.39, 367, 373; *Genuciae*, 208, 335–37, 345; *Hortensia*, 3, 132, 138, 157, 157 n.70, 165 n.97, 172 n.118, 198–99, 260, 337, 340, 351, 355, 362 n.30, 367–70, 373, 376–77; *Icilia de Aventino*, 177, 195; *Liciniae Sextiae*, 177, 190, 196, 200, 208, 208 n.23, 282, 336, 344, 350–51; *Maenia*, 340, 340 n.41; *Manilia*, 357 n.4; *de modo agrorum*, 362 n.27; *Ogulnia*, 171–72, 260 n.54, 279 n.42; *Ovinia*, 135, 164–65, 165 n.97, 168, 341, 346, 348; *Papiria*, 373 n.65; *de plebiscitis*, 207 n.20; *Poetilia Papiria*, 208 n.23, 237; *de provocatione*, 207 n.20; *repetundarum*, 157 n.69; *sacrata* of plebeians, 27 n.66, 218–19, 227, 285; *Titia*, 95; *Valeriae de provocatione*, 201, 331, 336–37, 355, 370 n.57; *Valeriae Horatiae*, 297, 297 n.85, 374–75. *See also* Law; *Rogatio*
Lexicographers, 9, 23, 24
Liberti, 253
Lictors, 79, 111, 128
Lists of magistrates, 53. *See also Fasti consulares*
Ludi: Plebei, 364, 364 n.38, 366, 372, 376; *Romani*, 364, 372
Luperci, 148, 164
Lynching, lynch law, 190, 197, 219, 295 n.77, 298, 298 n.88. *See also* Trials

Magister: equitum, 59, 184, 347, 366; *populi*, 183
Magistrates, magistracy, 21, 25, 25 n.59, 33–34, 38, 46, 88, 128, 135–36, 139, 164–66, 168, 190, 200, 204, 209 n.25, 219–20, 226–27, 229, 229 n.109, 233, 235, 240–42, 246, 270, 277 n.36, 279, 295, 336, 341, 354. *See also* Aediles; Consuls; Praetors; Quaestors; Tribunes
Maiestas populi Romani, 365
Manus, 147, 248, 249 n.17, 251, 252 n.23, 254–56, 258–60, 296, 298 n.91
Marriage, 147, 174, 225, 244–61, 357. *See also Confarreatio*; Intermarriage
Mensa, 308, 308 n.32
Merchants, 124, 191, 223–24. *See also* Trade

Mimesis, 270, 275–76
Mixed constitution, 374
Monarchy. *See* Kings
Mos, 157, 333, 333 n.20, 337, 345; *maiorum*, 58, 134, 141, 144

Names. *See* Gentilitial names; *Plebs*
Nexum, nexus, 76, 125–26, 177, 208, 213 n.42, 221, 237, 350. *See also* Debt, debt-bondage
Nobilis, nobiles, 132, 242, 347–48, 357, 360, 366–70, 373–74
Nobility. *See Nobilis*; Patricio-plebeian aristocracy
Nomen gentile. See Gentilitial names
Nominatio, 245 n.3, 257, 257 n.43
Nomos, 268 n.9, 333 n.20
Nota, 168 n.103
Novi homines, 132, 157, 202, 242, 347–49, 351–52, 368
Nundinae, 172 n.118, 369

Odyssey, 214
Office. *See* Magistrates
Oikos-economy, 110, 284
Optimates, 86, 90–93, 132, 177, 374 n.69
Opus tectorium, 307
Ordo: sacerdotum, 165 n.98; *senatorum*, 359; *equester. See* Equites

Paides amphithaleis, 147 n.45
Pater, patres, 107, 112, 120–24, 130–74, 182–83, 194, 196, 202, 231, 233 n.123, 239–40, 281, 328 n.32, 340, 357–58; *familias*, 33, 33 n.86; *patratus*, 158
Patria potestas, 33, 341 n.43, 358, 365
Patricians, 5, 21, 35 n.92, 44–46, 76, 78–100, 105–29, 130–74, 175, 177–78, 180–93, 196, 198–243, 244, 246–61, 279, 281–83, 295–99, 305, 326, 327–52, 353–58, 368; arbitrariness of, 206, 220, 235, 237, 238–39, 286, 287–89; closure of the patriciate, 124, 205, 228, 229 n.109, 230, 234–35, 241, 243, 253, 282; Greek influence on, 37; number of, 42, 44, 233 n.126; formation of, 66, 105–29, 228–35. *See also Patricius*
Patriciate. *See* Patricians
Patricio-plebeian aristocracy, 199, 234 n.126, 351, 355–56, 367, 372

Patricius, patricii, 107, 231, 240, 242, 276, 279; *magistratus*, 341
Patrimi et matrimi, 147–48, 250 n.20
Patroni, 182, 186, 196, 235, 284 n.52, 285–86, 298
Patrons. *See* Patroni
Patrum auctoritas, 131, 134–35, 138, 140–44, 173, 183, 229 n.109, 273 n.22, 340
Peace of Callias, 267 n.7
Perduellio, 372
Pestilence (plague), 68, 210
Phalanx. *See* Hoplites
Phylobasileis, 284 n.53
Pilumnus, 184
Plebeians. *See Plebs*
Plebiscitum, plebiscita, 131, 190, 260, 336–37, 340–41, 348, 351, 355, 364, 368–70, 374
Plebs, plebeians, 21, 35 n.92, 75–76, 78–100, 105–29, 130–74, 177–78, 180–93, 194, 196–97, 198–243, 244, 249, 263–64, 277, 277 n.36, 277 n.38, 279, 281–83, 285–86, 295–99, 305, 315, 326, 327–52, 353–77; composition of, 45, 124–28; elite, 5, 19, 206–8; formation of, 124–29; Greek influence on, 37; integration of, 207, 327–52; names of, 132, 138, 227–28; organization of, 21, 37–38, 46, 127 n.85, 184, 190–91, 197, 204, 217 n.60, 218–19, 224, 224 n.89, 230, 234–35, 285–86, 295, 298, 354; political objectives of, 206–8; revolution of, 5, 83
Poetry, oral, 63 n.32
Polis. See City-state
Politics, political, 31, 216, 224, 273, 278, 280, 286–88, 342–52, 354; power, 264, 279, 290, 293; reform, 306, 314–26
Pomerium, 69 n.49
Pontifex, pontifices, 12, 115, 140, 156–57, 161, 169, 171, 176, 220, 339, 371; *maximus*, 145, 151–52, 157, 169, 172, 250–51, 251 n.22, 255–56, 257 n.44, 371
Populares, 75, 86, 90–93, 101 n.75, 132, 177, 365 nn.38–39, 366, 371 n.59, 377
Population, 14 n.30; figures for Rome and Athens, 41–45; Roman, 69–72, 72 n.55, 106, 185, 233 n.126
Populor, 117 n.49, 184
Populus, 83, 117, 128, 169–70, 182–93, 194, 217 n.61, 355, 364, 368–69, 372
Potestas, 149, 236, 248, 259, 338
Pottery: Athenian monopoly and export of, 45, 45 n.125, 295 n.76; imported to Rome, 14, 65–66, 124

Praeteriti, 163, 168 n.103
Praetextati, 148, 148 n.47, 149, 168. See also *Toga: praetexta*
Praetors, praetorship, 172 n.118, 178, 275 n.30, 328, 334, 338; *maximus*, 25
Prata Flaminia, 364 n.38
Presbeis, 158
Priesthoods, priests, 130–74, 226, 240–41, 244–47, 261, 277 n.36, 279, 289 n.63, 339, 354. See also *Flamen*; *Pontifex*, etc.
"Primitive cultures," 28, 179, 324–26
Princeps senatus, 144, 340–41
Probouleusis, 34, 34 n.90
Procum patricium, 119
Proletarii, 82, 116, 119 n.57, 182, 194, 298, 298 n.91, 354, 367 n.45
Property, 80, 238, 264, 278, 281, 294, 294 n.72, 296–97
Prosopography, 342, 347 n.60
Provocatio, 19, 78–79, 98, 219 n.65, 336–37, 355, 370, 370 n.57

Quaestors, quaestorship, 165, 167–68
Quinqueviri mensarii, 350–51
Quirinalia, 108–9
Quirites, 108–10

Recuperatores, 161 n.83
Reform: agrarian, 86, 301; political, 316–26. See also Law; *Lex*
Regia, 179, 195
Religion, 9, 37, 39, 46, 130–74, 190, 207, 220, 224–26, 235, 240–41, 244–61, 268, 273, 311, 321, 324, 326, 334, 338–40, 354. See also Cults; Priesthoods
Republic, Roman, beginning of, 2, 4, 7, 124–28, 202
Restrictions, funerary. See Law: funerary
Revolution, plebeian. See Plebs
Rex sacrorum, 38–39, 135, 141, 151, 158 n.72, 163, 179, 244–47, 284 n.53
Rhetra, 267, 274
Rogatio: Terentilia, 122; *agraria*, of Spurius Cassius, 211 n.34

Sacer, 290
Sacramentum, 298 n.91
Sacred band, 218, 227
Sacrosanctitas, 219, 282, 297
Salii, 112, 148, 163–64, 244

Secessio plebis, 5, 122, 124–25, 127, 127 n.85, 180, 185, 207–8, 213, 218, 220–23, 237, 295 n.78, 297, 351, 353–54, 357, 367, 376
Seisachtheia. See Solon
Sella curulis, 111, 145
Senate, senator, 21, 76, 80, 86, 106–7, 111–12, 114, 120–24, 130–74, 178, 182–83, 187–88, 193, 216, 227, 232 n.122, 233, 239–40, 253, 279, 328, 334, 336, 338, 341, 351, 357, 358–64, 365 n.38, 366, 372–77; size of, 44–45, 166–67, 233 n.126
Senatores pedarii, 158 n.71, 161 n.84, 162–63, 202–3
"*Serrata del patriziato*." See Patricians: closure of the patriciate
"Servian Walls," 13 n.30
Shortage of land and food, 206, 211 n.34, 221. See also Flamen
Sibylline oracles, 191, 197, 210
Slavery, 30, 30 n.78, 31. See also Debt
Social aspects, factors, 204 n.12, 206, 216, 224, 225, 238–39, 268, 272, 273–74, 355
Societies: archaic, 28; archaic Italian, 26; "Homeric," 29 n.76. See also "Primitive cultures"
Sources, 5, 8, 199, 265–72. See also Archaeology
Stroma, 308
Suffragia, 334

Tabula Hebana, 257 n.43
Tabulae Iguvinae, 27 n.65
Talio, 298 n.91
Temples, 11, 13, 66, 124, 181, 189–91, 325; construction of, 14, 68, 190–91, 197, 213, 217 n.57; built by Servius Tullius, 15, 67; of Apollo, 326; of Castor, 189; of Ceres, Liber, and Libera, 189–91, 197, 210, 210 n.31, 326; of Diana, 271, 271 n.19; of Fortuna, 271; of Jupiter Capitolinus, 13, 13 n.29, 70–71, 189, 372; of Jupiter Libertas, 372; of Libertas, 372–73; of Mater Matuta, 271, 271 n.18; of Mercury, 189, 326; of Saturn, 189; Parthenon, 45; at Ardea, 189; at Lanuvium, 189; in Latium, 189; at Sant' Omobono, 15, 67, 88 n.33; at Satricum, 189; of southern Etruria, 189; at Veii, 189; at Volsinii, 189
Terminology, political, in archaic Rome, 25, 25 n.59, 29, 37, 37 n.98, 182, 196, 233, 347

Territory, Roman, 6, 24–25, 42, 42 n.113, 69, 69 n.47, 72 n.55
Testamenti factio, 109
"Themistocles Decree," 267 n.7
Theory, xviii–xix, 37; of law, 289–92
Time, 279 n.43
Timocracy, timocratic, 37, 226, 287
Toga: praetexta, 144–46, 168, 169 n.110; *virilis*, 145
Tomba Bernardini, 180, 191, 196
Tombs, 12, 181, 221, 305, 305 n.19, 307–8, 310, 310 n.37, 313, 318–22, 325 n.80
Trade, 12, 36, 36 n.95, 264, 281, 294; in archaic Rome, 45, 45 nn.126–27, 66, 120, 231–32
Traders. *See* Merchants
Tradition: annalistic, 52–76, 77–104, 84, 106–7, 118–19, 124–26, 188, 204–5, 268; Etruscan, 23; Greek, 2, 23, 309; Italic, 302, 309; literary, 52–76; oral, 2, 12, 49, 53, 62, 267–68, 332–34. *See also Annales*, annalists
Tragedy, Greek, 19
Trans Tiberim, 82, 289
Transitio ad plebem, 358 n.11
Treaty, 159; between Rome and Carthage, 70–71; of Tarentum, 95. *See also Foedus Cassianum*
Tresviri capitales, 368 n.46
Trials: capital, 83; plebeian, 190, 219. *See also* Lynching
Tribes, *tribus*, 37; Athenian, 115; Roman, 69, 71, 106, 115, 116, 126 n.81, 136, 169, 362 n.30; "gentilitial," 115; pre-Servian, 109–10, 135. *See also* Ramnes, Tities, Luceres
Tribunes, tribunate: of the *plebs*, 19, 75, 78–81, 91, 98–99, 127–28, 132, 132 n.6, 137, 145, 168, 184, 190, 218–19, 235, 276 n.34, 277, 277 n.38, 282, 285, 292, 297–98, 300, 315, 337, 341, 346, 349, 354–55, 358–59, 364 n.38, 366, 368, 370, 372, 374, 376; military, 127, 166, 184; military, with consular power, 204 n.13, 209 n.25, 229, 236 n.133, 339 n.35, 341
Tribuni celerum, 164 n.94
Tribuni militum. See Tribunes, tribunate: military
Tribuni militum consulari potestate. See Tribunes, tribunate: military, with consular power
Tribuni plebis. See Tribunes, tribunate: of the *plebs*
Tribus. See Tribes

Trinoctium. See Usurpatio trinoctii
Trittyes, 115
Triumvirate: first, 93–94, 102; second, 96–97, 104
Trojan War, 16, 16 n.38
Turmae, 117–18
Twelve Tables, 12, 25, 29 n.75, 41, 53, 78, 81–85, 171–72, 172 n.118, 174, 177–78, 182, 192, 197, 211, 219–20, 238, 252–55, 259, 261, 262–300, 354, 357; influence of Greek law on, 85 n.15, 192, 302, 304–5; tenth table, 302–26
Tyranny, tyrants, 13, 34, 34 n.90, 214–16, 216 n.56, 226, 243, 270 n.16, 275 n.29, 277–78, 282–83, 287 n.59, 292–93, 295, 304, 319, 321; decemvirs as, 79–80, 83, 85, 93, 97–98; Tarquins as, 119, 132

Univira, 147 n.44
Urbanization, 30, 66
Usucapio, 303
Usurpatio, 170, 171 n.113
Usurpatio trinoctii, 252 n.23, 254, 259, 296
Usus, 252 n.23, 254–55, 258–59
Usus auctoritas, 296–97

Values, aristocratic, 33, 227, 230
Vendetta, 293, 293 n.68
Vestals, 256 n.41
Via Flaminia, 364, 364 n.37
Viliora capita, 348–49
Vindex, 298 n.91
Violence, 31, 125, 287. *See also* Lynching
Voting, 219, 226, 334–35, 337

Warfare, in early Rome, 44 n.122, 76, 159, 189, 222
Wars, 11, 211–13, 233, 236, 264, 305; with the Aequi and Volsci, 190; with Carthage, 42, 328, 341, 372 n.65, 374–76; civil, 102; with the Gauls, 206, 236, 360–62; with the Latins, 207, 212, 212 n.37; with the Samnites, 2, 2 n.2, 19 n.47, 207, 334; with Veii, 44 n.122, 206, 208 n.23, 212, 236, 281

Zeugitai, 200

Index of Persons and Places

Aelius Paetus, Sex., 53
Aelius Tubero, L. and Q., 103–4
Aemilius Lepidus, M. (*cos.* 187), 160 n.80
Aemilius Lepidus, M. (triumvir), 95–96, 143, 143 n.33
Aemilius Lepidus Livianus, Mam. (*cos.* 77), 143 n.33
Aemilius Mamercinus, L. (*cos.* 366, 363), 343
Aemilius Papus, L. (*cens.* 220), 167
Aemilius Papus, Q. (*cos.* 282, 278), 346
Aemilius Paullus, L. (*cos.* 182, 168), 143 n.33
Aeneas: statuettes of at Veii, 179, 195; dedication to Lar Aeneas, 179
Aequi, 80, 190, 192
Aequimaelium, 60
Aglauros, 280 n.43
Alba Longa, 15, 114, 253
Alcaeus, 281
Alexander Severus (emp.), 255
Androtion, 330
Annia (wife of L. Cornelius Cinna), 258
Antiochus (of Syracuse), 176
Antonius, M. (triumvir), 96, 96 n.56, 97
Apollo, temple of. *See* Temples: of Apollo
Appian, 96
Ardea, 189, 357
Aricia, battle of, 212
Ariminum, 361, 364
Aristodemus (of Cumae), 26, 176, 195
Aristotle, 92, 127, 320, 330
Arruns (son of Porsenna), 26
Astarte, sanctuary of, discovered at Pyrgi, 179, 195
Ateius Capito Praetextatus, L. (author), 245 n.4, 250 n.20, 358–59
Athens, xv, 32 n.83, 34, 34 nn.90–91, 38, 40, 44–46, 82, 115–16, 191, 199–200, 211 n.34, 212, 214–16, 220–21, 226–27, 229 n.111, 239, 262–301, 330–32, 355; agora, 279 n.43; funerary legislation, 307–8, 317; public funeral orations at, 318; Roman embassy to, 12 n.26, 197, 302
Atilius Regulus, M. (*cos.* 217), 366 n.41
Attica, 34 n.90
Atticus. *See* Pomponius Atticus, T.
Augustine (Aurelius Augustinus), 375
Augustus, 95–96, 96 n.56, 149, 153, 153 n.58, 275 n.30; marriage laws of, 252 n.23, 261
Aurelia (mother of C. Julius Caesar), 257–58
Aurelius Cotta, C. (*pont. max.* 74), 150
Aurelius Papirius Dionysius, M. (*praef. Aeg.* 188–89, jurist), 255–56
Aventine Hill, 75, 81, 177, 354, 364 n.38, 372, 377 n.84

Baebius Herennius, Q. (*trib. pleb.* 216), 366, 366 n.42
Boeotia, Boeotians, 309

Caecilius Metellus Pius Scipio Nasica, Q. (*cos.* 52), 143, 143 n.32
Caelian Hill, 107
Caelius Vibenna, 15, 15 n.37
Caere, 191
Caesar. *See* Julius Caesar, C.
Caligula, 257 n.43
Callias, peace of, 267 n.7
Callimachus, 56

Calpurnius Piso Frugi, L. (*cos.* 122, historian), 2, 56, 59, 62
Camillus. *See* Furius Camillus, M.
Camillus, name for Mercury, 147
Campania, 40, 42, 43 n.116, 44 n.121
Cannae, battle of, 57, 359
Canuleius, C. (*trib. pleb.* 445), 260–61. *See also Lex, leges*: Canuleia de conubio
Carthage, Carthaginians, 8 n.19, 328, 376; collaboration of, with Etruscans, 179; interests in Italy, 70. *See also* Treaty: between Rome and Carthage
Carvilius Maximus, Sp. (*cos.* 293, 272), 368, 371
Cassius Hemina, C. (historian), 53
Cassius Vicellinus, Sp. (*cos.* 502, 493, 486), 17 n.44, 87, 88 n.30, 211 n.34, 243, 365 n.39
Castor and Pollux, 179, 189, 191, 195, 270 n.15. *See also* Temples: of Castor
Catiline. *See* Sergius Catilina, L.
Cato. *See* Porcius Cato Censorius, M.
Celts. *See* Gauls
Ceos, funerary legislation, 307–8, 317
Cerameicus, 313, 318–20
Ceres, Liber, and Libera, temple of. *See* Temples: of Ceres, Liber, and Libera
Charondas, funerary legislation of, 309 n.34, 312, 316–17
Cicero. *See* Tullius Cicero, M.
Cincinnatus. *See* Quinctius Cincinnatus, L.
Cincius Alimentus, L. (historian), 1, 59–60, 177
Cispian Hill, 107
Claudia (sister of P. Claudius Pulcher, *cos.* 249), 372
Claudii, Claudians. *See Gens, gentes*: Claudia
Claudius, Ap. (Clausus, Att(i)us), 45, 45 n.124, 122, 235
Claudius, L. (*rex sacr.* 57), 158 n.72
Claudius Caecus, Ap. (*cens.* 312), 5, 165, 165 n.97, 346, 347 n.60, 348
Claudius Crassus Inregillensis, Ap. (*dict.* 362), 339, 343
Claudius Crassus Inregillensis Sabinus, Ap. (*decemv.*), 79–81, 91–94, 189
Claudius Pulcher, Ap. (*interr.* 77), 143 n.33
Claudius Pulcher, Ap. (*cos.* 43), 93 n.45
Claudius Pulcher, P. (*cos.* 249), 371–72
Claudius Quadrigarius, Q. (historian), 18 n.46, 61
Cleisthenes, 30 n.79, 31 n.82, 34 n.90, 41 n.111, 115–16, 199–200, 279, 280 n.43, 286, 319
Clodius Pulcher, P. (*trib. pleb.* 58), 244
Cloelius, P., 356

Coelius Antipater, L. (historian), 54–55
Colophon, 303
Corinth, 295 n.76
Coriolanus. *See* Marcius Coriolanus, Cn.
Cornelia (wife of C. Julius Caesar), 150, 257
Cornelii, Cornelians. *See Gens, gentes*: Cornelia
Cornelius Cinna, L. (*cos.* 87–84), 94 n.48, 257 n.45
Cornelius Dolabella (*septemvir epulo*), 140 n.22
Cornelius Dolabella, L. (*duumvir nav.* 180–178), 151
Cornelius Lentulus, Ser. (*flam. Dial.* from 11), 149, 151–53
Cornelius Lentulus Niger, L. (*praet.* by 61), 258
Cornelius Merula, L. (*cos.* 87), 149–50
Cornelius Scipio Nasica Serapio, P. (*cos.* 138), 59
Cornelius Sulla Felix, L., 93, 94 n.48, 102, 150, 168, 202, 258, 275 n.30, 319, 323
Cornelius Tacitus, P. (historian), 149
Coruncanius, Ti. (*cos.* 280), 368, 371, 371 n.59
Cossutia, 257
Crassus (*triumvir*). *See* Licinius Crassus Dives, M.
Cremera, 45, 186, 196, 212
Cremona, 362
Crete, 266, 274 n.29
Cumae, 36 n.96, 176, 191
Curiatii, 253
Curius Dentatus, M'. (*cos.* 290, 275, 274), 340, 351, 362 n.30, 368, 368 n.47, 371
Cylon, 274, 281, 332
Cypselids, 304

Decius Mus, P. (*cos.* 340), 349
Delphi. *See* Labyadae
Demetrius (of Phalerum), funerary legislation of, 308, 313–14, 320
Demosthenes, 307
Diana, cult of, on Aventine, 177. *See also* Temples: of Diana
Diocles (of Peparethos), 56
Diodorus (of Athens), 320
Diodorus (Siculus), 61, 176, 317
Diogenes Laertius, 320–21
Dionysius (of Halicarnassus), 1, 3, 8, 11, 16, 17, 17 n.44, 19, 24–26, 52, 55, 59–62, 77–78, 89, 94–96, 98, 101–4, 109–10, 120–21, 127, 172, 177, 186, 201 n.5, 207, 211 n.33

Dioscuri. *See* Castor and Pollux
Domitius Ahenobarbus, Cn. (*cos.* 162), 153 n.56
Domitius Ahenobarbus, Cn. (*trib. pleb.* 104), 152, 169
Domitius (Ahenobarbus), L. (senator in 129), 153 n.56
Domitius Ahenobarbus, L. (*pont.* 50–48), 153 n.58
Domitius Calvinus, Cn. (*pont. c.* 45), 153 n.58
Draco, 82, 264, 274, 277, 280, 288, 292–93, 293 n.68
Dreros, 274 n.29
Duillius, C. (K?) (*quinquevir mens.* 352), 350 n.65
Duillius, K. (*cos.* 336), 350 n.65

Elagabalus (Aurelius Antoninus, M.), 255
Ennius, Q. (poet), 2
Ephialtes, 200
Esquiline Hill, 110
Etruria, xv, 25–26, 40, 83, 110, 110 n.23, 116, 189, 191, 216, 221, 241
Etruscans, 7, 27, 134, 140, 186, 192, 205, 212, 227, 230, 232, 232 n.120, 243, 309–10, 310 n.37; funerary practice of, 309–10; collaboration of, with Carthaginians, 179; in the *fasti*, 228

Fabii, Fabians. *See Gens, gentes: Fabia*
Fabius Ambustus, M. (*cos.* 360, 356), 343
Fabius Buteo, M. (*cos.* 245), 165
Fabius Maximus Verrucosus (Cunctator), Q. (*dict.* II 217), 151, 361, 364 n.36, 366
Fabius Pictor, Q. (historian), 1–2, 52–53, 53 n.1, 55–56, 62, 72–74, 85 n.16, 158 n.72, 176–77, 245 n.4, 361, 365, 365 n.39, 375
Fabricius Luscinus, C. (*cos.* 282, 278), 346, 368, 371
Faliscans, 158 n.72
Festus. *See* Pompeius Festus, Sex.
Flaminius, C. (*cos.* 223, 217), 167, 347, 349, 360–67, 372–76
Flavius, Cn. (*scriba* of Ap. Claudius Caecus), 170, 170 n.113
Folius Flaccinator, M. (*mag. equit.* 320, 314), 348
Fortuna, temple of. *See* Temples: of Fortuna
Forum, 66
Forum Boarium, 11, 15, 67
Fundanius Fundulus, C. (*cos.* 243), 372
Furius Camillus, M. (*dict.* 368), 88 n.30, 343

Gaius (jurist), 256 n.41
Gambreion, funerary legislation at, 309, 317
Gauls, 11 n.24, 178, 358, 360–62; aristocracy of, 254 n.27; invasion of Italy by, 6 n.14; sack of Rome by, 200, 206, 208 n.23, 236, 257 n.4, 267
Gellius, A. (antiquarian), 25
Gellius, Cn. (historian), 3
Gelon, 317, 317 n.59
Genucius Augurinus, M. (*cos.* 445), 122 n.68
Genucius Aventinensis, Cn. (*cos.* 363), 343
Genucius Aventinensis, L. (*cos.* 365, 362), 339, 343
Genucius, L. (*trib. pleb.* 342), 335–36
Gortyn, law code of, 255–66, 275 n.29
Gracchi, 87, 376. *See also* Sempronius Gracchus, C.; Sempronius Gracchus, Ti.
Granius Licinianus (historian), 369
Greece, Greeks, xv, xxii–xxiii, 29–46, 110, 116–17, 158, 192, 216, 220, 221 n.77, 223, 226–27, 230–31, 238–39, 243, 264, 268, 275, 284, 290 n.64, 302; connections between mainland and Magna Graecia, 270 n.15; Roman embassies to, 12 n.26, 85 n.15; of southern Italy, 27, 178; Greek accounts on early Rome, 56 n.13. *See also* City–state (*polis*); Influence: of Greeks on archaic Rome

Hannibal, 42, 86, 341, 374
Hercules, 170–71
Herdonius, Ap., 45 n.124
Hermodorus, 275
Hesiod, 35, 39, 198 n.1, 214, 219, 238–39, 280
Hieronymus (of Cardia), 56
Homer, 39, 214, 221
Horatii, 253
Horatius Barbatus, M. (*cos.* 449), 365 n.38
Hortensius, Q. (*dict.* 287), 337, 351
Hortensius Hortalus, Q. (*aug.* before 67–50), 152
Hostilius, Tullus (king), 107

Icilius, L. (*trib. pleb.* 456, 455, 449), 81, 91
India, 180, 252 n.23, 269
Ionia, 302
Iranians, 181
Ireland, 269
Isocrates, 267 n.7, 274 n.25
Israel, ancient, 28
Italic peoples, 178, 191
Italy: ancient, 3–4, 310; medieval, 28

Index of Persons and Places

Juba (historian), 246 n.4
Julius Caesar, C., 90–91, 102, 150, 150 n.50, 153, 164 n.94, 256–57, 257 n.44, 275 n.30, 311
Julius Caesar, Sex. (*praet. urb.* 123), 151 n.50
Junius Brutus, L. (*cos.* 509), 120, 134, 134 n.11
Jupiter, 241
Jupiter Capitolinus, temple of. *See* Temples: of Jupiter Capitolinus

Kallias. *See* Callias
Kerameikos. *See* Ceramicus
Kylon. *See* Cylon

Labyadae (Delphic phratry), funerary regulations of, 308, 310, 314, 317
Laelius Felix (jurist), 109, 368 n.50
Laetorius, M., 125 n.76
Lanuvium, 189
Latins, 7, 134, 177, 181, 207, 212, 232, 243, 253; relations with Servius Tullius, 271; Latin League, 236–37
Latium, 11, 40, 41 n.110, 42–43, 65, 69–70, 110, 189, 212, 216, 221, 232 n.118; tombs and burials in, 305, 310, 310 n.37, 322–23, 325
Lavinium, 179, 195
Leonidas, 186
Lepidus (*triumvir*). *See* Aemilius Lepidus, M.
Libertas, temple of. *See* Temples: of Libertas
Licinius Varus, P. (*praet. urb.* 208), 145
Licinius Crassus, C. (*trib. pleb.* 145), 169
Licinius Crassus, L. (*cos.* 95), 152
Licinius Crassus, M. (*cos.* 30), 152
Licinius Crassus, P. (*aug. c.* 55–53), 152
Licinius Crassus Dives, M. (*cos.* 70, 55), 93–94
Licinius Crassus Dives, P. (*pont. max.* 212–183), 145
Licinius Crassus Frugi, M. (*aug.*), 152
Licinius Lucullus, L. (*cos.* 74), 152
Licinius Macer, C. (*trib. pleb.* 73, historian), 3, 19, 55–56, 61, 103, 204 n.13, 377 n.84
Licinius Stolo (or Calvus), C. (*cos.* 364, 361), 343
Livius, T., 2–3, 8, 11, 16–21, 23, 25, 52, 54–55, 57, 59, 61–62, 77–78, 81, 81 n.1, 87–89, 92–104, 120, 132, 132 n.6, 135, 142, 142 n.31, 152, 176–77, 201–4, 207, 211 n.33, 218–19, 236 n.132, 260–61, 272, 302, 328, 329–32, 336, 337 n.32, 339, 344–45, 350–52, 353, 356–58, 364 n.38
Livy. *See* Livius, T.
Locri, Locris, 107, 270 n.15
Luceres. *See* Ramnes, Tities, Luceres
Lucretia, 73, 97, 175
Lutatius Catulus, Q. (*cos.* 78), 357 n.4
Lycurgus, 274, 307, 316
Lydia, 303

Macer. *See* Licinius Macer, C.
Machiavelli, Niccoló, 99–100
Macrobius, Ambrosius Theodosius, 147, 258, 258 n.48, 324
Maelius, Sp., 49, 58–61, 88 n.30
Maenius, C. (*dict.* 320, 314), 347–49
Magna Graecia, 191, 211 n.34, 270, 270 n.15, 275, 302. *See also* Greece, Greeks: of southern Italy
Maharbal, 57
Mamilius, L. (of Tusculum), 123, 235 n.129
Manlius Capitolinus Imperiosus, Cn. (*cos.* 359, 357), 343
Marathon, battle of, 44 n.120
Marcius, Ancus (king), 107, 114
Marcius Coriolanus, Cn., 212 n.33, 232 n.120
Marcius Rutilus, C. (*cos.* 357), 338, 343, 344, 344 n.50
Mark Antony. *See* Antonius, M.
Massilia, 36 n.96
Masurius Sabinus, 245 n.4
Mater Matuta. *See* Temples: of Mater Matuta
Megara, 225
Memmius, C. (*trib. pleb.* 111), 377 n.84
Menenius Lanatus, Agrippa (*cos.* 503), 180
Mercury: called Camillus, 147. *See also* Temples: of Mercury
Metilius, M. (*trib. pleb.* 217), 366
Minucius Augurinus, C. (*monetal. c.* 133–126), 60
Minucius Esquilinus Augurinus, L. (*praef. annon.* 440–39), 60, 60 n.23
Minucius Rufus, M. (*dict.* 217), 366
Mons Sacer, 354
Mytilene, 317

Naevius, Cn. (poet), 52–53
Naples, 191, 197
Numa. *See* Pompilius, Numa
Numicius Priscus, T. (*cos.* 469), 122 n.68

Index of Persons and Places 451

Octavian. *See* Augustus
Odysseus, 233 n.122
Oppian Hill, 107
Oscans and Umbrians, 27, 178

Palatine Hill, 11
Papirius, C. (*pont.* 241), 158 nn.72–73
Papirius Praetextatus, L. (*cens.* 272), 146, 171
Parthenon. *See* Temples: Parthenon
Paulus Diaconus, 120
Pausanias (Spartan leader), 116
Pausanias (geographer), 268, 319
Peisistratus, Peisistratids, 30 n.79, 283, 319
Pericles, 41, 282
Philip V of Macedon, 160, 319
Phoenicia, Phoenicians, xv, 28
Pinarius Natta, M. (*pont.*), 158 n.72
Pittacus, funerary legislation of, 307, 314, 317
Placentia, 362
Plato, 92, 274 n.25, 311–15, 320
Plautius Proculus, C. (*cos.* 358), 343
Plinius Secundus, C., 268
Pliny (the Elder). *See* Plinius Secundus, C.
Plutarch, 24, 309 n.34, 357, 357 n.4
Poetilius Libo Visolus, C. (*cos.* 360, 346, 326), 343
Polybius, 7, 18, 18 n.46, 70–71, 74, 146, 329, 360–62, 365, 374–75
Pompeius Festus, Sex. (grammarian), 164–65
Pompeius Magnus, Cn., 93–94, 143, 152
Pompeius Magnus, Sex., 95, 153
Pompey. *See* Pompeius Magnus, Cn.
Pompilius, Numa (king), 167, 303 n.10, 312, 322
Pomponius, Sex. (jurist), 84, 84 n.13
Pomponius Atticus, T., 315
Popillius Laenas, M. (*cos.* 359, 356), 154, 343, 344 n.50
Poplios Valesios. *See* Valerius Publicola, P.
Porcius Cato Censorius, M. (*cos.* 195, historian), 12 n.26, 25, 56–57, 74, 146, 177, 348 n.61, 362, 362 n.27
Porsenna, Lars, 26
Praeneste, 180, 191, 196
Publicia (wife of L. Cornelius Lentulus Niger), 258
Publilius Philo, Q. (*dict.* 339), 335, 340, 346–47
Pudicitia Patricia, cult of, 259
Pyrgi: gold tablets of, 11, 11 n.25, 70; sanctuary of Astarte, 179

Quinctius Cincinnatus, L. (*dict.* 458), 59, 60 n.23

Ramnes, Tities, Luceres, 113, 180
Regillus, Lake, battle of, 126 n.81, 127
Remus, 180
Rome. *See* City of Rome, size and early growth; Tarquins
Romulus, 106, 132, 134–35, 142, 202, 241
Rutilius, M., 356, 366

Sabines, 80, 134, 205, 232
Saguntum, 86
Sallust. *See* Sallustius Crispus, C.
Sallustius Crispus, C., 328, 375
Samnites, 2, 19 n.47, 27, 27 n.66, 207, 212, 218
Sant' Omobono, church of. *See* Temples: at Sant' Omobono
Satricum, 11, 189; *see also Lapis Satricanus*
Saturn, temple of. *See* Temples: of Saturn
Sempronius Gracchus, C. (*trib. pleb.* 123–22), 75, 92 n.44, 157, 177, 374, 377 n.84
Sempronius Gracchus, Ti. (*cos.* 238), 372
Sempronius Gracchus, Ti. (*trib. pleb.* 133), 59, 92, 92 n.44, 93 n.45, 361, 361 n.22, 374, 376
Sempronius Tuditanus, C. (*cos.* 129, historian), 103
Sena Gallica, 361
Sergius Catilina, L., 87, 93, 102
Servilius Ahala, C. (*mag. equit.* 439), 49, 59–60, 60 n.23
Servilius Ahala, Q. (*cos.* 365, 362), 343
Servilius Geminus, C. (*pont. max.* 183–180), 151, 358
Servilius Geminus, Cn. (*cos.* 217), 366 n.41
Servius (comment. on Virgil), 147–48
Servius Tullius. *See* Tullius, Servius
Sextius Sextinus Lateranus, L. (*cos.* 366), 343
Sicily, 191, 270 n.15
Solon, 18 n.44, 31 n.82, 34, 34 n.90, 35, 39–40, 118, 126, 198 n.1, 200, 211 n.34, 214–15, 217, 219 nn.6–7, 272, 274–77, 279 n.43, 280–81, 285, 292–95, 295 n.76, 299–300, 302, 309 n.34, 317, 319; funerary legislation, 304, 307, 314, 320–21; *seisachtheia*, 36 n.93, 273 n.23, 277 n.37
Sostratus (of Aegina), 15 n.37

452 *Index of Persons and Places*

Sparta, 232n.120, 234n.126, 316; funerary legislation, 307; *rhetra*, 267
Stobaeus, 312, 317
Strabo, 268
Strato, 321
Suetonius Tranquillus, C., 93–94, 256
Sulla. *See* Cornelius Sulla Felix, L.
Sulpicius Galba, C. (*pont.* before 73), 157n.71
Sulpicius Galba, Ser. (*pont.* 203–199), 160n.80
Sulpicius Galba Maximus, P. (*cos.* 200), 160
Sulpicius Peticus, C. (*cos.* 364, 361), 343, 344
Sulpicius Rufus, P. (*pont.* c. 47–42), 143–44
Sulpicius Rufus, Ser. (*trib. mil.* c. 388, 384, 383, 377), 139n.22
Sulpicius Rufus, Ser. (*cos.* 51), 143–44, 314
Syracuse, funerary legislation in, 309n.34, 317

Tacitus. *See* Cornelius Tacitus, P.
Tarquinius Priscus, L., 114–15, 122
Tarquinius Superbus, L., 119–21, 125, 202, 310
Tarquins, 2, 66, 70, 132, 137–38, 205, 209, 232nn.120–21, 233n.126, 253; "grande Roma dei Tarquini," 2, 4, 6n.14, 13, 14n.30, 42, 45, 65–72, 210n.30. *See also* Tarquinius Priscus *and* Tarquinius Superbus
Terentius Varro, C. (*cos.* 216), 348, 366
Terentius Varro, M. (antiquarian), 127, 178, 303n.12, 322n.67
Terracina, 70
Tertullian, 324
Thasos, 309n.34
Themistocles, 319
Theognis, 35, 36n.93, 214, 225, 232n.120, 281
Theophilus, 370n.55
Theophrastus, 56, 321
Thucydides, 284n.53
Tiber, 82–83
Tiberius (emp.), 149
Timaeus, 56, 176, 195
Tities. *See* Ramnes, Tities, Luceres
Troezen, 309n.34
Tullius Cicero, M., 25, 48n.130, 54, 59, 61, 74, 90–91, 152, 169, 169n.109, 183, 244, 253, 260, 279, 302, 307–8, 311–15, 317–20, 321n.67, 322–24, 339–41, 365n.39
Tullius, Servius (king), 15, 15n.36, 25, 42, 67, 69–70, 72, 74, 110–11, 115–19, 119n.58, 136, 177, 195, 223, 271, 271n.19, 286n.58, 354
Tusculum, 123, 235n.129
Tyrtaeus, 35

Umbrians. *See* Oscans and Umbrians

Valerius Antias (historian), 55–56, 61, 103–4, 331
Valerius Flaccus, C. (*flam. Dial.* 209–before 174), 145, 151–53, 163–64, 164n.95, 170
Valerius Flaccus, L. (*cos.* 86), 257n.45
Valerius Maximus (author), 365n.39
Valerius Messalla Niger, M. (*cos.* 61), 143
Valerius Publicola, P. (*cos.* 509), 15, 120, 134, 134n.11; name of Poplios Valesios on *lapis Satricanus*, 11, 15, 15n.37
Valerius Publicola Potitus, L. (*cos.* 449), 365n.38
Varro. *See* Terentius Varro, M.
Veii, 15, 15n.37, 44n.122, 83, 189, 206, 208n.23, 212, 236, 281
Velia, 191, 197
Velleius Paterculus (historian), 256, 257n.44
Verginia, 80–81, 85, 85n.16, 94, 97
Verginia (wife of L. Volumnius, *cos.* 296), 259
Verginius, L., 81
Verrius Flaccus, M. (grammarian), 120
Vibenna, A., 15, 15n.37, 179–80, 195
Volsci, 190, 192, 203, 212, 218
Volsinii, 189
Volumnius Flamma Violens, L. (*cos.* 296), 259
Volumnius, P. (*pont.* before 69), 157n.71
Vulci, 216

Xenophanes, 214, 303
Xenophon, 312

Zaleucus, 316n.50
Zonaras, 359

Index of Scholars

Alföldi, A., 9, 42, 42 n.113, 43, 55, 65, 71, 180–81, 194, 210 n.30
Altheim, F., 181
Ampolo, C., 12 n.27, 27, 43–44, 115 n.43, 228 n.107, 232 n.118
Angelini, P., 123 n.71
Appleton, C., 125
Aymard, A., 358 n.10

Badian, E., 270 n.16
Bauman, R. A., 336 n.29, 365 n.39, 372
Beloch, K. J., 14 n.30, 42, 43, 43 n.116, 69, 69 n.47, 85 n.16
Berchem, D. van, 305
Bernardi, A., 24 n.57
Bickerman, E. J., xvii, 28, 204 n.13, 229 n.112, 230 n.113
Bleicken, J., 4 n.7, 23 n.55, 274 n.25, 295 n.77, 369 n.53
Bonamente, M., 323 n.74
Bonfante, G. P., 179
Boni, G., 179
Botsford, G. W., 151 n.53
Brassloff, S., 245 n.3
Bredehorn, U., 86 n.18
Bringmann, K., 361
Brown, F. E., 179
Brunt, P. A., 42, 44 n.120, 54, 205
Burck, E., 90

Capogrossi Colognesi, L., xvii
Cassola, F., 342
Castagnoli, F., 13 n.29, 179
Catalano, P., 371 n.58

Coarelli, F., 13 n.29
Cohen, B., 119 n.57
Colonna, G. M., 27, 41 n.110, 305, 325
Combet-Farnoux, B., 124 n.76
Cornell, T. J., 12 nn.26–27, 14 n.30, 15, 21 n.53, 23 n.55, 47–51, 88, 88 n.30, 89 n.37, 204, 216 n.56, 224 n.89, 231 n.116, 322, 330 n.9
Crook, J., 136 n.13

Davies, J. K., 293 n.69
Dell'Oro, A., 181
De Martino, F., 4, 36 n.93, 42, 43 n.116
De Sanctis, G., 38, 124, 178, 188, 228
Develin, R., 23 n.55, 41 n.111, 47, 51, 88, 89 n.37, 132 n.7, 134 n.10, 359, 364 n.36, 365 n.39
Dumézil, G., 180–81, 252 n.23
Duncan-Jones, R., 44 n.120

Eder, W., 224 n.88, 238–39, 305
Ellul, J., 126 n.81

Ferenczy, E., 5, 6 n.12, 7 n.15, 29 n.75, 347 n.60
Feuvrier-Prévotat, C., 287 n.58
Finley, M. I., 18 n.44, 20 n.52, 28 n.71, 89 n.37, 214–15
Fraccaro, P., 44, 44 n.122, 72, 362–63
Frank, T., 42
Frier, B. W., 3, 16 n.41, 131 n.4
Fritz, K. von, 87–88, 273 n.20

Gabba, E., 87
Gagé, J., 24 n.57
Gelzer, M., 86
Gjerstad, E., 64–65, 65 n.36, 178, 180, 253 n.25
Gschnitzer, F., 233 n.122, 263, 263 n.2
Gomme, A. W., 43, 44 n.120
Guarducci, M., 179
Guarino, A., 5, 29 n.75, 132 n.7, 232 n.118

Hackl, U., 362 n.30
Hahm, D. E., 155 n.62
Hanell, K., 180
Harris, W. V., 160, 160 n.78
Heichelheim, F., 204
Heurgon, J., 4 n.9, 10
Heuss, A., 26, 199 n.3, 227 n.99
Humbert, M., 123, 126 n.81
Humphreys, S. C., 293 n.69, 305 n.19

Ihering, R. von, 373 n.65

Jacoby, F., 319–20
Jordan, H., 107

Kaser, M., 248, 259
Kienast, D., 253 n.25, 285 n.56, 298 n.88, 360 n.18
Koschaker, P., 247–48
Kretschmer, P., 108
Krüger, P., 356

Lange, L., 357
Lenel, O., 305, 305 n.20
Lewis, D. M., 268
Lewis, G. C., 64
Lewis, M. W. H., 153, 170
Linderski, J., 26, 236 n.133, 296
Luce, T. J., 101 n.76, 329

MacDowell, D. M., 159
Magdelain, A., 107, 241–42
Martin, J., 35 n.92
Mazzarino, S., 180, 303–4, 304 n.15
Meier, C., 360 n.18

Meister, K., 267 n.7
Meyer, Ed., 14 n.30
Meyer, J. C., 124 n.74, 213 n.40
Mitchell, R., 239–40, 242, 261 n.56, 338 n.33, 351
Momigliano, A., xvii, 4, 9, 22 n.54, 26, 37–39, 112, 118, 119 n.57, 122, 122 n.67, 133 n.9, 141–42, 144, 223 n.81, 224 n.89, 230–31, 276 n.32
Mommsen, Th., 87, 87 n.27, 97, 103, 106, 185, 247 n.7, 248–49, 295 n.78, 356–57
Müller-Karpe, H., 7 n.16
Münzer, F., 368 n.47

Nagy, G., 36 n.93
Nap, J. M., 357
Niebuhr, B. G., 63 n.32, 77, 101 n.72, 178
Nilsson, M. P., 304, 304 n.18
Noailles, P., 247–49
Norden, E., 317

Ogilvie, R. M., 89 n.35, 154 n.60, 159, 171–72, 261

Pacchioni, G., 178
Pais, E., 10, 64, 64 n.35, 106
Palmer, R. E. A., 106, 123 n.71, 154 n.60
Pasquali, G., 210 n.30
Peremans, W., 295 n.76
Petzold, K.-E., 98 n.64
Pflaum, H.-G., 255
Pleket, H., 304, 304 n.17
Poma, G., 101 n.76
Pouilloux, J., 309 n.34

Quinn-Schofield, W. K., 365 n.38

Raaflaub, K. A., 88 n.33, 131 n.4, 134 n.10, 137 n.15, 261 n.56, 330 n.9, 367 n.44
Ranouil, P. C., 106, 123, 123 n.71, 139 n.22
Rawson, E., 86
Richter, G., 319
Rilinger, R., 335 n.26, 344
Rouland, N., 337 n.31
Ruschenbusch, E., 43–44, 306 n.24

Ste. Croix, G. E. M. de, 222 n.79, 349 n.64
Saint-Hilaire, J. C., 287 n.58
Schulz, F., 156 n.66
Schwartz, Ed., 87
Scullard, H. H., 262–63
Seager, R., 90 n.39, 94 n.49, 376
Seel, O., 100
Snodgrass, A. M., 284 n.51
Spahn, P., 215
Starr, C. G., 215–16
Staveley, E. S., 242–43
Stupperich, R., 304 n.19

Täubler, E., 83, 87
Taylor, L. R., 376
Toher, M., 41, 172 n.118
Torelli, M., 27, 234 n.128
Toynbee, A. J., 343

Ungern-Sternberg, J. von, 49–50, 330 n.9, 347 n.59

Vanderpool, E., 318 n.56

Watson, A., 254–55
Werner, R., 83, 84 n.13
Westrup, C. W., 259
Wieacker, F., 82, 100 n.69, 305, 310, 369
Wiehemeyer, W., 88, 103 n.89
Wilamowitz-Moellendorff, U. von, 87
Will, Ed., 304, 304 n.16
Willems, P., 106–7
Winter, E. H., 136 n.13
Wiseman, T. P., 88, 103, 331 n.15, 365 n.38

Yeo, C., 204

Index of Sources

Aelian
  VH 5.14 .... 309 n.34
Anon. ad Bas.
  60.3.1 .... 370 n.54
Appian
  Bell. civ. 1.26 .... 75 n.61
  3.94 .... 153 n.58
  5.95 96
  Samn. 5 .... 351 n.67, 368 n.47
Apuleius
  Met. 5.26 .... 256 n.36
  10.29 .... 256 n.36
Aristotle
  Ath. Pol. 2.2 .... 294 n.74
  5ff. 216 n.53
  6.1 .... 294 n.74
  8.4 .... 279 n.43
  8.5 .... 293 n.70
  12.4 .... 294 n.74
  13.3 .... 292 n.67
  20ff. 279 n.41
  25 .... 279 n.41
  Pol. 2.1266b 14ff. 294 n.72
  2.1271a 26ff. 232 n.120
  2.1274b 15ff. 289 n.61
  4.1296a 21 316
  5.1310b 15 92
  6.1321a 13ff. 127 n.83
Arnobius
  Adv. gent. 4.20 .... 255 n.32
Ateius Capito
  Fr. suppl. 6a Str. 251 n.21
Athenaeus
  12.526a 303
Augustine
  De civ. D. 2.18 375
  3.17 .... 367 n.45

Augustus
  Res gest. 5.25 .... 149 n.47

Boethius
  on Cic. Top. 3.14 .... 255 n.32

Caesar
  Bell. Gall. 1.3.5 .... 254 n.27
  1.8.6–7 .... 254 n.27
Cassius Hemina
  Fr. 18 P 95 n.50
Cato
  De agr. praef. 2.4 .... 224 n.86
  Fr. 43 P 361, 362 n.29
  77 P 12 n.26, 210 n.31
  86 P 57 n.18
  167 ORF: 362 n.27
Cicero
  Acad. prior. 2.13 ...... 361 n.21, 363 n.35
  Att. 4.2.3–4 .... 140 n.25, 261 n.56
  6.1.8 .... 299 n.92
  10.1.2 .... 293 n.70
  12.35 .... 315, 319 n.59, 323 n.71
  12.36.1 315
  Balb. 23.53 195
  24.55 197
  Brut. 1.1 .... 152 n.54, 257 n.43
  11.42 .... 48 n.130
  14.55 ..... 340 n.41, 346 n.58, 368 n.47
  14.56 .... 344 n.50
  14.57 .... 362 n.29
  16.62 .... 89 n.37, 203 n.9
  19.75 .... 63 n.32
  31.117 .... 164 n.94

456

Caec. 19.54 .... 296 n.82
Cael. 34 .... 93 n.45
Cato Maior 11 ... 361, 362 n.29, 363 n.35,
                                  364 n.36
 56 .... 59 n.21, 60 n.23
De fin. 2.66 91
De inv. 2.52 .... 361 n.21, 363 n.35,
                           365 n.39, 374 n.68
De leg. 1.2.5 .... 48 n.130
 1.6f. 103
 2.4.9 .... 267 n.9
 2.23.59 .... 293 n.69
 2.25 .... 311, 313, 315
 2.25.63–26.66 .... 293 n.69
 2.27 312
 2.33 315
 2.33.59–35.64 .... 296 n.79
 2.40 312
 2.45 .... 314 n.44
 2.58 .... 314 n.44, 315
 2.59 .... 302 n.3, 303 n.9, 306 n.24, 311,
                                       313
 2.59–61 .... 302 n.6
 2.60 .... 303 n.11, 321, 324
 2.61 312
 2.62 .... 311, 312
 2.64–65 .... 307 n.27, 318
 2.65 314
 2.66 ...... 397 n.26, 308 n.31, 311, 313,
                        314, 314 n.47, 320
 2.67 .... 313 n.42
 3.4.11 .... 25 n.61, 297 n.87
 3.12.27 .... 166 n.99
 3.19 .... 98 n.62
 3.19.44 .... 297 n.87
 3.20 .... 361 n.21
 3.24 315
De off. 1.150f. 224 n.86
De orat. 1.240 .... 53 n.1
 2.36 .... 54 n.7
 3.73 .... 169 n.110
De re pub. 1.43 313
 2.2 .... 74 n.59
 2.14–16 .... 106 n.3
 2.16 .... 106 n.4
 2.20.35 .... 134 n.11
 2.22.39 339
 2.33 .... 114 n.39
 2.36.61 ..... 25 n.61, 279 n.40, 297 n.87
 2.36.61–37.63 .... 226 n.92
 2.37 192
 2.37.62 .... 297 n.86
 2.39 .... 117 n.50, 118 n.55
 2.39–40 .... 118 n.54
 2.40 116
 2.60 .... 365 n.39

 2.62 95
 2.63 .... 91, 253 n.24
 2.63.183 .... 282 n.47
Dom. 1 .... 140 n.25
 14.38 341
 38 .... 111 n.25, 135 n.12, 245 n.1
 101 .... 60 n.25
 118 .... 158 n.72
Fam. 6.18.1 .... 164 n.94
 9.21 .... 154 n.60
Flacc. 84 258
Har. resp. 12 .... 151 n.50
 13 .... 140 n.25
 21 .... 164 n.94
Lael. 11.39 346
 25.96 .... 169 n.108
 41 .... 92 n.44
Leg. agr. 2.7.16 .... 169 n.109
 2.18 .... 257 n.43
 2.73 362
Mur. 1.1 183
 11.25 .... 299 n.92
Phil. 2.2.4 .... 152 n.54
 2.4 .... 257 n.43
 9.17 .... 314, 323 n.72
 13.5.12 .... 152 n.54
Planc. 35 .... 335 n.25
Sest. 65 .... 297 n.87
 69.144 .... 146 n.40
Top. 4.23 .... 296 n.82
Tusc. 2.55 .... 303 n.9
 4.23 .... 63 n.32
Verr. 2.1.18 .... 157 n.71
CIL
 I² 587 .... 167 n.101
 I² 2500 .... 335 n.25
 VIII 2403 .... 148 n.47
 IX 338 (*ILS* 6121) 148 n.47
 X 6662 (*ILS* 1455) 255 n.34
Cincius Alimentus
 Fr. 6 P 59 n.22
Coelius Antipater
 Fr. 40 P 54 n.8

Demosthenes
 19.255 .... 274 n.27
 43.62 .... 306 n.24, 314 n.47
De Viris Illustribus
 7.7 .... 115 n.42
 30.10 .... 368 n.47
 34.3 .... 340 n.41, 346 n.58
Digesta
 1.2.2.3–4 84
 1.2.2.8 .... 368 n.50

Digesta (continued)
1.2.2.24 84
1.2.2.35 .... 371n.60
1.2.2.36 .... 171n.113
1.2.2.38 .... 371n.60

Dio Cassius
2.9.1 .... 114n.37
2.11.2–3 .... 121n.65
4.17.1–8 .... 125n.77
37.8 .... 311n.39
37.46.4 .... 167n.101
46.47.5 .... 153n.58
Fr. 37 368
Fr. 81 .... 45n.93

Diodorus Siculus
1.79.4 .... 294n.74
11.38.2 .... 309n.34, 317, 319n.59
12.24–25 94
12.24.2 91
12.25 .... 93n.47
12.26 94
34/35.28a 92n.44
37.9 .... 92n.44

Diogenes Laertius
1.58 .... 293n.70
5.53.61 320–21

Dionysius of Halicarnassus
Ant. Rom. 1.6.2 1
2.8.1–4 .... 106n.3
2.9–10 196
2.9.2 .... 106n.4
2.10 .... 284n.52, 298n.89
2.12.3 .... 120n.63
2.25 .... 251n.21
2.26.5 .... 365n.39
2.28.1 .... 224n.86
2.47.1 .... 113n.37, 120n.62
2.62.2 .... 114n.37
2.63–74 .... 164n.94
3.29.7 .... 114n.37
3.37.4 .... 114n.39
3.38.2–3 .... 114n.39
3.41.4 .... 114n.37
3.43.2 .... 114n.39
3.67.1 .... 134n.11
4.3.4 .... 114n.37
4.14.1–2 .... 115n.42
4.14.2 .... 110n.21
4.15.1 .... 115n.42
4.16.1–19.4 .... 118n.54
4.18.1 .... 117n.50, 118n.55
4.26 195
4.26.4 .... 271n.19
4.27.7 .... 271n.18
4.42.4 .... 121n.65
4.43.2 .... 120n.60
4.61 .... 70n.51
4.62 .... 164n.94
5.13.2 121
5.36 195
5.40.3 .... 45n.124, 134n.11
5.40.3–5 .... 297n.83
5.40.5 .... 122n.69, 196
5.63.1–67.3 .... 125n.77
5.70.1–5 .... 125n.77
6.7.12ff. 210n.31
6.10.2 .... 116, 127
6.17 197
6.22.1–29.1 .... 125n.77
6.34.1–44.3 .... 125n.77
6.94.3 .... 210n.31
7.2–12 .... 26n.63
7.59.2–10 .... 118n.54
8.87.6 .... 128n.87
9.15.3 .... 45n.124
9.25.2 .... 224n.86
10.14.1 .... 45n.124
10.32 195
10.51.5 .... 302n.5
10.54.7 .... 93n.46
10.55.1 .... 93n.46
10.57.4 .... 93n.46
10.58.1 .... 98n.62
10.58.3 .... 93n.46
10.58.4 197
10.59.2 94
10.60 .... 93n.47
10.60.5–6 .... 95n.51
11.2 .... 93n.47
11.4–21 .... 101n.76
11.4.2 .... 98n.64
11.5.2ff. 96n.57
11.6.4–5 .... 95n.51, 96n.57
11.15 .... 297n.85
11.22.6–7 .... 98n.63
11.43.6 .... 127n.85
11.62 .... 104n.90
12.1–4 .... 59n.21
12.1.14 61
12.4.2–5 .... 59n.22
12.4.6 .... 60nn.25–26

Festus
p. 6 L 120
p. 36 L 120
p. 65 L 250n.19
p. 82 L 111n.27
p. 100 L 72n.56, 196
p. 137 L 111n.25, 154n.60
p. 144 L 154n.60

p. 198 L 165 n.98
p. 224 L 117 n.49
p. 247 L 119 n.58
p. 262 L 106 n.4
p. 268 L 197
p. 290 L 119, 163 n.92, 165 n.96, 341
p. 304 L ... 109, 120, 120 n.62, 121 n.64,
                                    134 n.11, 182
p. 470 L 360 n.17
p. 487 L 195
p. 506 L 115 n.42
p. 821 L 147 n.45
p. 154 M 303 n.12, 322 n.67
p. 273 M 303 n.8
p. 274 M 302 n.7
Florus
1.10.3 .... 19 n.48
1.25 .... 282 n.47
2.4.4 .... 92 n.44
Frontinus
De aquis 2.129 .... 335 n.25
p. 131–32 Van den Hout 103 n.83

Gaius
Inst. 1.3 .... 368 n.50
1.110 .... 255 n.32
1.111 .... 254 n.29, 259
1.112 ...... 245 n.2, 249 n.17, 250 n.19,
         251 n.21, 252 n.23, 256 n.41
1.113 .... 256 n.41
1.115 .... 154 n.60
2.42 .... 296 n.82
4.14 .... 298 n.91
Gellius, Aulus
Noctes Atticae 1.12 .... 147 n.45
1.12.15 .... 151 n.52, 256 n.41
1.15.9 .... 171 n.113
1.23 .... 146 n.41
2.12.1 .... 293 n.70
2.24 .... 324 n.75
2.28.6 .... 210 n.31
3.2.11 .... 128 n.87
3.18.1 .... 163 n.92
6.13 196
6.13.3 .... 72 n.56
10.6.3 372
10.15 .... 150 n.49
10.15.4 .... 111 n.28
10.15.22–24 .... 245 n.4
10.24 .... 57 n.18
13.12.9 .... 128 n.87
14.7 .... 140 n.26
14.8.2 359
15.27.4 .... 368 n.50
15.27.5 .... 109 n.19

16.10.5 .... 298 n.90
16.10.8 .... 298 n.90
16.10.11 .... 116 n.45
20.1.45–49 .... 172 n.118
20.1.46–47 .... 289 n.61
20.1.47 .... 25 n.62
20.1.48–52 .... 289 n.61

Herodotus
1.65f. 274 n.28
4.152 .... 15 n.37
5.66ff. 34 n.89, 41
5.66.2 .... 279 n.41
5.78 .... 92 n.42
5.97.2 .... 44 n.120
8.53 .... 280 n.43
9.10 .... 116 n.46
9.28 .... 116 n.46
Hesiod
Works and Days 27ff. 214 n.43
202ff. 214 n.43
250 .... 288 n.60
221 .... 288 n.60
267ff. 214 n.43
Historia Augusta
Alex. Sev. 22.3 255
Homer
Il. 2.212ff. 227 n.102
16.384ff. 214 n.43
18.507f. 298 n.91
Od. 14.199ff. 233 n.122
19.109ff. 214 n.43
Horace
Epist. 2.2.74 .... 314 n.45
Sat. 1.62.42 .... 314 n.45

IG
IV 1607 .... 309 n.34
V 2 .... 309 n.34
V 4 .... 309 n.34
Isidorus
Orig. 9.4.11 .... 120 n.63

Justinian
Inst. 1.2.4 .... 368 n.50

Livy
1.8.3 .... 146 n.40
1.8.4–7 .... 106 n.3
1.15.8–16.8 .... 132 n.6

Livy (*continued*)
1.17 .... 132 n.6, 142 n.31
1.20.2 .... 111 n.27
1.24 .... 158 n.73
1.24.9 .... 54 n.4
1.25.2 .... 54 n.4
1.30.2 .... 114 n.37
1.33.1–2 .... 114 n.39
1.33.5 .... 114 n.39
1.35.6 .... 121, 134 n.11
1.36.3 .... 113 n.35
1.42.4–43.9 .... 118 n.54
1.43.8–9 .... 117 n.50
1.43.9 .... 113 n.35
1.44 .... 69 n.49
1.44.2 .... 72 n.57
1.45 .... 271 n.19
1.49.2–6 .... 121 n.65
2.1.10 120
2.1.10–11 .... 120 n.62
2.1.11 182
2.8.2 .... 202 n.6
2.14 195
2.16.3–6 .... 297 n.83
2.16.4 .... 45 n.124, 134 n.11
2.16.5 .... 122 n.69, 196
2.19.1 .... 69 n.47
2.20.12 195
2.21–23 .... 132 n.6
2.21.7 .... 69 n.46
2.23 .... 211 n.33
2.23.1–31.6 .... 125 n.77
2.27.10f. 222 n.79
2.28.5ff. 222 n.79
2.28.8–29.4 .... 222 n.79
2.31.7ff. 218 n.63
2.32.8 .... 203 n.9
2.33.1 .... 128 n.88, 277 n.38
2.34 .... 293 n.68
2.41 .... 211 n.34
2.41.3 .... 211 n.34
2.41.10 .... 365 n.39
2.42.5 195
2.43.1ff. 222 n.79
2.48.5–50.11 .... 282 n.46
2.49.4 .... 45 n.124
2.50 196
2.50.11 .... 45 n.124
2.55.1ff. 222 n.79
3.9.5 .... 276 n.34
3.10.10ff. 222 n.79
3.16.5 .... 45 n.124
3.16.5ff. 222 n.79
3.20.1ff. 222 n.79
3.25.9ff. 222 n.79
3.27.1 .... 112 n.33
3.29.6 .... 123, 235 n.129
3.30.1ff. 222 n.79
3.31 195
3.31.7f. 78, 203 n.8, 302 n.5
3.32 197
3.32.6f. 203 n.8
3.33.7 91
3.33.9 .... 112 n.33
3.34.6 .... 81, 272
3.34.8 .... 79, 98 n.61
3.35.4–5 91
3.35.11 197
3.36.1 93
3.36.7 .... 79, 93 n.47
3.36.9 .... 94 n.48
3.37 .... 290 n.65
3.37.1 .... 98 n.64
3.37.2–3 .... 80, 98 n.62
3.37.4 .... 80, 95
3.37.6–8 93
3.38.6 80
3.38.9–10 .... 80, 98 n.64
3.38.13 .... 98 n.64
3.39–41 .... 101 n.76
3.39.3ff. 96 n.57
3.40.12 .... 96 n.57
3.41.5–6 .... 80, 98 n.65
3.42.2 .... 80, 92 n.42
3.43 80
3.44.1 80
3.47.5 81
3.49.7 .... 98 n.64
3.50.13 81
3.51.2 .... 127 n.85
3.51.13 .... 96 n.57
3.54.15 .... 364 n.38
3.55 .... 297 n.85
3.55.4 .... 202 n.6
3.55.13 197
3.63.7 .... 364 n.38
4.1ff. 236 n.132
4.1.1–6.4 .... 282 n.47
4.1.2f. 203 n.8
4.2.5 261
4.4.5 192
4.4.7 .... 170 n.111
4.6.2–3 260
4.6.12 .... 98 n.64
4.7.1–2 .... 104 n.90
4.9–10 .... 17 n.43, 357
4.13–16 .... 59 n.21
4.16.1 .... 60 n.25
4.21.3–4 .... 60 n.23
4.23.1 .... 104 n.90
4.28.7 .... 54 n.4
5.12.8–11 .... 204 n.13

Index of Sources   461

5.19.6	271 n.18
6.5.8	237 n.136
6.11.9	237 n.138
6.14	211 n.33
6.31.2	237 n.137
6.32.1	237 n.138
6.34ff.	343
6.34.2	237 n.138
6.35	350
6.35–42	279 n.42
6.37.8	204 n.13
6.39.2	350
6.42.2	327 n.2
6.42.13f.	197
7.1	337 n.32
7.1.5	146 n.40
7.3.3	16 n.41
7.6.7ff.	339 n.35
7.6.12	343
7.15.12	345
7.17.6	338
7.17.10ff.	344 n.49
7.18.3–10	335, 344
7.19.5f.	344, 350
7.21	336, 344 n.51, 350 n.65
7.22.1ff.	345 n.52, 350
7.22.7–10	338, 344
7.22.10f.	345 n.53
7.24.11	345 n.54
7.28.9f.	345
7.42.2	328 n.8, 335
8.12.4–17	346
8.12.15	340 n.41
8.12.16	328 n.8
8.15.9	338, 346
8.18.12f.	16 n.41
8.22.13ff.	346 n.57
8.37	154 n.60
8.40	2 n.2
8.40.3–5	89
8.40.4	329–30
9.26.5ff.	347 n.60
9.30.2	168 n.103
9.33.3ff.	346
9.36.3	197
9.46.1ff.	348
9.46.5–6	299 n.92
10.6.4ff.	346
10.6–9	279 n.42
10.9.3–6	202 n.6
10.15.7ff.	346 n.58, 348
10.23	259
10.46.14	271 n.18
21.15.3–6	86
21.63.3–4	359
22.33.9ff.	348 n.61
22.34.7–8	366
22.49.16–18	165 n.98
22.51.2	57 n.17
22.57.3	171 n.113
23.22f.	328 n.4
23.22.9	141 n.26
23.23	165 n.98
23.23.6	359
23.30.15	311 n.39
23.31.7–14	339
24.16.19	372
25.12.10	183
27.8.1–3	112
27.8.4–10	111 n.27, 145 n.39, 163 n.93, 170 n.112, 256 n.41
27.11.12	168 n.103
27.11.22	163 n.92
27.21.10	358
27.37.13	146 n.40
29.27.13	54 n.8
29.38.6	256 n.41
30.19.9	358
30.26.7–10	151 n.51
31.6.4	366 n.42
31.8.3	160 n.80
31.50.4	311 n.39
31.50.7–10	164 n.95
33.42.1	169 n.110
33.42.6	151 n.51
33.44.5	163 n.92
34.7.2	146 n.40
34.44.5	141 n.26, 168 n.103
34.55.4–8	141 n.26
37.3.6	147 n.45
37.57.15	348 n.61
38.28.2	163 n.92, 168 n.103
39.32.5ff.	331 n.15
39.41.1ff.	348 n.61
39.46.2	311 n.39
39.47.9	168 n.103
40.42.7	151 n.51
40.42.8–11	151 n.53, 256 n.40
40.51.2	168 n.103
41.28.11	311 n.39
45.40.8	146 n.40
Epit. 61	75 n.61
89	167 n.101
Fr. 12 W	347 n.59, 356, 357 n.7, 366, 375 n.75
Per. 11	351 n.67, 367, 368 n.46
18	371

Lydus
Mag. 1.16, pp. 20–21 W 120 n.63
Lysias
   1.14 .... 309 n.34

Macrobius
Sat. 1.3.8 . . . . 128 n.87
1.6.12–14 . . . . 146 n.40
1.15.9 . . . . 299 n.92
1.16.30 . . . . 157 n.70, 369
3.8.7 . . . . 147 n.45
3.8.9 . . . . 141 n.27
3.11.6 . . . . 141 n.26
3.17 . . . . 324 n.75

Nonius
p. 371 . . . . 302 n.7

Orosius
5.17.6 . . . . 92 n.44
Ovid
Fasti 6.475ff. 271 n.18
6.569ff. 271 n.18
6.663–4 . . . . 323 n.72

Pausanias
1.18.2–3 . . . . 280 n.43
1.29.11 . . . . 320 n.61
Piso (L. Calpurnius P. Frugi)
Fr. 6 P 59 n.22
Plato
Leg. 4.717d7–e1 312
12.955e6–8 . . . . 314 n.44
12.955e8–56a2 314
12.958d6–e6 313
12.958e6–7 310
12.959c1ff. 312, 315
12.959e5–7 312
12.960a1–2 310
Rep. 566d–e 92
Pliny
Nat. Hist. 11.157 . . . . 303 n.9
14.88 . . . . 303 n.10, 322 n.69
16.37 . . . . 369 n.51
18.3.12 . . . . 293 n.68
18.15 . . . . 60 n.26
21.7 . . . . 303 n.11
33.1.17 . . . . 299 n.92
33.53 . . . . 311 n.39
34.21 . . . . 60 n.26
35.12.154 197
35.197f. 360 n.17
Plutarch
Apophth. Rom. 194e 362 n.30

Caes. 1 . . . . 150 n.50
De sera 550c 293 n.70
Fab. 1.5 . . . . 151 n.51
24.4 . . . . 151 n.51
C. Gracch. 15–16 . . . . 75 n.61
Ti. Gracch. 14 . . . . 92 n.44
Lyc. 2.6f. 274 n.28
13.1 . . . . 267 n.9
27.1 . . . . 307 n.25
Numa 1.2 . . . . 18 n.46
2.5 . . . . 114 n.37
12.1–2 . . . . 322 n.69
Per. 12 . . . . 41 n.111
Pomp. 30.4 . . . . 357 n.4
Publ. 11.2 . . . . 120 n.63
21 . . . . 196, 297 n.83
21.10 . . . . 122 n.69
Quaest. Gr. 296 F 24 . . . . 309 n.34
Quaest. Rom. 6 . . . . 357, 357 n.7, 376 n.81
50 . . . . 246 n.4
113 . . . . 111 n.27
Rom. 13.1–9 . . . . 106 n.3
13.7 . . . . 106 n.4
20.1 . . . . 114 n.37
Sol. 5.6 . . . . 290 n.65
13–15 . . . . 294 n.74
14ff. 216 n.53
17 . . . . 289 n.61
17.2 . . . . 293 n.68
19.1 . . . . 279 n.43
20.1 . . . . 293 n.70
21.5 . . . . 293 n.69
21.5–7 . . . . 306 n.24
21.7 . . . . 309 n.34
23.3 . . . . 212 n.36
24.4 . . . . 294 n.73
Sull. 10 . . . . 94 n.48
35 . . . . 319 n.59
35.3 . . . . 323 n.70
Polybius
2.21.8 . . . . 360 n.20
2.33.7f. 361 n.24
3.2.6 . . . . 361 n.23
3.20.3 . . . . 146 n.42
3.22 . . . . 70 n.52, 89 n.36
3.80.3 . . . . 360 n.20, 361 n.24
4.2.1–3 . . . . 2 n.2
6.10.14 . . . . 361 n.23
6.11 . . . . 74 n.59, 374 n.72
6.57 361
6.58.1 . . . . 361 n.23
12.5.6–8 . . . . 107 n.9
16.34.2 . . . . 160 n.80

Rhet. ad Herenn.
1.20 . . . . 257 n.43

Sallust
Ad Caes. sen. 2.8 . . . . 339 n.37
Hist. Fr. 1.11 M 125 n.77
Fr. 3.48 M 377 n.94
Fr. 11 M 328, 377 n.94
Iug. 31 . . . . 92 n.44, 377 n.94
Sempronius Asellio
Frs. 1–2 P 18 n.46
Sempronius Tuditanus
Fr. 7 P 95 n.50
Servius
on Aen. 6.609 . . . . 226 n.93, 298 n.89
7.303 . . . . 256 n.41
7.706 . . . . 122 n.69
8.663 . . . . 112 n.30
12.606 . . . . 303 n.9
on Georg. 1.31 . . . . 147 n.45
Servius Auctus
on Aen. 1.426 . . . . 120 n.63
4.29 . . . . 246 n.4
4.103 . . . . 245 n.2, 247 n.10
4.339 . . . . 245 n.2, 247 n.10
4.374 . . . . 245 n.2, 247 n.10, 250 n.19
8.552 . . . . 246 n.4, 258 n.49
on Georg. 1.31 . . . . 245 n.2, 250 n.20,
                              251 n.21, 255 n.32
Solon (Diehl)
Fr. 1.7ff. 294 n.75
Fr. 1.11 . . . . 278 n.39
Fr. 1.16 . . . . 278 n.39
Fr. 3.7ff. 214, 214 n.43, 294 n.75
Fr. 3.8 . . . . 278 n.39
Fr. 3.30–39 . . . . 274 n.27
Fr. 3.34 . . . . 278 n.39
Fr. 3.36 . . . . 288 n.60
Fr. 4 . . . . 294 n.75
Fr. 5.1–4 . . . . 279 n.43
Fr. 24 . . . . 294 n.74
Fr. 24.9f. 214 n.46, 294 n.75
Fr. 24.14 . . . . 278 n.39
Stobaeus
44.40 . . . . 309 n.34
Strabo
4.1.5 . . . . 271 n.19
Suetonius
Cal. 12 . . . . 257 n.43
Div. Aug. 38.2 . . . . 149 n.47
Div. Iul. 1 . . . . 150 n.50, 256 n.37

19.2 94
Tib. 1.2 . . . . 122 n.69
2.3 372
2.4 . . . . 93 n.45

Tacitus
Ann. 2.49 . . . . 210 n.31
3.58 . . . . 150 n.49
3.59 . . . . 150 n.49
4.16 . . . . 150 n.49, 256 nn.40–41
11.22 . . . . 167 n.101
11.25 . . . . 134 n.11
15.51 89
Hist. 3.72 . . . . 71 n.54
Tertullian
Apol. 6.1–6 . . . . 324 n.75
Theognis
31f. 226 n.92
101ff. 226 n.92
173ff. 232 n.120
Theophilus
ad Autol. 4.3.15 . . . . 370 n.54
Thucydides
1.13ff. 284 n.53
1.18.1 . . . . 274 n.28
Twelve Tables
I.1–3 . . . . 298 n.91
I.4 . . . . 298 n.90
I.6–7 . . . . 298 n.91
III 172 n.118
III.1–6 . . . . . 211 n.32, 217 n.58, 277 n.36
III.5–6 . . . . 25 n.62, 289 n.61
VI.3 . . . . 296 n.82
VIII.9 . . . . 293 n.68
VIII.21 . . . . 226 n.93, 298 n.89
IX.1–2 . . . . . . 25 n.61, 280 n.43, 297 n.87
X.2–10 . . . . 296 n.79
XI.1 . . . . 226 n.92

Ulpianus
Reg. 9.1 . . . . 245 n.2, 249 n.17
10.5 . . . . 256 n.41

Valerius Maximus
4.3.9 197
5.4.5 . . . . 362 n.29, 363 n.35, 365 n.39,
                                      374 n.68
6.3.1 . . . . 60 n.25

Varro
  Ling. 5.81 .... 127 n.85
    5.83–87 .... 164 n.94
    5.157 .... 60 n.25
    6.13 .... 108 n.17
  Rust. 2, *praef.* 1 .... 171 n.113
Velleius Paterculus
  2.4.4 .... 92 n.44
  2.6.2 .... 92 n.44
  2.6.4–7 .... 75 n.61
  2.9.6 .... 103 n.83
  2.41 .... 256 n.38, 258 n.47

Xenophanes
  Fr. 3 303

Xenophon
  Cyr. 8.7.25 312
  Oec. 14.4f. 289 n.61
  Rep. Lac. 10.7 .... 232 n.120

Zonaras
  7.7 .... 114 n.39
  7.8 .... 114 n.37
  7.11 .... 164 n.94
  7.13–14 .... 125 n.77
  7.15 .... 127 n.85, 359
  7.18 .... 91, 95
  7.20 .... 59 n.21
  8.2 368

           Designer: Janet Wood
         Compositor: G&S Typesetters, Inc.
              Text: 11/13 Baskerville
           Display: Baskerville
           Printer: Braun-Brumfield, Inc.
            Binder: Braun-Brumfield, Inc.